CW01084242

EVERYMAN'S LIBRARY

EVERYMAN,
I WILL GO WITH THEE,
AND BE THY GUIDE,
IN THY MOST NEED
TO GO BY THY SIDE

HORACE WALPOLE

SELECTED LETTERS

EDITED AND INTRODUCED BY
STEPHEN CLARKE

FROM A SELECTION BY
WILLIAM HADLEY

EVERYMAN'S LIBRARY
Alfred A. Knopf New York London Toronto

350

THIS IS A BORZOI BOOK
PUBLISHED BY ALFRED A. KNOPF

First included in Everyman's Library, 1926
Revised edition Copyright © 2017 by Everyman's Library
Introduction Copyright © 2017 by Stephen Clarke
Bibliography and Chronology Copyright © 2017 by Everyman's Library
Typography by Peter B. Willberg

www.randomhouse/everymans
www.everymanslibrary.co.uk

ISBN 978-1-101-90789-4 (US)
978-1-84159-350-0 (UK)

A CIP catalogue reference for this book is available from the
British Library

Book design by Barbara de Wilde and Carol Devine Carson
Typeset in the UK by Input Data Services, Bridgwater
Printed and bound in Germany by GGP Media GmbH, Pössneck

CONTENTS

———

CONTENTS

INTRODUCTION

___

HORACE WALPOLE AND
THE ART OF LETTER-WRITING

The letters of Horace Walpole have always been recognised as one of the most outstanding collections of correspondence in English literature. Throughout his long life Walpole maintained an extensive correspondence with a wide circle of friends – it is estimated that he may have written over seven thousand letters, of which some three thousand survive, and those figures exclude notes and letters of business. His letters open a window onto the eighteenth century and allow the reader to engage with the panorama of contemporary life: to listen to the talk, to hear the scandal, to participate in the debates, and to watch the events of the day unfold. What Walpole offers is a sense of immediacy, an unrivalled ability to re-create a scene and to tell a story, and that gift the modern reader can share with the letters' original recipients.

Walpole was insistent that letters should not be fine or studied, but should rather, as he explained to his friend Lady Ossory, be "extempore conversations upon paper".[1] But he was so well placed and had such broad interests that those conversations are extremely wide-ranging. As the son of Sir Robert Walpole, the prime minister, and a Member of Parliament himself for over twenty-five years, he knew and watched the politicians of the time and observed and participated in their schemes. As a young man on the Grand Tour he had thrown himself into ridottos and carnivals, and for the rest of his life he attended events of all kinds: from balls and routs to gatherings of the Bluestockings, and from the salons of Paris to Coronations and royal funerals and state trials. He moved

---

1 The Yale Edition of Horace Walpole's Correspondence, ed. W. S. Lewis (New Haven and London: Yale University Press, 1937–83), letter of 25 December 1781, Vol. 33, p. 318 [such a reference henceforth appearing as YE 33:318]. For Lady Ossory see heading to letter 221.

freely through London society, meeting familiarly with statesmen, writers, artists, actors, scholars, historians, courtiers, and
clerics. When he wrote about the unfolding dramas of his
time, whether foreign wars or political upheavals, he did so
with personal knowledge of many of the actors involved. We
can hear from him the conversation of the wits and celebrities
of the day, and observe its cultural life: as an historian and
writer he was engaged with and had informed views on
contemporary art and architecture, on the latest novel and
the newest play. In addition, the letters reveal much of his
own complex personality, of his friendships and achievements,
and of the extraordinary house that he created at Strawberry
Hill and filled with his collections.

The variety of Walpole's various correspondents reflected
the range of his contacts and activities, and each series of
letters has its own centre of gravity and dynamic. The letters
are as informal as any conversation with its asides and incid-
ental digressions, but there are recurrent themes to individual
correspondences, whether politics, or literature, or social life,
or antiquarianism. Perhaps the most striking example of this
is the largest of all Walpole's series of letters, that written to
Sir Horace Mann,[2] the British plenipotentiary at Florence.
From 1740 about two thousand letters passed between them.
Walpole did not see Mann after staying with him in Florence
in 1741, but they wrote to each other regularly until Mann's
death forty-five years later. Mann needed news of British
politics and policy, and of world affairs that might impact on
the court of the Duke of Tuscany. This Walpole supplied,
interspersing it with incident and entertaining detail on the
talking-points of the moment. Mann responded with a picture
of evolving Florentine society, of the cares of his official duties
(which included benignly overseeing the endless succession of
young men passing through Florence on their Grand Tour)
and the rigours of the gout to which, like Walpole, he was a
martyr. Walpole knew the charm and value of anecdotal
asides, and lamented that Mann's residence abroad meant he
could only employ them sparingly. He noted to Lady Ossory

2 See heading to letter 200.

(herself isolated from London society after a scandalous divorce) that "Nothing is so pleasant as the occurrences of society in a letter. I am always regretting in my correspondence with Madame du Deffand[3] and Sir Horace Mann, that I must not make use of them, as the one has never lived in England, and the other not these fifty years, and so any private stories would want notes as much as Petronius. Sir Horace and I have no acquaintance in common but the kings and queens of Europe."[4]

Principally, however, Walpole provided Mann with news, and his ability to provide news, or frustration in its absence, is a leitmotif throughout their correspondence. On occasion he plays with his correspondents, as when he suggests to Lord and Lady Hertford (newly arrived in Paris on Hertford's appointment as British Ambassador) in letter 207: "Consider you are in my power. You, by this time, are longing to hear from England, and depend upon me for the news of London. I shall not send you a tittle, if you are not very good, and do not (one of you, at least) write to me punctually." Similar gestures as to the power of giving or withholding information can be seen in the opening of letter 277 to Mann on the victory of Culloden ("You have bid me for some time to send you good news – well! I think I will. How good would you have it?"), and again in letter 293 to Hertford on the Wilkes riots, where Walpole opens his letter by asking "Well! but we have had a prodigious riot: are you not impatient to know the particulars?" It is through his access to news that Walpole controlled his correspondences – hence his irritation when in later life he became dependent on newspapers that were as readily available to his recipient.

The letters to Mann evolved into a prospect of the eighteenth-century world, as seen from London and Strawberry Hill and delivered to Florence. Walpole was aware of their significance, and from as early as 1748 asked Mann to give him back his letters: the first set was returned the following year, the last following Mann's death in 1786. From 1754

3 Madame du Deffand was Walpole's elderly French friend, for whom see heading to letter 215.
4 Letter of 22 September 1776 (YE 32:320).

Walpole started to prepare transcripts of the letters, on occasion pruning some of the text, and adding explanatory footnotes. He then delegated the task of transcription to his secretary Thomas Kirgate (who also conducted the printing press Walpole had established at Strawberry Hill), and ultimately there were six folio volumes of transcripts: it is these, rather than his original letters to Mann, which have survived. To the first of these volumes Walpole attached the following Advertisement:

The following collection of letters, written very carelessly by a young man, had been preserved by the person to whom they were addressed. The author, some years after the date of the first, borrowed them, on account of some anecdotes interspersed. On the perusal, among many trifling relations and stories which were only of consequence or amusing to the two persons concerned in the correspondence, he found some facts, characters and news, which, though below the dignity of history, might prove entertaining to many other people: and knowing how much pleasure, not only himself, but many other persons have often found in a series of private and familiar letters, he thought it worth his while to preserve these, as they contain something of the customs, fashions, politics, diversions and private history of several years; which, if worthy of any existence, can be properly transmitted to posterity, only in this manner.

This introductory note is typically Walpolian in its familiar, relaxed tone and its underlying seriousness. Walpole's letters were not studied, but neither were they ever careless. He employs a tone of self-deprecation, apologising for the trifling nature of some of the letters, but that self-deprecation was a mask he often wore when most earnest, and is a pose that appears recurrently in his correspondence. Compare, for example, the hauteur of his dismissal of authorship ("there is nothing I hold so cheap as a learned man, except an unlearned one") in letter 242 to his assessment of his limitations as an author in letter 124 ("I have learnt and have practised the humiliating task of comparing myself with great authors; and that comparison has annihilated all the flattery that self-love could suggest"). Walpole scorned the trade of authorship, and claimed to regret having ventured his reputation in the market-place, but was nonetheless fully aware of the value both of the works he published and the rich body of letters that he sent to his friends. He understood the significance of his correspondence with Mann and went to great trouble to preserve it, as he believed that "nothing gives so just an idea of an age as genuine letters; nay, history waits for its last seal from them".[5] But he also held it "cruel to publish private letters, while the persons concerned in them are living".[6] Consequently none of his letters was published in his lifetime, but he clearly envisaged publication for the Mann letters and at least some of the others, and hoped that what he described in letter 134 as "that undutiful urchin, Posterity" would value the portrait of his age he provided. In the words of R. W. Ketton-Cremer, still after over seventy-five years Walpole's finest and most sensitive biographer, "It is impossible to exaggerate either his solicitude for posterity, or the skill with which he ensured that his varied records should reach posterity in the most complete and attractive form."[7]

Walpole left his papers to the father of his young friend Mary Berry,[8] knowing that she would duly edit his collected works: five large quarto volumes appeared the year after his death. The last two volumes of the *Works* included Walpole's correspondence with Richard West and Thomas Gray, and his letters to his cousin Henry Conway, the artist Richard Bentley, the amateur architect John Chute, Lord Strafford, Lady Hervey, Lady Ailesbury, and Hannah More.[9] With the exception of More, all these correspondents had already died, and Walpole's letters to More, which respect her personal piety, were unexceptionable by any standards. The letters were lightly annotated by Berry as editor but also have a sprinkling of notes by Walpole, who clearly in old age planned

5 Letter to Lord Dalrymple, 30 November 1761 (YE 15:73).
6 Letter to Sir Horace Mann, 30 May 1767 (YE 22:524).
7 R. W. Ketton-Cremer, *Horace Walpole* (London: Duckworth, 1940), p. 19.
8 See heading to letter 228.
9 For West, see letter 1, note 1, and for Gray see the heading to letter 195; for Bentley see letter 15, note 1; for Lady Ailesbury see letter 20, note 1; and for Conway, Chute, Strafford, Hervey and More see the headings to letters 191, 210, 213, 214, and 226 respectively.

their forming a part of his published *Works*, the monument to his literary achievement.

But as a young man Walpole was not writing with publication in mind, and the charm of his letters lies in their unstudied informality and spontaneity. Walpole himself once admonished his friend George Montagu for praising his letters: "it sounds as if I wrote them to be fine and to have them printed, which might be very well for Mr. Pope who having wrote pieces carefully, which ought to be laboured, could carry off the affectation of having studied things that have no excuse but their being wrote flying".[10] Alexander Pope was known to have taken great trouble to prepare his literary correspondence for publication, and Walpole contrasts Pope's artifice with letters that should be "wrote flying". The minor adjustments he made in transcribing the Mann letters were modest indeed in comparison with the wholesale amendments undertaken not only by Pope, but also by other writers such as Anna Seward, a provincial author who left behind her carefully arranged correspondence in the vain hope that it would bolster her fading reputation, and Walpole's friend the Reverend William Mason,[11] who cut and even transferred text between letters when editing the correspondence of Thomas Gray. Such re-ordering was permissible by the standards of the day, but correspondence consciously prepared for publication inevitably loses the freshness of unguarded intimacy. Walpole celebrated that intimacy in a letter of 1777 to Lady Ossory, written at a time when he was distracted by the financial affairs of his nephew (see letters 185 to 188):

I have time to write to nobody, but on business, or to a few that are used to my ways, and with whom I don't mind whether I stand on my head or my heels – I beg your Honour's pardon, for you are one to whom I can write comfortably ... but since neither Aristotle nor Bossu[12] have laid down rules for letters, and consequently have left them to their native wildness, I shall persist in saying whatever comes

10 Letter of 12 June 1746 (YE 9:29). For Montagu see heading to letter 203.
11 For Mason see letter 93, p. 151, n. 1.
12 René le Bossu (1631–80), French writer and critic.

uppermost, and the less I am understood by anybody but the person I write to, so much the better.[13]

The artist Richard Bentley described both Walpole's ease and familiarity of tone, and his care to recover his original letters:

Mr. Bentley said that Walpole was the best letter-writer that ever took pen in hand; that he wrote with the greatest ease imaginable, with company in the room, and even talking to other people at the time: that he had a great loss when, some time ago, he demanded all his letters of him, which were sent to him, and refused returning those of his writing.[14]

Montagu, who lived in the depths of the country and rarely put himself to the trouble of travelling to London, similarly praised Walpole's correspondence, claiming:

Your last letter is always the best and most charming; if you would promise me to write every week I would never come to town as long as I lived. Think that I have a box full of them of above twenty years old; think what a treasure they will be a hundred years hence ... Look you, Sir, they are my property; you may burn your own works but you shall as soon burn me as make me burn them.[15]

Montagu was charming and witty, and Walpole was very fond of him, but he was also idle. His enthusiasm for receiving Walpole's effervescent dispatches of news and gossip faded, and his replies became more irregular (the opening of letter 111 and the conclusion of letter 122 show Walpole's mounting frustration) and eventually in 1770 died away. This does raise the question of what it must have been like to receive a steady flow of sparkling letters from Walpole: how could one compete? Dr. Johnson in his correspondence repeatedly lamented that the pleasure of receiving a letter was qualified by the sense of obligation that one must compose a letter

13 Letter of 8 October 1777 (YE 33:385).
14 See *Nichols's Illustrations of the Literary History of the Eighteenth Century* (1858), Volume 8, p. 573.
15 Letter from Montagu of 3 February 1760 (YE 9:275).

in reply. The letters of some of Walpole's correspondents, particularly those who were writers or scholars, are of real interest, but it has never been suggested that figures such as Lady Ossory, secluded in the Bedfordshire countryside, could even begin to match him for matter or manner.

Montagu and Ossory were both isolated in the provinces, and Walpole's letters provided them with news of the social life of London that they were denied. Walpole's correspondence with Lady Ossory only takes off in 1771, at least ten years after he had met her, but the year after his letters to Montagu finally dried up. It has been suggested that Walpole consciously chose his correspondents with a view to whatever aspect of his age his letters to them could display: when he lost Montagu, he found a replacement in Lady Ossory, so the record of contemporary life could be maintained. Beneath all this was an element of tension between Walpole's desire to record the incidents of the day, and his concern that the freedom of his letters would be curtailed if he felt that his letters were preserved and shown: "Can I say everything, that comes into my head, to Lady Ossory, if Posterity stands behind my chair and peeps over my shoulder?"[16]

It is true that his major series of letters do have distinct personalities: for example, he wrote to the Reverend William Cole[17] predominantly on antiquarian matters (as well as their shared sufferings from gout); and to the poet Gray, and after Gray's death to his editor and biographer Mason, he wrote on the world of literature. But it would be simplistic to see the disposition of the content of Walpole's letters in such mechanistic terms. A better approach is to see his letters as reflections of his varied interests, and those of his correspondents. There are many other antiquarians apart from Cole to whom he wrote on historical subjects, and his literary opinions are scattered widely. Any one letter may move from politics to a society wedding, from a painting bought for his collection to an anecdote or witticism heard and preserved, from foreign affairs to some example of domestic injustice. The letters to Mann appear more frequently in this selection

16 Letter to Lady Ossory of 27 September 1778 (YE 33:53–4).
17 For Cole see heading to letter 211.

not because this selection is focused on politics and world affairs, or even because more letters to Mann survive than to any other correspondent, but rather because their subject-matter is so diverse, and their quality so high.

Bruce Redford has noted that letters are essentially performances, theatrical events in which the writer compensates for physical absence by a series of rhetorical gestures and stylistic inflections.[18] Walpole certainly employs variety of manner, phrasing and tempi, and there is no question that the purpose of a Walpole letter is to engage and entertain, but the concept of performance suggests perhaps more premeditation than he would have recognised. His pose of familiar ease, of unstudied immediacy expressed in crystalline prose, is a performance of a very special kind, but not theatrical in the staged or histrionic sense. It is a conversation, brilliantly managed.

This mode of letter-writing relates back to classical models of which Walpole would have been fully aware. Of Roman writers, it is the natural style of Cicero that Walpole's most closely resembles. Cicero explained his epistolary style in a letter to Papirius Paetus:

But be that as it may, how do I strike you in my letters? Don't I seem to talk to you in the language of common folk? For I don't always adopt the same style. What similarity is there between a letter, and a speech in court or at a public meeting? Why, even in law-cases I am not in the habit of dealing with all of them in the same style. Private cases, and those petty ones too, I conduct in a more plain-spoken fashion, those involving a man's civil status or his reputation, of course, in a more ornate style; but my letters I generally compose in the language of everyday life.[19]

Walpole would not have expressed himself in tones quite so lofty, but in his letters the relaxed familiarity is the same, and

18 Bruce Redford, *The Converse of the Pen: Acts of Intimacy in the Eighteenth-Century Familiar Letter* (Chicago and London: Chicago University Press, 1986), p. 2.
19 *Cicero: The letters to his Friends*, trans. W. Glynn Williams (1927–9, reprinted Cambridge: Harvard University Press, 1952), Volume II, pp. 261, 263: Book ix, letter 21.

although he does not comment on Cicero or Seneca as letter-writers, his own are closer to the simplicity of Cicero than the wit of Seneca or the studied elegance of Pliny. Simplicity was widely recognised as the hallmark of good letter-writing: In number 152 of *The Rambler*, Johnson wrote that "The qualities of the epistolary stile most frequently required are ease and simplicity, an even flow of unlaboured diction, and an artless arrangement of obvious sentiments. But these directions are no sooner applied to use, than their scantiness and imperfection become evident." Walpole, who had no time for Johnson and thought his style ponderous, managed to supplement those directions with wit and vivacity – his reader never knows how a letter will develop, what anecdote or aside may deflect his attention, what new subject may be opened in the next paragraph. There is of course artifice in this: but Walpole is a writer exercising his art, and the model for his art lay in the French seventeenth century, in the charm and natural good spirits of Marie de Rabutin-Chantal, Marquise de Sévigné.

Walpole adored the memory of Madame de Sévigné. Born in 1626, she was an aristocrat, orphaned as a child but well educated by her uncle, and widowed when just twenty-five after her husband was mortally wounded in a duel over his mistress. Dividing her time between Paris and his family seat at Les Rochers in Brittany, she devoted herself to her son and daughter and developed a correspondence first with her cousin, Roger de Bussy-Rabutin, and latterly with her daughter, who had married and moved to Provence. That correspondence was maintained for twenty-five years, and moves easily between the domestic and the intimate, and court and Parisian life. Her letters were copied and circulated, and the first sample of them was published within thirty years of her death.

Walpole acknowledged to Mann that "there is scarce a book in the world I love so much as her letters", and while in France in 1766 made a pilgrimage to the seat of her uncle and guardian at Livry.[20] He admired her for her wit, her delicacy of feeling, her subtlety of expression and her dramatic skill in

20 Letter to Mann, 12 September 1749 (YE 20:90): and for the visit to Livry, see letter to Montagu, 3 April 1766 (YE 10:211–12).

painting and re-creating a scene. He summarised his response to her in a letter to the historian John Pinkerton (letter 175 in this selection), in which he concludes his discussion on grace as a literary quality with this tribute:

Madame de Sévigné shines both in grief and gaiety. There is too much of sorrow for her daughter's absence; yet it is always expressed by new turns, new images, and often by wit, whose tenderness has a melancholy air. When she forgets her concern, and returns to her natural disposition – gaiety, every paragraph has novelty: her allusions, her applications are the happiest possible. She has the art of making you acquainted with all her acquaintance, and attaches you even to the spots she inhabited. Her language is correct, though unstudied; and, when her mind is full of any great event, she interests you with the warmth of a dramatic writer, not with the chilling impartiality of an historian. Pray read her accounts of the death of Turenne, and of the arrival of King James in France, and tell me whether you do not know their persons as if you had lived at the time.

Walpole held that women were the best letter-writers, as men were "too jealous of the reputation of good sense, to condescend to hazard a thousand trifles and negligences, which give grace, ease and familiarity to correspondence":[21] and among women, Madame de Sévigné was unequalled.

In the opening of this selection, the first three letters, written when he was at the University at Cambridge, show Walpole straining for effect and making liberal use of classical quotations and references. But as early as letter 6 there is a typically revealing and wry Walpolian anecdote. It was sent from Paris at the beginning of his Grand Tour, and gives an account of the lying-in-state of the former Governor of Paris, where the monks charged with watching the body "fell asleep one night, and let the tapers catch fire of the rich velvet mantle lined with ermine and powdered with gold flower-de-luces, which melted the lead coffin, and burnt off the feet of the deceased before it awakened them". The combination of the solemnity of the occasion, the human frailty of the monks, and the absurdity of the outcome appealed to Walpole, and similar

21 Letter to Lord Strafford, 11 December 1783 (YE 35:381).

follies give piquancy to his great set-pieces, such as the behaviour of the Duke of Newcastle at the burial of George II (letter 43), or the incidents that enlivened the coronation of George III (letter 46). This second letter is a fine example of Walpole's art, describing a solemn and formal event by means of a succession of *tableaux vivants*: "My Lady Harrington, covered with all the diamonds she could borrow, hire, or tease", the Duchess of Richmond, "as pretty as nature and dress, with no pains of her own, could make her", and the King's Champion, who "dashed down his gauntlet with proud defiance", but was assisted by the Lord High Steward, who "piqued himself on backing his horse down the Hall, and not turning its rump towards the King, but he had taken such pains to dress it to that duty, that it entered backwards". Walpole was always alert to the ridiculous, but in his letters (unlike his harsher political Memoirs) his tone is amused, sharply observant and witty, but neither cynical nor carping. Take for example the opening of letter 296 on the trial of John Wilkes in 1768 amid scenes of serious public unrest:

Yesterday was fixed for the appearance of Wilkes in Westminster Hall. The judges went down by nine in the morning, but the mob had done breakfast still sooner, and was there before them; and as judges stuffed out with dignity and lambskins are not absolute sprites, they had much ado to glide through the crowd.

The wit here works on ludicrous images – a mob pausing to eat breakfast in the way that judges might formally take breakfast, and the idea of elderly judges in their finery trying to accelerate through an angry rabble.

Walpole was equally sensitive to landscape and place, as illustrated in his awed account to Richard West of crossing the Alps (letter 8):

But the road, West, the road! Winding round a prodigious mountain, and surrounded with others, all shagged with hanging woods, obscured with pines, or lost in clouds! Below, a torrent breaking through cliffs, and tumbling through fragments of rocks! Sheets of cascades forcing their silver speed down channelled precipices, and hasting into the roughened river at the bottom! Now and then an old foot-bridge, with a broken rail, a leaning cross, a cottage, or the ruin of an hermitage! This sounds too bombast and too romantic to one that has not seen it, too cold for one that has.

This early letter may still have some of the mannered exaggeration of the letters written to West from Cambridge, and the phrase "silver speed" stands out as self-consciously literary, but there is no question of the directness of his vision. Ketton-Cremer noted that Walpole's response was visual and aesthetic, whereas his companion Gray reacted on a different level, sensing the landscape as pregnant with religion and poetry.[22] But Walpole still captures the thrill of the act of seeing, and imbues what he sees with the resources of an active and sensitive imagination. The same can be said of the very different landscapes of southern and central England and their old houses and churches, which he visited on tours in the summers of the 1750s and 1760s and described evocatively to Bentley and Montagu. Take for example his portrayal in letter 86 of Drayton House, the seat of the Mordaunts, which was preserved by Lady Betty Germain throughout her long widowhood, "covered with portraits, crammed with old china, furnished richly, and not a rag in it under forty, fifty, or a thousand years old; but not a bed or chair that has lost a tooth, or got a grey hair, so well they are preserved. I rummaged it from head to foot, examined every spangled bed, and enamelled pair of bellows ..." The antiquarian in him has an almost visceral response to the atmosphere of the old mansion, a sleeping house dutifully preserved and waiting to reveal its riches to Walpole's sympathetic eye.

Walpole's letters, then, offer triumphs of description, expressed in supple prose that is vivid and unpredictable, making unexpected connections and allowing the reader the illusion of participation in a witty and sophisticated conversation. But they are also an extended study in friendship, using the letter form as a medium for intimacy with a necessarily disembodied recipient, a correspondent not physically present. George Haggerty has written of the depth of affection

22 Ketton-Cremer, pp. 59–60.

apparent in the correspondences with Mann, Conway, and Chute, and even in the ostensibly less fertile ground of Walpole's antiquarian exchanges with Cole.[23] Given Walpole's lifelong separation from Mann after 1741, their relationship, as Haggerty remarks, has no existence outside the letters. The series of letters to Montagu, perhaps the most animated of any, is in a sense about friendship, and dies as the friendship that has given it life fades away. And many of these friendships – with Montagu, Chute, Mann, and Gray – are with male correspondents.

Much has been written about the nature of Walpole's relationships and his sexual orientation, and much of what has been written is not particularly illuminating. Ketton-Cremer, in his 1940 biography, was carefully discreet but not misleading to the alert reader. The great Walpole scholar and collector Wilmarth Sheldon Lewis was more troubled, and in returning a verdict of "not proven" appeared to be expressing a need for a Walpole not openly compromised as what would now be described as "gay": indeed, there is a story that he once said to George Lam, his ablest researcher, that if Walpole could be proved to have been in bed with any woman, it would be the happiest discovery that George could make.[24]

But twentieth- and twenty-first century terms and criteria are of limited help in looking back over two-and-a-half centuries. Certainly Walpole's letters to Conway, and in particular his youthful letters to Lord Lincoln (not included in this selection),[25] are emotionally charged; and most of his principal correspondents were confirmed bachelors. His separation from Gray at Reggio on their Grand Tour in 1741 has become something of a litmus test not merely of their relationship but also of Walpole's sexual identity. For all the painfully honest yet managed accounts that Walpole provided in letters 197

23 George E. Haggerty, *Horace Walpole's Letters: Masculinity and Friendship in the Eighteenth Century* (Lewisburg: Bucknell University Press), 2011.
24 Warren Hunting Smith, manuscript memoir of Wilmarth Sheldon Lewis, 1990 (unpublished). Another version of the anecdote appears in his "Horace Walpole's Correspondence", *The Yale University Library Gazette*, Volume 58, Nos. 1–2, October 1983, p. 25.
25 Walpole's letters to Lord Lincoln are contained in Volume 30 of the Yale edition of Walpole's Correspondence.

and 198, it is hard not to see their parting as a dramatic end to a charged male relationship between the socially dominant but insensitive Walpole and the socially awkward but fiercely gifted Gray. Walpole's later life, when he channelled much of his emotional life into his letters to his closest friends and was noted for the amount of time he spent entertaining local dowagers, may seem slightly desiccated: but that would understate the richness of his networks of friendship, both with his male and his female correspondents. It also fails to take into account his infatuation at the end of his life with the Berry sisters, a relationship as inevitably unconsummated as Gray's infatuation in his last years with Charles Victor de Bonstetten. Walpole, like Gray, deserves to be judged by his art, not by historically anachronistic criteria.

Alongside the celebration of friendship, Walpole's political and social commentaries can have a sharper edge, a querulousness that is particularly visible in his correspondence with the poet Mason: this is partly a reflection of Mason's rather unattractive personality, and partly because Walpole, for all his airy disavowals of authorship and its prizes, was not at his most engaging when addressing writers he admired: the letters to Voltaire and Gibbon in this collection, numbers 167, 353, and 354, provide other and more obsequious examples, and that to Gibbon can be contrasted to letter 169 to Mason, where he describes their falling out.

Then there are the letters to women. Walpole can appear gallant in his letters to Lady Ossory, in figuratively taking her hand to escort her round the London season, and passing on to her the news and gossip of the moment. With Madame du Deffand his relationship was almost filial, while his anxious letters to the Berry sisters when they were travelling in Europe in 1790–91 can seem those of a fussing parent. With the elderly dowagers whose society he enjoyed, such as Lady Hervey and Lady Suffolk, his letters express old-fashioned politeness. But where he was most emotionally engaged, the letters become a vehicle for affectionate relations (a term used by Haggerty) with long-standing friends.[26]

26 Haggerty, pp. 49–50.

After the first appearance of some of Walpole's letters in his collected *Works* of 1798, further series were published from 1818 – Cole, Montagu (both 1818), Hertford (1825), Mann (1833–44), Ossory (1848), and Mason (1851). It was as a review of the first series of letters to Mann that Thomas Macaulay wrote his famous assault on Walpole in the *Edinburgh Review* of October 1833. It was a comprehensive demolition of Walpole's character as artificial and frivolous, his affectations of sincerity hiding mask upon mask, with nothing beneath. It is a *tour de force*, and by far the most influential account of Walpole ever written. Walpole is dismissed as "the most eccentric, the most artificial, the most fastidious, the most capricious, of men". His judgement of contemporary literature was perverted by his aristocratic feelings, he did not have a creative imagination or a pure taste, nor was he a great reasoner, his work was full of contradictory judgements, and his talk of liberty was cant. He recorded gossip and fancied that he was writing history, and had the soul of a gentleman usher. As for his letters, Macaulay's view was that they were his best performances simply because his faults were less offensive there than in the rest of his writings.

Readers of these letters will not find it hard to identify some of the qualities in Walpole that Macaulay so effectively dissected. His accounts of other writers can be tainted with aristocratic hauteur: see for example in letter 150 his description of Henry Fielding at dinner, where he depicts the author of *Tom Jones* (whom he did not admire), apparently living out one of his own low-life scenes. Similarly, it is revealing to compare the three references in this selection to his parliamentary constituency of King's Lynn. When in 1760 he was asked to transfer his seat to the populous town of King's Lynn from the family-controlled borough of Castle Rising, which had made no demands whatever of its sitting member, he wrote to Montagu how he dreaded having to make an appearance of civility to the voters there, "whose favour I never asked, nor care if I have or not" (letter 42). The following year he wrote again to Montagu of the horrors of presenting himself to the voters of Lynn as their candidate, of country dances and sixpenny whist and being required to admire aldermen's copies of Rubens and Carlo Maratta and their daughters' accomplishments on the harpsichord: "how comfortable it will be tomorrow, to see my parroquet, to play at loo, and not to be obliged to talk seriously!" (letter 19). Yet his letter to the Mayor of Lynn announcing his intended withdrawal from Parliament (no. 24) is a model of the polished politeness of the courtier, shot through with respectful sensibility of the honour of the town and corporation of Lynn, and of the merely trifling services that he had been able to render them. If this seems to support Macaulay's accusations of insincerity, the second of those three letters, after lamenting (not wholly unreasonably) the demands of electioneering, adds the balancing sentence "Yet to do the folks justice, they are sensible, and reasonable, and civilised; their very language is polished since I lived among them." Even though Walpole can hardly be said to have ever lived among the electors of King's Lynn, the sentiment is sincere: Macaulay's view was only ever partial.

Meanwhile, collected editions of Walpole's letters appeared from 1820, and the final volume of the collected edition of 1840 contained Mary Berry's response to Macaulay. It was dignified, balanced, and surprisingly restrained – but it was no match for Macaulay's dazzling prose, and passed almost unnoticed. Walpole's reputation continued to suffer: *The Castle of Otranto* always remained in print, but largely as a curiosity as the first Gothic novel, while with the exception of one edition of the *Anecdotes of Painting*, none of his other works that had been published during his lifetime was reprinted between 1833, the date of Macaulay's review, and the close of the nineteenth century. His house at Strawberry Hill was viewed with disdain as hopelessly frivolous by the standards of Victorian Gothic architecture; and when his collection was sold in the great Strawberry Hill sale of 1842, having been preserved effectively untouched for forty-five years since his death, it received distinctly mixed coverage in the press. But book collectors always sought out the productions of the Strawberry Hill Press, the private press he founded at the house, and more important, his letters were always read.

Between 1857 and 1859 the first edition of the letters

with any aspirations to completeness was edited by Peter Cunningham in nine volumes. Later writers such as Austin Dobson and Leslie Stephen, sympathetic to the eighteenth century, reintroduced a new generation to Walpole, and from 1884 a number of popular selections of the letters were published. Then Mrs. Paget Toynbee produced a comprehensive edition in sixteen volumes (1903–5). That was the position when an Everyman's Library selection of the letters was first mooted, although it did not appear until 1926, when it was edited by William Hadley (who had also edited their edition of William Cowper's letters). It was original in that it ordered the letters by topic rather than simply by date, or even by correspondent, but it was taken from a superseded mid-nineteenth-century text, and virtually all the notes were copied from early- and mid-nineteenth-century editions. Although it is that selection which appears here, it has been newly annotated and introduced, with the text corrected, and with those passages that previous editors had excised as uncharitable or improper restored.

The reader can accordingly choose between Walpole on politics, or the court, or other contemporary writers, or collecting, or a range of other issues, rather than being presented with a random assembly of reflections on disparate subjects to disparate correspondents. Within the topics – say, for example, the long-running saga of John Wilkes and Liberty (letters 292 to 299) or the American War of Independence (letters 300 to 329) – the reader is given a chronological sequence in which Walpole recounts events as they unfold. This selection gives 434 letters arranged thematically: these are listed in order in Appendix A. However, about ninety per cent of them are extracts: where in one letter Walpole covered a number of topics, only the relevant part of his letter may be reprinted. Many of his letters, of course, touch on a number of different subjects, and in sixteen cases separate portions of letters appear in two different sections of the book as illustrations of different themes: the letter to Mann of 3 May 1749, for example, appears as letter 54 describing the celebrations for the peace of Aix-la-Chappelle, and as letter 402 on the increasing popularity of Methodism, while two letters appear in three locations. This is shown in Appendix B, which orders the letters chronologically by correspondent, and also enables readers if they wish to follow the course of Walpole's letters with one particular correspondent. The fact that a letter is not complete is shown in all cases by a line of dots, which may appear at the beginning or end of an extract, or in the body of a letter.

Two other selections of Walpole's letters appeared in the same year as Hadley's. One was a selection of 147 letters edited by Dorothy M. Stuart; the other was far more significant, 149 letters edited by the young Walpole collector W. S. Lewis, handsomely printed for Oxford University Press, and illustrated by items from his collection. Lewis had discovered Walpole in 1924, and he built up an extraordinary body of manuscripts, books, prints and related Walpole material that is now held at the Lewis Walpole Library of Yale University, housed at Farmington, Connecticut. In 1929 Lewis first had the idea of a complete and comprehensive edition of the letters, an edition that would print a correct text, with letters to as well as from Walpole, and annotate it fully – so the reader could hear both sides of the conversation. That edition, the *Yale Edition of Horace Walpole's Correspondence* (1937–83), became a monument of twentieth-century scholarship. It extends to forty-eight large quarto volumes, and the rich and extensive annotation together with five volumes of index (itself of over three thousand pages) have made it an indispensable encyclopedia of eighteenth-century life. To its painstaking scholarship this book – though far more limited in purpose and scale – is inevitably greatly indebted, and readers will find repeated references in the notes to points made by the Yale editors. For those who wish to explore further, Appendix A also provides for each of the letters here printed a reference to where the full letter with its detailed annotation appears in the Yale edition. Where a letter that does not appear in this selection is quoted in any of the introductory sections, its Yale edition (YE) reference is given by volume and page number.

Yale's volumes are organised by correspondent: the letters to and from Mann, for example, fill eleven volumes, with their own index. Lewis's life work transformed Walpole's status as a writer and historian, but – partly because of his diversity, partly because of his aristocratic detachment, and partly also because of the equivocal literary status of familiar letters – Walpole remains an essentially marginal figure: celebrated in the history of collecting and the Gothic Revival and antiquarianism, and without par in the social art of letter-writing, but still not the staple of university courses.

The Yale edition is incomparable, but it is not portable, and the need for a selection of the letters remains. What this edition provides is the flexibility of arrangement by topic, giving readers the opportunity to follow Walpole's particular interests and the events of the day, and in some cases enabling them to compare how he adjusted his material for different recipients.[27] Within each section the letters are printed chronologically, and it is worth bearing in mind when individual letters were written – all are dated, but there are differences of tone as the decades pass.

So what is offered is over fifty years of correspondence, presenting the eighteenth century and its personalities in all their variety. It is the view from Strawberry Hill, and expresses Walpole's preferences and prejudices, but does so in prose of enviable brilliance. It can be read as a record of his age, but it is also a more personal record of the nature of friendship. It is, as Walpole no doubt intended, a unique and invaluable resource. But perhaps the last word should be given to W. S. Lewis, Walpole's most devoted champion. In introducing his first selection of Walpole's letters in 1926, he aptly summarised them with a lightness of touch befitting both Walpole as author and himself as editor: "This prologue will not attempt to cry up the charm and importance of Horace Walpole. The most indifferent reader may discover the first at a glance. To define and analyse his importance would be to rob the more thoughtful of a gradual and unfolding pleasure."

Stephen Clarke

27 See letters 162 and 163 on Goldsmith's *She Stoops to Conquer*, letters 165 and 166 on Sheridan's *The School for Scandal*, letters 332 and 333 on the Gordon Riots, and letters 347 and 348 on the French court and a Parisian dinner.

ACKNOWLEDGMENTS

I would like to acknowledge the generous support of Jamie and Julia Korner, which has made this edition possible; the consent of the Yale University Press, with whose edition of the letters this text has been collated for errors and omissions; the assistance of the Director and staff of the Lewis Walpole Library of Yale University; and also the advice of Peter Sabor and Jim McCue.

SELECT BIBLIOGRAPHY

BIOGRAPHY

"Short Notes on the life of Horatio Walpole, youngest son of Sir Robert Walpole, Earl of Orford, and of Catherine Shorter, his first wife", in the Yale Edition of *Horace Walpole's Correspondence* [for which see below under Letters], Volume 13, pp. 1–51.

John Pinkerton, *Walpoliana* (London: R. Phillips, 1799), 2 volumes: a "lounging miscellany" that gives some impression of Walpole's conversation and opinions.

Thomas Babington Macaulay, review of *Letters of Horace Walpole ... to Sir Horace Mann, Edinburgh Review*, October 1833, vol. 58, pp. 227–58.

Austin Dobson, *Horace Walpole: A Memoir* (New York: Dodd, Mead & Company, 1890); and 2nd edition (London: James R. Osgood, McIlvaine & Co, 1893); one of the most important elements in the revival of Walpole's critical fortunes in the late 19th century.

R. W. Ketton-Cremer, *Horace Walpole: A Biography* (London: Duckworth, 1940; most recently reprinted by Cornell University Press, 1966): despite its age and reticence still the most compelling biography.

Wilmarth Sheldon Lewis, *Horace Walpole: The A. W. Mellon Lectures in Fine Arts 1960* (London: Rupert Hart-Davis, 1961). The great Walpole collector's account of Walpole and his areas of interest, written *con amore* but based on a lifetime of study.

Horace Walpole Writer, Politician, and Connoisseur: Essays on the 250th Anniversary of Walpole's Birth, ed. Warren Hunting Smith (New Haven and London: Yale University Press, 1967).

Morris Brownell, *The Prime Minister of Taste: A Portrait of Horace Walpole* (New Haven and London: Yale University Press, 2001): more than an account of Walpole as collector, an exposition of Walpole's passion for portraits and portraiture.

"Horace Walpole: Beyond the Castle of Otranto", ed. Peter Sabor, special feature in *1650–1850: Ideas, Aesthetics, and Inquiries in the Early*

HORACE WALPOLE

Modern Era, Volume 16, 2009, pp. 191–361: a selection of essays on Walpole.

WALPOLE'S CIRCLE AND CORRESPONDENTS

Brian Fothergill, *The Strawberry Hill Set: Horace Walpole and his Circle* (London: Faber & Faber, 1983).

Richard Bentley
Loftus Jestin, *The Answer to the Lyre: Richard Bentley's Illustrations for Thomas Gray's Poems* (Philadelphia: University of Pennsylvania Press, 1990).

Mary Berry
Extracts of the Journal and Correspondence of Miss Berry from the year 1783 to 1852, ed. Lady Theresa Lewis (London: Longmans, Green, and Co., 1865), 3 volumes; and Virginia Surtees, *The Grace of Friendship: Horace Walpole and the Misses Berry* (Norwich: Michael Russell, 1995).

Thomas Chatterton
E. H. W. Meyerstein, *A Life of Thomas Chatterton* (London: Ingpen & Grant, 1930).

William Cole
W. M. Palmer, *William Cole of Milton* (Cambridge: Galloway and Porter Ltd., 1935); and William Cole, *A Journal of my Journey to Paris in the Year 1765*, ed. Francis Griffin Stokes (London: Constable & Co., 1931).

Anne Damer
Richard Webb, *Mrs. D: The Life of Anne Damer* (Studley: Brewin Books, 2013).

Madame du Deffand
Benedetta Craveri, *Madame du Deffand and her World* (London: Peter Halban, 1994). For Walpole and France more generally see Rex A. Barrell, *Horace Walpole and France* (Lewiston/Queenston/Lampeter: The Edwin Mellon Press, 1991).

Thomas Gray
R. W. Ketton-Cremer, *Thomas Gray: A Biography* (Cambridge: Cambridge University Press, 1955); and Robert L. Mack, *Thomas Gray: A Life* (New Haven and London: Yale University Press, 2000).

SELECT BIBLIOGRAPHY

Sir Horace Mann

Dr. Doran, *"Mann" and Manners at the Court of Florence 1740–1786: Founded on the letters of Horace Mann to Horace Walpole* (London: Richard Bentley, 1876), 2 volumes.

William Mason

John W. Draper, *William Mason: A Study in Eighteenth-Century Culture* (New York: New York University Press, 1924).

Hannah More:

M. G. Jones, *Hannah More 1745–1833* (Cambridge: Cambridge University Press, 1952); and Anne Stott, *Hannah More: the First Victorian* (Oxford: Oxford University Press, 2003).

George Selwyn

John Heneage Jesse, *George Selwyn and his Contemporaries* (London: Richard Bentley, 1843), 4 volumes; *George Selwyn: His Letters and His Life*, ed. E. S. Roscoe and Helen Clergue (London: T. Fisher Unwin, 1899).

WALPOLE'S WORKS

Original Editions

The Lessons for the Day. Being the First and Second Chapters of the Book of Preferment (London, 1742); *The Beauties. An Epistle to Mr. Eckardt, the Painter* (London, 1746); *Ædes Walpolianæ: or, a Description of the Collection of Pictures at Houghton-Hall in Norfolk* (London, 1747); *A Letter from Xo Ho, a Chinese Philosopher at London, to his Friend Lien Chi at Peking* (London, 1757); *A Catalogue of Royal and Noble Authors of England, with Lists of their Works* (Strawberry Hill, 1758), 2 volumes; *Fugitive Pieces in Verse and Prose* (Strawberry Hill, 1758); *Anecdotes of Painting in England* (Strawberry Hill, 1762–71), 5 volumes with the *Catalogue of Engravers*; *A Counter-Address to the Public on the late Dismission of a General Officer* (London, 1764); *The Castle of Otranto* (London, 1765); *An Account of the Giants lately discovered* (London, 1766); *Historic Doubts on the Life and Reign of King Richard the Third* (London, 1768); *The Mysterious Mother* (Strawberry Hill, 1768); *A Description of the Villa of Horace Walpole ... at Strawberry-Hill* (Strawberry Hill, 1774) [further expanded edition with illustrations, 1784]; *A Letter to the Editor of the Miscellanies of Thomas Chatterton* (Strawberry Hill, 1779); *Hieroglyphic Tales* (Strawberry Hill, 1785). [For Walpole's Letters and Memoirs, see below.]

Later Editions
The Castle of Otranto has been endlessly reprinted, one recent edition being edited by Nick Groom for Oxford World Classics (Oxford, 2014).

The Mysterious Mother and *Hieroglyphic Tales* were both printed in tiny numbers at Strawberry Hill: recent editions include *The Mysterious Mother*, ed. Frederick S. Frank (Peterborough: Broadway Press, 2002), and *Hieroglyphic Tales*, ed. Kenneth Gross (London: Pallas Athene, 2011).

Reminiscences Written by Mr. Horace Walpole in 1788 for the Amusement of Miss Mary and Miss Agnes Berry, first published in Volume IV of Walpole's *Works* (1798), was reprinted in an edition by Paget Toynbee (Oxford: Clarendon Press, 1924).

There were various 19th-century editions of the *Royal and Noble Authors* and the *Anecdotes of Painting*. These include *A Catalogue of the Royal and Noble Authors of England, Scotland, and Ireland*, ed. Thomas Park (London, 1806), 5 volumes, and *Anecdotes of Painting in England*, ed. the Rev. James Dallaway (London, 1828), 5 volumes.

"Horace Walpole's Journals of Visits to Country Seats", ed. Paget Toynbee, *Walpole Society*, Volume 16, 1927–8, pp. 8–80.

A further volume of Walpoles's notes on artists was edited by Frederick W. Hilles and Philip B. Daghlian under the title *Anecdotes of Painting in England (1760–1795) ... Volume the Fifth and Last* (New Haven and London: Yale University Press, 1937).

A finely produced facsimile of Charles Bedford's extra-illustrated copy of the *Description* of Strawberry Hill was edited by Nicolas Barker for the Roxburghe Club in 2010. There is also a working facsimile of the version of the *Description* as reprinted in the collected *Works* of 1798 (London: Pallas Athene, 2015).

For a general critical assessment of Walpole's writings see *Horace Walpole: The Critical Heritage*, ed. Peter Sabor (London and New York: Routledge & Kegan Paul, 1987).

Collected Works
The Works of Horatio Walpole, Earl of Orford (London, 1798), 5 volumes. Reprinted edition, ed. Peter Sabor (London: Pickering & Chatto, 1999), 5 volumes.

SELECT BIBLIOGRAPHY

LETTERS

Individual Correspondences

Walpole's letters to Richard West, Henry Conway, Richard Bentley, Thomas Gray, John Chute, the Earl of Strafford, Lady Hervey, the Countess of Ailesbury, and Hannah More were first published in Volumes IV and V of Walpole's *Works* (1798). Individual correspondences were then published as follows: *Letters from the Hon. Horace Walpole to George Montagu, Esq.*, ed. John Martin (London, 1818); *Letters from the Hon. Horace Walpole to the Rev. William Cole, and others*, ed. John Martin (London, 1818); *Letters from the Hon. Horace Walpole to the Earl of Hertford ... to which are added Mr. Walpole's Letters to the Rev. Henry Zouch*, ed. John Wilson Croker (London, 1825); *Letters of Horace Walpole ... to Sir Horace Mann*, ed. Lord Dover (London, 1833), 3 volumes; *Letters to Sir Horace Mann ... Concluding Series* (London, 1843–4), 4 volumes; *Letters addressed to the Countess of Ossory*, ed. R. Vernon Smith (London, 1848), 2 volumes; *The Correspondence of Horace Walpole ... with the Rev. William Mason*, ed. the Rev. J. Mitford (London, 1851), 2 volumes.

Collected Editions

Private Correspondence of Horace Walpole, Earl of Orford. Now first Collected (London, 1820), 4 volumes; *Correspondence of Horace Walpole with George Montagu* [and others] (London, 1837), 3 volumes; *The Letters of Horace Walpole, Earl of Orford: including numerous letters now first published from the Original Manuscripts*, ed. John Wright (London, 1840), 6 volumes; *The Letters of Horace Walpole, Earl of Orford ... now first Chronologically Arranged*, ed. Peter Cunningham (London, 1857–9), 9 volumes; *The Letters of Horace Walpole Fourth Earl of Orford Chronologically Arranged*, ed. Mrs. Paget Toynbee (Oxford: Clarendon Press, 1903–5), 16 volumes, with three supplemental volumes ed. Paget Toynbee, 1918–25.

All these are superseded by the Yale Edition of *Horace Walpole's Correspondence*, ed. W. S. Lewis (New Haven and London: Yale University Press, 1937–83), 48 volumes.

For a recent reading of the Letters see George E. Haggerty, *Horace Walpole's Letters: Masculinity and Friendship in the Eighteenth Century* (Lewisburg: Bucknell University Press, 2011).

HORACE WALPOLE

POLITICAL MEMOIRS

Original Editions
Memoires of the last ten years of the Reign of George the Second, ed. Lord Holland (London, 1822), 2 volumes; *Memoirs of the Reign of King George the Third*, ed. Sir Denis Le Marchant (London, 1845), 2 volumes; *Journal of the reign of King George the Third, from the year 1771 to 1783*, ed. Dr. Doran (London: 1859), 2 volumes.

Recent Editions
Memoirs of King George II, ed. John Brooke (New Haven and London: Yale University Press, 1985), 3 volumes; *Memoirs of the Reign of King George III*, ed. Derek Jarrett (New Haven and London: Yale University Press, 2000), 4 volumes.

STRAWBERRY HILL: THE HOUSE AND GROUNDS

Paget Toynbee, ed., *Strawberry Hill Accounts: A Record of Expenditure in Building, Furnishing, &c. Kept by Mr. Horace Walpole from 1747 to 1795* (Oxford: Clarendon Press, 1927).

W. S. Lewis, "The Genesis of Strawberry Hill", *Metropolitan Museum Studies*, Volume V, Part 1, June 1934, pp. 57–92.

Michael McCarthy, *The Origins of the Gothic Revival* (New Haven and London: Yale University Press, 1987), pp. 63–91.

Peter Guillery and Michael Snodin, "Strawberry Hill: Building and Site", *Architectural History*, Volume 38, 1995, pp. 102–28.

Anna Chalcraft and Judith Viscardi, *Strawberry Hill: Horace Walpole's Gothic Castle* (London: Frances Lincoln, 2007).

Marion Harney, *Place-Making for the Imagination: Horace Walpole and Strawberry Hill* (Farnham: Ashgate, 2013).

Peter Lindfield, *Georgian Gothic: Medievalist Architecture, Furniture and Interiors, 1730–1840* (Woodbridge: Boydell & Brewer, 2016).

Country Life articles: J. Mordaunt Crook, "Strawberry Hill Revisited", 1973, pp. 1598–1602, 1726–30, 1794–7; Tim Knox, "Strawberry Hill Twickenham", August 12, 2004, pp. 34–9; Roger White, "True Gothic Taste: Strawberry Hill, Twickenham", March 21, 2012, pp. 50–55.

SELECT BIBLIOGRAPHY

Isabel Wakelin Urban Chase, *Horace Walpole: Gardenist, An Edition of Walpole's* The History of the Modern Taste in Gardening *with an* Estimate of Walpole's Contribution to Landscape Architecture (Princeton: Princeton University Press, 1943).

Mavis Batey, "Horace Walpole as Modern Garden Historian", *Garden History*, 19:1, Spring 1991, pp. 1–11.

STRAWBERRY HILL: THE COLLECTION

The foundation of all studies of Walpole's collection lies in two books, Walpole's *Description* of Strawberry Hill [see under Walpole's Works above] and the Catalogue for the sale of his collection, *A Catalogue of the Classic Contents of Strawberry Hill collected by Horace Walpole* (George Robins, 1842).

Horace Walpole's Strawberry Hill, ed. Michael Snodin (New Haven and London: Yale University Press, 2009). This is the catalogue with supporting essays for the exhibition held at the Yale Center for British Art and the Victoria and Albert Museum in 2009–10 and is the best modern overview of Walpole's collection.

Clive Wainwright, *The Romantic Interior: the British Collector at Home 1750–1850* (New Haven and London: Yale University Press, 1989), pp. 70–107.

Anna Eavis and Michael Peover, "Horace Walpole's painted glass at Strawberry Hill", *The Journal of Stained Glass*, Volume 19, no. 3, 1994–5, pp. 280–313.

STRAWBERRY HILL PRESS

Journal of the Printing Office at Strawberry Hill, ed. Paget Toynbee (London: Constable & Co. and Boston: Houghton Mifflin Company, 1923).

Stephen Clarke, *The Strawberry Hill Press & Its Printing House* (New Haven: The Lewis Walpole Library, 2011).

[See under Bibliography for Hazen's Bibliography of the Press.]

HORACE WALPOLE

WALPOLE'S LIBRARY

Wilmarth Sheldon Lewis, *Horace Walpole's Library* (Cambridge: Cambridge University Press, 1958).

Allen T. Hazen, *A Catalogue of Horace Walpole's Library* (New Haven and London: Yale University Press, 1969), 3 volumes.

MISCELLANEOUS ANTIQUITIES

Miscellaneous Antiquities; or, a Collection of Curious Papers, Numbers I and II, ed. Horace Walpole (Strawberry Hill, 1772). The series was revived by W. S. Lewis in 1927, and he produced Numbers III to XVI between 1927 and 1940 as a series of keepsakes and short volumes, with print runs varying from 50 to 500 copies. It was revived again by the Lewis Walpole Library in 2004, and as at 2016 the most recent volume is Number XIX.

W. S. LEWIS

Wilmarth Lewis, *Collector's Progress* (New York: Alfred A. Knopf, 1951): a particularly fresh and engaging account of his Walpole collection.

Wilmarth S. Lewis, "Horace Walpole, Antiquary", *Essays presented to Sir Lewis Namier*, ed. Richard Pares and A. J. P. Taylor (London: Macmillan & Co., 1956), pp. 178–203: the best account of Walpole as antiquary.

Wilmarth Sheldon Lewis, *One Man's Education* (New York; Alfred A. Knopf, 1967): a more general autobiography, but without the lightness of touch of *Collector's Progress*.

Wilmarth S. Lewis, *Rescuing Horace Walpole* (New Haven: Yale University Press, 1978): an illuminating account of the highlights of his collection, if written with the indulgence of age.

SELECT BIBLIOGRAPHY

BIBLIOGRAPHY

A. T. Hazen, *A Bibliography of Horace Walpole* (Folkestone and London, Dawsons of Pall Mall, reprinted 1973).

A. T. Hazen, *A Bibliography of the Strawberry Hill Press* (Folkestone and London, Dawsons of Pall Mall, reprinted 1973).

Horace Walpole: A Reference Guide, ed. Peter Sabor (Boston: G. K. Hall & Co., 1984).

CHRONOLOGY

DATE	AUTHOR'S LIFE	LITERARY CONTEXT
1717	Walpole born in Arlington Street, Mayfair, 24 September.	
1718		
1720		
1721		
1724		
1725		Lord Burlington's Chiswick House erected (to 1729).
1726		Swift: *Gulliver's Travels*.
1727	Enters Eton College: "Quadruple Alliance" of Walpole, Thomas Gray, Richard West, and Thomas Ashton.	
1728		Gay: *The Beggar's Opera*. Pope: *The Dunciad*.
1731		Pope: *Moral Essays* (to 1735). Hogarth: *A Harlot's Progress*.
1733		Pope: *Essay on Man* (to 1734).
1734		Society of Dilettanti founded. Construction of Holkham Hall commences to design of William Kent. Voltaire: *Lettres philosophiques*.
1735	Enters King's College, Cambridge.	Hogarth: *A Rake's Progress*.
1737	Death of his mother.	
1738	His father Sir Robert Walpole marries Maria Skerrett (who dies later that year).	Johnson: *London*. Bolingbroke: *The Idea of a Patriot King*.
1739	Leaves on the Grand Tour, accompanied by Gray, staying in Paris and Rheims and in December reaching Florence; meets Horace Mann.	Hume: *A Treatise of Human Nature* (to 1740). Foundling Hospital created.
1740	In Rome and Naples, returning to Florence.	Richardson: *Pamela* (to 1741).
1741	Leaves Florence for Venice; rupture with Gray at Reggio;	London debut of David Garrick.

Walpole's father Robert Walpole resigns as Chancellor of the Exchequer.

Quadruple Alliance and war with Spain.
Treaty of the Hague concludes War of the Quadruple Alliance.
South Sea Bubble.
Robert Walpole returns to power, becoming effectively prime minister until 1742.

Robert Walpole is made a Knight of the Bath, and a Knight of the Garter in 1726.

Death of George I; accession of George II. Britain at war with Spain until 1729.

Excise crisis shakes Walpole's administration.

Death of Queen Caroline.
John Wesley experiences spiritual rebirth: origins of Methodism.

War of Jenkins' Ear with Spain.

War of the Austrian Succession (to 1748).

DATE	AUTHOR'S LIFE	LITERARY CONTEXT
1741 *cont.*	illness at Reggio, then visits Venice and returns to London in September. Elected M.P. for Callington.	"Capability" Brown begins his career at Stowe.
1742	*Letters for the Day*, Walpole's first publication.	Fielding: *Joseph Andrews.*
1743		First London performance of Handel's *Messiah.* Hogarth: *Marriage A-la-Mode.*
1745 1746	Death of Sir Robert Walpole.	
1747	*Ædes Walpolianæ.* Walpole rents Strawberry Hill.	Johnson: *The Plan of a Dictionary.* Richardson: *Clarissa* (to 1748).
1748		Smollett: *Roderick Random.* Gray: "Ode on the Death of a Favourite Cat ..." Montesquieu: *De l'esprit des lois.*
1749	Acquires freehold of Strawberry Hill and subsequently expands estate.	Johnson: *The Vanity of Human Wishes.* Fielding: *Tom Jones.*
1750		Johnson's *Rambler* (to 1752). Rousseau: *Discours sur les sciences et les arts.*
1751	Begins *Memoirs of the Reign of King George II.* Death of his brother Robert; his nephew George becomes 3rd Earl of Orford.	Gray: *Elegy Written in a Country Church-Yard.* First volume of the French *Encyclopédie*, ed. Diderot (to 1772). Voltaire: *Le Siècle de Louis XIV.*
1752	Original cottages at Strawberry Hill, re-cased and hall and staircase and rooms leading off them created (to 1753).	
1753	Arranges for publication of six poems by Gray illustrated by Richard Bentley.	Richardson: *Sir Charles Grandison* (to 1754). Wood and Dawkins: *The Ruins of Palmyra.*
1754	Great Parlour and Library added to Strawberry Hill. M.P. for Castle Rising	
1755 1756		Johnson: *Dictionary.*

CHRONOLOGY

Fall of Sir Robert Walpole, created Earl of Orford. Opening of Ranelagh Gardens.
Henry Pelham prime minister (to 1754). Battle of Dettingen.

Battle of Fontenoy. Jacobite rebellion and battle of Prestonpans.
Battle of Culloden crushes Jacobite rebellion. Trial and execution of the rebel Lords Balmarino and Kilmarnock.

Treaty of Aix-la-Chappelle.

Opening of Westminster Bridge.

Death of Frederick, Prince of Wales.

Gregorian calendar adopted: eleven days "lost".

Lord Hardwicke's Marriage Act to prevent clandestine marriages.

Duke of Newcastle prime minister (other than for eight months during 1756–7) until 1762.

Seven Years' War. Battle of Minorca.

DATE	AUTHOR'S LIFE	LITERARY CONTEXT
1757	Printing Office built and opens with publication of Gray's *Odes*. *A Letter from Xo Ho*. M.P. for King's Lynn.	Burke: *A Philosophical Enquiry . . . into the Sublime and Beautiful*.
1758	Little Cloister and Holbein Chamber added to Strawberry Hill. *Catalogue of Royal and Noble Authors* and *Fugitive Pieces* printed at Strawberry Hill Press.	
1759	Marriage of his niece Maria to Lord Waldegrave (who dies in 1763).	Voltaire: *Candide*. Johnson: *Rasselas*. Sterne: *Tristram Shandy* (to 1767). British Museum (est. 1753) opens at Montagu House.
1760	Great Cloister, Gallery, Round Tower and Tribune added to Strawberry Hill (to 1763).	Macpherson: *Fragments of Ancient Poetry* [Ossian].
1761		
1762	*The Anecdotes of Painting* (to 1771).	Stuart and Revett: *Antiquities of Athens*. Rousseau: *Du contrat social*; *Emile*.
1763		Boswell meets Johnson in Thomas Davies's bookshop.
1764	Dismissal of Henry Conway from court and his regiment. *A Counter-Address to the Public on the late Dismission of a General Officer*. *The Castle of Otranto*.	
1765	Visits Paris and meets Madame du Deffand. Spends time with William Cole there.	Percy: *Reliques of Ancient English Poetry*.
1766	Probable date of beginning of *Memoirs of the Reign of King George III*.	Goldsmith: *The Vicar of Wakefield*.
1768	Retires from Parliament. *Historic Doubts on the Life and Reign of King Richard III*. *The Mysterious Mother* printed at Strawberry Hill.	Boswell: *An Account of Corsica*. Royal Academy founded.
1769	Correspondence with Thomas Chatterton.	Garrick's Shakespeare Jubilee at Stratford. First Royal Academy exhibition.

CHRONOLOGY

Court martial and execution of Admiral Byng. William Pitt Secretary of State. Clive's victory at battle of Plassey.

The Year of Victories: battle of Minden (followed by court martial of Lord George Sackville); naval battles of Lagos, Quiberon Bay and Pondicherry; capture of Guadaloupe and Quebec.

Death of George II; accession of George III.

Resignation of Pitt; Lord Bute appointed Secretary of State. *The North Briton* founded by John Wilkes. Resignation of Newcastle; Bute prime minister. The Cock Lane Ghost.

Treaty of Paris concludes Seven Years' War. George Grenville prime minister. *North Briton* No. 45 published. Wilkes arrested under general warrant and released; flees to France.
Wilkes expelled from the House of Commons and outlawed.

Passing of the Stamp Act. The Marquis of Rockingham prime minister.

Repeal of the Stamp Act. William Pitt, now Earl of Chatham, prime minister.

The Duke of Grafton prime minister. Wilkes returns to England, elected M.P. for Middlesex, imprisoned (to 1770).

Wilkes expelled from the House of Commons and re-elected three times.

DATE	AUTHOR'S LIFE	LITERARY CONTEXT
1770	Great North Bedchamber added to Strawberry Hill (to 1772).	Death of Chatterton.
1771	Death of Thomas Gray.	
1772	His niece Maria, Lady Waldegrave, marries the Duke of Gloucester. Resigns from Society of Antiquaries. Chapel in the Woods added to Strawberry Hill (to 1774).	Junius: *Letters*.
1773	First attack of insanity of Lord Orford; Walpole manages his affairs until 1774.	Goldsmith: *She Stoops to Conquer*. Robert and James Adam: *Works in Architecture* (to 1779).
1774	*Description . . . of Strawberry-Hill* printed at the Strawberry Hill Press.	Warton: *The History of English Poetry* (to 1781). Chesterfield: *Letters*. Decision of Donaldson v. Beckett: House of Lords rejects common law copyright and upholds limited copyright by statute.
1775	Last visit to Paris.	The Poems and Memoirs of Gray, ed. William Mason. Johnson: *A Journey to the Western Islands of Scotland*. Sarah Siddons's debut at Drury Lane. Beaumarchais: *Le Barbier de Séville*. Sheridan: *The Rivals*.
1776	Beauclerk Tower added to Strawberry Hill.	Gibbon: *Decline and Fall of the Roman Empire* (to 1788). Smith: *The Wealth of Nations*.
1777	Second attack of insanity of Lord Orford (to 1778).	Sheridan: *The School for Scandal*. Chatterton's Rowley poems.
1778	*A Letter to the Editor of the Miscellanies of Thomas Chatterton* printed at the Strawberry Hill Press (the Chatterton controversy lasts from 1777 to 1782).	Burney: *Evelina*.
1779	Moves from Arlington Street to Berkeley Square. Sale of the Houghton pictures by his nephew to Catherine the Great.	Johnson: *Lives of the Poets* (to 1781). Death of Garrick.

HISTORICAL EVENTS

Lord North prime minister.

Captain Cook completes his circumnavigation.
Opening of the Pantheon.

Boston Tea Party. Warren Hastings Governor-General of India.

Coercive Acts. Death of Louis XV; accession of Louis XVI.

American Revolutionary War.

American Declaration of Independence.

Battle of Saratoga.

France enters war on the side of the American colonists. Death of Chatham.
Catholic Relief Act.

Spain enters war. Siege of Gibraltar.

DATE	AUTHOR'S LIFE	LITERARY CONTEXT
1780	Death of Madame du Deffand: Walpole inherits her papers and her dog Tonton.	First exhibition of Royal Academy at Somerset House.
1781		
1782		Burney: *Cecilia*. Rousseau: *Confessions* (to 1789).
1783		Crabbe: *The Village*.
1784	Expanded and illustrated edition of the *Description . . . of Strawberry-Hill* printed at the Strawberry Hill Press.	
1785	*Hieroglyphic Tales* printed at Strawberry Hill Press.	Boswell: *The Journal of a Tour to the Hebrides*. Cowper: *The Task*.
1786		Beckford: *Vathek*.
1787	Meets Mary and Agnes Berry.	
1788		
1789		Darwin: *The Loves of the Plants*. White: *The Natural History and Antiquities of Selborne*.
1790	The Berry sisters depart for Italy (returning in 1791).	Burke: *Reflections on the Revolution in France*.
1791	Death of his nephew George: Walpole becomes 4th Earl of Orford.	Boswell: *Life of Johnson*. Paine: *Rights of Man* (part 1).
1792		Wollstonecraft: *A Vindication of the Rights of Woman*. Gilpin: *Three Essays on the Picturesque*.
1793		Godwin: *Political Justice*.
1794		Radcliffe: *The Mysteries of Udolpho*.
1795		
1796		Lewis: *The Monk*. Burney: *Camilla*.
1797	Dies at Berkeley Square, 2 March.	Radcliffe: *The Italian*.
1798	Publication of Walpole's *Works*, edited by Mary Berry.	Wordsworth and Coleridge: *Lyrical Ballads*.

HISTORICAL EVENTS

Petitioning movement calls for economical reform (reforms to limit government patronage). Gordon Riots. Major John André hung as a spy.

Surrender at Yorktown. Herschel discovers Uranus.
North resigns; Rockingham becomes prime minister, succeeded on his death by the Earl of Shelburne. Burke's Civil Establishments Act. Battle of the Saintes.
Fox–North coalition. Siege of Gibraltar lifted. Peace of Paris concludes the American Revolutionary War. William Pitt the Younger becomes prime minister.

Society for Effecting the Abolition of the Slave Trade founded by Thomas Clarkson and Granville Sharp.
Trial of Warren Hastings (to 1795). George III suffers first bout of insanity; regency crisis.
French Revolution begins. Storming of the Bastille. Washington first President of the United States.

Civil constitution of the clergy in France. Abolition of nobility and titles.

The flight of Louis XVI to Varennes. Constitution of 1791. Wilberforce's motion to abolish slave trade defeated.

France at war with Prussia and Austria. September massacre of royalists. Abolition of monarchy.

Execution of Louis XVI. France declares war on Britain, Holland and Spain. Jacobins seize power; the Terror. Execution of Marie Antoinette.
Execution of Robespierre. Suspension of habeas corpus in Britain (to 1795).

Seditious Meetings and Treasonable Practices Act.
Abortive French invasion of Ireland. Napoleon overruns Italy.

Naval battles of Cape St. Vincent and Camperdown. Mutinies at Spithead and the Nore.
Rebellion in Ireland.

SELECTED LETTERS
OF HORACE WALPOLE

I
BOYHOOD AND THE GRAND TOUR

H ORACE WALPOLE WAS born on 24 September 1717 in
Arlington Street, London, youngest child of Robert Walpole,
the statesman, and his first wife Catherine Shorter.[1] The Walpoles
were Norfolk gentry, while Catherine came from a family of merchants – her grandfather had been Lord Mayor of London – with
aristocratic connections through her mother. Walpole was always
known as Horace ("Horry" to his friends) but he was christened
Horatio after his father's brother. His father became First Lord of
the Treasury (effectively prime minister) in April 1721 when Horace
was three and secured a knighthood in 1725; he remained in office
for twenty-one years.

Walpole was largely brought up by his mother – his parents led
separate lives and the attentions of his rather distant and increasingly
powerful father were diverted by his mistress, Maria Skerrett, who
lived with him openly at Richmond and in Norfolk. At the age of
nine he was sent to Eton, where he formed the "Quadruple Alliance"
with Thomas Gray, the poet; Richard West, another promising poet
who died young; and Thomas Ashton who took clerical orders and
became a Fellow of Eton. There was also a "Triumvirate" of Walpole, Charles Lyttelton, the future Bishop of Carlisle, and the
charming but ineffectual George Montagu, and lifelong friendships
with his cousins Henry and Francis Conway, the antiquarian
William Cole and the wit and gambler George Selwyn. Walpole
acknowledged himself as "never quite a schoolboy", unmoved by "an
expedition against bargemen, or a match at cricket".

1 A rumour that Walpole was in fact the son of Carr, Lord Hervey, was circulated
by Lady Louisa Stuart forty years after Walpole's death, in the Introductory Anecdotes to Lord Wharncliffe's edition of the *Letters and Works* of Lady Mary Wortley
Montagu (London, 1837). It is however unsupported by evidence and generally
believed to be malicious. Carr had died in 1723, "utterly ruind both in reputation and
fortune" according to his stepmother Lady Bristol [quoted in Robert Halsband, *Lord
Hervey: Eighteenth-Century Courtier* (Oxford, 1973), p. 51].

He went up to King's College, Cambridge in 1735, where little is known of his studies beyond the dismissive remarks of his professor of mathematics. He came under the influence of the theologian Conyers Middleton, acquiring his religious scepticism and later his collection of antiquities. In 1737 Walpole's mother died and six months later his father married his mistress. However, the second Lady Walpole died in childbirth only a few months later.

Walpole had been provided for by his father with several lucrative government sinecures for life. In the spring of 1739 he embarked on a Grand Tour, taking with him Thomas Gray, whose social circumstances were considerably more modest than his. The pair spent two months in Paris and a further three in Rheims. After travelling south through Dijon to Lyons, they received a letter from Sir Robert proposing that they extend their tour to Italy. They then made a detour to Geneva where they left Henry Conway (who had joined them in Paris), taking in the Grand Chartreuse en route. Walpole was unimpressed by the famous monastery but both he and Gray rhapsodised over the grandeur of the mountain scenery (letter 8).

Crossing the Alps into Italy (not without one exciting incident, see letter 9), they visited Turin, Genoa and Bologna and proceeded to Florence, where they arrived in December. During his stay in Florence Walpole threw himself into all the distractions of the city's carnival seasons, emerging as *cicisbeo* to the beautiful Signora Elisabetta Grifoni (an ambiguous role which might involve a sexual or a platonic relationship). He also made two important and lasting friendships, with Horace Mann, the British Resident, to whom over forty-six years he would write probably his greatest series of letters, and John Chute, an amateur architect who was to contribute significantly to the design of Strawberry Hill. From March 1740 he and Gray were in Rome for the papal election, though Gray's commitment to inspecting classical antiquities and works of art continued to be greater than Walpole's. After an excursion to Naples they returned in July to Florence, staying with Mann at the Casa Manetti, his house overlooking the Arno. They finally left in April 1741, travelling north towards Venice: but at Reggio they had a furious argument and separated.

A quarrel between two such ill-sorted travelling companions was perhaps inevitable. Walpole's own later account of it (letters 197 and 198) takes much of the blame. During their journey the pleasure-loving prime minister's son was everywhere courted and fêted; he was perhaps too emotionally detached to appreciate the financial and emotional dependence of the introspective Gray. After Gray left Reggio, Walpole fell seriously ill but was saved by the efforts of the literary scholar Joseph Spence, travelling in Italy as tutor to the Earl of Lincoln (a former school friend to whom the young Walpole wrote extravagantly affectionate letters). He then moved on to Venice, where he stayed with Chute. In July he left Venice in the company of Spence and Lincoln, returning to London by September. Gray returned to England alone save for one servant.

1. *College Professors.*

TO RICHARD WEST, ESQ.[1]

Dear West, King's College, 9 November 1735.

You expect a long letter from me, and have said in verse all that I intended to have said in far inferior prose. I intended filling three or four sides with exclamations against a University life; but you have showed me how strongly they may be expressed in three or four lines. I can't build without straw; nor have I the ingenuity of the spider, to spin fine lines out of dirt: a master of a college would make but a miserable figure as a hero of a poem, and Cambridge sophs are too low to introduce into a letter that aims not at punning:

> Haud equidem invideo vati, quem pulpita pascunt.[2]

But why mayn't we hold a classical correspondence? I can never forget the many agreeable hours we have passed in reading Horace and Virgil; and I think they are topics will never grow stale. Let us extend the Roman empire, and cultivate two barbarous towns o'er-run with rusticity and mathematics. The creatures are so used to a circle, that they plod on in the same eternal round, with their whole view confined to a *punctum, cujus nulla est pars:*

> Their time a moment, and a point their space.

> Orabunt causas melius, cœlique meatus
> Describent radio, et surgentia sidera dicent:

1 Richard West (1716–42), poet, son of the Lord Chancellor of Ireland. He was a close friend of Walpole at Eton, but died prematurely.
2 Broadly, "I cannot begrudge a poet who earns his living from the playhouse."

Tu coluisse novem musas, Romane, memento;
Hæ tibi erunt artes. . . .[1]

We have not the least poetry stirring here; for I can't call verses on the 5th of November and 30th of January[2] by that name, more than four lines on a chapter in the New Testament is an epigram. Tydeus[3] [Walpole himself] rose and set at Eton: he is only known here to be a scholar of King's. Orosmades [Gray] and Almanzor [West] are just the same; that is, I am almost the only person they are acquainted with, and consequently the only person acquainted with their excellencies. Plato [Ashton][4] improves every day; so does my friendship with him. These three divide my whole time, though I believe you will guess there is no quadruple alliance;[5] that was a happiness which I only enjoyed when you was at Eton. A short account of the Eton people at Oxford would much oblige,

My dear West, your faithful friend,

H. Walpole.

2. Eton.

TO GEORGE MONTAGU, ESQ.[6]

King's College, 6 May 1736.

Dear George,

I agree with you entirely in the pleasure you take in talking over old stories, but can't say but I meet every day with new circumstances, which will be still more pleasure to me to recollect. I think at our age 'tis excess of joy, to think, while we are running over past happinesses, that it is still in our power to enjoy as great. Narrations of the greatest actions of other people are tedious in comparison of

1 From Virgil, *Æneid* VI. 849–52, on the potential achievements and responsibilities of future Romans.
2 Guy Fawkes' day and the anniversary of the execution of Charles I, both marked by ceremonies at Cambridge.
3 Tydeus [Walpole], Orosmades [Gray], Almanzor [West] and Plato [Ashton] were names which had been given to them by some of their Eton schoolfellows. – BERRY.
4 Thomas Ashton (bap. 1715–75), later rector of St. Botolph, Bishopsgate and a Fellow of Eton. He and Walpole, to whom he owed much of his advancement, fell out in 1750.
5 Thus as boys they had called the intimacy formed at Eton between Walpole, Gray, West and Ashton – BERRY.
6 See heading to letter 203.

the serious trifles that every man can call to mind of himself while he was learning those histories. Youthful passages of life are the chippings of Pitt's diamond,[1] set into little heart-rings with mottos; the stone itself more worth, the filings more gentle and agreeable. – Alexander, at the head of the world, never tasted the true pleasure that boys of his own age have enjoyed at the head of a school. Little intrigues, little schemes, and policies engage their thoughts; and, at the same time that they are laying the foundation for their middle age of life, the mimic republic they live in furnishes materials of conversation for their latter age; and old men cannot be said to be children a second time with greater truth from any one cause, than their living over again their childhood in imagination. To reflect on the season when first they felt the titillation of love, the budding passions, and the first dear object of their wishes! how unexperienced they gave credit to all the tales of romantic loves! Dear George, were not the playing fields at Eton food for all manner of flights? No old maid's gown, though it had been tormented into all the fashions from King James to King George, ever underwent so many transformations as those poor plains have in my idea. At first I was contented with tending a visionary flock, and sighing some pastoral name to the echo of the cascade under the bridge. How happy should I have been, to have had a kingdom only for the pleasure of being driven from it, and living disguised in an humble vale! As I got further into Virgil and Clelia, I found myself transported from Arcadia to the garden of Italy; and saw Windsor Castle in no other view than the *Capitoli immobile saxum.*[2] I wish a committee of the House of Commons may ever seem to be the senate; or a bill appear half so agreeable as a billet-doux. You see how deep you have carried me into old stories; I write of them with pleasure, but shall talk of them with more to you. I can't say I am sorry I was never quite a schoolboy: an expedition against bargemen, or a match at cricket, may be very pretty things to recollect; but, thank my stars, I can remember things that are very near as pretty. The beginning of my Roman history was spent in the asylum, or conversing in Egeria's hallowed grove; not in thumping and pummelling king Amulius's herdsmen. I was

1   The Pitt diamond was purchased in India for £20,000 by Thomas Pitt (1653–1726), grandfather of Lord Chatham, and sold by him to the Duc d'Orléans for £125,000. Chippings from it were valued at some thousands of pounds.
2   Virgil, *Æneid* IX. 448: the Capitol's immobile stone.

sometimes troubled with a rough creature or two from the plough; one, that one should have thought, had worked with his head, as well as his hands, they were both so callous. One of the most agreeable circumstances I can recollect is the Triumvirate, composed of yourself, Charles,[1] and

Your sincere friend.

3. *School and College.*

TO RICHARD WEST, ESQ.

King's College, 17 August 1736.

Dear West,

Gray is at Burnham, and, what is surprising, has not been at Eton. Could you live so near it without seeing it? That dear scene of our quadruple-alliance would furnish me with the most agreeable recollections. 'Tis the head of our genealogical table, that is since sprouted out into the two branches of Oxford and Cambridge. You seem to be the eldest son, by having got a whole inheritance to yourself; while the manor of Granta is to be divided between your three younger brothers, Thomas of Lancashire [Ashton], Thomas of London [Gray the poet] and Horace. We don't wish you dead to enjoy your seat, but your seat dead to enjoy you. I hope you are a mere elder brother, and live upon what your father left you, and in the way you were brought up in, poetry: but we are supposed to betake ourselves to some trade, as logic, philosophy, or mathematics. If I should prove a mere younger brother, and not turn to any profession, would you receive me, and supply me out of your stock, where you have such plenty? I have been so used to the delicate food of Parnassus, that I can never condescend to apply to the grosser studies of Alma Mater. Sober cloth of syllogism colour suits me ill; or, what's worse, I hate clothes that one must prove to be of no colour at all. If the Muses *cœlique vias et sidera monstrent*, and *quâ vi maria alta tumescant*;[2] why *accipiant:* but 'tis thrashing, to study philosophy in the abstruse authors. I am not against cultivating these studies, as they are certainly useful; but then they quite neglect all polite literature, all knowledge of this world. Indeed, such people have not much

<hr>

1 Charles Lyttelton (1714–68), later Bishop of Carlisle.
2 Virgil, *Georgics* II. 475–80: show Heaven's way and the stars, and what powers swell the deep seas.

occasion for this latter; for they shut themselves up from it, and study till they know less than any one. Great mathematicians have been of great use; but the generality of them are quite unconversible: they frequent the stars, *sub pedibusque vident nubes*,[1] but they can't see through them. I tell you what I see; that by living amongst them, I write of nothing else: my letters are all parallelograms, two sides equal to two sides; and every paragraph an axiom, that tells you nothing but what every mortal almost knows. By the way, your letters come under this description; for they contain nothing but what almost every mortal knows too, that knows you – that is, they are extremely agreeable, which they know you are capable of making them: – no one is better acquainted with it than

Your sincere friend.

4. *Ignorance of Mathematics.*

TO SIR HORACE MANN[2]

Arlington Street, 13 December 1759.

That ever you should pitch upon me for a mechanic or geometric commission! How my own ignorance has laughed at me since I read your letter! I say, *your* letter, for as to Dr. Perelli's, I know no more of a Latin term in mathematics than Mrs. Goldsworthy had an idea of verbs.[3] I will tell you an early anecdote in my own life, and you shall judge. When I first went to Cambridge, I was to learn mathematics of the famous blind professor Sanderson. I had not frequented him a fortnight, before he said to me, "Young man, it is cheating you to take your money: believe me, you never can learn these things; you have no capacity for them." I can smile now, but I cried then with mortification. The next step, in order to comfort myself, was not to believe him: I could not conceive that I had not talents for anything in the world. I took, at my own expense, a private instructor, who came to me once a-day for a year. Nay, I took

1 Virgil, *Eclogues* V. 57: see the clouds beneath your feet.
2 Horace Mann (bap. 1706–86), the British resident in Florence: see heading to letter 200.
3 Tommaso Perelli (1704–83) was a famous Italian mathematician and astronomer. Walpole noted that Mrs. Goldsworthy was the wife of the English consul at Leghorn who, in trying to learn Italian, complained of Italian verbs as if unaware that there were verbs in English grammar.

infinite pains, but had so little capacity, and so little attention (as I have always had to anything that did not immediately strike my inclinations), that after mastering any proposition, when the man came the next day, it was as new to me as if I had never heard of it; in short, even to common figures, I am the dullest dunce alive. I have often said it of myself, and it is true, that nothing that has not a proper name of a man or a woman to it, affixes any idea upon my mind. I could remember who was King Ethelbald's great-aunt, and not be sure whether she lived in the year 500 or 1500. I don't know whether I ever told you, that when you sent me the seven gallons of drams, and they were carried to Mr. Fox by mistake for Florence wine, I pressed him to keep as much as he liked; for, said I, I have seen the bill of lading, and there is a vast quantity. He asked how much? I answered seventy gallons; so little idea I have of quantity. I will tell you one more story of myself, and you will comprehend what sort of a head I have! Mrs. Leneve[1] said to me one day, "There is a vast waste of coals in your house; you should make the servants take off the fires at night." I recollected this as I was going to bed, and, out of *economy*, put my fire out with a bottle of Bristol water! . . .

5. *Eton Revisited.*

TO GEORGE MONTAGU, ESQ.

Christopher Inn, Eton, *c.* 8 August 1746.

The Christopher.[2] Lord! how great I used to think anybody just landed at the Christopher! But here are no boys for me to send for – here I am, like Noah, just returned into his old world again, with all sorts of queer feels about me. By the way, the clock strikes the old cracked sound – I recollect so much, and remember so little – and want to play about – and am so afraid of my playfellows – and am ready to shirk Ashton – and can't help *making fun* of myself – and envy a dame over the way, that has just locked in her boarders, and is going to sit down in a little hot parlour to a very bad supper, so comfortably! and I could be so jolly a dog if I did not *fat*, which,

1 A Norfolk gentlewoman and dependant of the Walpole family who lived with Sir Robert to care for his youngest daughter after his wife's death, and later lived with Walpole.
2 The principal inn at Eton.

by the way, is the first time the word was ever applicable to me. In short, I should be out of all *bounds* if I was to tell you half I feel, how young again I am one minute, and how old the next. But do come and feel with me, when you will – to-morrow – for tonight I have so bad a pen, that you will think I deserve to be *flogged*. Adieu! If I don't compose myself a little more before Sunday morning, when Ashton is to preach,[1] I shall certainly *be in a bill for laughing at church;* but how to help it, to see him in the pulpit, when the last time I saw him here, was standing up funking over against a conduct to be catechised.[2]

Good night; yours.

6. *Paris.*

Dear West,   Paris, 21 April (N. S.)[3] 1739.[4]

You figure us in a set of pleasures, which, believe me, we do not find; cards and eating are so universal, that they absorb all variation of pleasures. The operas, indeed, are much frequented three times a week; but to me they would be a greater penance than eating maigre: their music resembles a gooseberry tart as much as it does harmony. We have not yet been at the Italian playhouse; scarce any one goes there. Their best amusement, and which, in some parts, beats ours, is the comedy; three or four of the actors excel any we have: but then to this nobody goes, if it is not one of the fashionable nights; and then they go, be the play good or bad – except on Molière's nights, whose pieces they are quite weary of. Gray and I have been at the

1 Ashton had taken orders in 1741.
2 Examples of Eton schoolboy slang: funking over against a conduct was flinching before a chaplain.
3 The designation N. S. (New Style) after the date of the letter – as opposed to O. S. (Old Style) – refers to the introduction of the Gregorian calendar in England in September 1752, when eleven days were skipped to compensate for the fractionally shorter year under the Julian calendar, and when the legal commencement of the year was moved from 25 March to 1 January. This and some other early letters sent by Walpole when on his Grand Tour are designated N. S., showing they complied with continental dating, which did not follow the Julian calendar. An alternative method of dating letters sent earlier in the year than 25 March was to show both years, as in letter 13 on p. 27, dated 4 February 1741–2.
4 Walpole and Thomas Gray left for Paris in March 1739.

Avare to-night; I cannot at all commend their performance of it.
Last night I was in the Place de Louis le Grand (a regular octagon,
uniform, and the houses handsome, though not so large as Golden
Square), to see what they reckoned one of the finest burials that ever
was in France. It was the Duke de Tresmes, governor of Paris and
marshal of France. It began on foot from his palace to his parish-
church, and from thence in coaches to the opposite end of Paris, to
be interred in the church of the Celestins, where is his family-vault.
About a week ago we happened to see the grave digging, as we went
to see the church, which is old and small, but fuller of fine ancient
monuments than any, except St. Denis, which we saw on the road,
and excels Westminster; for the windows are all painted in mosaic,
and the tombs as fresh and well preserved as if they were of yesterday.
In the Celestins' church is a votive column to Francis II., which says,
that it is one assurance of his being immortalised, to have had the
martyr Mary Stuart for his wife.[1] After this long digression, I return
to the burial, which was a most vile thing. A long procession of
flambeaux and friars; no plumes, trophies, banners, led horses,
scutcheons, or open chariots; nothing but

> friars,
> White, black, and grey, with all their trumpery.

This goodly ceremony began at nine at night, and did not finish till
three this morning; for, each church they passed, they stopped for a
hymn and holy water. By the bye, some of these choice monks, who
watched the body while it lay in state, fell asleep one night, and let
the tapers catch fire of the rich velvet mantle lined with ermine and
powdered with gold flower-de-luces, which melted the lead coffin,
and burnt off the feet of the deceased before it awakened them. The
French love show; but there is a meanness reigns through it all. At
the house where I stood to see this procession, the room was hung
with crimson damask and gold, and the windows were mended in
ten or a dozen places with paper. At dinner they give you three
courses; but a third of the dishes is patched up with sallads, butter,
puff-paste, or some such miscarriage of a dish. None, but Germans,
wear fine clothes; but their coaches are tawdry enough for the wedding of Cupid and Psyche. You would laugh extremely at their signs:

1 Mary, Queen of Scots, had in 1558 married Francis, the Dauphin of France, who
succeeded to the throne in 1559 and died a year later.

some live at the Y grec, some at Venus's toilette, and some at the sucking cat. You would not easily guess their notions of honour: I'll tell you one: it is very dishonourable for any gentleman not to be in the army, or in the king's service as they call it, and it is no dishonour to keep public gaming-houses: there are at least an hundred and fifty people of the first quality in Paris who live by it. You may go into their houses at all hours of the night, and find hazard, pharaoh, &c. The men who keep the hazard-table at the duke de Gesvres' pay him twelve guineas each night for the privilege. Even the princesses of the blood are dirty enough to have shares in the banks kept at their houses. We have seen two or three of them; but they are not young, nor remarkable but for wearing their red of a deeper dye than other women, though all use it extravagantly.

The weather is still so bad, that we have not made any excursions to see Versailles and the environs, not even walked in the Tuileries; but we have seen almost every thing else that is worth seeing in Paris, though that is very considerable. They beat us vastly in buildings, both in number and magnificence. The tombs of Richelieu and Mazarin at the Sorbonne and the College de Quatre Nations are wonderfully fine, especially the former. We have seen very little of the people themselves, who are not inclined to be propitious to strangers, especially if they do not play and speak the language readily. There are many English here: Lord Holderness, Conway and Clinton, and Lord George Bentinck; Mr. Brand, Offley, Frederic, Frampton, Bonfoy, &c. Sir John Cotton's son and a Mr. Vernon of Cambridge passed through Paris last week. We shall stay here about a fortnight longer, and then go to Rheims with Mr. Conway[1] for two or three months. When you have nothing else to do, we shall be glad to hear from you; and any news. If we did not remember there was such a place as England, we should know nothing of it: the French never mention it, unless it happens to be in one of their proverbs! Adieu!

                                                      Yours ever.

To-morrow we go to the Cid. They have no farces, but *petites pièces* like our 'Devil to Pay.'[2]

1 Walpole's cousin, close friend and correspondent Henry Seymour Conway: see heading to letter 191.
2 A ballad opera by Charles Coffey (d. 1745), first produced at Drury Lane in 1731. It became the most frequently performed afterpiece of the 18th century.

7. Versailles and Chartreux.

TO RICHARD WEST, ESQ.

Dear West,   From Paris, *c.* 15 May 1739.

I should think myself to blame not to try to divert you, when you tell me I can. From the air of your letter you seem to want amusement, that is, you want spirits. I would recommend to you certain little employments that I know of, and that belong to you, but that I imagine bodily exercise is more suitable to your complaint. If you would promise me to read them in the Temple garden, I would send you a little packet of plays and pamphlets that we have made up, and intend to dispatch to 'Dick's'[1] the first opportunity. – Stand by, clear the way, make room for the pompous appearance of Versailles le Grand! – But no: it fell so short of my idea of it, mine, that I have resigned to Gray the office of writing its panegyric.[2] He likes it. They say I am to like it better next Sunday; when the sun is to shine, the king is to be fine, the water-works are to play, and the new knights of the Holy Ghost are to be installed! Ever since Wednesday, the day we were there, we have done nothing but dispute about it. They say, we did not see it to advantage, that we ran through the apartments, saw the garden *en passant*, and slubbered over Trianon. I say, we saw nothing. However, we had time to see that the great front is a lumber of littleness, composed of black brick, stuck full of bad old busts, and fringed with gold rails. The rooms are all small, except the great gallery, which is noble, but totally wainscoted with looking-glass. The garden is littered with statues and fountains, each of which has its tutelary deity. In particular, the elementary god of fire solaces himself in one. In another, Enceladus,[3] in lieu of a mountain, is overwhelmed with many waters. There are avenues of water-pots, who disport themselves much in squirting up cascadelins. In short, 'tis a garden for a great child. Such was Louis Quatorze, who is here seen in his proper colours, where he commanded in person, unassisted by his armies and generals, and left to the pursuit of his own puerile ideas of glory.

1 A coffee-house on Fleet Street, near Temple Bar.
2 Gray (for whom see heading to letter 195) in fact described Versailles in a letter to West of 22 May 1739 as "a huge heap of littleness", recalling Pope's description of "what huge heaps of littleness around" at Timon's Villa in his *Moral Essays* IV. 109.
3 A giant in Greek mythology.

We saw last week a place of another kind, and which has more the air of what it would be, than anything I have yet met with: it was the convent of the Chartreux.[1] All the conveniences, or rather (if there was such a word) all the *adaptments* are assembled here, that melancholy, meditation, selfish devotion, and despair would require. But yet 'tis pleasing. Soften the terms, and mellow the uncouth horror that reigns here, but a little, and 'tis a charming solitude. It stands on a large space of ground, is old and irregular. The chapel is gloomy: behind it, through some dark passages, you pass into a large obscure hall, which looks like a combination-chamber for some hellish council. The large cloister surrounds their burying-ground. The cloisters are very narrow and very long, and let into the cells, which are built like little huts detached from each other. We were carried into one, where lived a middle-aged man not long initiated into the order. He was extremely civil, and called himself Dom Victor. We have promised to visit him often. Their habit is all white: but besides this he was infinitely clean in his person; and his apartment and garden, which he keeps and cultivates without any assistance, was neat to a degree. He has four little rooms, furnished in the prettiest manner, and hung with good prints. One of them is a library, and another a gallery. He has several canary-birds disposed in a pretty manner in breeding-cages. In his garden was a bed of good tulips in bloom, flowers and fruit-trees, and all neatly kept. They are permitted at certain hours to talk to strangers but never to one another, or to go out of their convent. But what we chiefly went to see was the small cloister, with the history of St. Bruno, their founder, painted by Le Sœur. It consists of twenty-two pictures, the figures a good deal less than life. But sure they are amazing! I don't know what Raphael may be in Rome, but these pictures excel all I have seen in Paris and England. The figure of the dead man who spoke at his burial, contains all the strongest and horridest ideas, of ghastliness, hypocrisy discovered, and the height of damnation, pain and cursing. A Benedictine monk, who was there at the same time, said to me of this picture: *C'est une fable, mais on la croyoit autrefois.* Another, who showed me relics in one of their churches, expressed as much ridicule for them. The pictures I have been speaking of are ill preserved, and some of the finest heads defaced, which was done at first

1 A convent on the site of what became part of the Luxembourg Gardens.

by a rival of Le Sœur's. Adieu! dear West, take care of your health; and some time or other we will talk over all these things with more pleasure than I have had in seeing them.

Yours ever.

8. *The Grande Chartreuse.*

TO RICHARD WEST, ESQ.

From a Hamlet among the Mountains of Savoy,
28 September (N. S.) 1739.

Precipices, mountains, torrents, wolves, rumblings, Salvator Rosa — the pomp of our park and the meekness of our palace! Here we are, the lonely lords of glorious, desolate prospects. I have kept a sort of resolution which I made, of not writing to you as long as I staid in France: I am now a quarter of an hour out of it, and write to you. Mind, 'tis three months since we heard from you. I begin this letter among the clouds; where I shall finish, my neighbour Heaven probably knows: 'tis an odd wish in a mortal letter, to hope not to finish it on this side the atmosphere. You will have a billet tumble to you from the stars when you least think of it; and that I should write it too! Lord, how potent that sounds! But I am to undergo many transmigrations before I come to "yours ever." Yesterday I was a shepherd of Dauphiné; to-day an Alpine savage; to-morrow a Carthusian monk; and Friday a Swiss Calvinist. I have one quality which I find remains with me in all worlds and in all æthers; I brought it with me from your world, and am admired for it in this – 'tis my esteem for you: this is a common thought among you, and you will laugh at it, but it is new here: as new to remember one's friends in the world one has left, as for you to remember those you have lost.

Aix in Savoy, Sept. 30th.

We are this minute come in here, and here's an awkward abbé this minute come in to us. I asked him if he would sit down. *Oui, oui, oui.* He has ordered us a radish soup for supper, and has brought a chess-board to play with Mr. Conway. I have left 'em in the act, and am set down to write to you. Did you ever see any thing like the prospect we saw yesterday? I never did. We rode three leagues to see the Grande Chartreuse; expected bad roads and the finest convent in the kingdom. We were disappointed pro and con. The building is large and plain, and has nothing remarkable but its primitive simplicity; they entertained us in the neatest manner, with eggs, pickled salmon, dried fish, conserves, cheese, butter, grapes, and figs, and pressed us mightily to lie there. We tumbled into the hands of a lay-brother, who, unluckily having the charge of the meal and bran, showed us little besides. They desired us to set down our names in the list of strangers, where, among others, we found two mottos of our countrymen, for whose stupidity and brutality we blushed. The first was of Sir J * * * D * * *, who had wrote down the first stanza of *Justum et tenacem*, altering the last line to *Mente quatit Carthusiana.* The second was of one D * *, *Cælum ipsum petimus stultitiâ*; and *Hic ventri indico bellum.*[1] The Goth! – But the road, West, the road! Winding round a prodigious mountain, and surrounded with others, all shagged with hanging woods, obscured with pines, or lost in clouds! Below, a torrent breaking through cliffs, and tumbling through fragments of rocks! Sheets of cascades forcing their silver speed down channelled precipices, and hasting into the roughened river at the bottom! Now and then an old foot-bridge, with a broken rail, a leaning cross, a cottage, or the ruin of an hermitage! This sounds too bombast and too romantic to one that has not seen it, too cold for one that has. If I could send you my letter post between two lovely tempests that echoed each other's wrath you might have some idea of this noble roaring scene, as you were reading it. Almost on the summit, upon a fine verdure, but without any prospect, stands the Chartreuse. We staid there two hours, rode back through this charming picture, wished for a painter, wished to be poets! Need I tell you we wished for you? Good night! . . .

9. *Tory and the Wolf.*

TO RICHARD WEST, ESQ.

Turin, 11 November (N. S.) 1739.

So, as the song says, we are in fair Italy! I wonder we are; for on the very highest precipice of Mount Cenis, the devil of discord, in the similitude of sour wine, had got amongst our Alpine savages,

---

1 These are principally inaccurately quoted passages of Horace.

and set them a-fighting with Gray and me in the chairs: they rushed
him by me on a crag, where there was scarce room for a cloven foot.
The least slip had tumbled us into such a fog, and such an eternity,
as we should never have found our way out of again. We were eight
days in coming hither from Lyons; the four last in crossing the Alps.
Such uncouth rocks, and such uncomely inhabitants! My dear West,
I hope I shall never see them again! At the foot of Mount Cenis we
were obliged to quit our chaise, which was taken all to pieces and
loaded on mules; and we were carried in low arm-chairs on poles,
swathed in beaver bonnets, beaver gloves, beaver stockings, muffs,
and bear-skins. When we came to the top, behold the snows fallen!
and such quantities, and conducted by such heavy clouds that hung
glouting, that I thought we could never have waded through them.
The descent is two leagues, but steep and rough as O * * * * father's
face, over which, you know, the devil walked with hobnails in his
shoes.[1] But the dexterity and nimbleness of the mountaineers are
inconceivable: they run with you down steeps and frozen precipices,
where no man, as men are now, could possibly walk. We had twelve
men and nine mules to carry us, our servants, and baggage, and were
above five hours in this agreeable jaunt! The day before, I had a cruel
accident; and so extraordinary an one, that it seems to touch upon
the traveller. I had brought with me a little black spaniel of King
Charles's breed; but the prettiest, fattest, dearest creature! I had let
it out of the chaise for the air, and it was waddling along close to the
head of the horses, on the top of the highest Alps, by the side of a
wood of firs. There darted out a young wolf, seized poor dear Tory
by the throat, and, before we could possibly prevent it, sprung up
the side of the rock and carried him off. The postilion jumped off
and struck at him with his whip, but in vain. I saw it and screamed,
but in vain; for the road was so narrow, that the servants that were
behind could not get by the chaise to shoot him. What is the extraordinary part is, that it was but two o'clock, and broad sunshine. It
was shocking to see anything one loved run away with to so horrid
a death. . . .

1 A reference to the "Character of a Certain Ugly Old Priest" by John Oldham
(1653–83).

10. *The Carnival at Florence.*

TO RICHARD WEST, ESQ.

Florence, 27 February (N. S.) 1740.

Well, West, I have found a little unmasqued moment to write to you; but for this week past I have been so muffled up in my domino, that I have not had the command of my elbows. But what have you been doing all the mornings? Could you not write then? – No, then I was masqued too; I have done nothing but slip out of my domino into bed, and out of bed into my domino. The end of the Carnival is frantic, bacchanalian; all the morn one makes parties in masque to the shops and coffee-houses, and all the evening to the operas and balls. *Then I have danced, good gods! how have I danced!*[1] The Italians are fond to a degree of our country dances: *Cold and raw* they only know by the tune; *Blowzybella* is almost Italian, and *Buttered peas* is *Pizelli al buro.* There are but three days more; but the two last are to have balls all the morning at the fine unfinished palace of the Strozzi; and the Tuesday night a masquerade after supper: they sup first, to eat *gras,* and not encroach upon Ash-Wednesday. What makes masquerading more agreeable here than in England, is the great deference that is showed to the disguised. Here they do not catch at those little dirty opportunities of saying any ill-natured thing they know of you, do not abuse you because they may, or talk gross bawdy to a woman of quality. I found the other day, by a play of Etheridge's, that we have had a sort of Carnival even since the Reformation; 'tis in '*She Would if She Could,*'[2] they talk of going a-mumming in Shrove-tide.—

After talking so much of diversions, I fear you will attribute to them the fondness I own I contract for Florence; but it has so many other charms, that I shall not want excuses for my taste. The freedom of the Carnival has given me opportunities to make several acquaintances; and if I have not found them refined, learned, polished, like some other cities, yet they are civil, good-natured, and fond of the English. Their little partiality for themselves, opposed to the violent vanity of the French, makes them very amiable in my eyes. I can give you a comical instance of their great prejudice about nobility;

1 Parody of a passage in Act I, Scene i of Nathaniel Lee's play *The Rival Queens*: "Then he will talk – good gods, how he will talk!"
2 A comedy of 1668 by Sir George Etherege.

it happened yesterday. While we were at dinner at Mr. Mann's,[1] word was brought by his secretary, that a cavalier demanded audience of him upon an affair of honour. Gray and I flew behind the curtain of the door. An elderly gentleman, whose attire was not certainly correspondent to the greatness of his birth, entered, and informed the British minister, that one Martin, an English painter,[2] had left a challenge for him at his house, for having said Martin was no gentleman. He would by no means have spoke of the duel before the transaction of it, but that his honour, his blood, his &c. would never permit him to fight with one who was no cavalier; which was what he came to inquire of his excellency. We laughed loud laughs, but unheard: his fright or his nobility had closed his ears. But mark the sequel: the instant he was gone, my very English curiosity hurried me out of the gate St. Gallo; 'twas the place and hour appointed. We had not been driving about above ten minutes, but out popped a little figure, pale but cross, with beard unshaved and hair uncombed, a slouched hat, and a considerable red cloak, in which was wrapped, under his arm, the fatal sword that was to revenge the highly injured Mr. Martin, painter and defendant. I darted my head out of the coach, just ready to say, "Your servant, Mr. Martin," and talk about the architecture of the triumphal arch that was building there; but he would not know me, and walked off. We left him to wait for an hour, to grow very cold and very valiant the more it grew past the hour of appointment. We were figuring all the poor creature's huddle of thoughts, and confused hopes of victory or fame, of his unfinished pictures, or his situation upon bouncing into the next world. You will think us strange creatures; but 'twas a pleasant sight, as we knew the poor painter was safe. I have thought of it since, and am inclined to believe that nothing but two English could have been capable of such a jaunt. I remember, 'twas reported in London, that the plague was at a house in the city, and all the town went to see it.

I have this instant received your letter. Lord! I am glad I thought of those parallel passages, since it made you translate them. 'Tis excessively near the original; and yet, I don't know, 'tis very easy too. – It snows here a little to-night, but it never lies but on the mountains. Adieu! Yours ever.

P.S. What is the history of the theatres this winter?

1 See heading to letter 200.
2 According to the Yale editors of Walpole's correspondence, untraced.

11. *Herculaneum.*

TO RICHARD WEST, ESQ.

Dear West,   Naples, 14 June (N. S.) 1740.

One hates writing descriptions that are to be found in every book
of travels; but we have seen something to-day that I am sure you
never read of, and perhaps never heard of. Have you ever heard of
a subterraneous town? a whole Roman town, with all its edifices,
remaining under ground? Don't fancy the inhabitants buried it there
to save it from the Goths: they were buried with it themselves; which
is a caution we are not told that they ever took. You remember in
Titus's time there were several cities destroyed by an eruption of
Vesuvius, attended with an earthquake. Well, this was one of them,
not very considerable, and then called Herculaneum.[1] Above it has
since been built Portici, about three miles from Naples, where the
King has a villa. This under-ground city is perhaps one of the noblest
curiosities that ever has been discovered. It was found out by chance,
about a year and half ago. They began digging, they found statues;
they dug further, they found more. Since that they have made a very
considerable progress, and find continually. You may walk the compass of a mile; but by the misfortune of the modern town being over-
head, they are obliged to proceed with great caution, lest they
destroy both one and t'other. By this occasion the path is very narrow, just wide enough and high enough for one man to walk upright.
They have hollowed, as they found it easiest to work, and have
carried their streets not exactly where were the ancient ones, but
sometimes before houses, sometimes through them. You would
imagine that all the fabrics were crushed together; on the contrary,
except some columns, they have found all the edifices standing
upright in their proper situation. There is one inside of a temple
quite perfect, with the middle arch, two columns, and two pilasters.
It is built of brick plastered over, and painted with architecture:
almost all the insides of the houses are in the same manner; and,
what is very particular, the general ground of all the painting is red.
Besides this temple, they make out very plainly an amphitheatre: the
stairs, of white marble, and the seats are very perfect; the inside was

1 Organised excavation by tunnelling had begun in 1738. Pompeii was not discovered
until 1748.

painted in the same colour with the private houses, and great part cased with white marble. They have found among other things some fine statues, some human bones, some rice, medals, and a few paintings extremely fine. These latter are preferred to all the ancient paintings that have ever been discovered. We have not seen them yet, as they are kept in the King's apartment, whither all these curiosities are transplanted; and 'tis difficult to see them – but we shall. I forgot to tell you, that in several places the beams of the houses remain, but burnt to charcoal; so little damaged that they retain visibly the grain of the wood, but upon touching crumble to ashes. What is remarkable, there are no other marks or appearance of fire, but what are visible on these beams.

There might certainly be collected great light from this reservoir of antiquities, if a man of learning had the inspection of it; if he directed the working, and would make a journal of the discoveries. But I believe there is no judicious choice made of directors. There is nothing of the kind known in the world; I mean a Roman city entire of that age, and that has not been corrupted with modern repairs. Besides scrutinising this very carefully, I should be inclined to search for the remains of the other towns that were partners with this in the general ruin. 'Tis certainly an advantage to the learned world, that this has been laid up so long. Most of the discoveries in Rome were made in a barbarous age, where they only ransacked the ruins in quest of treasure, and had no regard to the form and being of the building; or to any circumstances that might give light into its use and history. I shall finish this long account with a passage which Gray has observed in Statius, and which directly pictures out this latent city: –

> Hæc ego Chalcidicis ad te, Marcelle, sonabam
> Littoribus, fractas ubi Vestius egerit iras,
> Æmula Trinacriis volvens incendia flammis.
> Mira fides! credetne virûm ventura propago,
> Cum segetes iterum, cum jam hæc deserta virebunt,
> Infra urbes populosque premi?
>
> SYLV. lib. iv. epist. 4.

Adieu, my dear West! and believe me yours ever.

12. *The Return Home.*

TO THE HON. H. S. CONWAY[1]

My Dearest Harry,   London, *c.* 21 September 1741.

Before I thank you for myself, I must thank you for that excessive good nature you showed in writing to poor Gray.[2] I am less impatient to see you, as I find you are not the least altered, but have the same tender friendly temper you always had. I wanted much to see if you were still the same – but you are.

Don't think of coming before your brother; he is too good to be left for any one living: besides, if it is possible, I will see you in the country. Don't reproach me, and think nothing could draw me into the country: impatience to see a few friends has drawn me out of Italy; and Italy, Harry, is pleasanter than London. As I do not love living *en famille* so much as you (but then indeed my family is not like yours), I am hurried about getting myself a house; for I have so long lived single, that I do not much take to being confined with [words missing, but presumably a reference to his own family].

You won't find me much altered, I believe; at least, outwardly. I am not grown a bit shorter, or a bit fatter, but am just the same long lean creature as usual. Then I talk no French, but to my footman; nor Italian, but to myself. What inward alterations may have happened to me, you will discover best; for you know 'tis said, one never knows that one's self. I will answer, that that part of it that belongs to you, has not suffered the least change – I took care of that.

For virtù, I have a little to entertain you: it is my sole pleasure. – I am neither young enough nor old enough to be in love.

My dear Harry, will you take care and make my compliments to that charming Lady Conway, who I hear is so charming, and to Miss Jenny [Conway], who I know is so?[3] As for Miss Anne[4] and her love *as far as it is decent:* tell her, decency is out of the question between

1 See heading to letter 191.
2 This letter was written some three weeks after Gray had returned to London, and about four months after Walpole and Gray had quarrelled and separated at Reggio.
3 Isabella Fitzroy, daughter of the 2nd Duke of Grafton, who had earlier that year married Conway's elder brother Francis, later the Earl of Hertford (1718–94), another correspondent of Walpole's. For Hertford, see heading to letter 207. Jenny (Jane) was an older half-sister of the Conway brothers.
4 Anne Conway was the youngest sister of Walpole's cousins Francis and Henry Conway.

us, that I love her without any restriction. I settled it yesterday with Miss Conway, that you three are brothers and sister to me, and that if you had been so, I could not love you better. I have so many cousins, and uncles and aunts, and bloods that grow in Norfolk, that if I had portioned out my affections to them, as they say I should, what a modicum would have fallen to each! – So, to avoid fractions, I love my family in you three, their representatives. Adieu, my dear Harry! Direct to me at Downing Street. Good-b'ye! Yours ever.

II
WALPOLE AND POLITICS

WALPOLE ARRIVED BACK in England at the very end of his father's long premiership to find that he had been elected *in absentia* M.P. for Callington in Cornwall, a seat owned by relations; he would represent Callington for thirteen years without visiting it. His maiden speech, in March 1742, was in defence of his father's late administration, but he was not suited to the cut and thrust of active politics, the extemporary speeches and the detailed matters of business. He did, however, have an almost mischievous taste for faction. His political principles were those of a thoroughbred Whig, but his allegiances were personal, and he held in contempt any politician who had presumed to challenge Sir Robert Walpole.

After Sir Robert's fall from power – he resigned in February 1742 with the title of Earl of Orford – father and son spent an increasing amount of time together, at Arlington Street and at Houghton, the Earl's Palladian mansion in Norfolk, and enjoyed a much closer relationship.

In Parliament Walpole opposed the interests of Lord Carteret, his father's former adversary and *de facto* leader of the new government (1742–4), and allied himself with Henry Fox, rising politician and one of Sir Robert's most devoted supporters. After the Earl's death in 1745, he began to take a more independent line; he became increasingly disenchanted with government by the Pelhams – Henry Pelham (1744–54), his father's former protégé, whom he disliked, and his elder brother the Duke of Newcastle (1754–6 and 1757–62) whom he delighted to ridicule (see letters 14, 15, and 18). To Walpole's distaste, Henry Fox in 1755 became Secretary of State under Newcastle. The ministry under Newcastle was widely criticised for its role in the recall, court-martial and execution of Admiral Byng, the *cause célèbre* of 1756–7 (see letters 284 and 285) which aroused Walpole's sense of injustice and led to his writing the successful satirical pamphlet *A Letter from Xo Ho, a Chinese Philosopher at London, to his Friend Lien Chi, at Peking*. In the same year he was elected M.P.

for King's Lynn. For the previous three years he had held the seat for Castle Rising, a family-controlled pocket borough in Norfolk, but King's Lynn was different, a lively trading town where he had to participate in the exertions of elections and make some attempt to cultivate his constituents (see letter 19). Although living in an age marked by bribery and political jobbery, Walpole always maintained that his own record was uncompromised, and that "My votes have neither been dictated by favour nor influence" (letter 24).

He admired the oratorical powers of William Pitt the elder, Paymaster-General, remarking in 1755, "Pitt surpassed himself, and then I need not tell you that he surpassed Cicero and Demosthenes . . . He spoke above an hour and a half, with scarce a bad sentence."[1] He expressed some amazement at the formation of the Pitt–Newcastle coalition in 1757, but enjoyed the triumphs of 1759, Britain's "Year of Victories" during the Seven Years' War against France, for which successes Pitt, as Secretary of State, was in many ways responsible (letter 291). Two years later Pitt insisted on war with Spain, resigned when thwarted, and to Walpole's disgust accepted a pension and a peerage for his wife.

The accession of George III in 1760 was welcomed by Walpole, who was at first unperturbed by the swift rise to prominence of the royal favourite, Lord Bute, the young King's former tutor. Though pleased to see Bute replace Newcastle in 1762, he was soon critical of his government, disapproving of its attempts to muzzle the troublesome populist John Wilkes, whose journal the *North Briton* had been founded for the purpose of attacking the new prime minister (see letters 292 to 299). Bute resigned in 1763, but his successor George Grenville handled the matter no better.

The Wilkes affair was to provoke one of the most painful events in Walpole's political life. In 1764, his cousin Conway was at the behest of George III dismissed from his position at court and from his regiment for his opposition to the Grenville ministry's use of a general warrant to arrest Wilkes and others. Walpole, who almost hero-worshipped Conway and had long worked to promote his career, sprang to his defence in print and offered to share his fortune with him: but when the following year Conway was admitted to the government formed by the Marquis of Rockingham, Walpole was deeply offended not to be offered any position or sinecure as a reward for his support, and retreated hurt to Paris. From there he expressed

1 Letter to Richard Bentley, 16 November 1755 (YE 35:260).

his satisfaction when Rockingham's ministry repealed the Stamp Act of 1765 (letter 23), Grenville's misguided attempt to levy taxes from America, which had driven the colonists into active resistance. But he was already considering giving up public life and in 1767 he announced his intention of retiring from Parliament (letter 24).

Walpole continued to comment on politics until the end of his life, but his commentaries were increasingly those of a well-informed outsider. He opposed the provocative colonial policies of Lord North (1770–82), regarding the prosecution of the war with the American colonies as sheer folly. He supported the Rockingham Whigs, briefly in power again in 1782, who offered immediate peace terms to America, and was quick to spot the talents of both Charles James Fox and his future rival, William Pitt the younger. He was scandalised by the corrupt and exploitative practices of the East India Company, and relieved at the failure of bills to reform the British Parliament. But above all, in the last years of his life he was appalled by events in revolutionary France (see Section XV).

13. *Sir Robert Walpole's Resignation.*

TO SIR HORACE MANN

London, 4 February 1741–2.

I am miserable that I have not more time to write to you, especially as you will want to know so much of what I have to tell you; but for a week or fortnight I shall be so hurried, that I shall scarce know what I say. I sit here writing to you, and receiving all the town, who flock to this house; Sir Robert[1] has already had three levées this morning, and the rooms still overflowing – they overflow up to me. You will think this the prelude to some victory! On the contrary, when you receive this, there will be no longer a Sir Robert Walpole: you must know him for the future by the title of Earl of Orford. That other envied name expires next week with his Ministry!

Preparatory to this change, I should tell you, that last week we heard in the House of Commons the Chippenham election, when Jack Frederick and his brother-in-law, Mr. Hume, on our side,

---

1 Walpole's father Sir Robert Walpole (1676–1745) resigned as prime minister in February 1742.

petitioned against Sir Edmund Thomas and Mr. Baynton Rolt. Both sides made it the decisive question – but our people were not all equally true; and upon the previous question we had but 235 against 236, so lost it by one. From that time my brothers, my uncle, I, and some of his particular friends, persuaded Sir R. to resign. He was undetermined till Sunday night. Tuesday we were to finish the election, when we lost it by 16; upon which, Sir Robert declared to some particular persons in the House his resolution to retire, and had that morning sent the Prince of Wales notice of it. It is understood from the heads of the party, that nothing more is to be pursued against him. Yesterday (Wednesday) the King adjourned both Houses for a fortnight, for time to settle things. Next week Sir Robert resigns and goes into the House of Lords. The only change yet fixed, is, that Lord Wilmington[1] is to be at the head of the Treasury – but numberless other alterations and confusions must follow. The Prince will be reconciled, and the Whig-patriots will come in. There were a few bonfires last night, but they are very unfashionable, for never was fallen minister so followed. When he kissed the King's hand to take his first leave, the King fell on his neck, wept and kissed him, and begged to see him frequently. He will continue in town, and assist the Ministry in the Lords. Mr. Pelham has declared that he will accept nothing that was Sir Robert's; and this moment the Duke of Richmond has been here from Court to tell Sir R. that he had resigned the Mastership of the Horse, having received it from him, unasked, and that he would not keep it beyond his Ministry. This is the greater honour, as it was so unexpected, and as he had no personal friendship with the Duke. . . . Adieu! Yours, ever, and the same.

14. *The Duke of Newcastle.*

TO SIR HORACE MANN

14 July 1748.

. . . There are no good anecdotes yet arrived of the Duke of Newcastle's[2] travels, except that at a review which the Duke made for

1 Sir Spencer Compton, Earl of Wilmington, knight of the garter, and at this time lord president of the council. – WALPOLE.
2 Thomas Pelham-Holles, Duke of Newcastle (1693–1768), Whig statesman who

him, as he passed through the army, he hurried about with his glass up to his eye, crying, "Finest troops! finest troops! greatest General!" then broke through the ranks when he spied any Sussex man, kissed him in all his accoutrements, – my dear Tom such an one! chattered of Lewes races; then back to the Duke with "Finest troops! greatest General!" – and in short was a much better show than any review. The Duke is expected over immediately; I don't know if to stay, or why he comes – I mean, I do know, but am angry, and will not tell.

I have seen Sir James Grey, who speaks of you with great affection, and recommends himself extremely to me by it, when I am not angry with you;[1] but I cannot possibly be reconciled till I have finished this letter, for I have nothing but this quarrel to talk of, and I think I have worn that out – so adieu! you odious, shocking, abominable monster!

15. *Newcastle in Office.*

TO RICHARD BENTLEY, ESQ.[2]

Arlington Street, 17 March 1754.

In the confusion of things, I last week hazarded a free letter to you by the common post. The confusion is by no means ceased. However, as some circumstances may have rendered a desire of intelligence necessary, I send this by the coach, with the last volume of Sir Charles Grandison for its chaperon.

After all the world had been named for Chancellor of the Exchequer, and my Lord Chief Justice Lee, who is no part of the world, really made so *pro tempore;* Lord Hartington went to notify to Mr. Fox[3] that the cabinet council having given it as their unanimous opinion to the King that the Duke of Newcastle should be at the

---

had served under Sir Robert Walpole. He became prime minister on the death of his brother, Henry Pelham, in 1754, fell from power briefly in 1756 but returned the following year, forming a wartime ministry in conjunction with Pitt the Elder. He is a figure frequently ridiculed by Walpole.

1 The "quarrel" was in jest, as explained in the opening section of the letter, not here printed. Grey was a diplomat posted to Venice.

2 Richard Bentley (1708–82), designer and artist, a member of the Committee that advised Walpole on Strawberry Hill.

3 Henry Fox, later 1st Baron Holland (1705–74), with whom Walpole allied himself politically. He was the father of Charles James Fox.

head of the Treasury, and he (Mr. Fox) Secretary of State, with the management of the House of Commons; his grace, who had submitted to so *oracular* a sentence, hoped Mr. Fox would not refuse to concur in so salutary a measure; and assured him, that *though* the Duke would reserve the sole disposition of the secret service-money, his grace would bestow his entire confidence on Mr. Fox, and acquaint him with the most minute details of that service. Mr. Fox bowed and obeyed – and, as a preliminary step, received the Chancellor's[1] absolution. From thence he attended his and our new master. – But either grief for his brother's death, or joy for it, had so intoxicated the new *maître du palais*, that he would not ratify any one of the conditions he had imposed: and though my Lord Hartington's virtue interposed, and remonstrated on the purport of the message he had carried, the Duke persisted in assuming the whole and undivided power himself, and left Mr. Fox no choice but of obeying or disobeying, as he might choose. This produced the next day a letter from Mr. Fox, carried by my Lord Hartington, in which he refused Secretary of State, and pinned down the lie with which the new ministry is to commence. It was tried to be patched up at the Chancellor's on Friday night, though ineffectually: and yesterday morning Mr. Fox in an audience desired to remain Secretary at War. The Duke immediately kissed hands – declared, in the most unusual manner, universal minister. Legge was to be Chancellor of the Exchequer; but I can't tell whether that disposition will hold, as Lord Duplin is proclaimed the acting favourite. The German Sir Thomas Robinson was thought on for the Secretary's seals; but has just sense enough to be unwilling to accept them under so ridiculous an administration. – This is the first act of the comedy.

On Friday this august remnant of the Pelhams went to court for the first time. At the foot of the stairs he cried and sunk down: the yeomen of the guard were forced to drag him up under the arms. When the closet-door opened, he flung himself at his length at the King's feet, sobbed, and cried, "God bless your Majesty! God preserve your Majesty!" and lay there howling and embracing the King's knees, with one foot so extended, that my Lord Coventry, who was *luckily* in waiting, and begged the standers-by to retire, with – "For God's sake, gentlemen, don't look at a great man in distress,"

1 With whom he was at variance. – WALPOLE.

endeavouring to shut the door, caught his grace's foot, and made him roar out with pain.

You can have no notion of what points of ceremony have been agitated about the tears of the family. George Selwyn[1] was told that my Lady Catherine had not shed one tear: "And pray," said he, "don't she intend it?" It is settled that Mrs. Watson is not to cry till she is brought to bed.

You love George Selwyn's *bons-mots:* this crisis has redoubled them: here is one of his best. My Lord Chancellor is to be Earl of Clarendon: – "Yes," said Selwyn, from the very summit of the whites of his demure eyes; "and I suppose he will get the title of Rochester for his son-in-law, my Lord Anson."[2] Do you think he will ever lose the title of Lord Rochester?

I expected that we should have been over-run with elegies and panegyrics; indeed, I comforted myself that one word in all of them would atone for the rest – the *late* Mr. Pelham.[3] But the world seems to allow that their universal attachment and submission was universal interestedness; there has not been published a single encomium: Orator Henley alone has held forth in his praise – yesterday it was on *charming Lady Catherine*. Don't you think it should have been in these words, in his usual style? "Oratory-chapel. – Right reason; madness; charming Lady Catherine; hell-fire," &c.

Monday, 18 March.

Almost as extraordinary news as our political, is, that it has snowed ten days successively, and most part of each day. It is living in Muscovy, amid ice and revolutions; I hope lodgings will begin to let a little dear in Siberia! Beckford[4] and Delaval, two celebrated partisans, met lately at Shaftesbury, where they oppose one another: the latter said,

"Art thou the man whom men famed Beckford call?"

1 George Selwyn, wit, friend and correspondent of Walpole: see heading to letter 208.
2 Selwyn's joke contrasts the alleged impotence of Lord Anson with the sexual vigour of the Earl of Rochester, the Restoration rake.
3 Henry Pelham (1694–1754), protégé of Sir Robert Walpole and prime minister since 1744, had died 6 March. He was succeeded by his older brother, the Duke of Newcastle.
4 William Beckford (bap. 1709–70), West Indies plantation owner, Lord Mayor of London and father of William Beckford (1760–1844), writer and collector.

T'other replied,

> "Art thou the much more famous Delaval?"

But to leave politics and change of ministries, and to come to something of *real* consequence, I must apply you to my library ceiling, of which I send you some rudiments. I propose to have it all painted by Clermont; the principal part in *chiaroscuro,* on the design which you drew for the Paraclete; but as that pattern would be surfeiting, so often repeated in an extension of twenty feet by thirty, I propose to break and enliven it by compartments in colours, according to the enclosed sketch, which you must adjust and dimension. Adieu!

16. *Pitt and Single-speech Hamilton.*[1]

TO THE HON. H. S. CONWAY

Arlington Street, 15 November 1755.

... There was a young Mr. Hamilton who spoke for the first time, and was at once perfection: his speech was set, and full of antithesis, but those antitheses were full of argument: indeed his speech was the most argumentative of the whole day; and he broke through the regularity of his own composition, answered other people, and fell into his own track again with the greatest ease. His figure is advantageous, his voice strong and clear, his manner spirited, and the whole with the ease of an established speaker. You will ask, what could be beyond this? Nothing, but what was beyond what ever was, and that was Pitt![2] He spoke at past one, for an hour and thirty-five minutes: there was more humour, wit, vivacity, finer language, more boldness, in short, more astonishing perfections, than even you, who are used to him, can conceive. He was not abusive, yet very attacking on all sides: he ridiculed my Lord Hillsborough, crushed poor Sir George, terrified the Attorney, lashed my Lord Granville, painted my Lord of Newcastle, attacked Mr. Fox, and even hinted up to the Duke [of Cumberland]. A few of the Scotch were in the minority, and most

1 William Gerard Hamilton [died 1796]. It was this speech which, not being followed, as was naturally expected, by repeated exhibitions of similar eloquence acquired for him the name of *single-speech* Hamilton. – WALPOLE.
2 William Pitt (1708–78), later 1st Earl of Chatham.

of the Princess's people, not all: all the Duke of Bedford's in the majority. He himself spoke in the other House for the address (though professing incertainty about the treaties themselves), against my Lord Temple and Lord Halifax, without a division. My Lord Talbot was neuter; he and I were of a party: my opinion was strongly with the opposition; I could not vote for the treaties; I would not vote against Mr. Fox. It is ridiculous perhaps, at the end of such a debate, to give an account of my own silence; and as it is of very little consequence what I did, so it is very unlike me to justify myself. You know how much I hate *professions* of integrity; and my pride is generally too great to care what the generality of people say of me: but your heart is good enough to make me wish you should think well of mine. . . . Adieu!

17. *Coalition Between Pitt and Newcastle.*

TO SIR HORACE MANN

Strawberry Hill, 20 June 1757.

I renounce all prophesying; I will never suppose that I can foresee politically; I can foresee nothing, whatever I may foretell. Here is a Ministry formed of *all* the people who for these ten weeks have been giving each other exclusion! I will now not venture even to pronounce that they cannot agree together. On Saturday last, the 18th, Lord Hardwicke carried to Kensington the result of the last negotiations between Newcastle and Pitt, and the latter followed and actually kissed hands again for the seals.[1] Here is the arrangement as far as I know it, the most extraordinary part of which is, that they suffer Mr. Fox to be Paymaster – oh! no, it is more extraordinary that he will submit to be so. His grace returns to the Treasury, and replaces there his singular good friend Mr. Legge. Lord Holdernesse comes to life again as Secretary of State: Lord Anson reassumes the Admiralty, not with the present board, nor with his own, but with Mr. Pitt's, and this by Mr. Pitt's own desire. The Duke of Dorset retires with a pension of 4000*l.* a-year, to make room for Lord Gower, that he may make room for Lord Temple. Lord George Sackville forces out Lord Barrington from Secretary at War, who was going to resign

1 That is, kissed the King's hand on being appointed Secretary of State.

with the rest, for fear Mr. Fox should, and that this plan should not, take place. Lord Hardwicke, *young disinterested creature!* waits till something drops. Thus far all was smooth; but even this perfection of harmony and wisdom meets with rubs. Lord Halifax had often and lately been promised to be erected into a Secretary of State for the West Indies. Mr. Pitt says, "No, I will not part with so much power." Lord Halifax resigned on Saturday, and Lord Duplin succeeds him. The two Townshends are gone into the country in a rage; Lord Anson is made the pretence: Mr. Fox is the real sore to George, Lord G. Sackville to Charles. Sir George Lee, who resigned his Treasurership to the Princess against Mr. Pitt, and as the world says, wanting to bring Lord Bute into Doctors' Commons,[1] is succeeded by Lord Bute's brother Mackenzie; but to be sure, all this, in which there is no intrigue, no change, no policy, no hatred, no jealousy, no disappointment, no resentment, no mortification, no ambition, will produce the utmost concord! It is a system formed to last; and to be sure it will! In the mean time, I shall bid adieu to politics; my curiosity is satisfied for some months, and I shall betake myself to employments I love better, and to this place which I love best of all. . . . Adieu!

18. *Newcastle's Unpopularity.*

TO GEORGE MONTAGU, ESQ.

Arlington Street, 26 April 1759.

. . . The ball, at Bedford-house, on Monday, was very numerous and magnificent. The two Princes were there, deep hazard, and the Dutch deputies, who are a proverb for their dulness: they have brought with them a young Dutchman who is the richest man of Amsterdam. I am amazed Mr. Yorke has not married him! But the delightful part of the night was the appearance of the Duke of Newcastle, who is veering round again, as it is time to betray Mr. Pitt. The Duchess [of Bedford] was at the very upper end of the gallery, and though some of the Pelham court were there too, yet they showed so little cordiality to this revival of connection, that

---

1 Meaning the offence he took at Lord Bute's favour. Sir George Lee was a civilian. — WALPOLE.

Newcastle had nobody to attend him but Sir Edward Montagu, who kept pushing him all up the gallery. From thence he went into the hazard-room, and wriggled, and shuffled, and lisped, and winked, and spied, till he got behind the Duke of Cumberland, the Duke of Bedford, and Rigby; the first of whom did not deign to notice him; but he must come to it. You would have died to see Newcastle's piti-ful and distressed figure, – nobody went near him: he tried to flatter people, that were too busy to mind him; in short, he was quite dis-concerted; his treachery used to be so sheathed in folly, that he was never out of countenance; but it is plain he grows old. To finish his confusion and anxiety, George Selwyn, Brand, and I, went and stood near him, and in half whispers, that he might hear, said, "Lord, how he is broke! how old he looks!" then I said, "This room feels very cold: I believe there never is a fire in it." Presently afterwards I said, "Well, I'll not stay here; this room has been washed to-day." In short, I believe we made him take a double dose of Gascoign's powder when he went home. Next night Brand and I communicated this interview to Lord Temple, who was in agonies; and yesterday his chariot was seen in forty different parts of the town. I take for granted that Fox will not resist these overtures, and then we shall see the Paymastership, the Secretaryship of Ireland, and all Calcraft's regiments once more afloat. . . .

19. *At Lynn.*

TO GEORGE MONTAGU, ESQ.

Epping, 31 March 1761, addition to letter begun 25 March.

No, I have not seen him;[1] he loitered on the road, and I was kept at Lynn[2] till yesterday morning. It is plain I never knew for how many trades I was formed, when at this time of day I can begin electioneering, and succeed in my new vocation. Think of me, the subject of a mob, who was scarce ever before in a mob, addressing them in the town-hall, riding at the head of two thousand people through such a town as Lynn, dining with above two hundred of them, amid bumpers, huzzas, songs, and tobacco, and finishing with

1 Henry Conway.
2 King's Lynn, of which Walpole was M.P. from 1757 until his resignation in 1768.

country dancing at a ball and sixpenny whisk! I have borne it all cheerfully; nay, have sat hours in *conversation,* the thing upon earth that I hate; have been to hear misses play on the harpsichord, and to see an alderman's copies of Reubens and Carlo Marat. Yet to do the folks justice, they are sensible, and reasonable, and civilised; their very language is polished since I lived among them. I attribute this to their more frequent intercourse with the world and the capital, by the help of good roads and postchaises, which, if they have abridged the King's dominions, have at least tamed his subjects. Well, how comfortable it will be to-morrow, to see my parroquet, to play at loo, and not to be obliged to talk seriously! The Heraclitus of the beginning of this letter will be overjoyed on finishing it to sign himself your old friend

DEMOCRITUS.[1]

P.S. I forgot to tell you that my ancient aunt Hammond came over to Lynn to see me; not from any affection, but curiosity. The first thing she said to me, though we have not met these sixteen years, was, "Child, you have done a thing to-day, that your father never did in all his life; you sat as they carried you, – he always stood the whole time." "Madam," said I, "when I am placed in a chair, I conclude I am to sit in it; besides, as I cannot imitate my father in great things, I am not at all ambitious of mimicking him in little ones." I am sure she proposes to tell her remarks to my uncle Horace's ghost, the instant they meet.

20. *Pitt Accepts a Pension.*

TO THE COUNTESS OF AILESBURY[2]

Strawberry Hill, 10 October 1761.

I don't know what business I had, Madam, to be an economist: it was out of character. I wished for a thousand more drawings in

1 Walpole contrasts his more melancholic opening to the full letter, not here printed, with its more cheerful ending, by reference to two Greek philosophers, the melancholy Heraclitus and the cheerful Democritus.
2 Caroline Bruce, *née* Campbell (1721–1803), was the widow of the Earl of Ailesbury when she married Walpole's friend, cousin and correspondent Henry Seymour Conway in 1747. According to the custom of the day she continued to be known as Lady Ailesbury after her second marriage.

that sale at Amsterdam, but concluded they would be very dear; and not having seen them, I thought it too rash to trouble your ladyship with a large commission. . . .

I wish I could give you as good an account of your commission; but it is absolutely impracticable. I employed one of the most sensible and experienced men in the Custom-House; and all the result was, he could only recommend me to Mr. Amyand as the newest, and consequently the most polite of the commissioners – but the Duchess of Richmond had tried him before – to no purpose. There is no way of recovering any of your goods, but purchasing them again at the sale.

What am I doing, to be talking to you of drawings and chintzes, when the world is all turned topsy turvy? Peace, as the poets would say, is not only returned to heaven, but has carried her sister Virtue along with her! – Oh! no, Peace will keep no such company – Virtue is an errant strumpet, and loves diamonds as well as my Lady Harrington, and is as fond of a coronet as my Lord Melcombe.[1] Worse! worse! She will set men to cutting throats, and pick their pockets at the same time. I am in such a passion, I cannot tell you what I am angry about – why, about Virtue and Mr. Pitt; two errant cheats, gipsies! I believe he was a comrade of Elizabeth Canning, when he lived at Enfield-wash.[2] In short, the council were for making peace;

> But he, as loving his own pride and purposes
> Evades them with a bombast circumstance,
> Horribly stuff'd with epithets of war,
> And in conclusion – nonsuits my mediators.[3]

He insisted on a war with Spain, was resisted, and last Monday resigned. The City breathed vengeance on his opposers, the Council quaked, and the Lord knows what would have happened; but yesterday, which was only Friday, as this giant was stalking to seize the Tower of London, he stumbled over a silver penny, picked it up, carried it home to Lady Hester, and they are now as quiet, good sort of people, as my Lord and Lady Bath who lived in the vinegar-

1 Lady Caroline Fitzroy (1722–84), society beauty who married the Earl of Harrington; and George Bubb Dodington (1690/1–1762), Lord Melcombe, self-seeking politician.
2 Elizabeth Canning was a maidservant who claimed in a celebrated case to have been imprisoned in 1753 at a house at Enfield Wash. William Pitt had sometimes lived nearby at Enfield Chase. Canning was subsequently convicted of perjury.
3 *Othello* I, i, ll. 12–16.

bottle. In fact, Madam, this immaculate man has accepted the Barony of Chatham for his wife, with a pension of three thousand pounds a-year for three lives; and though he has not quitted the House of Commons, I think my Lord Abercorn would now be as formidable there. The pension he has left *us*, is a war for three thousand lives! perhaps, for twenty times three thousand lives! – But –

> Does this become a soldier? *this* become
> Whom armies follow'd, and a people loved?[1]

What! to sneak out of the scrape, prevent peace, and avoid the war! blast one's character, and all for the comfort of a paltry annuity, a long-necked peeress and a couple of Grenvilles! The City looks mighty foolish, I believe, and possibly even Beckford may blush. Lord Temple resigned yesterday: I suppose his virtue pants for a dukedom. Lord Egremont has the seals; Lord Hardwicke, I fancy, the Privy Seal; and George Grenville, no longer Speaker, is to be the cabinet minister in the House of Commons. Oh! Madam, I am glad you are inconstant to Mr. Conway, though it is only with a Barbette! If you piqued yourself on your virtue, I should expect you would sell it to the master of a Trechscoot.[2]

I told you a lie about the King's going to Ranelagh – No matter; there is no such thing as truth. The Duchess of Marlborough is dead, and Lady Berkeley has given up her jointure without dying – to avoid the ecclesiastical court.[3] Garrick exhibits the Coronation, and, opening the end of the stage, discovers a real bonfire and real mob: the houses in Drury-lane let their windows at threepence a head. Rich[4] is going to produce a finer Coronation, nay, than the real one; for there is to be a dinner for the Knights of the Bath and the Barons of the Cinque-ports, which Lord Talbot refused them.

I put your Caufields and Stauntons into the hands of one of the first heralds upon earth, and who has the entire pedigree of the Careys; but he cannot find a drop of Howard or Seymour blood in the least artery about them. Good night, Madam!

---

1 Edward Young, *The Revenge: A Tragedy*, III, i, ll. 335–6.
2 A barbette is a poodle, and a trechscoot is a Dutch canal boat.
3 The Yale editors note that Lady Berkeley, who had given birth to a child which her husband did not acknowledge as his, had been threatened by him with divorce if she did not give up her jointure.
4 John Rich (1692–1761), theatrical manager.

21. *Bute Resigns.*

TO GEORGE MONTAGU, ESQ.

Arlington Street, Friday night, late, 8 April 1763.

… If I had time or command enough of my thoughts, I could give you as long a detail of as unexpected a revolution in the political world. To-day has been as fatal to a whole nation, I mean to the Scotch, as to our family. Lord Bute resigned this morning. His intention was not even suspected till Wednesday, nor at all known a very few days before. In short, there is nothing, more or less, than a panic; a fortnight's opposition has demolished that scandalous but vast majority, which a fortnight had purchased; and in five months a plan of absolute power has been demolished by a panic. He pleads to the world bad health; to his friends, more truly, that the nation was set at him. He pretends to intend retiring absolutely, and giving no umbrage. In the mean time he is patching up a sort of ministerial legacy, which cannot hold even till next session, and I should think would scarce take place at all. George Grenville is to be at the head of the Treasury and Chancellor of the Exchequer; Charles Townshend to succeed him; and Lord Shelburne, Charles. Sir Francis Dashwood to have his barony of Despencer and the Great Wardrobe, in the room of Lord Gower, who takes the Privy Seal, if the Duke of Bedford takes the presidentship; but there are many *ifs* in this arrangement; the principal *if* is, if they dare stand a tempest which has so terrified the pilot. You ask what becomes of Mr. Fox? Not at all pleased with this sudden determination, which has blown up so many of his projects, and left him time to heat no more furnaces, he goes to France by the way of the House of Lords,[1] but keeps his place and his tools till something else happens. The confusion I suppose will be enormous, and the next act of the drama a quarrel among the Opposition who would be all-powerful if they could do what they cannot, hold together and not squabble for the plunder. As I shall be at a distance for some days, I shall be able to send you no more particulars of this interlude, but you will like a pun my brother made when he was told of this explosion: "Then," said he, "they must turn the *Jacks*[2] out of the drawing-room again, and

1 Fox was about to be created Baron Holland of Foxley.
2 The jack boot was the symbol used to mock Lord Bute.

again take them into the kitchen." Adieu! what a world to set one's heart on!

22. *Grenville Rebuked.*

TO THOMAS PITT, ESQ.[1]

Strawberry Hill, 5 June 1764.

Dear Sir,

... You know I went so far as to tell you that Mr. Conway[2] was, I firmly believed, not only not in opposition, but should he be ever so ill-used, and the Ministry should propose a question which he thought right for this country, he would vote for it. I remain exactly of the same opinion. He has been as ill, as hardly, and as unjustly used, as ever man was; and yet he will do what he thinks right, though his behaviour may serve his bitterest enemies; for he will never suffer his personal resentments to carry him to do a wrong thing, even to his foes, much less towards his country.

When I say he has been ill-used, I repeat with great sincerity – and you who have known, and are so good as to allow my real regard to Mr. Grenville, will believe me – that few things would give me more pleasure than to be assured that the dismission of Mr. Conway was without Mr. Grenville's consent or approbation.

You say that below the Bar of the House of Lords, Mr. Grenville told you and me that Mr. Conway had declared that he was not then engaged, nor did at that time intend to engage in any system of opposition; but at the same time desired not to be understood to intend to separate himself from the Dukes of Grafton and Devonshire, to whom he was obliged. This agrees with the message I myself delivered to Mr. Grenville from Mr. Conway, that he was in no opposition, nor thought of being in any; but in answer to Mr. Grenville's question, whether there was anything he would like, he declared he would accept nothing while those Dukes were dissatisfied with the Administration. Both your state of the case and mine, which agree together, do not at all coincide with Mr.

---

1 Thomas Pitt (1737–93), M.P., later Baron Camelford, nephew of William Pitt the Elder.
2 In April 1764 it had been made public that (at the King's behest) Walpole's cousin Conway was for political opposition dismissed from his regiment and from his position as Groom of the Bedchamber.

Grenville's letter to Lord Hertford, that he had found Mr. Conway's connections with his friends *unbounded*.

I have omitted, for the last, one passage, which I had forgotten in my own memorandums, which yet, from your assertion – who I am sure will adhere in every point to the strict matter of fact, let it affect whom it will – I am not only persuaded passed, but I think I recollect it myself, from the circumstance of the particular day on which it passed. You say Mr. Grenville told me that a regular system of opposition to Government would render any one unfit for a high rank in military command; and that in some instances, as in cases of tumults and insurrections, such a man would be more dangerous to the King and Commonwealth.

I am sure I do not remember the word *Commonwealth* being used; though if you assert it I cannot take upon me to say it was not used, for I remember this salvo but imperfectly. I know the day of the conversation was after the tumult on the burning of the "North Briton."[1] Mr. Grenville was much flustered, and very likely applied the case of the day to the subject we were discussing; and if he did, it probably made the less impression on me, because my mind had been already struck with the same singular words from you before the tumult happened; and therefore, when I heard them repeated by a Minister, it was natural for me to conclude you had heard them from his mouth, as you came to me with a message from him; and I am bold to declare, such words in the mouth of a Minister are to me exceedingly alarming. As such I have repeated them, and I leave you, who know me, to judge whether I will retract anything I have said, which I am particularly authorised, by having taken down the words, to affirm are true, and to the very substance of which you agree, as I am sure you will to the precise words, being thus put in mind of them, especially as you own you are not exact in the very words.

I love and honour Mr. Conway above any man in the world; I would lay down my life for him; and shall I see him every day basely and falsely traduced in newspapers and libels, and not say what I know is true, when it sets his character in so fair and noble a light? I am asked to discourage reports. I am ready to discourage such as are *not* true, and do *not* come from me.

---

1 The journal of the opposition politician John Wilkes (1725–97), on whose arrest under a general warrant Conway had voted against the government.

Mr. Grenville is welcome to publish this letter; it will be the fullest answer to anything that is said against him without foundation. Let Mr. Grenville, in his turn, discourage and disavow the infamous calumnies published against Mr. Conway, the authors of which, I daresay, are unknown to Mr. Grenville, but who, not content with seeing Mr. Conway's fortune ruined, would stab his reputation likewise. Thank God! they cannot fix a blemish upon it. I will certainly bear witness to it, as much as lies in me. Fear or favour will not intimidate or warp my friendship. . . .

23. *Stamp Act Repealed.*

TO SIR HORACE MANN

Paris, 21 March 1766.

You are not very just to me, my dear Sir, in suspecting me of neglecting you. Do you think Paris has turned my head, or could make me, what England never could, forget you? Was not it so when I first arrived here? and did not you find at last that it was the post's fault, not mine? . . . I shall be in London by the middle of April, and then I trust our correspondences will have no more interruptions: but sure you ought to distrust anything sooner than a friendship so unalterable as mine.

We do not yet actually know the last step of the repeal of the Stamp Act, but have all reason to conclude that it passed in the most satisfactory manner for the Ministry, as, on the second reading in the House of Lords, it was carried by a majority of thirty-four, though no greater majority was expected than of five or six. The blood-thirsty protested, and intended to protest again on the last stage; an evident symptom of their despair; and a most foolish step, as it is marking out their names to the odium of the nation, and delivering down an attestation of their tyrannic principles to posterity. Lord Lyttelton drew the first, and I hope it will be bound up hereafter with his Persian Letters, to show on what contradictory principles his lordship can oppose.

Grenville is fallen below contempt; Sandwich and his parson Anti-Sejanus[1] [are] hooted off the stage. Mr. Pitt's abilities, I am

1 One Scott, a clergyman, employed by Lord Sandwich to write in the newspapers against Mr. Pitt. He signed his papers Anti-Sejanus. – WALPOLE.

told, have shone with greater lustre than ever, and with more variety. There is a report here that he has actually accepted the Administration. I do not believe that he has yet, though I am sure no French *wishes* coined the report. I could not have believed, if I had not come hither, how much they dread him.

Well! all this paves the way to what I wish, liberty to my country and liberty to me. Tranquillity bounds my ambition. To see Grenville, and such wretches, grovelling in the mire, gilds the peaceable scene. How many wretches have I lived to see England escape! Thank God I am not philosopher enough not to be grateful for it! I would not wrestle like the *savants* here, against any powers beyond those of this world. I may spurn pigmies of my own size; but do not question what I cannot fathom. Gods of stone, or kings of flesh, are my derision; but of all gods that were ever invented, the most ridiculous is that old lumpish god of the Grecian sophists, whom the modern literati want to reinstate – the god Matter. It would be like a revolution in England in favour of the late Pretender after he was bedridden. . . .

If you receive any one of my letters, pray assure Sir James Macdonald that I have answered his; but when they miscarry to you, I have less hopes of one reaching him. Direct your next to Arlington-street.

24. *Walpole Retires from Parliament.*

TO WILLIAM LANGLEY, ESQ., MAYOR OF LYNN

Sir: Arlington Street, 13 March 1767.

The declining state of my health, and a wish of retiring from all public business, have, for some time, made me think of not offering my service again to the town of Lynn, as one of their representatives in Parliament. I was even on the point, above eighteen months ago, of obtaining to have my seat vacated, by one of those temporary places, often bestowed for that purpose; but I thought it more respectful, and more consonant to the great and singular obligations I have to the Corporation and Town of Lynn, to wait till I had executed their commands, to the last hour of the commission they had voluntarily intrusted to me.

Till then, Sir, I did not think of making this declaration; but hearing that dissatisfaction and dissensions have arisen amongst you (of which I am so happy as to have been in no shape the cause), that a warm contest is expected, and dreading to see, in the uncorrupted town of Lynn, what has spread too fatally in other places, and what, I fear, will end in the ruin of this constitution and country, I think it my duty, by an early declaration, to endeavour to preserve the integrity and peace of so great, so respectable, and so unblemished a borough.

My father was re-chosen by the free voice of Lynn, when imprisoned and expelled by an arbitrary Court and prostitute Parliament; and from affection to his name, not from the smallest merit in me, they unanimously demanded me for their member, while I was sitting for Castle-Rising. Gratitude exacts what in any other light might seem vain-glorious in me to say, but it is to the lasting honour of the town of Lynn I declare, that I have represented them in two Parliaments without offering, or being asked, for the smallest gratification by any one of my constituents. May I be permitted, Sir, to flatter myself they are persuaded their otherwise unworthy representative has not disgraced so free and unbiassed a choice?

I have sat above five and twenty years in Parliament; and allow me to say, Sir, as I am, in a manner, giving up my account to my constituents, that my conduct in Parliament has been as pure as my manner of coming thither. No man who is, or has been Minister, can say that I have ever asked or received a personal favour. My votes have neither been dictated by favour nor influence, but by the principles on which the Revolution was founded, the principles by which we enjoy the establishment of the present Royal Family, the principles to which the town of Lynn has ever adhered, and by which my father commenced and closed his venerable life. The best and only honours I desire, would be to find that my conduct has been acceptable and satisfactory to my constituents.

From your kindness, Sir, I must entreat to have this notification made in the most respectful and grateful manner to the Corporation and Town of Lynn. Nothing can exceed the obligation I have to them, but my sensibility to their favours; and be assured, Sir, that no terms can outgo the esteem I have for so upright and untainted a borough, or the affection I feel for all their goodness to my family and to me. My trifling services will be overpaid if they graciously accept my intention of promoting their union, and preserving their virtue; and though I may be forgotten, I never shall, or can, forget the obligations they have conferred on,

Sir, their and your
Most devoted humble servant.

25. *Lord North: Prime Minister.*

TO SIR HORACE MANN

Arlington Street, 30 January 1770.

I do not know how the year will end, but, to be sure, it begins with as many events as ever happened to any one of its predecessors. The Duke of Grafton has resigned: in a very extraordinary moment indeed; in the midst of his own measures, in the midst of a session, and undefeated. It is true, his last victory was far from being so complete as the former; and hence, as Horatio says,[1] *have the talkers of this populous city* taken occasion to impute this sudden retreat to as sudden a panic. You must know, that last Friday, upon a question on that endless topic the Middlesex election,[2] the Court had a majority, at past three in the morning, of only four and forty. The expulsion of the Chancellor, the resignation of Lord Granby, and of so many others, and much maladroitness in stating the question on the Court-side, easily accounted for that diminution in the numbers; and yet, though I believe that that defalcation determined this step, I know it was not a new thought. Whenever the current did not run smooth, his Grace's first thought has been to resign. When Mr. Yorke refused to accept, the fit returned violently: when he did accept, the wind changed; and I believe I gave you an obscure hint of the extreme importance of that acceptance. Mr. Yorke's precipitate death unhinged all again; the impossibility of finding another Chancellor fixed the wind in the resigning corner, and the slender majority overset the vessel quite. In short, it is over. A very bad temper, no conduct, and obstinacy always ill-placed, have put an end to his Grace's administration.

1 In Nicholas Rowe, *The Fair Penitent*, III, i, l. 122.
2 The long-running saga of Wilkes's election for the constituency of Middlesex: for Wilkes, see letters 292 to 299.

What will follow is impossible to say. In the meantime Lord North is first Minister.[1] He is much more able, more active, more assiduous, more resolute, and more fitted to deal with mankind. But whether the apparent, nay glaring timidity of the Duke may not have spread too general an alarm, is more than probable; and there is but the interval of to-day to take any measures, as the question of Friday must be reported to the House to-morrow; whence, at least, the lookers-out may absent themselves till the trump is turned up. The fear of a dissolution of Parliament may keep a large number together, and the fluctuation of probability between Lord North, Lord Chatham, and Lord Rockingham, may occasion a confusion of which the Government may profit. The King, in the meantime, is much to be pitied; abandoned where he had most confidence, and attacked on every other side. I write to-day, because the post goes out, and I choose to give you the earliest intelligence of such a material event; but the letter I shall certainly send you on Friday, will tread upon a little firmer ground. ... Adieu!

26. *Chatham's Last Speech.*

TO SIR HORACE MANN

Thursday, 9 April 1778.

I am not going to announce more war than by my last: it seems to sleep, like a paroli at Faro, and be reserved for another deal. Though I write oftener than usual, I have not a full cargo every time; but I have two novel events to send you. The newspapers indeed anticipate many of my articles; but, as I suppose you pay me the compliment of opening my letters before the Gazettes, I shall be the first to inform you, though but by five minutes. Lord Chatham has again appeared in the House of Lords, and probably for the last time. He was there on Tuesday, against the earnest remonstrance of his physician; and, I think, only to make confusion worse confounded. He had intended to be very hostile to the Ministers, and yet to force himself into all their places by maintaining the *sovereignty* of America, to which none of the Opposition but his own few followers

---

1 Frederick, Lord North (1732–92), who remained prime minister for the following twelve years.

adhere; and they cannot, like a strolling company in a barn, fill all the parts of a drama with four or five individuals. It appeared early in his speech that he had lost himself; he did not utter half he intended, and sat down: but, rising again to reply to the Duke of Richmond, he fell down in an apoplectic fit, and was thought dead. They transported him into the Jerusalem Chamber, and laid him on a table. In twenty minutes he recovered his senses, and was carried to a messenger's house adjoining, where he still remains. The scene was very affecting; his two sons, and son-in-law, Lord Mahon, were round him. The House paid a proper mark of respect by adjourning instantly. . . . Adieu!

27. Indictment of the Government.

TO SIR HORACE MANN

Strawberry Hill, 30 June 1779.

This letter will be of very ancient date when you receive it, and not have one very near it perhaps when it sets out. Your nephew called here two days ago, just as I was going to town on business, and told me, to my joy on your account, that he was going in a fortnight to make you a short visit — a very meritorious one when the journey is so long. He has promised to come and dine here *tête-à-tête* before he goes; but, lest he should surprise me, I prepare this, which therefore shall not contain news that would be antiquated, but give you as just a picture as I can in few words of our situation and prospect, and as impartial one as I can, considering my indignation at the ruin brought upon my country by both as worthless and incapable a set of men as ever had the front to call themselves politicians. They have hurried us, and then blundered us, into a civil war, a French war, a Spanish war. America is lost; Jamaica, the West Indian islands, Gibraltar, and Port Mahon, are scarcely to be saved; Ireland is in great danger, either from invasion or provocation.

Of this country I should have little fear, if men who conducted themselves so wretchedly were not still our governors![1] We are at this instant expecting a sea-battle between our fleet and the united one of France and Spain; in which, if the latter, who are the stronger,

---

1 The government of Lord North.

by a matter of nine ships, have the decided advantage, we conclude they will pour in troops, considerably into Ireland, – here probably in less detachments, to distract us. The nation is not so much alarmed as might be expected. What is infinitely more astonishing is, that the Spanish war, on which the Ministers lulled the country asleep even *till two days* before the declaration, has not excited general, scarcely any, indignation against the criminals. In short, the Court, aided by the Tories and clergy, the worst Tories, have infatuated the nation; and though the Opposition have yearly, daily, hourly, laboured to prevent, and foretold every individual step that has happened, the money of the Treasury, the industry of the Scotch, and the rancour of the Tories have persuaded the majority of the people that the Opposition have almost conjured up the storm; though they have not been strong enough to carry a single question, have deprecated every measure pursued, and have had every one of their prophecies verified. – I, who affirm all this, and appeal to facts, am still not partial to the Opposition. So far from thinking they have gone too far, I know they have been too inert, and, early at least in the American war, might have stemmed some of the torrent. Yet I will do them justice, – the fairness of their character checked them; a less conscientious Opposition might have saved the nation.

In this predicament then we stand; a good man scarcely knows what to wish. New misfortunes would level us to the dust. Success in such hands as we are in, would blow them up to the acme of insolence; and, as the whole scope of all our errors was despotism, it is greatly to be feared that, with the loss of our outlying dominions, our trade, influence, and credit, we might lose our freedom too.

There is the true secret. Prerogative has been whispered into the nation's ear, and taken root. The Tories scruple not to call for it. The Ministers, worthless and incapable wretches, and ill-connected with each other, and cohering from common danger, have little or no credit with their Master; and, no one being predominant, no particular odium rests on any one. Thus, though I am persuaded almost every one condemns the measures he promotes, and must have foreseen the precipice, not one has had the honest courage to withstand the Spanish war; which I firmly believe was by no means the Spanish King's intention, but turned solely on the refusal of the Closet to relinquish American dependence. Everything has been risked rather than waive prerogative; and so abandoned are the higher orders, that, for the emolument of salaries, they have staked their children and the future security of their estates!

Our late prodigious wealth, and our dissipation, have concurred to facilitate this delusion. We have excellent orators both in the Administration and Opposition, but no great man; and few, very few, virtuous men, even in the latter; who, though impudently charged still with acting from interested motives, have over and over rejected every offer of advantage. I mean, personally. Anything would have been granted to divide them. You will say, good sense, not integrity, checked their acceptance. Perhaps so: yet, as the Court would never have changed its system, nor would part with the lead; it is plain the Opposition did not intend to individual lucre, as every Minister had been gained by it. I believe that neither Lord Rockingham nor Lord Shelburne would be content without being first Minister; but honesty must have been the motive of the rest. ...

28. *The Younger Pitt.*

TO THE HON. H. S. CONWAY

Strawberry Hill, 3 June 1781.

... The rising generation does give one some hopes. I confine myself to some of this year's birds. The young William Pitt[1] has again displayed paternal oratory. The other day, on the Commission of Accounts, he answered Lord North, and tore him limb from limb. If Charles Fox could feel one should think such a rival, with an unspotted character, would rouse him. What if a Pitt and Fox should again be rivals! A still newer orator has appeared in the India business, a Mr. Bankes, and against Lord North too; and with a merit that the very last crop of orators left out of their rubric – modesty. As young Pitt is modest too, one would hope some genuine English may revive! ...

1   William Pitt (1759–1806) [Pitt the Younger], foreseen here by Walpole as the future rival of Charles James Fox.

29. *The Rockingham Ministry – Fox.*

TO SIR HORACE MANN

5 May 1782.

... Your last is of April the 13th. You had not then heard of the Revolution, but was still talking of Minorca; which was totally absorbed in the late change,[1] and has not emerged since, nor do I think it will, at least not from want of matter. Such a revulsion as the late one may stun; it does not compose. Virtue and reformation may give the new Ministers some momentary popularity, but it will not be equally durable with the resentment of the displaced and the cashiered; nor do I take the late crew to be so punctilious as the late Opposition: nor is the nation so very virtuously disposed, as to be genuine admirers of reformation. People must be wondrously changed, if they vote as readily from esteem as they used to do for pay. Esteem is no principle of union. When men are paid, they must vote for what they are bidden to vote. They will have a thousand vagaries when at liberty to vote for what they fancy right or not. The Ministers must continually propose or support popular questions, or even yield to those who are running races of popularity with them; while the advocates for prerogative are crying out against inroads made on it.

All this, I have no doubt, will happen, unless some master-genius gains the ascendant. Mr. Fox[2] alone seems to be such a man. He already shines as greatly in Place as he did in Opposition, though infinitely more difficult a task. He is now as indefatigable as he was idle. He has perfect temper, and not only good-humour but good-nature; and, which is the first quality in a Prime Minister in a free country, has more common sense than any man, with amazing parts, that are neither ostentatious nor affected. Lord North had wit and good-humour, but neither temper, nor feeling, nor activity, nor good-breeding. Lord Chatham was a blazing meteor that scattered war with success, but sunk to nothing in peace. Perhaps I am partial to Charles Fox, because he resembles my father in good-sense – I wish he had his excellent constitution too; yet his application to

1 The recent change of ministry, with Lord Rockingham as prime minister: Minorca had been lost to the French and Spanish in February 1782.
2 Charles James Fox (1749–1806), Whig politician and statesman.

business may preserve his life, which his former dissipation constantly endangered. Another advantage we have is in Mr. Conway's being at the head of the Army. With him nobody stands in competition. His military knowledge is unquestionably without a rival. His predecessor, Lord Amherst, was as much below all rivals. There is no word for him but downright stupidity. Had five thousand French landed while he commanded, he was totally incapable of preparing or putting in motion the least opposition. I could tell you facts that would not be believed, though known to every ensign in the army. The fleet will now be united, and want none of its best officers. Lord Sandwich, though certainly a man of abilities, was grown obstinate, peevish, intractable, and was not born for great actions. He loved subtlety and tricks and indirect paths, qualities repugnant to genius. Still, I conclude, as I used to do before the change, let us have peace! We certainly are so far nearer to it, that these Ministers will leave nothing vigorous unattempted while the war lasts. The last neither thought of peace, nor took one proper step towards success in the war. The nation must have been utterly undone, had they remained a year longer in power. They thought their power secure, and really cared about nothing else; and many of them and all their tools and creatures wished for, and talked for, arbitrary power, as a compensation for all our misfortunes and disgraces. Indeed, I tell you the truth. I have seen it and known it long, and have not the smallest private interest in my opinions. From my father's death to my own it will be evident, that I never received a favour for myself from any other Minister of whatever party.

30. *Young Pitt, Secretary of State.*

TO SIR HORACE MANN

Berkeley Square, 7 July 1782.

I do not pretend to be a prophet; at least, I confess I am one of that wary sort, who take care to be very sure of what will happen before they venture to foretell. I ordered you to expect to be surprised – no very wise way of surprising! In truth, I did foresee that Lord Rockingham's death would produce a very new scene; and so it has: but is it possible to give an account of what is only beginning? The few real facts that have actually happened are all that one can relate with certainty. They will open wide fields of conjectures to you, and, at your distance, probably not very just ones; nor, as I affect no sagacity, shall I offer you a clue that may lead you as much out of the way.

Lord Rockingham died on Monday. On Tuesday it was known amongst the Ministers, that Lord Shelburne was to succeed. This was not unforeseen; but did not please those the better who were disposed to dislike it. Lord John Cavendish, who had most unwillingly been dragged into the office of Chancellor of the Exchequer, declared, that nothing should make him retain it under any other man than his late friend, for whose sake he had undertaken it. Mr. Fox more directly protested against Lord Shelburne. The Duke of Richmond and General Conway endeavoured to prevent disunion in the new system, and on Wednesday night did not despair; but on Thursday, at Court, Mr. Fox arrived, took Lord Shelburne aside, asked him abruptly, if he was to be First Lord of the Treasury; and, being answered in the affirmative, said, "Then, my Lord, I shall resign" – went into the Closet, and left the Seals, which he had brought in his pocket, with the King.

The schism begun, has gone farther. Everybody knew that the Rockingham and Shelburne squadrons, who had never been cordial even in opposition, had with great difficulty been brought to coalesce in the formation of the Administration, and some knew that their conjunction had not proceeded with much amity. In the first moment it was still hoped by moderate men that the breach – I mean the present – would not go far; as many disapprove Mr. Fox's precipitation. But he and Lord John had not taken their part with indifference. A meeting of the late Marquis's friends was held yesterday at Lord Fitzwilliam's – the nephew or Octavius of the late Cæsar, but no more likely to be an Augustus, than the Marquis was a Julius.[1] After a debate of six hours the whole junto, except the Duke of Richmond, resolved to secede; but, by *whole junto,* you must not understand all who had been adherents to Lord Rockingham. Some who had been would not attend this novel institution of hereditary right, nor understand why the Government is to be permanent in two or three great families, like the Hebrew priesthood in one tribe;

1 Walpole suggests that Rockingham's nephew, Lord Fitzwilliam, a possible leader of the Rockingham faction after his uncle's death, had no more the characteristics of Julius Caesar's nephew and successor Octavius than Rockingham had of Julius Caesar.

General Conway, you may be sure, was not of that assembly. He never would attach himself to either or any faction; and, though they may change their note, the dissidents themselves yet allow that they have no claim to his allegiance, and that he always acts by the rule of right – they forget that that law ought to supersede the ties of party.

Mr. Fox's proclamation of his pretensions – which I allow are very good, if qualifications gave a right of succession (which he did not indeed directly claim, naming the Duke of Portland for successor to Lord Rockingham, who certainly would not degenerate if insufficience proved the true heir), – has called forth a rival, who, it was foreseen, must become so sooner or later. Don't you anticipate me, and cry out "What! Mr. William Pitt?" Yes! he is to be Secretary of State – at two-and-twenty – that is some glory![1]

What else is to be, I am sure I cannot tell you. Perhaps by Tuesday night more may be settled; for, as the Parliament is to rise on Wednesday, the posts that may be vacant will be filled up, for the new writs to issue. Guesses I do not name, not to be obliged to contradict them. The new Opposition will be weak in numbers, and have none at all but dignified cyphers in the House of Lords. Lord Rockingham's party was not numerous, though the strongest of any single faction; and it loses its real chief, the Duke of Richmond, and a few more. Fox and Burke are its only efficient men. There are other points on which you might wish to question me; but I do not choose to *write* more than might be in the newspapers, but with this difference, that I relate nothing but facts that have entity. . . .

31. *Pitt and Fox.*

TO H.R.H. THE DUCHESS OF GLOUCESTER [2]

Thursday, 13 March 1783.

Your Royal Highness may be surprised, Madam, that after announcing the fall of Lord Shelburne, I should not have told you

1 Pitt the Younger was appointed Chancellor of the Exchequer in Lord Shelburne's short-lived government.
2 Walpole's favourite niece, Maria, Countess Waldegrave (bap. 1736–1807), second daughter of Walpole's brother Sir Edward by his mistress Dorothy Clement, married (1) James, 2nd Earl Waldegrave (d. 1763), and (2) William Henry, Duke of Gloucester (1743–1805), son of Frederick, Prince of Wales. In this letter Walpole comments on the Fox–North coalition.

who was his successor. I had more reasons than one, like the Mayor of Orleans; though that one were sufficient, viz., his having no successor till yesterday. I knew Lord Cholmondeley had written to the Duke; and in truth I did not care to tell foreign Post-offices, though no secret, the confusion we were in. I had rather anybody should publish our disgraces than I. Nay, I should perhaps have sent false news, for several appointments of Premiers were believed, each for a day, and proved false the next. The post was certainly offered to and declined by young Mr. Pitt, to Lord North, Lord Gower, and, it was said, to Lord Thurlow. At last, after a vacancy of seventeen days, Lord North was summoned yesterday, and ordered to make his proposed arrangement; in consequence of which the Duke of Portland was sent for next, and is First Lord of the Treasury. I have not yet heard the other changes or dispositions, but suppose we shall know the principal before this shall set out to-morrow.

There have been cart-loads of abuse, satiric prints, and some little humour on the coalition of Lord North and Mr. Fox; nor has Lord Shelburne been spared before or since his exit. It is remarkable that the counties and towns are addressing thanks for the peace, which their representatives have condemned. George Selwyn has been happiest, as usual, in his *bons-mots*. He calls Mr. Fox and Mr. Pitt the Idle and Industrious Apprentices. It is a coarser and much poorer piece of wit, I don't know whose, that the Duke of Portland is a fit *block* to hang *Whigs* on. You have seen in the papers, Madam, the new peerages and pensions, and therefore I do not mention them. I very likely repeat what you hear from your daughters and others, but what can I tell but what everybody knows? . . .

32. *Pitt's Reform Bill Rejected.*

TO SIR HORACE MANN

Thursday morning, early, 8 May 1783.

I write, though I wrote but last week, and rather to gratify your nephew than you. Mr. William Pitt's motion for reform of the House of Commons was rejected at past two this morning by 293 to 149. I know no particulars yet, but from a hasty account in a newspaper; and to those intelligencers for the circumstances I refer you and him, as I shall not have time to-day probably to relate them after I have heard them, and must go to Strawberry Hill to-morrow morning to receive company, and this must go away to-morrow night.

This great majority will, I hope, at least check such attempts. Indeed, when 293 members dare to pronounce so firmly, it is plain that the spirit of innovation has gained but few counties; five or six at most, supposing Kent and Essex added to the *Quintuple* Alliance. That very epithet proves that the demand is confined to a small number. The object of altering the Representation I think most dangerous. We know pretty well what good or evil the present state of the House of Commons can do: what an enlargement might achieve, no man can tell. Nay, allowing the present construction to be bad, it is clear that on emergencies it will do right. Were the House of Commons now existing the worst that ever was, still it must be acceptable to our Reformers: for which House of Commons, since the Restoration, ever did more than tear two Prime Ministers from the Crown in one year? In short, the constitution of the House of Commons I see in the same light as I do my own constitution. The gout raises inflammations, weakens, cripples; yet it purges itself, and requires no medicines. To quack it would kill me. Besides, it prevents other illnesses and prolongs life. Could I cure the gout, should not I have a fever, a palsy, or an apoplexy? ... Adieu! I have not a moment more – but I believe there is nothing more worthy telling you.

33. *Fox's India Bill.*

TO SIR HORACE MANN

Berkeley Square, 2 December 1783.

... The politicians of London, who at present are not the most numerous corporation, are warm on a bill for a new regulation of the East Indies, brought in by Mr. Fox. Some even of his associates apprehended his being defeated, or meant to defeat him; but his marvellous abilities have hitherto triumphed conspicuously, and on two divisions in the House of Commons he had majorities of 109 and 114. On *that* field he will certainly be victorious: the forces will be more nearly balanced when the Lords fight the battle; but, though the Opposition will have more generals and more able, he is

confident that his troops will overmatch theirs; and, in Parliamentary engagements, a superiority of numbers is not vanquished by the
talents of the commanders, as often happens in more martial en-
counters. His competitor, Mr. Pitt, appears by no means an adequate
rival. Just like their fathers, Mr. Pitt has brilliant language, Mr. Fox
solid sense; and such luminous powers of displaying it clearly, that
mere eloquence is but a Bristol stone, when set by the diamond
Reason. . . .

5th.

P.S. The Opposition in the House of Commons were so humbled
by their two defeats, that, though Mr. Pitt had declared he would
contest every clause (of the India bill) in the committee, (where in
truth, if the bill is so bad as he says, he ought at least to have tried
to amend it), that he slunk from the contest, and all the blanks were
filled up without obstruction, the opponents promising only to resist
it in its last stage on Monday next; but really, having no hopes but
in the House of Lords, where, however, I do not believe they expect
to succeed. Mr. Pitt's reputation is much sunk; nor, though he is a
much more correct logician than his father, has he the same firmness
and perseverance. It is no wonder that he was dazzled by his own
premature fame; yet his late checks may be of use to him, and teach
him to appreciate his strength better, or to wait till it is confirmed.
Had he listed under Mr. Fox, who loved and courted him, he would
not only have discovered modesty, but have been more likely to
succeed him, than by commencing his competitor. But what [have]
I to do to look into futurity?

34. *Pitt's Administration.*

TO SIR HORACE MANN

Berkeley Square, 30 March 1784.

As I expect your nephew in town previously to his setting out for
Florence, and as his residence, I conclude, from his having let his
house in London, will be very short, I prepare a letter to send by
him, lest I should not have time to write it leisurely when he comes,
and is departing again instantly.

My letters, since the great change in the Administration, have been rare, and much less informing than they used to be. In a word, I was not at all glad of the Revolution, nor have the smallest connection with the new occupants. There has been a good deal of boldness on both sides. Mr. Fox, convinced of the necessity of hardy measures to correct and save India, and coupling with that rough medicine a desire of confirming the power of himself and his allies, had formed a great system, and a very sagacious one; so sagacious, that it struck France with terror. But as the new power was to be founded on the demolition of that nest of monsters, the East [India] Company, and their spawn of Nabobs, &c., they took the alarm; and the secret junto at Court rejoiced that they did. The Court struck the blow at the Ministers; but it was the gold of the Company that really conjured up the storm, and has diffused it all over England.

On the other hand, Mr. Pitt has braved the majority of the House of Commons, has dissolved the existent one, and, I doubt, given a wound to that branch of the Legislature, that, if the tide does not turn, may be very fatal to the Constitution. The nation is intoxicated, and has poured in Addresses of Thanks to the Crown for exerting the prerogative *against* the palladium of the people. The first consequence will probably be that the Court will have a considerable majority upon the new elections. The country has acted with such precipitation, and with so little knowledge of the question, that I do not doubt but thousands of eyes will be opened and wonder at themselves; but the mischief will be done! But, without talking of futurity and constitutional points, you may easily judge what detriment the nation must have received already. The first year after a war – and after so fatal a war! – was the moment to set about repairing what could be repaired. *That* year is already lost, totally lost! not a measure has been taken yet; and it will be the end of May before even the session can begin. Unanimity, too, was essential; instead of which, behold two parties revived with as much animosity as ever actuated factions, except in religious wars! It was deemed of the last urgency that the East India Bill should have gone by the ships in February! not a bill is yet in the egg-shell. The Cabinet of Versailles speak their opinion plainly, by being zealous for Mr. Pitt; a sad compliment to him! And they are sending a powerful fleet to India, accompanied by Spaniards and Dutch. Guess how near we are to peace with Holland! Add to all these difficulties the incapacity of the new Ministers. Mr. Pitt is certainly an extraordinary young man; but is he a supernatural one? Do not trust to me but believe the Foreign Ministers. There is but one voice amongst them on the marvellous superiority of Mr. Fox, and the unheard-of facility of doing business with him. *He* made the peace between the Turks and Russia; and Simonin, the latter's Minister, told the King himself so in the Drawing-room since Fox's fall. On the contrary, those foreigners talk loudly of the extreme ignorance of the new Secretaries. Our Ambassador at Paris is a proverb of insufficience. Lord Shelburne (who, by the way, seems likely to succeed one of his successors, Lord Sydney), said the other day, "Upon my word, I hear that the Duke of Dorset's letters are written very well; he talks of the ceded islands as if he knew where they are."

This is a brief sketch of part of our history; for particulars, I refer myself to your nephew, pray send me back this letter by him, and the preceding parcel. You, with whom I have conversed so freely for above forty years, could not want a clue to my sentiments on the present crisis. I never have changed my principles, nor am likely. I shall continue to write to you on great events, but without comments, which would be unnecessary after I have given you this key.

In a general view, I suppose we shall fall into all the distractions of a ruined country. The memory of what we have been so recently will exasperate our feelings; or we shall grow insensible, remain dissipated till totally impoverished, and perhaps imagine from indolence that submission is easy! I am so near the end of my course, that I bear these uncomfortable prospects with more indifference than I should have done some years ago. I take no part; for, when boys are on the stage, a veteran makes but an awkward figure: nor can I tap a new controversy, of which I shall probably see but little of the progress. Methinks one ought to be ready to go at one's time, and not be called away when one has much to do. I was enough engaged when the former Pitt[1] and Fox were the heroes of the scene. Were I to list under the son of the one or the other, I should feel as if I were reading the romance of "Amadis de Gaul," which continues through the adventures of his son. . . .

---

1 Mr. Pitt was second son of William Earl of Chatham, who was also a second son; as Charles Fox was of Lord Holland, a second son also. – WALPOLE.

35. *Quarrel of Burke and Fox.*

TO MARY BERRY[1]

Berkeley Square, 12 May 1791.

... The Prince is recovered: that is all the domestic news, except a most memorable debate last Friday, in the House of Commons. Mr. Fox had most imprudently thrown out a panegyric on the French revolution. His most considerable friends were much hurt, and protested to him against such sentiments. Burke went much farther, and vowed to attack these opinions. Great pains were taken to prevent such altercation, and the Prince of Wales is said to have written a dissuasive letter to Burke; but he was immovable; and on Friday, on the Quebec Bill, he broke out, and sounded a trumpet against the plot, which he denounced as carrying on here. Prodigious clamours and interruption arose from Mr. Fox's friends; but he, though still applauding the French, burst into tears and lamentations on the loss of Burke's friendship, and endeavoured to make atonement; but in vain, though Burke wept too. In short, it was the most affecting scene possible; and undoubtedly an *unique* one, for both the commanders were earnest and *sincere*. Yesterday a second act was expected; but mutual friends prevailed, that the contest should not be renewed: nay, on the same bill, Mr. Fox made a profession of his faith, and declared he would venture his life in support of the *present* constitution by Kings, Lords, and Commons. In short, I never knew a wiser dissertation, if the newspapers deliver it justly; and I think all the writers in England cannot give more profound sense to Mr. Fox than he possesses. I know no more particulars, having seen nobody this morning yet. ... What shall I tell you else? We have expected Mrs. Damer from last night; and perhaps she may arrive before this sets out to-morrow. ...

1 See heading to letter 228.

III
WALPOLE AND THE COURT

WALPOLE'S ATTITUDE TO the royal court was one of quiz-zical fascination. In 1788 when he was over seventy he wrote his *Reminiscences* for his young friends the Berry sisters, recalling how at the age of ten he had asked to see the King, George I: his mother obtained the co-operation of the Duchess of Kendal, the King's mistress, with the result that he was taken one evening to the chambers of the Duchess in St. James's Palace, and when the King joined her for supper, he was allowed to kneel before him and kiss his hand. This was two days before George I left England for Hanover, dying on the journey: sixty-one years later, Walpole insisted that "The person of the King is as perfect in my memory as if I saw him but yesterday."[1]

Walpole, who was steeped in the history of court life of the previous century, presents the scene as a historical tableau. He was a devotee of the *Mémoires of the Comte du Grammont* ("you know I am Grammont-mad"[2]), with its lively evocation of the courts of Charles II and Louis XIV, and printed an edition of the book at his Strawberry Hill press. The recollections of former courtiers who had charmed the courts of their youth – Lady Suffolk, Lady Hervey, Madame du Deffand – also appealed to him greatly. "Old castles, old pictures, old histories, and the babble of old people make one live back into centuries that cannot disappoint one", he wrote in 1766.[3] Hence his imaginative response to a scene at Hampton Court twelve years later, when strolling in the gardens one summer evening with his two nieces, they joined a party, one of whom sang for the company. To Lady Ossory he wrote:

> It was moonlight and late, and very hot, and the lofty façade of the palace, and the trimmed yews and canal, made me fancy myself of a party in Grammont's time – so you don't wonder that by the help of imagination I never passed an evening more deliciously. When by the aid of some historic vision and local

1 *Reminiscences Written by Mr. Horace Walpole in 1788*, ed. Paget Toynbee (Oxford: Clarendon Press, 1924), p. 12.
2 Letter to George Montagu, 8 October 1751 (YE 9:124).
3 Ibid, 5 January 1766 (YE: 10:192).

circumstance I can romance myself into pleasure, I know nothing transports me so much.[1]

However, he did not allow a pleasant nostalgia to blind him to
the stifling atmosphere and enforced idleness of court life, warning
Mary Berry in 1794 of "ambition, jealousy, envy, and thence hatred,
insincerity, little intrigues for credit . . ." in the royal household, particularly amongst the women.[2]

Walpole also affected republican sympathies. He kept a copy of
Charles I's death warrant on one side of his bed at Strawberry Hill,
and a copy of Magna Carta on the other, and called Damiens'
attempt on the life of Louis XV in 1757 an example of "the least bad
of all murders, that of a king".[3] Such sentiments, never profoundly
felt, did not survive the onset of the French Revolution, and by the
time Louis XVI was executed had been replaced by utter horror at
the sufferings imposed on "the most perfect character that ever sat
on a throne" (letter 384).

He appreciated the theatrical spectacle of courts, as can be seen
in his great set-piece descriptions of the burial of George II and the
coronation of George III (letters 43 and 46). But he also enjoyed
some of the intimacies of court life, playing cards with Princess
Amelia, daughter of George II, and on one occasion accompanying
her on a visit to Stowe (letter 66). He also received at Strawberry
Hill two successive Dukes of York (letter 51) and, at the end of his
life, Queen Charlotte (letter 52): "I am to wear a sword," he complained to Conway. "If I *fall*, as ten to one but I do, to be sure it will
be a superb tumble, at the feet of a Queen and eight daughters of
Kings; for besides the six Princesses, I am to have the Duchess of
York and the Princess of Orange! Woe is me, at seventy-eight, and
with scarce a hand and foot to my back!" Along with the apprehension, the sense of pride is palpable.

36. *George I.'s Will.*

TO THE REV. WILLIAM COLE

14 October 1778.

I think you take in no newspapers, nor I believe condescend to
read any more modern than the *Paris à la Main* at the time of the

1 Letter 11 August 1778 (YE 33:42).
2 Letter to Mary Berry, 7 October 1794 (YE 12:130).
3 Letter to Horace Mann, 20 April 1757 (YE 21:79).

Ligue;[1] consequently you have not seen a new scandal on my father, which you will not wonder offends me. You cannot be interested in his defence; but, as it comprehends some very curious anecdotes, you will not grudge my indulging myself to a friend in vindicating a name so dear to me.

In the accounts of Lady Chesterfield's death and fortune, it is said that the late King, at the instigation of Sir Robert Walpole, burnt his father's Will which contained a large legacy to that, his supposed, daughter, – and I believe his real one; for she was very like him, as her brother, General Schulembourg, is, in black, to the late King. The fact of suppressing the Will is indubitably true; the instigator most false, as I can demonstrate thus: –

When the news arrived of the death of George the First, my father carried the account from Lord Townshend to the then Prince of Wales. One of the first acts of royalty is for the new monarch to make a speech to the Privy Council. Sir Robert asked the King who he would please to have draw the Speech, which was, in fact, asking who was to be Prime Minister; to which his Majesty replied, Sir Spencer Compton. It is a wonderful anecdote, and but little known, that the new Premier, a very dull man, could not draw the Speech, and the person to whom he applied was the deposed Premier. The Queen, who favoured my father, observed how unfit a man was for successor, who was reduced to beg assistance of his predecessor. The Council met as soon as possible, the next morning at latest. There Archbishop Wake, with whom one copy of the Will had been deposited (as another was, I think, with the Duke of Wolfenbuttle, who had a pension for sacrificing it, which, *I know*, the late Duke of Newcastle transacted), advanced, and delivered the Will to the King, who put it into his pocket, and went out of Council without opening it, the Archbishop not having courage or presence of mind to desire it to be read, as he ought to have done.

These circumstances, which I solemnly assure you are strictly true, prove that my father neither advised, nor was consulted; nor is it credible that the King in one night's time should have passed from the intention of disgracing him, to make him his bosom confidant on so delicate an affair.

1 Walpole's correspondent the Rev. William Cole was an antiquary: see heading to letter 211.

I was once talking to the late Lady Suffolk,[1] the former mistress, on that extraordinary event. She said, "I cannot justify the deed to the legatees; but towards his father, the late King was justifiable, for George the First had burnt two Wills made in favour of George the Second." I suppose they were the testaments of the Duke and Duchess of Zell, parents of George the First's wife, whose treatment of her they always resented. . . . Yours ever.

37. *The King's Levee.*

TO SIR HORACE MANN

Arlington Street, 1 November 1742.

I have not felt so pleasantly these three months as I do at present, though I have a great cold with coming into an unaired house, and have been forced to carry that cold to the King's levee and the drawing-room. There were so many new faces that I scarce knew where I was; I should have taken it for Carlton House,[2] or my Lady Mayoress's visiting-day, only the people did not seem enough at home, but rather as admitted to see the King dine in public. 'Tis quite ridiculous to see the numbers of old ladies, who, from having been wives of patriots, have not been dressed these twenty years;[3] out they come in all the accoutrements that were in use in Queen Anne's days. Then the joy and awkward jollity of them is inexpressible! They titter, and wherever you meet them, are always going to court, and looking at their watches an hour before the time. I met several on the birth-day, (for I did not arrive time enough to make clothes,) and they were dressed in all the colours of the rainbow: they seem to have said to themselves twenty-years ago, "Well, if ever I do go to court again, I will have a pink and silver, or a blue and silver," and they keep their resolutions. But here's a letter from you sent to me back from Houghton; I must stop to read it. . . . I laughed at myself prodigiously the other day for a piece of absence; I was writing on the King's birth-day, and being disturbed with the mob in

1 Henrietta Howard, Countess of Suffolk (*c.* 1688–1767), former mistress of George II, friend of Pope, and later neighbour of Walpole at Marble Hill, Twickenham.
2 Then the residence of Frederick, Prince of Wales.
3 That is, had not been dressed for court in twenty years as their husbands had been in the opposition.

the street, I rang for the porter, and, with an air of grandeur, as if I was still at Downing Street, cried, "Pray send away those marrow-bones and cleavers!" The poor fellow, with the most mortified air in the world, replied, "Sir, they are not at *our* door, but over the way at my Lord Carteret's."[1] "Oh," said I, "then let them alone; may be, he does not dislike the noise!" I pity the poor porter, who sees all his old customers going over the way too. . . . Adieu!

38. *The King's Return from Dettingen.*

TO SIR HORACE MANN

London, 17 November 1743.

I would not write on Monday till I could tell you the King was come. He arrived at St. James's between five and six on Tuesday. We were in great fears of his coming through the city, after the treason that has been publishing for these two months; but it is incredible how well his reception was beyond what it had ever been before; in short, you would have thought that it had not been a week after the victory at Dettingen.[2] They almost carried him into the palace on their shoulders; and at night the whole town was illuminated and bonfired. He looks much better than he has for these five years, and is in great spirits. The Duke limps a little. The King's reception of the Prince, who was come to St. James's to wait for him, and who met him on the stairs with his two sisters and the privy councillors, was not so gracious – *pas un mot* – though the Princess[3] was brought to bed the day before,[4] and Prince George [George III.] is ill of the small pox. It is very unpopular! You will possibly, by next week, hear great things: hitherto, all is silence, expectation, struggle, and

1 John Carteret (1690–1763), later 2nd Earl Granville, politician, and rival of Sir Robert Walpole, becoming a Secretary of State on Walpole's fall. The crowd would have been outside his house (which like Sir Robert Walpole's was in Arlington Street) because he was a leading member of the new ministry.
2 The battle of Dettingen (June 1743), where the combined Allied armies, led by George II, defeated the French during the War of the Austrian Succession.
3 Princess Augusta (1719–72), wife of Frederick, Prince of Wales, and mother of George III.
4 Of a son, subsequently the Duke of Gloucester, who in 1766 married Walpole's niece Maria, Lady Waldegrave, following the death of her first husband.

ignorance. The birth-day is kept on Tuesday, when the Parliament was to have met; but that can't be yet. . . .

39. *Death of the Prince of Wales.*

TO SIR HORACE MANN

Arlington Street, 21 March 1751.

What, another letter, when I wrote to you but last week! – Yes – and with an event too big to be kept for a regular interval. You will imagine from the conclusion of my last letter that our King is dead – or, before you receive this, you will probably have heard by flying couriers that it is only our King that was to be. In short, the Prince died last night between nine and ten. If I don't tell you ample details, it is because you must content yourself with hearing nothing but what I know true. He had had a pleurisy, and was recovered. Last Tuesday was se'nnight he went to attend the King's passing some bills in the House of Lords; from thence to Carlton House, very hot, where he unrobed, put on a light unaired frock and waistcoat, went to Kew, walked in a bitter day, came home tired, and lay down for three hours, upon a couch in a very cold room at Carlton House, that opens into the garden. Lord Egmont told him how dangerous it was, but the Prince did not mind him. My father once said to this King, when he was ill and royally untractable, "Sir, do you know what your father died of? of thinking he could not die." In short, the Prince relapsed that night, has had three physicians ever since, and has never been supposed out of danger till yesterday: a thrush had appeared, and for the two or three last evenings he had dangerous suppressions of breath. However, his family thought him so well yesterday, that there were cards in his outward room. Between nine and ten he was seized with a violent fit of coughing. Wilmot, and Hawkins the surgeon, were present: the former said, "Sir, have you brought up all the phlegm? I hope this will be over in a quarter of an hour, and that your Royal Highness will have a good night." Hawkins had occasion to go out of the room, and said, "Here is something I don't like." The cough continued; the Prince laid his hand upon his stomach, and said, "*Je sens la mort!*" The page who held him up, felt him shiver, and cried out, "The Prince is going!" The Princess was at the feet of the bed; she catched up a candle and ran to him, but before she got to the head of the bed, he was dead.

Lord North was immediately sent to the King who was looking over a table, where Princess Emily, the Duchess of Dorset, and Duke of Grafton were playing. He was extremely surprised, and said, "Why, they told me he was better!" He bid Lord North tell the Princess he would do everything she could desire; and has this morning sent her a very kind message in writing. He is extremely shocked – but no pity is too much for the Princess; she has eight children, and is seven months gone with another. She bears her affliction with great courage and sense. They asked her if the body was to be opened; she replied, what the King pleased. ... Adieu! I have not time to write any longer to you; but you may well expect our correspondence will thicken.

40. *The New Prince of Wales.*

TO SIR HORACE MANN

1 April 1751.

... Now I will divert your private grief by talking to you of what is called the public. The King and Princess are grown as fond as if they had never been of different parties, or rather as people who always had been of different. She discountenances all opposition, and he *all ambition*. Prince George, who, with his two eldest brothers, is to be lodged at St. James's, is speedily to be created Prince of Wales. Ayscough, his tutor, is to be removed with her entire inclination as well as with everybody's approbation. They talk of a Regency to be established (in case of a minority) by authority of Parliament, even this session, with the Princess at the head of it. She and Dr. Lee, the only one she consults of the late cabal, very sensibly burned the late Prince's papers the moment he was dead. Lord Egmont, by seven o'clock the next morning, summoned (not very decently) the faction to his house: all was whisper! at last he hinted something of taking the Princess and her children under their protection, and something of the necessity of harmony. No answer was made to the former proposal. Somebody said, it was very likely indeed they should agree now, when the Prince could never bring it about; and so everybody went away to take care of himself. The imposthumation is supposed to have proceeded, not from his fall, last year, but from a blow with a tennis-ball some years ago. The grief for the dead brother is affectedly great; the aversion to the living one as affectedly displayed. They cried about an elegy,[1] and added, "Oh, that it were but his brother!" On 'Change they said, "Oh, that it were but the butcher!"[2] . . .

41. *Death of George II.*

TO GEORGE MONTAGU, ESQ.

Arlington Street, 25 October 1760.
I tell a lie, I am at Mr. Chute's.

Was ever so agreeable a man as King George the Second, to die the very day it was necessary to save me from a ridicule? I was to have kissed hands to-morrow – but you will not care a farthing about that now; so I must tell you all I know of departed majesty. He went to bed well last night, rose at six this morning as usual, looked, I suppose, if all his money was in his purse, and called for his chocolate. A little after seven, he went into the water-closet; the German *valet de chambre* heard a noise, louder than the royal wind, listened, heard something like a groan, ran in, and found the hero of Oudenarde and Dettingen on the floor, with a gash on his right temple, by falling against the corner of a bureau. He tried to speak, could not, and expired. Princess Emily was called, found him dead, and wrote to the Prince. I know not a syllable, but am come to see and hear as much as I can. I fear you will *cry and roar all night*, but one could not

---

1 The elegy was the following set of popular verses:
Here lies Fred,
Who was alive and is dead:
Had it been his father,
I had much rather;
Had it been his brother,
Still better than another;
Had it been his sister,
No one would have missed her;
Had it been the whole generation,
Still better for the nation:
But since 'tis only Fred,
Who was alive and is dead –
There's no more to be said.
2 William Augustus, Duke of Cumberland (1721–65), referred to as the butcher of Culloden.

keep it from you. For my part like a new courtier, I comfort myself, "considering what a gracious Prince comes next."¹ Behold my luck. I wrote to Lord Bute, thrust in all the *unexpecteds, want of ambition, disinteresteds*, &c. that I could amass, gilded with as much duty, affection, zeal, &c. as possible. I received a very gracious and sensible answer, and was to have been presented to-morrow, and the talk of the few people, that are in town, for a week. Now I shall be lost in the crowd, shall be as well there as I desire to be, have done what was right, they know I want nothing, may be civil to me very cheaply, and I can go and see the puppet-show for this next month at my ease: but perhaps, you will think all this a piece of art; to be sure, I have timed my court, as luckily as possible, and contrived to be the last person in England that made interest with the successor. You see virtue and philosophy always prove to know the world and their own interest. However, I am not so abandoned a patriot yet, as to desert my friends immediately; you shall hear now and then the events of the new reign – if I am not made secretary of state – if I am, I shall certainly take care to let you know it.

I had really begun to think that the lawyers for once talked sense, when they said the *King never dies*. He probably got his death, as he had liked to have done two years ago, by viewing the troops for the expedition from the wall of Kensington Garden. My Lady Suffolk told me about a month ago that he had often told her, speaking of the dampness of Kensington, that he would never die there. For my part, my man Harry will always be a favourite; he tells me all the amusing news; he first told me of the late Prince of Wales's death, and to-day of the King's. . . .

42. *Accession of George III.*

TO GEORGE MONTAGU, ESQ.

Arlington Street, 31 October 1760.

When you have changed the cypher of George the Second into that of George the Third, and have read the Addresses, and have shifted a few Lords and Grooms of the Bedchamber, you are master

1 A reference to Pope, *Epilogue to the Satires*, Dialogue I. 108, "Consid'ring what a gracious Prince was next".

of the history of the new reign, which is indeed but a new lease of the old one. The *Favourite*[1] took it up in a high style; but having, like my Lord Granville, forgot to ensure either house of Parliament, or the mob, the third house of Parliament, he drove all the rest to unite. They have united, and have notified their resolution of governing as before: not but the Duke of Newcastle cried for his old master, desponded for himself, protested he would retire, consulted everybody whose interest it was to advise him to stay, and has accepted to-day, thrusting the dregs of his ridiculous life into a young court, which will at least be saved from the imputation of childishness, by being governed by folly of seventy years' growth.

The young King has all the appearance of being amiable. There is great grace to temper much dignity and extreme good-nature, which breaks out on all occasions. He has shown neither inveteracy nor malice – in short we must have gained – he cannot be so unfeeling, so avaricious, or so German as his grandfather. Even the Household is not settled yet. . . . A week has finished my curiosity fully; I return to Strawberry to-morrow, and I fear go next week to Houghton, to make an appearance of civility to Lynn, whose favour I never asked, nor care if I have or not; but I don't know how to refuse this attention to my Lord Orford, who begs it.

I trust you will have approved my behaviour at Court, that is my mixing extreme politeness with extreme indifference. Our predecessors, the philosophers of ancient days, knew not how to be disinterested without brutality; I pique myself on founding a new sect. My followers are to tell kings, with excess of attention, that they don't want them, and to despise favour with more good breeding than others practise in suing for it. We are a thousand times a greater nation than the Grecians; why are we to imitate them? Our sense is as great, our follies greater; sure we have all the pretensions to superiority! Adieu! . . .

1 John Stuart (1713–92), 3rd Earl of Bute.

43. *Burial of George II. – The New King.*

TO GEORGE MONTAGU, ESQ.

Arlington Street, 13 November 1760.

Even the honeymoon of a new reign don't produce events every day. There is nothing but the common toying of addresses and kissing hands. The chief difficulty is settled; Lord Gower yields the Mastership of the Horse to Lord Huntingdon, and removes to the Great Wardrobe, from whence Sir Thomas Robinson was to have gone into Ellis's place, but he is saved. The City, however, have a mind to be out of humour; a paper has been fixed on the Royal Exchange with these words, "No petticoat Government, no Scotch Minister, no Lord George Sackville;" two hints totally unfounded, and the other scarce true.[1] No petticoat ever governed less, it is left at Leicester-house; Lord George's breeches are as little concerned; and, except Lady Susan Stuart and Sir Harry Erskine, nothing has yet been done for any Scots. For the King himself, he seems all good-nature, and wishing to satisfy everybody; all his speeches are obliging. I saw him again yesterday, and was surprised to find the levee-room had lost so entirely the air of the lion's den. This young man don't stand in one spot, with his eyes fixed royally on the ground, and dropping bits of German news; he walks about, and speaks to everybody. I saw him afterwards on the throne, where he is graceful and genteel, sits with dignity, and reads his answers to addresses well; it was the Cambridge address, carried by the Duke of Newcastle in his Doctor's gown, and looking like the *Médecin malgré lui*. He had been vehemently solicitous for attendance, for fear my Lord Westmoreland, who vouchsafes himself to bring the address from Oxford, should outnumber him. Lord Lichfield and several other Jacobites have kissed hands; George Selwyn says, "They go to St. James's because now there are so many *Stuarts*[2] there."

Do you know, I had the curiosity to go to the burying t'other night; I had never seen a royal funeral; nay, I walked as a rag of quality, which I found would be, and so it was, the easiest way of seeing it. It is absolutely a noble sight. The Prince's chamber, hung with

---

1 A reference to the influence of Princess Augusta of Saxe-Gotha and the power of Lord Bute, an issue on which Walpole was later to take a more critical view.
2 A reference to the favourite Lord Bute's family name of Stuart.

purple, and a quantity of silver lamps, the coffin under a canopy of purple velvet, and six vast chandeliers of silver on high stands, had a very good effect. The Ambassador from Tripoli and his son were carried to see that chamber. The procession, through a line of foot-guards, every seventh man bearing a torch, the horse-guards lining the outside, their officers with drawn sabres and crape sashes on horseback, the drums muffled, the fifes, bells tolling, and minute guns, – all this was very solemn. But the charm was the entrance of the Abbey, where we were received by the Dean and Chapter in rich robes, the choir and almsmen bearing torches; the whole Abbey so illuminated, that one saw it to greater advantage than by day; the tombs, long aisles, and fretted roof, all appearing distinctly, and with the happiest *chiaro scuro*. There wanted nothing but incense, and little chapels, here and there with priests saying mass for the repose of the defunct; yet one could not complain of its not being catholic enough. I had been in dread of being coupled with some boy of ten years old; but the heralds were not very accurate, and I walked with George Grenville, taller and older enough, to keep me in coun-tenance. When we came to the chapel of Henry the Seventh, all solemnity and decorum ceased; no order was observed, people sat or stood where they could or would; the yeoman of the guard were cry-ing out for help, oppressed by the immense weight of the coffin; the Bishop read sadly, and blundered in the prayers; the fine chapter, *Man that is born of a woman*, was chanted, not read; and the anthem, besides being immeasurably tedious, would have served as well for a nuptial. The real serious part was the figure of the Duke of Cum-berland, heightened by a thousand melancholy circumstances. He had a dark brown adonis,[1] and a cloak of black cloth, with a train of five yards. Attending the funeral of a father, how little reason soever he had to love him, could not be pleasant: his leg extremely bad, yet forced to stand upon it near two hours; his face bloated and distorted with his late paralytic stroke, which has affected, too, one of his eyes, and placed over the mouth of the vault, into which, in all probability, he must himself so soon descend; think how unpleasant a situation! He bore it all with a firm and unaffected countenance. This grave scene was fully contrasted by the burlesque Duke of Newcastle. He fell into a fit of crying the moment he came into the chapel, and

1 A long, bushy wig, more commonly white.

flung himself back in a stall, the Archbishop hovering over him with a smelling-bottle; but in two minutes his curiosity got the better of his hypocrisy, and he ran about the chapel with his glass to spy who was or was not there, spying with one hand, and mopping his eyes with the other. Then returned the fear of catching cold; and the Duke of Cumberland, who was sinking with heat, felt himself weighed down, and turning round, found it was the Duke of Newcastle standing upon his train, to avoid the chill of the marble. It was very theatric to look down into the vault, where the coffin lay, attended by mourners with lights. Clavering, the groom of the bedchamber, refused to sit up with the body, and was dismissed by the King's order.

I have nothing more to tell you, but a trifle, a very trifle. The King of Prussia has totally defeated Marshal Daun. This, which would have been prodigious news a month ago, is nothing to-day; it only takes its turn among the questions, "Who is to be groom of the bedchamber? what is Sir T. Robinson to have?" I have been to Leicesterfields to-day; the crowd was immoderate; I don't believe it will continue so. Good night. Yours ever.

44. *George III.'s Popularity.*

TO GEORGE MONTAGU, ESQ.

Strawberry Hill, Monday, 24 November 1760.

Unless I were to send you journals, lists, catalogues, computations of the bodies, tides, swarms of people that go to Court to present addresses, or to be presented, I can tell you nothing new. The day the King went to the House, I was three-quarters of an hour getting through Whitehall: there were subjects enough to set up half-a-dozen petty kings: the Pretender would be proud to reign over the footmen only; and, indeed, unless he acquires some of them, he will have no subjects left; all their masters flocked to St. James's. The palace is so thronged, that I will stay till some people are discontented. The first night the King went to the play, which was civilly on a Friday, not on the opera-night, as he used to do, the whole audience sung "God save the King" in chorus. For the first act, the press was so great at the door, that no ladies could go to the boxes, and only the servants appeared there, who kept places; at the end of the second act, the whole mob broke in, and seated themselves; yet all this zeal is not likely to last, though he so well deserves it. Seditious papers are again stuck up: one t'other day in Westminster Hall declared against a Saxe-Gothan Princess. The Archbishop, who is never out of the drawing-room, has great hopes from the King's goodness, that he shall make something of him, that is something bad of him. . . . Adieu!

45. *Queen Charlotte's Arrival.*

TO THE HON H. S. CONWAY

Arlington Street, 9 September 1761.

The date of my promise is now arrived, and I fulfil it – fulfil it with great satisfaction, for the Queen[1] is come; I have seen her, have been presented to her – and may go back to Strawberry. For this fortnight I have lived upon the road between Twickenham and London: I came, grew impatient, returned; came again, still to no purpose. The yachts made the coast of Suffolk last Saturday, on Sunday entered the road of Harwich, and on Monday morning the King's chief eunuch, as the Tripoline ambassador calls Lord Anson, landed the Princess. She lay that night at Lord Abercorn's at Witham [in Essex], the palace of silence; and yesterday at a quarter after three arrived at St. James's. In half an hour one heard of nothing but proclamations of her beauty: everybody was content, everybody pleased. At seven one went to court. The night was sultry. About ten the procession began to move towards the chapel, and at eleven they all came up into the drawing-room. She looks very sensible, cheerful, and is remarkably genteel.[2] Her tiara of diamonds was very pretty, her stomacher sumptuous; her violet-velvet mantle and ermine so heavy, that the spectators knew as much of her upper half as the King himself. You will have no doubts of her sense by what I shall tell you. On the road they wanted her to curl her toupet: she

1 Charlotte of Mecklenburg-Strelitz (1744–1818), who arrived at St. James' Palace on the afternoon of 8 September and married George III in the Chapel Royal the same evening.
2 It is reported that the Chamberlain to Queen Charlotte, who was not celebrated for her beauty when young, remarked of her in later life "I do think that the *bloom* of her ugliness is going off."

said she thought it looked as well as that of any of the ladies sent to fetch her; if the King bid her, she would wear a periwig, otherwise she would remain as she was. When she caught the first glimpse of the Palace, she grew frightened and turned pale; the Duchess of Hamilton[1] smiled – the Princess said, "My dear Duchess, you may laugh, you have been married twice, but it is no joke to me." Her lips trembled as the coach stopped, but she jumped out with spirit, and has done nothing but with good-humour and cheerfulness. She talks a great deal – is easy, civil, and not disconcerted. At first, when the bridemaids and the court were introduced to her, she said, "*Mon Dieu, il y en a tant, il y en a tant!*" She was pleased when she was to kiss the peeresses; but Lady Augusta[2] was forced to take her hand and give it to those that were to kiss it, which was prettily humble and good-natured. While they waited for supper, she sat down, sung, and played. Her French is tolerable, she exchanged much both of that and German with the King, the Duke [of Cumberland], and the Duke of York. They did not get to bed till two. To-day was a drawing-room: everybody was presented to her; but she spoke to nobody, as she could not know a soul. The crowd was much less than at a birth-day, the magnificence very little more. The King looked very handsome, and talked to her continually with great good-humour. It does not promise as if they two would be the two most unhappy persons in England, from this event. The bridemaids, especially Lady Caroline Russel, Lady Sarah Lenox, and Lady Elizabeth Keppel, were beautiful figures. With neither features nor air, Lady Sarah was by far the chief angel. The Duchess of Hamilton was almost in possession of her former beauty to-day; and your other Duchess, your daughter [Richmond], was much better dressed than ever I saw her. Except a pretty Lady Sutherland, and a most perfect beauty, an Irish Miss Smith,[3] I don't think the Queen saw much else to discourage her: my niece [Lady Waldegrave], Lady Kildare, Mrs. Fitzroy, were none of them there. There is a ball to-night, and two more drawing-rooms; but I have done with them. The Duchess of Queensbury and Lady Westmoreland were in the procession, and did credit to the ancient nobility.

1 The Duchess of Hamilton was a Lady of the Bedchamber to the Queen.
2 Princess Augusta, sister of George III.
3 Afterwards married to Mr. Mathew, now Lord Llandaff. – WALPOLE.

You don't presume to suppose, I hope, that we are thinking of you, and wars, and misfortunes, and distresses, in these festival times. Mr. Pitt himself would be mobbed if he talked of anything but clothes, and diamonds, and bridemaids. Oh! yes, we have wars, civil wars; there is a campaign opened in the Bed-chamber. Everybody is excluded but the ministers; even the Lords of the Bed-chamber, cabinet counsellors, and foreign ministers: but it has given such offence that I don't know whether Lord Huntingdon must not be the scapegoat. Adieu! I am going to transcribe most of this letter to your Countess [Lady Ailesbury].

46. *The Coronation.*

TO GEORGE MONTAGU, ESQ.

Arlington Street, 24 September 1761.

I am glad you arrived safe in Dublin,[1] and hitherto like it so well; but your trial is not begun yet. When your King comes, the ploughshares will be put into the fire. Bless your stars that your King [Halifax] is not to be married or crowned. All the vines of Bourdeaux, and all the fumes of Irish brains cannot make a town so drunk as a regal wedding, and coronation. I am going to let London cool, and will not venture into it again this fortnight. Oh! the buzz, the prattle, the crowds, the noise, the hurry! Nay, people are so little come to their senses, that though the Coronation was but the day before yesterday, the Duke of Devonshire had forty messages yesterday, desiring tickets for a ball that they fancied was to be at Court last night. People had sat up a night and a day, and yet wanted to see a dance. If I was to entitle ages, I would call this the *century of crowds*. For the Coronation, if a puppet-show could be worth a million, that is. The multitudes, balconies, guards, and processions, made Palace-yard the liveliest spectacle in the world: the Hall was the most glorious. The blaze of lights, the richness and variety of habits, the ceremonial, the benches of peers and peeresses, frequent and full, was as awful as a pageant can be: and yet for the King's sake and my own, I never wish to see another; nor am impatient to have my Lord

---

1 Montagu had been granted a position under his cousin Lord Halifax (1716–71), the Lord Lieutenant, in Dublin in 1761.

Effingham's[1] promise fulfilled. The King complained that so few precedents were kept for their proceedings. Lord Effingham owned, the Earl Marshal's office had been strangely neglected; but he had taken such care for the future, that the *next coronation* would be regulated in the most exact manner imaginable. The number of peers and peeresses present was not very great; some of the latter, with no excuse in the world, appeared in Lord Lincoln's gallery, and even walked about the hall indecently in the intervals of the procession. My Lady Harrington, covered with all the diamonds she could borrow, hire, or tease, and with the air of Roxana, was the finest figure at a distance; she complained to George Selwyn that she was to walk with Lady Portsmouth, who would have a wig, and a stick – "Pho," said he, "you will only look as if you were taken up by the constable." She told this everywhere, thinking the reflection was on my Lady Portsmouth. Lady Pembroke, alone at the head of the countesses, was the picture of majestic modesty; the Duchess of Richmond as pretty as nature and dress, with no pains of her own, could make her; Lady Spencer, Lady Sutherland, and Lady Northampton, very pretty figures. Lady Kildare, still beauty itself, if not a little too large. The ancient peeresses were by no means the worst party: Lady Westmoreland, still handsome, and with more dignity than all; the Duchess of Queensbury looked well, though her locks milk-white; Lady Albermarle very genteel; nay, the middle age had some good representatives in Lady Holdernesse, Lady Rochford, and Lady Strafford, the perfectest little figure of all. My Lady Suffolk ordered her robes, and I dressed part of her head, as I made some of my Lord Hertford's dress; for you know, no profession comes amiss to me, from a tribune of the people to a habit-maker. Don't imagine that there were not figures as excellent on the other side; old Exeter, who told the King he was the handsomest man she ever saw; old Effingham and a Lady Say and Seale, with her hair powdered and her tresses black, were an excellent contrast to the handsome. Lord B * * * *[2] put on rouge upon his wife and the Duchess of Bedford in the Painted Chamber; the Duchess of Queensbury told me of the

---

1 Thomas Howard (*c.* 1714–63), 2nd Earl of Effingham, deputy Earl Marshal, and responsible for organising the coronation.
2 Frederick St. John, 2nd Viscount Bolingbroke (1732–87). His wife, the former Lady Diana Spencer, remarried after their divorce in 1768 and became Lady Diana Beauclerk, the artist whose work Walpole greatly admired.

latter, that she looked like an orange-peach, half red and half yellow. The coronets of the peers and their robes disguised them strangely; it required all the beauty of the Dukes of Richmond and Marlborough to make them noticed. One there was, though of another species, the noblest figure I ever saw, the high-constable of Scotland, Lord Errol; as one saw him in a space capable of containing him, one admired him. At the wedding, dressed in tissue, he looked like one of the Giants in Guildhall, new gilt. It added to the energy of his person, that one considered him acting so considerable a part in that very Hall, where so few years ago one saw his father, Lord Kilmarnock, condemned to the block.[1] The Champion[2] acted his part admirably, and dashed down his gauntlet with proud defiance. His associates, Lord Effingham, Lord Talbot, and the Duke of Bedford, were woeful; Lord Talbot [the Lord High Steward] piqued himself on backing his horse down the Hall, and not turning its rump towards the King, but he had taken such pains to dress it to that duty, that it entered backwards: and at his retreat the spectators clapped, a terrible indecorum, but suitable to such Bartholomew-fair doings. He put me in mind of some King's fool, that would not give his right hand to the King of Spain, because he wiped his backside with it. He had twenty *demelés*, and came out of none creditably. He had taken away the table of the knights of the Bath, and was forced to admit two in their old place, and dine the others in the Court of Requests. Sir William Stanhope said, "We are ill-treated, for *some of us* are gentlemen." Beckford told the Earl, it was hard to refuse a table to the City of London, whom it would cost ten thousand pounds to banquet the King, and that his lordship would repent it, if they had not a table in the Hall; they had. To the barons of the Cinque-ports, who made the same complaint, he said, "If you come to me as Lord Steward, I tell you, it is impossible; if, as Lord Talbot, I am a match for any of you;" and then he said to Lord Bute, "If I were a minister, thus I would talk to France, to Spain, to the Dutch – none of your half measures." This has brought me to a melancholy topic. Bussy goes to-morrow, a Spanish war is hanging in the air, destruction is taking a new lease of mankind – of the remnant of mankind. I have no prospect of seeing Mr. Conway. Adieu! I will

1 Lord Kilmarnock, one of the rebel lords executed after the 1745 Jacobite rising.
2 John Dymoke (d. 1784), who as King's Champion rode into Westminster Hall and offered to challenge anyone who disputed the King's rights.

not disturb you with my forebodings. You I shall see again in spite
of war, and I trust in spite of Ireland.

Yours ever H. W.

I was much disappointed at not seeing your brother John: I kept a
place for him to the last minute, but have heard nothing of him.

47. *The King and America.*

TO THE HON. H. S. CONWAY

Strawberry Hill, 5 June 1779.

... I fear there is not more discretion in the treatment of Ireland
than of America. The Court seems to be infatuated, and to think
that nothing is of any consequence but a majority in Parliament –
though they have totally lost all power but that of provoking. Fortunate it had been for the King and kingdom, had the Court had no
majority for these six years! America had still been ours! – and all
the lives and all the millions we have squandered! A majority that
has lost thirteen provinces by bullying and vapouring, and the most
childish menaces, will be a brave countermatch for France and
Spain, and a rebellion in Ireland! In short, it is plain that there is
nothing a majority in Parliament can do, but outvote a minority;
and yet by their own accounts one would think they could not do
even that. I saw a paper t'other day that began with this Iriscism,
"As the minority have lost us thirteen provinces," &c. I know
nothing the minority have done, or been suffered to do, but restore
the Roman Catholic religion – and that too was by the desire of the
Court. ...

I know no private news: I have been here ever since Tuesday,
enjoying my tranquillity, as much as an honest man can do who sees
his country ruined. It is just such a period as makes philosophy wisdom. There are great moments when every man is called on to exert
himself – but when folly, infatuation, delusion, incapacity, and pro-
fligacy fling a nation away, and it concurs itself, and applauds its des-
troyers, a man who has lent no hand to the mischief, and can neither
prevent nor remedy the mass of evils, is fully justified in sitting aloof
and beholding the tempest rage, with silent scorn and indignant
compassion. Nay, I have, I own, some comfortable reflections.

I rejoice that there is still a great continent of Englishmen who will remain free and independent, and who laugh at the impotent majorities of a prostitute Parliament. I care not whether General Burgoyne and Governor Johnstone cross over and figure in, and support or oppose; nor whether Mr. Burke, or the superior of the Jesuits, is high commissioner to the kirk of Scotland. My ideas are such as I have always had, and are too plain and simple to comprehend modern confusions; and, therefore, they suit with those of few men. What will be the issue of this chaos, I know not, and, probably shall not see. I do see with satisfaction, *that what was meditated* has failed by the grossest folly; and when one has escaped the worst, lesser evils must be endured with patience. . . .

48. *Presentation at Court.*

TO SIR HORACE MANN

26 February 1782, addition to letter begun 25 February.

. . . How strange are the accidents of life! At ten years old I had set my heart on seeing George I., and, being a favourite child, my mother asked leave for me to be presented to him; which to the First Minister's wife was granted, and I was carried by the late Lady Chesterfield to kiss his hand as he went to supper in the Duchess of Kendal's apartment. This was the night but one before he left England the last time; and now, fifty years afterwards, one of his great-grandsons and one of his great-granddaughters are my great-nephew and niece! Yet how little had the first part to do with bringing about the second! When one considers these events abstractedly, as I do, the reflection is amusing; it makes the politician's arts trifling and ridiculous: no plan, no foresight, no industry could have ranged or accomplished what mere chance has effected. It would not be less entertaining, if a politician would talk as frankly on the projects he had planned and been disappointed of effecting; but a politician would not look on the *dénouement* with the same indifference.

49. *Princess Amelia.*

TO THE HON H. S. CONWAY

Sunday night, 18 June 1786.

I suppose you have been swearing at the east wind for parching your verdure, and are now weeping for the rain that drowns your hay. I have these calamities in common, and my constant and particular one, – people that come to see my house, which unfortunately is more in request than ever. Already I have had twenty-eight sets, have five more tickets given out; and yesterday, before I had dined, three German barons came. My house is a torment, not a comfort!

I was sent for again to dine at Gunnersbury[1] on Friday, and was forced to send to town for a dress-coat and a sword. There were the Prince of Wales, the Prince of Mecklenburg, the Duke of Portland, Lord Clanbrassil, Lord and Lady Clermont, Lord and Lady Southampton, Lord Pelham, and Mrs. Howe. The Prince of Mecklenburg went back to Windsor after coffee; and the Prince and Lord and Lady Clermont to town after tea, to hear some new French players at Lady William Gordon's. The Princess, Lady Barrymore, and the rest of us, played three pools at commerce till ten. I am afraid I was tired and gaped. While we were at the diary, the Princess insisted on my making some verses on Gunnesbury. I pleaded being superannuated. She would not excuse me. I promised she should have an Ode on her next Birthday, which diverted the Prince; but all would not do. So, as I came home, I made the following stanzas, and sent them to her breakfast next morning: –

> In deathless odes for ever green
>   Augustus' laurels blow;
> Nor e'er was grateful duty seen
>   In warmer strains to flow.
>
> Oh! why is Flaccus not alive,
>   Your favourite scene to sing?
> To Gunnersbury's charms could give
>   His lyre immortal spring.
>
> As warm as his my zeal for you,
>   Great princess! could I show it:
> But though you have a Horace too –
>   Ah, Madam! he's no poet.

1   Gunnersbury Park, Middlesex, was from 1761 the country seat of Princess Amelia (1711–86), daughter of George II.

If they are but poor verses, consider I am sixty-nine, was half asleep, and made them almost extempore – and by command! However, they succeeded, and I received this gracious answer: –

> "I wish I had a name that could answer your pretty verses. Your yawning yesterday opened your vein for pleasing me; and I return you my thanks, my good Mr. Walpole, and remain sincerely your friend,
>
> > "AMELIA."

I think this is very genteel at seventy-five. . . .

50. *Views on Kingship.*

TO HANNAH MORE [1]

Strawberry Hill, 22 September 1788.

. . . Now you have told me the behaviour of a certain great dame, I will confess to you that I have known it some months by accident – nay, and tried to repair it. I prevailed on Lady * * * * *,[2] who as readily undertook the commission, and told the Countess of her treatment of you. Alas! the answer was, "It is too late; I have no money." No! but she has, if she has a diamond left. I am indignant; yet, do you know, not at this duchess, or that countess, but at the invention of ranks, and titles, and pre-eminence. I used to hate that king and t'other prince; but, alas! on reflection I find the censure ought to fall on human nature in general. They are made of the same stuff as we, and dare we say what we should be in their situation? Poor creatures! think how they are educated, or rather corrupted, early, how flattered! To be educated properly they should be led through hovels, and hospitals, and prisons. Instead of being reprimanded (and perhaps immediately after *sugar-plum'd*) for not learning their Latin or French grammar they now and then should be kept fasting; and, if they cut their finger, should have no plaster till it festered. No part of a royal brat's memory which is good enough, should be burthened but with the remembrance of human sufferings. In short, I fear our nature is so liable to be corrupted and perverted by greatness, rank, power, and wealth, that I am inclined to think that virtue is the compensation to the poor for the want of

---

1   See heading to letter 226.
2   The great dame, Lady * * * * *, is not identified.

riches: nay, I am disposed to believe that the first footpad or high-wayman had been a man of quality, or a prince, who could not bear having wasted his fortune, and was too lazy to work; for a beggar-born would think labour a more natural way of getting a livelihood than venturing his life. I have something a similar opinion about common women. No modest girl thinks of many men, till she has been in love with *one*, been ruined by him, and abandoned. But to return to my theme, and it will fall heavy on yourself. Could the milkwoman[1] have been so bad, if you had merely kept her from starving, instead of giving her opulence? The soil, I doubt, was bad; but it could not have produced the rank weed of ingratitude, if you had not dunged it with gold, which rises from rock, and seems to meet with a congenial bed when it falls on the human heart. . . . Your most sincere friend.

51. *The Duke of York's Visit.*

TO THE COUNTESS OF UPPER OSSORY[2]

Strawberry Hill, 24 September 1788.

. . . New game, or village anecdotes, I have none to send you, Madam; nor from my own narrow circle, but that I have had a sort of *impromptu* visit from the Duke of York. He sent me word, one evening, that if I were alone he would come with some company and see my house; but it proving too late, he appointed the next day, and came. As I had never been presented to him, I asked leave at the door to kiss his hand, but he would not suffer it; and indeed the whole time he stayed, which was about an hour, it was impossible to be more gracious, or to say more obliging things. His uncle, the late Duke, surprised me still more suddenly eight-and-twenty years ago. Two Dukes of York, at such a distance of time, make me seem to have lived till the same adventures come round again to me in different reigns. You must not wonder, Madam, if I give myself the airs of a patriarch, when I am so like Abraham, who at very distant periods had exactly the same incidents happen to him twice from two princes about his wife; for Sarah's charms, it seems, remained

1 Ann Yearsley (bap. 1753–1806), the Bristol milkwoman, a poet supported by Hannah More, but with whom she subsequently fell out.
2 See heading to letter 221.

in fashion as long as Strawberry's, though one should have thought that young princes would not have an appetite for anything so Gothic as either.

I have answered; I have related; and I have not a syllable more to say, but good night, my dear Lady. . . .

52. *The Queen at Strawberry Hill.*

TO THE HON. H. S. CONWAY

Strawberry Hill, 2 July 1795.

I will write a word to you, though scarce time to write one, to thank you for your great kindness about the soldier, who shall get a substitute if he can. As you are, or have been in town, your daughter will have told you in what a bustle I am, preparing – not to resist, but to receive an invasion of royalties to-morrow; and cannot even escape them like Admiral Cornwallis, though seeming to make a semblance; for I am to wear a sword, and have appointed two aides-de-camp, my nephews, George and Horace Churchill. If I *fall*, as ten to one but I do, to be sure it will be a superb tumble, at the feet of a Queen and eight daughters of Kings; for, besides the six Princesses, I am to have the Duchess of York and the Princess of Orange! Woe is me, at seventy-eight, and with scarce a hand and foot to my back! Adieu! Yours, &c.

A POOR OLD REMNANT.[1]

---

1 Walpole reported to Conway on 5 July 1795 (YE 39:511) on the result of the royal visit. "The Queen was uncommonly condescending and gracious, and deigned to drink my health when I presented her with the last glass, and to thank me for all my attentions. Indeed my memory *de vieille cour* was but once in default. As I had been assured that her Majesty would be attended by her Chamberlain, yet was not, I had no glove ready when I received her at the step of her coach: yet she honoured me with her hand to lead her up stairs; nor did I recollect my omission when I led her down again. Still, though gloveless, I did not squeeze the royal hand, as Vice-chamberlain Smith did to Queen Mary."

IV
THE MAN ABOUT TOWN

IMMEDIATELY AFTER WALPOLE'S return from his continental tour with Gray, we find him plunging eagerly into the busy round of social pleasures of the man of fashion. Accounts of visits to theatres and operas, descriptions of balls, masquerades, ridottos, and fashionable assemblies henceforth take up a considerable space in his correspondence. Ranelagh opened in May 1742, and soon vied with Vauxhall in popularity; within two years it was preferred by the upper classes. Walpole became one of its earliest frequenters; he took his father there after his fall from office that year to test his popularity with the crowd. Thirty years later the Pantheon was built, and claimed its share of popularity.

Walpole, during these days, kept fashionable hours. Rising about noon, he dined about four (except in such unforeseen circumstances as described in letter 63) and retired in the early hours of the morning: "Good night! The Watchman cries three," he writes on one occasion in 1764.[1] He could not resist invitations to balls, even after a severe attack of gout or rheumatism.

Walpole's letters shed light on the state of society in the eighteenth century. He was *au courant* with the latest piece of scandal – the elopement of Lady Wentworth with her footman or that of Lord Ilchester's daughter with an Irish actor (letter 60); the cruelty of this nobleman, or the dissipations of that – each finds its place in his correspondence. He was singularly temperate in an age of heavy drinking and excessive gambling. Fabulous sums were won and lost at whist (a game that Walpole never liked), at faro, loo, and other card games. Any excuse was good enough for a wager: Walpole recounted to Mann in 1750 an occasion at White's (Walpole's own club), when a man dropped dead at the door, "the club immediately made bets whether he was dead or not, and when they were going to bleed him, the wagerers for his death interposed, and said it would affect the fairness of the bet".[2]

Particularly interesting are Walpole's references to the theatre

1 Letter to the Earl of Hertford, 27 May 1764 (YE 38:394).
2 Letter of 1 September 1750 (YE 20:185).

and the opera. The audience was difficult to control and hard to please, and riotous scenes were not uncommon. These disturbances were not always created by the gallery: we read of Lord Hobart's attempts to damn the play called *The Foundling*; his aristocratic followers "went armed with syringes charged with stinking oil, and with sticking plasters", but Garrick held his ground.[1] Occasionally a manager courted disaster, as did Fleetwood at Drury Lane when he tried to force a pantomime on his audience by intimidating them with "bruisers" (letter 72). In his judgment on some of the most celebrated actors and actresses of the day, Walpole was decidedly prejudiced: Mrs. Woffington, in his opinion, is "a bad actress; but she has life";[2] he grudgingly admits Garrick "was a real genius in his way", though "In declamation, I confess, he never charmed me; nor could he be a gentleman" (letter 74). Although he also later became personally acquainted with Mrs. Siddons, he was never one of her devotees: "I do not admire her in cool declamation, and find her voice very hollow and defective."[3] In later life he looked fondly back to the actors of his youth, to Quin as Falstaff, to Kitty Clive and Mrs. Pritchard. He took great interest in the opera and was more than once a subscriber, but was not enamoured of Handel's attempt, in 1743, to popularize the oratorio.

1. THE BEAU MONDE

53. *Opening of Ranelagh.*

TO SIR HORACE MANN

Downing Street, 26 May 1742.

To-day calls itself May the 26th, as you perceive by the date; but I am writing to you by the fire-side, instead of going to Vauxhall. If we have one warm day in seven, "we bless our stars, and think it luxury." And yet we have as much water-works and fresco diversions, as if we lay ten degrees nearer warmth. Two nights ago Ranelagh-gardens were opened at Chelsea; the Prince, Princess, Duke, much nobility, and much mob besides, were there. There is a vast amphitheatre, finely gilt, painted, and illuminated, into which everybody that loves eating, drinking, staring, or crowding, is admitted for twelve-pence. The building and disposition of the gardens cost sixteen thousand pounds. Twice a-week there are to be Ridottos, at

1 Letter to Mann, 11 March 1748 (YE 19:469).
2 Ibid, 22 October 1741 (YE 17:176).
3 Letter to Lady Ossory, 15 January 1788 (YE 34:2).

guinea-tickets, for which you are to have a supper and music. I was there last night, but did not find the joy of it. Vauxhall is a little better; for the garden is pleasanter, and one goes by water. Our operas are almost over; there were but three-and-forty people last night in the pit and boxes. There is a little simple farce at Drury Lane, called "Miss Lucy in Town,"[1] in which Mrs. Clive[2] mimics the Muscovita admirably, and Beard,[3] Amorevoli tolerably. But all the run is now after Garrick, a wine-merchant, who is turned player, at Goodman's-fields. He plays all parts, and is a very good mimic. His acting I have seen, and may say to you, who will not tell it again here, I see nothing wonderful in it;[4] but it is heresy to say so; the Duke of Argyll says, he is superior to Betterton. Now I talk of players, tell Mr. Chute, that his friend Bracegirdle breakfasted with me this morning. As she went out, and wanted her clogs, she turned to me, and said, "I remember at the playhouse, they used to call Mrs. Oldfield's chair! Mrs. Barry's clogs! and Mrs. Bracegirdle's pattens!"[5] . . .

54. *Peace Celebrations at Ranelagh.*

TO SIR HORACE MANN

Strawberry Hill, 3 May 1749.

I am come hither for a few days, to repose myself after a torrent of diversions, and am writing to you in my charming bow-window with a tranquillity and satisfaction which, I fear, I am grown old enough to prefer to the hurry of amusements, in which the whole world has lived for this last week. We have at last celebrated the Peace,[6] and that as much in extremes as we generally do everything,

1 *Miss Lucy in Town*, a one-act ballad opera by Henry Fielding (1707–54) that had first been produced at Drury Lane three weeks before the date of this letter.
2 Catherine (Kitty) Clive (1711–85), celebrated actress, who became Walpole's tenant and neighbour at Little Strawberry Hill in about 1754.
3 John Beard (1716/17–91), actor, singer, and manager.
4 The first performance of David Garrick (1717–79), as Richard III, had been at the theatre at Goodman's Fields the previous October. Thomas Gray shared Walpole's reservations, telling John Chute in a letter of 24 May 1742 that "the Town are horn-mad after [him], there are a dozen Dukes of a night at Goodman's-fields sometimes, & yet I am stiff in the opposition."
5 Anne Bracegirdle (bap. 1671–1748), actress, Anne Oldfield (1683–1730), actress, and Elizabeth Barry (1656/8–1713), actress and manager.
6 The treaty of Aix-la-Chapelle (1748), which concluded the War of the Austrian Succession.

whether we have reason to be glad or sorry, pleased or angry. Last Tuesday it was proclaimed: the King did not go to St. Paul's, but at night the whole town was illuminated. The next day was what was called "a jubilee-masquerade in the Venetian manner" at Ranelagh: it had nothing Venetian in it, but was by far the best understood and the prettiest spectacle I ever saw: nothing in a fairy tale ever surpassed it. One of the proprietors, who is a German, and belongs to court, had got my Lady Yarmouth to persuade the King to order it. It began at three o'clock, and, about five, people of fashion began to go. When you entered, you found the whole garden filled with masks and spread with tents, which remained all night *very commodely.* In one quarter was a May-pole dressed with garlands, and people dancing round it to a tabor and pipe and rustic music, all masqued, as were all the various bands of music that were disposed in different parts of the garden; some like huntsmen with French-horns, some like peasants, and a troop of harlequins and scaramouches in the little open temple on the mount. On the canal was a sort of gondola, adorned with flags and streamers, and filled with music, rowing about. All round the outside of the amphitheatre were shops, filled with Dresden china, japan, &c., and all the shop-keepers in mask. The amphitheatre was illuminated; and in the middle was a circular bower, composed of all kinds of firs in tubs, from twenty to thirty feet high: under them orange-trees with small lamps in each orange, and below them all sorts of the finest auriculas in pots; and festoons of natural flowers hanging from tree to tree. Between the arches too were firs, and smaller ones in the balconies above. There were booths for tea and wine, gaming-tables and dancing, and about two thousand persons. In short, it pleased me more than anything I ever saw. It is to be once more, and probably finer as to dresses, as there has since been a subscription-masquerade, and people will go in their rich habits. The next day were the fireworks, which by no means answered the expense, the length of preparation, and the expectation that had been raised: indeed, for a week before, the town was like a country fair, the streets filled from morning to night, scaffolds building wherever you could or could not see, and coaches arriving from every corner of the kingdom. This hurry and lively scene, with the sight of the immense crowd in the Park and on every house, the guards, and the machine itself, which was very beautiful, was all that was worth seeing. The rockets, and whatever was thrown up into the air, succeeded mighty well; but the wheels, and all that was to compose the principal part, were pitiful and ill-conducted, with no changes of coloured fires and shapes: the illumination was mean, and lighted so slowly that scarce any body had patience to wait the finishing; and then, what contributed to the awkwardness of the whole, was the right pavilion catching fire, and being burnt down in the middle of the show. The King, the Duke, and Princess Emily saw it from the Library, with their courts: the Prince and Princess, with their children, from Lady Middlesex's; no place being provided for them, nor any invitation given to the library. The Lords and Commons had galleries built for them and the chief citizens along the rails of the Mall: the Lords had four tickets a-piece, and each Commoner, at first, but two, till the Speaker bounced and obtained a third. Very little mischief was done, and but two persons killed: at Paris, there were forty killed and near three hundred wounded, by a dispute between the French and Italians in the management, who, quarrelling for precedence in lighting the fires, both lighted at once and blew up the whole. Our mob was extremely tranquil, and very unlike those I remember in my father's time, when it was a measure in the Opposition to work up everything to mischief, the Excise and the French players, the Convention and the Gin-Act. We are as much now in the opposite extreme, and in general so pleased with the peace, that I could not help being struck with a passage I read lately in Pasquier, an old French author, who says, "that in the time of Francis I. the French used to call their creditors 'Des Anglois,' from the facility with which the English gave credit to them in all treaties, though they had broken so many." . . .

55. *A Visit to Vauxhall.*

TO GEORGE MONTAGU, ESQ.

Dear George,

Arlington Street, 23 June 1750.

. . . As jolly and as abominable a life as she may have been leading,[1] I defy all her enormities to equal a party of pleasure that I had t'other night. I shall relate it to you to show you the manners of the age, which are always as entertaining to a person fifty miles off as to

1 A joke on Montagu's sister in the earlier part of this letter, not here printed.

one born an hundred and fifty years after the time. I had a card from Lady Caroline Petersham to go with her to Vauxhall. I went accordingly to her house, and found her and the little Ashe, or the Pollard Ashe, as they call her; they had just finished their last layer of red, and looked as handsome as crimson could make them. On the cabinet-door stood a pair of Dresden candlesticks, a present from the virgin hands of Sir John Bland: the branches of each formed a little bower over a cock and hen, yes, literally. We issued into the Mall to assemble our company, which was all the town, if we could get it; for just so many had been summoned, except Harry Vane, whom we met by chance. We mustered the Duke of Kingston, whom Lady Caroline says she has been trying for these seven years; but alas! his beauty is at the fall of the leaf; Lord March, Mr. Whitehed, a pretty Miss Beauclerc, and a very foolish Miss Sparre. These two damsels were trusted by their mothers for the first time of their lives to the matronly care of Lady Caroline. As we sailed up the Mall with all our colours flying, Lord Petersham,[1] with his hose and legs twisted to every point of crossness, strode by us on the outside, and repassed again on the return. At the end of the Mall she called to him; he would not answer: she gave a familiar spring, and, between laugh and confusion, ran up to him, "My lord, my lord! why, you don't see us!" We advanced at a little distance, not a little awkward in expectation how all this would end, for my lord never stirred his hat, or took the least notice of anybody: she said, "Do you go with us, or are *you going anywhere else?*" – "I don't go with you, I am going *somewhere else;*" and away he stalked, as sulky as a ghost that nobody will speak to first. We got into the best order we could, and marched to our barge, with a boat of French horns attending, and little Ashe singing. We paraded some time up the river, and at last debarked at Vauxhall: there, if we had so pleased, we might have had the vivacity of our party increased by a quarrel; for a Mrs. Lloyd, who is supposed to be married to Lord Haddington, seeing the two girls following Lady Petersham and Miss Ashe, said aloud, "Poor girls, I am sorry to see them in such bad company!" Miss Sparre, who desired nothing so much as the fun of seeing a duel, – a thing which, though she is fifteen, she has never been so lucky to see, –

1 William Stanhope, Lord Petersham (1719–79), army officer and politician, afterwards 2nd Earl of Harrington. He was known by his gait as "Peter Shambles".

took due pains to make Lord March resent this; but he, who is very lively and agreeable, laughed her out of this charming frolic with a great deal of humour. Here we picked up Lord Granby, arrived very drunk from Jenny's Whim;[1] where, instead of going to old Strafford's catacombs[2] to make honourable love, he had dined with Lady Fitzroy,[3] and left her and eight other women and four other men playing at Brag. He would fain have made over his honourable love upon any terms to poor Miss Beauclerc, who is very modest, and did not know at all what to do with his whispers or his hands. He then addressed himself to the Sparre, who was very well disposed to receive both; but the tide of champagne turned, he hiccupped at the reflection of his marriage (of which he is wondrous sick), and only proposed to the girl to shut themselves up and rail at the world for three weeks. If all the adventures don't conclude as you expect in the beginning of a paragraph, you must not wonder, for I am not making a history, but relating one strictly as it happened, and I think with full entertainment enough to content you. At last, we assembled in our booth, Lady Caroline in the front, with the vizor of her hat erect, and looking gloriously jolly and handsome. She had fetched my brother Orford from the next box, where he was enjoying himself with his Norsa[4] and his *petite partie*, to help us to mince chickens. We minced seven chickens into a china dish, which Lady Caroline stewed over a lamp with three pats of butter and a flagon of water, stirring, and rattling, and laughing, and we every minute expecting to have the dish fly about our ears. She had brought Betty, the fruit-girl,[5] with hampers of strawberries and cherries from Rogers's, and made her wait upon us, and then made her sup by us at a little table. The conversation was no less lively than the whole transaction. There was a Mr. O'Brien arrived from Ireland, who would get the Duchess of Manchester from Mr. Hussey, if she were still at liberty.

1 A tavern in Chelsea.
2 A gathering of "about a dozen antediluvian dowagers", who met regularly at Lady Strafford's.
3 Lady Fitzroy, *née* Elizabeth Cosby (*c.* 1715–88), mother of the 3rd Duke of Grafton.
4 Hannah Norsa (*c.* 1715–85), the mistress of Walpole's brother Lord Orford, a former actress who had made her debut to great acclaim in 1732 as Polly Peachum in Gay's *Beggar's Opera*, succeeding Lavinia Fenton in the role.
5 Elizabeth (Betty) Neale (*c.* 1730–97), who for many years traded from a fruit-shop in St. James's Street. She was known for her manners, news and conversation, and had many aristocratic customers. Rogers was presumably a grocer.

I took up the biggest haut-boy in the dish, and said to Lady Caroline, "Madam, Miss Ashe desires you would eat this O'Brien strawberry;" she replied immediately, "I won't, you hussey." You may imagine the laugh this reply occasioned. After the tempest was a little calmed, the Pollard said, "Now, how anybody would spoil this story that was to repeat it, and say, I won't, you jade!" In short, the whole air of our party was sufficient, as you will easily imagine, to take up the whole attention of the garden; so much so, that from eleven o'clock till half an hour after one we had the whole concourse round our booth: at last, they came into the little gardens of each booth on the sides of ours, till Harry Vane took up a bumper, and drank their healths, and was proceeding to treat them with still greater freedom. It was three o'clock before we got home. I think I have told you the chief passages. Lord Granby's temper had been a little ruffled the night before; the Prince had invited him and Dick Lyttelton to Kew, where he won eleven hundred pounds of the latter, and eight of the former, then cut, and told them he would play with them no longer, for he saw they played so idly, that they were capable of "losing more than they would like."

Adieu! I expect in return for this long tale that you will tell me some of your frolics with Robin Cursemother, and some of Miss Marjoram's *bons-mots*. . . .

56. *The Cock Lane Ghost.*[1]

TO GEORGE MONTAGU, ESQ.

Arlington Street, 2 February 1762.

. . . We set out from the Opera, changed our clothes at Northumberland-house, the Duke of York, Lady Northumberland, Lady Mary Coke, Lord Hertford, and I, all in one hackney coach, and drove to the spot: it rained torrents; yet the lane was full of mob, and the house so full we could not get in; at last they discovered it was the Duke of York, and the company squeezed themselves into one another's pockets to make room for us. The house which is borrowed, and to which the ghost has adjourned, is wretchedly small

1 A *cause célèbre* of 1762, a supposed haunting in a house in Cock Lane, near Smithfield.

and miserable; when we opened the chamber, in which were fifty people, with no light but one tallow candle at the end, we tumbled over the bed of the child to whom the ghost comes, and whom they are murdering by inches in such insufferable heat and stench. At the top of the room are ropes to dry clothes. I asked, if we were to have rope-dancing between the acts? We had nothing; they told us, as they would at a puppet-show, that it would not come that night till seven in the morning, that is, when there are only 'prentices and old women. We stayed, however, till half an hour after one. The Methodists have promised them contributions; provisions are sent in like forage, and all the taverns and ale-houses in the neighbourhood make fortunes. The most diverting part is to hear people wondering *when it will be found out*, as if there was anything to find out – as if the actors would make their noises when they can be discovered. However, as this pantomime cannot last much longer, I hope Lady Fanny Shirley will set up a ghost of her own at Twickenham, and then you shall *hear* one. The Methodists, as Lord Aylesford assured Mr. Chute two nights ago at Lord Dacre's, have attempted ghosts three times in Warwickshire. There, how good I am!

57. *A Firework Display.*

TO THE HON. H. S. CONWAY

Arlington Street, 21 May 1763.

... The Queen's real birthday, you know, is not kept; this Maid of Honour[1] kept it – nay, while the Court is in mourning, expected people to be out of mourning; the Queen's family really was so, Lady Northumberland having desired leave for them. A scaffold was erected in Hyde-park for fireworks. To show the illuminations without to more advantage, the company were received in an apartment totally dark, where they remained for two hours. – If they gave rise to any more birth-days, who could help it? The fireworks were fine, and succeeded well. On each side of the court were two large scaffolds for the Virgin's tradespeople. When the fireworks ceased, a large scene was lighted in the court, representing their Majesties;

1 "The Virgin Chudleigh", whose ball Walpole is describing: Elizabeth Chudleigh (*c.* 1720–88), later Duchess of Kingston, and later still in 1776 convicted of bigamy by the House of Lords.

on each side of which were six obelisks, painted with emblems, and illuminated; mottos beneath in Latin and English: 1. For the Prince of Wales, a ship, *Multorum spes.* 2. For the Princess Dowager, a bird of paradise, and *two* little ones, *Meos ad sidera tollo.* People smiled. 3. Duke of York, a temple, *Virtuti et honori.* 4. Princess Augusta, a bird of paradise, *Non habet parem* – unluckily this was translated, *I have no peer.* People laughed out, considering where this was exhibited. 5. The three younger princes, an orange-tree, *Promittit et dat.* 6. The two younger princesses, the flower crown-imperial. I forget the Latin: the translation was silly enough, *Bashful in youth, graceful in age.* The lady of the house made many apologies for the poorness of the performance, which she said was only oil-paper, painted by one of her servants; but it really was fine and pretty. The Duke of Kingston was in a frock, *comme chez lui.* Behind the house was a cenotaph for the Princess Elizabeth, a kind of illuminated cradle; the motto, *All the honours the dead can receive.* This burying-ground was a strange codicil to a festival; and, what was more strange, about one in the morning, this sarcophagus burst out into crackers and guns. The Margrave of Anspach began the ball with the Virgin. The supper was most sumptuous. . . . Adieu!

58. *A Masquerade.*

TO SIR HORACE MANN

Strawberry Hill, 7 June 1763, addition to letter begun 5 June.

. . . Last night we had a magnificent entertainment at Richmond House, a masquerade and fireworks. As we have consciences no wiser than his Modenese Highness's,[1] a masquerade was a new sight to the young people, who had dressed themselves charmingly, without having the fear of an earthquake before their eyes, though Prince William and Prince Henry[2] were not suffered to be there. The Duchesses of Richmond and Grafton, the first as a Persian Sultana, the latter as Cleopatra, – and such a Cleopatra! were glorious figures, in very different styles. Mrs. Fitzroy[3] in a Turkish dress, Lady George Lenox and Lady Bolingbroke in Grecian girls', Lady Mary

1 Francis III, Duke of Modena, whom Walpole had met on his Grand Tour.
2 Afterwards Dukes of Gloucester and Cumberland. – WALPOLE.
3 Eldest daughter of Sir Peter Warren. – WALPOLE.

Coke as Imoinda, and Lady Pembroke as a pilgrim, were the principal beauties of the night. The whole garden was illuminated, and the apartments. An encampment of barges decked with streamers in the middle of the Thames, kept the people from danger, and formed a stage for the fireworks, which were placed, too, along the rails of the garden. The ground rooms lighted, with suppers spread, the houses covered and filled with people, the bridge, the garden full of masks, Whitehall crowded with spectators to see the dresses pass, and the multitude of heads on the river who came to light by the splendour of the fire-wheels, composed the gayest and richest scene imaginable, not to mention the diamonds and sumptuousness of the habits. The Dukes of York and Cumberland, and the Margrave of Anspach, were there, and about six hundred masks. Adieu!

59. *The Fashionable Round.*

TO THE EARL OF HERTFORD [1]

Arlington Street, 29 December 1763.

You are sensible, my dear lord, that any amusement from my letters must depend upon times and seasons. We are a very absurd nation (though the French are so good at present as to think us a very wise one, only because they, themselves, are now a very weak one); but then that absurdity depends upon the almanac. Posterity, who will know nothing of our intervals, will conclude that this age was a succession of events. I could tell them that we know as well when an event, as when Easter, will happen. Do but recollect these last ten years. The beginning of October, one is certain that everybody will be at Newmarket, and the Duke of Cumberland will lose, and Shafto[2] win, two or three thousand pounds. After that, while people are preparing to come to town for the winter, the Ministry is suddenly changed, and all the world comes to learn how it happened, a fortnight sooner than they intended; and fully persuaded that the new arrangement cannot last a month. The Parliament opens; everybody is bribed; and the new establishment is perceived to be composed of adamant. November passes, with two or three self-murders, and a new play. Christmas arrives; everybody goes out of

1   See heading to letter 207.
2   Jenison Shafto, M.P., a well-known sportsman and racehorse owner.

town; and a riot happens in one of the theatres. The Parliament meets again; taxes are warmly opposed; and some citizen makes his fortune by a subscription.[1] The opposition languishes; balls and assemblies begin; some master and miss begin to get together, are talked of, and give occasion to forty more matches being invented; an unexpected debate starts up at the end of the session, that makes more noise than anything that was designed to make a noise, and subsides again in a new peerage or two. Ranelagh opens and Vauxhall; one produces scandal, and t'other a drunken quarrel. People separate, some to Tunbridge, and some to all the horse-races in England; and so the year comes again to October. I dare to prophesy, that if you keep this letter, you will find that my future correspondence will be but an illustration of this text; at least, it is an excuse for my having very little to tell you at present, and was the reason of my not writing to you last week. . . .

60. *An Elopement.*

TO THE EARL OF HERTFORD

Arlington Street, 12 April 1764.

. . . You will have heard of the sad misfortune that has happened to Lord Ilchester by his daughter's [Lady Susan Fox's] marriage with O'Brien the actor.[2] But, perhaps, you do not know the circumstances, and how much his grief must be aggravated by reflection on his own credulity and negligence. The affair has been in train for eighteen months. The swain had learned to counterfeit Lady Sarah Bunbury's hand so well, that in the country Lord Ilchester has himself delivered several of O'Brien's letters to Lady Susan; but it was not till about a week before the catastrophe that the family was apprised of the intrigue. Lord Cathcart went to Miss Read's, the paintress: she said softly to him, "My lord, there is a couple in next room that I am sure ought not to be together, I wish your lordship

1 The Yale editors suggest this was probably a subscription to a lottery.
2 Lady Susan Sarah Fox-Strangeways (1743–1827), the daughter of Lord Ilchester and cousin of Charles James Fox, married William O'Brien, related to the O'Briens, Viscounts Kildare, who had lost their fortune supporting the Stuarts. O'Brien was a popular actor in Garrick's company, and despite the scandal he and his wife (eventually reconciled to Lord Ilchester) remained happily married until O'Brien's death in 1815.

would look in." He did, shut the door again, and went directly and informed Lord Ilchester. Lady Susan was examined, flung herself at her father's feet, confessed all, vowed to break off – but – what a *but!* – desired to see the loved object, and take a last leave. You will be amazed – even this was granted. The parting scene happened the beginning of the week. On Friday she came of age, and on Saturday morning – instead of being under lock and key in the country – walked down stairs, took her footman, said she was going to breakfast with Lady Sarah, but would call at Miss Read's; in the street, pretended to recollect a particular cap in which she was to be drawn, sent her footman back for it, whipped into a hackney chair, was married at Covent-garden church, and set out for Mr. O'Brien's villa at Dunstable. My Lady – my Lady Hertford! what say *you* to permitting young ladies to act plays, and go to painters by themselves?

Poor Lord Ilchester is almost distracted; indeed, it is the completion of disgrace – even a footman were preferable; the publicity of the hero's profession perpetuates the mortification. *Il ne sera pas milord, tout comme un autre.* I could not have believed that Lady Susan would have stooped so low. She may, however, still keep good company, and say, "nos numeri sumus" – Lady Mary Duncan, Lady Caroline Adair, Lady Betty Gallini[1] – the shopkeepers of next age will be mighty wellborn. . . .

61. *An Engagement.*

TO THE EARL OF HERTFORD

Strawberry Hill, 8 June 1764.

To be sure, you have heard the event of this last week? Lord Tavistock has flung his handkerchief, and, except a few jealous *sultanas*, and some *sultanas valides*[2] who had marketable daughters, everybody is pleased that the lot is fallen on Lady Elizabeth Keppel.

The house of Bedford came to town last Friday. I supped with them that night at the Spanish Ambassador's, who has made Powis-

---

1 Married respectively a doctor, a surgeon, and a dancing master.
2 In the Ottoman empire the Valide Sultan, mother of the reigning Sultan, was second only to the Sultan and exercised considerable power, particularly over the court and harem. Francis Russell, Marquis of Tavistock (1739–67) was the eldest son of the 4th Duke of Bedford.

house magnificent. Lady Elizabeth was not there, nor mentioned.
On the contrary, by the Duchess's conversation, which turned on
Lady Betty Montagu, there were suspicions in her favour. The next
morning Lady Elizabeth received a note from the Duchess of
Marlborough [Lord Tavistock's sister], insisting on seeing her that
evening. When she arrived at Marlborough-house, she found
nobody but the Duchess and Lord Tavistock. The Duchess cried,
"Lord! they have left the window open in the next room!" went to
shut it, and shut the lovers in too, where they remained for three
hours. The same night all the town was at the Duchess of Richmond's. Lady Albemarle [Lady Elizabeth's mother] was at tredille;[1]
the Duke of Bedford came up to the table, and told her he must
speak to her as soon as the pool was over. You may guess whether
she knew a card more that she played. When she had finished, the
Duke told her he should wait on her the next morning, to make the
demand in form. She told it directly to me and my niece Waldegrave,
who was in such transport for her friend, that she promised the
Duke of Bedford to kiss him, and hurried home directly to write to
her sisters. The Duke asked no questions about fortune, but has
since slipped a bit of paper into Lady Elizabeth's hand, telling her,
he hoped his son would live, but if he did not, there was something
for her; it was a jointure of three thousand pounds a-year, and six
hundred pounds pin-money. I dined with her the next day at Monsieur de Guerchy's, and as I hindered the company from wishing her
joy, and yet joked with her myself, Madame de Guerchy said, she
perceived I would let nobody else tease her, that I might have all
the teasing to myself. She has behaved in the prettiest manner in the
world, and would not appear at a vast assembly at Northumberland-
house on Tuesday, nor at a great haymaking at Mrs. Pitt's[2] [at
Wandsworth-hill] on Wednesday. Yesterday they all went to
Woburn, and to-morrow the ceremony is to be performed; for the
Duke has not a moment's patience till she is breeding.

You would have been diverted at Northumberland-house;
besides the sumptuous liveries, the illuminations in the garden, the
pages, the two chaplains in waiting in their gowns and scarves, à
l'Irlandaise,[3] and Dr. Hill and his wife, there was a most delightful

1 A card game.
2 Wife of George Pitt, afterwards Lord Rivers, a distant relation of Lord Chatham.
3 Lord Northumberland was Lord Lieutenant of Ireland.

Countess, who has just imported herself from Mecklenburgh. She is an absolute Princess of Monomotapa;[1] but I fancy you have seen her, for her hideousness and frantic accoutrements are so extraordinary, that they tell us she was hissed in the Tuileries. She crossed the drawing-room on the birth-day [4 June] to speak to the Queen *en amie*, after standing with her back to Princess Amalie. The Queen was so ashamed of her, that she said cleverly, "This is not the dress at Strelitz; but this woman always dressed herself as capriciously there, as your Duchess of Queensberry does here."

The haymaking at Wandsworth-hill[2] did not succeed, from the excessive cold of the night; I proposed to bring one of the cocks into the great room, and make a bonfire. All the beauties were disappointed, and all the Macaronies afraid of getting the toothache.

The Guerchys are gone to Goodwood, and were to have been carried to Portsmouth, but Lord Egmont[3] refused to let the ambassador see the place. The Duke of Richmond was in a rage, and I do not know how it has ended, for the Duke of Bedford defends the refusal, and says, they certainly would not let you see Brest. The Comte d'Ayen is going a longer tour. He is liked here. The three great ambassadors danced at court – the Prince of Masserano they say well; he is extremely in fashion, and is a sensible, very good-humoured man, though his appearance is so deceitful. They have given me the honour of a bon-mot, which, I assure you, does not belong to me, that I never saw a man so full of *orders* and *disorders*. He and his suite, and the Guerchys and theirs, are to dine here next week. Poor little Strawberry never thought of such fêtes. I did invite them to breakfast, but they confounded it, and understood that they were asked to dinner, so I must do as well as I can. Both the Ambassadors [France and Spain] are in love with my niece [Waldegrave]; therefore, I trust they will not have unsentimental stomachs. . . .

---

1 A kingdom in East Africa: fantastical.
2 At Mrs. Pitt's villa.
3 John Perceval (1711–70), 2nd Earl of Egmont, was First Lord of the Admiralty, and Claude-Louis-François de Régnier, Comte de Guerchy (1715–67) was the French ambassador to England from 1763 to 1767.

62. *Almack's.*

TO THE EARL OF HERTFORD

14 February 1765, addition to letter begun 12 February.

The new Assembly Room at Almack's[1] was opened the night before last, and they say is very magnificent, but it was empty; half the town is ill with colds, and many were afraid to go, as the house is scarcely built yet. Almack advertised that it was built with hot bricks and boiling water – think what a rage there must be for public places, if this notice, instead of terrifying, could draw anybody thither. They tell me the ceilings were dropping with wet – but can you believe me, when I assure you the Duke of Cumberland was there? – Nay, had had a levee in the morning, and went to the Opera before the assembly! There is a vast flight of steps, and he was forced to rest two or three times. If he dies of it, – and how should he not? – it will sound very silly when Hercules or Theseus ask him what he died of, to reply "I caught my death on a damp staircase at a new club-room." ...

63. *A Late Dinner.*

TO THE EARL OF HERTFORD

7 April 1765.

... Now, for my disaster; you will laugh at it, though it was woful to me. I was to dine at Northumberland-house, and went a little after four: there I found the Countess, Lady Betty Mackenzie, Lady Strafford; my Lady Finlater, who was never out of Scotland before; a tall lad of fifteen, her son; Lord Drogheda, and Mr. Worseley. At five, arrived Mr. Mitchell, who said the Lords had begun to read the Poor-bill, which would take at least two hours, and perhaps would debate it afterwards. We concluded dinner would be called for, it not being very precedented for ladies to wait for gentlemen: – no such thing. Six o'clock came, – seven o'clock came, – our coaches came, – well! we sent them away, and excuses were we were engaged. Still the Countess's heart did not relent, nor uttered a syllable of apology.

1 William Almack's Assembly Rooms in King Street, St. James's, from 1871 known as Willis's Rooms.

We wore out the wind and the weather, the Opera and the Play, Mrs. Cornelys's and Almack's, and every topic that would do in a formal circle. We hinted, represented – in vain. The clock struck eight: my Lady, at last, said, she would go and order dinner; but it was a good half-hour before it appeared. We then sat down to a table for four-teen covers: but instead of substantials, there was nothing but a pro-fusion of plates striped red, green, and yellow, gilt plate, blacks and uniforms! My Lady Finlater, who had never seen these embroidered dinners, nor dined after three, was famished. The first course stayed as long as possible, in hopes of the Lords: so did the second. The dessert at last arrived, and the middle dish was actually set on when Lord Finlater and Mr. Mackay arrived! – would you believe it? – the dessert was remanded, and the whole first course brought back again! – Stay, I have not done: – just as this second first course had done its duty, Lord Northumberland, Lord Strafford, and Macken-zie came in, and the whole began a third time! Then the second course and the dessert! I thought we should have dropped from our chairs with fatigue and fumes! When the clock struck eleven, we were asked to return to the drawing-room, and drink tea and coffee, but I said I was engaged to supper, and came home to bed. My dear lord, think of four hours and a half in a circle of mixed company, and three great dinners, one after another, without interruption; – no, it exceeded our day at Lord Archer's! . . .

64. A Typical Day.

TO THE RIGHT HON. LADY HERVEY[1]

Strawberry Hill, 11 June 1765.

I am almost as much ashamed, Madam, to plead the true cause of my faults towards your ladyship, as to have been guilty of any neg-lect. It is scandalous, at my age, to have been carried backwards and forwards to balls and suppers and parties by very young people, as I was all last week. My resolutions of growing old and staid are admirable: I wake with a sober plan, and intend to pass the day with my friends – then comes the Duke of Richmond, and hurries me down to Whitehall to dinner – then the Duchess of Grafton sends

---

1 See heading to letter 214.

for me to loo in Upper Grosvenor-street – before I can get thither,
I am begged to step to Kensington, to give Mrs. Anne Pitt my opinion about a bow-window – after the loo, I am to march back to
Whitehall to supper – and after that, am to walk with Miss Pelham
on the terrace till two in the morning, because it is moonlight and
her chair is not come. All this does not help my morning laziness;
and, by the time I have breakfasted, fed my birds and my squirrels,
and dressed, there is an auction ready. In short, Madam, this was my
life last week, and is I think every week, with the addition of forty
episodes. – Yet, ridiculous as it is, I send it your ladyship, because
I had rather you should laugh at me than be angry. I cannot offend
you in intention, but I fear my sins of omission are equal to many a
good Christian's. Pray forgive me. I really will begin to be between
forty and fifty by the time I am fourscore: and I truly believe I will
bring my resolutions within compass; for I have not chalked out any
particular business that will take me above forty years more; so that,
if I do not get acquainted with the grandchildren of all the present
age, I shall lead a quiet sober life yet before I die. . . .

65. *A Ridotto at Vauxhall.*

TO GEORGE MONTAGU, ESQ.

Arlington Street, 11 May 1769.

. . . I cannot say last night was equally agreeable. There was what
they called a *ridotto al fresco* at Vauxhall, for which one paid half-a-
guinea, though, except some thousand more lamps and a covered
passage all round the garden, which took off from the gardenhood,
there was nothing better than on a common night. Mr. Conway and
I set out from his house at eight o'clock; the tide and torrent of
coaches was so prodigious, that it was half-an-hour after nine before
we got half way from Westminster-bridge. We then alighted; and
after scrambling under bellies of horses, through wheels, and over
posts and rails, we reached the gardens, where were already many
thousand persons. Nothing diverted me but a man in a Turk's dress
and two nymphs in masquerade without masks, who sailed amongst
the company, and, which was surprising, seemed to surprise nobody.
It had been given out that people were desired to come in fancied
dresses without masks. We walked twice round and were rejoiced to

come away, though with the same difficulties as at our entrance; for we found three strings of coaches all along the road, who did not move half a foot in half-an-hour. There is to be a rival mob in the same way at Ranelagh to-morrow; for the greater the folly and imposition the greater is the crowd. I have suspended the vestimenta that were torn off my back to the god of repentance, and shall stay away. Adieu! I have not a word more to say to you. Yours ever.

P.S. I hope you will not regret paying a shilling for this packet.

66. *A Princess Entertained.*

TO GEORGE MONTAGU, ESQ.

Strawberry Hill, Saturday night, 7 July 1770.

After making an inn of your house, it is but decent to thank you for my entertainment, and to acquaint you with the result of my journey. The party passed off much better than I expected. A Princess[1] at the head of a very small set for five days together did not promise well. However, she was very good-humoured and easy, and dispensed with a large quantity of etiquette. Lady Temple is good-nature itself, my Lord was very civil, Lord Besborough is made to suit all sorts of people, Lady Mary Coke respects royalty too much not to be very condescending, Lady Anne Howard and Mrs. Middleton filled up the drawing-room, or rather made it out, and I was so determined to carry it off as well as I could, and happened to be in such good spirits, and took such care to avoid politics, that we laughed a great deal, and had not a cloud the whole time.

We breakfasted at half an hour after nine; but the Princess did not appear till it was finished; then we walked in the garden, or drove about it in cabriolets, till it was time to dress; dined at three, which, though properly proportioned to the smallness of company to avoid ostentation, lasted a vast while, as the Princess eats and talks a great deal; then again into the garden till past seven, when we came in, drank tea and coffee, and played at pharaoh till ten, when the Princess retired, and we went to supper, and before twelve to bed. You

1 Princess Amelia (see letter 49, p. 80, n. 1), who with a small party was visiting Stowe, of which Lady Temple was châtelaine. Lord Temple had erected an arch in the grounds in honour of the Princess's visit.

see there was great sameness and little vivacity in all this. It was a little broken by fishing, and going round the park one of the mornings; but, in reality, the number of buildings and variety of scenes in the garden, made each day different from the rest, and my meditations on so historic a spot prevented my being tired. Every acre brings to one's mind some instance of the parts or pedantry, of the taste or want of taste, of the ambition or love of fame, or greatness or miscarriages, of those that have inhabited, decorated, planned, or visited the place. Pope, Congreve, Vanburgh, Kent, Gibbs, Lord Cobham, Lord Chesterfield, the mob of nephews, the Lytteltons, Grenvilles, Wests, Leonidas Glover, and Wilkes, the late Prince of Wales, the King of Denmark, Princess Amelia, and the proud monuments of Lord Chatham's services, now enshrined there, then anathematised there, and now again commanding there, with the Temple of Friendship,[1] like the Temple of Janus, sometimes open to war, and sometimes shut up in factious cabals – all these images crowd upon one's memory, and add visionary personages to the charming scenes, that are so enriched with fanes and temples, that the real prospects are little less than visions themselves.

On Wednesday night, a small Vauxhall was acted for us at the grotto in the Elysian fields, which was illuminated with lamps, as were the thicket and two little barks on the lake. With a little exaggeration I could make you believe that nothing ever was so delightful. The idea was really pretty; but, as my feelings have lost something of their romantic sensibility, I did not quite enjoy such an entertainment *al fresco* so much as I should have done twenty years ago. The evening was more than cool, and the destined spot anything but dry. There were not half lamps enough, and no music but an ancient militia-man, who played cruelly on a squeaking tabor and pipe. As our procession descended the vast flight of steps into the garden, in which was assembled a crowd of people from Buckingham and the neighbouring villages to see the Princess and the show, the moon shining very bright, I could not help laughing as I surveyed our troop, which, instead of tripping lightly to such an

1 The Temple of Friendship, designed by James Gibbs and finished in 1739, was dedicated to the group of opposition Whigs that included the future Lord Chatham. The Temple of Janus at Rome had doors at either end that were kept open in times of war, and were closed in times of peace: Walpole reflects on the shifting disputes among Whig politicians.

Arcadian entertainment, were hobbling down by the balustrades, wrapped up in cloaks and great-coats, for fear of catching cold. The Earl, you know, is bent double, the Countess very lame; I am a miserable walker, and the Princess, though as strong as a Brunswick lion, makes no figure in going down fifty stone stairs. Except Lady Anne [Howard], and by courtesy Lady Mary [Coke], we were none of us young enough for a pastoral. We supped in the grotto, which is as proper to this climate as a sea-coal fire would be in the dog-days at Tivoli. . . .

67. *The Pantheon.*

TO SIR HORACE MANN

Arlington Street, 26 April 1771.

. . . If we laugh at the French, they stare at us. Our enormous luxury and expense astonishes them. I carried their Ambassador, and a Comte de Levi, the other morning to see the new winter-Ranelagh [The Pantheon][1] in Oxford Road, which is almost finished. It amazed me myself. Imagine Balbec in all its glory! The pillars are of artificial *giallo antico*. The ceilings, even of the passages, are of the most beautiful stuccos in the best taste of grotesque. The ceilings of the ball-rooms and the panels painted like Raphael's *loggias* in the Vatican. A dome like the pantheon, glazed. It is to cost fifty thousand pounds. Monsieur de Guisnes said to me, "Ce n'est qu'à Londres qu'on peut faire tout cela." It is not quite a proof of the same taste, that two views of Verona, by Canaletti,[2] have been sold by auction for five hundred and fifty guineas, and, what is worse, it is come out that they are copies by Marlow, a disciple of Scott. Both master and scholar are indeed better painters than the Venetian; but the purchasers did not mean to be so well cheated. . . .

1 The Pantheon, designed by James Wyatt (1746–1813) at the beginning of his career, was to open to great acclaim the following January as a rival to Vauxhall and Ranelagh.
2 Bernardo Bellotto, the nephew of Canaletto.

68. *Lord Stanley's Ball.*

TO THE COUNTESS OF UPPER OSSORY

Arlington Street, 3 April 1773.

... Besides the gout for six months, which makes some flaws in the bloom of elderly Arcadians, I have been so far from keeping sheep for the last ten days, that I have kept nothing but bad hours; and have been such a rake that I put myself in mind of a poor old cripple that I saw formerly at Hogarth's auction: he bid for the 'Rake's Progress,' saying, "I *will* buy my own progress," though he looked as if he had no more title to it than I have, but by limping and sitting up. In short, I have been at four balls since yesterday se'n-night, though I had the prudence not to stay supper at Lord Stanley's.[1] That festival was very expensive, for it is the fashion now to make romances rather than balls. In the hall was a band of French horns and clarionets in laced uniforms and feathers. The dome of the staircase was beautifully illuminated with coloured glass lanthorns; in the anteroom was a bevy of vestals in white habits, making tea; in the next, a drapery of sarcenet, that with a very funereal air crossed the chimney, and depended in vast festoons over the sconces. The third chamber's doors were heightened with candles in gilt vases, and the ball-room was formed into an oval with benches above each other, not unlike pews, and covered with red serge, above which were arbours of flowers, red and green pilasters, more sarcenet, and Lord March's glasses[2] which he had lent, as an upholsterer asked Lord Stanley 300*l.* for the loan of some. He had burst open the side of the wall to build an orchestra, with a pendant mirror to reflect the dancers, *à la Guisnes;* and the musicians were in scarlet robes, like the candle-snuffers who represent the senates of Venice at Drury Lane. There were two more chambers at which I never arrived for the crowd. The seasons, danced by himself, the younger Storer, the Duc de Lauzun and another, the youngest Miss Stanley, Miss Poole, the youngest Wrottesley and another Miss, who is likewise anonymous in my memory, were in errant shepherdly dresses without invention, and Storer and Miss Wrottesley in banians with furs, for

1 At Derby House, Grosvenor Square. The decorations for the ball were provided by the brothers Adam.
2 Pier-glasses, as mirrors for the room.

winter, cock and hen. In six rooms below were magnificent suppers. I was not quite so sober last night at Mons. de Guisnes', where the evening began with a ball of children from eighteen to four years old. They danced amazingly well, yet disappointed me, so many of them were ugly; but Mr. Delawarr's two eldest daughters and the Ancaster infanta performed a *pas de trois* as well as Mdlle. Heinel, and the two eldest were pretty; yet I promise you, Madam, the next age will be a thousand degrees below the present in beauty. The most interesting part was to observe the anxiety of the mothers while their children danced or supped: they supped at ten in three rooms. I should not omit telling you that the Vernons,[1] especially the eldest, were not the homeliest part of the show. The former quadrilles then came again upon the stage, and Harry Conway the younger was so astonished at the agility of Mrs. Hobart's bulk, that he said he was sure she must be hollow. The tables were again spread in five rooms, and at past two in the morning we went to supper. To excuse *we*, I must plead that both the late and present Chancellor, and the solemn Lord Lyttelton, my predecessors by some years, stayed as late as I did, – and in good sooth the watchman went four as my chairman knocked at my door.

Such is the result of good resolutions! I determined during my illness to have my colt's tooth drawn, and lo! I have cut four new in a week. Well! at least I am as grave as a judge, looked as rosy as Lord Lyttelton, and much soberer than my Lord Chancellor. To show some marks of grace, I shall give up the opera, (indeed it is very bad,) and go and retake my doctor's degrees among the dowagers at Lady Blandford's; and intending to have no more diversions than I have news to tell your ladyship, I think you shall not hear from me again till we meet, as I shall think it, in heaven.

69. *"Dansant Comme Un Charme!"*

TO THE COUNTESS OF UPPER OSSORY

Strawberry Hill, 25 July 1781.

Poor human nature, what a contradiction it is! to-day it is all rheumatism and morality, and sits with a death's head before it:

1 Daughters of Richard Vernon, Esq., by Lady Evelyn Leveson, widow of John Fitzpatrick, first Earl of Upper Ossory. – WALPOLE.

to-morrow it is dancing! – Oh! my lady, my Lady, what will you say, when the next thing you hear of me after my last letter is, that I have danced three country-dances with a whole set, forty years younger than myself! Shall not you think I have been chopped to shreds and boiled in Medea's kettle? Shall not you expect to see a print of Vestris teaching me? – and Lord Brudenell dying with envy?[1] You may stare with all your expressive eyes, yet the fact is true. Danced – I do not absolutely say, *danced* – but I swam down three dances very grace-fully, with the air that was so much in fashion after the battle of Oudenarde, and that was still taught when I was fifteen, and that I remember General Churchill practising before a glass in a gouty shoe.

To be sure you die with impatience to know the particulars. You must know then – for all my revels must out – I not only went five miles to Lady Aylesford's ball last Friday, but my nieces the Walde-graves desired me there to let them come to me for a few days, as they had been disappointed about a visit they were to make at another place; but that is neither here nor there. Well, here they are, and last night we went to Lady Hertford at Ditton. Soon after, Lady North and her daughters arrived, and besides Lady Elizabeth and Lady Bel Conways, there were their brothers Hugh and George. All the *jeunesse* strolled about the garden. We ancients, with the Earl and Colonel Keene, retired from the dew into the drawing-room. Soon after, the two youths and seven nymphs came in, and shut the door of the hall. In a moment we heard a burst of laughter, and thought we distinguished something like the scraping of a fiddle. My curiosity was raised, I opened the door and found four couples and a half standing up, and a miserable violin from the ale-house. "Oh," said I, "Lady Bel shall not want a partner;" I threw away my stick, and *me voilà dansant comme un charme!* At the end of the third dance, Lord North and his son, in boots, arrived. "Come," said I, "my Lord, you may dance, if I have" – but it ended in my *resigning my place* to his son.

Lady North has invited us for to-morrow, and I shall reserve the rest of my letter for the second volume of my regeneration; however, I declare I will not *dance*. I will not make myself too cheap; I should have the Prince of Wales sending for me three or four times a week

1 Vestris was a dancer and dancing master, much admired by Lord Brudenell.

to hops in Eastcheap. As it is, I feel I shall have some difficulty to return to my old dowagers, at the Duchess of Montrose's, and shall be humming the Hempdressers; when they are scolding me for playing in flush.

Friday, 27 February.

I am not only a prophet, but have more command of my passions than such impetuous gentry as prophets are apt to have. We found the fiddles as I foretold; and yet I kept my resolution and did *not* dance, though the Sirens invited me, and though it would have shocked the dignity of old Tiffany Ellis,[1] who would have thought it an indecorum. The two younger Norths and Sir Ralph Payne supplied my place. I played at cribbage with the matrons, and we came away at midnight. So if I now and then do cut a colt's tooth, I have it drawn immediately. I do not know a paragraph of news – the nearer the minister, the farther from politics. . . .

70. *The Boat Race.*

TO MARY BERRY

Berkeley Square, Tuesday, 23 August 1791.

. . . On Monday was the boat-race [at Richmond]. I was in the great room at the Castle,[2] with the Duke of Clarence, Lady Di.,[3] Lord Robert Spencer, and the House of Bouverie, to see the boats start from the bridge to Thistleworth, and back to a tent erected on Lord Dysart's meadow, just before Lady Di.'s windows; whither we went to see them arrive, and where we had breakfast. For the second heat, I sat in my coach on the bridge; and did not stay for the third. The day had been coined on purpose, with my favourite south-east wind. The scene, both up the river and down, was what only Richmond upon earth can exhibit. The crowds on those green velvet meadows and on the shores, the yachts, barges, pleasure and small boats, and the windows and gardens lined with spectators, were so

1 According to the Yale editors a reference to Welbore Ellis (1713–1802), politician, as being flimsy and over-decorous.
2 The Castle Hotel, facing the Thames at Richmond.
3 Lady Diana Beauclerk (1734–1808) was an artist and friend of Walpole. She was the widow of Topham Beauclerk, for whom see letter 224, p. 319, n. 2.

delightful, that when I came home from that vivid show, I thought Strawberry looked as dull and solitary as a hermitage. At night there was a ball at the Castle, and illuminations, with the Duke's cypher, &c., in coloured lamps, as were the houses of his Royal Highness's tradesmen. I went again in the evening to the French ladies on the Green, where there was a bonfire; but, you may believe, not to the ball. . . . Adieu!

2. THE THEATRE

71. *Handel.*

TO SIR HORACE MANN

Arlington Street, 24 February 1743.

. . . But to come to more *real* contests; Handel has set up an Oratorio against the Operas, and succeeds. He has hired all the goddesses from farces and the singers of *Roast Beef*[1] from between the acts at both theatres, with a man with one note in his voice, and a girl without ever an one; and so they sing, and make brave hallelujahs; and the good company encore the recitative, if it happens to have any cadence like what they call a tune. I was much diverted the other night at the opera; two gentlewomen sat before my sister, and not knowing her, discoursed at their ease. Says one, "Lord! how fine Mr. W. is!" "Yes," replied the other, with a tone of saying sentences, "some men love to be particularly so, your *petit-maîtres* – but they are not always the brightest of their sex." – Do thank me for this period! I am sure you will enjoy it as much as we did.

I shall be very glad of my things, and approve entirely of your precautions; Sir R. will be quite happy, for there is no telling you how impatient he is for his Dominichin.[2] Adieu!

1 It was customary at this time for the galleries to call for a ballad called "The Roast Beef of Old England" between the acts, or before or after the play. – WALPOLE.
2 A painting of the Madonna and Child that Mann was acquiring for Sir Robert Walpole's collection. Walpole had convinced himself it was by Domenichino even though it was signed on the back by the lesser artist Sassoferrato, to whom it is now assigned.

72. *Pantomimes Unpopular.*

TO SIR HORACE MANN

Arlington Street, 26 November 1744.

... If you are not as detached from everything as I am, you will wonder at my tranquillity, to be able to write such variety in the midst of hurricanes. It costs me nothing! so I shall write on, and tell you an adventure of my own. The town has been trying all this winter to beat Pantomimes off the stage, very boisterously; for it is the way here to make even an affair of taste and sense a matter of riot and arms. Fleetwood,[1] the master of Drury-Lane, has omitted nothing to support them, as they supported his house. About ten days ago,[2] he let into the pit great numbers of Bear-garden *bruisers* (that is the term), to knock down everybody that hissed. The pit rallied their forces, and drove them out: I was sitting very quietly in the side-boxes, contemplating all this. On a sudden the curtain flew up, and discovered the whole stage filled with blackguards, armed with bludgeons and clubs, to menace the audience. This raised the greatest uproar; and among the rest, who flew into a passion, but your friend the philosopher? In short, one of the actors, advancing to the front of the stage to make an apology for the manager, he had scarce begun to say, "Mr. Fleetwood —" when your friend, with a most audible voice and dignity of anger, called out, "He is an impudent rascal!" The whole pit huzzaed, and repeated the words. Only think of my being a popular orator! But what was still better, while my shadow of a person was dilating to the consistence of a hero, one of the chief ringleaders of the riot, coming under the box where I sat, and pulling off his hat, said, "Mr. Walpole, what would you please to have us do next?" It is impossible to describe to you the confusion into which this apostrophe threw me. I sank down into the box, and have never since ventured to set my foot into the playhouse. The next night, the uproar was repeated with greater violence, and nothing was heard but voices calling out, "Where's Mr. W.? where's Mr. W.?" In short, the whole town has been entertained with my prowess, and Mr. Conway has given me the name of Wat Tyler; which,

1 Charles Fleetwood (d. 1747), controversial manager of Drury Lane theatre.
2 The Yale editors note that this was at a performance of Steele's *Conscious Lovers* and *The Fortune Tellers.*

I believe, would have stuck by me, if this new episode of Lord Granville had not luckily interfered.

We every minute expect news of the Mediterranean engagement; for, besides your account, Birtles has written the same from Genoa. We expect good news, too, from Prince Charles, who is driving the King of Prussia before him. In the mean time, his wife the Archduchess is dead, which may be a signal loss to him.

I forgot to tell you that, on Friday, Lord Charles Hay,[1] who has more of the parts of an Irishman than of a Scot, told my Lady Granville at the drawing-room on her seeing so full a court, "that people were come out of curiosity." The Speaker [Onslow] is the happiest of any man in these bustles: he says, "this Parliament has torn two favourite ministers from the throne." His conclusion is, that the power of the Parliament will in the end be so great, that nobody can be minister but their own Speaker.

I must tell you a good application by Winnington: there was a man kept one Betty Warner: on his deathbed he swore her never to lie with any other man: the last Lord Warwick piqued himself upon having her before the man was buried; and had. Winnington says, "Just so my Lord Chesterfield and Pitt will have places before old Marlborough's legacy to them for being patriots is paid." My compliments to the family of Suares on the Vittorina's marriage. Adieu!

73. *At the Opera.*

TO THE EARL OF HERTFORD

Strawberry Hill, 25 November 1764.

How could you be so kind, my dear lord, as to recollect Dr. Blanchard, after so long an interval. It will make me still more cautious of giving recommendations to you, instead of drawing upon the credit you give me. I saw Mr. Stanley last night at the Opera, who made his court extremely to me by what he said of you. It was our first opera, and I went to town to hear Manzoli,[2] who did not quite answer my expectation, though a very fine singer; but his voice *has*

1 Brother of Lord Tweeddale. – WALPOLE.
2 Giovanni Manzuoli (*c.* 1720–82), Italian castrato, who had arrived in London in 1764 to sing for the season.

been younger, and wants the touching tones of Elisi. However, the audience was not so nice, but applauded him immoderately, and *encored* three of his songs. The first woman was advertised for a perfect beauty, with no voice; but her beauty and voice are by no means so unequally balanced: she has a pretty little small pipe, and only a pretty little small person, and share of beauty, and does not act ill. There is Tenducci,[1] a moderate tenor, and all the rest intolerable. If you don't make haste and send us Doberval, I don't know what we shall do. The dances were not only hissed, as truly they deserved to be, but the gallery, *a-la-Drury-Lane*, cried out, "Off! off!" The boxes were empty, for so is the town, to a degree. The person who ordered me to write to you for Doberval, was reduced to languish in the Duchess of Hamilton's box. My Duchess [Grafton] does not appear yet – I fear. . . .

74. *Garrick.*

TO THE COUNTESS OF UPPER OSSORY

1 February 1779.

When Lord Ossory is in town, Madam, I do not presume to think of writing. He is more in the world, and hears everything sooner than I do; nor would it be fair to him, to divide a moment of your time with him. However, there were such interesting topics in the letter I had the honour of receiving this evening, that I must answer it directly. But I shall waive the first subject, which concerns myself, to come to the last, that touches your Ladyship; and can I but admire your goodness in thinking of me, when an angel[2] is inoculated? You must now continue it, for you have promised I shall hear how she goes on. Sweet little love! you must be anxious, though inoculation now can scarce be called a hazard. It is as sure, as a cheat of winning, though a strange run of luck may once in two thousand times disappoint him.

The pictures at Houghton, I hear, and I fear, are sold:[3] what can I say? I do not like even to think on it. It is the most signal

1 Giusto Fernando Tenducci (*c.* 1736–90), Italian castrato, known as Il Senesino.
2 Lady Gertrude Fitzpatrick, Lady Ossory's daughter.
3 Sir Robert Walpole's collection of pictures, sold (to Walpole's great distress) by his nephew the 3rd Earl of Orford to Catherine the Great in 1779.

mortification to my idolatry for my father's memory, that it could receive. It is stripping the temple of his glory and of his affection. A mad man excited by rascals has burnt his Ephesus. I must never cast a thought towards Norfolk more; nor will hear my nephew's name if I can avoid it. Him I can only pity; though it is strange he should recover any degree of sense, and never any of feeling! I could have saved my family but cannot repent the motives that bound my hands. If any unhappy lunatic is ever the better for my conduct and example, it is preferable to a collection of pictures.

Yes, Madam, I do think the pomp of Garrick's funeral perfectly ridiculous.[1] It is confounding the immense space between pleasing talents and national services. What distinctions remain for a patriot hero, when the most solemn have been showered on a player? – but when a great empire is on its decline, one symptom is, there being more eagerness on trifles than on essential objects. Shakspeare, who *wrote* when Burleigh counselled and Nottingham fought, was not rewarded and honoured like Garrick who only *acted*, when – indeed I do not know who has counselled and who has fought.

I do not at all mean to detract from Garrick's merit, who was a real genius in his way, and who, I believe, was never equalled in both tragedy and comedy. Still I cannot think that acting, however perfectly, what others have written, is one of the most astonishing talents: yet I will own as fairly that Mrs. Porter and Mademoiselle Dumenil have struck me so much, as even to reverence them. Garrick never affected me quite so much as those two actresses, and some few others in particular parts, as Quin, in Falstaff; King, in Lord Ogleby; Mrs. Pritchard, in Maria, in the Nonjuror; Mrs. Clive, in Mrs. Cadwallader; and Mrs. Abington, in Lady Teazle. They all seemed the very persons: I suppose that in Garrick I thought I saw more of his art; yet his Lear, Richard, Hotspur

---

1 Garrick was buried at the foot of Shakespeare's statue in Westminster Abbey in a funeral of great splendour. Lord Ossory, Walpole's correspondent, made a memorandum that "In Italy I became acquainted with Garrick, and from my earliest youth having admired him on the stage, was happy to be familiarly acquainted with him, cultivated his society from that time till his death, and then accompanied him to his grave as one of his pallbearers. He and Mrs. Garrick (I think it was in 1777) have been with us in the country; Gibbon and Reynolds, at the same time, all three delightful in society. The vivacity of the great actor, the keen sarcastic wit of the great historian, and the genuine pleasantry of the great painter, mixed up well together, and made a charming party. Garrick's mimicry of the mighty Johnson was excellent."

(which the town had not taste enough to like), Kitely, and Ranger, were as capital and perfect as action could be. In declamation, I confess, he never charmed me; nor could he be a gentleman; his Lord Townley and Lord Hastings were mean, but then too the parts are indifferent, and do not call for a master's exertion.

I should shock Garrick's *devotees* if I uttered all my opinion: I will trust your Ladyship with it – it is, that Le Texier is twenty times the genius. What comparison between the powers that do the fullest justice to a single part, and those that instantaneously can fill a whole piece, and transform themselves with equal perfection into men and women, and pass from laughter to tears, and make you shed the latter at both? Garrick, when he made one laugh, was not always judicious, though excellent. What idea did his Sir John Brute give of a Surly Husband. His Bayes was no less entertaining; but it was a Garretteer-bard. Old Cibber preserved the solemn coxcomb; and was the caricature of a great poet, as the part was designed to be.

Half I have said I know is heresy, but fashion had gone to excess, though very rarely with so much reason. Applause had turned his head, and yet he was never content even with that prodigality. His jealousy and envy were unbounded; he hated Mrs. Clive, till she quitted the stage, and then cried her up to the skies, to depress Mrs. Abington. He did not love Mrs. Pritchard, and with more reason, for there was more spirit and originality in her Beatrice than in his Benedick. . . .

75. *Mrs. Siddons – Pantomime.*

TO THE COUNTESS OF UPPER OSSORY

Strawberry Hill, 3 November 1782.

Our mutual silence, Madam, has had pretty nearly the same cause, want of matter; for though my nominal wife, Lady Browne, has not left me like your Lord, I have led almost as uneventful a life as your Ladyship in your lonely woods, except that I have been for two days in town, and seen Mrs. Siddons.[1] She pleased me beyond

1 Walpole saw Sarah Siddons (1755–1831) as Isabella in Garrick's version of Southerne's tragedy *The Fatal Marriage*, in which role he had long before seen Mrs. Porter.

my expectation, but not up to the admiration of the *ton*, two or three of whom were in the same box with me; particularly Mr. Boothby, who, as if to disclaim the stoic apathy of Mr. Meadows in 'Cecilia,' was all bravissimo. Mr. Crawfurd, too, asked me if I did not think her the best actress I ever saw? I said, "By no means; we old folks were apt to be prejudiced in favour of our first impressions." She is a good figure, handsome enough, though neither nose nor chin according to the Greek standard beyond which both advance a good deal. Her hair is either red, or she has no objection to its being thought so, and had used red powder. Her voice is clear and good; but I thought she did not vary its modulations enough, nor ever approach enough to the familiar – but this may come when more habituated to the awe of the audience of the capital. Her action is proper, but with little variety; when without motion, her arms are not genteel. Thus you see, Madam, all my objections are very trifling; but what I really wanted, but did not find, was originality, which announces genius, and without both which I am never intrinsically pleased. All Mrs. Siddons did, good sense or good instruction might give. I dare to say, that were I one-and-twenty, I should have thought her marvellous; but alas; I remember Mrs. Porter and the Dumesnil – and remember every accent of the former in the very same part. Yet this is not entirely prejudice: don't I equally recollect the whole progress of Lord Chatham and Charles Townshend, and does it hinder my thinking Mr. Fox a prodigy? – Pray don't send him this paragraph too. . . .

I am glad to hear so good an account of Hatfield from our Lord. I have been invited thither; but I have done with terrestrial journeys. I have not philosophy enough to stand stranger servants staring at my broken fingers[1] at dinner. I hide myself like spaniels that creep into a hedge to die; yet, having preserved my eyes and all my teeth, among which is a colt's, not yet decayed, I treated it and my eyes, not only with Mrs. Siddons but a harlequin farce. But there again my ancient prejudices operated: how unlike the pantomimes of Rich, which were full of wit, and coherent, and carried on a story! What I now saw was Robinson Crusoe: how Aristotle and Bossu, had they ever written on pantomimes, would swear! It was a heap of contradictions and violations of the costume. *Friday* is turned into

1 A reference to his gout.

Harlequin, and falls down at an old man's feet that I took for Pantaloon, but they told me it was *Friday's* father. I said, "Then it must be *Thursday*," yet still it seemed to be Pantaloon. I see I understand nothing from astronomy to a harlequin – farce! . . .

V
VIRTUOSO AND ANTIQUARIAN

IN HIS VILLA, every apartment is a museum, every piece of furniture is a curiosity; there is something strange in the form of the shovel; there is a long story belonging to the bell-rope. We wander among a profusion of rarities, of trifling intrinsic value, but so quaint in fashion, or connected with such remarkable names and events, that they may well detain our attention for a moment. A moment is enough. Some new relic, some new unique, some new carved work, some new enamel, is forthcoming in an instant. One cabinet of trinkets is no sooner closed than another is opened.

So wrote Thomas Macaulay in the *Edinburgh Review* for October 1833, a brilliant and devastating article which, while ostensibly reviewing the first series of Walpole's letters to Horace Mann, delivered a crushing blow to Walpole's posthumous reputation. It is effective because it has a sufficient veneer of truth to make it plausible. When Walpole's collection was sold nine years later the journalists of the day had fun with those items valued by Walpole for their associations – the pipe case of Admiral van Tromp, the hat of Cardinal Wolsey, and the spurs worn by King William III at the battle of the Boyne (for Walpole's awed reception of which see letter 91). But Macaulay's account now seems more dated and inaccurate in its description of Walpole as collector than perhaps in any other area.

In his youth, Walpole knew intimately and wrote on his father's great collection of Italian, Dutch and Flemish masters at Downing Street and Houghton, but his own could not have been more different. Its essence lay in the historical portraits, including a particularly fine group of miniatures. For Walpole the persons portrayed were perhaps more important than the artists. As well as paintings he also collected antiquities, ceramics, stained glass, armour, books and prints, furniture and curiosities. Despite the contempt he expressed for the Society of Antiquaries, which he described as a body of men "who seldom do anything but grow antiquated themselves"[1] – he resigned his membership after a dispute in 1772 – Walpole himself

1 Letter to Mason, 9 February 1781 (YE 29:107).

was essentially an antiquary. A subjective, imaginative relationship with the past lay at the heart of his collecting.

There is a sense in which he inhabited the collection – it filled his house, it inspired some of his writing (see letters 118 and 119 for the genesis of *The Castle of Otranto*), and on one occasion it even animated his entertaining: letter 111 describes how he wore "a cravat of Gibbons's carving, and a pair of gloves embroidered up to the elbows that had belonged to James I" in the course of greeting distinguished French visitors to Strawberry Hill. Walpole was innovative and influential in his concern for provenance, which in the preface to the *Description* of his collection he defined as "the genealogy of the objects of vertù – not so noble as those of the peerage, but on a par with those of race-horses". The origins of art and what he saw as primitive civilisations, though, had little appeal for him, as illustrated in letter 425.

Walpole began collecting in Italy – "I would buy the Coliseum if I could," he averred.[1] At home he attended auctions, sometimes picking up bargains: the Vandyck that he describes buying for twenty-nine guineas in 1764 (letter 87) fetched eight times that sum when his collection was dispersed at the Strawberry Hill sale in 1842. He became well known and widely consulted as an art connoisseur, and items from Walpole's collection are now prized for their Strawberry Hill provenance. His travels around England in the 1750s and early 1760s are recorded in some of the most delightful of his letters, which give an insight into his architectural taste (see letters 79, 80, and 82 to 86). He might stay at the country houses of friends, or sometimes at the local inn – on one occasion (letter 80) finding it full of smugglers. His account in letter 83 of the local clergyman's increasing wonder when encountering him at Ragley Hall (Lord Hertford's seat in Warwickshire) first on the floor of the lumber room, "all over cobwebs and dirt and mortar", then up a ladder identifying a portrait in the clergyman's own bedroom, then romping with the children of the family "in my slippers and without a hat", and at the end of the day sitting next to Lady Hertford at dinner, gives an engaging picture of Walpole the antiquarian at work and at play.

This section concludes with a revealing letter (number 94) to the antiquary Richard Gough in 1789 on the radical renovations being carried out by James Wyatt at Salisbury Cathedral, showing Walpole as an incipient conservationist.

1   Letter to Conway, 23 April 1740 (YE 37:57).

76. *Purchases in Italy.*

TO RICHARD WEST, ESQ.

Dear West,   Florence, 2 October (N.S.) 1740.

... I made but small collections, and have only bought some bronzes and medals, a few busts, and two or three pictures; one of my busts is to be mentioned; 'tis the famous Vespasian in touchstone,[1] reckoned the best in Rome, except the Caracalla of the Farnese: I gave but twenty-two pounds for it at Cardinal Ottoboni's sale. One of my medals is as great a curiosity: 'tis of Alexander Severus, with the amphitheatre in brass; this reverse is extant on medals of his, but mine is a *medagliuncino*, or small medallion, and the only one with this reverse known in the world: 'twas found by a peasant while I was in Rome, and sold by him for sixpence to an antiquarian, to whom I paid for it seven guineas and an half; but to virtuosi 'tis worth any sum.[2]

As to Tartini's[3] musical compositions, ask Gray; I know but little in music. ...

I am most sincerely
Yours.

77. *Genealogical Studies.*

TO GEORGE MONTAGU, ESQ.

Strawberry Hill, 11 August 1748.

I am arrived at great knowledge in the annals of the house of Vere, but though I have twisted and twined their genealogy and my own a thousand ways, I cannot discover, as I wished to do, that I am descended from them any how but from one of their Christian names; the name of Horace having travelled from them into Norfolk by the marriage of a daughter of Horace Lord Vere of Tilbury with a Sir Roger Townshend, whose family baptised some of us with it. But

1 The bust of Vespasian in basaltes, kept by Walpole in the gallery at Strawberry Hill and sold at the Strawberry Hill sale for 210 guineas.
2 The medal was struck when the Coliseum was restored in A.D. 223. It was with other medals exchanged by Walpole in 1772 for Lord Rockingham's carved silver bell (then believed to be by Cellini) one of Walpole's principal treasures.
3 Giuseppe Tartini (1692–1770), Italian Baroque composer and violinist.

I have made a really curious discovery! the lady with the strange dress at Earl's Colne, which I mentioned to you, is certainly Lancerona, the Portuguese; for I have found in Rapin, from one of the old chronicles, that Anne of Bohemia, to whom she had been Maid of Honour, introduced the fashion of *piked horns*, or high heads, which is the very attire on this tomb, and ascertains it to belong to Robert de Vere, the great Earl of Oxford, made Duke of Ireland by Richard II., who, after the banishment of this Minister, and his death at Louvain, occasioned by a boar at a hunting match, caused the body to be brought over, would have the coffin opened once more to see his favourite, and attended it himself in high procession to its interment at Earl's Colne. I don't know whether the "Craftsman" some years ago would not have found out that we were descended from this Vere, at least from his name and ministry: my comfort is, that Lancerona was Earl Robert's second wife. But in this search I have crossed upon another descent, which I am taking great pains to verify (I don't mean a pun), and that is a probability of my being descended from Chaucer, whose daughter, the Lady Alice, before her espousals with Thomas Montacute, Earl of Salisbury, and afterwards with William de la Pole, the great Duke of Suffolk (another famous favourite), was married to a Sir John Philips, who I hope to find was of Picton Castle, and had children by her; but I have not yet brought these matters to a consistency; Mr. Chute[1] is persuaded I shall, for he says any body with two or three hundred years of pedigree may find themselves descended from whom they please; and thank my stars and my good cousin, the present Sir J[ohn] Philips, I have a sufficient pedigree to work upon; for he drew us up one by which *Ego et rex meus* are derived hand in hand from Cadwallader, and the English Baronetage says from the Emperor Maximus (by the Philips's, who are Welsh, *s'entend*). These Veres have thrown me into a deal of this old study: t'other night I was reading to Mrs. Leneve and Mrs. Pigot, who has been here a few days, the description in Hall's Chronicle of the meeting of Harry VIII. and

---

1   Walpole's friend and correspondent John Chute of The Vyne, Hampshire, and a member of the Committee that advised on Walpole's building works at Strawberry Hill: see heading to letter 210.

Francis I. which is so delightfully painted in your Windsor.[1] We came to a paragraph, which I must transcribe; for though it means nothing in the world, it is so ridiculously worded in the old English that it made us laugh for three days.

> And the wer the twoo kynges served with a banket and after mirthe, had communication in the banket time, and there shewed the one the other their pleasure.

Would not one swear that old Hal showed all that is showed in the Tower? I am now in the act of expecting the house of Pritchard, Dame Clive, and Mrs. Metheglin to dinner. I promise you the Clive, and I will not show one another our pleasure during the banket time nor afterwards. In the evening, we go to a play at Kingston, where the places are two pence a head. Our great company at Richmond and Twickenham has been torn to pieces by civil dissensions, but they continue acting. Mr. Lee, the ape of Garrick, not liking his part, refused to play it, and had the confidence to go into the pit as spectator. The actress, whose benefit was in agitation, made her complaints to the audience, who obliged him to mount the stage; but since that he has retired from the company. I am sorry he was such a coxcomb, for he was the best. . . .

78. Interest in Heraldry.

TO GEORGE MONTAGU, ESQ.

Strawberry Hill, 20 July 1749.

I am returned to my Strawberry, and find it in such beauty, that I shall be impatient till I see you and your sisters here. They must excuse me if I don't marry for their reception; for it is said the Drax's have impeached fifteen more damsels, and till all the juries of matrons have finished their inquest, one shall not care to make one's choice:[2] I was going to say, "throw one's handkerchief," but at present that term would be a little equivocal.

As I came to town [from Mistley] I was extremely entertained with some excursions I made out of the road in search of antiquities.

1 The Windsor painting was of the Field of the Cloth of Gold. Hall's Chronicle was *The union of the two noble and illustre famelies of Lancastre and Yorke*, by Edward Hall, 1548.
2 The subject of this gossip is not known.

At Layer Marney is a noble old remnant of the palace of the Lords Marney, with three very good tombs in the church well preserved. At Messing I saw an extreme fine window of painted glass in the church: it is the duties prescribed in the Gospel, of visiting the sick and prisoners, &c. I mistook, and called it the seven deadly sins. There is a very old tomb of Sir Robert Messing, that built the church. The hall-place is a fragment of an old house belonging to Lord Grimston; Lady Luckyn his mother, of fourscore and six, lives in it with an old son and daughter. The servant who showed it told us much history of another brother that had been parson there: this history was entirely composed of the anecdotes of the doctor's drinking, who, as the man told us, had been a *blood*. There are some Scotch arms taken from the rebels in the '15, and many old coats of arms on glass brought from Newhall, which now belongs to Olmius. Mr. Conyers bought a window[1] there for only a hundred pounds, on which was painted Harry the Eighth and one of his queens at full length: he has put it up at Copthall, a seat which he has bought that belonged to Lord North and Grey. You see I persevere in my heraldry. T'other day the parson of Rigby's parish dined with us; he has conceived as high an opinion of my skill in genealogies, as if I could say the first chapter of Matthew by heart. Rigby drank my health to him, and that I might come to be garter king at arms: the poor man replied with great zeal, "I wish he may with all my heart." Certainly, I am born to preferment; I gave an old woman a penny once, who prayed that I might live to be Lord Mayor of London! What pleased me most in my travels was Dr. Sayer's parsonage at Witham, which, with Southcote's[2] help, whose old Roman Catholic father lives just by him, he has made one of the most charming villas in England. There are sweet meadows falling down a hill, and rising again on t'other side of the prettiest little winding stream you ever saw. . . .

---

1 Now the east window of St. Margaret's Church, Westminster. It had been purchased by John Conyers (*c.* 1718–75) of Copt Hall, M.P., or by his father Edward Conyers (d. 1742).
2 Philip Southcote (1697/8–1758) of Woburn Farm, Chertsey, whose celebrated gardens he laid out.

79. *Travels in England.*

TO GEORGE MONTAGU, ESQ.

Daventry, 22 July 1751.

You will wonder in what part of the county of Twicks lies this Daventry. It happens to be in Northamptonshire. My letter will scarce set out till I get to London, but I choose to give it its present date lest you should admire, that Mr. Usher of the Exchequer,[1] the lord treasurer of pen, ink, and paper, should write with such coarse materials. I am on my way from Ragley,[2] and if ever the waters subside and my ark rests upon dry land again, I think of stepping over to Tonghes: but your journey has filled my post-chaise's head with such terrible ideas of your roads, that I think I shall let it have done raining for a month or six weeks, which it has not done for as much time past, before I begin to grease my wheels again, and lay in a provision of French books, and tea, and blunderbusses, for my journey.

Before I tell you a word of Ragley, you must hear how busy I have been upon Grammont.[3] You know I have long had a purpose of a new edition, with notes, and cuts of the principal beauties and heroes, if I could meet with their portraits. I have made out all the people at all remarkable, except *my Lord Janet*, whom I cannot divine unless he be *Thanet*. Well, but what will entertain you is, that I have discovered the *philosophe Whitnell;* and what do you think his real name was? Only Whetenhall! Pray do you call cousins?[4] Look in Collins's Baronets, and under the article *Bedingfield* you will find that he was an *ingenious gentleman*, and *la blanche* Whitnell, *though one of the greatest beauties of the age, an excellent wife.* I am persuaded the Bedingfields crowded in these characters to take off the ridicule in Grammont; they have succeeded to a miracle. Madame de Mirepoix told me t'other day, that she had known a daughter of the Countess de Grammont, an Abbess in Lorrain, who, to the ambassadress's great scandal, was ten times more vain of the blood of Hamilton than of an equal quantity of that of Grammont. She had

1 The sinecure office held by Walpole was Usher of the Exchequer.
2 The seat of Walpole's cousin and correspondent, Lord Hertford.
3 Walpole's edition of the *Mémoires* of the Comte du Grammont was produced by his Strawberry Hill Press in 1772.
4 A sister of Mr. Montagu's was married to Nathaniel Whetenhall, Esq. – WALPOLE.

told her much of her sister my Lady Stafford, whom I remember to have seen when I was a child. She used to live at Twickenham when Lady Mary Wortley and the Duke of Wharton lived there; she had more wit than both of them. What would I give to have had Strawberry Hill twenty years ago! I think any thing but twenty years. Lady Stafford used to say to her sister, "Well, child, I have come without my wit to-day;" that is, she had not taken her opium, which she was forced to do if she had any appointment, to be in particular spirits. This rage of Grammont carried me a little while ago to old Marlborough's at Wimbledon,[1] where I had heard there was a picture of Lady Denham; it is a charming one. The house you know stands in a hole, or, as the whimsical old lady said, seems to be making a curtsey. She had directed my Lord Pembroke not to make her go up any steps; "I won't go up steps;" – and so he dug a saucer to put it in, and levelled the first floor with the ground. There is a bust of Admiral Vernon, erected I suppose by Jack Spencer, with as many lies upon it as if it was a tombstone; and a very curious old picture upstairs, that I take to be Louis Sforza the Moor, with his nephew Galeazzo. There are other good pictures in the house, but perhaps you have seen them. As I have formerly seen Oxford and Blenheim, I did not stop till I came to Stratford-upon-Avon, the wretchedest old town I ever saw, which I intended for Shakspeare's sake to find snug, and pretty, and antique, not old. His tomb, and his wife's, and John à Combes', are in an agreeable church, with several other monuments; as one of the Earl of Totness, and another of Sir Edward Walker, the Memoirs writer. There are quantities of Cloptons, too; but the bountiful corporation have exceedingly bepainted Shakspeare and the principal personages[2] – Lady Caroline Petersham is not more vermilion.

I was much struck with Ragley; the situation is magnificent; the house far beyond anything I have seen of that bad age: for it was begun, as I found by an old letter in the library from Lord Ranelagh to Earl Conway, in the year 1680. By the way, I have had, and am to have, the rummaging of three chests of pedigrees and letters to that secretary Conway, which I have interceded for and saved from the flames. The prospect is as fine as one destitute of a navigated river

1 Sarah Churchill, Dowager Duchess of Marlborough (1660–1744), had a house at Wimbledon. It was destroyed by fire in 1785.
2 Shakespeare's bust was repainted by the Corporation of Stratford in 1748.

can be, and hitherto totally unimproved; so is the house, which is but just covered in, after so many years. They have begun to inhabit the naked walls of the attic story; the great one is unfloored and unceiled; the hall is magnificent, sixty by forty, and thirty-eight high. I am going to pump Mr. Bentley[1] for designs. The other apartments are very lofty, and in quantity, though I had suspected that this leviathan hall must have devoured half the other chambers.

The Hertfords carried me to dine at Lord Archer's,[2] an odious place. . . . On my return, I saw Warwick, a pretty old town, small, and thinly inhabited, in the form of a cross. The castle is enchanting; the view pleased me more than I can express; the river Avon tumbles down a cascade at the foot of it. It is well laid out by one Brown,[3] who has set up on a few ideas of Kent and Mr. Southcote. One sees what the prevalence of taste does; little Brooke, who would have chuckled to have been born in an age of clipt hedges and cockle-shell avenues, has submitted to let his garden and park be natural. Where he has attempted gothic in the castle, he has failed woefully; and has indulged himself in a new apartment, that is paltry. The chapel is very pretty, and smugged up with tiny pews, that look like *étuis* for the Earl and his diminutive Countess. I shall tell you nothing of the glorious chapel of the Beauchamps in St. Mary's church, for you know it is in Dugdale; nor how ill the fierce bears and ragged staves are succeeded by puppets and corals. As I came back another road, I saw Lord Pomfret's [Easton Neston] by Towcester, where there are a few good pictures, and many masked statues; there is an exceeding fine Cicero, which has no fault, but the head being modern. I saw a pretty lodge [Wakefield Lodge], just built by the Duke of Grafton, in Whittleberry-forest; the design is Kent's, but, as was his manner, too heavy. I ran through the gardens at Stowe, which I have seen before, and had only time to be charmed with the variety of scenes. I do like that Albano[4] glut of buildings, let them be ever so much condemned.

1 There is no trace of Walpole's friend the designer Richard Bentley providing designs for Ragley.
2 Umberslade, near Henley-in-Arden, the seat of Thomas Archer (1695–1768), Baron Archer.
3 Lancelot "Capability" Brown (bap. 1716–83), the celebrated landscape gardener, here noticed by Walpole near the beginning of his career.
4 Francesco Albano or Albani (1578–1660), an Italian painter of landscapes and buildings.

80. *Kent and Sussex.*

TO RICHARD BENTLEY, ESQ.

Battel, Wednesday, 5 August 1752.

Here we are, my dear Sir, in the middle of our pilgrimage; and lest we should never return from this holy land of abbeys and Gothic castles, I begin a letter to you, that I hope some charitable monk, when he has buried our bones, will deliver to you. We have had piteous distresses, but then we have seen glorious sights! You shall hear of each in their order.

Monday, Wind S.E. – at least that was our direction. – While they were changing our horses at Bromley, we went to see the Bishop of Rochester's palace; not for the sake of anything there was to be seen, but because there was a chimney, in which had stood a flower-pot, in which was put the counterfeit plot against Bishop Sprat.[1] 'Tis a paltry parsonage, with nothing of antiquity but two panes of glass, purloined from Islip's chapel in Westminster Abbey, with that abbot's rebus, an eye and a slip of a tree. In the garden there is a clear little pond, teeming with gold fish. The Bishop is more prolific than I am.

From Sevenoaks we went to Knowle.[2] The park is sweet, with much old beech, and an immense sycamore before the great gate, that makes me more in love than ever with sycamores. The house is not near so extensive as I expected: the outward court has a beautiful decent simplicity that charms one. The apartments are many, but not large. The furniture throughout, ancient magnificence; loads of portraits, not good nor curious; ebony cabinets, embossed silver in vases, dishes, &c., embroidered beds, stiff chairs, and sweet bags lying on velvet tables, richly worked in silk and gold. There are two galleries, one very small; an old hall, and a spacious great drawing-room. There is never a good staircase. The first little room you enter has sundry portraits of the times; but they seem to have been bespoke by the yard, and drawn all by the same painter: one should be happy if they were authentic; for among them there is Dudley,

1 Thomas Sprat (bap. 1635–1713), Bishop of Rochester. The reference is to the plot of 1692 which sought without foundation to implicate Sprat in an attempt to restore James II to the throne.
2 Knole, Kent, the seat of Lionel Sackville, 1st Duke of Dorset (1688–1765).

Duke of Northumberland, Gardiner of Winchester, the Earl of Surrey the poet, when a boy, and a Thomas, Duke of Norfolk; but I don't know which. The only fine picture is of Lord Goring and Endymion Porter by Vandyke. There is a good head of the Queen of Bohemia, a whole-length of Duc d'Espernon, and another good head of the Clifford, Countess of Dorset,[1] who wrote that admirable haughty letter to Secretary Williamson, when he recommended a person to her for member for Appleby: "I have been bullied by an usurper, I have been neglected by a court, but I won't be dictated to by a subject: your man shan't stand. Ann Dorset, Pembroke and Montgomery." In the chapel is a piece of ancient tapestry; Saint Luke in his first profession is holding an urinal. Below stairs is a chamber of poets and players, which is proper enough in that house; for the first Earl wrote a play,[2] and the last Earl was a poet, and I think married a player. Major Mohun and Betterton are curious among the latter, Cartwright and Flatman among the former. The arcade is newly enclosed, painted in fresco, and with modern glass of all the family matches. In the gallery is a whole-length of the unfortunate Earl of Surrey,[3] with his device, a broken column, and the motto *Sat superest*. My father had one of them, but larger, and with more emblems, which the Duke of Norfolk bought at my brother's sale. There is one good head of Henry VIII., and divers of Cranfield, Earl of Middlesex, the citizen who came to be Lord Treasurer, and was very near coming to be hanged.[4] His countess, a bouncing kind of lady-mayoress, looks pure awkward amongst so much good company. A visto cut through the wood has a delightful effect from the front; but there are some trumpery fragments of gardens that spoil the view from the state apartments.

We lay that night at Tunbridge town, and were surprised with the ruins of the old castle. The gateway is perfect, and the inclosure formed into a vineyard by a Mr. Hooker, to whom it belongs, and the walls spread with fruit, and the mount on which the keep stood,

---

1 The indomitable Lady Anne Clifford (1590–1676), Baroness de Clifford in her own right, and through her two husbands Countess of Dorset, Pembroke and Montgomery.
2 Thomas Sackville, 1st Earl of Dorset (*c.* 1536–1608), the joint author of the tragedy of *Gorboduc*, produced in 1561.
3 Executed in 1547.
4 Lionel Cranfield (1575–1645), Earl of Middlesex. He had been impeached for corruption in 1624.

planted in the same way. The prospect is charming, and a breach in the wall opens below to a pretty Gothic bridge of three arches over the Medway. We honoured the man for his taste – not but that we wished the committee at Strawberry Hill were to sit upon it, and stick cypresses among the hollows – But, alas! he sometimes makes eighteen sour hogs-heads, and is going to disrobe "the ivy-mantled tower," because it harbours birds!

Now begins our chapter of woes. The inn was full of farmers and tobacco; and the next morning, when we were bound for Penshurst, the only man in the town who had two horses would not let us have them, because the roads, as he said, were so bad. We were forced to send to the Wells for others, which did not arrive till half the day was spent – we all the while up to the head and ears in a market of sheep and oxen. A mile from the town we climbed up a hill to see Summer Hill, the residence of Grammont's Princess of Babylon.[1] There is now scarce a road to it: the Paladins of those times were too valorous to fear breaking their necks; and I much apprehend that *la Monsery* and the fair Mademoiselle Hamilton[2] must have mounted their palfreys and rode behind their gentlemen-ushers upon pillions to the Wells. The house is little better than a farm, but has been an excellent one, and is entire, though out of repair. I have drawn the front of it to show you, which you are to draw over again to show me. It stands high, commands a vast landscape beautifully wooded, and has quantities of large old trees to shelter itself, some of which might be well spared to open views.

From Summer Hill we went to Lamberhurst to dine; near which, that is, at the distance of three miles, up and down impracticable hills, in a most retired vale, such as Pope describes in the last Dunciad,

> "Where slumber abbots, purple as their vines,"[3]

we found the ruins of Bayham Abbey, which the Barrets and Hardings bid us visit. There are small but pretty remains, and a neat little

---

1 Lady Margaret de Burgh (d. 1698), variously Lady Muskerry and Lady Purbeck, of Somerhill, near Tonbridge. The Yale editors note that according to Grammont's *Mémoires* as printed at Strawberry Hill, she was called the Princess of Babylon after a costume she wore at a masquerade to which she had been invited as a joke.
2 Elizabeth Hamilton (1641–1708) was the wife of Philibert, Comte du Grammont.
3 Pope, *Dunciad* IV. 302 (though the Yale editors note that the correct reading is "wines" not "vines").

Gothic house built near them by their nephew Pratt. They have found a tomb of an abbot, with a crozier, at length on the stone.

Here our woes increase. The roads grew bad beyond all badness, the night dark beyond all darkness, our guide frightened beyond all frightfulness. However, without being at all killed, we got up, or down, – I forget which, it was so dark, – a famous precipice called Silver Hill, and about ten at night arrived at a wretched village called Rotherbridge. We had still six miles hither, but determined to stop, as it would be a pity to break our necks before we had seen all we intended. But, alas! there was only one bed to be had: all the rest were inhabited by smugglers, whom the people of the house called mountebanks; and with one of whom the lady of the den told Mr. Chute he might lie. We did not at all take to this society, but, armed with links and lanthorns, set out again upon this impracticable journey. At two o'clock in the morning we got hither to a still worse inn, and that crammed with excise officers, one of whom had just shot a smuggler. However, as we were neutral powers, we have passed safely through both armies hitherto, and can give you a little farther history of our wandering through these mountains, where the young gentlemen are forced to drive their curricles with a pair of oxen. The only morsel of good road we have found, was what even the natives had assured us was totally impracticable; these were eight miles to Hurst Monceaux. It is seated at the end of a large vale, five miles in a direct line to the sea, with wings of blue hills covered with wood, one of which falls down to the house in a sweep of a hundred acres. The building, for the convenience of water to the moat, sees nothing at all; indeed it is entirely imagined on a plan of defence, with draw-bridges actually in being, round towers, watch-towers mounted on them, and battlements pierced for the passage of arrows from long bows. It was built in the time of Henry VI., and is as perfect as the first day. It does not seem to have been ever quite finished, or at least that age was not arrived at the luxury of white-wash; for almost all the walls, except in the principal chambers, are in their native *brick-hood*. It is a square building, each side about two hundred feet in length; a porch and cloister, very like Eton College; and the whole is much in the same taste, the kitchen extremely so, with three vast funnels to the chimneys going up on the inside. There are two or three little courts for offices, but no magnificence of apartments. It is scarcely furnished with a few necessary beds and chairs: one side has been sashed, and a drawing-room and dining-room and two or three rooms wainscoted by the Earl of Sussex, who married a natural daughter of Charles II. Their arms with delightful carvings by Gibbons, particularly two pheasants, hang over the chimneys. Over the great drawing-room chimney is the coat-armour of the first Leonard, Lord Dacre, with all his alliances. Mr. Chute was transported, and called cousin with ten thousand quarterings. The chapel is small, and mean: the Virgin and seven long lean saints, ill done, remain in the windows. There have been four more, but seem to have been removed for light; and we actually found St. Catherine, and another gentlewoman with a church in her hand, exiled into the buttery. There remain two odd cavities, with very small wooden screens on each side the altar, which seem to have been confessionals. The outside is a mixture of grey brick and stone, that has a very venerable appearance. The draw-bridges are romantic to a degree; and there is a dungeon, that gives one a delightful idea of living in the days of soccage and under such goodly tenures. They showed us a dismal chamber which they called *Drummer's*-hall, and suppose that Mr. Addison's comedy is descended from it. In the windows of the gallery over the cloisters, which leads all round to the apartments, is the device of the Fienneses, a wolf holding a baton with a scroll, *Le roy le veut* – an unlucky motto, as I shall tell you presently, to the last peer of that line. The estate is two thousand a year, and so compact as to have but seventeen houses upon it. We walked up a brave old avenue to the church, with ships sailing on our left hand the whole way. Before the altar lies a lank brass knight, hight William Fienis, chevalier, who obiit c.c.c.c.v. that is in 1405. By the altar is a beautiful tomb, all in our trefoil taste, varied into a thousand little canopies and patterns, and two knights reposing on their backs. These were Thomas, Lord Dacre, and his only son Gregory [Thomas] who died sans issue. An old grey-headed beadsman of the family talked to us of a blot in the scutcheon; and we had observed that the field of the arms was green instead of blue, and the lions ramping to the right, contrary to order. This and the man's imperfect narrative let us into the circumstances of the personage before us; for there is no inscription. He went in a Chevy-chase style to hunt in *a Mr. Pelham's*,[1] park at Lawton: the keepers opposed, a

1 At the date of this letter Mr. Pelham was prime minister. – BERRY.

fray ensued, a man was killed. The haughty baron took the death upon himself, as most secure of pardon; but however, though there was no Chancellor of the Exchequer in the question, he was condemned to be hanged: *Le roy le vouloist.*

Now you are fully master of Hurst Monceaux, I shall carry you on to Battel. – By the way, we bring you a thousand sketches, that you may show us what we have seen. Battel Abbey stands at the end of the town, exactly as Warwick Castle does of Warwick; but the house of Webster have taken due care that it should not resemble it in any thing else. A vast building, which they call the old refectory, but which I believe was the original church, is now barn, coach-house, etc. The situation is noble, above the level of abbeys: what does remain of gateways and towers is beautiful, particularly the flat side of a cloister, which is now the front of the mansion-house. A Miss of the family has clothed a fragment of a portico with cockle-shells! The grounds, and what has been a park, lie in a vile condition. In the church is the tomb of Sir Anthony Browne, Master of the Horse for life to Harry VIII.; from whose descendants the estate was purchased. The head of John Hammond, the last abbot, is still perfect in one of the windows. Mr. Chute says, "What charming things we should have done if Battel Abbey had been to be sold at Mrs. Chenevix's, as Strawberry was!"[1] Good-night. . . .

81. *Bentley's Paintings Criticised.*

TO RICHARD BENTLEY, ESQ.

Arlington Street, 23 February 1755

Your *Argosie* is arrived safe; thank you for shells, trees, cones; but above all, thank you for the landscape.[2] As it is your first attempt in oils, and has succeeded so much beyond my expectation, (and being against my advice too, you may believe the sincerity of my praises) I must indulge my Vasarihood,[3] and write a dissertation upon it. You have united and mellowed your colours, in a manner to make it look

1 Walpole first acquired Strawberry Hill from Mrs. Chenevix, the keeper of a celebrated toy shop.
2 It is now at Strawberry Hill. – WALPOLE.
3 Walpole as historian of art, after the Renaissance artist and biographer Giorgio Vasari.

like an old picture; yet there is something in the tone of it that is not quite right. Mr. Chute thinks that you should have exerted more of your force in tipping with light the edges on which the sun breaks: my own opinion is, that the result of the whole is not natural, by your having joined a Claude Lorrain summer sky to a wintry sea, which you have drawn from the life. The water breaks finely, but the distant hills are too strong, and the outlines much too hard. The greatest fault is the trees (not apt to be your stumbling-block); they are not of a natural green, have no particular resemblance, and are out of all proportion too large for the figures. Mend these errors, and work away in oil. I am impatient to see some gothic ruins of your painting. This leads me naturally to thank you for the sweet little *cul-de-lampe* to the Entail: it is equal to any thing you have done in perspective and for taste; but the boy is too large.

For the block of granite I shall certainly think a louis well bestowed – provided I do but get the block, and that you are sure it will be equal to the sample you sent me. My room remains in want of a table; and as it will take so much time to polish it, I do wish you would be a little expeditious in sending it. . . . Adieu!

82. *A Tour in the North.*

TO RICHARD BENTLEY, ESQ.

Wentworth Castle, August 1756.

I always dedicate my travels to you. My present expedition has been very amusing, sights are thick sown in the counties of York and Nottingham; the former is more historic, and the great lords live at a prouder distance: in Nottinghamshire there is a very Heptarchy of little kingdoms[1] elbowing one another, and the barons of them want nothing but small armies to make inroads into one another's parks, murder deer, and massacre park-keepers. But to come to particulars: the Great Road as far as Stamford is superb; in any other country it would furnish medals, and immortalise any drowsy monarch in whose reign it was executed. It is continued much farther, but is more rumbling. I did not stop at Hatfield and Burleigh to see the

1 "The Dukeries", containing the ducal estates of Welbeck, Clumber, Worksop and Thoresby.

palaces of my great-uncle-ministers, having seen them before.
Bugden palace¹ surprises one prettily in a little village; and the
remains of Newark castle, seated pleasantly, began to open a vein
of historic memory. I had only transient and distant views of Lord
Tyrconnel's at Belton [in Lincolnshire], and of Belvoir. The borders
of Huntingdonshire have churches instead of milestones, but the
richness and extent of Yorkshire quite charmed me. Oh! what quarries for working in Gothic!

This place is one of the very few that I really like; the situation,
woods, views, and the improvements, are perfect in their kinds;
nobody has a truer taste than Lord Strafford. The house is a pompous front screening an old house; it was built by the last lord² on a
design of the Prussian architect Bott, who is mentioned in the King's
Mémoires de Brandenburg, and is not ugly: the one pair of stairs is
entirely engrossed by a gallery of 180 feet, on the plan of that in the
Colonna palace at Rome: it has nothing but four modern statues and
some bad portraits, but, on my proposal, is going to have books at
each end. The hall is pretty, but low; the drawing-room handsome;
there wants a good eating-room and staircase: but I have formed a
design for both, and I believe they will be executed – that my plans
should be obeyed when yours are not! I shall bring you a ground-
plot for a Gothic building, which I have proposed that you should
draw for a little wood, but in the manner of an ancient market-cross.
Without doors all is pleasing: there is a beautiful (artificial) river,
with a fine semicircular wood overlooking it, and the temple of Tivoli placed happily on a rising towards the end. There are obelisks,
columns, and other buildings, and, above all, a handsome castle in
the true style, on a rude mountain, with a court and towers: in the
castle-yard, a statue of the late lord who built it. Without the park
is a lake on each side, buried in noble woods. Now contrast all this,
and you may have some idea of Lord Rockingham's.³ Imagine a most
extensive and most beautiful modern front erected before the great

1 Or Buckden Palace, Huntingdonshire, formerly belonging to the Bishops of
Lincoln.
2 Thomas Wentworth (1672–1739), 1st Earl of Strafford (2nd creation). Walpole was
staying with his friend the 2nd Earl (for whom see heading to letter 213) at his seat,
Wentworth Castle.
3 Wentworth Woodhouse, the very substantial Palladian mansion by Flitcroft, Carr
and others, a neighbour to Wentworth Castle. It was the seat of Charles Watson-
Wentworth (1730–82), 2nd Marquis of Rockingham, statesman.

Lord Strafford's old house, and this front almost blocked up with hills, and everything unfinished round it, nay within it. The great apartment, which is magnificent, is untouched: the chimney-pieces lie in boxes unopened. The park is traversed by a common road between two high hedges – not from necessity. Oh! no; this lord loves nothing but horses, and the enclosures for them take place of everything. The bowling-green behind the house contains no less than four obelisks, and looks like a Brobdignag nine-pin-alley: on a hill near, you would think you saw the York-buildings water-works[1] invited into the country. There are temples in corn-fields; and in the little wood, a window-frame mounted on a bunch of laurel, and intended for an hermitage. In the inhabited part of the house, the chimney-pieces are like tombs: and on that in the library is the figure of this lord's grandfather, in a night-gown of plaster and gold. Amidst all this litter and bad taste, I adored the fine Vandyck of Lord Strafford and his secretary, and could not help reverencing his bed-chamber. With all his faults and arbitrary behaviour, one must worship his spirit and eloquence: where one esteems but a single royalist, one need not fear being too partial. When I visited his tomb in the church (which is remarkably neat and pretty, and enriched with monuments) I was provoked to find a little mural cabinet, with his figure three feet high kneeling. Instead of a stern bust (and his head would furnish a nobler than Bernini's Brutus) one is peevish to see a plaything that might have been bought at Chenevix's. There is a tender inscription to the second Lord Strafford's wife, written by himself; but his genius was fitter to coo over his wife's memory than to sacrifice to his father's. . . .

During my residence here I have made two little excursions, and I assure you it requires resolution; the roads are insufferable; they mend them – I should call it spoil them – with large pieces of stone. At Pomfret I saw the remains of that memorable castle "where Rivers, Vaughan, and Grey lay shorter by the head;" and on which Gray says –

> "And thou, proud boy, from Pomfret's walls shalt send
> A groan, and envy oft thy happy grandsire's end!"[2]

1 A prominent water tower between the Strand and the River Thames.
2 Rivers, Vaughan and Grey were executed at Pontefract (or Pomfret) Castle in 1483 under the orders of Richard III.

The ruins are vanishing, but well situated; there is a large demolished church, and a pretty market-house. We crossed a Gothic bridge of eight arches at Ferrybridge, where there is a pretty view, and went to a large old house of Lord Huntingdon's at Ledstone, which has nothing remarkable but a lofty terrace, a whole-length portrait of his grandfather in tapestry, and the having belonged to the great Lord Strafford. We saw [Kippax Park] that monument of part of poor Sir John Bland's extravagance, his house and garden, which he left orders to make without once looking at either plan. The house is a bastard Gothic, but of not near the extent I had heard. We lay at Leeds, a dingy large town; and through very bad black roads (for the whole country is a colliery, or a quarry), we went to Kirkstall abbey, where are vast Saxon[1] ruins, in a most picturesque situation, on the banks of a river that falls in a cascade among rich meadows, hills, and woods: it belongs to Lord Cardigan: his father pulled down a large house here, lest it should interfere with the family seat, Deane. We returned through Wakefield, where is a pretty Gothic chapel on a bridge, erected by Edward IV. in memory of his father, who lived at Sandal castle just by, and perished in the battle here. There is scarce anything of the castle extant, but it commanded a rich prospect. . . .

83. *The Conway Papers.*

TO GEORGE MONTAGU, ESQ.

Strawberry Hill, 20 August 1758.

. . . I have been journeying much since I heard from you: first to the Vine, where I was greatly pleased with the alterations; the garden is quite beautified and the house dignified. We went over to the Grange,[2] that sweet house of my Lord Keeper's, that you saw too. The pictures are very good, and I was particularly pleased with the procession, which you were told was by Rubens, but is certainly Vandyke's sketch for part of that great work, that he was to have executed in the Banquetting-house. You did not tell me of a very fine Holbein, a woman, who was evidently some princess of the White Rose.

1 Actually Norman.
2 The Vyne, the seat of John Chute, and the Grange, Alresford. At the time of Walpole's visit the Grange was the seat of Sir Robert Henley (*c.* 1708–72), the Lord Keeper, and later Lord Chancellor.

I am just now returned from Ragley, which has had a great deal done to it since I was there last. Browne has improved both the ground and the water, though not quite to perfection. This is the case of the house; where there are no striking faults, but it wants a few Chute or Bentley touches. I have recommended some dignifying of the saloon with Seymours and Fitzroys, Henry the Eighths, and Charles the Seconds. They will correspond well to the proudest situation imaginable. I have already dragged some ancestors out of the dust there, written their names on their portraits; besides which, I have found and brought up to have repaired an incomparable picture of Van Helmont by Sir Peter Lely. But now for recoveries – think what I have in part recovered! Only the state papers, private letters, &c. &c. of the two Lords Conway, Secretaries of State. How you will rejoice and how you will grieve! They seem to have laid up every scrap of paper they ever had, from the middle of Queen Elizabeth's reign to the middle of Charles the Second's. By the accounts of the family there were whole rooms full; all which, during the absence of the last and the minority of the present lord, were by the ignorance of a steward consigned to the oven and to the uses of the house. What remained, except one box that was kept till almost rotten in a cupboard, were thrown loose into the lumber room, where, spread on the pavement, they supported old marbles and screens and boxes. From thence I have dragged all I could, and have literally, taking all together, brought away a chest near five feet long, three wide and two deep, brim full. Half are bills, another part rotten, another gnawed by rats; yet I have already found enough to repay my trouble and curiosity, not enough to satisfy it. I will only tell you of three letters of the great Strafford, and three long ones of news of Mr. Garrard, Master of the Charterhouse; all six written on paper edged with green, like modern French paper. There are handwritings of everybody, all their seals perfect, and the ribands with which they tied their letters. The original Proclamations of Charles the First, signed by the privy council; a letter to King James from his son-in-law of Bohemia, with his seal; and many, very many letters of negociation from the Earl of Bristol in Spain, Sir Dudley Carleton, Lord Chichester, and Sir Thomas Roe. – What say you? will not here be food for the *press*?

I have picked up a little painted glass too, and have got a promise of some old statues, lately dug up, which formerly adorned the

cathedral of Lichfield. You see I continue to labour in my vocation,
of which I can give you a comical instance: – I remembered a rose
in painted glass in a little village going to Ragley, which I remarked
passing by five years ago; told Mr. Conway on which hand it would
be, and found it in the very spot. I saw a very good and perfect tomb
at Alcester of Sir Fulke Greville's father and mother, and a wretched
old house with a very handsome gateway of stone at Colton, belonging to Sir Robert Throckmorton. There is nothing else tolerable but
twenty-two coats of the matches of the family painted glass. – You
cannot imagine how astonished a Mr. Seward, a learned clergyman,
was, who came to Ragley while I was there. Strolling about the
house, he saw me first sitting on the pavement of the lumber room
with Louis,[1] all over cobwebs and dirt and mortar; then found me
in his own room on a ladder writing on a picture: and half an hour
afterwards lying on the grass in the court with the dogs and the children, in my slippers and without my hat. He had had some doubt
whether I was the painter or the factotum of the family; but you
would have died at his surprise when he saw me walk into dinner
dressed and sit by Lady Hertford. Lord Lyttelton was there, and
the conversation turned on literature: finding me not quite ignorant
added to the parson's wonder; but he could not contain himself any
longer, when after dinner he saw me go to romps and jumping with
the two boys; he broke out to my Lady Hertford, and begged to
know who and what sort of man I really was, for he had never met
with anything of the kind. Adieu!

84. *Oxford and Blenheim.*

TO GEORGE MONTAGU, ESQ.

Strawberry Hill, 19 July 1760.

Mr. Conway, as I told you, was with me at Oxford, and I returned
with him to Park-place, and to-day hither. I am sorry you could not
come to us; we passed four days most agreeably, and I believe saw
more antique holes and corners than Tom Hearne[2] did in threescore
years. You know my rage for Oxford; if King's-college would not

1 Walpole's Swiss servant.
2 Thomas Hearne (bap. 1678–1735), Oxford antiquary.

take it ill, I don't know but I should retire thither, and profess Jacobitism, that I might enjoy some venerable set of chambers. Though
the weather has been so sultry, I ferreted from morning to night,
fatigued that strong young lad Lord Beauchamp, and harassed his
tutors till they were forced to relieve one another. With all this,
I found nothing worth seeing, except the colleges themselves,
painted glass, and a couple of crosiers. Oh, yes! in an old buttery at
Christ Church I discovered two of the most glorious portraits by
Holbein in the world. They call them Dutch heads. I took them
down, washed them myself, and fetched out a thousand beauties.
We went to Blenheim and saw all Vanbrugh's[1] quarries, all the acts
of parliament and Gazettes on the Duke in inscriptions, and all the
old flock chairs, wainscot tables, and gowns and petticoats of Queen
Anne, that old Sarah could crowd among blocks of marble. It looks
like the palace of an auctioneer, who has been chosen King of
Poland, and furnished his apartments with obsolete trophies, rub-
bish that nobody bid for, and a dozen pictures, that he had stolen
from the inventories of different families. The place is as ugly as the
house, and the bridge, like the beggars at the old Duchess's gate,
begs for a drop of water, and is refused. We went to Ditchley, which
is a good house, well furnished, has good portraits, a wretched
saloon, and one handsome scene behind the house. There are portraits of the Lichfield hunt, in *true blue* frocks, with ermine capes.
One of the colleges has exerted this loyal pun, and made their east
window entirely of blue glass. But the greatest pleasure we had, was
in seeing Sir Charles Cottrell's at Rousham [in Oxfordshire]; it has
reinstated Kent with me; he has nowhere shown so much taste. The
house is old, and was bad; he has improved it, stuck as close as *he*
could to Gothic, has made a delightful library, and the whole is comfortable. The garden is Daphne in little; the sweetest little groves,
streams, glades, porticoes, cascades and river, imaginable; all the
scenes are perfectly classic. Well, if I had such a house, such a library,
so pretty a place, and so pretty a wife, I think I should let King
George send to Herenhausen for a Master of the Ceremonies.[2] . . .
Adieu! Your most sincerely.

1 Sir John Vanbrugh (1664–1726), dramatist and architect of Blenheim Palace for the
Duke of Marlborough.
2 The Cottrells, or Cottrell-Dormers, were the hereditary Masters of the Ceremonies, responsible for receiving foreign dignitaries and presenting them at court.

85. Lichfield – Sheffield – Chatsworth – Hardwicke.

TO GEORGE MONTAGU, ESQ.

Arlington Street, 1 September 1760.

... My tour has been extremely agreeable. I set out with winning a good deal at Loo at Ragley; the Duke of Grafton was not so successful, and had some high words with Pam.[1] I went from thence to Offley's at Whichnovre, the individual manor of the flitch of bacon, which has been growing rusty for these thirty years in his hall.[2] I don't wonder; I have no notion that one could keep in good humour with one's wife for a year and a day, unless one was to live on the very spot, which is one of the sweetest scenes I ever saw. It is the brink of a high hill; the Trent wriggles through a lovely meadow at the foot; Lichfield and twenty other churches and mansions decorate the view. Mr. Anson has bought an estate [Shugborough] close by, whence my Lord used to cast many a wishful eye, though without the least pretensions even to a bit of lard.

I saw Lichfield cathedral, which has been rich, but my friend Lord Brooke and his soldiery treated poor St. Chad[3] with so little ceremony, that it is in a most naked condition. In a niche at the very summit they have crowded a statue of Charles the Second, with a special pair of shoe-strings, big enough for a weathercock. As I went to Lord Strafford's I passed through Sheffield, which is one of the foulest towns in England in the most charming situation; there are two-and-twenty thousand inhabitants making knives and scissors; they remit eleven thousand pounds a week to London. One man there has discovered the art of plating copper with silver; I bought a pair of candlesticks for two guineas that are quite pretty. Lord Strafford has erected the little Gothic building, which I got Mr. Bentley to draw; I took the idea from Chichester Cross. It stands on a high bank in the menagerie, between a pond and a vale, totally bowered over with oaks. I went with the Straffords to Chatsworth,

1 Presumably the Duchess, whom the Yale editors note had a passion for gambling which contributed to their estrangement.
2 The lord of this manor (Whichnor) was required to give a flitch of bacon to any man who swore that for a year and a day he had never regretted marrying his wife and would marry her again: no successful claimants are recorded.
3 Robert Greville (1607–43), 2nd Baron Brooke, seriously damaged Lichfield Cathedral in his siege of the city, in which siege he was killed.

and stayed there four days; there were Lady Mary Coke, Lord
Besborough and his daughters, Lord Thomond, Mr. Boufoy, the
Duke, the old Duchess, and two of his brothers. Would you believe
that nothing was ever better humoured than the ancient Grace?[1] She
stayed every evening till it was dark in the skittle-ground, keeping
the score; and one night, that the servants had a ball for Lady Dorothy's birth-day, we fetched the fiddles into the drawing-room, and
the dowager herself danced with us! I never was more disappointed
than at Chatsworth, which, ever since I was born, I have condemned. It is a glorious situation; the vale rich in corn and verdure,
vast woods hang down the hills, which are green to the top, and the
immense rocks only serve to dignify the prospect. The river runs
before the door, and serpentises more than you can conceive in the
vale. The Duke is widening it, and will make it the middle of his
park; but I don't approve an idea they are going to execute, of a fine
bridge with statues under a noble cliff. If they will have a bridge
(which by the way will crowd the scene), it should be composed of
rude fragments, such as the giant of the Peak would step upon, that
he might not be wetshod. The expense of the works now carrying
on will amount to forty thousand pounds. A heavy quadrangle of
stables is part of the plan, is very cumbrous, and standing higher
than the house, is ready to overwhelm it. The principal front of the
house is beautiful, and executed with the neatness of wrought plate;
the inside is most sumptuous, but did not please me; the heathen
gods, goddesses, Christian virtues, and allegoric gentlefolks, are
crowded into every room, as if Mrs. Holman[2] had been in heaven
and invited everybody she saw. The great apartment is trist; painted
ceilings, inlaid floors, and unpainted wainscots make every room
sombre. The tapestries are fine, but not fine enough, and there are
few portraits. The chapel is charming. The great *jet d'eau* I like, nor
would I remove it; whatever is magnificent of the kind in the time it
was done, I would retain, else all gardens and houses wear a tiresome
resemblance. I except that absurdity of a cascade tumbling down
marble steps, which reduces the steps to be of no use at all. I saw
Haddon, an abandoned old castle of the Rutlands, in a romantic
situation, but which never could have composed a tolerable

1 That is, "the old Duchess", Catherine Cavendish, *née* Hoskins (*c.* 1700–77), widow
of the 3rd Duke of Devonshire.
2 Mrs. Holman (fl. 1750–64) was a neighbour of Walpole's who held assemblies.

dwelling. The Duke sent Lord John [Cavendish] with me to Hard-wicke, where I was again disappointed; but I will not take relations from others; they either don't see for themselves, or can't see for me. How I had been promised that I should be charmed with Hard-wicke, and told that the Devonshires ought to have established there! never was I less charmed in my life. The house is not Gothic, but of that betweenity, that intervened when Gothic declined and Palladian was creeping in – rather, this is totally naked of either. It has vast chambers – aye, vast, such as the nobility of that time delighted in, and did not know how to furnish. The great apartment is exactly what it was when the Queen of Scots was kept there. Her council-chamber, the council-chamber of a poor woman, who had only two secretaries, a gentleman-usher, an apothecary, a confessor, and three maids, is so outrageously spacious, that you would take it for King David's, who thought, contrary to all modern experience, that in the multitude of counsellors there is wisdom. At the upper end is a [chair of] state, with a long table, covered with a sumptuous cloth, embroidered and embossed with gold, – at least what was gold; so are all the tables. Round the top of the chamber runs a mon-strous frieze, ten or twelve feet deep, representing stag-hunting in miserable plastered relief. The next is her dressing-room hung with patch-work on black velvet; then her state bed-chamber. The bed has been rich beyond description, and now hangs in costly golden tatters. The hangings, part of which they say her Majesty worked, are composed of figures as large as life, sewed and embroidered on black velvet, white satin, &c., and represent the virtues that were necessary for her, or that she was forced to have, as Patience and Temperance, &c. The fire-screens are particular; pieces of yellow velvet, fringed with gold, hang on a cross-bar of wood, which is fixed on the top of a single stick, that rises from the foot. The only furni-ture which has any appearance of taste are the table and cabinets, which are all of oak, richly carved. There is a private chamber within, where she lay, her arms and style over the door; the arras hangs over all the doors; the gallery is sixty yards long, covered with bad tapes-try, and wretched pictures of Mary herself, Elizabeth in a gown of sea-monsters, Lord Darnley, James the Fifth and his Queen, curious, and a whole history of Kings of England, not worth six-pence a-piece. There is an original of old Bess of Harwicke herself, who built the house. Her estates were then reckoned at sixty thousand pounds a-year, and now let for two hundred thousand pounds. Lord John Cavendish told me, that the tradition in the family is, that it had been prophesied to her that she should never die as long as she was building; and that at last she died in a hard frost, when the labourers could not work. There is a fine bank of old oaks in the park over a lake; nothing else pleased me there. . . .

86. *Drayton and Fotheringhay.*

TO GEORGE MONTAGU, ESQ.

Stamford, Saturday night, 23 July 1763.

"Thus far our arms have with success been crowned," bating a few mishaps, which will attend long marches like ours. We have con-quered as many towns as Louis Quatorze in the campaign of sev-enty-two: that is, seen them, for he did little more, and into the bargain he had much better roads, and a dryer summer. . . . Well! we hurried away and got to Drayton[1] an hour before dinner. Oh! the dear old place! you would be transported with it. In the first place, it stands in as ugly a hole as Boughton: well! that is not its beauty. The front is a brave strong castle wall, embattled and loop-holed for defence. Passing the great gate, you come to a sumptuous but narrow modern court, behind which rises the old mansion, all towers and turrets. The house is excellent; has a vast hall, ditto dining-room, king's chamber, trunk gallery at the top of the house, handsome chapel, and seven or eight distinct apartments, besides closets and conveniences without end. Then it is covered with portraits, crammed with old china, furnished richly, and not a rag in it under forty, fifty, or a thousand years old; but not a bed or chair that has lost a tooth, or got a grey hair, so well they are preserved. I rummaged it from head to foot, examined every spangled bed, and enamelled pair of bellows, for such there are; in short, I do not believe the old mansion was ever better pleased with an inhabitant, since the days of Walter de Drayton except when it has received its divine old mis-tress. If one could honour her more than one did before, it would be to see with what religion she keeps up the old dwelling and customs,

1 Drayton House, Northamptonshire, a courtyard house of medieval origins then owned by Lady Betty Germain (1680–1769).

as well as old servants, who you may imagine do not love her less than other people do. The garden is just as Sir John Germain brought it from Holland; pyramidal yews, treillages, and square cradle walks with windows clipped in them. Nobody was there, but Mr. Beauclerc and Lady Catherine, and two parsons: the two first suffered us to ransack and do as we would, and the last two assisted us, informed us, and carried us to every tomb in the neighbourhood. I have got every circumstance by heart, and was pleased beyond my expectation, both with the place and the comfortable way of seeing it. We stayed here till after dinner to-day, and saw Fotheringhay in our way hither. The castle is totally ruined.[1] The mount, on which the keep stood, two door-cases, and a piece of the moat, are all the remains. Near it is a front and two projections of an ancient house, which, by the arms about it, I suppose was part of the palace of Richard and Cicely, Duke and Duchess of York. There are two pretty tombs for them and their uncle Duke of York in the church, erected by order of Queen Elizabeth. The church has been very fine, but is now intolerably shabby; yet many large saints remain in the windows, two entire, and all the heads well painted. You may imagine we were civil enough to the Queen of Scots, to feel a feel of pity for her, while we stood on the very spot where she was put to death; my companion [Mr. Cole], I believe, who is a better royalist than I am, felt a little more. There, I have obeyed you. To-morrow we see Burleigh and Peterborough, and lie at Ely; on Monday I hope to be in town, and on Tuesday I hope much more to be in the gallery at Strawberry Hill, and to find the gilders laying on the last leaf of gold. Good night! . . .

87. *Buying Pictures.*

TO GEORGE MONTAGU, ESQ.

Arlington Street, 10 May 1764.

I hope I have done well for you, and that you will be content with the execution of your commission. I have bought you two pictures. No. 14, which is by no means a good picture, but it went so cheap and

1 Fotheringhay Castle, scene of the execution of Mary, Queen of Scots in 1587. It was dismantled in the 1630s.

looked so old-fashionably, like landscapes over chimneys in ancient mansions, that I ventured to give eighteen shillings for it. The other is very pretty, No. 17; two sweet children, undoubtedly by Sir Peter Lely. This costs you four pounds ten shillings; what shall I do with them – how convey them to you? The picture of Lord Romney[1] which you are so fond of, was not in this sale, but I suppose remains with Lady Sidney. I bought for myself much the best picture in the auction, a fine Vandyck of the famous Lady Carlisle and her sister Leicester in one piece: it cost me nine-and-twenty guineas.[2]

In general the pictures did not go high, which I was glad of; that the vulture[3] who sells them may not be more enriched than could be helped. There was a whole-length of Sir Henry Sidney, which I should have liked, but it went for fifteen guineas. Thus ends half the glory of Penshurst! Not one of the miniatures was sold.

I go to Strawberry to-morrow for a week. When do you come to Frogmore? I wish to know, because I shall go soon to Park-place, and would not miss the visit you have promised me. Adieu!

88. *A Fashionable Craze.*

TO SIR HORACE MANN

Strawberry Hill, 6 May 1770.

. . . There has lately been an auction of stuffed birds; and, as natural history is in fashion, there are physicians and others who paid forty and fifty guineas for a single Chinese pheasant: you may buy a live one for five. After this, it is not extraordinary that pictures should be dear. We have at present three exhibitions. One West,[4] who paints history in the taste of Poussin, gets three hundred pounds for a piece not too large to hang over a chimney. He has merit, but is hard and heavy, and far unworthy of such prices. The rage to see

---

1 Henry Sidney (1641–1704), politician and army officer, mentioned in Grammont's *Mémoires.*
2 Van Dyck's double portrait of the Percy sisters – Dorothy Sidney, Countess of Leicester and Lucy Hay, Countess of Carlisle – hung over the chimney piece of the Round Drawing Room at Strawberry Hill. It was sold in 1842 at the Strawberry Hill sale for 220 guineas.
3 The vulture was Anne, *née* Howard (d. 1775), Lady Yonge, who had inherited part of Penshurst.
4 Benjamin West (1738–1820), later second President of the Royal Academy.

these exhibitions is so great, that sometimes one cannot pass through the streets where they are. But it is incredible what sums are raised by mere exhibitions of anything; a new fashion, and to enter at which you pay a shilling or half-a-crown. Another rage, is for prints of English portraits: I have been collecting them above thirty years, and originally never gave for a mezzotinto above one or two shillings. The lowest are now a crown; most, from half a guinea to a guinea. Lately, I assisted a clergyman [Granger][1] in compiling a catalogue of them; since the publication, scarce heads in books, not worth threepence, will sell for five guineas. Then we have Etruscan vases, made of earthenware, in Staffordshire, [by Wedgwood] from two to five guineas; and *or moulu*, never made here before, which succeeds so well, that a tea-kettle, which the inventor offered for one hundred guineas, sold by auction for one hundred and thirty. In short, we are at the height of extravagance and improvements, for we do improve rapidly in taste as well as in the former. I cannot say so much for our genius. Poetry is gone to bed, or into our prose; we are like the Romans in that too. If we have the arts of the Antonines, – we have the fustian also. … Adieu!

89. *The Antiquarian Society.*

TO THE REV. WILLIAM COLE

Dear Sir,   Strawberry Hill, 28 July 1772.

I am anew obliged to you, as I am perpetually, for the notice you give me of another intended publication against me in the Archæologia, or Old Woman's Logic. By your account, the author will add much credit to their Society! For my part, I shall take no notice of any of his *handycrafts*. However, as there seems to be a willingness to carp at me, and as gnats may on a sudden provoke one to give a slap, I choose to be at liberty to say what I think of the learned Society; and therefore I have taken leave of them, having so good an occasion presented as their council on Whittington and his Cat, and

---

1 Rev. James Granger (bap. 1723–76), print collector, biographer and author of *A Biographical History of England* (1769).

the ridicule that Foote has thrown on them.[1] They are welcome to say anything on my writings, but that they are the works of a fellow of so foolish a Society.

I am at work on the Life of Sir Thomas Wyat, but it does not please me; nor will it be entertaining, though you have contributed so many materials towards it. You must take one trouble more: – it is to inquire and search for a book that I want to see. It is 'The Pilgrim'; was written by William Thomas, who was executed in Queen Mary's time; but the book was printed under, and dedicated to, Edward VI. I have only an imperfect memorandum of it, and cannot possibly recall to mind from whence I made it. All I think I remember is, that the book was in the King's Library. I have sent to the Museum to inquire after it; but I cannot find it mentioned in Ames's "History of English Printers." Be so good as to ask all your antiquarian friends if they know such a work. ... I am, dear Sir,

Your most faithful humble servant,

H. W.

90. *Berkeley and Thornbury Castles.*

TO THE REV. WILLIAM COLE

Dear Sir,   Matson,[2] near Gloucester, 15 August 1774.

... To-day I have been at Berkeley[3] and Thornbury Castles. The first disappointed me much, though very entire. It is much smaller than I expected, but very entire, except a small part burnt two years ago, while the present Earl was in the house. The fire began in the housekeeper's room, who never appeared more; but as she was strict over the servants, and not a bone of her was found, it was supposed that she was murdered, and the body conveyed away. The situation is not elevated nor beautiful, and little improvements made of late, but some silly ones *à la Chinoise*, by the present Dowager. In good sooth, I can give you but a very imperfect account; for, instead of the

1 *Archæologia*, the journal of the Society of Antiquaries. Walpole was offended by criticisms published by them of his *Historic Doubts on the Life and Reign of King Richard III* (1768) and used the satire of antiquaries in Samuel Foote's play *The Nabob* (1772) as his excuse for resigning from the Society.
2 The seat of George Selwyn.
3 Berkeley Castle, the seat of the earls of Berkeley, and scene of the murder of Edward II.

lord's being gone to dine with the mayor of Gloucester, as I expected, I found him in the midst of all his captains of the Militia. I am so sillily shy of strangers and youngsters, that I hurried through the chambers, and looked for nothing but the way out of every room. I just observed that there were many bad portraits of the family, but none ancient; as if the Berkeleys had been commissaries, and raised themselves in the last war. There is a plentiful addition of those of Lord Berkeley of Stratton, but no knights templars, or barons as old as Edward I.; yet are there three beds on which there may have been as frisky doings three centuries ago, as there probably have been within these ten years. The room shown for the murder of Edward II., and the shrieks of an agonising king, I verily believe to be genuine. It is a dismal chamber, almost at top of the house, quite detached, and to be approached only by a kind of foot-bridge, and from that descends a large flight of steps that terminate on strong gates; exactly a situation for a *corps de garde*. In that room they show you a cast of a face in plaster, and tell you it was taken from Edward's. I was not quite so easy of faith about that; for it is evidently the face of Charles I.

The steeple of the church, lately rebuilt handsomely, stands some paces from the body; in the latter are three tombs of the old Berkeleys, with cumbent figures. The wife of the Lord Berkeley, who was supposed to be privy to the murder, has a curious head-gear; it is like a long horse-shoe, quilted in quatrefoils; and, like Lord Foppington's wig, allows no more than the breadth of a half-crown to be discovered of the face. Stay, I think I mistake; the husband was a conspirator against Richard II., not Edward. But in those days, loyalty was not so rife as at present.

From Berkeley Castle I went to Thornbury, of which the ruins are half ruined. It would have been glorious, if finished.[1] I wish the Lords of Berkeley had retained the spirit of deposing till Henry the VIIIth's time! The situation is fine, though that was not the fashion; for all the windows of the great apartment look into the inner court. The prospect was left to the servants. Here I had two adventures. I could find nobody to show me about. I saw a paltry house that I took for the sexton's, at the corner of the close, and bade my servant

---

1 Thornbury Castle, not completed when its owner Edward Stafford (1478–1521), Duke of Buckingham, was executed on the orders of Henry VIII.

ring, and ask who could show me the Castle. A voice in a passion flew from a casement, and issued from a divine. "What! was it his business to show the Castle? Go look for somebody else! What did the fellow ring for as if the house was on fire?" The poor Swiss came back in a fright, and said, the doctor had sworn at him. Well – we scrambled over a stone stile, saw a room or two glazed near the gate, and rung at it. A damsel came forth, and satisfied our curiosity. When we had done seeing, I said, "Child, we don't know our way, and want to be directed into the London road; I see the Duke's steward yonder at the window, pray desire him to come to me, that I may consult him." She went – he stood staring at us at the window, and sent his footman. I do not think courtesy is resident at Thornbury. As I returned through the close, the divine came running out of breath, and without his beaver or band, and calls out, "Sir, I am come to justify myself: your servant says I swore at him: I am no swearer – Lord bless me! (dropping his voice) it is Mr. Walpole!" "Yes, Sir, and I think you was Lord Beauchamp's tutor at Oxford, but I have forgot your name." "Holwell,[1] Sir." "Oh! yes –" and then I comforted him, and laid the ill-breeding on my footman's being a foreigner; but could not help saying, I really had taken his house for the sexton's. "Yes, Sir, it is not very good without, won't you please to walk in?" I did, and found the inside ten times worse, and a lean wife, suckling a child. He was making an Index to Homer, is going to publish the chief beauties, and I believe had just been reading some of the delicate civilities that pass between Agamemnon and Achilles, and that what my servant took for oaths, were only Greek compliments. Adieu! Yours ever.

You see I have not a line more of paper.

91. *William III.'s Spurs.*

TO THE EARL OF HARCOURT[2]

Strawberry Hill, 8 October 1777.

I will never believe in impulses more; no, for I tore open the sacred box with as much impatience and as little reverence as Lady

1 Rev. William Holwell (1726–98), vicar of Thornbury and Chaplain to George III.
2 George Simon Harcourt (1736–1809), 2nd Earl Harcourt, of Nuneham Courtenay, amateur artist and friend of Walpole's correspondent the Rev. William Mason.

Barrymore could have done if she expected a new coiffeur from
Paris. No holy frisson, no involuntary tear warned me that there was
but a piece of paper between my sacrilegious fingers and the most
precious relics in the world. Alas! Why am not I a Gregory or a Boni-
face, and possess treasures enough to found a Casa Santa over the
invaluable offering your Lordship has sent me. You enriched my
museum before; you have now enriched me, for who is not rich, who
possesses what the world cannot buy? You have done more, my
Lord; you have given me a talisman that will for ever keep off
Macpherson[1] and evil spirits from entering my dwelling; you have
shown generosity, too, in the highest sense, for you have given me
what I know you value so much. I have seriously kissed each spur[2]
devoutly, and think them more lovely than Cellini's Bell. You could
have bestowed your bounty on no man living who could worship it
more, nor is there any man living whom I should not envy the possession except General Washington. If he *gains his spurs* I think
I could cede them. Thanks are poor, words could ill express my gratitude. The muse of the Dispensary would alone be capable of doing
justice to your Lordship as she did to the Hero who wore these ines-
timable trophies. . . . How can I say how much I am, &c.

92. *Westminster Abbey.*

TO THE REV. WILLIAM COLE

Berkeley Square, 5 January 1780.

. . . The picture found near the altar in Westminster Abbey, about
three years ago, was of King Sebert. I saw it, and it was well preserved, with some others worse; but they have foolishly buried it
again behind their new altar-piece; and so they have a very fair tomb
of Anne of Cleves, close to the altar, which they did not know till
I told them whose it was, though her arms are upon it, and though
there is an exact plate of it in Sandford.[3] They might at least have

1 James Macpherson (1736–96), the author of *Ossian*, whom Walpole considered had
Jacobite sympathies.
2 The spurs worn by William III at the battle of the Boyne (1690), displayed
by Walpole in the Glass Closet in the Great North Bedchamber at Strawberry
Hill. Walpole compares the spurs to the carved silver bell in his collection, then
attributed to Cellini, and now in the British Museum.
3 Francis Sandford's *Genealogical History of the Kings of England* (1677).

cut out the portraits and removed the tomb to a conspicuous situation; but though this age is grown so antiquarian, it has not gained a grain more of sense in that walk: witness as you instance in Mr. Grose's "Legends," and in the Dean and Chapter reburying the crown, robes, and ornaments of Edward I. There would surely have been as much piety in preserving them in their treasury, as in consigning them again to decay. I did not know that the salvation of robes and crowns depended on receiving Christian burial. At the same time, the Chapter transgress that Prince's will, like all their antecessors; for he ordered his tomb to be opened every year or two years, and receive a new cere-cloth or pall; but they boast now of having enclosed him so substantially, that his ashes cannot be violated again.

It was the present Bishop-Dean[1] who showed me the pictures and Anne's tomb, and consulted me on the new altar-piece. I advised him to have a light octangular canopy, like the cross at Chichester, placed over the table or altar itself, which would have given dignity to it, especially if elevated by a flight of steps; and from the side arches of the octagon, I would have had a semicircle of open arches that should have advanced quite to the seats of the prebends, which would have discovered the pictures; and through the octagon itself you would have perceived the shrine of Edward the Confessor, which is much higher than the level of the choir – but men who ask advice seldom follow it, if you do not happen to light on the same ideas with themselves.

P.S. The Houghton pictures are not lost – but to Houghton and England![2]

1 John Thomas (bap. 1712–93), Bishop of Rochester and Dean of Westminster.
2 See Letters 74 and 190.

93. *The Royal Academy.*

TO THE REV. WILLIAM MASON[1]

19 May 1780.

... You know, I suppose, that the Royal Academy at Somerset House is opened.[2] It is quite a Roman palace, and finished in perfect taste as well as boundless expense. It would have been a glorious apparition at the conclusion of the great war; now it is an insult on our poverty and degradation. There is a sign-post by West of his Majesty holding the memorial of his late campaign, lest we should forget that he was at Coxheath when the French fleet was in Plymouth Sound. By what lethargy of loyalty it happened I do not know, but *there* is also a picture of Mrs. Wright modelling the head of Charles the First, and their Majesties contemplating it.[3] Gainsborough has five landscapes there, of which one especially is worthy of any collection, and of any painter that ever existed. ...

94. *Vandalism.*

TO RICHARD GOUGH, ESQ.[4]

Strawberry Hill, 24 August 1789.

I shall heartily lament with you, Sir, the demolition of those beautiful chapels at Salisbury.[5] I was scandalised long ago at the ruinous state in which they were indecently suffered to remain. It appears as strange, that, when a spirit of restoration and decoration has taken place, it should be mixed with barbarous innovation. As much as taste has improved, I do not believe that modern execution will equal our models. I am sorry that I can only regret, not prevent. I do not know the Bishop of Salisbury[6] even by sight, and certainly have no credit to obstruct any of his plans. Should I get sight of

---

1 Rev. William Mason (1725–97), poet, garden designer, Walpole's correspondent, and friend and biographer of Thomas Gray.
2 The first exhibition was held in May 1780.
3 Patience Wright (1725–1826), American modeller in wax.
4 Richard Gough (1735–1809), antiquary and writer.
5 James Wyatt's extensive work at Salisbury (1787–93) included the dismantling of the Hungerford and Beauchamp chantries and much other work.
6 Shute Barrington (1734–1826), Bishop of Salisbury, who commissioned Wyatt's work, and commissioned Wyatt again on his translation to Durham.

Mr. Wyatt, which it is not easy to do, I will remonstrate against the intended alteration; but, probably, without success, as I do not suppose he has authority enough to interpose effectually: still, I will try.

It is an old complaint with me, Sir, that when families are extinct, Chapters take the freedom of removing ancient monuments, and even of selling over again the sites of such tombs. A scandalous, nay, dishonest abuse, and very unbecoming clergymen! Is it very creditable for divines to traffic for consecrated ground, and which the church had already sold? I do not wonder that magnificent monuments are out of fashion when they are treated so disrespectfully. You, Sir, alone, have placed several out of the reach of such a kind of simoniacal abuse; for to buy into the church, or to sell the church's land twice over, breathes a similar kind of spirit. Perhaps, as the subscription indicates taste, if some of the subscribers could be persuaded to object to the removal of the two beautiful chapels, as contrary to their view of beautifying, it might have good effect; or, if some letter were published in the papers against the destruction, as barbarous and the result of bad taste, it might divert the design. I zealously wish it were stopped, but I know none of the Chapter or subscribers.

VI
STRAWBERRY HILL

IN 1747 WALPOLE rented a former coachman's cottage on a site called Strawberry Hill Shot at Twickenham, a fashionable village on the Thames near Richmond. Its previous tenant had been a Mrs. Chenevix, who had a toy shop near Pall Mall. In 1749 he managed to acquire the freehold, and over the next four decades he added to the estate, which eventually extended to forty-six acres. In 1750 he wrote to Horace Mann, "I am going to build a little Gothic castle at Strawberry Hill. If you can pick me up any fragments of old painted glass, arms or anything, I shall be excessively obliged to you."[1] He then undertook a series of building campaigns over nearly thirty years to convert a modest cottage into what became the most famous icon of the early Gothic Revival.

His first main campaign was the conversion in 1753 of the existing rooms around a highly original Gothic hall, staircase, and armoury designed by Richard Bentley, who with John Chute formed the "Committee" that advised Walpole as the works progressed. This transformed Mrs. Chenevix's rooms into the Little Parlour hung with Gothic paper; the Beauty Room with its copies of Lely's paintings of the beauties of the court of Charles II (see letter 114); the Blue Bedchamber with portraits of Walpole, his parents and his friends; and the Red Bedchamber, together with a first-floor Breakfast Room with a view across the Thames towards Richmond Hill, "the room where we always live". Walpole described this eloquently to Mann in letter 100, and in letter 99 provided Mann with an explanation of his Gothic vision, and his concern that the garden should be given over to the gaiety of nature. Strawberry Hill was by no means all Gothic "gloomth" (a word of Walpole's invention), and in a manuscript now at the Fitzwilliam Museum Walpole wrote about the effects he strove to achieve by the careful management of light and shade and colour in the different rooms of the house.[2] The

1 Letter of 10 January 1750 (YE 20:III).
2 See Appendix 4 to *Horace Walpole's Strawberry Hill*, ed. Michael Snodin (New Haven: Yale Univeristy Press, 2009).

exterior, decorative Gothic with ogee-headed windows, was at this stage symmetrical and with no aspirations to archaeological correctness. It was painted a striking and very ungloomy white.

In 1754 Walpole added two large rooms to the north of the house: on the ground floor the Great Parlour for dining, hung with family portraits and furnished with Gothic chairs and a Gothic side table provided by Bentley; above it the Library, ranged round with arched Gothic bookshelves designed by Chute, based on a print of a side door of the choir of Old St. Paul's taken from Dugdale's *History of St. Paul's Cathedral* (1658). Both rooms had highly decorative chimney pieces, that in the Library combining details copied from the tombs of John of Eltham in Westminster Abbey and of the Duke of Clarence at Canterbury Cathedral – typical of the Committee's use of medieval precedents for the decorative work in the house. Between 1757 and 1763 Walpole cleared some outbuildings to the west, built a new cottage in the stable-yard for his printing house, and once again expanded the house. The first extension was the Little Cloister by the entrance door and the Holbein Chamber above, a room designed for the display of furniture and pictures intended to evoke the Tudor court; then came the Great Cloister with above it the Gallery and Tribune, or Cabinet, and beyond it the Round Tower. These rooms were markedly larger and more decorative than the converted rooms in the original cottage, and Gray, writing to Thomas Warton in 1763, described the Gallery as "all Gothicism, & gold, & crimson, & looking-glass", adding that Walpole had purchased at auction in Suffolk "ebony-chairs and old moveables enough to load a waggon".[1]

In 1770–72 Walpole added the Great North Bedchamber: like the main room in the Round Tower (which was finished in 1771), this was a mixture of medieval references and modern comfort – Walpole had written in the Preface to his *Description* of Strawberry Hill that "I did not mean to make my house so Gothic as to exclude convenience, and modern refinements in luxury." The final addition to the house was the Beauclerk Tower of 1776 (designed by the Cambridge architect James Essex to house and celebrate Lady Beauclerk's drawings for Walpole's play *The Mysterious Mother*), though Walpole also built a Gothic chapel in the garden, and some offices designed by James Wyatt. The overall effect was of the irregular growth by

---

1 Letter of 5 August 1763, *Correspondence of Thomas Gray*, ed. Paget Toynbee and Leonard Whibley (Oxford: Clarendon Press, 1955), vol. 2, p. 805.

accretion of an old seat, what Walpole playfully described to Montagu as "the castle (I am building) of my ancestors".[1]

Walpole principally used the house in the summer months, and was often there alone with his servants, but Strawberry was also the setting for entertainments. No expense was spared for an afternoon and evening party held in May 1769 for some visitors from France, described in letter III in terms that recall a *fête galante* by Watteau. As a piece of gallantry, his printing press could be called into service to flatter his guests (letters 106 and III). But such occasions were in contrast to the regular activity of showing the house. Its celebrity was such that between sixty and one hundred parties of visitors a year were allowed to see the house on application – usually escorted by the housekeeper, occasionally by Walpole's secretary and printer Thomas Kirgate, and in the case of distinguished guests by Walpole himself. He printed tickets for admission from at least 1774, and Rules for arranging visits (parties of not more than four, and no children) in 1784. Walpole was both flattered and exasperated by the steady stream of visitors, of whom he exclaimed to Mann, "I am tormented all day and every day by people that come to see my house, and have no enjoyment of it in summer".[2] But the torment was relative and there were ample compensations, as illustrated in letter 110.

Surprisingly this fragile house survives, has been magnificently restored, and in 2010 was again opened to visitors.

95. *Strawberry Hill Acquired.*

TO THE HON. H. S. CONWAY

Twickenham, 8 June 1747.

You perceive by my date that I am got into a new camp, and have left my tub at Windsor. It is a little play-thing-house that I got out of Mrs. Chenevix's shop, and is the prettiest bauble you ever saw. It is set in enamelled meadows, with filigree hedges:

> A small Euphrates through the piece is roll'd,
> And little finches wave their wings in gold.[3]

Two delightful roads, that you would call dusty, supply me continually with coaches and chaises: barges as solemn as Barons of the Exchequer move under my window; Richmond Hill and Ham walks

1 Letter of 11 June 1753 (YE 9:149).
2 Letter of 30 July 1783 (YE 25:423).
3 Pope, *Moral Essays*, Epistle V, ll. 29–30.

bound my prospect; but, thank God! the Thames is between me and the Duchess of Queensberry.[1] Dowagers as plenty as flounders inhabit all around, and Pope's ghost is just now skimming under my window by a most poetical moonlight. I have about land enough to keep such a farm as Noah's, when he set up in the ark with a pair of each kind; but my cottage is rather cleaner than I believe his was after they had been cooped up together forty days. The Chenevixes had tricked it out for themselves: up two pair of stairs is what they call Mr. Chenevix's library, furnished with three maps, one shelf, a bust of Sir Isaac Newton, and a lame telescope without any glasses. Lord John Sackville *predecessed* me here, and instituted certain games called *cricketalia*, which have been celebrated this very evening in honour of him in a neighbouring meadow. . . . Adieu, dear Harry! Yours ever.

96. *Improvements.*

TO SIR HORACE MANN

Strawberry Hill, 26 December 1748.

Did you ever know a more absolute country-gentleman? Here am I come down to what you call keep my Christmas! indeed it is not in all the forms; I have stuck no laurel and holly in my windows, I eat no turkey and chine, I have no tenants to invite, I have not brought a single soul with me. The weather is excessively stormy, but has been so warm, and so entirely free from frosts the whole winter, that not only several of my honeysuckles are come out, but I have literally a blossom upon a nectarine-tree, which I believe was never seen in this climate before on the 26th of December. I am extremely busy here planting; I have got four more acres, which makes my territory prodigious in a situation where land is so scarce, and villas as abundant as formerly at Tivoli and Baiæ. I have now about fourteen acres, and am making a terrace the whole breadth of my garden on the brow of a natural hill, with meadows at the foot, and commanding the river, the village, Richmond-hill, and the park, and part of Kingston – but I hope never to show it you. . . .

---

1   The celebrated and eccentric Duchess of Queensberry, Catherine (Kitty) Douglas, *née* Hyde (*c.* 1701–77), patroness of the poet John Gay, had a house at Petersham.

97. Painted Glass and Text.

Strawberry Hill, 28 September 1749.

I am much obliged to you, dear Sir, and agree with your opinion about the painting of Prince Edward, that it cannot be original and authentic, and consequently not worth copying. Lord Cholmondeley is, indeed, an original; but who are the wise people that build for him? Sir Philip Hoby seems to be the only person likely to be benefited by this new extravagance. I have just seen a collection of tombs like those you describe – the house of Russell robed in alabaster and painted. There are seven monuments in all; one is immense, in marble, cherubim'd and seraphim'd, crusted with bas-reliefs and titles, for the first Duke of Bedford and his Duchess. All these are in a chapel of the church at Cheneys,[1] the seat of the first Earls. There are but piteous fragments of the house remaining, now a farm, built round three sides of a court. It is dropping down, in several places without a roof, but in half the windows are beautiful arms in painted glass. As these are so totally neglected, I propose making a push, and begging them of the Duke of Bedford. They would be magnificent for Strawberry-castle. Did I tell you that I have found a text in Deuteronomy to authorise my future battlements? "When thou buildest a new house, then shalt thou make a battlement for thy roof, that thou bring not blood upon thy house, if any man fall from thence." ... My compliments to your sisters.

98. The Housebreaker.

Strawberry Hill, 6 June 1752.

I have just been in London for two or three days, to fetch an adventure, and am returned to my hill and my castle. I can't say I lost my labour, as you shall hear. Last Sunday night, being as wet a night as you shall see in a summer's day, about half an hour after twelve, I was just come home from White's, and undressing to step into bed,

---

1 Chenies, Buckinghamshire, where the church monuments include that of William Russell (1616–1700), 1st Duke of Bedford, and his wife Lady Anne Carr (1615–84).

I heard Harry,[1] who you know lies forwards, roar out, "Stop thief!" and run down stairs. I ran after him. Don't be frightened; I have not lost one enamel, nor bronze, nor have been shot through the head again. A gentlewoman, who lives at Governor Pitt's,[2] next door but one to me, and where Mr. Bentley used to live, was going to bed too, and heard people breaking into Mr. Freeman's house, who, like some acquaintance of mine in Albemarle Street, goes out of town, locks up his doors, and leaves the community to watch his furniture. N.B. It was broken open but two years ago, and I and all the chairmen vow they shall steal his house away another time, before we will trouble our heads about it. Well, madam called out "watch;" two men, who were centinels, ran away, and Harry's voice after them. Down came I, and with a posse of chairmen and watchmen found the third fellow in the area of Mr. Freeman's house. Mayhap you have seen all this in the papers, little thinking who commanded the detachment. Harry fetched a blunderbuss to invite the thief up. One of the chairmen, who was drunk, cried, "Give me the blunderbuss, I'll shoot him!" But as the general's head was a little cooler, he prevented military execution, and took the prisoner without bloodshed, intending to make his triumphal entry into the metropolis of Twickenham with his captive tied to the wheels of his post-chaise. I find my style rises so much with the recollection of my victory, that I don't know how to descend to tell you that the enemy was a carpenter, and had a leather apron on. The next step was to share my glory with my friends. I despatched a courier to White's for George Selwyn, who, you know, loves nothing upon earth so well as a criminal, except the execution of him. It happened very luckily that the drawer, who received my message, has very lately been robbed himself, and had the wound fresh in his memory. He stalked up into the club-room, stopped short, and with a hollow trembling voice said, "Mr. Selwyn! Mr. Walpole's compliments to you, and he has got a house-breaker for you!" A squadron immediately came to reinforce me, and having summoned Moreland with the keys of the fortress, we marched into the house to search for more of the gang. Col. Seabright with his sword drawn went first, and then I, exactly the figure of Robinson Crusoe, with a candle and lanthorn in my hand, a

---

1 Harry or Henry Jones appears to have been Walpole's steward or butler.
2 George Morton Pitt (d. 1756), M.P., and formerly Governor of Fort St. George.

carbine upon my shoulder, my hair wet and about my ears, and in a linen night-gown and slippers. We found the kitchen shutters forced, but not finished; and in the area a tremendous bag of tools, a hammer large enough for the hand of a Jael, and six chisels! All which *opima spolia*, as there was no temple of Jupiter Capitolinus in the neighbourhood, I was reduced to offer on the altar of Sir Thomas Clarges.[1]

I am now, as I told you, returned to my plough with as much humility and pride as any of my great predecessors. We lead quite a rural life, have had a sheep-shearing, a haymaking, a syllabub under the cow, and a fishing of three gold fish out of Poyang,[2] for a present to Madam Clive. They breed with me excessively, and are grown to the size of small perch. Everything grows, if tempests would let it; but I have had two of my largest trees broke to-day with the wind, and another last week. I am much obliged to you for the flower you offer me, but by the description it is an Austrian rose, and I have several now in bloom. Mr. Bentley is with me, finishing the drawings for Gray's Odes;[3] there are some mandarin-cats fishing for gold fish, which will delight you; *au reste*, he is just where he was; he has heard something about a journey to Haughton, to the great Cu of Haticu-leo [the Earl of Halifax], but it don't seem fixed, unless he hears farther. ... Adieu! My compliments to Miss Montagu.

99. *The Building Progressing.*

TO SIR HORACE MANN

Strawberry Hill, 27 April 1753.

I have brought two of your letters hither to answer: in town there are so many idle people besides oneself, that one has not a minute's time: here I have whole evenings, after the labours of the day are ceased. Labours they are, I assure you; I have carpenters to direct, plasterers to hurry, papermen to scold, and glaziers to help: this last is my greatest pleasure: I have amassed such quantities of painted

1 Sir Thomas Clarges (1688–1759), presumably a local Justice of the Peace.
2 The Chinese name given by Walpole to his goldfish pond.
3 Bentley's drawings were published in *Designs by Mr. R. Bentley, for Six Poems by Mr. T. Gray* (1753), one of the most celebrated English illustrated books of the 18th century.

glass, that every window in my castle will be illuminated with it: the adjusting and disposing it is vast amusement. I thank you a thousand times for thinking of procuring me some Gothic remains from Rome; but I believe there is no such thing there; I scarce remember any morsel in the true taste of it in Italy. Indeed, my dear Sir, kind as you are about it, I perceive you have no idea what Gothic is; you have lived too long amidst true taste, to understand venerable barbarism. You say, "You suppose my garden is to be Gothic too." That can't be; Gothic is merely architecture; and as one has a satisfaction in imprinting the gloomth of abbeys and cathedrals on one's house, so one's garden, on the contrary, is to be nothing but *riant*, and the gaiety of nature. I am greatly impatient for my altar, and so far from mistrusting its goodness, I only fear it will be too good to expose to the weather, as I intend it must be, in a recess in the garden. I was going to tell you that my house is so monastic, that I have a little hall decked with long saints in lean arched windows and with taper columns, which we call the Paraclete, in memory of Eloisa's cloister.[1] ... Adieu!

100. *Description of the Castle.*

TO SIR HORACE MANN

Strawberry Hill, 12 June 1753

I could not rest any longer with the thought of your having no idea of a place of which you hear so much, and therefore desired Mr. Bentley to draw you as much idea of it as the post would be persuaded to carry from Twickenham to Florence. The enclosed enchanted little landscape, then, is Strawberry Hill; and I will try to explain so much of it to you as will help to let you know whereabouts we are when we are talking to you; for it is uncomfortable in so intimate a correspondence as ours not to be exactly master of every spot where one another is writing, or reading, or sauntering. This view of the castle[2] is what I have just finished, and is the only side that will be at all regular. Directly before it is an open grove, through which you see a field, which is bounded by a serpentine wood of all

1 The Oratory of the Paraclete was the Benedictine monastery founded by Abelard, and subsequently a convent of which Héloïse d'Argenteuil, or Eloisa, was Abbess.
2 It was a view of the south side, towards the north-east. – WALPOLE.

kind of trees, and flowering shrubs, and flowers. The lawn before
the house is situated on the top of a small hill, from whence to the
left you see the town and church of Twickenham encircling a turn
of the river, that looks exactly like a seaport in miniature. The opposite shore is a most delicious meadow, bounded by Richmond Hill,
which loses itself in the noble woods of the park to the end of the
prospect on the right, where is another turn of the river, and the
suburbs of Kingston as luckily placed as Twickenham is on the left:
and a natural terrace on the brow of my hill, with meadows of my
own down to the river, commands both extremities. Is not this a
tolerable prospect? You must figure that all this is perpetually
enlivened by a navigation of boats and barges, and by a road below
my terrace, with coaches, post-chaises, waggons, and horsemen constantly in motion, and the fields speckled with cows, horses, and
sheep. Now you shall walk into the house. The bow-window below
leads into a little parlour hung with a stone-colour Gothic paper and
Jackson's Venetian prints, which I could never endure while they
pretended, infamous as they are, to be after Titian, &c., but when
I gave them this air of barbarous bas-reliefs, they succeeded to a miracle: it is impossible at first sight not to conclude that they contain
the history of Attila or Tottila, done about the very æra. From hence,
under two gloomy arches, you come to the hall and staircase, which
it is impossible to describe to you as it is the most particular and
chief beauty of the castle. Imagine the walls covered with (I call it
paper, but it is really paper painted in perspective to represent)
Gothic fretwork: the lightest Gothic balustrade to the staircase,
adorned with antelopes (our supporters) bearing shields; lean windows fattened with rich saints in painted glass, and a vestibule open
with three arches on the landing-place, and niches full of trophies
of old coats of mail, Indian shields made of rhinoceros's hides,
broadswords, quivers, long bows, arrows, and spears – all *supposed* to
be taken by Sir Terry Robsart[1] in the holy wars. But as none of this
regards the enclosed drawing, I will pass to that. The room on the
ground-floor nearest to you is a bedchamber, hung with yellow paper
and prints, framed in a new manner, invented by Lord Cardigan;
that is, with black and white borders printed. Over this is
Mr. Chute's bedchamber, hung with red in the same manner. The

---

1 An ancestor of Sir Robert Walpole, who was knight of the garter. – WALPOLE.

bow-window room one pair of stairs is not yet finished; but in the tower beyond it is the charming closet where I am now writing to you. It is hung with green paper and water-colour pictures; has two windows; the one in the drawing looks to the garden, the other to the beautiful prospect; and the top of each glutted with the richest painted glass of the arms of England, crimson roses, and twenty other pieces of green, purple, and historic bits. I must tell you, by the way, that the castle, when finished, will have two-and-thirty windows enriched with painted glass. In this closet, which is Mr. Chute's College of Arms, are two presses with books of heraldry and antiquities, Madame Sevigné's Letters, and any French books that relate to her and her acquaintance. Out of this closet is the room where we always live,[1] hung with a blue and white paper in stripes adorned with festoons, and a thousand plump chairs, couches, and luxurious settees covered with linen of the same pattern, and with a bow-window commanding the prospect, and gloomed with limes that shade half each window, already darkened with painted glass in chiaroscuro, set in deep blue glass. Under this room is a cool little hall, where we generally dine, hung with paper to imitate Dutch tiles.

I have described so much, that you will begin to think that all the accounts I used to give you of the diminutiveness of our habitation were fabulous; but it is really incredible how small most of the rooms are. The only two good chambers I shall have are not yet built: they will be an eating-room and a library, each twenty by thirty, and the latter fifteen feet high. For the rest of the house, I could send it you in this letter as easily as the drawing, only that I should have nowhere to live till the return of the post. The Chinese summer-house, which you may distinguish in the distant landscape, belongs to my Lord Radnor. We pique ourselves upon nothing but simplicity, and have no carvings, gildings, paintings, inlayings, or tawdry businesses. . . . Adieu! my dear child; I think this is a very tolerable letter for summer!

---

1 The Breakfast Room, above the Waiting Room, with views east across the Thames towards Richmond Hill.

101. *Further Progress.*

TO RICHARD BENTLEY, ESQ.

My Dear Sir, Arlington Street, 18 May 1754.

... The little that I believe you would care to know relating to the Strawberry annals is, that the great tower is finished on the outside, and the whole whitened, and has a charming effect, especially as the verdure of this year is beyond what I have ever seen it: the grove nearest the house comes on much; you know I had almost despaired of its ever making a figure. The bow-window room over the supper-parlour is finished; hung with a plain blue paper, with a chintz bed and chairs; my father and mother over the chimney in the Gibbons frame,[1] about which you know we were in dispute what to do. I have fixed on black and gold, and it has a charming effect over your chimney with the two dropping points, which is executed exactly; and the old grate of Henry VIII. which you bought, is within it. In each panel round the room is a single picture; Gray's, Sir Charles Williams's,[2] and yours, in their black and gold frames; mine is to match yours; and, on each side the door, are the pictures of Mr. Churchill and Lady Mary,[3] with their son, on one side; Mr. Conway and Lady Ailesbury on the other. You can't imagine how new and pretty this furniture is. – I believe I must get you to send me an attestation under your hand that you knew nothing of it, that Mr. Rigby[4] may allow that at least this one room was by my own direction. As the library and great parlour grow finished, you shall have exact notice. ... Adieu!

1 By Eckardt and Wootton, hung by Walpole in the Blue Bedchamber. The decorative carved frame to the painting (now at the Lewis Walpole Library, Yale University) is not by Grinling Gibbons.
2 Sir Charles Hanbury Williams (1708–59), diplomat, wit and poet. Walpole provided notes for his *Works*, published in 1822.
3 Lady Mary (Maria) Walpole (*c.* 1725–1801), Walpole's illegitimate half-sister, who married Colonel Charles Churchill.
4 Richard Rigby (1722–88), a young and ambitious politician, who ultimately secured the position of Paymaster-General of the Forces. The Yale editors note that Walpole had been intimate with him but that the friendship later cooled.

102. *The Flood.*

TO RICHARD BENTLEY, ESQ.

Wednesday, 11 June 1755, addition to letter begun 10 June.

I was prevented from finishing my letter yesterday, by what do you think? By no less magnificent a circumstance than a deluge. We have had an extraordinary drought, no grass, no leaves, no flowers; not a white rose for the festival of yesterday! About four arrived such a flood, that we could not see out of the windows: the whole lawn was a lake, though situated on so high an Ararat: presently it broke through the leads, drowned the pretty blue bedchamber, passed through ceilings and floor into the little parlour, terrified Harry, and opened all Catherine's water-gates and speech-gates. I had but just time to collect two dogs, a couple of sheep, a pair of bantams, and a brace of gold fish; for, in the haste of my zeal to imitate my ancestor Noah, I forgot that fish would not easily be drowned. In short, if you chance to spy a little ark with pinnacles sailing towards Jersey,[1] open the skylight, and you will find some of your acquaintance. You never saw such desolation! A pigeon brings word that Mabland has fared still worse: it never came into my head before, that a rainbow-office for insuring against water might be very necessary. This is a true account of the late deluge.

> Witness our hands,
>
>   HORACE NOAH.
>   CATHERINE NOAH, her X mark.
>   HENRY SHEM.
>   LOUIS JAPHET.
>   PETER HAM, &c. . . .

103. *The Printing-Press.*

TO SIR HORACE MANN

Strawberry Hill, 4 August 1757.

. . . Shall I tell you what, more than distance, has thrown me out of attention to news? A little packet which I shall give your brother for you, will explain it. In short, I am turned printer, and have

---

1 Where Bentley was then living, to escape his creditors.

converted a little cottage here into a printing-office. My abbey is a perfect college or academy. I keep a painter [Müntz] in the house, and a printer [Robinson] – not to mention Mr. Bentley, who is an academy himself. I send you two copies (one for Dr. Cocchi)[1] of a very honourable opening of my press – two amazing Odes of Mr. Gray; they are Greek, they are Pindaric, they are sublime! consequently I fear a little obscure; the second particularly, by the confinement of the measure and the nature of prophetic vision, is mysterious. I could not persuade him to add more notes; he says whatever wants to be explained, don't deserve to be. I shall venture to place some in Dr. Cocchi's copy, who need not be supposed to understand Greek and English together, though he is so much master of both separately. To divert you in the mean time, I send you the following copy of a letter written by my printer[2] to a friend in Ireland. I should tell you that he has the most sensible look in the world; Garrick said he would give any money for four actors with such eyes – they are more Richard the Third's than Garrick's own; but whatever his eyes are, his head is Irish. Looking for something I wanted in a drawer, I perceived a parcel of strange romantic words in a large hand beginning a letter; he saw me see it, yet left it, which convinces me it was left on purpose: it is the grossest flattery to me, couched in most ridiculous scraps of poetry, which he has retained from things he has printed; but it will best describe itself: –

"SIR,
    "I date this from shady bowers, nodding groves, and amaranthine shades – close by old Father Thames's silver side – fair Twickenham's luxurious shades – Richmond's near neighbour, where great George the King resides. You will wonder at my prolixity – in my last I informed you that I was going into the country to transact business for a private gentleman. – This gentleman is the Hon. Horatio Walpole, son to the late great Sir Robert Walpole, who is very studious, and an admirer of all the liberal arts and sciences; amongst the rest he admires printing. He has fitted out a complete printing-house at this his country seat, and has done me the favour to make me sole manager and operator (there being no one but myself). All men of genius resorts his house, courts his company, and admires his understanding – what with his own and their writings, I believe I shall be pretty well employed. I have pleased him, and I hope to continue so to do. Nothing can be more warm than the weather has been here this time past; they have in London, by the help of glasses, roasted in the Artillery-ground fowls and quarters of lamb. The coolest days that I have felt since May last, are equal to, nay, far

1 Antonio Cocchi (1695–1758), Italian physician, antiquarian, and friend of Mann.
2 William Robinson, first printer to the press at Strawberry Hill. – WALPOLE.

exceed the warmest I ever felt in Ireland. The place I am in now is all my
comfort from the heat – the situation of it is close to the Thames, (and is
Richmond Gardens if you were ever in them) in miniature, surrounded by
bowers, groves, cascades, and ponds, and on a rising ground, not very common in this part of the country – the building elegant, and the furniture of a
peculiar taste, magnificent and superb. He is a bachelor, and spends his time
in the studious rural taste – not like his father, tossed in the weather-beaten
vessel of state – many people censured, but his conduct was far better than
our late pilot's at the helm, and more to the interest of England – they follow
his advice now, and court the assistance of Spain, instead of provoking a war,
for that was ever against England's interest."

I laughed for an hour at this picture of myself, which is much
more like to the studious magician in the enchanted opera of Rin-
aldo: not but Twickenham has a romantic genteelness that would
figure in a more luxurious climate. It was but yesterday that we had
a new kind of auction – it was of the orange-trees and plants of your
old acquaintance, Admiral Martin. It was one of the warm days of
this jubilee summer, which appears only once in fifty years – the
plants were disposed in little clumps about the lawn; the company
walked to bid from one to the other, and the auctioneer knocked
down the lots on the orange tubs. Within three doors was an auction
of China. You did not imagine that we were such a metropolis!
Adieu!

104. *Extensions.*

TO SIR HORACE MANN

Strawberry Hill, 9 September 1758.

. . . I am again got into the hands of builders, though this time to
a very small extent; only the addition of a little cloister and bedchamber. A day may come that will produce a gallery, a round tower,
a larger cloister, and a cabinet, in the manner of a little chapel: but
I am too poor for these ambitious designs yet, and I have so many
ways of dispersing my money, that I don't know when I shall be
richer. However, I amuse myself infinitely; besides my printing-
house, which is constantly at work, besides such a treasure of taste
and drawing as my friend Mr. Bentley, I have a painter [Mr. Müntz]
in the house, who is an engraver too, a mechanic, and everything.
He was a Swiss engineer in the French service; but his regiment
being broken at the peace, Mr. Bentley found him in the isle of Jersey

and fixed him with me. He has an astonishing genius for landscape, and added to that, all the industry and patience of a German. We are just now practising, and have succeeded surprisingly in a new method of painting, discovered at Paris by Count Caylus, and intended to be the encaustic method of the ancients. My Swiss has painted, I am writing the account,[1] and my press is to notify our improvements. As you will know that way, I will not tell you here at large. In short, to finish all the works I have in hand, and all the schemes I have in my head, I cannot afford to live less than fifty years more. What pleasure it would give me to see you here for a moment! I should think I saw you and your dear brother at once! Can't you form some violent secret expedition against Corsica or Port-Mahon, which may make it necessary for you to come and settle here? Are we to correspond till we meet in some unknown world? Alas! I fear so; my dear Sir, you are as little likely to save money as I am – would you could afford to resign your crown and be a subject at Strawberry Hill! Adieu! . . .

105. The "Shell."

TO GEORGE MONTAGU, ESQ.

2 June 1759.

Strawberry Hill is grown a perfect Paphos; it is the land of beauties. On Wednesday the Duchesses of Hamilton and Richmond, and Lady Ailesbury dined there; the two latter stayed all night. There never was so pretty a sight as to see them all three sitting in the shell;[2] a thousand years hence, when I begin to grow old, if that can ever be, I shall talk of that event, and tell young people how much handsomer the women of my time were than they will be then: I shall say, "Women alter now; I remember Lady Ailesbury looking handsomer than her daughter, the pretty Duchess of Richmond, as they were sitting in the shell on my terrace with the Duchess of Hamilton, one of the famous Gunnings." Yesterday t'other more famous Gunning [Coventry] dined there. She has made a friendship with my charming niece, to disguise her jealousy of the new

1 Müntz left Mr. Walpole, and published another account himself. – WALPOLE.
2 The shell bench, designed by Bentley, in the grounds of Strawberry Hill.

Countess's beauty: there were they two, their lords, Lord Buckingham, and Charlotte. You will think that I did not choose men
for my parties so well as women. I don't include Lord Waldegrave
in this bad election. . . .

106. *French Visitors.*

TO GEORGE MONTAGU, ESQ.

Strawberry Hill, 17 May 1763.

"On vient de nous donner une très jolie fête au château de Strab-
erri: tout étoit tapissé de narcisses, de tulipes, et de lilacs; des cors
de chasse, des clarionettes; des petits vers galants faits par des fées,
et qui se trouvoient sous la presse; des fruits à la glace, du thé, du
caffé, des biscuits, et force hot-rolls." – This is not the beginning of
a letter to you, but of one that I might suppose sets out to-night for
Paris, or rather, which I do not suppose will set out thither; for
though the narrative is circumstantially true, I don't believe the
actors were pleased enough with the scene, to give so favourable an
account of it.

The French do not come hither to see. *A l'Anglaise* happened to
be the word in fashion; and half a dozen of the most fashionable
people have been the dupes of it. I take for granted that their next
mode will be *à l'Iroquaise*, that they may be under no obligation of
realising their pretensions. Madame de Boufflers[1] I think will die a
martyr to a taste, which she fancied she had, and finds she has not.
Never having stirred ten miles from Paris, and having only rolled in
an easy coach from one hotel to another on a gliding pavement, she
is already worn out with being hurried from morning till night from
one sight to another. She rises every morning so fatigued with the
toils of the preceding day, that she has not strength, if she had
inclination, to observe the least, or the finest thing she sees! She
came hither to-day to a great breakfast I made for her, with her eyes
a foot deep in her head, her hands dangling, and scarce able to support her knitting-bag. She had been yesterday to see a ship launched,
and went from Greenwich by water to Ranelagh. Madame Dusson,[2]

1 The Comtesse de Boufflers, born Marie-Charlotte-Hippolyte de Campet de Sau-
jon (1725–1800). For Walpole's account of her see letter 352.
2 Noted by the Yale editors as the wife of Victor-Timoléon, Comte d'Usson.

who is Dutch-built, and whose muscles are pleasure-proof, came with her; there were besides, Lady Mary Coke, Lord and Lady Holdernesse, the Duke and Duchess of Grafton, Lord Hertford, Lord Villiers, Offley, Messieurs de Fleury, D'Eon,[1] et Duclos. The latter is author of the Life of Louis Onze; dresses like a dissenting minister, which I suppose is the livery of a *bel esprit*, and is much more impetuous than agreeable. We breakfasted in the great parlour, and I had filled the hall and large cloister by turns with French horns and clarionettes. As the French ladies had never seen a printing-house, I carried them into mine; they found something ready set, and desiring to see what it was, it proved as follows: –

The Press speaks –

FOR MADAME DE BOUFFLERS.

The graceful fair, who loves to know,
Nor dreads the north's inclement snow;
Who bids her polish'd accent wear
The British diction's harsher air;
Shall read her praise in every clime
Where types can speak or poets rhyme.

FOR MADAME DUSSON.

Feign not an ignorance of what I speak;
You could not miss my meaning were it Greek:
'Tis the same language Belgium utter'd first,
The same which from admiring Gallia burst.
True sentiment a like expression pours;
Each country says the same to eyes like yours.

You will comprehend that the first speaks English, and that the second does not; that the second is handsome, and the first not; and that the second was born in Holland. This little gentilesse pleased, and atoned for the popery of my house, which was not serious enough for Madame de Boufflers, who is Montmorency, *et du sang du premier Chrétien;* and too serious for Madame Dusson, who is a Dutch Calvinist. The latter's husband was not here, nor Drumgold, who have both got fevers, nor the Duc de Nivernois, who dined at Claremont. The Gallery is not advanced enough to give them any idea at all, as they are not apt to go out of their way for one; but the Cabinet, and the glory of yellow glass at top, which had a charming

1 The Chevalier d'Eon (1728–1810), French diplomat, spy, and transvestite, who was at the time chargé d'affaires in London.

sun for a foil, did surmount their indifference, especially as they were animated by the Duchess of Grafton, who had never happened to be here before, and who perfectly entered into the air of enchantment and fairyism, which is the tone of the place, and was peculiarly so to-day – *à-propos*, when do you design to come hither? Let me know, that I may have no measures to interfere with receiving you and your grandsons. . . .

107. *The Gallery is Finishing.*

TO GEORGE MONTAGU, ESQ.

Strawberry Hill, 1 July 1763.

Mr. Chute and I intend to be with you on the seventeenth or eighteenth; but as we are wandering swains, we do not drive one nail into one day of the almanack irremovably. Our first stage is to Bletchley, the parsonage of venerable Cole,[1] the antiquarian of Cambridge. Bletchley lies by Fenny Stratford; now can you direct us how to make Horton[2] in our way from Stratford to Greatworth?[3] If this meander engrosses more time than we propose, do not be disappointed, and think we shall not come, for we shall. The journey you must accept as a great sacrifice either to you or to my promise, for I quit the Gallery almost in the critical minute of consummation.[4] Gilders, carvers, upholsterers and picture-cleaners are labouring at their several forges, and I do not love to trust a hammer or a brush without my own supervisal. This will make my stay very short, but it is a greater compliment than a month would be at another season; and yet I am not profuse of months. Well, but I begin to be ashamed of my magnificence; Strawberry is growing sumptuous in its latter day; it will scarce be any longer like the fruit of its name, or the modesty of its ancient demeanour, both which seem to have been in Spenser's prophetic eye, when he sung of

> . . . the blushing strawberries
> Which lurk, close-shrouded from high-looking eyes,
> Showing that sweetness low and hidden lies.

1 Walpole's correspondent the Rev. William Cole: see heading to letter 211.
2 Horton Hall, Northamptonshire, a seat of the Montagus, earls of Halifax, to whom George Montagu was related: demolished in 1936.
3 The house in Northamptonshire where Montagu lived.
4 The Gallery at Strawberry Hill was finished the following month, August 1763.

In truth, my collection was too great already to be lodged humbly; it has extended my walls, and pomp followed. It was a neat, small house; it now will be a comfortable one, and, except one fine apartment, does not deviate from its simplicity. Adieu! I know nothing about the world, and am only Strawberry's and yours sincerely.

108. *Lord Herbert's Life Printed.*

TO GEORGE MONTAGU, ESQ.

Strawberry Hill, 16 July 1764.

... I want to send you something from the Strawberry press; tell me how I shall convey it; it is nothing less than the most curious book that ever set its foot into the world. I expect to hear you scream hither: if you don't I shall be disappointed, for I have kept it as a most profound secret from you, till I was ready to surprise you with it; I knew your impatience, and would not let you have it piecemeal. It is the Life of the great philosopher, Lord Herbert, written by himself.[1] Now are you disappointed? Well, read it – not the first forty pages, of which you will be sick – I will not anticipate it, but I will tell you the history. I found it a year ago at Lady Hertford's, to whom Lady Powis had lent it. I took it up, and soon threw it down again, as the dullest thing I ever saw. She persuaded me to take it home. My Lady Waldegrave was here in all her grief; Gray and I read it to amuse her. We could not get on for laughing and screaming. I begged to have it to print: Lord Powis, sensible of the extravagance, refused – I insisted – he persisted. I told my Lady Hertford, it was no matter, I would print it, I was determined. I sat down and wrote a flattering dedication to Lord Powis, which I knew he would swallow: he did, and gave up his ancestor. But this was not enough; I was resolved the world should not think I admired it seriously, though there are really fine passages in it, and good sense too: I drew up an equivocal preface, in which you will discover my opinion, and sent it with the dedication. The Earl gulped down the one under the palliative of the other, and here you will have all. Pray take notice of

---

1 *The Life of Edward Lord Herbert of Cherbury, Written by Himself,* edited by Walpole and published at the Strawberry Hill Press in 1764.

the pedigree, of which I am exceedingly proud;[1] observe how I have clearly arranged so involved a descent: one may boast of one's heraldry. I shall send you, too, Lady Temple's Poems. Pray keep both under lock and key, for there are but two hundred copies of Lord Herbert, and but one hundred of the Poems suffered to be printed. . . .

109. *Royal Visitors Refused.*

TO THE EARL OF HERTFORD

3 August 1764.

. . . I have been much distressed this morning. The royal family reside chiefly at Richmond, whither scarce necessary servants attend them, and no mortal else but Lord Bute. The King and Queen have taken to going about to see places; they have been at Oatlands and Wanstead. A quarter before ten to-day, I heard the bell at the gate ring, – truth is, I was not up, for my hours are not reformed, either at night or in the morning, – I inquired who it was? the Prince of Mecklenburgh and De Witz had called to know if they could see the house; my two Swiss, Favre and Louis, told them I was in bed, but if they would call again in an hour, they might see it. I shuddered at this report, – and would it were the worst part! The Queen herself was behind, in a coach: I am shocked to death, and know not what to do! It is ten times worse just now than ever at any other time: it will certainly be said, that I refused to let the Queen see my house. See what it is to have republican servants! When I made a tempest about it, Favre said, with the utmost *sang froid*, "Why could not he tell me he was the Prince of Mecklenburgh?" I shall go this evening and consult my oracle, Lady Suffolk. If she approves it, I will write to De Witz, and pretend I know nothing of anybody but the Prince, and beg a thousand pardons, and assure him how proud I should be to have his master visit my castle at Thundertentronk.[2] . . .

---

1 Walpole subsequently realised there were a number of inaccuracies in his genealogy.
2 The childhood home of Voltaire's Candide.

110. *Strawberry Hill by Night.*

TO GEORGE MONTAGU, ESQ.

Strawberry Hill, 10 June 1765. Eleven at night.

I am just come out of the garden in the most oriental of all evenings, and from breathing odours beyond those of Araby. The acacias, which the Arabians have the sense to worship, are covered with blossoms, the honeysuckles dangle from every tree in festoons, the seringas are thickets of sweets, and the new-cut hay in the field tempers the balmy gales with simple freshness; while a thousand sky-rockets launched into the air at Ranelagh or Marybone illuminate the scene, and give it an air of Haroun Alraschid's paradise. I was not quite so content by daylight; some foreigners dined here, and, though they admired our verdure, it mortified me by its brownness – we have not had a drop of rain this month to cool the tip of our daisies. My company was Lady Lyttelton, Lady Schaub, a Madame de Juliac from the Pyreneans, very handsome, not a girl, and of Lady Schaub's mould; the Comte de Caraman, nephew of Madame de Mirepoix, a Monsieur de Clausonnette, and General Schouallow, the favourite of the late Czarina; absolute favourite for a dozen years, without making an enemy. . . .

111. *Visitors to Strawberry Hill.*

TO GEORGE MONTAGU, ESQ.

Arlington Street, 11 May 1769.

You are so wayward, that I often resolve to give you up to your humours. Then something happens with which I can divert you, and my good-nature returns. Did not you say you should return to London long before this time? At least, could you not tell me you had changed your mind? why am I to pick it out from your absence and silence, as Dr. Warburton found a future state in Moses's saying nothing of the matter![1] I could go on with a chapter of severe interrogatories, but I think it more cruel to treat you as a hopeless reprobate; yes, you are graceless, and as I have a respect for my own scolding, I shall not throw it away upon you.

1 A slighting reference to *The Divine Legation of Moses Demonstrated* (1737–41) by the Rev. William Warburton (1698–1779), friend of Pope and later Bishop of Gloucester.

Strawberry has been in great glory; I have given a festino there that will almost mortgage it. Last Tuesday all France dined there: Monsieur and Madame du Châtelet, the Duc de Liancourt, three more French ladies, whose names you will find in the enclosed paper, eight other Frenchmen, the Spanish and Portuguese ministers, the Holdernesses, Fitzroys, in short we were four and twenty. They arrived at two. At the gates of the castle I received them, dressed in the cravat of Gibbons's carving, and a pair of gloves embroidered up to the elbows that had belonged to James I.[1] The French servants stared, and firmly believed this was the dress of English country gentlemen. After taking a survey of the apartments, we went to the printing-house, where I had prepared the enclosed verses, with translations by Monsieur de Lille, one of the company. The moment they were printed off, I gave a private signal, and French horns and clarionets accompanied this compliment. We then went to see Pope's grotto and garden, and returned to a magnificent dinner in the refectory. In the evening we walked, had tea, coffee, and lemon-ade in the Gallery, which was illuminated with a thousand, or thirty candles, I forget which, and played at whisk and loo till midnight. Then there was a cold supper, and at one the company returned to town, saluted by fifty nightingales, who, as tenants of the manor, came to do honour to their lord. . . .

112. *Armour and Chapel.*

TO THE REV. WILLIAM COLE

Strawberry Hill, 23 October 1771.

. . . I am making a very curious purchase at Paris, the complete armour of Francis the First. It is gilt in relief, and is very rich and beautiful. It comes out of the Crozat Collection. I am building a small chapel, too, in my garden, to receive two valuable pieces of antiquity, and which have been presents singularly lucky for me.[2] They are the window from Bexhill [in Sussex] with the portraits of Henry III. and his Queen, procured for me by Lord Ashburnham.

1 The Grinling Gibbons limewood cravat and the gloves of James I still survive, at the Victoria and Albert Museum and the Fashion Museum, Bath, respectively.
2 The armour of Francis I (actually very fine parade armour of *c.* 1600) still survives, as does Walpole's Chapel in the Woods.

The other, great part of the tomb of Capoccio, mentioned in my "Anecdotes of Painting" on the subject of the Confessor's shrine, and sent to me from Rome by Mr. Hamilton, our minister at Naples. It is very extraordinary that I should happen to be master of these curiosities. After next summer, by which time my castle and collection will be complete (for if I buy more I must build another castle for another collection), I propose to form the Catalogue[1] and description, and shall take the liberty to call on you for your assistance. In the mean time there is enough new to divert you at present.

113. *An Explosion.*

TO THE HON. H. S. CONWAY

Late Strawberry Hill, 7 January 1772.

You have read of my calamity without knowing it, and will pity me when you do. I have been blown up; my castle is blown up; Guy Fawkes has been about my house; and the 5th of November has fallen on the 6th of January! In short, nine thousand powder-mills broke loose yesterday morning on Hounslow-heath;[2] a whole squadron of them came hither, and have broken eight of my painted-glass windows; and the north side of the castle looks as if it had stood a siege. The two saints in the hall have suffered martyrdom! they have had their bodies cut off, and nothing remains but their heads. The two next great sufferers are indeed two of the least valuable, being the passage-windows to the library and great parlour – a fine pane is demolished in the round-room; and the window by the gallery is damaged. Those in the cabinet, and Holbein-room, and gallery, and blue-room, and green-closet, &c. have escaped. As the storm came from the north-west, the china-closet was not touched, nor a cup fell down. The bow-window of brave old coloured glass, at Mr. Hindley's, is massacred; and all the north sides of Twickenham and Brentford are shattered. At London it was proclaimed an earthquake, and half the inhabitants ran into the street.

1 A reference to Walpole's catalogue of his collection, the *Description* of Strawberry Hill, printed 1774, revised and reprinted 1784.
2 Two powder mills on Hounslow Heath, about two and a half miles from Strawberry Hill, blew up on 6 January 1772. As Lieutenant of the Ordnance Conway would have had some ultimate responsibility for the army's supply of gunpowder.

As Lieutenant-General of the Ordnance, I must beseech you to give strict orders that no more powder-mills may blow up. My aunt, Mrs. Kerwood, reading one day in the papers that a distiller's had been burnt by the head of the still flying off, said, she wondered they did not make an act of parliament against the heads of stills flying off. Now, I hold it much easier for you to do a body this service; and would recommend to your consideration, whether it would not be prudent to have all magazines of powder kept under water till they are wanted for service. In the mean time, I expect a pension to make me amends for what I have suffered under the government. Adieu! Yours.

114. *The Beauty Room.*

TO THE HON. H. S. CONWAY

Strawberry Hill, 30 June 1776.

I was very glad to receive your letter, not only because always most glad to hear of you, but because I wished to write to you, and had absolutely nothing to say till I had something to answer. I have lain but two nights in town since I saw you; have been, else, constantly here, very much employed, though doing, hearing, knowing exactly nothing. I have had a Gothic architect [Mr. Essex] from Cambridge to design me a gallery, which will end in a mouse,[1] that is, in an hexagon closet of seven feet diameter. I have been making a Beauty Room, which was effected by buying two dozen of small copies of Sir Peter Lely, and hanging them up; and I have been making hay, which is not made, because I put it off for three days, as I chose it should adorn the landscape when I was to have company; and so the rain is come, and has drowned it. However, as I can even turn calculator when it is to comfort me for not minding my interest, I have discovered that it is five to one better for me that my hay should be spoiled than not; for, as the cows will eat it if it is damaged, which horses will not, and as I have five cows and but one horse, is not it plain that the worse my hay is the better? Do not you with your refining head go, and, out of excessive friendship, find out

1 The Beauclerk Tower, designed by James Essex (bap. 1722–84), just over nine feet in diameter, contained the Beauclerk Closet, created by Walpole to house Lady Diana Beauclerk's drawings.

something to destroy my system. I had rather be a philosopher than a rich man; and yet have so little philosophy, that I had much rather be content than be in the right.

Mr. Beauclerk and Lady Di. have been here four or five days – so I had both content and exercise for my philosophy. I wish Lady Ailesbury was as fortunate! The Pembrokes, Churchills, Le Texier, as you will have heard, and the Garricks have been with us. Perhaps, if alone, I might have come to you; but you are all too healthy and harmonious. I can neither walk nor sing; nor, indeed, am fit for anything but to amuse myself in a sedentary trifling way. What I have most certainly not been doing, is writing anything: a truth I say to you, but do not desire you to repeat. I deign to satisfy scarce anybody else. Whoever reported that I was writing anything, must have been so totally unfounded, that they either blundered by guessing without reason, or knew they lied – and that could not be with any kind intention; though saying I am going to do what I am not going to do, is wretched enough. Whatever is said of me without truth, anybody is welcome to believe that pleases.

In fact, though I have scarce a settled purpose about anything, I think I shall never write any more. I have written a great deal too much, unless I had written better, and I know I should now only write still worse. One's talent, whatever it is, does not improve at near sixty – yet, if I liked it, I dare to say a good reason would not stop my inclination; – but I am grown most indolent in that respect, and most absolutely indifferent to every purpose of vanity. Yet without vanity I am become still prouder and more contemptuous. I have a contempt for my countrymen that makes me despise their approbation. The applause of slaves and of the foolish mad is below ambition. Mine is the haughtiness of an ancient Briton, that cannot write what would please this age, and would not, if he could. . . .

115. *The Vase.*

TO THE COUNTESS OF UPPER OSSORY

Strawberry Hill, 2 August 1786.

. . . The vase for which your Ladyship is so good as to interest yourself, was not the famous Cat's *lofty vase*, nor one of any consequence, but a vase and dish of Florentine Fayence, that stood under the table in the Round Chamber;[1] nor had I the least concern but for the company who were so grieved at the accident. With the troops that come, I am amazed I have not worse damage; however, I am sometimes diverted too. Last week a scientific lady was here, and exactly at the moment that I opened the cabinet of enamels, she turned to a gentleman who came with her, and entered into a discussion of the ides and calends. Another gentlewoman was here two days ago, who had seen a good half century: she said, "Well, I must live another *forty* years to have time to see all the curiosities of this house." These little incidents of character do not make me amends for being the master of a puppet-show, for though I generally keep behind the scenes, I am almost as much disturbed as if I constantly exhibited myself and

"Ev'n Sunday shines no Sabbath day to me!"[2] . . .

1 A vase in the Round Chamber damaged by visitors to the house, distinguished from the vase that was the subject of Gray's "Ode on the Death of a Favourite Cat", which was kept in the Little Cloister.
2 Pope, *Epistle to Dr. Arbuthnot*, line 12.

VII
HIS LITERARY WORKS

THE STRAWBERRY HILL press was established in 1757 (see letter 103) and it was this event that led Walpole to become something more than an occasional writer. Up to that date his literary output had been mainly confined to some minor poems, a few contributions to periodicals such as Dodsley's *The World*, and political pamphlets. He continued to write occasional verses, some of which were printed at his press (see letters 106 and 111), but far more important were his historical and antiquarian works and his writings on art history. The earliest of these, the *Ædes Walpolianæ*, was an account of his father's collection of pictures at Houghton, with an introduction that surveyed the history of European painting with all the confidence of youth. One hundred copies were printed in 1747 for private distribution. Walpole had the antiquary's urge to record: in 1758 he printed at Strawberry Hill the *Catalogue of the Royal and Noble Authors of England* (see letter 116); later, more importantly, he arranged the painter George Vertue's chaotic manuscript material into *The Anecdotes of Painting in England* (1762–71), a biographical survey that was to become a founding text of English art historical studies (see letter 117). In 1774 he produced a *Description of the Villa of Horace Walpole ... at Strawberry-Hill* (of which he printed an expanded and illustrated edition in 1784). This was not offered for sale, but he directed that copies of the later edition be distributed to a number of friends after his death. It remains the vital record of both the house that he created and the treasures with which he filled it.

The most important function of the Strawberry Hill press was to enable Walpole as an amateur to print and circulate whatever he wished outside the London book trade, creating editions which, as he explained to Mason, "have all the beautiful negligence of a gentleman".[1] Of the thirty-four books and pamphlets (excluding ephemera) printed at the press, half were written by Walpole. He could print a few copies for friends, or extend the print-run and pass them to the trade to sell. With other titles, such as the *Historic*

1 Letter of 15 May 1773 (YE 28:88).

Doubts on the Life and Reign of King Richard the Third (1768), he
would have the booksellers publish them (see letters 120 and 121). It
is disdain for commercial publishing, tinged with the fear of ridicule
and the defensive tendency to self-deprecation which were always
part of Walpole's character, that lie beneath the sentiments expressed
in letters 124 and 125.

Walpole wrote little fiction, but his principal foray into the genre,
The Castle of Otranto, created a considerable stir. "It makes some of
us cry a little, and all in general afraid to go to bed o' nights," wrote
Gray in December 1764.[1] It was not until the second edition was
published commercially the following year that Walpole acknowledged that the romance, alleged to have been translated from an
Italian black-letter printing of the year 1529, was in reality his own
composition. Now regarded as the first Gothic novel, it has been
influential beyond measure. There are other fictions that should not
be overlooked, in particular *The Mysterious Mother* (1768), his unper-
formable tragedy on the theme of double incest. This greatly
shocked Frances Burney when she started reading it at court in November 1786, but impressed Byron, who praised Walpole as the author
of the first romance [*Otranto*] and the last tragedy in our language.
Also worth looking out are his strange, surreal fantasies or riddles
known as the *Hieroglyphic Tales* (1785).

Much of Walpole's writing remained unpublished until after his
death in 1797. His letters, for which he is best known today, began
to appear in the collected *Works* (1798), edited by Mary Berry: these
are discussed in the general introduction. Finally, there are his political Memoirs, twenty-three folio volumes covering the years 1746 to
1791, which he directed to be sealed up after his death. The bulk of
them were published in three instalments between 1822 and 1859.
They have always had a mixed reception, painting as they do a far
harsher portrait of humanity than the letters. Walpole insisted that
his sole purpose in writing them was to use his position as an
informed participant and observer to provide an objective record of
political events for posterity. Others have thought differently, and
felt that Walpole was not above the factional arguments over which
he presumed to preside. John Wilson Croker said in 1824 that Walpole had poisoned the sources of history,[2] and the introduction to
the most recent edition of the *Memoirs of the Reign of King George
III* (Yale, 2000) reaches a conclusion that is no more charitable.

1 Letter from Gray of 30 December 1764 (YE 14:137).
2 *Horace Walpole: The Critical Heritage*, ed. Peter Sabor (London: Routledge, 1987),
p. 202.

116. "A Catalogue of Royal and Noble Authors."

TO GEORGE MONTAGU, ESQ.

Arlington Street, 4 May 1758.

... My book[1] is marvellously in fashion, to my great astonishment. I did not expect so much truth and such notions of liberty would have made their fortune in this our day. I am preparing an edition for publication, and then I must expect to be a little less civilly treated. My Lord Chesterfield tells everybody that he subscribes to all my opinions; but this mortifies me about as much as the rest flatter me; I cannot, because it is my own case, forget how many foolish books he has diverted himself with commending. The most extraordinary thing I have heard about mine is, that it being talked of at Lord Arran's table, Doctor King (the Dr. King of Oxford) said of the passage on my father; "It is very modest, very genteel, and VERY TRUE." I asked my Lady Cardigan if she would forgive my making free with her grandmother;[2] she replied very sensibly, "I am sure she would not have hindered anybody from writing against me; why should I be angry at any writing against her?" ...

117. "Anecdotes of Painting."

TO THE REV. HENRY ZOUCH[3]

Sir,   12 January 1759.

... You love to be troubled, and therefore I will make no apology for troubling you. Last summer, I bought of Virtue's widow forty volumes of his MS. collections relating to English painters, sculptors, gravers, and architects. He had actually begun their lives: unluckily he had not gone far, and could not write grammar. I propose to digest and complete this work (I mean after the Conway Papers).[4] In the mean time, Sir, shall I beg the favour of you just to

---

1 *A Catalogue of the Royal and Noble Authors of England, with Lists of their Works* was compiled by Walpole and published at the Strawberry Hill Press in April 1758.
2 Sarah, Duchess of Marlborough. – WALPOLE.
3 Rev. Henry Zouch of Wakefield (*c*. 1725–95), antiquary and social reformer, Justice of the Peace, and later political agent for Lord Rockingham.
4 Virtue's MSS. were the basis for the *Anecdotes of Painting*. Walpole had discovered the Conway Papers at Ragley (see letter 83) but never published them.

mark down memorandums of the pages where you happen to meet with anything relative to these subjects, especially of our antienter buildings, paintings, and artists. I would not trouble you for more reference, if even that is not too much. . . . Sir, most sincerely yours,

Hor. Walpole.

118. *"The Castle of Otranto."*

TO THE REV. WILLIAM COLE

Strawberry Hill, 28 February 1765.

Dear Sir,

. . . I have lately had an accession to my territory here, by the death of good old Franklin,[1] to whom I had given for his life the lease of the cottage and garden cross the road. Besides a little pleasure in planting and in crowding it with flowers, I intend to make, what I am sure you are antiquarian enough to approve, a bower, though your friends the abbots did not indulge in such retreats, at least not under that appellation: but though we love the same ages, you must excuse worldly me for preferring the romantic scenes of antiquity. If you will tell me how to send it, and are partial enough to me to read a profane work in the style of former centuries, I shall convey to you a little story-book, which I published some time ago, though not boldly with my own name: but it has succeeded so well, that I do not any longer *entirely* keep the secret. Does the title 'The Castle of Otranto,'[2] tempt you? I shall be glad to hear you are well and happy.

119. *Origin of Novel.*

TO THE REV. WILLIAM COLE

Strawberry Hill, 9 March 1765.

Dear Sir,

I had time to write but a short note with the 'Castle of Otranto,' as your messenger called on me at four o'clock, as I was going to dine

1 Richard Francklin (*c.* 1696–1765), the printer of *The Craftsman*, the opposition paper to Sir Robert Walpole's government, who in later life had become Walpole's tenant.
2 *The Castle of Otranto* was published in December 1764, the title page (dated 1765) claiming it was translated by a fictitious William Marshal from an Italian book of 1529. After the success of the first edition, Walpole acknowledged authorship in the second edition, published in April 1765.

abroad. Your partiality to me and Strawberry have, I hope, inclined you to excuse the wildness of the story. You will even have found some traits to put you in mind of this place. When you read of the picture quitting its panel, did not you recollect the portrait of Lord Falkland, all in white, in my Gallery?[1] Shall I even confess to you, what was the origin of this romance! I waked one morning, in the beginning of last June, from a dream, of which, all I could recover was, that I had thought myself in an ancient castle (a very natural dream for a head filled like mine with Gothic story), and that on the uppermost bannister of a great staircase I saw a gigantic hand in armour. In the evening I sat down, and began to write, without knowing in the least what I intended to say or relate. The work grew on my hands, and I grew fond of it – add, that I was very glad to think of anything, rather than politics. In short, I was so engrossed with my tale, which I completed in less than two months, that one evening, I wrote from the time I had drunk my tea, about six o'clock, till half an hour after one in the morning, when my hand and fingers were so weary, that I could not hold the pen to finish the sentence, but left Matilda and Isabella talking, in the middle of a paragraph. You will laugh at my earnestness; but if I have amused you, by retracing with any fidelity the manners of ancient days, I am content, and give you leave to think me as idle as you please. . . .

120. *"Historic Doubts on Richard III."*

TO SIR DAVID DALRYMPLE[2]

Strawberry Hill, 17 January 1768.

. . . I will beg to know how I may convey my "Richard" to you, which will be published to-morrow fortnight. I do not wonder you could not guess the discovery I have made. It is one of the most marvellous that ever was made. In short, it is the original Coronation Roll of Richard the Third, by which it appears that very magnificent robes were ordered for Edward the Fifth, and that he did, or was

---

1 Sir Henry Cary (*c.* 1575–1633), 1st Viscount Falkland, by Vansomer, a full-length portrait which hung on the window wall of the Gallery.
2 Sir David Dalrymple, Lord Hailes (1726–92), Scottish judge and antiquary.

to have walked at his uncle's Coronation.[1] This most valuable monument is in the Great Wardrobe. It is not, though the most extraordinary, the only thing that will surprise you in my work. But I will not anticipate what little amusement you may find there. I am, Sir, &c.

121. *The Same.*

TO THOMAS GRAY[2]

Arlington Street, 18 February 1768.

... It would be affected, even to you, to say I am indifferent to fame. I certainly am not, but I am indifferent to almost anything I have done to acquire it. The greater part are mere compilations; and no wonder they are, as you say, incorrect, when they are commonly written with people in the room, as "Richard" and the "Noble Authors" were. But I doubt there is a more intrinsic fault in them: which is, that I cannot correct them. If I write tolerably, it must be at once; I can neither mend nor add. The articles of Lord Capel and Lord Peterborough, in the second edition of the "Noble Authors," cost me more trouble than all the rest together: and you may perceive that the worst part of "Richard," in point of ease and style, is what relates to the papers you gave me on Jane Shore, because it was tacked on so long afterwards, and when my impetus was chilled. If some time or other you will take the trouble of pointing out the inaccuracies of it, I shall be much obliged to you: at present I shall meddle no more with it. It has taken its fate: nor did I mean to complain. I found it was condemned indeed beforehand, which was what I alluded to. Since publication (as has happened to me before) the success has gone beyond my expectation. ...

The Duke of Richmond and Lord Lyttelton agree with you, that I have not disculpated Richard of the murder of Henry VI. I own to you, it is the crime of which in my own mind I believe him most guiltless. Had I thought he committed it, I should never have taken the trouble to apologize for the rest. I am not at all positive or

1 The document was not in fact a "coronation roll", but a wardrobe account, and so did not support Walpole's argument that Edward V, one of the Princes in the Tower, survived to walk at the coronation of Richard III.

2 See heading to letter 195.

obstinate on your other objections, nor know exactly what I believe on many points of this story. And I am so sincere, that, except a few notes hereafter, I shall leave the matter to be settled or discussed by others. As you have written much too little, I have written a great deal too much, and think only of finishing the two or three other things I have begun – and of those, nothing but the last volume of Painters is designed for the present public. What has one to do when turned fifty, but really think of *finishing*?

I am much obliged and flattered by Mr. Mason's approbation, and particularly by having had almost the same thought with him. I said, "People need not be angry at my excusing Richard; I have not diminished their fund of hatred, I have only transferred it from Richard to Henry." . . .

122. *"The Mysterious Mother."*

TO GEORGE MONTAGU, ESQ.

Strawberry Hill, 15 April 1768.

I have finished my Tragedy ["The Mysterious Mother"], but as you would not bear the subject, I will say no more of it, but that Mr. Chute, who is not easily pleased, likes it, and Gray, who is still more difficult, approves it. I am not yet intoxicated enough with it to think it would do for the stage, though I wish to see it acted; but, as Mrs. Pritchard[1] leaves the stage next month, I know nobody could play the Countess; nor am I disposed to expose myself to the impertinences of that jackanapes Garrick, who lets nothing appear but his own wretched stuff, or that of creatures still duller, who suffer him to alter their pieces as he pleases. I have written an epilogue in character for the Clive, which she would speak admirably: but I am not so sure that she would like to speak it. Mr. Conway, Lady Ailesbury, Lady Lyttelton, and Miss Rich, are to come hither the day after to-morrow, and Mr. Conway and I are to read my play to them; for I have not strength enough to go through the whole alone. . . .

Adieu! though I am very angry with you, I deserve all your friendship, by that I have for you, witness my anger and disappointment. Yours ever.

---

1 Hannah Pritchard (1709–68), celebrated actress, the Lady Macbeth to Garrick's Macbeth, and the Beatrice to his Benedick.

123. *To be Published.*

TO THE REV. WILLIAM MASON

6 May 1781.

Do you know that I am in great distress? My "Mysterious Mother" has wandered into the hands of booksellers, and has been advertised with my name without my knowledge. Like a legislator I have held out both rewards and punishments to prevent its appearance, but at last have been forced to advertise it myself; but unless the spurious edition appears, I shall keep it back till everybody is gone out of town, and then it will be forgotten by the winter. I intend, too, to abuse it myself in a short advertisement prefixed. It is hard that when one submits to be superannuated, it is not permitted. At first I had a mind to add your magic alterations, which in the compass of ten lines makes it excusable;[1] but then I thought it would look like wishing to have it brought on the stage as it might be. If I do publish it, I shall like with your leave to print your alterations hereafter, for I think them, as I said, performed by a *coup de baguette*, and that nothing is a greater proof of your superiority. Pray send me another copy, for in moving from Arlington Street to Berkeley Square I mislaid them, and cannot find them directly, though I saw them but last year, and have treasured them up so safely, as I did Gray's "Candidate," that I don't know where they are.

124. *An Edition of His Works.*

TO JOHN PINKERTON, ESQ.[2]

27 October 1784.

I would not answer your letter, Sir, till I could tell you that I had put your play into Mr. Colman's hands, which I have done. He desired my consent to his carrying it into the country to read it deliberately: you shall know as soon as I receive his determination. I am much obliged to you for the many civil and kind expressions in your letter, and for the friendly information you give me. Partiality, I fear,

1 Walpole never adopted the alterations Mason had suggested to the play, of which he privately disapproved. He did manage to forestall the unauthorised publication.
2 John Pinkerton (1758–1826), Scots antiquary and historian.

dictated the former; but the last I can only ascribe to the goodness of your heart. I have published nothing of any size but the pieces you mention, and one or two small tracts now out of print and forgotten. The rest have been prefaces to some of my Strawberry editions, and to a few other publications; and some fugitive pieces which I reprinted some years ago in a small volume, and which shall be at your service, with the "Catalogue of Noble Authors."

With regard to the bookseller who has taken the pains of collecting my writings for an edition (amongst which I do not doubt but he will generously bestow on me many that I did not *write*, according to the liberal practice of such compilers), and who also intends to write my life to which (as I never did anything worthy of the notice of the public) he must likewise be a volunteer contributor, it would be vain for me to endeavour to prevent such a design. Whoever has been so unadvised as to throw himself on the public, must pay such a tax in a pamphlet or magazine when he dies; but, happily, the insects that prey on carrion are still more short-lived than the carcases were, from which they draw their nutriment. Those momentary abortions live but a day, and are thrust aside by like embryos. Literary characters, when not illustrious, are known only to a few literary men; and, amidst the world of books, few readers can come to my share. Printing, that secures existence (in libraries) to indifferent authors of any bulk, is like those cases of Egyptian mummies which in catacombs preserve bodies of one knows not whom, and which are scribbled over with characters that nobody attempts to read, till nobody understands the language in which they were written.

I believe therefore it will be most wise to swim for a moment on the passing current, secure that it will soon hurry me into the ocean where all things are forgotten. To appoint a biographer is to bespeak a panegyric; and I doubt whether they who collect their works for the public, and, like me, are conscious of no intrinsic worth, do but beg mankind to accept of talents (whatever they were) in lieu of virtues. To anticipate spurious publications by a comprehensive and authentic one, is almost as great an evil: it is giving a body to scattered atoms; and such an act in one's old age is declaring a fondness for the indiscretions of youth, or for the trifles of an age which, though more mature, is only the less excusable. It is most true, Sir, that, so far from being prejudiced in favour of my own writings, I am persuaded that, had I thought early as I think now, I should never have appeared as an author. Age, frequent illness and pain, have given me as many hours of reflection in the intervals of the two latter, as the two latter have disabled from reflection; and, besides their showing me the inutility of all our little views, they have suggested an observation that I love to encourage in myself from the rationality of it. I have learnt and have practised the humiliating task of comparing myself with great authors; and that comparison has annihilated all the flattery that self-love could suggest. I know how trifling my own writings are, and how far below the standard that constitutes excellence: for the shades that distinguish the degrees of mediocrity, they are not worth discrimination; and he must be very modest, or easily satisfied, who can be content to glimmer for an instant a little more than his brethren glow-worms. Mine, therefore, you find, Sir, is not humility, but pride. When young, I wished for fame; not examining whether I was capable of attaining it, nor considering in what lights fame was desirable. There are two sorts of honest fame; *that* attendant on the truly great, and that better sort that is due to the good. I fear I did not aim at the latter; nor discovered, till too late, that I could not compass the former. Having neglected the best road, and having, instead of the other, strolled into a narrow path that led to no good worth seeking, I see the idleness of my journey, and hold it more graceful to abandon my wanderings to chance or oblivion, than to mark solicitude for trifles, which I think so myself.

I beg your pardon for talking so much of myself; but an answer was due to the unmerited attention which you have paid to my writings. I turn with more pleasure to speak on yours. . . .

125. *Self-Criticism.*

TO HANNAH MORE

Strawberry Hill, 12 July 1788.

Won't you repent having opened the correspondence, my dear Madam, when you find my letters come so thick upon you? In this instance, however, I am only to blame in part, for being too ready to take advice, for the sole reason for which advice ever is taken, — because it fell in with my inclination.

You said in your last that you feared you took up time of mine to the prejudice of the public; implying, I imagine, that I might employ it in composing. Waving both your compliment and my own vanity, I will speak very seriously to you on that subject, and with exact truth. My simple writings have had better fortune than they had any reason to expect; and I fairly believe, in a great degree, because gentlemen-writers, who do not write for interest, are treated with some civility if they do not write absolute nonsense. I think so, because I have not unfrequently known much better works than mine much more neglected, if the name, fortune, and situation of the authors were below mine. I wrote early from youth, spirits, and vanity; and from both the last when the first no longer existed. I now shudder when I reflect on my own boldness; and with mortification, when I compare my own writings with those of any great authors. This is so true, that I question whether it would be possible for me to summon up courage to publish anything I have written, if I could recall time past, and should yet think as I think at present. So much for what is over and out of my power. As to writing now, I have totally forsworn the profession, for two solid reasons. One I have already told you; and it is, that I know my own writings are trifling and of no depth. The other is, that, light and futile as they were, I am sensible they are better than I could compose now. I am aware of the decay of the middling parts I had, and others may be still more sensible of it. How do I know but I am superannuated? nobody will be so coarse as to tell me so; but if I published dotage, all the world would tell me so. And who but runs that risk who is an author after seventy? What happened to the greatest author of this age, and who certainly retained a very considerable portion of his abilities for ten years after my age? Voltaire, at eighty-four, I think, went to Paris to receive the incense, in person, of his countrymen, and to be witness of their admiration of a tragedy he had written at that Methusalem age. Incense he did receive till it choked him; and, at the exhibition of his play, he was actually crowned with laurel in the box where he sat. But what became of his poor play? It died as soon as he did – was buried with him; and no mortal, I dare to say, has ever read a line of it since, it was so bad.

As I am neither by a thousandth part so great, nor a quarter so little, I will herewith send you a fragment that an accidental rencontre set me upon writing, and which I found so flat, that I would not finish it. Don't believe that I am either begging praise by the stale artifice of hoping to be contradicted; or that I think there is any occasion to make you discover my caducity.[1] No; but the fragment contains a curiosity – English verses written by a French Prince of the blood,[2] and which at first I had a mind to add to my "Royal and Noble Authors;" but as he was not a royal author of ours, and as I could not please myself with an account of him, I shall revert to my old resolution of not exposing my pen's grey hairs.

Of one passage I must take notice; it is a little indirect sneer at our crowd of authoresses. My choosing to send this to *you*, is a proof that I think you an author, that is, a classic. But, in truth, I am nauseated by the Madams Piozzi, &c., and the host of novel-writers in petticoats, who think they imitate what is inimitable, "Evelina" and "Cecilia." Your candour, I know, will not agree with me, when I tell you I am not at all charmed with Miss Seward and Mr. Hayley piping to one another: but *you* I exhort, and would encourage to write; and flatter myself you will never be royally gagged and promoted to fold muslins, as has been lately wittily said on Miss Burney, in the List of five hundred living authors. *Your* writings promote virtues; and their increasing editions prove their worth and utility. If you question my sincerity, can you doubt my admiring you, when you have gratified my self-love so amply in your "Bas Bleu"?[3] Still, as much as I love your writings, I respect yet more your heart and your goodness. You are so good that I believe you would go to heaven, even though there were no Sunday, and only six *working* days in the week. Adieu, my best Madam!

---

1 Senility.
2 Charles (1394–1465), Duc d'Orléans, taken prisoner at Agincourt and then imprisoned in England for 25 years.
3 Hannah More published in 1784 *The Bas Bleu*, a verse celebration of the Blue Stockings, in which Walpole is featured.

VIII
HIS LITERARY CRITICISM

WALPOLE WAS WIDELY read in English, French and classical literature; his collection of books at Strawberry Hill grew to about eight thousand volumes, and by the end of his life was distributed between his main library and three other book rooms. He was an active annotator; many of his books are covered with marginalia, adding information or marking with a succession of dashes, crosses, asterisks, and exclamation marks his interest or disapproval. We have detailed records of the books in the library, which naturally reflect Walpole's interests: antiquities and topography, biography, poetry, the arts and belles-lettres. He ordered new books as they were published and frequently discussed them in his letters.

Walpole did not consider that he was living in a golden age of literature (letter 174), finding much contemporary poetry vapid and dismissing a variety of novels that are now considered canonical: his criticism is far from being unbiased. He had an aristocratic disdain for those writers who were compelled to earn their livelihood by their pen, relating with zest a scabrous tale of Fielding (letter 150) and dismissing Richardson's novels as "deplorably tedious lamentations ... pictures of high life as conceived by a bookseller" (letter 149). Sterne's *Tristram Shandy*, the talk of the town in 1760, he found "insipid" – "the humour is for ever attempted and missed" – and the clergyman author's fame and financial success are treated with scorn (letter 151); Goldsmith is merely "silly".[1] Like so many of his contemporaries Walpole was enthusiastic about Burney's *Evelina*, but less sympathetic towards her longer, later novels, which suffered in his view from Johnson's baleful influence on her prose (letter 152). He also commented regularly on contemporary drama, and particularly admired Sheridan's *The School for Scandal* (letters 165 and 166).

Johnson epitomised almost everything that Walpole disliked about contemporary literature (letters 153 to 158). He was a Tory, a hack writer, ill-mannered and puffed up by the praise of his circle of admirers (a number of whom Walpole knew socially). Walpole thought his prose style "teeth-breaking" (letter 134), measuring it by Addisonian standards of ease and fluidity. "The more one learns of

1 Letter to Cole, 27 April 1773 (YE 1:310).

Johnson, the more preposterous assemblage he appears of strong sense, of the lowest bigotry and prejudices, of pride, brutality, fretfulness, and vanity," he observed to Conway in 1785, having just read Boswell's newly published *Journal of a Tour to the Hebrides*.[1] Boswell himself, meanwhile, was "that quintessence of busybodies" (letter 160), whose adulation of Johnson Walpole found contemptible.

Always a warm partisan of the artistic achievements of his friends, Walpole extravagantly compared Lady Beauclerk to Michelangelo and his cousin the sculptor Anne Damer to Praxiteles. He praised the poetry of William Mason, whom posterity has consigned to obscurity, but also championed the genius of Thomas Gray (see heading to letter 195), predicting "what he published during his life will establish his fame as long as our language lasts" (letter 132). However, his praise was not unqualified. He offers his criticism of the *Odes* in letter 130 to Lord Lyttelton, concluding, "Your Lordship sees that I am no enthusiast to Mr. Gray: his great lustre hath not dazzled me, as his obscurity seems to have blinded his contemporaries."

Walpole had little interest in the roots of culture. Of medieval writers he took the sweeping view that "there is not a gleam of poetry in their compositions between the Scalds [Old Norse] and Chaucer" (letter 145). Chaucer he preferred in the modern dress of Dryden. But he was initially excited by two examples of medieval poetry that were in fact forgeries. The Gaelic poems of Ossian, purportedly translated by James Macpherson, were published between 1760 and 1763 and created a sensation at home and abroad (both Goethe and Napoleon would be admirers). Walpole, however, soon appreciated that they could not be authentic (letters 137 to 139). With the gifted and tragic Thomas Chatterton his dealings were short, but had farreaching consequences. In 1769 Chatterton had written from Bristol offering Walpole the enticing bait of an English medieval treatise on oil painting, together with some verses. Walpole's immediate response was encouraging (letter 140), but was followed once he had realised the manuscript was a forgery by a lost letter, which he always insisted was a gentle rebuttal. The following year the seventeen-year-old Chatterton committed suicide, and as the controversy over the poems raged back and forth over the following decade, Walpole had to deal with quite unfounded accusations that he bore some moral responsibility for Chatterton's death (letters 141 to 144).

1 Letter of 6 October 1785 (YE 39:437–8).

Returning to Walpole's other critical judgements, he was among the first to appreciate the greatness of Gibbon's masterpiece, *The Decline and Fall of the Roman Empire*: "You have, unexpectedly, given the world a classic history," he wrote in February 1776, though his relations with the author subsequently chilled (letters 167 to 169). The *Reflections on the Revolution in France*, he praised lavishly, no doubt because he shared its sentiments, but he also recognised the durable achievement of Burke's political pamphlet: "It is sublime, profound, and gay," he said, "the wit and satire are equally brilliant ... I should think it would be a classic book in all countries, except in *present* France" (letter 171). The last letter in this section analyses the quality of "grace" in writing, and concludes with a celebration of the letters of Madame de Sévigné. It may read as something of a lament for a lost age, but it also articulates some of the elements that make Walpole's own letters so engaging.

1. POPE

126. *Pope Publishes Bolingbroke.*

TO SIR HORACE MANN

17 May 1749.

... There is a Preface to this famous book,[1] which makes much more noise than the work itself. It seems, Lord Bolingbroke had originally trusted Pope with the copy, to have half-a-dozen printed for particular friends. Pope, who loved money infinitely beyond any friend, got fifteen hundred copies printed privately, intending to outlive Bolingbroke, and make great advantage of them: and not only did this, but altered the copy at his pleasure, and even made different alterations in different copies. Where Lord Bolingbroke had strongly flattered their common friend Lyttelton, Pope suppressed the panegyric: where, in compliment to Pope, he had softened the satire on Pope's great friend, Lord Oxford, Pope reinstated the abuse. The first part of this transaction is recorded in the Preface; the two latter facts are reported by Lord Chesterfield and Lyttelton, the latter of whom went to Bolingbroke to ask how he

---

1 Bolingbroke's *Letters on the Spirit of Patriotism; on the Idea of a Patriot King; and on the State of Parties at the Accession of King George the First* had been published a few weeks before Walpole's letter.

had forfeited his good opinion. In short, it is comfortable to us people of moderate virtue to hear these demigods, and patriots, and philosophers, inform the world of each other's villainies. What seems to make Lord Bolingbroke most angry, and I suppose does, is Pope's having presumed to correct his work. As to his printing so many copies, it certainly was a compliment, and the more profit (which however could not be immense) he expected to make, the greater opinion he must have conceived of the merit of the work: if one had a mind to defend Pope, should not one ask if any body ever blamed Virgil's executors for not burning the Æneid,[1] as he ordered them? Warburton, I hear, does design to defend Pope; and my uncle Horace[2] to answer the book: his style, which is the worst in the world, must be curious, in opposition to the other. . . .

2. SWIFT

127. *The Journal to Stella.*

TO GEORGE MONTAGU, ESQ.

Strawberry Hill, 20 June 1766.

. . . There are two new volumes, too, of Swift's Correspondence,[3] that will not amuse you less in another way, though abominable, for there are letters of twenty persons now alive; fifty of Lady Betty Germain, one that does her great honour, in which she defends her friend my Lady Suffolk,[4] with all the spirit in the world, against that brute, who hated everybody that he hoped would get him a mitre, and did not. There is one [letter] to his Miss Van Homrigh [Vanessa], from which I think it plain he lay with her, notwithstanding his supposed incapacity, yet not doing much honour to that capacity, for he says he can drink coffee but once a week, and I think

1 Walpole noted that the analogy of Virgil came from a pamphlet published in defence of Pope's conduct, *An Apology for the Late Mr. Pope* (1749,) which Walpole attributed to Joseph Spence (1699–1768), friend of Pope and collector of literary anecdotes.
2 Walpole's uncle Horatio Walpole (1678–1757), Baron Walpole of Wolterton, politician and diplomatist. William Warburton (see letter III, p. 173, n. 1) was Pope's executor and editor, and a celebrated controversialist.
3 *Letters Written by the late Jonathan Swift, D.D., Dean of St. Patrick's, Dublin*, forming volumes 10 to 13 of John Hawkesworth's quarto edition of Swift's *Works* (1755–68).
4 See letter 36, p. 63, n. 1.

you will see very clearly what he means by coffee. His own journal sent to Stella during the four last years of the Queen, is a fund of entertainment. You will see his insolence in full colours, and, at the same time, how daily vain he was of being noticed by the Ministers he affected to treat arrogantly. His panic at the Mohocks[1] is comical; but what strikes one, is bringing before one's eyes the incidents of a curious period. He goes to the rehearsal of "Cato," and says the *drab* that acted Cato's daughter could not say her part. This was only Mrs. Oldfield. I was saying before George Selwyn, that this journal put me in mind of the present time, there was the same indecision, irresolution, and want of system; but I added, "There is nothing new under the sun." "No," said Selwyn, "nor under the grandson." ... Yours ever.

3. BERKELEY

128. *Tar Water.*

TO SIR HORACE MANN

29 May 1744.

... We are now mad about tar-water, on the publication of a book that I will send you, written by Dr. Berkeley, Bishop of Cloyne.[2] The book contains every subject from tar-water to the Trinity; however, all the women read, and understand it no more than they would if it were intelligible. A man came into an apothecary's shop the other day, "Do you sell tar-water?" "Tar-water!" replied the apothecary, "why, I sell nothing else!" Adieu!

1 A London street gang of violent but allegedly well-born criminals.
2 George Berkeley (1685–1753), Bishop of Cloyne and philosopher. His book had first been published the previous month under the title *Siris: A Chain of Philosophical Reflections and Inquiries Concerning the Virtues of Tar Water.*

4. THOMSON AND AKENSIDE

129. *"Tame Genius's."*

TO SIR HORACE MANN

Arlington Street, 29 March 1745.

... The town flocks to a new play of Thomson's called "Tancred and Sigismunda:"[1] it is very dull; I have read it. I cannot bear modern poetry; these refiners of the purity of the stage, and of the incorrectness of English verse, are most wofully insipid. I had rather have written the most absurd lines in Lee, than "Leonidas" or "The Seasons;" as I had rather be put into the round-house for a wrong-headed quarrel, than sup quietly at eight o'clock with my grandmother. There is another of these tame genius's, a Mr. Akenside, who writes Odes: in one he has lately published, he says, "Light the tapers, urge the fire." Had not you rather make gods "jostle in the dark," than light the candles for fear they should break their heads? One Russel, a mimic, has a puppet-show to ridicule Operas; I hear, very dull, not to mention its being twenty years too late: it consists of three acts, with foolish Italian songs burlesqued in Italian.

There is a very good quarrel on foot between two duchesses: she of Queensberry sent to invite Lady Emily Lenox[2] to a ball: her Grace of Richmond, who is wonderfully cautious since Lady Caroline's elopement [with Mr. Fox], sent word, "she could not determine." The other sent again the same night: the same answer. The Queensberry then sent word, that she had made up her company, and desired to be excused from having Lady Emily's; but at the bottom of the card wrote, "Too great a trust." You know how mad she is, and how capable of such a stroke. There is no declaration of war come out from the other Duchess; but, I believe it will be made a national quarrel of the whole illegitimate royal family.

It is the present fashion to make conundrums: there are books of them printed, and produced at all assemblies: they are full silly enough to be made a fashion. I will tell you the three most renowned: "Why is my Lord Granville like a fumbler? Because he is half in and

---

1 *Tancred and Sigismunda*, a tragedy by the poet James Thomson (1700–48), author of *The Seasons*.
2 Second daughter of Charles, Duke of Richmond. – WALPOLE. The 2nd Duke of Richmond was the son of an illegitimate son of Charles II. For the Duchess of Queensberry, see letter 95, p. 156, n. 1.

half out." "Why is my uncle Horace like two people conversing? –
Because he is both teller and auditor." This was Winnington's.
"Why is my Lady Sandys like a man in armour? Because she carries
a cuirass: i.e. queer-arse."

Well, I had almost forgot to tell you a most extraordinary impertinence of your Florentine Marquis Riccardi. About three weeks
ago, I received a letter by Monsieur Wasner's footman from the marquis. He tells me most cavalierly, that he has sent me seventy-seven
antique gems to sell for him, by the way of Paris, not caring it should
be known in Florence. He will have them sold altogether, and the
lowest price two thousand pistoles. You know what no-acquaintance
I had with him. I shall be as frank as he, and not receive them. If
I did, they might be lost in sending back, and then I must pay his
two thousand *doppie di Spagna*. The refusing to receive them is positively all the notice I shall take of it.

I inclose what I think a fine piece on my father: it was written by
Mr. Ashton,[1] whom you have often heard me mention as a particular
friend. You see how I try to make out a long letter, in return for your
kind one, which yet gave me great pain by telling me of your fever.
My dearest Sir, it is terrible to have illness added to your other
distresses!

I will take the first opportunity to send Dr. Cocchi his translated
book; I have not yet seen it myself.

Adieu! my dearest child! I write with a house full of relations, and
must conclude. Heaven preserve you and Tuscany.

5. GRAY

130. *The Odes Criticised.*

TO GEORGE LORD LYTTELTON[2]

My Lord,   Strawberry Hill, 25 August 1757.

It is a satisfaction one can't often receive, to show a thing of great
merit to a man of great taste. Your Lordship's approbation is

1 Ashton's *A Character of the Life and Administration of the Late . . . Earl of Orford.* For
Ashton see letter 1, p. 6, n. 4. Walpole noted that it was printed in the public papers.
2 George, 1st Baron Lyttelton (1709–73), politician, writer, and creator of the landscape garden at Hagley Hall, Worcestershire.

conclusive, and it stamps a disgrace on the age, who have not given themselves the trouble to see any beauties in these Odes of Mr. Gray.[1] They have cast their eyes over them, found them obscure, and looked no further, yet perhaps no compositions ever had more sublime beauties than are in each. I agree with your Lordship in preferring the last upon the whole; the three first stanzas and half, down to *agonising King*, are in my opinion equal to anything in any language I understand. Yet the three last of the first Ode please me very near as much. The description of Shakespeare is worthy Shakespeare: the account of Milton's blindness, though perhaps not strictly defensible, is very majestic. The character of Dryden's poetry is as animated as what it paints. I can even like the epithet *Orient;* as the East is the empire of fancy and poesy, I would allow its livery to be erected into a colour. I think *blue-eyed Pleasures* is allowable: when Homer gave eyes of what hue he pleased to his Queen-Goddesses, sure Mr. Gray may tinge those of their handmaids.

In answer to your Lordship's objection to *many-twinkling*, in that beautiful epode, I will quote authority to which you will yield. As Greek as the expression is, it struck Mrs. Garrick, and she says, on that whole picture, that Mr. Gray is the only poet who ever understood dancing.[2]

These faults I think I can defend, and can excuse others; even the general obscurity of the latter, for I do not see it in the first; the subject of it has been taken for music, – it is the Power and Progress of Harmonious Poetry. I think his objection to prefixing a title to it was wrong – that Mr. Cooke published an ode with such a title. If the Louis the Great, whom Voltaire has discovered in Hungary, had not disappeared from history himself, would not Louis Quatorze have annihilated him? I was aware that the second would at first have darknesses, and prevailed for the insertion of what notes there are, and would have had more. Mr. Gray said, whatever wanted explanation did not deserve it, but that sentence was never so far from being an axiom as in the present case. Not to mention how he had shackled himself with strophe, antistrophe, and epode[3] (yet acquitting himself nobly), the nature of prophecy forbade him naming his kings. To me they are apparent enough – yet I am far from thinking either

1 *Odes by Mr. Gray* (1757) was the first production of the Strawberry Hill Press.
2 David Garrick's wife Eva Maria Veigel (1724–1822) was a dancer.
3 The three elements of the Pindaric Ode.

piece perfect, though with what faults they have, I hold them in the first rank of genius and poetry. The second strophe of the first Ode is inexcusable, nor do I wonder your Lordship blames it; even when one does understand it, perhaps the last line is too turgid. I am not fond of the antistrophe that follows. In the second Ode he made some corrections for the worse. *Brave Urion* was originally *stern;* brave is insipid and common-place. In the third antistrophe, *leave me unblessed, unpitied*, stood at first, *leave your despairing Caradoc.* But the capital faults in my opinion are these – what punishment was it to Edward I. to hear that his grandson would conquer France? or is so common an event as Edward III. being deserted on his death-bed, worthy of being made part of a curse that was to avenge a nation. I can't cast my eye here, without crying out on those beautiful lines that follow, *Fair smiles the morn!* Though the images are extremely complicated, what painting in the whirlwind, likened to a lion lying in ambush for his evening prey, *in grim repose.* Thirst and hunger mocking Richard II. appear to me too ludicrously like the devils in "The Tempest," that whisk away the banquet from the shipwrecked Dukes. From thence to the conclusion of Queen Elizabeth's portrait, which he has faithfully copied from Speed, in the passage where she humbled the Polish Ambassador, I admire. I can even allow that image of Rapture hovering like an ancient grotesque, though it strictly had little meaning: – but there I take my leave – the last stanza has no beauties for me. I even think its obscurity fortunate, for the allusions to Spenser, Shakespeare, Milton, are not only weak, but the two last returning again, after appearing so gloriously in the first Ode, and with so much fainter colours, enervate the whole conclusion.

Your Lordship sees that I am no enthusiast to Mr. Gray: his great lustre hath not dazzled me, as his obscurity seems to have blinded his contemporaries. Indeed, I do not think that they ever admired him, except in his Churchyard, though the Eton Ode was far its superior, and is certainly not obscure. The Eton Ode is perfect: these of more masterly execution have defects, yet not to admire them is total want of taste. I have an aversion to tame poetry; at best, perhaps, the art is the sublimest of the *difficiles nugæ;* to measure or rhyme prose, is trifling without being difficult. ... Your Lordship's Admirer

And obedient humble Servant

131. *The Norse Odes.*

Arlington Street, 12 March 1768.

... Sterne has published two little volumes, called "Sentimental Travels." They are very pleasing, though too much dilated, and infinitely preferable to his tiresome "Tristram Shandy," of which I never could get through three volumes. In these there is great good-nature and strokes of delicacy. Gray has added to his poems three ancient Odes from Norway and Wales.[1] The subjects of the two first are grand and picturesque, and there is *his* genuine vein in them; but they are not interesting, and do not, like his other poems, touch any passion. Our human feelings, which he masters at will in his former pieces, are here not affected. Who can care through what horrors a Runic savage arrived at all the joys and glories they could conceive, the supreme felicity of boozing ale out of the skull of an enemy in Odin's hall? Oh! yes, just now perhaps these Odes would be tasted at many a contested election. Adieu! Yours ever.

132. *Immortality Assured.*

Arlington Street, 28 January 1772.

... Mr. Mason has shown me the relics of poor Mr. Gray. I am sadly disappointed at finding them so very inconsiderable. He always persisted, when I enquired about his writings, that he had nothing by him. I own I doubted. I am grieved he was so very near exact – I speak of my own satisfaction; as to his genius, what he published during his life will establish his fame as long as our language lasts, and there is a man of genius left. There is a silly fellow, I don't know who, that has published a volume of Letters on the English Nation, with characters of our modern authors.[2] He has talked such

1 Gray's three Odes, "The Fatal Sisters", "The Descent of Odin", and "The Triumphs of Owen", were published in his *Poems by Mr. Gray* (London, 1768). *A Sentimental Journey* by Laurence Sterne (1713–68) had been published on 27 February.
2 The anonymous author of *Letters Concerning the Present State of England* (1772) criticised Gray for learned obscurity, and praised Walpole as "one of the most agreeable, spirited and lively writers that this age has produced".

nonsense on Mr. Gray, that I have no patience with the compliments he has paid me. He must have an excellent taste! and gives me a woful opinion of my own trifles, when he likes them, and cannot see the beauties of a poet that ought to be ranked in the first line. . . .

133. *Gray's Letters.*

TO THE REV. WILLIAM MASON

Arlington Street, 14 December 1773.

. . . I communicated to you the reflections that naturally arose to my mind on reading your Work – but I prefer truth and justice to myself, and for a selfish reason too. I mean, I had rather exercise those virtues, than have my vanity gratified; for I doubt whether even you and la Rochefoucault will not find that the love of virtue itself is founded on self-love – at least I can say with the strictest veracity, that I never envied Gray or West their talents. I admired Gray's poetry as much as man ever did or will; I do wish that I had no more faults than they had! I must say too, that though I allow he loved me sincerely in the beginning of our friendship, I wish he had felt a little more patience for errors that were not meant to hurt him, and for that want of reflection in me which I regret as much as he condemned.[1] I have now done with that subject and will say no more on it. As I mean to be docile to your advice, whenever I have the pleasure of seeing you, we will read over the remainder of the letters together, and burn such as you disapprove of my keeping. Several of them I own I think worth preserving. They have infinite humour and wit, are the best proofs of his early and genuine parts, before he arrived at that perfection at which he aimed, and which thence appear to me the more natural. I have kept them long with pleasure, may have little time to enjoy them longer, but hereafter they may appear with less impropriety than they would in your work, which is to establish the rank of his reputation. At least I admire them so very much, that I should trust to the good taste of some few (were they mine) and despise any criticisms. . . .

---

1 See letters 197 and 198 for Walpole's account of the quarrel with Gray. Walpole provided Mason with letters from Gray that Mason used in his *Memoirs* of Gray (1775).

134. *Publication of Works.*

TO THE REV. WILLIAM MASON

Arlington Street, 3 April 1775.

Well! your book ["Memoirs of Gray"] is walking the town in midday. How it is liked, I do not yet know. Were I to judge from my own feelings, I should say there never was so entertaining or interesting a work: that it is the most perfect model of biography; and must make Tacitus, and Agricola too, detest you. But as the world and simple I are not often of the same opinion, it will perhaps be thought very dull. If it is, all we can do is to appeal to that undutiful urchin, Posterity, who commonly treats the judgment of its parents with contempt, though it has so profound a veneration for its most distant ancestors. As you have neither imitated the teeth-breaking diction of Johnson, nor coined slanders against the most virtuous names in story, like modern historians [Dalrymple and Macpherson], you cannot expect to please the *reigning* taste. Few persons have had time, from their politics, diversions, and gaming, to have read much of so large a volume, which they will keep for the summer, when they have full as much of nothing to do. Such as love poetry, or think themselves poets, will have hurried to the verses and been disappointed at not finding half a dozen more "Elegies in a Churchyard." A few fine gentlemen will have read one or two of the shortest letters, which not being exactly such as they write themselves, they will dislike or copy next post; they who wish or intend to find fault with Gray, you, or even me, have, to be sure, skimmed over the whole, except the Latin for even spite, *non est tanti* –. The Reviewers, no doubt, are already writing against you; not because they have read the whole, but because one's own name is always the first thing that strikes one in a book. The Scotch will be more deliberate, but not less angry; and if not less angry, not more merciful. Every Hume,[1] however spelt, will I don't know what do; I should be sorry to be able to guess what. I have already been asked, why I did not prevent publication of the censure on David? The truth is (as you know) I never saw the whole together till now, and not that part; and if I had, why ought I to have prevented it? Voltaire will cast an *imbelle*

---

1   A reference to the playwright and historian John Home (1722–1808) as opposed to the philosopher and historian David Hume (1711–76).

javelin *sine ictu* at Gray, for he loves to depreciate a *dead* great author, even when unprovoked, – even when he has commended him alive, or before he was so vain and so envious as he is now. The Rousseaurians will imagine that I interpolated the condemnation of his Eloise. In short, we shall have many sins laid to our charge, of which we are innocent; but what can the malicious say against the innocent but what is not true?

I am here in brunt to the storm; you sit serenely aloof and smile at its sputtering. So should I too, were I out of sight, but I hate to be stared at, and the object of whispers before my face. The Maccaronis will laugh out, for you say I am still in the fashionable world. – What! they will cry, as they read while their hair is curling, – that old soul; for old and old-fashioned are synonymous in the vocabulary of mode, alas! Nobody is so sorry as I to be in the world's fashionable purlieus; still, in truth, all this is a joke and touches me little. I seem to myself a Strulbrug, who have lived past my time, and see almost my own life written before my face while I am yet upon earth, and as it were the only one of my contemporaries with whom I began the world. Well; in a month's time there will be little question of Gray, and less of me. America and feathers and masquerades will drive us into libraries, and there I am well content to live as an humble companion to Gray and you; and, thank my stars, not on the same shelf with the Macphersons and Dalrymples. . . .

135. *Comparative Merits.*

TO THE REV. WILLIAM COLE

Strawberry Hill, 10 December 1775.

I was very sorry to have been here, dear Sir, the day you called on me in town. It is so difficult to uncloister you, that I regret not seeing you when you are out of your own *ambry*. I have nothing new to tell you that is very old; but you can inform me of something within your own district. Who is the author, E. B. G. of a version of Mr. Gray's Latin Odes into English, and of an Elegy on my wolf-devoured dog, poor Tory?[1] a name you will marvel at in a dog of mine; but his

---

1 *The Latin Odes of Mr. Gray, in English Verse, with an Ode on the Death of a favourite Spaniel* (1775), by Edward Burnaby Greene (d. 1788).

godmother was the widow of Alderman Parsons, who gave him at
Paris to Lord Conway, and he to me. The author is a poet; but he
makes me blush, for he calls Mr. Gray and me *congenial pair*. Alas!
I have no genius; and if any symptom of talent, so inferior to Gray's,
that Milton and Quarles might as well be coupled together. We rode
over the Alps in the same chaise, but Pegasus drew on his side, and
a cart-horse on mine. I am too jealous of his fame to let us be coupled
together. This author says he has lately printed at Cambridge a Latin
translation of the Bards; I should be much obliged to you for it. . . .

6. PERCY

136. *The Reliques.*

TO THE REV. WILLIAM COLE

Strawberry Hill, 9 March 1765.

. . . In return for your obliging offer, I can acquaint you with a
delightful publication of this winter, A Collection of Old Ballads
and Poetry, in three volumes, many from Pepys's Collection at Cambridge.[1] There were three such published between thirty and forty
years ago, but very carelessly, and wanting many in this set: indeed,
there were others, of a looser sort, which the present editor [Dr.
Percy], who is a clergyman, thought it decent to omit. . . .

7. OSSIAN

137. *Ossian and Ballads.*

TO SIR DAVID DALRYMPLE

Strawberry Hill, 3 February 1760.

I am much obliged to you, Sir, for the Irish poetry:[2] they are
poetry, and resemble that of the East; that is, they contain natural
images and natural sentiment elevated, before rules were invented
to make poetry difficult and dull. The transitions are as sudden as

---

1 *Reliques of Ancient English Poetry* (1765) edited by Thomas Percy (1729–1811), later
Bishop of Dromore. The earlier *Collection of Old Ballads* (1723–5) was edited by
Ambrose Philips.
2 Specimens of the poems attributed to Ossian by James Macpherson, which were
to be published in Edinburgh in *Fragments of Ancient Poetry* (1760).

those in Pindar, but not so libertine; for they start into new thoughts on the subject, without wandering from it. I like particularly the expression of calling Echo, "Son of the Rock." The Monody is much the best. ... You have mentioned, Sir, Mr. Dyer's "Fleece." I own I think it a very insipid poem. His "Ruins of Rome" had great pictur-esque spirit, and his "Grongar Hill" was beautiful.[1] His "Fleece" I could never get through; and from thence I suppose never heard of Dr. Mackenzie.

Your idea of a collection of ballads for the cause of liberty is very public spirited. I wish, Sir, I could say I thought it would answer your view. Liberty, like other good and bad principles, can never be taught the people but when it is taught them by faction. The mob will never sing Lillibullero[2] but in opposition to some other mob. However, if you pursue the thought, there is an entire treasure of that kind in the library of Magdalen College, Cambridge.[3] It was collected by Pepys, Secretary of the Admiralty, and dates from the battle of Agincourt. Give me leave to say, Sir, that it is very comfort-able to me to find gentlemen of your virtue and parts attentive to what is so little the object of public attention now. The extinction of faction, that happiness to which we owe so much of our glory and success, may not be without some inconveniences. A free nation, perhaps, especially when arms are become so essential to our exist-ence as a free people, may want a little opposition: as it is a check that has preserved us so long, one cannot wholly think it dangerous; and though I would not be one to tap new resistance to a government with which I have no fault to find, yet it may not be unlucky hereafter if those who do not wish so well to it, would a little show themselves. They are not strong enough to hurt; they may be of service by keep-ing Ministers in awe. But all this is speculation, and flowed from the ideas excited in me by your letter, that is full of benevolence both to public and private. Adieu! Sir; believe that nobody has more esteem for you than is raised by each letter. ...

1 John Dyer (bap. 1699–1757) author of "The Fleece", a blank-verse poem in four books based on sheep and the wool trade, "The Ruins of Rome", and "Grongar Hill", an important poem in celebrating locality and prospect.
2 A popular 17th-century song, mocking the Irish: whistled by Uncle Toby in Sterne's *Tristram Shandy.*
3 The library of Samuel Pepys, with its collection of ballads, is still at Magdalene College, Cambridge.

138. *Inquiries.*

Strawberry Hill, 4 April 1760.

Sir,

As I have very little at present to trouble you with myself, I should have deferred writing till a better opportunity, if it were not to satisfy the curiosity of a friend; a friend whom you, Sir, will be glad to have made curious, as you originally pointed him out as a likely person to be charmed with the old Irish poetry you sent me. It is Mr. Gray, who is an enthusiast about those poems, and begs me to put the following queries to you; which I will do in his own words, and I may say truly, *Poeta loquitur.*

"I am so charmed with the two specimens of Erse poetry, that I cannot help giving you the trouble to inquire a little farther about them, and should wish to see a few lines of the original, that I may form some slight idea of the language, the measures and the rhythm.

"Is there anything known of the author or authors, and of what antiquity are they supposed to be?

"Is there any more to be had of equal beauty, or at all approaching to it?

"I have been often told, that the poem called Hardykanute[1] (which I always admired and still admire) was the work of somebody that lived a few years ago. This I do not at all believe, though it has evidently been retouched in places by some modern hand; but, however, I am authorised by this report to ask, whether the two poems in question are certainly antique and genuine. I make this inquiry in quality of an antiquary, and am not otherwise concerned about it; for if I were sure that any one now living in Scotland had written them, to divert himself and laugh at the credulity of the world, I would undertake a journey into the Highlands only for the pleasure of seeing him."

You see, Sir, how easily you may make our greatest southern bard travel northward to visit a brother. The young translator has nothing to do but to own a forgery, and Mr. Gray is ready to pack up his lyre, saddle Pegasus, and set out directly. But seriously, he, Mr. Mason, my Lord Lyttelton, and one or two more, whose taste the world

---

1   "Hardicanute", written by Elizabeth Halket (bap. 1677–1727).

allows, are in love with your Erse elegies: I cannot say in general they are so much admired – but Mr. Gray alone is worth satisfying. ...

139. *A Forgery.*

TO GEORGE MONTAGU, ESQ.

Arlington Street, 8 December 1761.

... Fingal is come out;[1] I have not yet got through it; not but it is very fine – yet I cannot at once compass an epic poem now. It tires me to death to read how many ways a warrior is like the moon, or the sun, or a rock, or a lion, or the ocean. Fingal is a brave collection of similes, and will serve all the boys at Eton and Westminster for these twenty years. I will trust you with a secret, but you must not disclose it; I should be ruined with my Scotch friends; in short, I cannot believe it genuine; I cannot believe a regular poem of six books has been preserved, uncorrupted, by oral tradition, from times before Christianity was introduced into the island. What! preserved unadulterated by savages dispersed among mountains, and so often driven from their dens, so wasted by wars civil and foreign! Has one man ever got all by heart? I doubt it; were parts preserved by some, other parts by others? Mighty lucky, that the tradition was never interrupted, nor any part lost – not a verse, not a measure, not the sense! luckier and luckier. I have been extremely qualified myself lately for this Scotch memory; we have had nothing but a coagulation of rains, fogs, and frosts, and though they have clouded all understanding, I suppose, if I had tried, I should have found that they thickened, and gave great consistence to my remembrance. ...

---

1 Macpherson's epic poem *Fingal*, whose authenticity as a Gaelic poem was the subject of immediate controversy, had just been published.

8. CHATTERTON

140. *A Courteous Letter.*

TO MR. THOMAS CHATTERTON[1]

Arlington Street, 28 March 1769.

Sir,

I cannot but think myself singularly obliged by a gentleman with whom I have not the pleasure of being acquainted, when I read your very curious and kind letter, which I have this minute received. I give you a thousand thanks for it, and for the very obliging offer you make me, of communicating your MSS. to me. What you have already sent me is very valuable, and full of information; but instead of correcting you, Sir, you are far more able to correct me. I have not the happiness of understanding the Saxon language, and without your learned notes should not have been able to comprehend Rowley's text.

As a second edition of my Anecdotes was published but last year, I must not flatter myself that a third will be wanted soon; but I shall be happy to lay up any notices you will be so good as to extract for me, and send me at your leisure; for, as it is uncertain when I may use them, I would by no means borrow and detain your MSS.

Give me leave to ask you where Rowley's poems are to be found? I should not be sorry to print them; or at least, a specimen of them, if they have never been printed.

The Abbot John's verses that you have given me, are wonderful for their harmony and spirit, though there are some words I do not understand.

You do not point out exactly the time when he lived, which I wish to know, as I suppose it was long before John Ab Eyck's discovery of oil-painting. If so, it confirms what I had guessed, and have hinted in my Anecdotes, that oil-painting was known here much earlier than that discovery or revival.

I will not trouble you with more questions now, Sir, but flatter myself from the humanity and politeness you have already shown me, that you will sometimes give me leave to consult you. I hope,

---

1 This letter is Walpole's initial enthusiastic response to the manuscript account of the rise of painting in England, allegedly written by Thomas Rowley in 1469, sent to Walpole by the then 16-year-old Thomas Chatterton (1752–70) – and before he had shown the manuscripts to Gray and Mason, who confirmed that they were forgeries.

too, you will forgive the simplicity of my direction, as you have
favoured me with no other.

I am, Sir,

Your much obliged

And obedient humble servant,

Hor. Walpole.

141. *Tyrrwhit's Edition.*

TO THE REV. WILLIAM MASON

17 February 1777.

I do not know whether you will value the execution of a promise,
when the letter is observed and not the spirit. I write only because
you desired it, and that I said I would; neither the literary nor political world furnish much matter. I have read the Goat's Beard: the
lines on Charles II. are very good, and there is true humour here and
there; but the humour is often missed, and I think the whole much
too long – it is far inferior to "Variety."[1] Mr. Tyrrwhit has at last
published the Bristol poems.[2] He does not give up the antiquity, yet
fairly leaves everybody to ascribe them to Chatterton, if they please,
which I think the internal evidence must force every one to do,
unless the amazing prodigy of Chatterton's producing them should
not seem a larger miracle than Rowley's and Canning's anticipation
of the style of very modern poetry. Psalmanazar alone seems to
have surpassed the genius of Chatterton, and when that lad could
perform such feats, as he certainly did, what difficulty is there in
believing that Macpherson forged the cold skeleton of an epic
poem, that is more insipid than "Leonidas"? Mr. Tyrrwhit seems to
have dreaded drawing himself into a controversy, which joys me,
who dreaded being drawn into one too. . . .

---

1 "The Goat's Beard" and "Variety" were both poems by William Whitehead (bap.
1715–85), Poet Laureate. Mason in 1788 provided a Memoir of Whitehead to a third
and concluding volume of Whitehead's poems, which he probably edited.
2 Thomas Tyrwhitt (1730–86) edited *Poems, Supposed to have been Written at Bristol
in the Fifteenth Century* . . . (1777), in which he reserved judgement as to the poems'
authenticity. He later accepted them as forgeries. George Psalmanazar (1679–1763)
was a literary forger.

142. Accusation Refuted.

TO THE REV. WILLIAM COLE

Strawberry Hill, 19 June 1777.

I thank you for your notices, dear Sir, and shall remember that on Prince William.[1] I did see the "Monthly Review,"[2] but hope one is not guilty of the death of every man who does not make one the dupe of a forgery. I believe M'Pherson's success with "Ossian" was more the ruin of Chatterton than I. Two years passed between my doubting the authenticity of Rowley's poems and his death. I never knew he had been in London till some time after he had undone and poisoned himself there. The poems he sent me were transcripts in his own hand, and even in that circumstance he told a lie: he said he had them from the very person at Bristol to whom he had given them. If any man was to tell you that monkish rhymes had been dug up at Herculaneum, which was destroyed several centuries before there was any such poetry, should you believe it? Just the reverse is the case of Rowley's pretended poems. They have all the elegance of Waller and Prior, and more than Lord Surrey – but I have no objection to anybody believing what he pleases. I think poor Chatterton was an astonishing genius – but I cannot think that Rowley foresaw metres that were invented long after he was dead, or that our language was more refined at Bristol in the reign of Henry V. than it was at Court under Henry VIII. One of the chaplains of the Bishop of Exeter has found a line of Rowley in Hudibras – the monk might foresee that too! The prematurity of Chatterton's genius is, however, full as wonderful, as that such a prodigy as Rowley should never have been heard of till the eighteenth century. The youth and industry of the former are miracles, too, yet still more credible. There is not a symptom in the poems, but the old words, that savours of Rowley's age – change the old words for modern, and the whole construction is of yesterday. . . .

1 An antiquarian query about a medieval tomb on which Cole had been assisting Walpole.
2 Cole had told Walpole of the *Monthly Review* for May 1777, which claimed misleadingly that Chatterton had committed suicide "soon after" Walpole had written to Chatterton questioning the authenticity of his manuscripts.

143. *Answer to Critics.*

TO THE REV. WILLIAM MASON

Strawberry Hill, 24 July 1778.

. . . It is not unlucky that I have got something to divert my mind; for I can think on other subjects when I have them. I am at last forced to enter into the history of the supposed Rowley's Poems. I must write on it, nay, what is more, print, not directly, controversially, but in my own defence. Some jackanapes at Bristol (I don't know who) has published Chatterton's Works;[1] and I suppose to provoke me to tell the story, accuses me of treating that marvellous creature with contempt; which having supposed, contrary to truth, he invites his readers to feel indignation at me. It has more than once before been insinuated that his disappointment from me contributed to his horrid fate. You know how gently I treated him. He was a consummate villain, and had gone enormous lengths before he destroyed himself. It would be cruel indeed, if one was to be deemed the assassin of every rogue that miscarries in attempting to cheat one; in short the attack is now too direct not to be repelled. Two months ago I did draw up an account of my share in that affair. That Narrative and an Answer to this insult which I wrote last night I will publish, signed with my name, but not advertised by it.[2] It will reach all those that take part in the controversy, and I do not desire it should go farther. These things I will have transcribed, and ask your leave to send you before they go to the press. I am in no hurry to publish, nor is the moment a decent one; yet I embrace it, as I shall be the less talked over. I hate controversy, yet to be silent now, would be interpreted guilt; and it is impossible to be more innocent than I was in that affair. Being innocent, I take care not to be angry. Mr. Tyrwhitt, one of the enthusiasts to Rowley, has recanted, and published against the authenticity of the Poems. The new publisher of Chatterton's undisputed works seems to question the rest too, so his attack on me must be mere impertinent curiosity. One satisfaction will arise from all this; the almost incredible genius of Chatterton

1 *Miscellanies in Prose and Verse by Thomas Chatterton* (1778), edited by John Broughton.
2 *A Letter to the Editor of the Miscellanies of Thomas Chatterton*, printed at the Strawberry Hill Press in 1778.

will be ascertained. He had generally genuine powers of poetry; often wit, and sometimes natural humour. I have seen reams of his writing, besides what is printed. He had a strong vein of satire, too, and very irascible resentment; yet the poor soul perished before he was nineteen![1] He had read, and written, as if he was fourscore, yet it cannot be discovered when or where. He had no more principles than if he had been one of all our late Administrations. He was an instance that a complete genius and a complete rogue can be formed before a man is of age. The world has generally the honour of their education, but it is not necessary; you see by Chatterton, that an individual could be as perfect as a senate! Adieu!

144. *Chattertonian Controversy.*

TO THE REV. WILLIAM COLE

Berkeley Square, 30 December 1781.

. . . You will be surprised when I tell you, that I have only dipped into Mr. Bryant's book, and lent the Dean's before I had cut the leaves, though I had peeped into it enough to see that I shall not read it.[2] Both he and Bryant are so diffuse on our antiquated litera-ture, that I had rather believe in Rowley than go through their proofs. Mr. Warton and Mr. Tyrwhitt have more patience, and intend to answer them – and so the controversy will be two hundred years out of my reach. Mr. Bryant, I did find, begged a vast many questions, which proved to me his own doubts. Dr. Glynn's foolish evidence made me laugh, and so did Mr. Bryant's sensibility *for me;* he says Chatterton treated me very *cruelly* in one of his writings. I am sure I did not feel it so. I suppose Bryant means under the title of Baron of Otranto, which is written with humour.[3] I must have been the sensitive plant if anything in that character had hurt me! Mr. Bryant too, and the Dean, as I see by extracts in the papers, have decorated Chatterton with sanctimonious honour – think of that

1 Chatterton was only 17 at the time of his death.
2 Jacob Bryant's *Observations upon the Poems of Thomas Rowley* (1781) and Dean Jere-miah Milles's *Poems . . . by Thomas Rowley* (1782) both argued for the authenticity of the poems.
3 Chatterton lampooned Walpole in his "Memoirs of a Sad Dog" (1770) as "the redoubted Baron Otranto, who has spent his whole life in conjectures".

young rascal's note, when, summing up his gains and losses by writing for and against Beckford, he says, "Am glad he is dead by 3*l.* 13*s.* 6*d.*" *There* was a lad of too nice honour to be capable of forgery! and a lad who, they do not deny, forged the poems in the style of "Ossian," and fifty other things. In the parts I did read, Mr. Bryant, as I expected, reasons admirably, and staggered me; but when I took up the poems called Rowley's again, I protest I cannot see the smallest air of antiquity but the old words. The whole texture is conceived on ideas of the present century. The liberal manner of thinking of a monk so long before the Reformation is as stupendous; and where he met with Ovid's Metamorphoses, Eclogues, and plans of Greek tragedies, when even Caxton, a printer, took Virgil's "Æneid" for so rare a novelty, are not less incomprehensible: though on these things I speak at random, nor have searched for the era when the Greek and Latin classics came again to light – at present I imagine long after our Edward the Fourth.

Another thing struck me in my very cursory perusal of Bryant. He asks where Chatterton could find so much knowledge of English events? I could tell him where he might, by a very natural hypothesis, though merely an hypothesis. It appears by the evidence, that Canninge left six chests of manuscripts, and that Chatterton got possession of some or several. Now, what was therein *so probably* as a diary drawn up by Canninge himself, or some churchwarden or wardens, or by a monk or monks? Is anything more natural than for such a person, amidst the events at Bristol, to set down such other public facts as happened in the rest of the kingdom? Was not such almost all the materials of our ancient story? There is actually such an one, with some curious collateral facts, if I am not mistaken, – for I write by memory, – in the "History of Furnese" or "Fountain's Abbey," I forget which: if Chatterton found such an one, did he want the extensive literature on which so much stress is laid? Hypothesis for hypothesis, – I am sure this is as rational an one as the supposition that six chests were filled with poems never else heard of.

These are my indigested thoughts on this matter – not that I ever intend to digest them – for I will not, at sixty-four, sail back into the fourteenth and fifteenth centuries, and be drowned in an ocean of monkish writers of those ages or of this! Yours most sincerely.

9. WARTON

145. *"History of Poetry"* – *Goldsmith's Death.*

TO THE REV. WILLIAM MASON

Strawberry Hill, 7 April 1774.

Well, I have read Mr. Warton's book;[1] and shall I tell you what I think of it? I never saw so many entertaining particulars crowded together with so little entertainment and vivacity. The facts are overwhelmed by one another, as Johnson's sense is by words: they are all equally strong. Mr. Warton has amassed all the parts and learning of four centuries, and all the impression that remains is, that those four ages had no parts or learning at all. There is not a gleam of poetry in their compositions between the Scalds and Chaucer: nay I question whether they took their metres for anything more than rules for writing prose. In short, it may be the genealogy of versification with all its intermarriages and anecdotes of the family; but Gray's and your plan might still be executed. I am sorry Mr. Warton has contracted such an affection for his materials, that he seems almost to think that not only Pope, but Dryden himself have added few beauties to Chaucer.

The republic of Parnassus has lost a member; Dr. Goldsmith is dead of a purple fever, and I think might have been saved if he had continued James's powder, which had had much effect, but his physician interposed. His numerous friends neglected him shamefully at last, as if they had no business with him when it was too serious to laugh. He had lately written Epitaphs for them all, some of which hurt, and perhaps made them not sorry that his own was the first necessary.[2] The poor soul had sometimes parts, though never common sense. . . .

---

1 *The History of English Poetry* (1774–81) by Thomas Warton (1728–90), of which the first volume had been published the previous month.
2 Oliver Goldsmith had died three days earlier. James's Powder was a popular fever powder. Goldsmith's Epitaphs were in "Retaliation", which though written in February would not be published until later in April: Walpole may have seen a manuscript copy.

10. CHURCHILL

146. *His Death.*

TO SIR HORACE MANN

Arlington Street, 15 November 1764.

Churchill the poet[1] is dead, – to the great joy of the Ministry and the Scotch, and to the grief of very few indeed, I believe; for such a friend is not only a dangerous, but a ticklish possession. The next revolution would have introduced the other half of England into his satires, for no party could have promoted him, and woe had betided those who had left him to shift for himself on Parnassus! He had owned that his pen itched to attack Mr. Pitt and Charles Townshend; and neither of them are men to have escaped by their steadiness and uniformity. This meteor blazed scarce four years; for his "Rosciad" was subsequent to the accession of the present King, before which his name was never heard of; and what is as remarkable, he died in nine days after his antagonist, Hogarth. Were I Charon, I should without scruple, give the best place in my boat to the latter, who was an original genius. Churchill had great powers; but, besides the facility of outrageous satire, almost all his compositions were wild and extravagant, executed on no plan, and void of the least correction. Many of his characters were obscure even to the present age; and some of the most known were so unknown to *him*, that he has missed all resemblance; of which Lord Sandwich is a striking instance. He died of a drunken debauch at Calais,[2] on a visit to his friend Wilkes, who is going to write notes to his Works. But he had lived long enough for himself at least for his reputation and his want of it, for his works began to decrease considerably in vent. But he has left some Sermons, for he wrote even sermons; but lest they should do any good, and for fear they should not do some hurt, he had prepared a Dedication of them to Bishop Warburton, whose arrogance and venom had found a proper corrector in Churchill. I don't know whether this man's fame had extended to Florence; but you may judge of the noise he made in this part of the world by the following trait, which is a pretty instance of that good breeding on

1 Charles Churchill (1732–64), poet and political satirist, who had a public dispute with the artist William Hogarth, by whom he was caricatured as a drunken bear.
2 Actually Boulogne.

which the French pique themselves. My sister[1] and Mr. Churchill are in France; a Frenchman asked him if he was Churchill *le fameux poete*? "Non" – "Ma foi, monsieur, tant pis pour vous!" ...

11. DARWIN

147. *"The Botanic Garden."*

TO HANNAH MORE

Berkeley Square, 22 April 1789.

Dear Madam,
    As perhaps you have not yet seen the "Botanic Garden"[2] (which I believe I mentioned to you), I lend it you to read. The poetry, I think, you will allow most admirable; and difficult it was, no doubt. If you are not a naturalist, as well as a poetess, perhaps you will lament that so powerful a talent has been wasted to so little purpose; for where is the use of describing in verse what nobody can understand without a long prosaic explanation of every article? It is still more unfortunate that there is not a symptom of plan in the whole poem. The lady-flowers and their lovers enter in pairs or trios, or &c., as often as the couples in Cassandra, and you are not a whit more interested about one heroine and her swain than about another. The similes are beautiful, fine, and sometimes sublime: and thus the episodes will be better remembered than the mass of the poem itself, which one cannot call *the subject;* for could one call it a subject, if anybody had composed a poem on the matches formerly made in the Fleet, where, as Waitwell says, in "The Way of the World,"[3] they stood like couples in rows ready to begin a country dance? Still, I flatter myself, you will agree with me that the author is a great poet and could raise the passions, and possesses all the requisites of the art. I found but a single bad verse: in the last canto one line ends *e'relong.* You will perhaps be surprised at meeting a truffle converted into a nymph, and inhabiting a palace studded with emeralds and rubies like a saloon in the Arabian Nights! I had a more

1 Lady Maria Walpole, only child of Sir Robert Walpole Earl of Orford by his second wife, and married to Charles, son of General Charles Churchill. – WALPOLE.
2 *The Botanic Garden*, Part II (1789) by Erasmus Darwin (1731–1802).
3 Waitwell was the valet in William Congreve's comedy *The Way of the World* (1700). The Fleet prison was the venue for innumerable irregular weddings until they were stopped by Act of Parliament in 1753.

particular motive for sending this poem to *you:* you will find the bard espousing your poor Africans. There is besides, which will please you too, a handsome panegyric on the apostle of humanity, Mr. Howard.[1] . . .

12. RICHARDSON

148. *"Sir Charles Grandison."*

TO RICHARD BENTLEY, ESQ.

Arlington Street, 19 December 1753.

. . . There are two more volumes come out of "Sir Charles Grandison." I shall detain them till the last is published, and not think I postpone much of your pleasure. For my part, I stopped at the fourth; I was so tired of sets of people getting together, and saying, "Pray, Miss, with whom are you in love?" and of mighty good young men that convert your Mr. M*****'s in the twinkling of a sermon! – You have not been much more diverted, I fear, with Hogarth's book – 'tis very silly! – Palmyra[2] is come forth, and is a noble book; the prints finely engraved, and an admirable dissertation before it. My wonder is much abated: the Palmyrene empire which I had figured shrunk to a small trading city with some magnificent public buildings out of proportion to the dignity of the place.

The operas succeed pretty well; and music has so much recovered its power of charming, that there is started up a burletta at Covent Garden, that has half the vogue of the old Beggar's Opera: indeed there is a soubrette, called the Nicolina[3] who, besides being pretty, has more vivacity and variety of humour than ever existed in any creature.

1 John Howard (*c.* 1726–90), prison reformer.
2 The books discussed in this letter are Samuel Richardson's *Sir Charles Grandison*, of which volumes 5 and 6 had been published earlier that month; William Hogarth's *The Analysis of Beauty*; and Robert Wood's *The Ruins of Palmyra*, both very recently published.
3 Nicolina Giordani, who had appeared at Covent Garden in a comic Italian opera two nights before.

149. *Tedious Novels.*

Arlington Street, 20 December 1764.

... There is a Madame de Beaumont[1] who has lately written a very pretty novel, called "Lettres du Marquis du Roselle." It is imitated, too, from an English standard, and in my opinion a most woeful one; I mean the works of Richardson, who wrote those deplorably tedious lamentations, "Clarissa" and "Sir Charles Grandison," which are pictures of high life as conceived by a bookseller,[2] and romances as they would be spiritualised by a Methodist teacher: but Madame de Beaumont has almost avoided sermons, and almost reconciled sentiments and common sense. Read her novel – you will like it.

13. FIELDING
150. *Fielding at Supper.*

Arlington Street, 18 May 1749.

Dear George,
... Rigby[3] gave me as strong a picture of nature: he and Peter Bathurst t'other night carried a servant of the latter's, who had attempted to shoot him, before Fielding; who, to all his other vocations, has, by the grace of Mr. Lyttelton, added that of Middlesex justice. He sent them word he was at supper, that they must come next morning. They did not understand that freedom, and ran up, where they found him banqueting with a blind man, three Irishmen, and a whore, on some cold mutton and a bone of ham, both in one dish, and the cursedest dirty cloth! He never stirred nor asked them to sit. Rigby, who had seen him so often come to beg a guinea of Sir C. Williams, and Bathurst, at whose father's he had lived for victuals, understood that dignity as little, and pulled themselves chairs; on which he civilised.[4]

1 Wife of Monsieur Elie de Beaumont, a celebrated lawyer. – WALPOLE.
2 Richardson was not a bookseller but a printer. – WALPOLE.
3 For Richard Rigby see letter 101, p. 163, n. 4.
4 Sir Walter Scott described this anecdote of the novelist Henry Fielding as "humiliating", but its accuracy has been questioned. Walpole is the sole authority for it. The

Millar the bookseller has done very generously by him: finding
Tom Jones, for which he had given him six hundred pounds, sell so
greatly, he has since given him another hundred. . . .

14. STERNE

151. *"Tristram Shandy."*

TO SIR DAVID DALRYMPLE

Strawberry Hill, 4 April 1760.

. . . At present, nothing is talked of, nothing admired, but what
I cannot help calling a very insipid and tedious performance: it is a
kind of novel, called "The Life and Opinions of Tristram Shandy";[1]
the great humour of which consists in the whole narration always
going backwards. I can conceive a man saying that it would be droll
to write a book in that manner, but have no notion of his persevering
in executing it. It makes one smile two or three times at the beginning, but in recompense makes one yawn for two hours. The characters are tolerably kept up, but the humour is for ever attempted and
missed. The best thing in it is a Sermon, oddly coupled with a good
deal of bawdy, and both the composition of a clergyman. The man's
head, indeed, was a little turned before, now topsy-turvy with his
success and fame. Dodsley has given him six hundred and fifty
pounds for the second edition and two more volumes (which I suppose will reach backwards to his great-great-grandfather); Lord
Fauconberg, a donative of one hundred and sixty pounds a-year; and
Bishop Warburton gave him a purse of gold and this compliment
(which happened to be a contradiction), "that it was quite an original
composition, and in the true Cervantic vein": the only copy that ever
was an original, except in painting, where they all pretend to be so.[2]
Warburton, however, not content with this, recommended the book

---

blind man may have been Fielding's blind half-brother, the magistrate Sir John
Fielding (1721–80).
1 The first two volumes of Laurence Sterne's *The Life and Opinions of Tristram
Shandy, Gentleman* had been published by Robert Dodsley in early April 1760, having
been previously issued in York at the end of December 1759.
2 Thomas Belayse, 1st Earl Fauconberg of Newburgh (1699–1774), who according to
Sterne gave him £160 a year, was the patron of Sterne's living at Coxwold. The Yale
editors suggest that Warburton's gift may have been intended to discourage Sterne
from satirising him in future volumes.

to the bench of bishops, and told them Mr. Sterne, the author, was the English Rabelais. They had never heard of such a writer. Adieu!

15. FRANCES BURNEY
152 *"Cecilia."*

1 October 1782.

... "Cecilia,"[1] I did read, but, besides its being immeasurably long, and written in Dr. Johnson's unnatural phrase, I liked it far less than "Evelina." I did delight in Mr. Briggs, and in the droll names he calls the proud gentleman, whose name I forget. Morris, too, is well, and Meadows tolerable, and Lady Something Something and Miss Something; but all the rest are *outrés*. The great fault is that the authoress is so afraid of not making all her *dramatis personæ* act in character, that she never lets them say a syllable but what is to mark their character, which is very unnatural, at least in the present state of things, in which people are always aiming to disguise their ruling passions, and rather affect opposite qualities, than hang out their propensities. The old religious philosopher is a lunatic, and contributing nothing to the story, might be totally omitted, and had better be so. But I am most offended at the want of poetical justice. The proud gentleman and his proud wife ought to be punished and humbled; whereas the wife is rather exhibited as an amiable character. To say the truth, the last volume is very indifferent. ...

16. JOHNSON
153. *"Tour to the Western Isles."*

Arlington Street, 19 January 1775.

No; I will never read nonsense again with a settled resolution of being diverted! The "Miscellany" from Bath-Easton is ten degrees duller than a Magazine, and, which is wondrous, the Noble Authors

---

1 *Cecilia, or Memoirs of an Heiress*, the second novel of Frances Burney (1752–1840), had been published in June 1782.

it adds to my "Catalogue" are the best of this foolish Parnassus. There is one very pretty copy by Lord Palmerston; and the Duchess of Northumberland has got very jollily through her task.[1] I have scarce been better diverted by Dr. Johnson's "Tour to the Western Isles." What a heap of words to express very little! and though it is the least cumbrous of any style he ever used, how far from easy and natural! He hopes nobody but is glad that a boatful of sacrilege, a diverting sin! was shipwrecked. He believes in second sight, and laughs at poor Pennant for credulity![2] The King sent for the book in MS., and then wondering, said, "I protest, Johnson seems to be a Papist and a Jacobite!" – so he did not know why he had been made to give him a pension! . . .

154. Triple Tautology.

TO THE COUNTESS OF UPPER OSSORY

1 February 1779.

. . . I have always thought that he[3] was just the counterpart of Shakespeare; this, the first of writers, and an indifferent actor; that, the first of actors, and a woeful author. Posterity would believe me, who will see only his writings; and who will see those of another modern idol, far less deservedly enshrined, Dr. Johnson. I have been saying this morning, that the latter deals so much in triple tautology,[4] or the fault of repeating the same sense in three different phrases, that I believe it would be possible, taking the ground-work for all three, to make one of his "Ramblers" into three different papers, that

1 Henry Temple, 2nd Viscount Palmerston (1739–1802) and Elizabeth Percy, *née* Seymour (1716–76), Duchess of Northumberland, as members of the nobility, would qualify for inclusion in Walpole's *Catalogue of Royal and Noble Authors* (1758) on the strength of their appearance in *Poetical Amusements at a Villa near Bath*, an anthology of poems written for the literary salon of Anna Riggs Miller (1741–81) – later Lady Miller – at Batheaston, and published in January 1775. For Walpole's visit to her villa see letter 409.
2 Samuel Johnson's *A Journey to the Western Islands of Scotland* was published on 18 January 1775. It appeared to applaud the deaths of thieves lost at sea in a boat loaded with lead they had stolen from the roofs of Scottish cathedrals. Thomas Pennant (1726–98) was a writer and naturalist.
3 David Garrick.
4 Walpole collected his strictures on Johnson's prose style in his "General Criticism of Dr. Johnson's Writings", published in volume 4 of his collected *Works* (1798), pp. 361–2.

should all have exactly the same purport and meaning, but in different phrases. It would be a good trick for somebody to produce one and read it; a second would say, "Bless me, I have this very paper in my pocket, but in quite other diction"; and so a third. . . .

155. *"Life of Gray."*

TO THE REV. WILLIAM MASON

Berkeley Square, 27 January 1781.

. . . Mr. Gilpin[1] has sent me his book and dedication. I thank you for the latter being so moderate, yet he talks of my researches, which makes me smile; I know, as Gray would have said, how little I have *researched*, and what slender pretensions are mine to so pompous a term. *A-propos* to Gray, "Johnson's Life," or rather criticism on his Odes, is come out; a most wretched, dull, tasteless, *verbal* criticism, – yet, timid too.[2] But he makes amends, he admires Thomson and Akenside, and Sir Richard Blackmore, and has reprinted Dennis's "Criticism on Cato," to save time and swell his pay. In short, as usual, he has proved that he has no more ear than taste. Mrs. Montagu and all her Mænades intend to tear him limb from limb for despising their moppet Lord Lyttelton. . . .

156. *"Lives of the Poets."*

TO THE REV. WILLIAM MASON

Berkeley Square, 3 February 1781.

With Mr. Palgrave's leave I will answer the essential parts of your letter before I attend to his entertainment,[3] for which I am poorly qualified at present.

1 The 3rd edition of the *Essay on Prints* by William Gilpin (1724–1804), the writer on the picturesque, was dedicated to Walpole.
2 Johnson's Life of Gray in his *Prefaces, Biographical and Critical, to the Works of the English Poets* [*Lives of the Poets*], was not in fact published until May 1781 and Walpole must have seen an advance copy or transcript. Its trenchant criticisms of Gray caused considerable controversy.
3 In a recent letter Mason had asked Walpole to send him letters with which he could entertain William Palgrave, a Fellow of Pembroke College, Cambridge, who had arranged to stay with Mason at Mason's vicarage in Yorkshire.

I have not Dr. Johnson's "Lives": I made a conscience of not buying them. However, having a mind to be possessed of these last volumes (I never even dipped into their predecessors), I inquired if I could buy the "Lives" separately from the edition of the Poems; no, the whole are sixty volumes. My purse made a conscience of laying out so much money for criticisms I despise, and for bodies of poetry that I never shall read again, and printed in so small a type that I could not read them if I would. I will try if I can borrow Gray's "Life" for you, and will send it with Mr. Conway's pamphlet, and will consult Mr. Stonhewer. I think you will not deem the dull comment on Gray worth your notice; if you do, pray do not forget Soame Jenyns's "Ode" that is levelled at you both. . . .

157. *Feeble Criticism.*

TO THE REV. WILLIAM MASON

19 February 1781.

. . . I have not yet been able to get you "Gray's Life" [by Johnson]. My bookseller had blundered, and after trusting to him so long, he brought me the preceding volumes: but I am on a new scent, and hope at least to send you a transcript of that single life; though I wish you to see the whole set, nay, those old ones; I dipped into them and found that the tasteless pedant admires that wretched buffoon Dr. King, who is but a Tom Brown in rhyme; and says that "The Dispensary," that *chef d'œuvre*, can scarce make itself read. This is prejudice on both sides, equal to that monkish railer Père Garasse.[1] But Dr. Johnson has indubitably neither taste nor ear, criterion of judgment, but his old woman's prejudices; where they are wanting, he has no rule at all; he prefers Smith's poetic, but insipid and undramatic "Phædra and Hippolitus" to Racine's "Phédre," the finest tragedy in my opinion of the French Theatre, for, with Voltaire's leave, I think it infinitely preferable to "Iphigenie," and so I own I do "Britannicus," "Mahomet," "Alzire," and some others; but I will allow Johnson to dislike Gray, Garth, Prior – ay, and every genius we have had, when he cries up Blackmore, Thomson, Akenside, and Dr. King; nay, I am

1 William King (1663–1712) was a miscellaneous writer; *The Dispensary* by Samuel Garth (1660/1–1719) was first published in 1699 and was often reprinted; François Garasse (1585–1631) was a French Jesuit who was considered a virulent controversialist.

glad that the measure of our dulness is full. I would have this era stigmatise itself in every respect, and be a proverb to the nations around, and to future ages. We want but Popery to sanctify every act of blindness. Hume should burn the Works of Locke, and Johnson of Milton, and the Atheist and the Bigot join in the same religious rites, as they both were pensioned by the same piety. Oh! let us not have a ray of sense or throb of sensation left to distinguish us from brutes! let total stupefaction palliate our fall,[1] and let us resemble the Jews, who when they were to elect a God, preferred a calf! . . .

158. *"Life of Pope."*

TO THE REV. WILLIAM MASON

Strawberry Hill, 14 April 1781.

. . . Sir Joshua Reynolds has lent me Dr. Johnson's "Life of Pope,"[2] which Sir Joshua holds to be a *chef d'œuvre*. It is a most trumpery performance, and stuffed with all his crabbed phrases and vulgarisms, and much trash as anecdotes; you shall judge yourself. He says, that all he can discover of Pope's correspondent, Mr. Cromwell, is that he used to hunt in a tie-wig. The "Elegy on the Unfortunate Lady," he says, "signifies the amorous fury of a raving girl"; and yet he admires the subject of Eloisa's Epistle to Abelard. The machinery in "The Rape of the Lock," he calls "combinations of skilful genius with happy casuality," in English I guess a "lucky thought": publishing proposals is turned into "emitting" them. But the 66th page is still more curious: it contains a philosophic solution of Pope's not transcribing the whole "Iliad" as soon as he thought he should, and it concludes with this piece of bombast nonsense, "he that runs against time has an antagonist not subject to casualties." Pope's house here he calls "the house to which his residence afterwards procured so much celebration," and that "his vanity produced a grotto where necessity enforced a passage"; and that, "of his intellectual character, the constituent and fundamental principle was good sense, a prompt and intuitive perception of consonance and

1　Walpole's lament at the triumph of dullness among contemporary writers is reminiscent of Pope's *Dunciad*.
2　An advance copy or transcript, as Johnson's Life of Pope was published in volume 7 of the *Prefaces, Biographical and Critical* the following month.

propriety." Was poor good sense ever so unmercifully overlaid by a babbling old woman? How was it possible to marshal words so ridiculously? He seems to have read the ancients with no view but of pilfering polysyllables, utterly insensible to the graces of their simplicity, and these are called standards of biography! I forgot, he calls Lord Hervey's challenging Pulteney, "summoning him to a duel." Hurlothrumbo[1] talked plain English in comparison of this wight on stilts, but I doubt I have wearied you, – send me something to put my mouth in taste again.

17. BOSWELL

159. *"Account of Corsica."*

TO THOMAS GRAY

Arlington Street, 18 February 1768.

... Pray read the new Account of Corsica. What relates to Paoli will amuse you much.[2] There is a deal about the island and its divisions that one does not care a straw for. The author, Boswell, is a strange being, and, like Cambridge,[3] has a rage of knowing anybody that ever was talked of. He forced himself upon me at Paris in spite of my teeth and my doors, and I see has given a foolish account of all he could pick up from me about King Theodore.[4] He then took an antipathy to me on Rousseau's[5] account, abused me in the newspapers, and exhorted Rousseau to do so too: but as he came to see me no more, I forgave all the rest. I see he now is a little sick of

1 Hurlothrumbo, who was the main character and walked on stilts in a bombastic nonsense play of 1729.
2 *An Account of Corsica*, by James Boswell (1740–95), with its celebration of the achievements of the Corsican leader Pascal Paoli (1725–1807) had just been published, and the Yale editors note that Boswell sent Walpole a presentation copy later that month.
3 This name was not supplied in the first printing of this letter, but some editors have proposed Richard Owen Cambridge (1717–1802), poet, essayist, gossip, and near neighbour of Walpole.
4 Theodor von Neuhoff (1694–1756), an adventurer who was King of Corsica for six months in 1736, and later a prisoner in the Fleet, a debtors' prison. Walpole attempted to support him and erected a tablet to his memory.
5 Walpole had written a mock letter to Jean-Jacques Rousseau two years previously, purporting to be from the King of Prussia, Frederick the Great: see letter 351.

Rousseau himself; but I hope it will not cure him of his anger to me. However, his book will I am sure entertain you.[1] ...

160. *An Unwanted Caller.*

TO THE REV. WILLIAM MASON

22 May 1781.

... It was not from me, I assure you, that you have received any defence of Milton, nor do I know anything of it, but what you tell me, that it is in the "Memoirs of Hollis."[2] Boswell, that quintessence of busybodies, called on me last week, and was let in, which he should not have been, could I have foreseen it. After tapping many topics, to which I made as dry answers as an unbribed oracle, he vented his errand. "Had I seen Dr. Johnson's 'Lives of the Poets'?" I said, slightly, "No, not yet"; and so overlaid his whole impertinence. As soon as he could recover himself, with Caledonian sincerity, he talked of Macklin's new play ["The True-Born Scotchman"], and pretended to like it, which would almost make one suspect that he knows a dose of poison has already been administered; though, by the way, I hear there is little good in the piece, except the likeness of Sir Pertinax[3] to twenty thousand Scots. ...

161. *"Life of Johnson."*

TO MARY BERRY

Berkeley Square, 26 May 1791.

... The rest of my letter must be literary; for we have no news. Boswell's book is gossiping; but, having numbers of proper names, would be more readable, at least by me, were it reduced from two

1 To this Gray replied on 25 February, "The pamphlet proves what I have always maintained, that any fool may write a most valuable book by chance, if he will only tell us what he heard and saw with veracity. Of Mr. Boswell's truth I have not the least suspicion, because I am sure he could invent nothing of this kind. The true title of this part of his work is, 'A Dialogue between a Green-goose and a Hero'" (YE 14:174).
2 Mason had been under the misapprehension that a book he had received, reprinting an already published critical account of Johnson's Life of Milton, had been sent to him by Walpole.
3 The leading character in the play was a scheming Scotsman.

volumes to one: but there are woful longueurs, both about his hero and himself, the *fidus Achates;*[1] about whom one has not the smallest curiosity. But I wrong the original Achates: one is satisfied with his fidelity in keeping his master's secrets and weaknesses, which modern led-captains betray for their patron's glory and to hurt their own enemies; which Boswell has done shamefully, particularly against Mrs. Piozzi, and Mrs. Montagu, and Bishop Percy. Dr. Blagdon says justly, that it is a new kind of libel, by which you may abuse anybody, by saying some dead person said so and so of somebody alive.[2] Often, indeed, Johnson made the most brutal speeches to living persons; for though he was good-natured at bottom, he was very ill-natured at top. He loved to dispute to show his superiority. If his opponents were weak, he told them they were fools; if they vanquished him, he was scurrilous – to nobody more than to Boswell himself, who was contemptible for flattering him so grossly, and for enduring the coarse things he was continually vomiting on Boswell's own country, Scotland. I expected, amongst the excommunicated, to find myself, but am very gently treated.[3] I never would be in the least acquainted with Johnson; or, as Boswell calls it, had not a just value for him; which the biographer imputes to my resentment for the Doctor's putting bad arguments (purposely, out of Jacobitism,) into the speeches which he wrote fifty years ago for my father, in the "Gentleman's Magazine"; which I did not read then, or ever knew Johnson wrote till Johnson died, nor have looked at since. Johnson's blind Toryism and known brutality kept me aloof; nor did I ever exchange a syllable with him: nay, I do not think I ever was in a room with him six times in my days. The first time I think was at the Royal Academy. Sir Joshua said, "Let me present Dr. Goldsmith to you"; he did. "Now I will present Dr. Johnson to you." – "No," said I, "Sir Joshua, for Dr. Goldsmith, pass – but you shall *not* present Dr. Johnson to me."

Some time after, Boswell came to me, said Dr. Johnson was writing the "Lives of the Poets," and wished I would give him anecdotes

---

1 Loyal Achates, the companion of Aeneas in the *Æneid*.
2 Dr. Charles Blagdon or Blagden (1748–1820), physician, scientist and F.R.S., knighted in 1792. Boswell quotes Johnson criticising Hester Thrale Piozzi, Elizabeth Montagu, and Bishop Percy.
3 At p. 314 of volume 4 of the Hill Powell edition of *Boswell's Life of Johnson*, Boswell quotes Johnson as saying (somewhat disdainfully) that Walpole "got together a great many curious little things, and told them in an elegant manner".

of Mr. Gray. I said, very coldly, I had given what I knew to Mr. Mason. Boswell hummed and hawed, and then dropped, "I suppose you know Dr. Johnson does not admire Mr. Gray." Putting as much contempt as I could into my look and tone, I said, "Dr. Johnson don't! – humph!" – and with that monosyllable ended our interview.[1] After the Doctor's death, Burke, Sir Joshua Reynolds, and Boswell sent an ambling circular-letter to me, begging subscriptions for a Monument for him – the two last, I think, impertinently; as they could not but know my opinion, and could not suppose I would contribute to a Monument for one who had endeavoured, poor soul! to degrade my friend's superlative poetry. I would not deign to write an answer; but sent down word by my footman, as I would have done to parish officers with a brief, that I would not subscribe. In the two new volumes Johnson says, and very probably did, or is made to say, that Gray's poetry is *dull*, and that he was a *dull* man! The same oracle dislikes Prior, Swift, and Fielding. If an elephant could write a book perhaps one that had read a great deal would say, that an Arabian horse is a very clumsy ungraceful animal. Pass to a better chapter! . . .

18. GOLDSMITH

162. *"She Stoops to Conquer."*

TO THE COUNTESS OF UPPER OSSORY

Strawberry Hill, 27 March 1773.

What play makes you laugh very much, and yet is a very wretched comedy? Dr. Goldsmith's "She Stoops to Conquer." Stoops indeed! – so she does, that is the Muse; she is draggled up to the knees, and has trudged, I believe, from Southwark fair. The whole view of the piece is low humour, and no humour is in it. All the merit is in the situations, which are comic; the heroine has no more *mauvaise honte* than Lady Bridget,[2] and the author's wit is as much *manqué* as the

---

1 The Yale editors quote Boswell's description in his Journals of Walpole, "just the same as ever: genteel, fastidious, priggish", after visiting him three years before this encounter, on 25 April 1788: *Boswell: the English Experiment 1785–1789* (London: Heinemann, 1986), p. 217.
2 No more modesty than Lady Bridget Fox-Lane, *née* Henley (d. 1796), whom Walpole criticised elsewhere as indiscreet.

lady's; but some of the characters are well acted, and Woodward speaks a poor prologue, written by Garrick, admirably.

You perceive, Madam, that I have boldly sallied to a play; but the heat of the house and of this sultry March half killed me, yet I limp about as if I was young and pleased. From the play I travelled to Upper Grosvenor Street, to Lady Edgecumbe's, supped at Lady Hertford's and that Maccaroni rake, Lady Powis,[1] who is just come to her estate and spending it, calling in with news of a fire in the Strand at past one in the morning, Lady Hertford, Lady Powis, Mrs. Howe, and I, set out to see it, and were within an inch of seeing the Adelphi buildings burnt to the ground.[2] I was to have gone to the Oratorio next night for Miss Linley's[3] sake, but, being engaged to the French ambassador's ball afterwards, I thought I was not quite Hercules enough for so many labours, and declined the former....

163. *A Low Farce.*

TO THE REV. WILLIAM MASON

Strawberry Hill, 27 March 1773.

... Dr. Goldsmith has written a Comedy ["She Stoops to Conquer"] – no, it is the lowest of all farces. It is not the subject I condemn, though very vulgar, but the execution. The drift tends to no moral, no edification of any kind. The situations, however, are well imagined, and make one laugh, in spite of the grossness of the dialogue, the forced witticisms, and total improbability of the whole plan and conduct. But what disgusts me most is, that though the characters are very low, and aim at low humour, not one of them says a sentence that is natural or marks any character at all. It is set up in opposition to sentimental comedy, and is as bad as the worst of them. Garrick would not act it, but bought himself off by a poor prologue. I say nothing of Home's "Alonzo" and Murphy's "Alzuma," because

1 The Yale editors note that Barbara Herbert, Countess of Powis (1735–86), had been recently widowed and was accused of incurring large losses at cards. Macaronis were fashionable, affected men, fastidious, usually young and sometimes given to gambling.
2 The Adelphi, a building speculation of the Adam brothers sited between the Strand and the Thames.
3 Elizabeth Linley (1754–92), singer, who some two weeks after the date of this letter married Richard Brinsley Sheridan.

as the latter is sense and poetry compared to the former, you cannot want an account of either. . . .

164. *A Butt.*

TO THE COUNTESS OF UPPER OSSORY

Arlington Street, 14 December 1773.

. . . I dined and passed Saturday at Beauclerk's, with the Edgecumbes, the Garricks, and Dr. Goldsmith, and was most thoroughly tired, as I knew I should be, I who hate the playing off a butt. Goldsmith is a fool, the more wearing for having some sense. It was the night of a new comedy, called "The School for Wives,"[1] which was exceedingly applauded, and which Charles Fox says is execrable. Garrick has at least the chief hand in it. I never saw anybody in a greater fidget, nor more vain when he returned, for he went to the play-house at half-an-hour after five, and we sat waiting for him till ten, when he was to act a speech in "Cato" with Goldsmith! that is, the latter sat in t'other's lap, covered with a cloak, and while Goldsmith spoke, Garrick's arms that embraced him, made foolish actions. How could one laugh when one had expected this for four hours? . . .

19. SHERIDAN

165. *"The School for Scandal." – Advice.*

TO ROBERT JEPHSON, ESQ.[2]

Strawberry Hill, 13 July 1777.

. . . Instead of hurrying "The Law of Lombardy," which, however, I shall delight to see finished, I again wish you to try comedy. To my great astonishment there were more parts performed admirably in "The School for Scandal,"[3] than I almost ever saw in any play. Mrs.

1 A comedy by Hugh Kelly (1739–77), a miscellaneous writer. The Yale editors speculate that Garrick's unease may have been caused by fear of pro-Wilkes riots at the theatre, as Kelly was known as an opponent of Wilkes.
2 Robert Jephson (1736/7–1803), playwright, author of *The Law of Lombardy*, *Braganza* (for which Walpole wrote the Epilogue) and in 1781 *The Count of Narbonne*, based on Walpole's *The Castle of Otranto*.
3 Sheridan's *The School for Scandal* had been first performed two months earlier.

Abington was equal to the first of her profession, Yates (the husband), Parsons, Miss Pope, and Palmer, all shone. It seemed a marvellous resurrection of the stage. Indeed, the play had as much merit as the actors. I have seen no comedy that comes near it since the "Provoked Husband."[1]

I said I was jealous of your fame as a poet, and I truly am. The more rapid your genius is, labour will but the more improve it. I am very frank, but I am sure that my attention to your reputation will excuse it. Your facility in writing exquisite poetry may be a disadvantage; as it may not leave you time to study the other requisites of tragedy so much as is necessary. Your writings deserve to last for ages; but to make any work last, it must be finished in all parts to perfection. You have the first requisite to that perfection, for you can sacrifice charming lines, when they do not tend to improve the whole. I admire this resignation so much, that I wish to turn it to your advantage. Strike out your sketches as suddenly as you please, but retouch and retouch them, that the best judges may for ever admire them. The works that have stood the test of ages, and been slowly approved at first, are not those that have dazzled contemporaries and borne away their applause, but those whose intrinsic and laboured merit have shone the brighter on examination. I would not curb your genius, Sir, if I did not trust it would recoil with greater force for having obstacles presented to it. . . .

166. *An Excellent Play.*

TO THE REV. WILLIAM MASON

16 May 1777.

. . . I have seen Sheridan's new comedy ["The School for Scandal"], and liked it much better than any I have seen since "The Provoked Husband." There is a great deal of wit and good situations, but it is too long, has two or three bad scenes that might easily be omitted, and seemed to me to want nature and truth of character; but I have not read it, and sat too high to hear it well. It is admirably

---

1 *The Provoked Husband*, a comedy of 1728 by Colley Cibber (1671–1757) based on a fragment by Sir John Vanbrugh.

acted. Burke has published a pamphlet on the American War,[1] and an Apology for his own secession and that of his friends. I have not had time to look at it, but I do not believe I shall agree with him on the latter part so much as on the first. Do not return me the "Incas"; I shall never read it. I hear your "Garden" was criticised in the "Morning Post." Continue to plant

> Flowers worthy of paradise, –

and do not mind their being trampled on in such a soil as this.[2] Adieu! I wish I had leisure to chat with you longer.

20. GIBBON

167. *A Classic History.*

TO EDWARD GIBBON, ESQ.

14 February 1776.

After the singular pleasure of reading you, Sir, the next satisfaction is to declare my admiration.[3] I have read great part of your volume, and cannot decide to which of its various merits I give the preference, though I have no doubt of assigning my partiality to one virtue of the author, which, seldom as I meet with it, always strikes me superiorly. Its quality will naturally prevent your guessing which I mean. It is your amiable modesty. How can you know so much, judge so well, possess your subject, and your knowledge, and your power of judicious reflection so thoroughly, and yet command yourself and betray no dictatorial arrogance of decision? How unlike very ancient and very modern authors! You have, unexpectedly, given the world a classic history. The fame it must acquire will tend every day

---

1 Edmund Burke (1730–97): *A Letter from Edmund Burke, Esq. . . . on the Affairs of America*: Walpole thought he was more likely to agree with Burke's opposition to the war with the American colonists than he was to be persuaded that the policy of "secession" – boycotting Parliament to show disapproval of the policies under discussion – was an effective way of opposing the government's suspension of Habeas Corpus in America.
2 *Les Incas* by Jean-François Marmontel (1723–99) had been lent unread by Walpole to Mason. The second book (of four) of Mason's blank-verse poem *The English Garden* had been published the previous month. The quotation is from *Paradise Lost*, IV, 241.
3 Edward Gibbon (1737–94) had presented Walpole with a copy of the first volume of his *History of the Decline and Fall of the Roman Empire*.

to acquit this panegyric of flattery. The impressions it has made on me are very numerous. The strongest is the thirst of being better acquainted with you; but I reflect that I have been a trifling author, and am in no light profound enough to deserve your intimacy, except by confessing your superiority so frankly, that I assure you honestly, I already feel no envy, though I did for a moment. The best proof I can give you of my sincerity, is to exhort you, warmly and earnestly, to go on with your noble work: the strongest, though a presumptuous mark of my friendship, is to warn you never to let your charming modesty be corrupted by the acclamations your talents will receive. The native qualities of the man should never be sacrificed to those of the author, however shining. I take this liberty as an older man, which reminds me how little I dare promise myself that I shall see your work completed! But I love posterity enough to contribute, if I can, to give them pleasure through you.

I am too weak to say more, though I could talk for hours on your History. But one feeling I cannot suppress, though it is a sensation of vanity. I think, nay, I am sure I perceive, that your sentiments on government agree with my own. It is the only point on which I suspect myself of any partiality in my admiration. It is a reflection of a far inferior vanity that pleases me in your speaking with so much distinction of that, alas! wonderful period, in which the world saw five good monarchs succeed each other.[1] I have often thought of treating that Elysian era. Happily it has fallen into better hands!

I have been able to rise to-day, for the first time, and flatter myself that if I have no relapse, you will in two or three days more give me leave, Sir, to ask the honour of seeing you. In the mean time, be just; and do not suspect me of flattering you. You will always hear that I say the same of you to everybody. I am, with the greatest regard, Sir, &c.

---

1 In a letter to John Chute begun on 5 August 1771 (YE 35:127) Walpole had suggested that the world would not again see "a succession of five good emperors, like Nerva, Trajan, Adrian, and the two Antonines". They ruled the Roman Empire from A.D. 96 to A.D. 180.

168. *An Unsuspected Genius.*

TO THE REV. WILLIAM MASON

18 February 1776.

... Lo, there is just appeared a truly classic work: a history, not majestic like Livy, nor compressed like Tacitus; not stamped with character like Clarendon; perhaps not so deep as Robertson's "Scotland," but a thousand degrees above his "Charles"; not pointed like Voltaire, but as accurate as he is inexact; modest as he is *tranchant* and sly as Montesquieu without being so *recherché.* The style is as smooth as a Flemish picture, and the muscles are concealed and only for natural uses, not exaggerated like Michael Angelo's to show the painter's skill in anatomy; nor composed of the limbs of clowns of different nations, like Dr. Johnson's heterogeneous monsters.[1] This book is Mr. Gibbon's "History of the Decline and Fall of the Roman Empire." He is son of a late foolish alderman,[2] is a Member of Parliament, and called a whimsical one because he votes variously as his opinion leads him; and his first production was in French, in which language he shines too. I know him a little, never suspected the extent of his talents, for he is perfectly modest, or I want penetration, which I know too, but I intend to know him a great deal more – there! there is food for your residence at York. ...

169. *Quarrel with Gibbon.*

TO THE REV. WILLIAM MASON

27 January 1781.

... You will be diverted to hear that Mr. Gibbon has quarrelled with me. He lent me his second volume in the middle of November. I returned it with a most civil panegyric. He came for more incense, I gave it, but alas! with too much sincerity; I added, "Mr. Gibbon, I am sorry *you* should have pitched on so disgusting a subject as the Constantinopolitan History. There is so much of the Arians and Eunomians, and semi-Pelagians; and there is such a strange

---

1 An expression of Walpole's rooted antipathy to Johnson's prose style.
2 The Yale editors suggest that Walpole may have thought Gibbon's father foolish because of his Tory or Jacobite leanings.

contrast between Roman and Gothic manners, and so little harmony between a Consul Sabinus and a Ricimer, Duke of the palace, that though you have written the story as well as it could be written, I fear few will have patience to read it." He coloured; all his round features squeezed themselves into sharp angles; he screwed up his button-mouth, and rapping his snuff-box, said, "It had never been put together before" – *so well* he meant to add – but gulped it. He meant *so well* certainly, for Tillemont, whom he quotes in every page, has done the very thing. Well, from that hour to this I have never seen him, though he used to call once or twice a week; nor has sent me the third volume, as he promised. I well knew his vanity, even about his ridiculous face and person, but thought he had too much sense to avow it so palpably. The "History" is admirably written, especially in the characters of Julian and Athanasius, in both which he has piqued himself on impartiality – but the style is far less sedulously enamelled than the first volume, and there is flattery to the Scots that would choke anything but Scots, who can gobble feathers as readily as thistles. David Hume and Adam Smith are *legislators* and sages, but the homage is intended for his patron, Lord Lough-borough.[1] . . .

21. BURKE

170. *American Speeches.*

TO THE REV. WILLIAM MASON

27 May 1775.

. . . Burke has printed a second speech,[2] which I prefer much to his first. It is grave, solid, temperate, and chaster from exuberant imagination. If his fancy breaks out, it does not soar above the third heaven and come tumbling down flat. *Apropos* to authors, the husband of Mrs. Montagu of Shakespeareshire is dead, and has left her an estate of seven thousand pounds a year in her own power.

---

1 The Yale editors suggest that the affronted Walpole exaggerates both Gibbon's reliance on the French author Tillemont, and Gibbon's praise of the Scots. Alexander Wedderburn (1733–1805), Lord Loughborough, later Lord Chancellor, had helped Gibbon obtain his appointment as a Lord of Trade in 1779.
2 Burke's speech was on conciliation with the American colonies.

Will you come and be a candidate for her hand?[1] I conclude it will be given to a champion at some Olympic games, and were I she, I would sooner marry you than Pindar. . . . Adieu! I remove to Strawberry to-morrow,

Yours ever,
H. W.

171. *"Reflections on the French Revolution."*

TO MARY BERRY

Park Place, 8 November 1790.

. . . The third volume of news, expected, but not yet in the press, is a counter-revolution in France. Of that I know nothing but rumour; yet it certainly is not the most incredible event that rumour ever foretold. In this country the stock of the National Assembly is fallen down to bankruptcy. Their only renegade, aristocrat Earl Stanhope, has, with Lord W. Russel, scratched his name out of the Revolution Club;[2] but the fatal blow has been at last given by Mr. Burke. His pamphlet[3] came out this day se'nnight, and is far superior to what was expected, even by his warmest admirers. I have read it twice; and though of three hundred and fifty pages, I wish I could repeat every page by heart. It is sublime, profound, and gay. The wit and satire are equally brilliant; and the whole is wise, though in some points he goes too far: yet in general there is far less want of judgment than could be expected from *him*. If it could be translated, – which, from the wit and metaphors and allusions, is almost impossible, – I should think it would be a classic book in all countries, except in *present* France. To their tribunes it speaks daggers; though, unlike them, it uses none. Seven thousand copies have been taken

1 Elizabeth Montagu (1718–1800), author of *An Essay on the Writings and Genius of Shakespeare* (1769), who managed her late husband's substantial mining and other interests. In 1778 a mezzotint caricature titled "Abelard and Eloisa" was published showing Mason as suitor for Montagu.
2 The Revolution Society was a society of political reformers formed in London on the centenary of the 1688 Revolution. It supported the early stages of the French Revolution, but died away by 1793. Charles Stanhope, 3rd Earl of Stanhope (1753–1816) served as its chairman. Although he resigned in 1790 he continued to be involved in radical politics.
3 Burke's *Reflections on the Revolution in France.*

off by the booksellers already, and a new edition is preparing. I hope you will see it soon. There ends my gazette. . . .

172. *The Same.*

Strawberry Hill, 1 December 1790.

Indeed, my too indulgent Lady, my letters are written so idly, and filled with such trifles as occur, as Arabian tales, &c., that they are very unfit to be seen by any but yourselves, for whose amusement I send them; and being generally only answers to yours, they must be Hebrew to anybody else. This is merely a reply to your last. Madame de Sillery's protest against the *Monseigneur* was no panic, but an emanation of that *poissarde* cant that her recreant protector has adopted. When the late Emperor died, she forbade her pupils to mourn for him. The Duc de Chartres obeyed. The Duc de Montpensier, the second son, about seventeen, would not, but bespoke a black coat. La Gouvernante said to him, "Quelle fantaisie est-ce cela?" "Fantaisie!" cried the Prince, "est-ce une fantaisie que de vouloir porter le deuil de l'Empereur?" "Well, then!" said the mock Minerva, "you shall have no other coat till that is worn out." Would not one think that the Duc de Chartres was *her* son, and the two others sprung from Henri Quatre by the *Duchess* of Orleans?[1]

One word more about Mr. Burke's book: I know the tirade on the Queen of France is condemned, and yet I must avow I admire it much. It paints her exactly as she appeared to me the first time I saw her when Dauphiness. She was going after the late King to chapel, and shot through the room like an aerial being, all brightness and grace, and without seeming to touch earth – *vera incessu patuit dea!*[2] Had I Mr. Burke's powers, I would have described her in his words. I like "the swords leaping out of their scabbards"; in short, I am not more charmed with his wit and eloquence, than with his enthusiasm.

1 Mme. de Sillery (1746–1830), otherwise Mme. de Genlis, was the former mistress of the Duc d'Orléans (Philippe Egalité), and subsequently became governor of his sons by his marriage to Louise de Bourbon, including the Duc de Chartres (later King Louis-Philippe) and the Duc de Montpensier. The emperor who died was Joseph II, Holy Roman Emperor and brother of Marie Antoinette.
2 From Virgil, *Æneid* I. 405, of Venus: each step revealed her as a goddess.

Every page shows how sincerely he is in earnest – a wondrous merit in a political pamphlet. All other party writers *act* zeal for the public, but it never seems to flow from the heart. That cordiality like a phial of spirits, will preserve his book, when some of his doctrines would have evaporated in fume. Lord Stanhope's were the ravings of a lunatic, imagining he could set the world on fire with phosphorus. Lord Lansdowne, I hear, said there was some good sense in that rant. How fortunate that Price[1] and his adherents were intoxicated by their own hopes, and flattered themselves that Europe was in so combustible a temper, that by throwing their farthing squibs from a pulpit, they should set even this country in a blaze, and like the wretches hanged last week for burning houses, should plunder some silver candlesticks from the altars in our churches, to which *the rights of men*[2] entitle them. That proclamation of the "Rights of Men," is *ipso facto* a dissolution of all society, into which men entered for the defence of the rights of every individual. The consequence of universal equality would be, that the industrious only would labour, the idle not. Who then would be to maintain the inactive? Must the produce of the labours of the laborious be shared with the indolent? Oh, but there should be some government – then the governed would not be equal with the governors; but it is idle to confute nonsense! All the blessed liberty the French seemed to have gained is, that every man or woman, if *poissardes* are women, may hang whom they please. Dr. Price adopting such freedom, opened the nation's eyes – *Honi soit qui mal y pense!* . . .

22. CHESTERFIELD
173. *His Letters.*

TO THE REV. WILLIAM MASON

Strawberry Hill, 9 April 1774, addition to letter begun 7 April.

I was too late for the post on Thursday, and have since got Lord Chesterfield's Letters,[3] which, without being well entertained, I sat

1 Richard Price (1723–91), a radical dissenter attacked by Burke in his *Reflections*.
2 The French National Assembly had issued the Declaration of the Rights of Man in August 1789.
3 Philip Dormer Stanhope (1694–1773), 4th Earl of Chesterfield, politician and wit. *Letters Written by the Late Right Honourable Philip Dormer Stanhope, Earl of Chesterfield, to his Son, Philip Stanhope, Esq.* had been published two days previously.

up reading last night till between one and two, and devoured above 140. To my great surprise they seem really written from the heart, not for the honour of his head, and in truth do no great honour to the last, nor show much feeling in the first, except in wishing for his son's fine gentlemanhood. He was sensible what a cub he had to work on, and whom two quartos of licking could not mould, for cub he remained to his death. The repetitions are endless and tiresome. The next volume, I see, promises more amusement, for in turning it over, I spied many political names. The more curious part of all is that one perceives by what infinite assiduity and attention his lordship's own great character was raised and supported; and yet in all that great character what was there worth remembering but his bons mots? His few fugitive pieces that remain show his genteel turn for songs and his wit: from politics he rather escaped well, than succeeded by them. In short, the diamond owed more to being brillianted and polished, and well set, than to any intrinsic worth or solidity.[1]

23. GENERAL CRITICISM

174. *Present Dearth of Literary Genius.*

TO THE REV. WILLIAM MASON

Dear Sir,   Strawberry Hill, 21 July 1772.

. . . Mr. Cole has told me of somebody else, I forgot who it is, that is going to republish old historians à la Hearne.[2] This taste of digging up antiquated relics flourishes abundantly, unless Foote's last new piece blows us up. He has introduced the Learned Society in Chancery-lane, sitting as they really did, on Whittington and his Cat; and as I do not love to be answerable for any fooleries, but my own, I think I shall scratch my name out of their books.[3] Oxford has lately contributed to the mass the Lives of Leland, Hearne, and Wood. In the latter's journal one of the most important entries is,

1 Walpole in 1774 wrote three letters parodying Chesterfield's Letters, with an Introduction: see his *Works* (1798), volume 4, pp. 355–60. At pp. 535–8 of volume 1 of the *Works* is his account of Chesterfield as an author.
2 Thomas Hearne (see letter 84, pp. 137, n. 2).
3 Walpole used Samuel Foote's mockery of antiquaries in his play *The Nabob* as an excuse to withdraw from the Society of Antiquaries.

This day old Joan began to make my bed. What a figure will this our Augustan age make; Garrick's prologues, epilogues, and verses, Sir W[illiam] Chambers's gardening, Dr. Nowel's sermon, Whittington and his Cat, Sir John Dalrymple's History, and the Life of Henry II. What a library of poetry, taste, good sense, veracity and vivacity! ungrateful Shebbear! indolent Smollett! trifling Johnson! piddling Goldsmith! how little have they contributed to the glory of a period in which all arts, all sciences are encouraged and rewarded. Guthrie buried his mighty genius in a Review, and Mallet died of the first effusions of his loyalty.[1] The retrospect makes one melancholy, but Ossian has appeared, and were Paradise once more lost, we should not want an Epic Poem. Adieu! dear Sir,

> Yours ever,
>
> H. W.

175. *Critical Opinions.*

TO JOHN PINKERTON, ESQ.

26 June 1785.

I have sent your book to Mr. Colman, Sir, and must desire you in return to offer my grateful thanks to Mr. Knight,[2] who has done me an honour, to which I do not know how I am entitled, by the present of his poetry, which is very classic, and beautiful, and tender, and of chaste simplicity.

To *your* book, Sir, I am much obliged on many accounts; particularly for having recalled my mind to subjects of delight, to which it was grown dulled by age and indolence. In consequence of your reclaiming it, I asked myself whence you feel so much disregard for certain authors whose fame is established: you have assigned good reasons for withholding your approbation from some, on the plea of their being imitators: it was natural, then, to ask myself again, whence they had obtained so much celebrity. I think I have discovered a cause, which I do not remember to have seen noted; and

---

1 William Guthrie (1708–70) and David Mallet (1701/2–65) were miscellaneous writers: Walpole had been abused by the first, and disapproved of the political writings of the second.
2 Samuel Knight (1755–1829), author of *Elegies and Sonnets* (1785), was a friend of Pinkerton whose book here referred to was *Letters of Literature* (also 1785).

that cause I suspect to have been, that certain of those authors possessed grace: – do not take me for a disciple of Lord Chesterfield,
nor imagine that I mean to erect grace into a capital ingredient of
writing, but I do believe that it is a perfume that will preserve from
putrefaction, and is distinct even from style, which regards expression. *Grace*, I think, belongs to *manner*. It is from the charm of grace
that I believe some authors, not in your favour, obtained part of their
renown; Virgil, in particular: and yet I am far from disagreeing with
you on his subject in general. There is such a dearth of invention in
the *Æneid*, (and when he did invent, it was often so foolishly,) so
little good sense, so little variety, and so little power over the passions, that I have frequently said, from contempt for his matter, and
from the charm of his harmony, that I believe I should like his poem
better, if I was to hear it repeated, and did not understand Latin. On
the other hand, he has more than harmony: whatever he utters is said
gracefully, and he ennobles his images, especially in the Georgics; or,
at least, it is more sensible there, from the humility of the subject.
A Roman farmer might not understand his diction in agriculture;
but he made a Roman courtier understand farming, the farming of
that age, and could captivate a lord of Augustus's bedchamber, and
tempt him to listen to themes of rusticity. On the contrary, Statius
and Claudian, though talking of war, would make a soldier despise
them as bullies. That graceful manner of thinking in Virgil seems
to me to be more than style, if I do not refine too much: and I admire,
I confess, Mr. Addison's phrase, that Virgil "tossed about his dung
with an air of majesty." A style may be excellent without grace: for
instance, Dr. Swift's. Eloquence may bestow an immortal style, and
one of more dignity; yet eloquence may want that ease, that genteel
air that flows from or constitutes grace. Addison himself was master
of that grace, even in his pieces of humour, and which do not owe
their merit to style; and from that combined secret he excels all men
that ever lived, but Shakspeare, in humour, by never dropping into
an approach towards burlesque and buffoonery, when even his
humour descended to characters that in other hands would have
been vulgarly low. Is not it clear that Will Wimble[1] was a gentleman,
though he always lived at a distance from good company? Fielding

---

1   Will Wimble, a country gentleman and younger son without estate or profession,
as described in no. 108 of *The Spectator*.

had as much humour, perhaps, as Addison; but, having no idea of grace, is perpetually disgusting. His innkeepers and parsons are the grossest of their profession; and his gentlemen are awkward when they should be at their ease.

The Grecians had grace in everything; in poetry, in oratory, in statuary, in architecture, and probably, in music and painting. The Romans, it is true, were their imitators; but, having grace too, imparted it to their copies, which gave them a merit that almost raises them to the rank of originals. Horace's "Odes" acquired their fame, no doubt, from the graces of his manner and purity of his style, – the chief praise of Tibullus and Propertius who certainly cannot boast of more meaning than Horace's "Odes."

Waller, whom you proscribe, Sir, owed his reputation to the graces of his manner, though he frequently stumbled, and even fell flat; but a few of his smaller pieces are as graceful as possible: one might say that he excelled in painting ladies in enamel, but could not succeed in portraits in oil, large as life. Milton had such superior merit, that I will only say, that if his angels, his Satan, and his Adam have as much dignity as the Apollo Belvidere, his Eve has all the delicacy and graces of the Venus of Medicis; as his description of Eden has the colouring of Albano. Milton's tenderness imprints ideas as graceful as Guido's Madonnas: and the "Allegro," "Penseroso," and "Comus" might be denominated from the three Graces; as the Italians gave similar titles to two or three of Petrarch's best sonnets.

Cowley, I think, would have had grace (for his mind was graceful) if he had had any ear, or if his taste had not been vitiated by the pursuit of wit; which, when it does not offer itself naturally, degenerates into tinsel or pertness. Pertness is the mistaken affectation of grace, as pedantry produces erroneous dignity; the familiarity of the one, and the clumsiness of the other, distort or prevent grace. Nature, that furnishes samples of all qualities, and in the scale of gradation exhibits all possible shades, affords us types that are more apposite than words. The eagle is sublime, the lion majestic, the swan graceful, the monkey pert, the bear ridiculously awkward. I mention these as more expressive and comprehensive than I could make definitions of my meaning; but I will apply the swan only, under whose wings I will shelter an apology for Racine, whose pieces give me an idea of that bird. The colouring of the swan is pure; his attitudes are graceful; he never displeases you when sailing on his proper element. His feet may be ugly, his notes hissing, not musical, his walk not natural; he can soar, but it is with difficulty – still, the impression the swan leaves is that of grace. So does Racine.

Boileau may be compared to the dog, whose sagacity is remarkable, as well as its fawning on its master, and its snarling at those it dislikes. If Boileau was too austere to admit the pliability of grace, he compensates by good sense and propriety. He is like (for I will drop animals) an upright magistrate, whom you respect, but whose justice and severity leave an awe that discourages familiarity. His copies of the ancients may be too servile: but, if a good translator deserves praise, Boileau deserves more. He certainly does not fall below his originals; and, considering at what period he wrote, has greater merit still. By his imitations he held out to his countrymen models of taste, and banished totally the bad taste of his predecessors. For his "Lutrin," replete with excellent poetry, wit, humour, and satire, he certainly was not obliged to the ancients. Excepting Horace, how little idea had either Greeks or Romans of wit and humour! Aristophanes and Lucian, compared with moderns, were, the one a blackguard, and the other a buffoon. In my eyes, the "Lutrin," the "Dispensary," and the "Rape of the Lock,"[1] are standards of grace and elegance, not to be paralleled by antiquity; and eternal reproaches to Voltaire, whose indelicacy in the "Pucelle" degraded him as much, when compared with the three authors I have named, as his "Henriade" leaves Virgil, and even Lucan, whom he more resembles, by far his superiors.

"The Dunciad" is blemished by the offensive images of the games; but the poetry appears to me admirable; and, though the fourth book has obscurities, I prefer it to the three others: it has descriptions not surpassed by any poet that ever existed, and which surely a writer merely ingenious will never equal. The lines on Italy, on Venice, on Convents, have all the grace for which I contend as distinct from poetry, though united with the most beautiful; and the "Rape of the Lock," besides the originality of great part of the invention, is a standard of graceful writing.

In general, I believe that what I call grace, is denominated

---

1 Boileau's *Le Lutrin* (1674), Samuel Garth's *The Dispensary* (1699) and Pope's *The Rape of the Lock* (1712 as first published).

elegance; but by grace I mean something higher. I will explain myself by instances – Apollo is graceful, Mercury is elegant. Petrarch, perhaps, owed his whole merit to the harmony of his numbers and the graces of his style. They conceal his poverty of meaning and want of variety. His complaints, too, may have added an interest, which, had his passion been successful, and had expressed itself with equal sameness, would have made the number of his sonnets insupportable. Melancholy in poetry, I am inclined to think, contributes to grace, when it is not disgraced by pitiful lamentations, such as Ovid's and Cicero's in their banishments. We respect melancholy, because it imparts a similar affection, pity. A gay writer, who should only express satisfaction without variety, would soon be nauseous.

Madame de Sévigné[1] shines both in grief and gaiety. There is too much of sorrow for her daughter's absence; yet it is always expressed by new turns, new images, and often by wit, whose tenderness has a melancholy air. When she forgets her concern, and returns to her natural disposition – gaiety, every paragraph has novelty: her allusions, her applications are the happiest possible. She has the art of making you acquainted with all her acquaintance, and attaches you even to the spots she inhabited. Her language is correct, though unstudied; and, when her mind is full of any great event, she interests you with the warmth of a dramatic writer, not with the chilling impartiality of an historian. Pray read her accounts of the death of Turenne, and of the arrival of King James in France,[2] and tell me whether you do not know their persons as if you had lived at the time.

For my part, if you will allow me a word of digression, (not that I have written with any method,) I have the cold impartiality recommended to Historians: "Si vis me flere, dolendum est primùm ipsi tibi":[3] but, that I may not wander again, nor tire, nor contradict you any more, I will finish now, and shall be glad if you will dine at Strawberry Hill next Sunday, and take a bed there, when I will tell you how many more parts of your book have pleased me, than have startled my opinions, or, perhaps, prejudices. I am, Sir, Your obedient humble servant. . . .

1 Marie de Rabutin-Chantal, Mme. de Sévigné (1626–96), whose correspondence was greatly admired by Walpole: see general Introduction.
2 In her letters of 31 July to 9 August 1675 and 10 January 1689.
3 Horace, *Ars poetica*, lines 102–3: if you want me to weep, you must first feel grief yourself.

IX
HIS FAMILY

Walpole was deeply devoted to his mother and her memory; her death in 1737 while he was studying at Cambridge was a heavy blow to him, and his friends became concerned for his health. The inscription on her tomb in Westminster Abbey was his own composition and he kept the plaster cast of the statue in the Tribune at Strawberry Hill. For his father he had a profound admiration. Writing at the age of sixty-two he said: "My father is ever before my eyes – not to attempt to imitate him, for I have none of his matchless wisdom, or unsullied virtues, or heroic firmness."[1] Of his father's statesmanship he had the highest opinion: in 1780, when England was at war with America and her European allies, he sighed for the "twenty years of peace, and credit, and happiness, and liberty" that the nation enjoyed under his father – "I look about for a Sir Robert Walpole – but where is he to be found?"[2] The worldly Sir Robert and the somewhat effete son largely brought up by the statesman's estranged wife would seem to have had little in common; letter 407 shows the young man's sense of isolation amongst his father's supporters and neighbours in Norfolk. Nonetheless, their relationship grew more affectionate during Sir Robert's retirement.

Walpole had little time for his father's brother, the diplomat Horatio Walpole, known as "Old Horace", who was created Baron Walpole of Wolterton in 1756. On this event his nephew remarked, "My uncle's ambition and dirt are crowned at last; he is a peer"[3] – but not for long, as he died the following year. Neither did he enjoy cordial relations with his own brothers. He disapproved of Robert, the eldest, who succeeded to the earldom in 1745 and installed as his mistress ("my brother's concubine") the actress Hannah Norsa (she is mentioned in letter 55), his wife, Margaret Rolle, having "run to Italy after lovers and books".[4] Walpole was on no better terms with his second brother Edward. They quarrelled after their father's death because Horace had not nominated Edward as member of

1 Letter to Mann, 19 August 1779 (YE 24:507).
2 Ibid, 13 January 1780 (YE 25:7).
3 Ibid 27 May 1756 (YE 20:556).
4 Letter to Conway, 5 May 1752 (YE 333–4).

Parliament for Castle Rising when a vacancy occurred, and Edward was jealous of his younger brother's friendship with Henry Fox.

Sir Edward (he was knighted in 1753) never married but had three daughters and a son by his mistress Dorothy Clement, a milliner's apprentice, who died young around 1739. To these children their uncle was much attached. The eldest, Laura, married Frederick Keppel who afterwards became Bishop of Exeter; the youngest, Charlotte, married the future Earl of Dysart; Edward, the only son, remained single. The second daughter, Maria, a beauty and her uncle's favourite, became the wife of James, Earl Waldegrave. When he died of small-pox in 1763 Maria retired to Twickenham with her three small daughters to be near Walpole (letters 182 and 183). She soon caught the eye of the Duke of Gloucester, brother of George III, and Walpole was one of the few who knew before it was openly acknowledged that they had secretly been married in 1766. Maria, a commoner and illegitimate, would not have been considered a suitable wife for royalty. The Royal Marriages Act of 1772 drove the Duke to confess to the King and make the match public (letter 184); Walpole's pride is undisguised, though predictably Gloucester was banished from court and even when he was forgiven the Duchess was never received there.

It is Maria's three daughters by Lord Waldegrave – Elizabeth Laura, Charlotte Maria and Anna Horatia – who appear as "The Ladies Waldegrave" in the famous group portrait by Sir Joshua Reynolds (1780), commissioned by Walpole for Strawberry Hill and now at the Scottish National Gallery. Elizabeth Laura, the eldest, married her cousin the fourth Earl Waldegrave; she inherited Strawberry Hill in 1811.

Walpole's nephew George, son of his eldest brother Robert, became the third Earl of Orford in 1751. George was a cause of despair to his uncle. An obsessive sportsman, he ate and drank to excess, spent wildly, lost a fortune on the turf and other sporting extravagancies, and became subject to periodical fits of insanity. The estate at Houghton was allowed to fall into ruin, and as "the most signal mortification to my idolatry for my father's memory, that it could receive" (letter 74), Walpole watched helplessly as in 1779 his nephew sold Sir Robert's great collection of paintings to Catherine the Great of Russia. Letters 185 to 190 describe the unfolding saga and Walpole's efforts to control his nephew's affairs while he was incapacitated. In spite of this, "his only acknowledgment of my existence", Walpole complained in November 1791, was "an annual present of two boxes of pewit's eggs with a line and half *in his own hand* on a folio sheet, simply notifying the donation".[1] Two weeks later George was dead, leaving to his uncle, aged seventy-four, an empty title and a devastated estate, of which he wrote, "I do not understand the management, and am too old to learn".[2]

After Walpole's death, Houghton passed to the descendants of his older sister, Mary, who had married into the Cholmondeley family but died young in 1731. He also had a younger half-sister – Maria, also known as Mary – by his father's mistress Maria Skerrett. After his ennoblement in 1742 the new Earl of Orford had persuaded George II to grant Maria the rank of an Earl's daughter in spite of her illegitimate birth. She married Charles Churchill, illegitimate son of her father's friend General Churchill. Walpole was fond of her and she and her husband were frequent visitors at Strawberry Hill.

1. SIR ROBERT WALPOLE, HIS FATHER

176. *Biography of his Father.*

TO THE REV. HENRY ZOUCH

Sir,   Strawberry Hill, 21 October 1758.

… When I speak my opinion to you, Sir, so frankly about what I dare say you care as little for as I do, (for what is the merit of a mere man of letters?) it is but fit I should answer you as sincerely on a question about which you are so good as to interest yourself. That my father's life is likely to be written, I have no grounds for believing. I mean I know nobody that thinks of it.[3] For myself, I certainly shall not, for many reasons, which you must have the patience to hear. A reason to me myself is, that I think too highly of him, and too meanly of myself, to presume I am equal to the task. They who do not agree with me in the former part of my position, will undoubtedly allow the latter part. In the next place, the very truths that I should relate

1 Letter to Lady Ossory, 23 November 1791 (YE 34:130).
2 Letter to John Pinkerton, 26 December 1791 (YE 16:313).
3 Sir Robert Walpole's biography, *Memoirs of the Life and Administration of Sir Robert Walpole, Earl of Orford*, was written by the Rev. William Coxe and published in three volumes in 1798.

would be so much imputed to partiality, that he would lose of his due praise by the suspicion of my prejudice. In the next place, I was born too late in his life to be acquainted with him in the active part of it. Then I was at school, at the university, abroad, and returned not till the last moments of his administration. What I know of him I could only learn from his own mouth in the last three years of his life; when, to my shame, I was so idle, and young, and thoughtless, that I by no means profited of his leisure as I might have done; and, indeed, I have too much impartiality in my nature to care, if I could, to give the world a history, collected solely from the person himself of whom I should write. With the utmost veneration for his truth, I can easily conceive, that a man who had lived a life of party, and who had undergone such persecution from party, must have had greater bias than he himself could be sensible of. The last, and that a reason which must be admitted, if all the others are not – his papers are lost. Between the confusion of his affairs, and the indifference of my elder brother to things of that sort, they were either lost, burnt, or what we rather think, were stolen by a favourite servant of my brother, who proved a great rogue, and was dismissed in my brother's life; and the papers were not discovered to be missing till after my brother's death. Thus, Sir, I should want vouchers for many things I could say of much importance. I have another personal reason that discourages me from attempting this task, or any other, besides the great reluctance that I have to being a voluminous author. Though I am by no means the learned man you are so good as to call me in compliment; though, on the contrary, nothing can be more superficial than my knowledge, or more trifling than my reading, – yet I have so much strained my eyes, that it is often painful to me to read even a newspaper by daylight. In short, Sir, having led a very dissipated life, in all the hurry of the world and pleasure, I scarce ever read, but by candlelight, after I have come home late at nights. As my eyes have never had the least inflammation or humour, I am assured I may still recover them by care and repose. I own I prefer my eyes to anything I could ever read, much more to anything I could write. However, after all I have said, perhaps I may now and then, by degrees, throw together some short anecdotes of my father's private life and particular story, and leave his public history to more proper and more able hands, if such will undertake it. . . .

177. *Sir Robert's Character.*

TO GOVERNOR POWNALL[1]

Strawberry Hill, 27 October 1783.

I am extremely obliged to you, Sir, for the valuable communication you have made to me.[2] It is extremely so to me, as it does justice to a memory I revere to the highest degree; and I flatter myself that it would be acceptable to that part of the world that loves truth; and that part will be the majority, as fast as *they* pass away who have an interest in preferring falsehood. Happily, truth is longer-lived than the passions of individuals; and, when mankind are not misled, they can distinguish white from black. I myself do not pretend to be unprejudiced; I must be so to the best of fathers: I should be ashamed to be quite impartial. No wonder, then, Sir, if I am greatly pleased with so able a justification; yet I am not so blinded, but that I can discern solid reasons for admiring your defence. You have placed that defence on sound and *new* grounds; and, though very briefly, have very learnedly stated and distinguished the landmarks of our constitution, and the encroachments made on it, by justly referring the principles of liberty to the Saxon system, and by imputing the corruptions of it to the Norman. This was a great deal too deep for that superficial mountebank, Hume,[3] to go; for a mountebank he was. He mounted a tréteau[4] in the garb of a philosophic empiric, but dispensed no drugs but what he was authorised to vend by a royal patent, and which were full of Turkish opium. He had studied nothing relative to the English constitution before Queen Elizabeth, and had selected her most arbitrary acts to countenance those of the Stuarts: and even hers he misrepresented; for her worst deeds were levelled against the nobility, those of the Stuarts against the people. Hers, consequently, were rather an obligation to the people; for the most heinous part of common despotism is, that it produces a

---

1 Thomas Pownall (1722–1805), former Lieutenant-Governor of New Jersey and Governor of Massachusetts.
2 Pownall's "Character Sketch of Sir Robert Walpole" was printed in the 3rd volume of William Coxe's *Memoirs* of Sir Robert Walpole (1798).
3 David Hume, in his *History of England* (1754–62).
4 Trestle: that is, an inadequate working surface on which to support his philosophical system.

thousand despots instead of one. Muley Moloch[1] cannot lop off many heads with his own hands; at least, he takes those in his way, those of his courtiers: but his bashaws and viceroys spread destruction everywhere. The flimsy, ignorant, blundering manner in which Hume executed the reigns preceding Henry VII., is a proof how little he had examined the history of our constitution.

I could say much, much more, Sir, in commendation of your work, were I not apprehensive of being biassed by the subject. Still, that it would not be from flattery, I will prove, by taking the liberty of making two objections; and they are only to the last page but one. Perhaps you will think that my first objection does show that I am too much biassed. I own I am sorry to see my father compared to Sylla.[2] The latter was a sanguinary usurper, a monster; the former the mildest, most forgiving, best-natured of men, and a *legal* minister. Nor, I fear, will the only light in which you compare them, stand the test. Sylla resigned his power voluntarily, insolently; perhaps timidly, as he might think he had a better chance of dying in his bed, if he retreated, than by continuing to rule by force. My father did not retire by his own option. He had lost the majority of the House of Commons. Sylla, you say, Sir, retired unimpeached; it is true, but covered with blood. My father was not *impeached*, in our strict sense of the word; but, to my great joy, he was in effect. A Secret Committee, a worse inquisition than a jury, was named; not to try him, but to sift his life for crimes: and out of such a jury, chosen in the dark, and not one of whom he might challenge, he had some determined enemies, many opponents, and but two he could suppose his friends. And what was the consequence? A man charged with every state crime almost, for twenty years, was proved to have done – what? Paid some writers much more than they deserved, for having defended him against ten thousand and ten thousand libels, (some of which had been written by his inquisitors,) all which libels were confessed to have been lies by his inquisitors themselves; for they could not produce a shadow of one of the crimes with which they have charged him! I must own, Sir, I think that Sylla and my father ought to be set in opposition rather than paralleled.

My other objection is still more serious; and if I am so happy as

1 Muley Moloch, a 16th-century ruler of Morocco.
2 Lucius Cornelius Sulla (*c.* 138–78 B.C.), Roman tyrant, who had abdicated.

to convince you, I shall hope that you will alter the paragraph; as it seems to impute something to Sir Robert, of which he was not only most innocent, but of which, if he had been guilty, I should think him extremely so, for he would have been very ungrateful. You say he had not the comfort to see that he had established his own family by anything which he received from the gratitude of that Hanover family, or from the gratitude of that country, which he had saved and served! Good Sir, what does this sentence seem to imply, but that either Sir Robert himself, or his family, thought or think, that the Kings George I. and II., or England, were ungrateful in not rewarding his services? Defend him and us from such a charge! He nor we ever had such a thought. Was it not rewarding him to make him Prime Minister, and maintain and support him against his enemies for twenty years together? Did not George I. make his eldest son a peer, and give to the father and son a valuable patent place in the Custom-House for three lives? Did not George II. give my elder brother the Auditor's place, and to my other brother and me other rich places for our lives; for, though in the gift of the First Lord of the Treasury, do we not owe them to the King who made him so? Did not the late King make my father an Earl, and dismiss him with a pension of 4000*l.* a-year for his life? Could he or we not think these ample rewards? What rapacious sordid wretches must he and we have been, and be, could we entertain such an idea? As far have we all been from thinking him neglected by his country. Did not his country see and know these rewards? and could it think these rewards inadequate? Besides, Sir, great as I hold my father's services, they were solid and silent, not ostensible. They were of a kind to which I hold your justification a more suitable reward than pecuniary recompenses. To have fixed the House of Hanover on the throne, to have maintained this country in peace and affluence for twenty years, with the other services you record, Sir, were actions, the *éclat* of which must be illustrated by time and reflection; and whose splendour has been brought forwarder than I wish it had, by comparison with a period very dissimilar! If Sir Robert had not the comfort of leaving his family in affluence, it was not imputable to his King or his country. Perhaps I am proud that he did not. He died forty thousand pounds in debt. That was the wealth of a man that had been taxed as the plunderer of his country! Yet, with all my adoration of my father, I am just enough to own that it was his own fault if he died so poor. He had made Houghton much too magnificent for the moderate estate which he left to support it; and, as he never – I repeat it with truth, *never* – got any money but in the South Sea and while he was Paymaster, his fondness for his paternal seat, and his boundless generosity, were too expensive for his fortune. I will mention one instance, which will show how little he was disposed to turn the favour of the Crown to his own profit. He laid out fourteen thousand pounds of his own money on Richmond New Park.[1] I could produce other reasons too why Sir Robert's family were not in so comfortable a situation, as the world, deluded by misrepresentation, might expect to see them at his death. My eldest brother had been a very bad economist during his father's life, and died himself fifty thousand pounds in debt, or more; so that to this day neither Sir Edward nor I have received the five thousand pounds a-piece which Sir Robert left us as our fortunes. I do not love to charge the dead; therefore will only say that Lady Orford[2] (reckoned a vast fortune, which till she died she never proved,) wasted vast sums; nor did my brother or father *ever* receive but the twenty thousand pounds which she brought at first, and which were spent on the wedding and christening; I mean, including her jewels.

I beg pardon, Sir, for this tedious detail, which is minutely, perhaps too minutely, true; but, when I took the liberty of contesting any part of a work which I admire so much, I owed it to you and to myself to assign my reasons. I trust they will satisfy you; and, if they do, I am sure you will alter a paragraph against which it is the duty of the family to exclaim. Dear as my father's memory is to my soul, I can never subscribe to the position that he was unrewarded by the House of Hanover. . . .

1 In 1727 Sir Robert Walpole had secured the Rangership of Richmond Park for his eldest son, later 2nd Earl of Orford.
2 Margaret Rolle, wife of the 2nd Earl of Orford, daughter-in-law to Sir Robert.

178. *The Same.*

Strawberry Hill, 26 August 1785.

... On *this* day, about an hundred years ago (look at my date), was born the wisest man[1] I have seen. He kept this country in peace for twenty years, and it flourished accordingly. He injured no man; was benevolent, good-humoured, and did nothing but the common necessary business of the State. Yet was H E burnt in effigy too; and so traduced, that his name is not purified yet! – Ask why his memory is not in veneration? You will be told, from libels and trash, that he was *the Grand Corrupter* – What! did he corrupt the nation to make it happy, rich, and peaceable? Who was oppressed during his administration? Those saints Bolingbroke and Pulteney were kept out of the Paradise of the Court; ay, and the Pretender was kept out and was kept quiet. Sir Robert fell: a Rebellion ensued in four years, and the crown shook on the King's head. The nation, too, which had been tolerably corrupted before his time, and which, with all its experience and with its eyes opened, has not cured itself of being corrupt, is not quite so prosperous as in the day of that man, who, it seems, poisoned its morals. Formerly it was the most virtuous nation on earth!

Under Henry VIII. and his children there was no persecution, no fluctuation of religion: their Ministers shifted their faith four times, and were sincere honest men! There was no servility, no flattery, no contempt of the nation abroad, under James I. No tyranny under Charles I. and Laud; no factions, no civil war! Charles II., however, brought back all the virtues and morality, which, somehow or other, were missing! His brother's was a still more blessed reign, though in a different way! King William was disturbed and distressed by no contending factions, and did not endeavour to bribe them to let him pursue his great object of humbling France! The Duke of Marlborough was not overborne in a similar and more glorious career by a detestable Cabal! – and if Oxford and Bolingbroke did remove him, from the most patriot motives, they, good men! used no corruption!

1 Sir Robert Walpole. In an ironic summary of English political history Walpole contrasts the beneficent rule of his father with the state of the country before and after his ministry.

Twelve Peerages showered at once, to convert the House of Lords, were no bribes; nor was a shilling issued for secret services; nor would a member of either House have received it!

Sir R. Walpole came, and, strange to tell, found the whole Parliament, and every Parliament, at least a great majority of every Parliament, ready to take his money. For what? – to undo their country! – which, however, wickedly as he meant, and ready as they were to concur, he left in every respect in the condition he found it, except in being improved in trade, wealth, and tranquillity; till *its friends* who expelled him, and dipped their poor country in a war; which was far from mending its condition. Sir Robert died, foretelling a Rebellion, which happened in less than six months, and for predicting which he had been ridiculed: and in detestation of a maxim ascribed to him by his enemies, that *every man has his price*, the tariff of every Parliament since has been as well known as the price of beef and mutton; and the universal electors, who cry out against that traffic, are not a jot less vendible than their electors. – Was not Sir Robert Walpole an abominable Minister? ...

2. SIR EDWARD WALPOLE, HIS BROTHER

179. *An Angry Brother.*

HORACE WALPOLE TO SIR EDWARD WALPOLE[1]

Dear Brother,   17 May 1745.

You have used me very ill without any provocation or any pretence. I have always made it my study to deserve your friendship, as you yourself own, and by a submission which I did not owe you. For consulting you in what you had nothing to do, I certainly did not, nor ever will, while you profess so much aversion for me. I am still ready to live with you upon any terms of friendship and equality; but I don't mind your anger, which can only hurt yourself, when you come to reflect with what strange passion you have treated me, who have always loved you, have always tried to please you, have always spoken of you with regard, and who will yet be, if you will let me,

Your affectionate brother and humble servant,

Hor. Walpole.

1 Sir Edward Walpole (1706–84), second son of Sir Robert Walpole.

180. *Sir Edward's Envy.*

TO SIR HORACE MANN

23 March 1749.

... If I had more paper or time, I could tell you an excellent long history of my brother Ned's [Sir Edward's] envy, which was always up at high-water-mark, but since the publication of my book of Houghton[1] (one should have thought a very harmless performance), has overflowed on a thousand ridiculous occasions. Another great object of his jealousy is my friendship with Mr. Fox: my brother made him a formal visit at nine o'clock the other morning, and in a set speech of three quarters of an hour, begged his pardon for not attending the last day of the Mutiny-bill, which, he said, was so particularly brought in by him, though Mr. Fox assured him that he had no farther hand in it than from his office. Another instance: when my brother went to live at Frogmore, Mr. Fox desired him to employ his tradesmen at Windsor, by way of supporting his interest in that borough. My brother immediately went to the Duke of St. Albans, to whom he had never spoke (nor indeed was his acquaintance with Mr. Fox much greater), and notified to him, that if seven years hence his grace should have any contest with Mr. Fox about that borough, he should certainly espouse the latter. Guess how the Duke stared at so strange and unnecessary a declaration! ... Adieu!

181. *His Death.*

TO THE REV. WILLIAM MASON

Berkeley Square, 2 February 1784.

I thank you for your condolence on the death of my brother,[2] and on the considerable diminution of my own fortune, though neither are events to which I am not perfectly reconciled. My brother was seventy-seven, had enjoyed perfect health and senses to that age, did not even begin to break till last August, suffered no pain, saw death advance gradually though fast, with the coolest tranquillity, did not

---

1 *Ædes Walpolianæ* (1747), Walpole's account of his father's collection.
2 Sir Edward Walpole.

even wish to live longer, and died both with indifference and without affectation; is that a termination to lament?

I do lose fourteen hundred a-year by his death,[1] but had I reason to expect to keep it so long? I had twice been offered the reversion for my own life, and positively refused to accept it, because I would receive no obligation that might entangle my honour and my gratitude, and set them at variance. I never did ask or receive a personal favour from my own most intimate friends when in power, though they were too upright to have laid me under the same difficulties, and have always acted an uniform and honest part; but though I love expense, I was content with a fortune far above any merit I can pretend to, and knew I should be content with it were it much lessened. As it would be contemptible to regret the diminution at sixty-six, there is no merit in being quite easy under the loss. But you do me honour I do not deserve in complimenting me on not loving money. I have always loved what money would purchase, which is much the same thing; and the whole of my philosophy consists in reconciling myself to buying fewer baubles for a year or two that I may live, and when the old child's baby-house is quite full of playthings. . . .

3. MARIA, HIS NIECE[2]

182. *Her First Marriage.*

TO GEORGE MONTAGU, ESQ.

16 May 1759.

. . . Well! Maria was married yesterday. Don't we manage well? the original day was not once put off: lawyers and milliners were all ready canonically. It was as sensible a wedding as ever was. There was neither form nor indecency, both which generally meet on such occasions. They were married at my brother's in Pall-Mall, just before dinner, by Mr. Keppel; the company, my brother, his son, Mrs. Keppel, and Charlotte, Lady Elizabeth Keppel, Lady Betty Waldegrave, and I. We dined there; the Earl and new Countess got into their post-chaise at eight o'clock, and went to Navestock [in Essex] alone, where they stay till Saturday night: on Sunday she is

---

1 Walpole's enjoyment of the sinecure of Collector of the Customs lapsed with his brother's death.
2 Maria, Lady Waldegrave (see letter 31, p. 53, n. 2).

to be presented, and to make my Lady Coventry[1] distracted, who, t'other day, told Lady Anne Connolly how she dreaded Lady Louisa's arrival; "But," said she, "now I have seen her, I am easy."

Maria was in a white silver night gown, with a hat very much pulled over her face; what one could see of it was handsomer than ever; a cold maiden blush gave her the sweetest delicacy in the world. I had liked to have demolished the solemnity of the ceremony by laughing, when Mr. Keppel read the words, "Bless thy servant and thy handmaid"; it struck me how ridiculous it would have been, had Miss Drax[2] been the handmaid, as she was once to have been. . . .

Lord Weymouth is to be married on Tuesday, or, as he said himself, to be turned off.[3] George Selwyn told him he wondered that he had not been turned off before, for he still sits up drinking all night and gaming. . . .

183. *Her Husband's Death.*

TO SIR HORACE MANN

Strawberry Hill, 10 April 1763.

At a time when the political world is in strange and unexpected disorder, you would wonder that I should be here, and be so for some days; but I am come on a very melancholy occasion. Lord Waldegrave is just dead of the small-pox, and I have brought my poor unhappy niece hither till he is buried. He was taken ill on the Wednesday, the distemper showed itself on the Friday a very bad sort, and carried him off that day se'nnight. His brother and sister were inoculated but it was early in the practice of that great preservative, which was then devoutly opposed; he was the eldest son, and weakly. He never had any fear of it, nor ever avoided it. We scarce feel this heavy loss more than it is felt universally. He was one of

1 Lady Coventry (bap. 1732–60) was Maria, one of the two Gunning sisters, famous for their beauty. Lady Louisa was Lady Louisa Connolly, *née* Lennox, daughter-in-law of the Lady Anne Connolly to whom Lady Coventry was speaking. On the Sunday Lady Waldegrave was to be presented at court.
2 The Yale editors note that Harriet Drax had been deserted by Lord Waldegrave for Maria Walpole, and that George II, who clearly had no good opinion of Miss Drax, was said to have remarked that "he had prevented him marrying a Whore, and now he had wedded a Bastard".
3 "Turned off", used colloquially for both hanged, and (of a servant) dismissed.

those few men whose good-nature silenced even ill-nature. His strict honour and consummate sense made him reverenced as much as beloved. He died as he lived, the physicians declaring that if anything saved him, it would be his tranquillity; I soon saw by their ignorance and contradictions that *they* would not. Yet I believe James's powder[1] would have preserved him. He took it by my persuasion, before I knew what his disorder was. But James was soon chased away, to make room for regular assassins. In the course of the illness nobody would venture to take on them so important a hazard as giving the powder again; yet in his agonies it was given, and even then had efficacy enough to vomit him; but too late! My niece has nothing left but a moderate jointure of a thousand pounds a-year, three little girls,[2] a pregnancy, her beauty, and the testimonial of the best of men, who expressed no concern but for her, and who has given her as much as he could, and ratified her character by making her sole executrix. Her tenderness, which could not be founded on any charms in his person, shows itself in floods of tears, in veneration for his memory, and by acting with just such reason and propriety as he would wish her to exert; yet it is a terrible scene! She loses in him a father, who formed her mind, and a lover whose profusion knew no bounds. From his places his fortune was very great – that is gone! From his rank and consideration with all parties, she was at the summit of worldly glory – that is gone too! Four short years were all their happiness. Since the death of Lady Coventry, she is allowed the handsomest woman in England; as she is so young, she may find as great a match and a younger lover – but she never can find another Lord Waldegrave! . . .

1 A popular fever powder patented by Dr. Robert James (bap. 1703–76).
2 The three girls, Walpole's great-nieces, became the three Ladies Waldegrave as painted for him by Reynolds (now in the National Gallery of Scotland). Of these, Elizabeth Laura (1760–1816), in the centre of Reynolds's painting, married her cousin the 4th Earl Waldegrave and was the residuary legatee of Strawberry Hill, inheriting it in 1811 when the sculptor Anne Seymour Damer (see letter 193, p. 273, n. 1) relinquished her life tenancy.

184. *Duchess of Gloucester.*

TO SIR HORACE MANN

Strawberry Hill, 20 September 1772.

There is an end of palliating, suppressing, or disbelieving: the marriage (my niece's marriage) is formally notified to the King by the Duke of Gloucester.[1] Many symptoms had convinced me of late that so it would be. Last Wednesday night I received a letter signed *Maria Gloucester*, acquainting me that the declaration has been made, and been received by his Majesty with grief, tenderness, and justice. I say justice, *tout oncle* as I am, for it would have been very unjust to the Duke of Cumberland to have made any other distinction between two brothers equally in fault, than what affection without overt acts cannot help making. This implies that the Duke of Gloucester must undergo the same prohibition[2] as his brother did, which I am told is to be the case, though the step is not yet taken.

Having acted so rigorously while I could have any doubt of any sort left, it was but decent now to show that respect, nay gratitude, for so great an honour done to the family, which was due to the Prince, and still more to his honour and justice. I accordingly begged the Duchess to ask leave for me to kiss his Royal Highness's hand, which was immediately granted. I went directly to the Pavilions at Hampton Court, where they were, and the Duke received me with great goodness, even drawing an arm-chair for me himself when I refused to continue sitting by the Duchess, or even to sit at all. He entered into the detail of his reasons for declaring the marriage, which he knew, by a former letter to the Duchess, I had approved their not publishing so far as her taking the title; and by something that dropped apropos to the title, I am persuaded that my having obstinately avoided all connexion with him, had been a principal cause of his anger, though I do not doubt but some who were averse to the marriage had said everything they could to the disadvantage of the family; and as I had shown most disapprobation of the connexion, impressions against me naturally took the easiest root. Well

1 William Henry (1743–1805), Duke of Gloucester, brother of George III.
2 Both the Duke of Gloucester and the Duke of Cumberland were banned from the royal presence for marrying commoners without the King's permission: Gloucester and Maria Waldegrave had been married privately six years earlier.

here ends my part of this history; I neither shall be, nor seek to be a favourite, and as little a counsellor. Were I to advise, it should be to submit themselves entirely to the King. A Prince of the Blood, especially of a character so esteemed, may give great trouble, but whom do they hurt but their own family? The Duke of Cumberland was slighted by the Opposition, because he married the sister of the man in England [Colonel Luttrell][1] the most obnoxious to them. To them the Duke of Gloucester is a very different case, and they are not likely not to make the distinction; but I shall think the Duchess very ill-advised, if she does not dissuade everything that can displease the King. Her temper is warm, but she has an admirable understanding and a thousand virtues. . . .

4. GEORGE, THE THIRD EARL OF ORFORD,[2] HIS NEPHEW

185. *His Insanity.*

TO SIR HORACE MANN

Arlington Street, 17 February 1773.

. . . I have a melancholy tale to tell you of another branch of it,[3] my Lord Orford. He had a cutaneous or some scorbutic eruption. By advice of his *groom*, he rubbed his body all over with an ointment of sulphur and hellebore. This poison struck in the disease. By as bad advice as his groom's, I mean his own, he took a violent antimonial medicine, which sweated him immoderately; and then he came to town, went to Court, took James's pills, without telling him of the quack drops, sat up late, and, though ordered by James to keep at home, returned into the country the next day. The cold struck all his nostrums and ails into his head, and the consequence is – insanity! To complete the misfortune, he is in a public inn, on the great road to Newmarket and Norfolk. His mother, the only proper directress, is in Italy; I am in the state of pain and weakness you know; and my

1 Henry Luttrell (1737–1821), John Wilkes's opponent in the contested Middlesex election of 1769.
2 George, 3rd Earl of Orford (1730–91), son of Walpole's eldest brother. He was troubled by periodic bouts of insanity. In 1779 he sold the Houghton collection of paintings to Catherine the Great.
3 Walpole's family.

brother [Sir Edward Walpole] has so long shut himself up in his own house, that no consideration could draw him out of it. I need but tell you, that his daughter, the Duchess [of Gloucester], even in summer, could not prevail on him to wait on the Duke. It is an additional distress, that Lord Orford has for so many years dropped all connexion, all decency, with both my brother and me, that nothing but tenderness for his lamentable position could bear us out in assuming the least authority in what regards him. We have the precaution, however, not to take a single step but at the request of his physicians, or with the advice and approbation of his own most particular friends. His life, we are assured, is safe, and we have hopes given us of the recovery of his reason. His death would be the completion of the family's ruin: his continuance as he is, dreadful to himself and his friends: his total recovery liable to dismal moments for his own mind. His case is a heavy addition to my sufferings, and the anxiety I am under on every step I take in concert with my brother, lest, one way or other, we should be censured, cannot accelerate my recovery. . . .

186. *Walpole Manages the Estate.*

TO SIR HORACE MANN

Strawberry Hill, 13 July 1773.

. . . When my mind reposes a little, I smile at myself. I intended to trifle out the remnant of my days; and lo! they are invaded by lawyers, stewards, physicians, and jockeys![1] Yes; this whole week past I have been negotiating a sale of race-horses at Newmarket, and, to the honour of my transactions, the sale has turned out greatly. My Gothic ancestors are forgotten; I am got upon the turf. I give orders about game, dispark Houghton, have plans of farming, vend colts, fillies, bullocks, and sheep, and have not yet confounded terms, nor ordered pointers to be turned to grass. I read the part of the newspapers I used to skip, and peruse the lists of sweepstakes: not the articles of intelligence, nor the relations of the shows at Portsmouth for the King, or at Oxford for the Viceroy North.[2] I must leave

1 Walpole was administering his nephew's estate during his nephew's temporary insanity.
2 Frederic Lord North, Prime Minister, and Chancellor of Oxford. – WALPOLE.

Europe and its Kings and Queens to you; we do not talk of such folks at the Inns of Court. I sold *Stoic*[1] for five hundred guineas: I shall never get five pence by the Monarchs of the Empire, and therefore we jockeys of the Temple, and we lawyers of Newmarket, hold them to be very insignificant individuals. The only political point that touches me at present is what does occasion much noise and trouble, – the new Act that decries guineas under weight. Though I have refused to receive a guinea myself of Lord Orford's income, yet I must see it all paid into my Lady's banker's hands, and I am now in a fright lest the purchase-money of the racers should be made in light coin,[2] – not from suspicion of such *honourable* men, but from their inattention to money. . . .

187. *Desolation of Houghton.*

TO THE HON. H. S. CONWAY

Arlington Street, 30 August 1773.

I returned last night from Houghton, where multiplicity of business detained me four days longer than I intended, and where I found a scene infinitely more mortifying than I expected; though I certainly did not go with a prospect of finding a land flowing with milk and honey. Except the pictures, which are in the finest preservation, and the woods, which are become forests, all the rest is ruin, desolation, confusion, disorder, debts, mortgages, sales, pillage, villainy, waste, folly and madness. I do not believe that five thousand pounds would put the house and buildings into good repair. The nettles and brambles in the park are up to your shoulders; horses have been turned into the garden, and banditti lodged in every cottage. The perpetuity of livings that come up to the park-pales have been sold – and every farm let for half its value. In short, you know how much family pride I have, and consequently may judge how much I have been mortified! Nor do I tell you half, or *near* the worst circumstances. I have just stopped the torrent – and that is all. I am very uncertain whether I must not fling up the trust; and some of the difficulties in my way seem insurmountable, and too dangerous

1 Name of a race-horse. – WALPOLE.
2 The Act was against clipped coinage. Walpole was accounting for the proceeds of his sales to the bankers for Lady Orford, his nephew's mother.

not to alarm even my zeal; since I must not ruin myself, and hurt those for whom I must feel, too, only to restore a family that will end with myself, and to retrieve an estate from which I am not likely ever to receive the least advantage.

If you will settle with the Churchills your journey to Chalfont, and will let me know the day, I will endeavour to meet you there; I hope it will not be till next week. I am overwhelmed with business – but, indeed, I know not when I shall be otherwise! I wish you joy of this endless summer.

188. *Another Attack.*

TO SIR HORACE MANN

Barton Mills, 28 April 1777.

... After an interval of three years, in which my nephew remained as much in his senses as he was *supposed* to be before his declared phrenzy, he was seized a fortnight ago with a fever which soon brought out the colour of his blood. In two days he was furious. The low wretches by whom in his *sensible* hours he has always been sur-rounded, concealed the symptoms till they were terrifying. I received no notice till the sixth day, and then – by the stage-coach! I set out directly for the hovel where he is – a *pasnidge*-house, as the reverend proprietor[1] called it to me, on the edge of the fens, which my Lord hires, and is his usual residence. The single chamber without a bed is a parlour seven feet high, directly under my Lord's bedchamber, without shutters, and so smoky that there is no sitting in it unless the door is open. I am forced to lie here, five miles off, in an inn – a palace to *his* dwelling. The morning after my arrival, a physician I had sent for from Norwich, forty miles from hence, coming down to tell me how he had found my Lord, we were alarmed with a scream and a bustle. The doctor had ordered the window to be opened to let out the smoke, and, the moment he had quitted his patient, my Lord attempted to fling himself out of the window, but was prevented by his keeper and servants, who flung him on the bed. You will scarcely believe that, on my arrival, his mistress, his steward, and a neighbouring parson of the confederacy, on my declaring

1 One Ball, Minister of Eriswell, a jockey-parson. – WALPOLE.

I should remove him directly to London for proper assistance, cried out, that I should kill him if I conveyed him from that Paradise in which was all his delight, and where he has so long swallowed every apple that every serpent has offered to him. The very day before he had asked where he was.

At the desire of the Norwich physician, I sent for Dr. Jebb[1] from London. Before he came, the fever was gone, and an interval of sense was returned. Yet, as before, he would only speak in a whisper, and could not be persuaded to show his tongue to Dr. Jebb, though he made rational answers. Dr. Jebb pronounced, that he had neither fever nor understanding. He has had a slight return of the former, and no delirium. Yet both his physicians, the apothecary, and even his mistress, think his disorder will still last some weeks. Perhaps it may not; nor is it the worst consideration that he will have these relapses: as this arrived in very cold weather, and from no apparent cause, the madness is evidently constitutional, and leaves both himself and his family with all their apprehensions. Mine are, that as both now and formerly he has betrayed mischievous designs, he will after some lucid interval destroy himself; and I have seen that the crew about him will not call in help till perhaps too late. They had not even sent for a physician; because, as they told me, my Lord (a lunatic) has no opinion of physicians. Judge of my distress! My brother and I have too much tenderness and delicacy to take out the statute of lunacy. All my care and attention to him, his mistress, and fortune, in his former illness, have not made the smallest impression. I have not even seen him these three years, though he declared on his recovery that he approved all I had done; and I must say that I meant to set an example of tenderness which, I believe, was never seen before in a parallel case. I cannot resent it from him; for his misfortune acquits him of everything. I had greatly improved his fortune, and should have effected much more, had he not instantly taken everything out of my hands.

This treatment, and many such reasons, had determined me never more to meddle with his affairs: indeed, the fatigue, joined to my apprehension, had half killed me. I had done everything at my own risk, and some things at my own cost. Thus, without the sanction of law, which I will not claim for my Lord's sake, I could

1   Sir Richard Jebb (1729–87), physician.

not undertake his affairs again. I now declared I would take on me the care of his person and health, but never of his fortune – what will become of that, I know not! . . .

I shall stay here to see the physician from Norwich to-morrow. If he pronounces, as I expect, that my Lord is recovered, I shall take my leave, and resign him to the rudder of his own poor brain. I pity him, but it must be so. My character and Sir Edward's are at stake, and to preserve them we must obey the law literally. The last time, the moment the physicians pronounced him sane, we submitted and threw open his doors; though neither of us were of that opinion. I attended him to Houghton, and saw nothing but evidence of distraction. The gentlemen of the country came to congratulate him on his recovery; yet, for more than six weeks, he would do nothing but speak in the lowest voice, and would whisper to them at the length of the table, when the person next to him could not distinguish what he said. Every evening, precisely at the same hour, sitting round a table, he would join his forehead to his mistress's (who is forty, red-faced, and with black teeth, and with whom he has slept every night these twenty years), and there they would sit for a quarter of an hour, like two parroquets, without speaking. Every night, from seven to nine, he regularly, for the whole fortnight, made his secretary of militia, an old drunken, broken tradesman, read "Statius"[1] to the whole company, though the man could not hiccup the right quantity of the syllables. Imagine what I suffered! One morning I asked the company before my Lord was up, how they found him? They answered, just as he had always been. Then, thought I, he has always been distracted. . . . Adieu!

189. *Reply to Letter of Thanks.*

TO THE EARL OF ORFORD

My Dear Lord,   Strawberry Hill, 5 October 1778.

Your Lordship is very good in thanking[2] me for what I could not claim any thanks, as in complying with your request, and assisting you to settle your affairs, according to my Father's Will, was not only

1 Roman poet of the first century A.D.
2 Written in response to a letter from Lord Orford of 1 October 1778 thanking Walpole for his assistance during his indisposition and inviting him to Houghton.

my duty, but to promote your service and benefit, to re-establish the affairs of my family, and to conform myself to the views of the excellent man, the glory of human nature, who made us all what we are, has been constantly one of the principal objects of my whole life. If my labours and wishes have been crowned with small success, it has been owing to my own inability in the first place, and next to tenderness, and to the dirt and roguery of wretches below my notice. For your Lordship, I may presume to say, I have spared no thought, industry, solicitude, application, or even health, when, I had the care of your affairs. What I did, and could have done, and should have done, if you had not thought fit to prefer a most conceited and worthless fellow, I can demonstrate by reams of paper, that may, one day or other, prove what I say; and which, if I have not yet done, it proceeds from the same tenderness that I have ever had for your Lordship's tranquillity and repose. To acquiesce afterwards in the arrangement you have proposed to me, is small merit indeed. My honour is much dearer to me than fortune, and to contribute to your Lordship's enjoying your fortune with credit and satisfaction, is a point I would have purchased with far greater compliances; for, my Lord, as I flatter myself that I am not thought an interested man, so all who know me know, that to see the lustre of my family restored to the consideration to which it was raised by Sir Robert Walpole, shining in you, and transmitted to his and your descendants, was the only ambition that ever actuated me. No personal advantage entered into those views; and if I say thus much of myself with truth, I owe still greater justice to my brother, who has many more virtues than I can pretend to, and is as incapable of forming any mean and selfish wishes as any man upon earth. We are both old men now, and without sons to inspire us with future visions. We wish to leave your Lordship in as happy and respectable situation as you was born to, and we have both given you all the proof in our power, by acquiescing in your proposal immediately.

For me, my Lord, I should with pleasure accept the honour of waiting on you at Houghton at the time you mention, if my lameness and threats of the gout did not forbid my taking so long a journey at this time of the year. At sixty-one, it would not become me to talk of another year: perhaps I may never go to Houghton again, till I go thither for ever; but without affectation of philosophy, even the path to that journey will be sweetened to me, if I leave Houghton the

flourishing monument of one of the best Ministers that ever blest
this once flourishing country.

I am, my dear Lord,
Yours most affectionately,
Hor. Walpole.

190. *The Houghton Pictures Sold.*

TO SIR HORACE MANN

Strawberry Hill, 4 August 1779.

... Private news we have none, but what I have long been bidden
to expect, the completion of the sale of the pictures at Houghton
to the Czarina. The sum stipulated is forty or forty-five thousand
pounds, I neither know nor care which;[1] nor whether the picture-
merchant ever receives the whole sum, which probably he will not
do, as I hear it is to be discharged at three payments – a miserable
bargain for a mighty empress! Fresh lovers, and fresh, will perhaps
intercept the second and third payments. Well! adieu to Houghton!
about its mad master I shall never trouble myself more. From the
moment he came into possession, he has undermined every act of
my father that was within his reach, but, having none of that great
man's sense or virtues, he could only lay wild hands on lands and
houses; and, since he has stript Houghton of its glory, I do not care
a straw what he does with the stone or the acres. The happiness my
father entailed on this country has been thrown away in as distracted
a manner, but his fame will not be injured by the insanity of any of
his successors. We have paid a fine for having cut off the entail, but
shall not so easily suffer a recovery. ...

---

1   The price was £40,555. The paintings are now in the Hermitage and other Russian
collections.

X
HIS FRIENDS AND CORRESPONDENTS

1. HENRY CONWAY

Henry Seymour Conway (1719–95), soldier and statesman, was Walpole's cousin, their mothers being sisters. From Eton days Conway was perhaps Walpole's most intimate friend, and their correspondence, which runs from 1737 to Conway's death in 1795, contains repeated expressions of Walpole's deep affection. Recent commentators have speculated about a sexual element in their relationship – a possibility that did not escape his contemporaries, as witness the taunts of William Guthrie's *Reply to the Counter-Address*, a scurrilous Grub Street pamphlet of 1764; this was circulated after Conway was dismissed from his regiment and his place at court for voting against the government and Walpole had staunchly defended his cousin's conduct. Walpole's disarming response was to send the pamphlet to Conway, commenting "They have nothing better to say, than that I am in love with you, have been so these twenty years, and am no giant. I am a very constant old swain: they might have made the years above thirty; it is so long I have had the same unalterable friendship for you, independent of being near relations and bred up together."[1]

Walpole's immediate reaction to Conway's downfall was to offer to share his fortune with him (letter 192), repeating the generous offer he had made twenty years previously when Conway was contemplating marriage to Lady Caroline Fitzroy (letter 191). Conway instead married in 1747 Caroline Bruce, Lady Ailesbury, and they had one child, Anne Seymour Damer the sculptor. Walpole was a great admirer of her talents and in his will gave her a life interest in Strawberry Hill, where she lived until 1811.

Conway accompanied Walpole and Gray on part of their Grand

---

[1] Letter of 1 September 1764 (YE 38:437).

Tour in 1739. He had obtained a commission in the Dragoons in 1737, and became an M.P. in 1741. During the War of the Austrian Succession he distinguished himself in the battle of Fontenoy (1745); promoted to colonel, he fought against the Jacobite army at Culloden the following year. During 1751–2 he visited Florence and Rome with his wife, and on their return he bought as his country seat Park Place, near Henley, Berkshire, where he made extensive improvements to both house and grounds. He was unexpectedly made Chief Secretary for Ireland in 1755; in 1757 he was appointed a Groom of the Bedchamber to George II, but in the same year his reputation was damaged by his involvement in the unsuccessful expedition to capture Rochefort, an incident in the Seven Years' War. In 1764, during the Wilkes affair, he had felt strongly enough on the question of general warrants to vote against Grenville's government on their use, but his consequent fall from grace, so grievous to his cousin, was short-lived. The following year he was Secretary of State in Rockingham's administration, and continued to serve under Chatham's ministry, eventually resigning in 1768, though at the King's request remaining in the Cabinet until 1770. He was Lieutenant-General of the Ordnance (resulting in Walpole's delightful letter 113) from 1767 until 1772, when he was appointed Governor of Jersey.

Conway was an outspoken opponent of the American war, and in 1782 returned to government under Lords Rockingham and Shelburne and (having resumed his military career in 1768) was appointed Commander-in-Chief and a member of the Cabinet. He resigned on the fall of the Shelburne ministry in 1783, retiring to Park Place.

Walpole told Conway in letter 192 "You have ever been the dearest person to me in the world", but the closeness of his friendship is equally well demonstrated by letter 218, in which he asks favours of his cousin in relation to Madame du Deffand – Conway was in Paris at the time – clearly confident of his unconditional co-operation.

191. *A Generous Offer.*

TO THE HON. H. S. CONWAY

Arlington Street, 20 July 1744.

My Dearest Harry,

... You must see why I don't care to say more on this head.[1] My wishing it could be right for you to break off with her[2] (for, without it is right, I would not have you on any account take such a step) makes it impossible for me to advise it; and, therefore, I am sure you will forgive my declining an act of friendship which your having put in my power gives me the greatest satisfaction. But it does put something else in my power, which I am sure nothing can make me decline, and for which I have long wanted an opportunity. Nothing could prevent my being unhappy at the smallness of your fortune, but its throwing it into my way to offer you to share mine. As mine is so precarious, by depending on so bad a constitution, I can only offer you the immediate use of it. I do that most sincerely. My places still (though my Lord Walpole has cut off three hundred pounds a-year to save himself the trouble of signing his name ten times for once) brings me in near two thousand pounds a-year. I have no debts, no connections indeed; no way to dispose of it particularly. By living with my father, I have little real use for a quarter of it. I have always flung it away all in the most idle manner; but, my dear Harry, idle as I am, and thoughtless, I have sense enough to have real pleasure in denying myself baubles, and in saving a very good income to make a man happy, for whom I have a just esteem and most sincere friendship. I know the difficulties any gentleman and man of spirit must struggle with, even in having such an offer made him, much more in accepting it. I hope you will allow there are some in making it. But hear me: if there is any such thing as friendship in the world, these are the opportunities of exerting it, and it can't be exerted without it is accepted. I must talk of myself to prove to you that it will be right for you to accept it. I am sensible of having more follies

---

1 In the earlier part of the letter Walpole had been discussing Conway's attachment to Lady Caroline Fitzroy, whose sister had married Conway's elder brother, later Earl of Hertford.

2 This was an early attachment of Mr. Conway's. By his having complied with the wishes and advice of his friend on this subject, and got the better of his passion, he probably felt that he, in some measure, owed to Mr. Walpole the subsequent happiness of his life, in his marriage with another person. – WALPOLE.

and weaknesses, and fewer real good qualities, than most men. I sometimes reflect on this, though I own too seldom. I always want to begin acting like a man, and a sensible one, which I think I might be if I would. Can I begin better, than by taking care of my fortune for one I love? You have seen (I have seen you have) that I am fickle, and foolishly fond of twenty new people; but I don't really love them – I have always loved you constantly: I am willing to convince you and the world, what I have always told you, that I loved you better than anybody. If I ever felt much for any thing, (which I know may be questioned,) it was certainly for my mother. I look on you as my nearest relation[1] by her, and I think I can never do enough to show my gratitude and affection to her. For these reasons, don't deny me what I have set my heart on – the making your fortune easy to you. * * *

[The rest of this letter is wanting.]

192. *A Further Offer.*

TO THE HON. H. S. CONWAY

Strawberry Hill, Saturday night, eight o'clock, 21 April 1764.

I write to you with a very bad head-ache; I have passed a night, for which George Grenville and the Duke of Bedford shall pass many an uneasy one! Notwithstanding I heard from everybody I met, that your Regiment, as well as Bedchamber, were taken away, I would not believe it, till last night the Duchess of Grafton told me, that the night before the Duchess of Bedford said to her, "Are not you very sorry for poor Mr. Conway? He has lost everything." When the Witch of Endor pities, one knows she has raised the devil.

I am come hither alone to put my thoughts into some order, and to avoid showing the first sallies of my resentment, which I know you would disapprove; nor does it become your friend to rail. My anger shall be a little more manly, and the plan of my revenge a little deeper laid than in peevish bons mots. You shall judge of my indignation by its duration.

In the meantime, let me beg you, in the most earnest and most

1 Walpole's mother Catherine Shorter (*c.* 1682–1737), whose memory he cherished, was Conway's aunt.

sincere of all professions, to suffer me to make your loss as light as it is in my power to make it: I have six thousand pounds in the funds; accept all, or what part you want. Do not imagine I will be put off with a refusal. The retrenchment of my expenses, which I shall from this hour commence, will convince you that I mean to re-place your fortune as far as I can. When I thought you did not want it, I had made another disposition. You have ever been the dearest person to me in the world. You have shown that you deserve to be so. You suffer for your spotless integrity. Can I hesitate a moment to show that there is at least one man who knows how to value you? The new will, which I am going to make, will be a testimonial of my own sense of virtue.

One circumstance has heightened my resentment. If it was *not* an accident, it deserves to heighten it. The very day on which your dismission was notified, I received an order from the Treasury for the payment of what money was due to me there. Is it possible that they could mean to make any distinction between us? Have I separated myself from you? Is there that spot on earth where I can be suspected of having paid court? Have I even left my name at a Minister's door since you took your part? If they have dared to hint this, the pen that is now writing to you will bitterly undeceive them.

I am impatient to see the letters you have received, and the answers you have sent. Do you come to town? If you do not, I will come to you to-morrow se'nnight, that is, the 29th. I give no advice on anything, because you are cooler than I am – not so cool, I hope, as to be insensible to this outrage, this villany, this injustice! You owe it to your country to labour the extermination of such ministers!

I am so bad a hypocrite, that I am afraid of showing how deeply I feel this. Yet last night I received the account from the Duchess of Grafton with more temper than you believe me capable of: but the agitation of the night disordered me so much, that Lord John Cavendish, who was with me two hours this morning, does not, I believe, take me for a hero. As there are some who I know would enjoy my mortification, and who probably designed I should feel my share of it, I wish to command myself – but that struggle shall be added to their bill. I saw nobody else before I came away but Legge,[1] who sent for me and wrote the enclosed for you. He would have said

---

1 Henry Legge (1708–64), politician. Lady Ailesbury was Conway's wife.

more both to you and Lady Ailesbury, but I would not let him, as he is so ill: however, he thinks himself that he shall live. I hope he will! I would not lose a shadow that can haunt these ministers.

I feel for Lady Ailesbury, because I know she feels just as I do – and it is not a pleasant sensation. I will say no more, though I could write volumes. Adieu! Yours, as I ever have been and ever will be.

193. *Mr. Damer's*[1] *Suicide.*

TO SIR HORACE MANN

Strawberry Hill, 20 August 1776.

You will have concluded, on the sight of another letter so soon, that you are to hear of a battle in America. Not so, though you are going to hear a dismal story, and, which is worse, relative to friends of mine. Indeed the newspapers will have told it to you already, and you have known the principal actor, Mr. Damer, Lord Milton's eldest son, and who married General Conway's only daughter. I think I told you in my last that he and his two brothers most unexpectedly notified to their father that they owed above seventy thousand pounds. The proud lord, for once in the right, refused to pay the debt, or see them. The two eldest were to retire to France, and Mrs. Damer was to accompany them, without a murmur, and with the approbation, though to the great grief, of Mr. Conway and Lady Ailesbury. She was, luckily, gone to take her leave of them, and to return to town last Friday morning. On Thursday, Mr. Damer supped at the Bedford Arms in Covent Garden, with four common women, a blind fiddler, and no other man. At three in the morning he dismissed his seraglio, bidding each receive her guinea at the bar, and ordering Orpheus to come up again in half-an-hour. When he returned, he found a dead silence, and smelt gunpowder. He called, the master of the house came up, and found Mr. Damer sitting in his chair, dead, with a pistol by him, and another in his pocket! The ball had not gone through his head, nor made any report. On the table lay a scrap of paper with these words, "The people of the house

---

1 The Hon. John Damer (1744–76), who had married Conway's daughter Anne Seymour Conway (1749–1828) in 1767. Walpole had recommended him to Mann when as a young man Damer had visited Florence in 1765. Anne Damer later became a sculptor and, on Walpole's death, life tenant of Strawberry Hill.

are not to blame for what has happened, which was my own act."
This was the sole tribute he paid to justice and decency!

What a catastrophe for a man at thirty two, heir to two and
twenty thousand a year! We are persuaded lunacy, not distress, was
the sole cause of his fate. He has often, and even at supper that night,
hinted at such an exploit – the very reason why one should not expect
it. His brothers have gamed – he never did. He was grave, cool,
reasonable, and reserved; but passed his life as he died, with troops
of women and the blind fiddler – an odd companion in such scenes!
One good springs out of this evil, the leeches, the Jews, and extor-
tioners, will lose very considerably. Lord Milton, whom anything
can petrify and nothing soften, will not only not see his remaining
sons, but wrecks his fury on Mrs. Damer, though she deserves only
pity, and shows no resentment. He insists on selling her jewels,
which are magnificent, for discharge of just debts. This is all the hurt
he can do her; she must have her jointure of 2500*l*. a-year. . . .

194. *Mutual Affection.*

TO THE HON. H. S. CONWAY

Strawberry Hill, 16 September 1781.

I am not surprised that such a mind as yours cannot help
expressing gratitude:[1] it would not be your mind, if it could command that sensation as triumphantly as it does your passions. Only
remember that the expression is unnecessary. I do know that you feel
the entire friendship I have for you; nor should I love you so well if
I was not persuaded of it. There never was a grain of anything
romantic in my friendship for you. We loved one another from children, and as so near relations; but my friendship grew up with your
virtues, which I admired, though I did not imitate. We had scarce
one in common but disinterestedness. Of the reverse we have both,
I may say, been so absolutely clear, that there is nothing so natural
and easy as the little monied transactions between us; and therefore,
knowing how perfectly indifferent I am upon that head, and remembering the papers I showed you, and what I said to you when I saw

1 The Yale editors speculate that Walpole had provided Conway with some financial
assistance.

you last, I am sure you will have the complaisance never to mention thanks more. – Now, to answer your questions.

As to coming to you, as that *feu grégeois* Lord George Gordon[1] has given up the election, to my great joy, I can come to you on Sunday next. It is true, I had rather you visited your regiment first, for this reason: I expect summons to Nuneham every day; and besides, having never loved two journeys instead of one, I grow more covetous of my time, as I have little left, and therefore had rather take Park-place, going and coming, on my way to Lord Harcourt.

I don't know a word of news, public or private. I am deep in my dear old friend's [Madame du Deffand] papers. There are some very delectable; and though I believe – nay, know – I have not quite all, there are many which I almost wonder, after the little delicacy they[2] have shown, ever arrived to my hands. I dare to say they will not be quite so just to the public; for though I consented that the correspondence with Voltaire should be given to the editors of his works, I am persuaded that there are many passages at least which they will suppress, as very contemptuous, to his chief votaries, – I mean, of the votaries to his sentiments; for, like other heresiarchs, he despised his tools. If I live to see the edition, it will divert me to collate it with what I have in my hands.

You are the person in the world the fittest to encounter the meeting you mention for the choice of a bridge.[3] You have temper and patience enough to bear with fools and false taste. I, so unlike you, have learned some patience with both sorts too, but by a more summary method than by waiting to instil reason into them. Mine is only by leading them to their own vagaries, and by despairing that sense and taste should ever extend themselves. Adieu! . . .

1 Lord George Gordon (1751–93), religious and political agitator, described in the light of the anti-Catholic Gordon riots of 1780 as a firebrand. See letters 330 to 334 for the Gordon Riots.
2 The executors of Mme. du Deffand, who permitted some documents to be removed before her papers were, in accordance with her will, sent to Walpole. For Mme. du Deffand see heading to letter 215.
3 The bridge over the river Thames at Henley-on-Thames, near Conway's seat of Park Place. Conway contributed to the design, and his daughter Anne Damer provided the sculpted keystones.

2. THOMAS GRAY

The nature of Walpole's relationship with Thomas Gray has been much debated, with Walpole contributing to the debate. Gray (1716–71) was the son of a London scrivener. His mother, a milliner, paid for him to go to Eton in 1725, where he later joined Walpole's "Quadruple Alliance" of school friends. The early correspondence suggests an element of emotional dependence, Gray's admiration of the sophisticated prime minister's son paralleling Walpole's admiration for his cousin Conway. Gray preceded Walpole to Cambridge, where he studied at Peterhouse, and accompanied him on the Grand Tour in 1739. They separated in acrimonious circumstances in Reggio in 1741, and even after their reconciliation four years later, Walpole remained conscious of his friend's social failings, observing critically to George Montagu in 1748: "He is the worst company in the world – from a melancholy turn, from living reclusely, and from a little too much dignity, he never converses easily – all his words are measured and chosen, and formed into sentences; his writings are admirable; he himself is not agreeable."[1]

Gray, who passed most of his life at Cambridge, spent time with Walpole on his visits to London. Their correspondence resumed, though their exchanges were more literary and antiquarian than personal. Walpole had the highest opinion of Gray's poetry and could be possessive about it (see letter 195). In 1753 he arranged for Dodsley to publish a sumptuous edition of six poems illustrated by his protégé the designer Richard Bentley, and in 1757 he printed at Strawberry Hill the first edition of Gray's two Pindaric Odes. He always acknowledged Gray's superior literary talents, writing to Cole in 1775 of their Grand Tour: "We rode over the Alps in the same chaise, but Pegasus drew on his side, and a cart-horse on mine" (letter 135).

After Gray's death a correspondence blossomed between Walpole and his literary executor, the Reverend William Mason, who was preparing an edition of the poems with a life of Gray (published in 1775). Walpole's three letters to Mason (133, 197 and 198) show him looking back on his quarrel with Gray and on their relationship with frankness: the layered tone of self-deprecation he often employed is present, but accompanied by a frank appraisal of Gray's awkward dignity and by an analysis of his own motivations and insensitivity that is almost brutal in its dignified honesty.

1 Letter of 3 September 1748 (YE 9:76).

195. *His Secretiveness.*

TO THOMAS GRAY

Arlington Street, 18 February 1768.

You have sent me a long and very obliging letter, and yet I am extremely out of humour with you. I saw *Poems* by *Mr. Gray*[1] advertised: I called directly at Dodsley's to know if this was to be more than a new edition? He was not at home himself, but his foreman told me he thought there were some new pieces, and notes to the whole. It was very unkind, not only to go out of town without mentioning them to me, without showing them to me, but not to say a word of them in this letter. Do you think I am indifferent, or not curious about what you write? I have ceased to ask you, because you have so long refused to show me anything. You could not suppose I thought that you never write. No; but I concluded you did not intend, at least yet, to publish what you had written. As you did intend it, I might have expected a month's preference. You will do me the justice to own that I had always rather have seen your writings than have shown you mine; which you know are the most hasty trifles in the world, and which, though I may be fond of the subject when fresh, I constantly forget in a very short time after they are published. This would sound like affectation to others, but will not to you. . . .

196. *His Death.*

TO JOHN CHUTE, ESQ.

13 August 1771, addition to letter begun 5 August.

Mr. Edmonson has called on me; and, as he sets out to-morrow, I can safely trust my letter to him. I have, I own, been much shocked at reading Gray's death[2] in the papers. 'Tis an hour that makes one forget any subject of complaint, especially towards one with whom I lived in friendship from thirteen years old. As self lies so rooted in

---

1 James Dodsley's edition of Gray's *Poems* was published in March 1768. See letter 131, p. 200, n. 1 for the new pieces.
2 Gray had died on 30 July 1771, six days after suffering a seizure in the hall of Pembroke College, Cambridge. Walpole, in Paris, only learned of this twelve days later.

self, no doubt the nearness of our ages made the stroke recoil to my own breast; and having so little expected his death, it is plain how little I expect my own. Yet to you, who of all men living are the most forgiving, I need not excuse the concern I feel. I fear most men ought to apologise for their want of feeling, instead of palliating that sensation when they have it. I thought that what I had seen of the world had hardened my heart; but I find that it had formed my language, not extinguished my tenderness. In short, I am really shocked – nay, I am hurt at my own weakness, as I perceive that when I love anybody, it is for my life; and I have had too much reason not to wish that such a disposition may very seldom be put to the trial. You, at least, are the only person to whom I would venture to make such a confession.

Adieu! my dear Sir! Let me know when I arrive, which will be about the last day of the month, when I am likely to see you. I have much to say to you. Of being here I am most heartily tired, and nothing but this dear old woman[1] should keep me here an hour – I am weary of them to death – but that is not new! Yours ever.

197. *The Quarrel.*

TO THE REV. MR. MASON

2 March 1773.

... What shall I say? how shall I thank you for the kind manner in which you submit your papers to my correction?[2] But if you are friendly I must be just: I am so far from being dissatisfied, that I must beg leave to sharpen your pen, and in that light only, with regard to myself, would make any alterations in your text. I am conscious, that in the beginning of the differences between Gray and me, the fault was mine. I was too young, too fond of my own diversions, nay, I do not doubt, too much intoxicated by indulgence, vanity, and the insolence of my situation, as a Prime Minister's son, not to have been inattentive and insensible to the feelings of one I thought below me; of one, I blush to say it, that I knew was obliged to me; of one whom

---

1 Mme. du Deffand.
2 Mason had on 23 February sent Walpole "three or four paragraphs where your name must necessarily be mentioned [dealing with the rupture between Walpole and Gray at Reggio in 1741], which I would choose to alter entirely to your satisfaction".

presumption and folly perhaps made me deem not my superior *then* in parts, though I have since felt my infinite inferiority to him. I treated him insolently: he loved me, and I did not think he did. I reproached him with the difference between us, when he acted from conviction of knowing he was my superior. I often disregarded his wishes of seeing places, which I would not quit other amusements to visit, though I offered to send him to them without me. Forgive me, if I say that his temper was not conciliating; at the same time that I will confess to you that he acted a more friendly part, had I had the sense to take advantage of it – he freely told me of my faults. I declared I did not desire to hear them, nor would correct them. You will not wonder that with the dignity of his spirit, and the obstinate carelessness of mine, the breach must have grown wider, till we became incompatible. After this confession, I fear you will think I fall far short of the justice I promised him, in the words which I should wish to have substituted to some of yours. If you think them inadequate to the state of the case, as I own they are, preserve this letter, and let some future Sir John Dalrymple[1] produce it to load my memory; but I own I do not desire that any ambiguity should aid his invention to forge an account for me. If you have no objection, I would propose your narrative should run thus, and contain no more, till a more proper time shall come for stating the truth, as I have related it to you. While I am living, it is not pleasant to read one's private quarrels discussed in magazines and newspapers.[2] . . .

198. *Genius of Gray and West.*

TO THE REV. WILLIAM MASON

Dear Sir,   Arlington Street, 27 November 1773.

    Mr. Stonhewer has sent me, and I have read, your first part of Gray's Life, which I was very sorry to part with so soon. Like every thing of yours, I like it ten times better upon reading it again. You have with most singular art displayed the talents of my two departed

---

1 John Dalrymple (1673–1747), soldier and diplomat, disliked by Walpole as a former opponent of his father.
2 Walpole then provides Mason with his proposed amended account of his separation from Gray, more self-critical than Mason's original draft. Mason adopted Walpole's text for his *Memoirs* of Gray.

friends[1] to the fullest advantage; and yet there is a simplicity in your manner, which, like the frame of a fine picture, seems a frame only, and yet is gold. I should say much more in praise if, as I have told Mr. Stonhewer, I was not aware that I myself must be far more interested in the whole of the narrative than any other living mortal, and therefore may suppose it will please the world still more than it will——. And yet if wit, parts, learning, taste, sense, friendship, information, can strike or amuse mankind, must not this work have that effect? – and yet, though *me* it may affect far more strongly, self-love certainly has no share in my affection to many parts. Of my two friends and me, I only make a most indifferent figure. I do not mean with regard to parts or talents – I never one instant of my life had the superlative vanity of ranking myself with them. They not only possessed genius, which I have not, great learning which is to be acquired, and which I never acquired; but both Gray and West had abilities marvellously premature. What wretched boyish stuff would my contemporary letters to them appear, if they existed; and which they both were so good-natured as to destroy! What unpoetic things were mine at that age, some of which unfortunately do exist, and which I yet could never surpass; but it is not in that light I consider my own position. We had not got to Calais before Gray was dissatisfied, for I was a boy, and he, though infinitely more a man, was not enough so to make allowances. Hence am I never mentioned once with kindness in his letters to West. This hurts me for him, as well as myself. For the oblique censures on my want of curiosity, I have nothing to say. The fact was true; my eyes were not purely classic; and though I am now a dull antiquary, my age then made me taste pleasures and diversions merely modern: I say this to you, and to you only, in confidence. I do not object to a syllable. I know how trifling, how useless, how blameable I have been, and submit to hear my faults, both because I have had faults, and because I hope I have corrected some of them; and though Gray hints at my unwillingness to be told them, I can say truly that to the end of his life he neither spared the reprimand nor mollified the terms, as you and others know, and I believe have felt.

These reflections naturally arose on reading his letters again, and

1 Gray and Richard West. Mason's *Memoirs* of Gray was not to be published until April 1775.

arose in spite of the pleasure they gave me, for self will intrude, even where self is not so much concerned. I am sorry to find I disobliged Gray so very early. I am sorry for him that it so totally obliterated all my friendship for him; a remark the world probably, and I hope, will not make, but which it is natural for me, dear Sir, to say to you. I am so sincerely zealous that all possible honour should be done to my two friends, that I care not a straw for serving as a foil to them. And as confession of faults is the only amendment I can now make to the one disobliged, I am pleased with myself for having consented and for consenting as I do, to that public reparation. I thank you for having revived West and his, alas! stifled genius and for having extended Gray's reputation. If the world admires them both as much as they deserved, I shall enjoy their fame; if it does not, I shall comfort myself for standing so prodigiously below them, as I do even without comparison.

There are a few false printings I could have corrected, but of no consequence, as Grotto del Cane, for Grotta, and a few notes I could have added, but also of little consequence. Dodsley [James], who is printing Lord Chesterfield's Letters, will hate you for this publication. I was asked to write a Preface – *Sic notus Ulysses?*[1] I knew Ulysses too well. Besides, I have enough to burn without adding to the mass. Forgive me, if I differ with you, but I cannot think Gray's Latin Poems inferior even to his English, at least as I am not a Roman. I wish too that in a note you had referred to West's Ode on the Queen[2] in "Dodsley's Miscellanies." Adieu! go on and prosper. My poor friends have an historian worthy of them, and who satisfies their and your friend ...

Hor. Walpole.

---

1 Virgil, *Æneid* II. 44: Is that how Ulysses is known? Walpole had refused the request of Mrs. Eugenia Stanhope, the wife of Chesterfield's natural son, to introduce the publication of his *Letters*.
2 West's "Monody on the Death of Queen Caroline", published in the second volume of Dodsley's *Collection of Poems by Several Hands*, which included one quatrain that is echoed in Gray's "Elegy Written in a Country Church-Yard".

199. *"The Candidate."*

TO THE REV. WILLIAM MASON

Strawberry Hill, 16 September 1774.

What is the commonest thing in the world? – Lord! how can you be so dull as not to guess? why to be sure, to hunt for a thing forty times, and give it over, and then find it when you did not look for it, exactly where you had hunted forty times. This happened to me this very morning, and overjoyed I am. I suppose you don't guess what I have found? Really, Mr. Mason, you great poets are so absent, and so unlike the rest of the world! Why what should I have found,[1] but the thing in the world that was most worth finding? a hidden treasure – a hidden fig; no, Sir, not the certificate of the Duchess of Kingston's first marriage, nor the lost books of Livy, nor the longitude, nor the philosopher's stone, nor all Charles Fox has lost.[2] I tell you it is, what I have searched for a thousand times, and had rather have found than the longitude, if it was a thousand times longer. Oh! you do guess, do you? I thought I never lost anything in my life. I was sure I had them, and so I had; and now am I not a good soul, to sit down and send you a copy incontinently? Don't be too much obliged to me neither. I am in a panic till there are more copies than mine, and as the post does not go till to-morrow, I am in terror lest the house should be burnt to-night. I have a mind to go and bury a transcript in the field; but then if I should be burnt too! nobody would know where to look for it. Well, here it is! I think your decorum will not hold it proper to be printed in the Life, nor would I have it. We will preserve copies, and the devil is in it, if some time or other it don't find its way to the press. My copy is in his own handwriting; but who could doubt it: I know but one man[3] upon earth who could have written it but Gray. . . .

---

1 Walpole had found, and was sending Mason a transcript of, Gray's MS. poem "The Candidate", a satire on the candidacy of John Montagu, 4th Earl of Sandwich (1718–92), for the High Stewardship of Cambridge University. Lord Sandwich (who had led the prosecution of his former associate John Wilkes) was known as Jemmy Twitcher after the character in Gay's *Beggar's Opera* who betrayed his friend.
2 Including references to the bigamous Duchess of Kingston (see letter 57, p. 92, n. 1) and to Charles James Fox's gambling debts.
3 That is, Mason himself.

3. SIR HORACE MANN

Walpole first met his distant cousin Horace Mann (1706–86) in Florence in December 1739. Mann, who had travelled to Italy in the early 1730s, was by 1738 assisting the British Resident at the court of the Grand Duke of Tuscany. He became chargé d'affaires when the Resident returned to Britain in 1738, and in 1740 was formally confirmed as his successor through the influence of Sir Robert Walpole. He remained in Florence for the rest of his life. Horace Walpole helped research into his genealogy ("there is not a pipe of good blood in the kingdom but we will tap for you"[1]) in order to impress the Florentine grandees. He was knighted in 1755, achieved his baronetcy (long an ambition) in 1768, and finally in 1782 was elevated to Envoy-Extraordinary and Minister-Plenipotentiary. All this time he kept a watchful eye on the succession of British youths making their way through Florence on their Grand Tour, and (as Britain had no diplomatic representative in the Papal States) an even more watchful eye on the movements of the Stuart court. Mann was a dedicated hypochondriac, described as finical and effeminate, but also widely praised for his politeness and his hospitality.

When Walpole left Florence in 1740 there ensued what he was to describe in 1784 as "a correspondence of near half a century . . . not to be paralleled in the annals of the Post Office", which terminated only with Mann's death two years later.[2] Walpole's letters to Mann comprise nearly one-third of his extant correspondence, and in their detailed discussion of current topics for the benefit of a permanent exile from England, they are amongst the most valuable historical documents of the eighteenth century. Mann's own letters, unkindly described as "absolutely unreadable" by Walpole's editor Peter Cunningham in 1857, have no pretensions to literary merit but do provide an illuminating picture of Florentine society against a background of European political events.

Walpole was aware of the importance of this correspondence as a record of the times. As early as 1748 he was asking Mann to return his letters to him, and with the help of his amanuensis Thomas Kirgate he prepared transcripts from 1754 and added notes to them. Looking back in 1778, Walpole could exclaim to Mann "What scenes my letters to you have touched on for eight and thirty years!"[3]

1 Letter to Mann, 17 August 1749 (YE 20:88).
2 Ibid, 25 August 1784 (YE 25:520).
3 Ibid, 18 February 1778 (YE 24:356).

200. *Galfridus Mann's Illness.*

TO SIR HORACE MANN

Arlington Street, 5 February 1756.

I think I can give you a little better account of your brother,[1] who is so dear to both of us; I put myself on a foot with you, for nothing can love him better than I do. I have been a week at Strawberry Hill, in order to watch and see him every day. The Duke's physician, Dr. Pringle, who now attends him, has certainly relieved him much: his cough is in a manner gone, his fever much abated, his breath better. His strength is not yet increased; and his stitches, which they impute to wind, are not removed. But both his physicians swear that his lungs are not touched. His worst symptom is what they cannot, but *I* must and will remove: in short, his wife is killing him, I can scarce say slowly. Her temper is beyond imagination, her avarice monstrous, her madness about what she calls cleanliness, to a degree of distraction; if I had not first, and then made your brother Ned interpose in form, she would once or twice a week have the very closet *washed* in which your brother sleeps after dinner. It is certainly very impertinent to interfere in so delicate a case, but your brother's life makes me blind to every consideration: in short, we have made Dr. Pringle declare that the moment the weather is a little warmer, and he can be moved, change of air is absolutely necessary, and I am to take him to Strawberry Hill, where you may imagine he will neither be teased nor neglected: the physicians are strong for his going abroad, but I find that will be a very difficult point to carry even with himself. His affairs are so extensive, that as yet he will not hear of leaving them. Then the exclusion of correspondence by the war with France would be another great objection with him to going thither; and to send him to Naples by sea, if we could persuade him, would hardly be advisable in the heat of such hostilities. I think by this account you will judge perfectly of your brother's situation: you may depend upon it, it is not desperate, and yet it is what makes me very unhappy. Dr. Pringle says, that in his life he never knew a person for whom so many people were concerned. I go to him again to-morrow. . . .

1 Galfridus Mann (1706–56), Horace Mann's twin brother, who died in December 1756. Richard Bentley designed his monument in Linton Church, Kent.

Adieu! Pray for your brother: I need not say talk him over and over with Dr. Cocchi, and hope the best of the war.

201. *A Long Correspondence.*

TO SIR HORACE MANN

Berkeley Square, 26 March 1784.

... To the present drama, Elections, I shall totally shut my ears. Such subjects as, however noisy, one is sure to hear of no more the moment they are over, are to me insupportable. I hated elections forty years ago; and, when I went to White's, preferred a conversation on Newmarket to one on elections: for the language of the former I did not understand, and, consequently, did not listen to; the other, being uttered in common phrase, made me attend, whether I would or not. When such subjects are on the tapis,[1] they make me a very insipid correspondent. One cannot talk of what one does not care about; and it would be jargon to you, if I did: however, do not imagine but I allow a sufficient quantity of dulness to my time of life. I have kept up a correspondence with you with tolerable spirit for three-and-forty years together, without our once meeting. Can you wonder that my pen is worn to the stump? You see it does not abandon you; nor, though conscious of its own decay, endeavour to veil it by silence. The Archbishop of Gil Blas has long been a lesson to me to watch over my own ruins;[2] but I do not extend that jealousy of vanity to commerce with an old friend. You knew me in my days of folly and riotous spirits; why should I hide my dotage from you, which is not equally my fault and reproach? I take due care that nobody should hear of me but two or three, who persuade me that I still live in their memories; by the rest I had rather be forgotten.

---

1 On the table, or under consideration.
2 In Le Sage's *Gil Blas* the Archbishop of Grenada dismissed Gil Blas for presuming to suggest that a sermon delivered by him after recovery from apoplexy revealed failing powers.

202. *Gratitude.*

TO SIR HORACE MANN

22 June 1786.

I have not yet received your letter by Mrs. Damer,[1] my dear Sir; but I have that of June 3rd, which announces it. I lament the trouble your cough gives you, though I am quite persuaded that it is medicinal, and diverts the gout from critical parts. I have felt so much, and consequently have observed so much, of chronical disorders, that I don't think I deceive myself. Should you tell me your complaint is not gouty, I should reply, that all chronical distempers are or ought to be gout; and, when they do not appear in their proper form, are only deviations. Coughs in old persons clear the lungs; and, as I have told you, I know two elderly persons who are never so well as when they have a cough.

I love Mrs. Damer for her attention to you; but I shall scold her, instead of you, for letting you send me the Cameo. To you I will not say a cross word, when you are weak; but why will you not let me love you without being obliged to it by gratitude? You make me appear in my own eyes interested; a dirty quality, of which I flattered myself I was totally free. Gratitude may be a virtue; but what is a man who consents to have fifty obligations to be so virtuous? I have always professed hating presents: must not I appear a hypocrite, when I have accepted so many from you? Well! as I have registered them all in the printed catalogue of my collection,[2] I hope I shall be called a mercenary wretch. I deserve it. . . .

I talked of gratitude, but recollect that I have not even thanked you for your Cameo. I hope this looks like not being delighted with it: – how can I say such a brutal thing? I am charmed with your kindness though I wished for no more proofs of it. In short, I don't know how to steer between my inclination for expressing my full sense of your friendship, and my pride, that is not fond of being obliged – and so very often obliged – by those I love most. Oh! but I have a much worse vice than pride (which, begging the clergy's pardon, I don't think a very heinous one, as it is a counter-poison to

1 Anne Damer travelled in Italy in 1785–6.
2 Walpole's *Description* of Strawberry Hill, of which he printed the expanded edition in 1786.

meanness) – I am monstrously ungrateful; I have received a thousand valuable presents from you, and yet never made you one! I shall begin to think I am avaricious too. In short, my dear Sir, your Cameo is a mirror in which I discover a thousand faults, of which I did not suspect myself, besides all those which I did know: no, no, I will not lecture Mrs. Damer, but myself. I absolve you, and am determined to think myself a prodigy of rapacity! I see there is no merit in not loving money, if one loves playthings. I have often declaimed against collectors, who will do anything mean to obtain a rarity they want: pray, is that so bad as accepting curiosities, and never making a return? Oh! I am the most ungrateful of all virtuosos, as you are the most generous of all friends! Well! the worse I think of myself, the better I think of you, and that is some compensation for the contempt I have for myself; and I will be content to serve as a foil to you. Adieu![1]

4. GEORGE MONTAGU

George Montagu (c. 1713–80) was a scion of the aristocratic Montagu family and lived a life of cheerful and indolent dependence. He was at Eton with Walpole, then at Trinity College, Cambridge. He made the Grand Tour, and met Walpole and Gray in Rheims in August 1739. When in 1761 his cousin Lord Halifax became Lord Lieutenant of Ireland, he accompanied him as Gentleman Usher of the Black Rod; when Lord North, also a cousin, became Chancellor of the Exchequer in 1767, he offered Montagu as a sinecure the post of private secretary. Essentially, though, his life was one of obscurity, and he seldom stirred from his house at Greatworth in Northamptonshire.

Yet this apparently insubstantial figure inspired one of the most appealing of Walpole's correspondences. Montagu was witty and good company, and Walpole's letters to him exude gaiety and charm. Some of them are accounts of Walpole's visits to country houses (see letters 79 and 83 to 86), but principally they are a record of the social life of the capital, sparkling with amusing anecdote and sharp observation (letters 55, 65 and 66). The correspondence fades away by 1770, a victim of Montagu's lethargy.

1 This is the last surviving letter from Walpole to Mann. Mann wrote to Walpole on 5 September and died in November, concluding a correspondence of over 46 years.

203. *Condolence.*

TO GEORGE MONTAGU, ESQ.

Arlington Street, 7 October 1755.

My Dear Sir,

Nobody living feels more for you than I do: nobody knows better either the goodness or tenderness of your heart, or the real value of the person you have lost.[1] I cannot flatter myself that anything I could say would comfort you under an affliction so well founded; but I should have set out, and endeavoured to share your concern, if Mrs. Trevor had not told me that you were going into Cheshire. I will only say, that if you think change of place can contribute at all to divert your melancholy, you know where you would be most welcome; and whenever you will come to Strawberry Hill, you will, at least, if you do not find a comforter, find a most sincere friend that pities your distress, and would do anything upon earth to alleviate your misfortune. If you can listen yet to any advice, let me recommend to you to give up all thoughts of Greatworth; you will never be able to support life there any more: let me look out for some little box for you in my neighbourhood. You can live nowhere where you will be more beloved; and you will there always have it in your power to enjoy company or solitude, as you like. I have long wished to get you so far back into the world, and now it is become absolutely necessary for your health and peace. I will say no more, lest too long a letter should be either troublesome or make you think it necessary to answer; but do not, till you find it more agreeable to vent your grief this way than in any other. I am, my good Sir, with hearty concern and affection, yours most sincerely.

204. *A Gift of Venison.*

TO GEORGE MONTAGU, ESQ.

Arlington Street, 16 December 1766.

I wrote to you last post on the very day I ought to have received yours; but being at Strawberry did not get it in time. Thank you for your offer of a doe; you know when I dine at home here it is quite alone, and venison frightens my little meal; yet, as half of it is

1 Montagu's unmarried sister Harriet had died.

designed for *dimidium animæ meæ*[1] Mrs. Clive (a pretty round half), I must not refuse it. Venison will make such a figure at her Christmas gambols! only let me know when and how I am to receive it, that she may prepare the rest of her banquet; I will convey it to her.

I don't like your wintering so late in the country. Adieu!

205. *Friends in Old Age.*

TO GEORGE MONTAGU, ESQ.

Arlington Street, 15 November 1768.

You cannot wonder when I receive such kind letters from you, that I am vexed our intimacy should be reduced almost to those letters. It is selfish to complain, when you give me such good reasons for your system: but I grow old; and the less time we have to live together, the more I feel a separation from a person I love so well; and that reflection furnishes me with arguments in vindication of my peevishness. Methinks, though the contrary is true in practice, prudence should be the attribute of youth, not of years. When we approach to the last gate of life, what does it signify to provide for new furnishing one's house? Youth should have all those cares; indeed, charming youth is better employed. It leaves foresight to those that have little occasion for it. You and I have both done with the world, the busy world, and therefore I would smile with you over what we have both seen of it, and luckily we can smile both, for we have quitted it willingly, not from disgust nor mortifications. However, I do not pretend to combat your reasons, much less would I draw you to town a moment sooner than it is convenient to you, though I shall never forget your offering it. Nay, it is not so much in town that I wish we were nearer, as in the country. Unless one lives exactly in the same set of company, one is not much the better for one's friends being in London. I that talk of giving up the world, have only given up the troubles of it, as far as that is possible. I should speak more properly in saying, that I have retired out of the world into London. I always intend to place some months between me and the moroseness of retirement. We are not made for solitude. It gives us prejudices, it indulges us in our own humours, and at last we cannot live without them. . . . Adieu! Yours ever.

1 Half of my soul, of his neighbour and tenant Catherine Clive.

206. *Death of Montagu.*

TO THE REV. WILLIAM COLE

Berkeley Square, 11 May 1780.

Mr. Godfrey, the engraver, told me yesterday that Mr. Tyson[1] is dead. I am sorry for it, though he had left me off. A much older friend of mine died yesterday; but of whom I must say the same, George Montagu, whom you must remember at Eton and Cambridge. I should have been exceedingly concerned for him a few years ago, but he had dropped me, partly from politics and partly from caprice, for we never had any quarrel; but he was grown an excessive humourist, and had shed almost all his friends as well as me. He had parts, and infinite vivacity and originality till of late years; and it grieved me much that he had changed towards me, after a friendship of between thirty and forty years. . . .

5. THE EARL OF HERTFORD

Francis Seymour Conway (1718–94), Earl and subsequently Marquis of Hertford, was the elder brother of Henry Conway. He was ambassador in Paris from 1763 to 1765, Lord Lieutenant of Ireland from 1765 to 1766, a Knight of the Garter, and Lord Chamberlain of the Household. His distinguished career as diplomat and courtier was marred by allegations of avarice (Walpole makes mention of his love of money) and it appears that the respect and kindness that Walpole showed to him and his family were not fully reciprocated. But he was a cousin and a Conway, and consequently remained the recipient of Walpole's affection and letters.

207. *In Paris.*

TO THE EARL OF HERTFORD

Arlington Street, 18 October 1763.

My Dear Lord,

I am very impatient for a letter from Paris, to hear of your outset, and what my Lady Hertford thinks of the new world she is got into,

---

1 Rev. Michael Tyson (1740–80), artist and antiquary.

and whether it is better or worse than she expected.[1] Pray tell me all:
I mean of that sort, for I have no curiosity about the family compact,
nor the harbour of Dunkirk. It is your private history – your audi-
ences, reception, comforts or distresses, your way of life, your company – that interests me; in short, I care about my cousins and
friends, not, like Jack Harris,[2] about my Lord Ambassador. Consider you are in my power. You, by this time, are longing to hear from
England, and depend upon me for the news of London. I shall not
send you a tittle, if you are not very good, and do not (one of you,
at least) write to me punctually.

This letter, I confess, will not give you much encouragement, for
I can absolutely tell you nothing. I dined at Mr. Grenville's to-day,
where, if there had been anything to hear, I should have heard it;
but all consisted in what you will see in the papers – some diminutive
battles in America, and the death of the King of Poland, which you
probably knew before we did. The town is a desert; it is like a vast
plain, which, though abandoned at present, is in three weeks to have
a great battle fought upon it. One of the colonels, I hear, is to be in
town to-morrow, the Duke of Devonshire.[3] I came myself but this
morning, but as I shall not return to Strawberry till the day after to-
morrow, I shall not seal my letter till then. In the mean time, it is
but fair to give you some more particular particulars of what I expect
to know. For instance, of Monsieur de Nivernois's cordiality; of
Madame Dusson's affection for England; of my Lord Holland's joy
at seeing you in France, especially without your secretary; of all my
Lady Hertford's cousins at St. Germains; and I should not dislike a
little anecdote or two of the late embassy, of which I do not doubt
you will hear plenty. I must trouble you with many compliments to
Madame de Boufflers, and with still more to the Duchesse de
Mirepoix,[4] who is always so good as to remember me. Her brother,

---

1 Lord Hertford had arrived in Paris as British Ambassador.
2 Lord Hertford's brother-in-law.
3 Walpole contrasts two recent battles between the British and the Indians in America with the impending parliamentary battles. The Duke of Devonshire is returning
to London for the opening of the new session.
4 Anne-Marguerite-Gabrielle de Beauvau (1707–91), Duchesse de Mirepoix. Her
husband had been French Ambassador. Both Mme. Dusson and Mme. de Boufflers
had visited Strawberry Hill earlier that year, and had verses printed for them at the
Strawberry Hill Press (see letter 106). For Walpole's account of both Mme. de
Mirepoix and Mme. de Boufflers, see letter 352.

Prince de Beauvau, I doubt has forgotten me. In the disagree-
ableness of taking leave, I omitted mentioning these messages.
Good night for to-night – Oh! I forgot – pray send me some *café au
lait:* the Duc de Picquigny (who by the way is somebody's son, as
I thought) takes it for snuff, and says it is the new fashion at Paris;
I suppose they drink rappee[1] after dinner. . . .

6. GEORGE SELWYN

George Augustus Selwyn (1719–91) was a society wit whose *bons mots*
Walpole was fond of quoting. Another of Walpole's Eton contemporaries, Selwyn held several lucrative sinecures, and inherited from
his father an important parliamentary interest both in Gloucester
and at Ludgershall in Wiltshire, a two-member borough where he
controlled both seats. These he would offer – when not occupying
one of them himself – for a suitable price, to whichever was the
administration of the day. He sat as M.P. for Gloucester from 1754
to 1780, but despite some forty-four years in Parliament, he never
spoke in debate.

As for his humour, presumably much of it lay in the delivery.
Contemporaries commented on his listless manner (and on his
tendency to fall asleep both in the House of Commons and in company), and this, together with a solemn countenance, no doubt
heightened the impact of his witticisms. Also widely remarked upon
was his macabre obsession with executions, referred to in letter 98.

As a young man Selwyn spent much of his time in Paris and was
well-known at the French court where he was a favourite of Louis
XV's queen, Marie Leszczynska. He never married, but adopted as
his daughter "Mie-Mie", Maria Emily Fagnani (1770/1–1856), who
was probably the daughter of his friend the Duke of Queensberry.
She later married the third Marquis of Hertford.

1   A coarse snuff.

208. *Morbid Tastes.*

TO THE HON. H. S. CONWAY

Dear Harry,   Arlington Street, 16 April 1747.

... You have heard that old Lovat's[1] tragedy is over: it has been succeeded by a little farce, containing the humours of the Duke of Newcastle and his man Stone. The first event was a squabble between his Grace and the Sheriff about holding up the head on the scaffold – a custom that has been disused, and which the Sheriff would not comply with, as he received no order in writing. Since that, the Duke has burst ten yards of breeches strings[2] about the body, which was to be sent into Scotland; but it seems it is customary for vast numbers to rise to attend the most trivial burial. The Duke, who is always at least as much frightened at doing right as at doing wrong, was three days before he got courage enough to order the burying in the Tower. I must tell you an excessive good story of George Selwyn: Some women were scolding him for going to see the execution, and asked him, how he could be such a barbarian to see the head cut off? "Nay," says he, "if that was such a crime, I am sure I have made amends, for I went to see it sewed on again." When he was at the undertaker's, as soon as they had stitched him together, and were going to put the body into the coffin, George, in my Lord Chancellor's [Hardwicke's] voice, said, "My Lord Lovat, your lordship may rise." ... Adieu!

209. *His Death.*

TO THE COUNTESS OF UPPER OSSORY

Berkeley Square, 28 January 1791.

You and Lord Ossory have been so very good to me, Madam, that I must pay you the first tribute of my poor reviving fingers[3] – I believe they never will be their own men again; but as they have lived so long in your Ladyship's service, they shall show their attachment to the last, like Widdrington on his stumps. I have had another

1 The Jacobite rebel Lord Lovat (1667/8–1747) had been beheaded on 9 April.
2 Alluding to a trick of the Duke of Newcastle's. – WALPOLE.
3 Injured by repeated attacks of gout.

and grievous memento, the death of poor Selwyn! His end was lovely, most composed and rational. From eight years old I had known him intimately without a cloud between us; few knew him so well, and consequently few knew so well the goodness of his heart and nature. But I will say no more – *Mon. Chancelier vous dira le reste.*[1] – No, my chancellor shall put an end to the session, only concluding, as Lord Bacon would have done for King James, with an apologue, "His Majesty's recovery has turned the corner, and exceeding the old fable, has proved that the stomach can do better without the limbs than they could without him."[2] – Adieu, Madam.

7. JOHN CHUTE

John Chute, born in 1701, was sixteen years older than Walpole, but from their first meeting in Florence in the summer of 1740 the two became devoted friends. "We passed many hours together without saying a syllable to each other; for we were both above ceremony . . . Half is gone; the other remains solitary . . . To me he was the most faithful and secure of friends and a delightful companion," wrote Walpole, paying tribute to that friendship after Chute's death in 1776 (letter 210).

Chute was an amateur architect and connoisseur who, although the youngest of ten children, unexpectedly inherited the family estate of the Vyne in Hampshire. He and his young cousin Francis Whithed (Walpole called them the Chuteheds) lived in Italy between 1740 and 1746. Chute, with Richard Bentley and Walpole himself formed "the Committee" that worked on the design of Strawberry Hill, and was described by Walpole in letter 210 as "the genius that presided over poor Strawberry". Walpole also said of Chute that he was "an able geometrician and was an exquisite architect of the purest taste both in the Grecian and Gothic styles";[3] this can be seen in the library at Strawberry Hill, and in the Gothic chapel and ante-room and the highly accomplished and theatrical main staircase at the Vyne. He also designed Donnington Grove, Berkshire, in a delicate Gothic style. Affected in manner, he was physically frail and short-sighted, and despite an abstemious diet a

1 Walpole's printer and secretary Thomas Kirgate (1734/5–1810) wrote the letter from this point.
2 A reference to a fable by Æsop, "The Belly and the Other Members".
3 See volume 35 of the Yale edition of Walpole's Correspondence, Appendix 1, p. 642.

victim of the gout. He was a frequent visitor to Strawberry Hill, where the Red Bedchamber was known as Mr. Chute's bedchamber.

210. *A Grievous Loss.*

Strawberry Hill, 27 May 1776.

This fatal year puts to the proof the nerves of my friendship! I was disappointed of seeing you when I had set my heart on it; and now I have lost Mr. Chute![1] It is a heavy blow; but such strokes reconcile one's self to parting with this pretty vision, life! What is it, when one has no longer those to whom one speaks as confidentially as to one's own soul? Old friends are the great blessing of one's latter years – half a word conveys one's meaning. They have memory of the same events, and have the same mode of thinking. Mr. Chute and I agreed invariably in our principles; he was my counsel in my affairs, was my oracle in taste, the standard to whom I submitted my trifles, and the genius that presided over poor Strawberry! His sense decided me in everything; his wit and quickness illuminated everything. I saw him oftener than any man; to him in every difficulty I had recourse, and him I loved to have here, as our friendship was so entire, and we knew one another so entirely, that he alone never was the least constraint to me. We passed many hours together without saying a syllable to each other; for we were both above ceremony. I left him without excusing myself, read or wrote before him, as if he were not present. Alas! alas! and how *self* presides even in our grief! I am lamenting myself, not him! – no, I am lamenting my other self. Half is gone; the other remains solitary. Age and sense will make me bear my affliction with submission and composure – but for ever – that little *for ever* that remains, I shall miss him. My first thought will always be, *I will go talk to Mr. Chute on this;* the second, *alas! I cannot;* and therefore judge how my life is poisoned! I shall only seem to be staying behind one who is set out a little before me.

Mr. Chute for these last two or three years was much broken by his long and repeated shocks of gout, yet was amazingly well, considering that he had suffered by it from twenty to seventy-three! Still

1 John Chute, Esq., of the Vine, in Hampshire; the last of the male line. – WALPOLE.

as he never had had it in his head or stomach; I never was alarmed
till last summer when he had a low lingering fever, and sickness and
pain in his breast, with returns of an excessive palpitation at his
heart, which formerly much alarmed me, but of which he had been
free for some years. He got better and went to the Bath, which gave
him the gout, and he returned quite well; so well, that, alarmed at
our situation, he thought of drawing some money out of the Stocks
and buying an annuity, saying, that he thought his life as good as
any man's for five years. I am sure I thought so too. On Thursday
last, being surprised at his not calling on me for three days, which
was unusual, I went to him and was told that he was very ill. I found
him in bed; he had so violent a pain in his breast that two days before
he had sent for Dr. Thomas, whom he had consulted in the summer,
though of all men the most averse to physicians. Thomas had given
him an hundred drops of laudanum and asafœtida. Mr. Chute said,
*it is not the gout; I have had my palpitation, and fear it is something of
a polypus.* Thus, perfectly reasonable, though with much more indifference than he who was all spirit and eagerness used to have,
I attributed it to the laudanum, and indeed he desired me to leave
him, as he was heavy, and wanted to sleep. He dozed all that evening,
and had no return of pain. On Friday morning, still without pain,
I saw him again. He had taken more asafœtida, but no more laudanum; yet, when I said, I trusted the pain was gone, he said, *I do not
know; the effects of the laudanum are not yet gone.* I said, I thought that
impossible; that the pain would have surmounted the laudanum by
that time, if the pain were not removed. I was coming hither on business, and charged his valet to send for me if the pain returned. On
Saturday morning I rejoiced at not receiving even a letter by the post,
and concluded all was well.

This dream of satisfaction lasted all that day and Saturday night.
I knew he would take no more laudanum, unless the pain returned,
and that then I should be advertised. But, oh, unhappy! yesterday,
just as I had breakfasted, and was in the garden, I heard the bell at
the gate ring, and wondered, as it was but ten o'clock, who could
come to me so early. I went to see, and met my valet-de-chambre,
with a letter in his hand, who said, *Oh, Sir, Mr. Chute is dead!* In a
word, he had continued quite easy till three that morning, when he
said, *Who is in the room?* His own valet replied, *I, Sir!* and, going to
the bed, found him very ill, ran to call help, and, returning as quickly

as possible, saw him dead! It was certainly a polypus; his side immediately grew black as ink. A charming death for him, dearest friend!
And why should I lament? His eyes, always short-sighted, were
grown dimmer, his hearing was grown imperfect, his hands were all
chalk-stones and of little use, his feet very lame – yet how not
lament? The vigour of his mind was strong as ever; his power of
reasoning clear as demonstration; his rapid wit astonishing as at
forty, about which time you and I knew him first. Even the impetuosity of his temper was not abated, and all his humane virtues had
but increased with his age. He was grown sick of the world; saw very,
very few persons; submitted with unparalleled patience to all his sufferings; and, in five-and-thirty years, I never once saw or heard him
complain of them, nor, passionate as he was, knew him fretful. His
impatience seemed to proceed from his vast sense, not from his temper: he saw everything so clearly, and immediately, that he could not
bear a momentary contradiction from folly or defective reasoning.
Sudden contempt broke out, particularly on politics, which, having
been fixed in him by a most sensible father, and matured by deep
reflection, were rooted in his inmost soul. His truth, integrity, honour, spirit, and abhorrence of all dirt, confirmed his contempt; and
even I, who am pretty warm and steady, was often forced to break
off politics with him, so impossible was it to be zealous enough to
content him when I most agreed with him. Nay, if I disputed with
him, I learnt something from him, and always saw truth in a stronger
and more summary light.

His possession of the quintessence of argument reduced it at once
into axioms, and the clearness of his ideas struck out flashes of the
brightest wit. He saw so suddenly and so far, that, as Mr. Bentley
said of him long ago, *his wit strikes the more you analyse it, and more
than at first hearing; he jumps over two or three intermediate ideas, and
couples the first with the third or fourth.* Don't wonder I pour out my
heart to you; you knew him, and know how faithfully true all I say
of him. My loss is most irreparable. To me he was the most faithful
and secure of friends, and a delightful companion. I shall not seek
to replace him. Can I love any that are old, more than I have had
reason for loving them? and is it possible to love younger, as one
loved an habitual old friend of thirty-five years' standing? I have
young relations that may grow upon me, for my nature is affectionate, but can they grow *old* friends? My age forbids that. Still less can

they grow companions. Is it friendship to explain half one says? One must relate the history of one's memory and ideas; and what is that to the young, but old stories? No, my dear sir, *you* could be that resource, but I must not think of it – I must not be selfish. I must do what I ought to do, while I remain here; pass my time as amusingly as I can; enjoy the friends I have left; drink my grief in silence – it is too sincere for parade and what cares the world about my private sensations? Or what has an old man to do but to be forgotten; and to remember how soon he will be so? Forgive this expansion of my heart; it was necessary to me. I will not often mention poor Mr. Chute even to you. His loss is engraven on my soul, and real grief does not seek for applause. Could the world's plaudit comfort me, sit with me, hear me, advise me? Did it know Mr. Chute's worth as well as I did? Does it love me as well? When it does, I will beg its compassion. I have done, and will now show you that I am master of myself, and remember *you*, and consider that at this distance of time you cannot feel what I do, and must be anxious about public affairs. If I indulged my own feelings, I should forswear thinking of the public. *He* is gone to whom I ran with ever scrap of news I heard; but I promised to forget myself: I will go take a walk, shed a tear, and return to you more composed. . . . Adieu!

8. THE REVEREND WILLIAM COLE

An antiquarian of note, William Cole was born in 1714, the son of a gentleman farmer. He met Walpole at Eton and preceded him to Cambridge, moving from Clare College to King's, where private means enabled him to remain for seventeen years. He was ordained in 1745 and eventually left the university in 1753 to become rector of Bletchley in Buckinghamshire. He performed his duties conscientiously and his Journal gives an entertaining picture of his fellow clergymen and his somewhat chaotic household – the scatterbrained servants of whom he was very fond, his fat dun horse, his dog and his parrot. Though he mixed with the great and the learned he was equally happy to join his labourers in the hayfields. During his life he made several excursions on the continent and in 1765 spent a month in Paris with Walpole, who helped to discourage him from emigrating and converting to Roman Catholicism. In 1767 he resigned the Bletchley living in favour of his patron's grandson and took a poorly paid curacy in the Fen country (hence Walpole's remarks in letter 211). Three years later he retired to the village of Milton, near Cambridge. His correspondence with Walpole had begun in 1762 when Cole sent him detailed comments on the first two volumes of the *Anecdotes of Painting*, and continued until Cole's death in 1782. It was, fittingly, to Cole that Walpole sent an account of the composition of his medieval fantasy *The Castle of Otranto* (see letters 118 and 119). As well as their shared antiquarian interests, they both suffered badly from gout, which became another recurrent theme in their letters.

Political differences – Cole was a High Tory – did not undermine their friendship, which was also unaffected by Walpole's quarrel with the Antiquarian Society: "I exempt you entirely from my general censure on antiquaries, both for your singular modesty in publishing nothing yourself, and for collecting stone and brick for others to build with" (letter 212). The old-fashioned bachelor scholar described his manuscript collections to Walpole as "my only delight – they are my wife and children – they have been, in short, my whole employ and amusement for these twenty or thirty years"[1]. He left them to the British Museum, and they have been mined by generations of grateful researchers. Along with his important collections for a history of Cambridgeshire and for an *Athenæ Cantabrigiensis* they include two accounts of visits to Walpole at Strawberry Hill.[2]

211. *An Invitation.*

TO THE REV. WILLIAM COLE

Dear Sir,   Strawberry Hill, Monday 26 June 1769.

Oh! yes, yes, I shall like Thursday or Friday, 6th or 7th, exceedingly; I shall like your staying with me two days exceedinglier; and longer exceedingliest: and I will carry you back to Cambridge on our pilgrimage to Ely. But I should not at all like to be catched in the glories of an installation,[3] and find myself a doctor, before I knew

1 Letter from Cole of 17 March 1765 (YE 1:92).
2 Printed as Appendices 5 and 6 on pp. 368–75 of volume 2 of the Yale edition of Walpole's Correspondence.
3 The installation as Chancellor of the University of Cambridge of Augustus Henry Fitzroy (1735–1811), 3rd Duke of Grafton and prime minister (who had been the first husband of Walpole's correspondent Lady Ossory).

where I was. It will be much more agreeable to find the whole *caput* asleep, digesting turtle, dreaming of bishoprics, and humming old catches of Anacreon, and scraps of Corelli. I wish Mr. Gray may not be set out for the north; which is rather the case than setting out for the summer. We have no summers, I think, but what we raise, like pine-apples, by fire. My hay is an absolute *water-soochy*, and teaches me how to feel for you. You are quite in the right so sell your fief in Marshland. I should be glad if you would take one step more, and *quit* Marshland. We live, at least, on terra firma in this part of the world, and can saunter out without stilts. Then we do not wade into pools, and call it going upon the water, and get sore throats. I trust yours is better; but I recollect this is not the first you have complained of. Pray be not incorrigible, but come to shore.

Be so good as to thank Mr. Smith, my old tutor, for his corrections. If ever the "Anecdotes" are reprinted, I will certainly profit of them.

I joked, it is true, about Joscelin de Louvain,[1] and his Duchess; but not at all in advising you to make Mr. Percy pimp for the plate. On the contrary, I wish you success, and think this an infallible method of obtaining the benefaction. It is right to lay vanity under contribution; for then both sides are pleased.

It will not be easy for you to dine with Mr. Granger[2] from hence, and return at night. It cannot be less than six or seven-and-twenty miles to Shiplake. But I go to Park-place to-morrow, which is within two miles of him, and I will try if I can tempt him to meet you here. Adieu!

212. Antiquarians.

TO THE REV. WILLIAM COLE

1 September 1778.

I have now seen the "Critical Review," with Lord Hardwicke's note, in which I perceive the sensibility of your friendship for me, dear Sir, but no rudeness on his part. Contemptuous it was to reprint

1 The Duke of Northumberland: Sir Hugh Smithson (bap. 1712–86), who like his medieval predecessor Joscelin de Louvain had married into the Percy family and assumed the name and arms of Percy.
2 For the Rev. James Granger see letter 88, p. 145, n. 1.

Jane Shore's letter without any notice of my having given it before: the apology, too, is not made to me – but I am not affected by such incivilities, that imply more ill-will than boldness. As I expected more from your representation, I believe I expressed myself with more warmth than the occasion deserved; and, as I love to be just, I will, now I am perfectly cool, be so to Lord Hardwicke. His dislike of me was meritorious in him, as I conclude it was founded on my animosity to *his* father, as mine had been, from attachment to *my own*, who was basely betrayed by the late Earl. The present has given me formerly many peevish marks of enmity; and I suspect, I don't know if justly, that he was the mover of the cabal in the Anti-quarian Society[1] against me; but all their misunderstandings were of a size that made me smile rather than provoke me. The Earl, as I told you, has since been rather wearisome in applications to me; which I received very civilly, but encouraged no farther. When he wanted me to be his printer, I own I was not good Christian enough, not to be pleased with refusing, and yet in as well-bred excuses as I could form, pleading, what was true at the time, as you know, that I had laid down my press – but so much for this idle story. I shall think no more of it, but adhere to my specific system.

The Antiquarians will be as ridiculous as they used to be; and, since it is impossible to infuse taste into them, they will be as dry and dull as their predecessors. One may revive what perished, but it will perish again, if more life is not breathed into it than it enjoyed originally. Facts, dates, and names will never please the multitude, unless there is some style and manner to recommend them, and un-less some novelty is struck out from their appearance. The best merit of the Society lies in their prints; for their volumes, no mortal will ever touch them but an antiquary. Their Saxon and Danish dis-coveries are not worth more than monuments of the Hottentots; and for Roman remains in Britain, they are upon a foot with what ideas we should get of Inigo Jones, if somebody was to publish views of huts and houses, that our officers run up at Senegal and Goree. Bishop Lyttelton used to torment me with bar-rows and Roman camps, and I would as soon have attended to the turf graves in our churchyards. I have no curiosity to know how

---

1 Walpole had resigned from the Society of Antiquaries in 1772: see letter 174, p. 239, n. 3.

awkward and clumsy men have been in the dawn of arts, or in their decay.

I exempt you entirely from my general censure on antiquaries, both for your singular modesty in publishing nothing yourself, and for collecting stone and brick for others to build with. I wish your materials may ever fall into good hands – perhaps they will! our empire is falling to pieces! we are relapsing to a little island. In that state, men are apt to inquire how great their ancestors have been; and, when a kingdom is past doing anything, the few that are studious look into the memorials of past time; nations, like private persons, seek lustre from their progenitors, when they have none in themselves, and the farther they are from the dignity of their source. When half its colleges are tumbled down, the ancient University of Cambridge will revive from your Collections,[1] and you will be quoted as a living witness that saw it in its splendour. . . .

9. THE EARL OF STRAFFORD

William Wentworth (1722–91), second Earl of Strafford, was an amateur architect who designed the Palladian south wing of Wentworth Castle, his country seat in Yorkshire. Walpole was enthusiastic, describing this as the model of "the most perfect taste in architecture, where grace softens dignity, and lightness attempers magnificence", using it in the concluding paragraph of his *Essay on Modern Gardening* (1780) to illustrate the triumph of English architecture and landscape. He was fond of both Strafford and his wife, Lady Anne Campbell; they also had a house at Twickenham, and so for part of the year were Walpole's neighbours.

213. *Current News.*

TO THE EARL OF STRAFFORD

Strawberry Hill, 5 August 1762.

My Dear Lord,

As you have correspondents of better authority in town, I don't pretend to send you great events, and I know no small ones. Nobody

1 At his death Cole left his substantial manuscript collections to the British Museum.

talks of anything under a revolution. That in Russia alarms me, lest Lady Mary should fall in love with the Czarina, who has deposed *her* Lord Coke, and set out for Petersburgh.[1] We throw away a whole summer in writing Britons and North Britons; the Russians change sovereigns faster than Mr. Wilkes can choose a motto for a paper. What years were spent here in controversy on the abdication of King James, and the legitimacy of the Pretender! Commend me to the Czarina. They doubted, that is, her husband did, whether her children were of genuine blood-royal. She appealed to the Preobazinski guards, excellent casuists; and, to prove Duke Paul heir to the crown, assumed it herself. The proof was compendious and unanswerable.

I trust you know that Mr. Conway has made a figure by taking the castle of Waldeck. There has been another action to Prince Ferdinand's advantage, but no English were engaged.

You tantalise me by talking of the verdure of Yorkshire; we have not had a teacup full of rain till to-day for these six weeks. Corn has been reaped that never wet its lips; not a blade of grass; the leaves yellow and falling as in the end of October. In short, Twickenham is rueful; I don't believe Westphalia looks more barren. Nay, we are forced to fortify ourselves too. Hanworth was broken open last night, though the family was all there. Lord Vere lost a silver standish, an old watch, and his writing-box with fifty pounds in it. They broke it open in the park, but missed a diamond ring, which was found, and the telescope, which by the weight of the case they had fancied full of money. Another house in the middle of Sunbury has had the same fate. I am mounting cannon on my battlements.

Your chateau I hope, proceeds faster than mine. The carpenters are all associated for increase of wages; I have had but two men at work these five weeks. You know, to be sure, that Lady Mary Wortley cannot live.[2] Adieu, my dear Lord!

1 Walpole draws a parallel between Strafford's sister-in-law Lady Mary Coke (1727–1811), who in 1749 brought a suit for divorce against her husband, Viscount Coke, and Catherine the Great of Russia, who had recently deposed her husband Peter III and assumed the crown. Lady Mary, a keen traveller, had left for France in June.
2 Lady Mary Wortley Montagu (bap. 1689–1762), writer, traveller, friend and then enemy of Pope, died later that month.

10. LADY HERVEY

Mary (or Molly) Lepell (1699/1700–1768) at the age of fourteen or fifteen was appointed Maid of Honour to Caroline of Ansbach, wife of the future George II, and became one of the brightest ornaments of the "alternative" court set up by the Prince and Princess of Wales at Leicester House. Admired for her beauty, charm, and vivacity, she was also very well educated, and was soon drawn into the literary circle forming around Caroline, which included Alexander Pope, John Gay, John Arbuthnot, Lord Chesterfield and Henrietta Howard, later Countess of Suffolk. Many of her friends celebrated her in verse; Voltaire, too, wrote his one known English poem in her honour. In 1720 she secretly married the handsome John Hervey, second son of the Earl of Bristol. Notwithstanding his bisexuality, the couple had eight children, and while Pope in his *Epistle to Dr. Arbuthnot* (1735) caricatured Hervey as Sporus – the youth Nero had castrated before marrying – she appeared to tolerate her husband's affairs with men and even made a friend of his greatest *amorato*, Stephen Fox. Both she and her husband involved themselves in politics, not always in the same cause, and were prominent at the court of George II during the 1730s when Lord Hervey held the post of Vice-Chamberlain. Lady Hervey was widowed in 1743. She began to spend long periods in France and developed pronounced Francophile, Catholic (and also, allegedly, Jacobite) sympathies. Walpole was fascinated by her as a link with the early Hanoverian court, and shared her love of France.

214. *A Gift.*

10 November 1764.

Soh! Madam, you expect to be thanked, because you have done a very obliging thing![1] But I won't thank you, and I won't be obliged. It is very hard one can't come into your house and commend anything, but you must recollect it and send it after one! I will never dine in your house again; and, when I do, I will like nothing; and when I do, I will commend nothing; and when I do, you shan't

---

1 Lady Hervey, it is supposed, had sent Mr. Walpole some potted pilchards. – BERRY.

remember it. You are very grateful indeed to Providence that gave you so good a memory, to stuff it with nothing but bills of fare of what everybody likes to eat and drink! I wonder you are not ashamed – I wonder you are not ashamed! Do you think there is no such thing as gluttony of the memory? – You a Christian! A pretty account you will be able to give of yourself! – Your fine folks in France may call this friendship and attention, perhaps, but sure, if I was to go to the devil, it should be for thinking of nothing but myself, not of others, from morning to night. I would send back your temptations; but, as I will not be obliged to you for them, verily I shall retain them to punish you; ingratitude being a proper chastisement for sinful friendliness. Thine in the spirit,

PILCHARD WHITFIELD.[1]

11. MADAME DU DEFFAND

"This best and sincerest of friends who loves me as much as my mother did." – So Walpole in letter 216 describes Madame du Deffand, whose acquaintance he first made in Paris in 1765. Born Marie de Vichy-Chamrond in 1696, she was married to her cousin, the Marquis du Deffand, but finding him dull soon sought diversion at court in the scandalous circle of the regent, Philippe, Duc d'Orléans. She became his mistress in 1721, though only for a fortnight, and shed her husband a year later. For many years she frequented the brilliant court of the Duchesse du Maine at Sceaux, where she formed a lasting relationship with the writer and historian Charles-Jean-François Hénault, President of the Paris *parlement*. Her Paris salon, held from 1747 in her rooms at the Convent of Saint Joseph, enjoyed great renown, attracting both aristocrats and intellectuals including Voltaire, Montesquieu, Fontenelle and D'Alembert. After 1764, however, it was in decline. She had quarrelled with her niece and protégée Julie de Lespinasse, who left to set up a rival salon to which D'Alembert and the *philosophes* defected.

Walpole always enjoyed the company of elderly dowagers who could regale him with tales of the courts of their youth, and Madame du Deffand still retained much of her former charm in spite of her seventy years and total blindness. He visited her in alternate years

1 A joke at the expense of the Methodist preacher George Whitfield (1714–70).

until 1771 and finally in 1775, and they wrote at least once a week to each other, always in French. Clever and cynical, she was a sharp observer of character, but a troubled personality, craving constant stimulation and companionship to stave off the existential horror of what she described as "an ennui such as to extinguish all light from her mind"; a condition on which Voltaire, with whom she maintained a celebrated correspondence for nearly thirty years, had tried in vain to reason with her. She was a demanding correspondent and Walpole's deflection of her intense outpourings of affection was perhaps unkind; he feared ridicule, and letter 217 records his embarrassed concern to recover his letters to her. Nonetheless he always spoke of her with admiration and fondness. Her versatility and her wonderful activity amazed him: "She makes songs, sings them, remembers all that ever were made . . . She humbles the learned, sets right their disciples, and finds conversation for everybody. Affectionate as Madame de Sévigné, she has none of her prejudices, but a more universal taste" (letter 216). In 1766 she sent him a snuffbox with a letter in the name of his idol Madame de Sévigné, addressed to him from the Elysian Fields, as one great letter-writer's tribute to another: in letter 215 Walpole refers to the gift, and to his rather ungallantly having scolded her for the embarrassment it caused him while he tried to identify the giver. At her death in 1780 she bequeathed to Walpole all her manuscripts and at his request entrusted to him her little dog Tonton, who became as great a pet with his new master as he had been with his old mistress.

215. *The Snuff-Box.*

TO THE RIGHT HON. LADY HERVEY

Strawberry Hill, 28 June 1766.

It is consonant to your ladyship's long experienced goodness, to remove my error as soon as you could. In fact, the same post that brought Madame d'Aiguillon's letter to you, brought me a confession from Madame du Deffand of her guilt.[1] I am not the less

---

1 Madame du Deffand had sent Mr. Walpole a snuff-box, in which was a portrait of Madame de Sévigné, accompanied by a letter written in her name from the Elysian Fields, and addressed to Mr. Walpole; who did not at first suspect Madame du Deffand as the author, but thought both the present and letter had come from the Duchess of Choiseul. – BERRY.

obliged to your ladyship for *informing* against the true criminal. It is well for me, however, that I hesitated, and did not, as Monsieur de Guerchy pressed me to do, constitute myself prisoner. What a ridiculous vain-glorious figure I should have made at Versailles with a laboured letter and my present! I still shudder when I think of it, and have scolded Madame du Deffand black and blue. However, I feel very comfortable; and though it will be imputed to my own vanity, that I showed the box as Madame de Choiseul's present, I resign the glory, and submit to the shame with great satisfaction. I have no pain in receiving this present from Madame du Deffand, and must own have great pleasure that nobody but she could write that most charming of all letters.[1] Did not Lord Chesterfield think it so, Madam? I doubt our friend Mr. Hume must allow that not only Madame de Boufflers, but Voltaire himself, could not have written so well. When I give up Madame de Sévigné herself, I think his sacrifices will be trifling. . . .

216. *Her Wonderful Vitality.*

TO GEORGE MONTAGU, ESQ.

Paris, 7 September 1769.

. . . My dear old friend [Madame du Deffand] was charmed with your mention of her, and made me vow to return you a thousand compliments. She cannot conceive why you will not step hither. Feeling in herself no difference between the spirits of twenty-three and seventy-three, she thinks there is no impediment to doing whatever one will, but the want of eyesight. If she had that I am persuaded no consideration would prevent her making me a visit at Strawberry Hill. She makes songs, sings them, remembers all that ever were made; and, having lived from the most agreeable to the most reasoning age, has all that was amiable in the last, all that is sensible in this, without the vanity of the former, or the pedant impertinence of the latter. I have heard her dispute with all sorts of people, on all sorts of subjects, and never knew her in the wrong. She humbles the learned, sets right their disciples, and finds conversation for

1 Mme. du Deffand's letter was written to Walpole in the name of Mme. de Sévigné, as from the Elysian Fields.

everybody. Affectionate as Madame de Sévigné, she has none of her
prejudices, but a more universal taste; and, with the most delicate
frame, her spirits hurry her through a life of fatigue that would kill
me, if I was to continue here. If we return by one in the morning
from suppers in the country, she proposes driving to the Boulevard
or to the Foire St. Ovide, because it is too early to go to bed. I had
great difficulty last night to persuade her, though she was not well,
not to sit up till between two or three for the comet; for which purpose she had appointed an astronomer to bring his telescopes to the
president Henault's, as she thought it would amuse me. In short, her
goodness to me is so excessive, that I feel unashamed at producing
my withered person in a round of diversions, which I have quitted
at home. I tell a story; I do feel ashamed, and sigh to be in my quiet
castle and cottage; but it costs me many a pang, when I reflect that
I shall probably never have resolution enough to take another journey to see this best and sincerest of friends, who loves me as much
as my mother did! but it is idle to look forward – what is next year?
– a bubble that may burst for her or me, before even the flying year
can hurry to the end of its almanack! To form plans and projects in
such a precarious life as this, resembles the enchanted castles of fairy
legends, in which every gate was guarded by giants, dragons, &c.
Death or diseases bar every portal through which we mean to pass;
and, though we may escape them and reach the last chamber, what
a wild adventurer is he that centres his hopes at the end of such an
avenue! I sit contented with the beggars at the threshold, and never
propose going on, but as the gates open of themselves. . . .

217. *Conway's Visit.*

TO THE HON. H. S. CONWAY

Strawberry Hill, 28 September 1774.

Lady Ailesbury brings you this,[1] which is not a letter, but a paper
of directions, and the counterpart of what I have written to Madame
du Deffand. I beg of you seriously to take a great deal of notice of
this dear old friend of mine. She will, perhaps, expect more attention

---

1 Mr. Conway ended his military tour at Paris; whither Lady Ailesbury and Mrs.
Damer went to meet him, and where they spent the winter together. – WALPOLE.

from *you*, as my friend, and as it is her own nature a little, than will be quite convenient to you: but you have an infinite deal of patience and good-nature, and will excuse it. I was afraid of her importuning Lady Ailesbury, who has a vast deal to see and do, and, therefore, I have prepared Madame du Deffand, and told her Lady Ailesbury loves amusements, and that, having never been at Paris before, she must not confine her: so you must pay for both – and it will answer: and I do not, I own, ask this only for Madame du Deffand's sake, but for my own, and a little for yours. Since the late King's [Louis XV.] death she has not dared to write to me freely, and I want to know the present state of France exactly, both to satisfy my own curiosity, and for her sake, as I wish to learn whether her pension, &c. is in any danger from the present ministry, some of whom are not her friends. She can tell you a great deal if she will – by that I don't mean that she is reserved, or partial to her own country against ours – quite the contrary; she loves me better than all France together – but she hates politics: and therefore, to make her talk on it, you must tell her it is to satisfy me, and that I want to know whether she is well at Court, whether she has any fears from the government, particularly from Maurepas and Nivernois: and that I am eager to have Monsieur de Choiseul[1] and *ma grandmaman*, the Duchess, restored to power. If you take it on this foot easily, she will talk to you with the utmost frankness and with amazing cleverness. I have told her you are strangely absent, and that, if she does not repeat it over and over, you will forget every syllable: so I have prepared her to joke and be quite familiar with you at once. She knows more of personal characters, and paints them better, than anybody: but let this be between ourselves, for I would not have a living soul suspect that I get any intelligence from her, which would hurt her; and, therefore, I beg you not to let any human being know of this letter, nor of your conversation with her, neither English nor French.

Madame du Deffand hates *les philosophes;* so you must give them up to her. She and Madame Geoffrin[2] are no friends: so, if you go

1 Étienne-François de Choiseul-Stainville, Duc de Choiseul (1719–85), Louis XV's chief minister between 1758 and 1770, was not reinstated. Jean-Frédéric Phélypeaux (1701–81), Comte de Maurepas, who had been Secretary of State for the Marine from 1723 to 1749, was recalled from exile by Louis XVI as first minister, a post he held until 1781: Nivernois was his brother-in-law.
2 Marie-Thérèse Rodet Geoffrin (1699–1777) held a celebrated salon at her house in the Rue Saint-Honoré. For Walpole's account of her, see letter 352.

thither, don't tell her of it. Indeed you would be sick of that house, whither all the pretended *beaux esprits* and *faux savants* go, and where they are very impertinent and dogmatic.

Let me give you one other caution, which I shall give Lady Ailesbury too. Take care of your papers at Paris, and have a very strong lock to your *porte-feuille*. In the *hôtels garnis* they have double keys to every lock, and examine every drawer and paper of the English they can get at. They will pilfer, too, whatever they can. I was robbed of half my clothes there the first time, and they wanted to hang poor Louis [his Swiss servant] to save the people of the house who had stolen the things.

Here is another thing I must say. Madame du Deffand has kept a great many of my letters, and, as she is very old, I am in pain about them. I have written to her to beg she will deliver them up to you to bring back to me, and I trust she will. If she does, be so good to take great care of them. If she does not mention them, tell her just before you come away, that I begged you to bring them; and if she hesitates, convince her how it would hurt me to have letters written in very bad French, and mentioning several people, both French and English, fall into bad hands, and, perhaps, be printed.

Let me desire you to read this letter more than once, that you may not forget my requests, which are very important to me; and I must give you one other caution, without which all would be useless. There is at Paris a Mademoiselle de l'Espinasse,[1] a pretended *bel esprit*, who was formerly an humble companion of Madame du Deffand; and betrayed her and used her very ill. I beg of you not to let anybody carry you thither. It would disoblige my friend of all things in the world, and she would never tell you a syllable; and I own it would hurt me, who have such infinite obligations to her, that I should be very unhappy, if a particular friend of mine showed her this disregard. She has done everything upon earth to please and serve me, and I owe it to her to be earnest about this attention. Pray do not mention it; it might look simple in me, and yet I owe it to her, as I know it would hurt her: and, at her age, with her misfortunes, and with infinite obligations on my side, can I do too much to show my gratitude, or prevent her any new mortification? I dwell

1 Julie de Lespinasse (1732–76), illegitimate niece of Mme. du Deffand, who after ten years as companion to her aunt set up a rival salon. Now celebrated for her letters.

upon it, because she has some enemies so spiteful that they try to carry all English to Mademoiselle de l'Espinasse. . . .

218. *Walpole in Paris Again.*

TO THE HON. H. S. CONWAY

Paris, 8 September 1775.

The delays of the post, and its departure before its arrival, saved me some days of anxiety for Lady Ailesbury, and prevented my telling you how concerned I am for her accident; though I trust, by this time, she has not even pain left. I feel the horror you must have felt during her suffering in the dark, and on the sight of her arm;[1] and though nobody admires her needlework more than I, still I am rejoiced that it will be the greatest sufferer. However, I am very impatient for a further account. Madame du Deffand, who, you know, never loves her friends by halves, and whose impatience never allows itself time to inform itself, was out of her wits, because I could not explain exactly how the accident happened, and where. She wanted to write directly, though the post was just gone; and, as soon as I could make her easy about the accident, she fell into a new distress about her fans for Madame de Marchais, and concludes they have been overturned, and broken too. In short, I never saw anything like her. She has made engagements for me till Monday se'nnight, in which are included I don't know how many journeys into the country; and as nobody ever leaves her without engaging them for another time, all these parties will be so many polypuses, that will shoot out into new ones every way. Madame de Jonsac, a great friend of mine, arrived the day before yesterday, and Madame du Deffand has pinned her down to meeting me at her house four times before next Tuesday, all parentheses, that are not to interfere with our other suppers; and from those suppers I never get to bed before two or three o'clock. In short, I need have the activity of a squirrel, and the strength of a Hercules, to go through my labours – not to count how many *démêlés* I have had to *raccommode*, and how many *mémoires* to present against Tonton,[2]

1 Lady Ailesbury had been overturned in her carriage at Park-place, and dislocated her wrist. – WALPOLE.
2 Mme. du Deffand's dog, who until his death in 1789 was cared for by Walpole.

who grows the greater favourite the more people he devours. As I am the only person who dare correct him, I have already insisted on his being confined in the Bastile every day after five o'clock. T'other night he flew at Lady Barrymore's face and I thought would have torn her eye out; but it ended in biting her finger. She was terrified; she fell into tears. Madame du Deffand, who has too much parts not to see everything in its true light, perceiving that she had not beaten Tonton half enough, immediately told us a story of a lady, whose dog, having bitten a piece out of a gentleman's leg, the tender dame, in a great fright, cried out, "Won't it make my dog sick?" . . .

I used to scold you about your bad writing, and perceive I have written in such a hurry, and blotted my letter so much, that you will not be able to read it: but consider how few moments I have to myself. I am forced to stuff my ears with cotton to get any sleep. – However, my journey has done me good. I have thrown off at least fifteen years. Here is a letter for my dear Mrs. Damer from Madame de Cambis, who thinks she dotes on you all. Adieu! . . .

219. *Her Death.*

TO SIR HORACE MANN

Strawberry Hill, 9 October 1780, addition to letter begun 7 October.

Since I wrote the above, I have heard from Paris of the death of my dear old friend Madame du Deffand, whom I went so often thither to see. It was not quite unexpected, and was softened by her great age, eighty-four, which forbad distant hopes; and, by what I dreaded more than her death, her increasing deafness, which, had it become, like her blindness, total, would have been living after death. Her memory only *began* to impair; her amazing sense and quickness, not at all. I have written to her once a week for these last fifteen years, as correspondence and conversation could be her only pleasures. You see that I am the most faithful letter-writer in the world – and, alas! never see those I am so constant to! One is forbidden common-place reflections on these misfortunes, because they *are* common-place; but is not that because they are natural? But you never having known that dear old woman is a better reason for not making you the butt of my concern.

Lord George Gordon[1] has just got a neighbour – I believe, not a companion; for state-prisoners are not allowed to be very sociable. Laurens, lately President of the Congress, has been taken by a natural son of the last Lord Albemarle, and brought to England, to London, to the Tower. He was going Ambassador to Holland, and his papers are captured too. I should think they would tell us but what we learnt a fortnight ago; and (which is more wonderful, what we would not believe *till a* fortnight ago) that there is an end of our American dream! Perhaps they will give us back a cranny in exchange for their negotiator.

I go again to-morrow to see General Conway, and hope to find him out of bed; and I finish my letter, that I may not run into meditations on what is uppermost in my mind, – mortality and its accidents! ...

220. *Her Will.*

TO THE COUNTESS OF UPPER OSSORY

Berkeley Square, 1 November 1780.

... As I have been returned above a fortnight I should have written had I had a syllable to tell you; but what could I tell you from that melancholy and very small circle at Twickenham Park,[2] almost the only place I do go to in the country, partly out of charity, and partly as I have scarce any other society left which I prefer to it; for, without entering on too melancholy a detail, recollect, Madam, that I have outlived most of those to whom I was habituated, Lady Hervey, Lady Suffolk, Lady Blandford – my dear old friend [Madame du Deffand], I should probably never have seen again – yet that is a deeper loss, indeed! She has left me all her MSS. – a compact between us – in one word I had, at her earnest request, consented to accept them, on condition she should leave me nothing else. She had, indeed, intended to leave me her little all, but I declared I would never set foot in Paris again (this was ten years ago) if she did not engage to retract that destination. To satisfy her, I at last agreed to

1 He had been committed to the Tower in June after the Gordon Riots. Henry Laurens was captured after sailing from Philadelphia.
2 Twickenham Park, the seat of the widowed Duchess of Montrose (*c.* 1717–88), a neighbouring dowager visited by Walpole.

accept her papers, and one thin gold box with the portrait of her dog.[1] I have written to beg her dog itself, which is so cross, that I am sure nobody else would treat it well; and I have ordered her own servant who read all letters to her to pick out all the letters of living persons, and restore them to the several writers without my seeing them. . . .

12. THE COUNTESS OF UPPER OSSORY

Anne Fitzpatrick, Lady Ossory (1738–1804) was the recipient of some of Walpole's most brilliant letters, admired for their depiction of eighteenth-century society – a society from which she was largely excluded. She had at eighteen married the Duke of Grafton. In 1761, when she and her husband were going to Florence, Walpole described her to Horace Mann as "a passion of mine – not a regular beauty, but one of the finest women you ever saw, and with more dignity and address. She is one of our first great ladies."[2]

The marriage was not happy; the Duke disapproved of his wife's gambling, and indulged himself with a succession of mistresses. They separated in 1765. In 1766 the Duchess met Lord Ossory, by whom she had a daughter in 1768: she was divorced from the Duke (who was by then prime minister) the following year, whereupon she married Ossory, who was seven years her junior. He was an M.P., an enthusiast for horse-racing, and also a member of the Literary Club, though Boswell records hardly any contribution made by him to their discussions. Nonetheless, Walpole thought the marriage "made two persons happier than Venus's son generally does".[3]

Walpole's correspondence with Lady Ossory really begins in 1771, when she was living in the country at Ossory's seat, Ampthill Park, Bedfordshire. It has often been noted that the combination of her isolation after a scandalous divorce, and the falling away of Walpole's correspondence with the indolent George Montagu – who had been as secluded in Northamptonshire as Lady Ossory was at Ampthill – provided Walpole with the opportunity of a new recipient for his sparkling chronicle of London news and society. Her letters do not survive, but Walpole wrote to her for some thirty-six years,

1 Tonton: see letter 218, p. 311, n. 2.
2 Letter of 14 May 1761 (YE 21:506).
3 Letter to Lady Ossory, 12 September 1775 (YE 32:262).

culminating in his much-quoted letter of 15 January 1797 (letter 240), six weeks before his death; the gentlest of admonitions for her showing his "idle notes" to friends, it provides a poignant envoi to her and to the art of letter-writing.

221. *Advancing Years.*

TO THE COUNTESS OF UPPER OSSORY

Strawberry Hill, 14 June 1774.

Virgin Mary! offended at you, Madam! I have crossed myself forty times since I read the impious words, never to be pronounced by human lips, – nay, and to utter them, when I am seemingly to blame, – yet, believe me, my silence is not owing to negligence, or to that most wicked of all sins, inconstancy. I have thought on you waking or sleeping, whenever I have thought at all, from the moment I saw you last; and if there was an echo in the neighbourhood besides Mr. Cambridge,[1] I should have made it repeat your Ladyship's name, till the parish should have presented it for a nuisance. I have begun twenty letters, but the naked truth is, I found I had absolutely nothing to say. You yourself owned, Madam, that I am grown quite lifeless, and it is very true. I am none of your Glastonbury thorns that blow at Christmas. I am a remnant of the last age, and have nothing to do with the present. I am an exile from the sunbeams of drawing-rooms; I have quitted the gay scenes of Parliament and the Antiquarian Society; I am not of Almack's; I don't understand horse-races; I never go to reviews; what can I have to talk of? I go to no *fêtes champêtres*, what can I have to think of? I know nothing but about myself, and about myself I know nothing. I have scarce been in town since I saw you, have scarce seen anybody here, and don't remember a tittle but having scolded my gardener twice, which, indeed, would be as important an article as any in Montaigne's Travels, which I have been reading, and if I was tired of his Essays, what must one be of these! What signifies what a man thought, who never thought of anything but himself; and what signifies what a man did, who never did anything? ...

Thank Heaven the age is as dull as I am! Pray tell me, Madam,

1 A reference to Cambridge's reputation as a gossip: see letter 159, p. 225, n. 3.

some of Lady Anne's[1] *bons-mots* to enliven me a little. I am expecting Lords Ashburnham, March, Digby, Williams, and George Selwyn.[2] . . .

222. *A Welcome Gift.*

TO THE COUNTESS OF UPPER OSSORY

Arlington Street, 1 January 1775.

This morning, Madam, as soon as my eyes opened, Philip [his servant] stood before me, bearing in one hand a shining vest, and in the other a fair epistle,[3] written in celestial characters, which, however, it was given me to understand.

The present, I saw, came from no mortal hand, and seemed to be the boon of all the gods, or rather of all the goddesses; for there was taste, fancy, delicacy, flattery, wit, and sentiment in it, and so artfully blended, that no celestial in breeches could possibly have mixed so bewitching a potion. Venus had chosen the pattern, Flora painted the roses after those at Paphos, Minerva had worked the tambour part, Clio wrote the ode, and Thalia took off the majestic stiffness of the original sketch by breathing her own ease all over it.

These visions naturally presented themselves. I told you, Madam, I was but just awake, and at that hour, somehow or other, one's head is very apt to be full of Venus and such pretty figures. Vanity soon took their place, and, not to be unworthy of my visitants, I held up my head, and thought it became so favoured a personage as myself to assume a loftier port, and behave like my predecessors who had been honoured in the same manner.

Was I more like Æneas when his mother brought him armour of heavenly temper, or like Paris when three divinities exerted all their

1 One of Lady Ossory's daughters.
2 Lord Ashburnham (1724–1812) was a courtier, Lord March (1725–1810) was later the Duke of Queensberry ["Old Q"], Henry, Lord Digby (1731–93) was a former Lord of the Admiralty, and Williams was "Gilly" Williams (*c.* 1719–1805), soon to be appointed Receiver-General of Excise, friend of Walpole and correspondent of Selwyn. Williams, Selwyn, and Richard Edgcumbe (for whom see letter 272, p. 374, n. 2) were portrayed by Reynolds at Strawberry Hill in "The Out of Town Party", which hung over the chimney in the Great Parlour.
3 Lady Ossory had sent Walpole a (presumably New Year's) present of a waistcoat she had embroidered, with some verses.

charms and all their artifices to ensnare his partiality? To be sure I could have been simple enough to be content with the character of Horatius Flaccus, with which my patronesses had hailed me; but when I ordered Philip to reach me my lyre, that I might pour out a rapturous epode or secular hymn in gratitude, he said, "Lord! sir, you know Horace's lyre is at Ampthill."

What follows is more melancholy. I rose; the first object was to examine more attentively the inspired vest in the full sun against which it shone gorgeously; but, alas! as I crept to the window, in the glass I beheld – what do you think, Madam? – such an emaciated, wan, wrinkled, poor skeleton, that – O! adieu, visions, goddesses, odes, vests of roses, and immortal Strawberry! – I thought I saw a thinner Don Quixote[1] attired by the Duchess for sport. Shocked, sunk from my altitudes, and shrinking into myself, I bade Philip Pança fold up the vest, and vowed never to dress up my ghost-like Adonis, but to consecrate the dear work of dear fingers to the single word (I will believe in the charming ode) Friendship; and may the memory of that word, the vest and the ode, exist when Strawberry Hill, its tinsel glories and its master, are remembered no where else!

223. *Minister to George V.*

TO THE COUNTESS OF UPPER OSSORY

Strawberry Hill, 22 August 1776.

I perceive at last, Madam, that it is very foolish to live out of the world, and a good deal alone; one contracts the strangest prejudices! one fancies one grows old, because one is near threescore; that it is absurd to lay plans for ten or twenty years hence; that one shall not govern the next generation as one did their grandfathers and grandmothers; in short, one imagines one is not immortal. Nay, though there never was an age in which youth thought it so right to anticipate all its prerogatives, and declare us veterans Strulbrugs[2] a little before our time, we silly folks in the country despair of recovering the province of wisdom, that is, keeping young people for ever in

1 In Don Quixote, the knight is presented with fine clothes by the Duchess: Walpole's servant Philip [Columb] becomes Sancho Panza.
2 In Swift's *Gulliver's Travels*, the Struldbrugs are humans who can grow old, but not die.

leading-strings, while we enjoy the world and dispose of all its blessings over our bottle.

The picture of St. George[1] has opened my eyes. I will launch into
the world again, and propose to be Prime Minister to King George
V., and lay a plan for governing longer than Cardinal Fleury, by surfeiting all the young nobility at Eton and Westminster Schools with
sugar-plums. In the meantime if I grow deaf, like the late or present
governor, I will have Master George V. taught to talk to me upon
his fingers, which will teach both him and me to spell, for it would
not be proper to have him bawling secrets of State to me through a
speaking-trumpet: and when I come to be Minister, I will secure the
attachment of all the young senators by getting drunk with them
every night till six in the morning; and if I should never be sober
enough to give away places, which is the only real business of a Minister, I will marry a Scotch wife, who shall think of nothing else. I
will do still more, and what no Minister yet could ever compass,
I will prevent all clamour, by adopting St. George's motto, – "*Honi
soit qui mal y pense*," which, if inscribed on the picture now in agitation, will certainly hinder anybody's smiling at it. As one cannot
entirely divest one's self of one's character,

> But find the ruling passion strong in death,[2]

I propose to conclude my career in a manner worthy of an antiquary,
as I was in the last century, and when I am satiated with years and
honours, and arrived at a comfortable old age, to break my neck out
of a cherry-tree in robbing an orchard, like the Countess of
Desmond at an hundred and forty; but don't mention this last idea,
Madam, lest that roguish lad, the first Lord of the Admiralty[3]
should steal the thought from me. . . .

1 Reynolds's painting of "The Bedford Family", a fancy piece showing the children
of the family as St. George and attendants slaying the dragon.
2 From Pope, *Moral Essays*, Epistle I. 263.
3 Lord Sandwich, First Lord of the Admiralty, was in fact only a year younger than
Walpole.

224. *News, True and False.*

TO THE COUNTESS OF UPPER OSSORY

Berkeley Square, 14 November 1779.

I must be equitable; I must do the world justice; there are really some hopes of its amendment; I have not heard one lie these four days; but then, indeed, I have heard nothing. Well, then, why do you write? Stay, Madam; my letter is not got on horseback yet; nor shall it mount till it has something to carry. It is my duty, as your gazetteer, to furnish you with news, true or false, and you would certainly dismiss me if I did not, at least, tell you something that was impossible. The whole nation is content with hearing anything new, let it be ever so bad. Tell the first man you meet that Ireland has revolted; away he runs, and tells everybody he meets, – everybody tells everybody, and the next morning they ask for more news. Well, Jamaica is taken; oh! Jamaica is taken. Next day, what news? Why, Paul Jones is landed in Rutlandshire, and has carried off the Duchess of Devonshire and a squadron is fitting out to prevent it; and I am to have a pension for having given the earliest intelligence; and there is to be a new farce called the *Rutlandshire Invasion*, and the King and Queen will come to town to see it, and the Prince of Wales will not, because he is not old enough to understand pantomimes.

Well, Madam; having despatched the nation and its serious affairs, one may chat over private matters. I have seen Lord Macartney, and do affirm that he is shrunk, and has a *soupçon* of black that was not wont to reside in his complexion. George is so engrossed by the Board of Trade, that I have seen him but the morning after his arrival.[1]

Mr. Beauclerk[2] has built a library in Great Russell Street [Bloomsbury] that reaches half way to Highgate. Everybody goes to see it; it has put the Museum's nose quite out of joint.

Now I return to politics. Sir Ralph Payne and Dr. Johnson are answering General Burgoyne, and they say the words are to be so long that the reply must be printed in a pamphlet as large as an atlas,

1 Lord Macartney (1737–1806) had been released by the French after being captured while Governor of Grenada. George was Walpole's friend George Selwyn, though he held an office in the Board of Works, not the Board of Trade.
2 Topham Beauclerk (1739–80), book collector, friend of Dr. Johnson, and husband of Walpole's friend the artist Lady Diana Beauclerk.

but in an Elzevir type, or the first sentence would fill twenty pages in octavo. You may depend upon the truth of it, for Mr. Cumberland[1] told it in confidence to one with whom he is not at all acquainted, who told it to one whom I never saw; so you see, Madam, there is no questioning the authority.

I will not answer so positively for what I am going to tell you, as I had it only from the person himself. The Duke of Gloucester was at Bath with the Margrave of Anspach. Lord Nugent came up and would talk to the Duke, and then asked if he might take the liberty of inviting his Royal Highness to dinner? I think you will admire the quickness and propriety of the answer: – the Duke replied, "My Lord, I make no acquaintance but in London," where you know, Madam, he only has levees. The Irishman continued to talk to him even after that rebuff. He certainly hoped to have been very artful – to have made court there, and yet not have offended anywhere else by not going in town, which would have been a gross affront to the Duke had he accepted the invitation.

I was at Blackheath t'other morning, where I was grieved. There are eleven Vander Werffs that cost an immense sum: half of them are spoiled since Sir Gregory Page's[2] death by servants neglecting to shut out the sun. There is another room hung with the history of Cupid and Psyche, in twelve small pictures by Luca Giordano, that are sweet. There is, too, a glorious Claude, some fine Teniers, a noble Rubens and Snyders, two beautiful Philippo Lauras, and a few more, – and several very bad. The house is magnificent, but wounded me; it was built on the model of Houghton, except that three rooms are thrown into a gallery.

Now I have tapped the chapter of pictures, you must go and see Zoffani's "Tribune at Florence,"[3] which is an astonishing piece of work, with a vast deal of merit.

There too you will see a delightful piece of Wilkes looking – no, squinting tenderly at his daughter.[4] It is a caricature of the Devil

1   Richard Cumberland (1732–1811), Secretary to the Board of Trade from 1776 to 1782, playwright and novelist.
2   Sir Gregory Page (1689–1775), art collector, whose house at Blackheath was designed by the architect John James (c. 1672–1746).
3   Walpole had just seen Zoffany's "Tribuna" in the artist's studio: it was subsequently bought for the Royal Collection.
4   Zoffany's double portrait of Wilkes and his daughter Mary (now in the National Portrait Gallery) flatters neither of them.

acknowledging Miss Sin in Milton. I do not know why, but they are under a palm-tree, which has not grown in a free country for some centuries. . . .

225. *The Monkey and the Parrot.*

TO THE COUNTESS OF UPPER OSSORY

Friday Night, 10 February 1786.

. . . To divert the theme, how do you like, Madam, the following story? A young Madame de Choiseul is inloved with by Monsieur de Coigny and Prince Joseph of Monaco. She longed for a parrot that should be a miracle of eloquence: every other shop in Paris sells mackaws, parrots, cockatoos, &c. No wonder one at least of the rivals soon found a Mr. Pitt, and the bird was immediately declared the nymph's first minister: but as she had two passions as well as two lovers, she was also enamoured of General Jackoo at Astley's.[1] The unsuccessful candidate offered Astley ingots for his monkey, but Astley demanding a *terre* for life, the paladin was forced to desist, but fortunately heard of another miracle of parts of the Monomotapan race, who was not in so exalted a sphere of life, being only a *marmiton*[2] in a kitchen, where he had learnt to pluck fowls with inimitable dexterity. This dear animal was not invaluable, was bought, and presented to Madame de Choiseul, who immediately made him the *secretaire de ses commandemens*. Her caresses were distributed equally to the animals, and her thanks to the donors. The first time she went out, the two former were locked up in her bed-chamber: how the two latter were disposed of, history is silent. Ah! I dread to tell the sequel. When the lady returned and flew to her chamber, Jackoo the second received her with all the *empressement* possible – but where was Poll? – found at last under the bed, shivering and cowering – and without a feather, as stark as any Christian. Poll's presenter concluded that his rival had given the monkey with that very view, challenged him, they fought, and both were wounded; and an heroic adventure it was!

I have not paper or breath to add more, Madam, but to thank you

1 A French performing monkey that was exhibited at Astley's Amphitheatre.
2 Scullion.

for inverting the story of Poll, and feathering my Venus. I hope
I shall have occasion to send you no more letters; but that if I cannot
wait on you, you will have charity enough to come and visit the
chalk-pits[1] in Berkeley Square.

13. HANNAH MORE

A friendship between Walpole and the pious bluestocking Hannah
More (1745–1833) may seem surprising, but was nonetheless sincere.
They met in 1781, just as More was beginning to withdraw from the
pleasures of London society to which David Garrick had introduced
her (her tragedy, *Percy*, was acted with great success at Covent Garden in 1777) as a result of a gradual conversion to Evangelical Christianity. In 1785 she built a cottage near Bristol at Cowslip Green –
the cousin, Walpole declared, to Strawberry Hill – and with two of
her sisters set about establishing a network of Sunday schools and
women's benefit clubs in the district. Through her friendship with
the Bishop of London, Beilby Porteus, and with fellow Evangelical
William Wilberforce she became involved with the movement to
end the slave trade. From this time onward her writings were generally on religious, moral, and occasionally political subjects. Like
Walpole she was appalled by the French Revolution, taking up the
cause of French *émigré* clergy, and launching in 1795 her Cheap
Repository Tracts which were widely circulated and hugely popular.
    Walpole was apprehensive of her growing Sabbatarianism, but
respected her philanthropy. He enjoyed teasing her for her earnest
sense of propriety, for "that bead-roll of virtues that make you so
troublesome and amiable" (see letter 253), and addressed her as "My
dear Saint Hannah" and "My holy Hannah". For her part, she
acknowledged in a letter of 7 February 1786 to her sister that "Except
the delight he has in teasing me for what he calls over strictness,
I have never heard a sentence from him which savoured of infidel-
ity"[2] – a tribute more to Walpole's breeding and discretion than an
illustration of shared spiritual values.

1 A reference to Walpole's gouty fingers.
2 YE 31:242, n.7.

226. *A Dedicated Poem.*

TO HANNAH MORE

Berkeley Square, 9 February 1786.

It is very cruel, my dear Madam, when you send me such charming lines,[1] and say such kind and flattering things to me and of me, that I cannot even thank you with my own poor hand; and yet my hand is as much obliged to you as my eye, and ear, and understanding. My hand was in great pain when your present arrived. I opened it directly, and set to reading, till your music and my own vanity composed a quieting draught that glided to the ends of my fingers, and lulled the throbs into the deliquium that attends opium when it does not put one absolutely to sleep. I don't believe that the deity who formerly practised both poetry and physic, when gods got their livelihood by more than one profession, ever gave a recipe in rhyme; and therefore, since Dr. Johnson has prohibited application to pagan divinities, and Mr. Burke has not struck medicine and poetry out of the list of sinecures,[2] I wish you may get a patent for life for exercising both faculties. It would be a comfortable event for me: for, since I cannot wait on you to thank you, nor dare ask you

> to call your doves yourself,

and visit me in your Parnassian quality, I might send for you as my *physicianess.* Yet why should not I ask you to come and see me? You are not such a prude as to

> blush to show compassion,

though it should

> not chance this year to be the fashion.

And I can tell you, that powerful as your poetry is, and old as I am, I believe a visit from you and Mrs. Garrick would do me as much good almost as your verses. In the mean time, I beg you to accept of

---

1 The poem of "Florio," dedicated to Mr. Walpole. – BERRY. The lines quoted by Walpole below come from the poem.
2 An allusion to Johnson's objections to mythological references in modern poetry, and to Burke's denouncement of sinecures (he had abolished many of them in his Civil Establishments Act while Paymaster-General in 1782).

an addition to your Strawberry editions;[1] and believe me to be, with the greatest gratitude, your too much honoured and most obliged humble servant.

227. *A Present.*

TO HANNAH MORE

Berkeley Square, 1 January 1787.

Do not imagine, dear Madam, that I pretend in the most distant manner to pay you for charming poetry with insipid prose; much less that I acquit a debt of gratitude for flattering praise and compliments by a meagre tale that does not even aim at celebrating you. No; I have but two motives for offering you the accompanying trifle:[2] the first, to prove that the moment I have finished anything, *you* are of the earliest in my thoughts: the second, that, coming from my press, I wish it may be added to your Strawberry editions. It is so far from being designed for the public, that I have printed but forty copies; which I do not mention to raise its value, though it will with mere collectors, but lest you should lend it and lose it, when I may not be able to supply its place.

Christina, indeed, has some title to connection with you, both from her learning and her moral writings; as you are justly entitled to a lodging in her "Cité des Dames," where, I am sure, her three patronesses would place you, as a favourite *élève* of some of their still more amiable sisters, who must at this moment be condoling with their unfortunate sister Gratitude, whose vagabond foundling has so basely disgraced her and herself. You fancied that Mrs. Lactilla[3] was a spurious issue of a Muse; and to be sure, with all their immortal virginity, the parish of Parnassus has been sadly charged with their

---

1 The Yale editors suggest that Walpole's gift may have been the Duc de Nivernois' translation of his *Essay on Modern Gardening*, printed at the Strawberry Hill Press the previous year.

2 Walpole's *Postscript* to his *Royal and Noble Authors*, printed at the Strawberry Hill Press in 1786, which had a frontispiece engraving showing Reason, Rectitude and Justice appearing to Christine de Pisan and promising to assist her in writing *Le Trésor de la Cité des Dames*.

3 The poet Ann Yearsley, known as the Bristol Milkwoman, for whom see letter 50, p. 82, n. 1.

bantlings; and, as nobody knows the fathers, no wonder some of the misses have turned out woful reprobates! . . .

14. MARY AND AGNES BERRY

Mary and Agnes Berry lightened the last decade of Walpole's life. They were twenty-four and twenty-three respectively when they moved to Twickenham with their father in 1787. Walpole was seventy. Robert Berry had been disinherited in circumstances explained in letter 228; his daughters had been brought up with the help of their grandmother, first in Yorkshire, and then in Chiswick. In 1783 their father took them on a continental tour for two years to France and Italy. Walpole was entranced by their company, by Mary's literary accomplishments and good sense, and by her sister's skill as an artist. They became frequent visitors to Strawberry Hill, and in 1791 they moved into the adjoining property Little Strawberry Hill, formerly occupied by the retired actress Mrs. Clive.

Walpole was fully aware of the potential for ridicule in his affection for two women young enough to be his grandchildren: he described them jokingly as his "wives" and there was a rumour that he had offered marriage to each in succession, a rumour firmly scotched when it resurfaced in 1843 by an elderly but indignant Mary Berry.[1] When the Berry family travelled abroad again in 1790–91 they were followed across Europe by Walpole's letters, ever concerned for their safety and well-being – not wholly unreasonably, given events in France. Some of Walpole's family – his niece, the Duchess of Gloucester, and his half-sister Lady Mary Churchill – were concerned by his emotional dependence on this new attachment, while Walpole's cousin the sculptor Anne Damer (already the subject of satires for her sexual orientation) complicated matters further by falling in love with Mary.

Walpole's correspondence was essentially with Mary rather than Agnes. In his will he left the sisters Little Strawberry Hill, £4,000 each and all his published and unpublished works, ostensibly to be edited by their father but in practice by Mary, who produced five large quarto volumes in 1798, thus securing his literary inheritance.

1   Charles Greville, *A Journal of the Reign of Queen Victoria from 1837 to 1852* (London, 1885), volume 2, p. 202.

In this selection of Walpole's letters the historic notes that have been preserved are those supplied either by Walpole himself, or by Mary Berry.

Mary wrote a comedy, *Fashionable Friends*, which was produced at Drury Lane in 1802 but ran for only three nights. As well as editing in 1810 Madame du Deffand's letters to Walpole (with some of her letters to Voltaire) she wrote an account of Rachel Wriothesley, Lady Russell (1819), and two books comparing the social life of England and France (1828–31). The two sisters never married, though Mary had in 1795 been engaged to General O'Hara, the Governor of Gibraltar. From 1824 they lived together in Curzon Street in Mayfair, receiving young writers and society figures of the day including William Makepeace Thackeray. Both survived until their late eighties, dying within ten months of each other in 1852.

228. *Introduction.*

TO THE COUNTESS OF UPPER OSSORY

Strawberry Hill, 11 October 1788.

... I have made a much more, to me, precious acquisition. It is the acquaintance of two young ladies of the name of Berry, whom I first saw last winter, and who accidentally took a house here with their father for this season. Their story is singular enough to entertain you. The grandfather,[1] a Scot, had a large estate in his own country, 5000*l.* a year it is said; and a circumstance I shall tell you makes it probable. The eldest son married for love a woman with no fortune. The old man was enraged and would not see him. The wife died and left these two young ladies. Their grandfather wished for an heir male, and pressed the widower to re-marry, but could not prevail; the son declaring he would consecrate himself to his daughters and their education. The old man did not break with him again, but much worse, totally disinherited him, and left all to his second son, who very handsomely gave up 800*l.* a year to his elder brother. Mr. Berry has since carried his daughters for two or three years to France and Italy, and they are returned the best-informed and the most perfect creatures I ever saw at their age. They are exceedingly

1 Actually the maternal uncle of Robert Berry, the Berry sisters' father.

sensible, entirely natural and unaffected, frank, and, being qualified to talk on any subject, nothing is so easy and agreeable as their conversation – not more apposite than their answers and observations. The eldest, I discovered by chance, understands Latin and is a perfect Frenchwoman in her langauge. The younger draws charmingly, and has copied admirably Lady Di.'s gypsies,[1] which I lent, though the first time of her attempting colours. They are of pleasing figures; Mary, the eldest, sweet, with fine dark eyes, that are very lively when she speaks, with a symmetry of face that is the more interesting from being pale; Agnes, the younger, has an agreeable sensible countenance, hardly to be called handsome, but almost. She is less animated than Mary, but seems, out of deference to her sister, to speak seldomer, for they dote on each other, and Mary is always praising her sister's talents. I must even tell you they dress within the bounds of fashion, though fashionably; but without the excrescences and balconies with which modern hoydens overwhelm and barricade their persons. In short, good sense, information, simplicity, and ease characterise the Berrys; and this is not particularly mine, who am apt to be prejudiced, but the universal voice of all who know them. The first night I met them I would not be acquainted with them, having heard so much in their praise that I concluded they would be all pretension. The second time, in a very small company, I sat next to Mary, and found her an angel both inside and out. Now I do not know which I like best, except Mary's face, which is formed for a sentimental novel, but is ten times fitter for a fifty times better thing, genteel comedy. This delightful family comes to me almost every Sunday evening, as our region is too *proclamatory*[2] to play at cards on the seventh day. I do not care a straw for cards, but I do disapprove of this partiality to the youngest child of the week; while the other poor six days are treated as if they had no souls to save. I forgot to tell you that Mr. Berry is a little merry man with a round face, and you would not suspect him of so much feeling and attachment. I make no excuse for such minute details; for, if your Ladyship

1 Lady Diana Beauclerk's drawing of gypsies telling a country girl's fortune, prized by Walpole and now at the Victoria and Albert Museum.
2 A royal proclamation the previous year had admonished playing dice or cards on Sundays.

insists on hearing the humours of my district, you must for once indulge me with sending you two pearls[1] that I found in my path.

229. *Delight in their Society.*

TO MARY BERRY

2 February 17— and 71[2] [1789].

I am sorry, in the sense of that word before it meant, like a Hebrew word, glad or sorry, that I am engaged this evening; and I am at your command on Tuesday, as it is always my inclination to be. It is a misfortune that words are become so much the current coin of society, that, like King William's shillings, they have no impression left; they are so smooth, that they mark no more to whom they first belonged than to whom they do belong, and are not worth even the twelvepence into which they may be changed: but if they mean too little, they may seem to mean too much too, especially when an old man (who is often synonymous for a miser) parts with them. I am afraid of protesting how much I delight in your society, lest I should seem to affect being gallant; but if two negatives make an affirmative, why may not two ridicules compose one piece of sense? and therefore, as I am in love with you both, I trust it is a proof of the good sense of your devoted,

H. Walpole.

230. *Departure for Italy.*

TO MARY BERRY

Sunday, 10 October 1790. The day of your departure.

Is it possible to write to my beloved friends, and refrain from speaking of my grief for losing you; though it is but the continuation of what I have felt ever since I was stunned by your intention of going abroad this autumn? Still I will not tire you with it often. In happy days I smiled, and called you my dear wives: now I can only think

1 Walpole contrasts his growing friendship with the Berry sisters to the base Indian who threw away a pearl richer than all his tribe: *Othello* V. ii. 347–8. Walpole has held on to the pearls he has found, whereas the Indian discarded his.
2 The date is thus put alluding to his age, which, in 1789, was seventy-one. – BERRY.

on you as darling children of whom I am bereaved! As such I have loved and do love you; and, charming as you both are, I have had no occasion to remind myself that I am past seventy-three. Your hearts, your understandings, your virtues, and the cruel injustice of your fate,[1] have interested me in everything that concerns you; and so far from having occasion to blush for any unbecoming weakness, I am proud of my affection for you, and very proud of your condescending to pass so many hours with a very old man, when everybody admires you, and the most insensible allow that your good sense and information (I speak of both) have formed you to converse with the most intelligent of our sex as well as your own; and neither can tax you with airs of pretension or affectation. Your simplicity and natural ease set off all your other merits – all these graces are lost to me, alas! when I have no time to lose.

Sensible as I am to my loss, it will occupy but part of my thoughts, till I know you safely landed, and arrived safely at Turin. Not till you are there, and I learn so, will my anxiety subside and settle into steady, selfish sorrow. I looked at every weathercock as I came along the road to-day, and was happy to see every one point north-east. May they do so to-morrow!

I found here the frame for Wolsey,[2] and to-morrow morning Kirgate will place him in it; and then I shall begin pulling the little parlour to pieces, that it may be hung anew to receive him. I have also obeyed Miss Agnes, though with regret; for, on trying it, I found her Arcadia would fit the place of the picture she condemns,[3] which shall therefore be hung in its room; though the latter should give way to nothing else, nor shall be laid aside, but shall hang where I shall see it almost as often. I long to hear that its dear paintress is well; I thought her not at all so last night. You will tell me the truth, though she in her own case, and in that alone, allows herself mental reservation.

Forgive me for writing nothing to-night but about you two and myself. Of what can I have thought else? I have not spoken to a single person but my own servants since we parted last night. I found

1 This alludes to Miss Berry's father having been disinherited by an uncle, to whom he was heir at law, and a large property left to his younger brother. – BERRY.
2 A copy in watercolours by Agnes Berry of William Lock's "The Death of Cardinal Wolsey".
3 "Arcadia" and the picture condemned by Agnes Berry were both pictures by her.

a message here from Miss Howe[1] to invite me for this evening – do you think I have not preferred staying at home to write to you, as this must go to London to-morrow morning by the coach to be ready for Tuesday's post? My future letters shall talk of other things, whenever I know anything worth repeating; or perhaps any trifle, for I am determined to forbid myself lamentations that would weary you; and the frequency of my letters will prove there is no forgetfulness. If I live to see you again, you will then judge whether I am changed; but a friendship so rational and so pure as mine is, and so equal for both, is not likely to have any of the fickleness of youth, when it has none of its other ingredients. It was a sweet consolation to the short time that I may have left, to fall into such a society; no wonder then that I am unhappy at that consolation being abridged. I pique myself on no philosophy, but what a long use and knowledge of the world had given me – the philosophy of indifference to most persons and events. I do pique myself on not being ridiculous at this very late period of my life; but when there is not a grain of passion in my affection for you two, and when you both have the good sense not to be displeased at my telling you so, (though I hope you would have despised me for the contrary,) I am not ashamed to say that your loss is heavy to me; and that I am only reconciled to it by hoping that a winter in Italy, and the journeys and sea air, will be very beneficial to two constitutions so delicate as yours. Adieu! my dearest friends: it would be tautology to subscribe a name to a letter, every line of which would suit no other man in the world but the writer.

231. My "Wives."

TO THE COUNTESS OF UPPER OSSORY

Berkeley Square, 29 May [1792] in the evening.

I returned from Strawberry too late yesterday, Madam, to answer your Ladyship's letter incontinently, and this morning I was hindered by business and company; but my gratitude is not cooled by being postponed. I am indeed much obliged for the transcript of the letter on my "Wives." Miss Agnes has a *finesse* in her eyes and

---

1 An unmarried sister of Richard Howe, 1st Earl Howe, the admiral, then living at Richmond.

countenance that does not propose itself to you, but is very engaging on observation, and has often made herself preferred to her sister, who has the most exactly fine features, and only wants colour to make her face as perfect as her graceful person; indeed neither has good health nor the air of it. Miss Mary's eyes are grave, but she is not so herself; and, having much more application than her sister, she converses readily, and with great intelligence, on all subjects. Agnes is more reserved, but her compact sense very striking, and always to the purpose. In short, they are extraordinary beings, and I am proud of my partiality for them; and since the ridicule can only fall on me, and not on them, I care not a straw for its being said that I am in love with one of them – people shall choose which: it is as much with both as either, and I am infinitely too old to regard the *qu'en dit on*.

XI
HIS LATER YEARS

IN 1779, FOLLOWING the expiry of the lease of his house in Arlington Street, Walpole moved into Berkeley Square – "a charming situation, and a better house than I wanted" (letter 235) – which remained his home in London for the rest of his life.

He suffered his first attack of gout as early as 1760, before his forty-third birthday. Gout was to become a dominant theme in his correspondence, particularly with Cole, a fellow-sufferer. It frustrated Walpole's social activities, curtailed his travels, and despite his abstemious habits afflicted him for the rest of his life.

Another favourite theme was his age, and the reader may sometimes feel that Walpole protests too much, picturing himself as the desiccated relic of an era long past. But someone so alert to the dynamics of social and political life could hardly fail to be sensitive to a new generation carving its own path. He was also very much aware that having left Parliament in 1769 he had lost his privileged position as conveyor of news from the heart of government, and it saddened him to have to rely on newspapers. Eventually he came in a sense to resemble one of those antediluvian dowagers whom he had in earlier years so enjoyed visiting for their tales of old courts and old scandals.

As already noted, succession to the earldom in 1791 was entirely unwelcome and onerous, but it made no essential difference to his mode of life and he declined to take up his seat in the House of Lords. His last years were cheered by the society of the Berry sisters (letters 228 to 231), but not all of his protégées accorded him the respect that might have been expected as he faded: in 1795, when he failed to deal sympathetically with the news of Mary Berry's engagement to General O'Hara, Anne Damer noted ungenerously to Berry how "when I think of *what* his dinners are, and *how* he eats them, I wonder he and his cat are not sick together every day for their dessert".[1]

1 *Berry Papers*, ed. Lewis Melville (London, 1914) p. 159.

Old age and physical infirmities did not lessen his cheerfulness: in a letter written in 1796 he said, "This (gout) constitutes me totally a prisoner. But ... I thank God, I have vast blessings; I have preserved my eyes, ears and teeth; I have no pain left; and I would bet with any dormouse that day or night it cannot outsleep me" (letter 239).

Walpole died on 2 March 1797: at the very end he lost his memory, and thought himself neglected, a sad fate for this most social of beings.

232. *The Gout.*

TO GEORGE MONTAGU, ESQ.

Strawberry Hill, 12 August 1760.

In what part of the island you are just now, I don't know; flying about somewhere or other, I suppose. Well, it is charming to be so young! Here am I, lying upon a couch, wrapped up in flannels, with the gout in both feet – oh yes, gout in all the forms. Six years ago I had it, and nobody would believe me – now they may have proof. My legs are as big as your cousin Guilford's, and they don't use to be quite so large. I was seized yesterday se'nnight; have had little pain in the day, but most uncomfortable nights; however, I move about again a little with a stick. If either my father or mother had had it, I should not dislike it so much. I am herald enough to approve it if descended genealogically; but it is an absolute upstart in me, and what is more provoking, I had trusted to my great abstinence for keeping me from it: but thus it is, if I had any gentleman-like virtue, as patriotism or loyalty, I might have got something by them; I had nothing but that beggarly virtue temperance, and she had not interest enough to keep me from a fit of the gout. Another plague is, that everybody that ever knew anybody that had it, is so good as to come with advice, and direct me how to manage it; that is, how to continue to have it for a great many years. I am very refractory; I say to the gout, as great personages do to the executioners, "Friend, do your work as quick as you can." They tell me of wine to keep it out of my stomach; but I will starve temperance itself; I will be virtuous indeed – that is, I will stick to virtue, though I find it is not its own reward.

This confinement has kept me from Yorkshire; I hope, however, to be at Ragley by the 20th, from whence I shall still go to Lord Strafford's, and by this delay you may possibly be at Greatworth by my return, which will be about the beginning of September. Write me a line as soon as you receive this; direct it to Arlington Street, it will be sent after me. Adieu. . . .

233. *A Visit to Houghton.*

TO GEORGE MONTAGU, ESQ.

Houghton, 25–30 March 1761.

Here I am at Houghton! and alone! in this spot, where (except two hours last month) I have not been in sixteen years! Think, what a crowd of reflections! No; Gray, and forty churchyards, could not furnish so many; nay, I know one must feel them with greater indifference than I possess, to have patience to put them into verse. Here I am, probably for the last time of my life, though not for the last time: every clock that strikes tells me I am an hour nearer to yonder church – that church, into which I have not yet had courage to enter, where lies that mother on whom I doated, and who doated on me! There are the two rival mistresses of Houghton, neither of whom ever wished to enjoy it! There too lies he who founded its greatness, to contribute to whose fall Europe was embroiled; there he sleeps in quiet and dignity, while his friend and his foe, rather his false ally and real enemy, Newcastle and Bath, are exhausting the dregs of their pitiful lives in squabbles and pamphlets.

The surprise the pictures gave me is again renewed; accustomed for many years to see nothing but wretched daubs and varnished copies at auctions, I look at these as enchantment. My own description of them seems poor;[1] but shall I tell you truly, the majesty of Italian ideas almost sinks before the warm nature of Flemish colouring. Alas! don't I grow old? My young imagination was fired with Guido's ideas: must they be plump and prominent as Abishag[2] to warm me now? Does great youth feel with poetic limbs, as well as see with poetic eyes? In one respect I am very young, I cannot satiate myself with looking: an incident contributed to make me feel this

1 His father's picture collection, which he had described in *Ædes Walpolianæ*. It would be sold 18 years later.
2 The virgin brought to warm the ageing King David, in I Kings 1: 1–4.

more strongly. A party arrived, just as I did, to see the house, a man
and three women in riding dresses, and they rode past through the
apartments. I could not hurry before them fast enough; they were
not so long in seeing for the first time, as I could have been in one
room, to examine what I knew by heart. I remember formerly being
often diverted with this kind of *seers;* they come, ask what such a
room is called, in which Sir Robert lay, write it down, admire a lob-
ster or a cabbage in a market-place, dispute whether the last room
was green or purple, and then hurry to the inn for fear the fish should
be over-dressed. How different my sensations! not a picture here but
recalls a history; not one, but I remember in Downing-street or
Chelsea, where queens and crowds admired them, though seeing
them as little as these travellers!

When I had drunk tea, I strolled into the garden; they told me it
was now called the *pleasure-ground.* What a dissonant idea of pleasure! those groves, those *allées,* where I have passed so many charming
moments, are now stripped up or overgrown – many fond paths
I could not unravel, though with a very exact clew in my memory:
I met two gamekeepers, and a thousand hares! In the days when all
my soul was tuned to pleasure and vivacity (and you will think, perhaps, it is far from being out of tune yet), I hated Houghton and its
solitude; yet I loved this garden, as now, with many regrets I love
Houghton; Houghton, I know not what to call it, a monument of
grandeur or ruin! How I have wished this evening for Lord Bute![1]
how I could preach to him! For myself, I do not want to be preached
to; I have long considered, how every Balbec must wait for the
chance of a Mr. Wood.[2] The servants wanted to lay me in the great
apartment – what, to make me pass my night as I have done my
evening! It were like proposing to Margaret Roper[3] to be a duchess
in the court that cut off her father's head, and imagining it would
please her. I have chosen to sit in my father's little dressing-room,
and am now by his scrutoire, where, in the height of his fortune, he
used to receive the accounts of his farmers, and deceive himself, or
us, with the thoughts of his economy. How wise a man at once, and

---

1 Lord Bute, then prime minister, who the following year commissioned Robert
Adam to build Lansdowne House in Berkeley Square, and in 1767 Luton Hoo,
Bedfordshire, in neither of which he lived as finished houses.
2 *The Ruins of Balbec* by Robert Wood (1716/17–71) had been published in 1757.
3 The daughter of Sir Thomas More.

how weak! For what has he built Houghton? for his grandson to annihilate, or for his son to mourn over. If Lord Burleigh could rise and view his representative driving the Hatfield stage,[1] he would feel as I feel now. Poor little Strawberry! at least it will not be stripped to pieces by a descendant![2] ...

234. *The Gout Again.*

TO THE EARL OF STRAFFORD

Strawberry Hill, Monday, 10 October 1768.

I give you a thousand thanks, my dear Lord, for the account of the ball at Welbeck. I shall not be able to repay it with a relation of the Masquerade to-night;[3] for I have been confined here this week with the gout in my foot, and have not stirred off my bed or couch since Tuesday. I was to have gone to the great ball at Sion on Friday, for which a new road, paddock, and bridge were made, as other folks make a dessert. I conclude Lady Mary Coke has, and will tell you of all these pomps which Health thinks so serious, and Sickness with her grave face tells one are so idle. Sickness may make me moralise, but I assure you she does not want humour. She has diverted me extremely with drawing a comparison between the repose (to call neglect by its dignified name) which I have enjoyed in this fit, and the great anxiety in which the whole world was when I had the last gout, three years ago – you remember my friends were then coming into power.[4] Lord Weymouth was so good as to call at least once every day, and inquire after me; and the foreign ministers insisted that I should give them the satisfaction of seeing me, that they might tranquillise their sovereigns with the certainty of my not being in any danger. The Duke and Duchess of Newcastle were so kind, though very nervous themselves, as to send messengers and long messages every day from Claremont. I cannot say this fit has alarmed

1 Lord Burghley's descendant, the 6th Earl of Salisbury (1713–80), had an obsession with driving stage coaches.
2 Though Strawberry Hill was stripped by George, 7th Earl Waldegrave (1816–46), the grandson of Walpole's residuary legatee, in the Strawberry Hill sale of 1842.
3 A masquerade given at the Opera House by the King of Denmark, before he left England.
4 In 1765, when Henry Conway was appointed Secretary of State in Lord Rocking-ham's government and Walpole was disappointed not to be offered any position.

Europe quite so much. I heard the bell ring at the gate, and asked with much majesty if it was the Duke of Newcastle had sent? "No, Sir, it was only the butcher's boy." The butcher's boy is, indeed, the only courier I have had. Neither the King of France nor King of Spain appears to be under the least concern about me.

My dear Lord, I have had so many of these transitions in my life, that you will not wonder they divert me more than a masquerade. I am ready to say to most people, "Mask, I know you." I wish I might choose their dresses!

When I have the honour of seeing Lady Strafford, I shall beseech her to tell me all the news; for I am too nigh and too far to know any. Adieu, my dear Lord!

235. *Removal to Berkeley Square.*

TO SIR HORACE MANN

11 October 1779.

... Of late – indeed, for the entire summer – I have been much out of order, and thought my constitution breaking fast; but it exerted its internal strength, and, when I was lowest, threw out the gout in several joints. In short, I have stamina of iron, in a case, as I used to call yours, of wet brown paper. I am now taking the bark, and find great benefit from it: nay, I am removing into a new house in London, that I bought last winter, as if I believed I had several years to come. It is in Berkeley Square, whither for the future you must direct. It is a charming situation, and a better house than I wanted – in short, I would not change my two pretty mansions for any in England: but I do not shut my eyes on the transitory tenure of them; though, if mortals did not coin visions for themselves, they would sit with folded arms, and take no thought for the morrow! I hold visions to be wisdom; and would deny them only to ambition, which exists by destruction of the visions of everybody else. Like Vesuvius, it overwhelms the fair face of the world, though to reign over cinders, and only lift its head above the desolation it has occasioned, and cannot enjoy.

236. *A Vivid Description.*

TO THE COUNTESS OF UPPER OSSORY

Berkeley Square, 27 December 1784.

I am told that I am in a prodigious fine way; which, being trans-lated into plain English, means, that I have suffered more sharp pain these two days than in all the moderate fits together that I have had for these last nine years: however, Madam, I have one great blessing, there is drowsiness in all the square hollows of the red-hot bars of the gridiron on which I lie, so that I scream and fall asleep by turns like a babe that is cutting its first teeth. I can add nothing to this exact account, which I only send in obedience to your Ladyship's commands, which I received just now: I did think on Saturday that the worst was over.

237. *Old Age Brings Content.*

TO HANNAH MORE

Strawberry Hill, 2 July 1789.

. . . My fall, for which you so kindly concern yourself, was not worth mentioning; for as I only bruised the muscles of my side, instead of breaking a rib, camphire infused in arquebusade took off the pain and all consequences in five or six days: and one has no right to draw on the compassion of others for what one *has* suffered and is past. Some love to be pitied on that score; but forget that they only excite, in the best-natured, joy on their deliverance. You commend me too for not complaining of my chronical evil; but, my dear Madam, I should be blameable for the reverse. If I would live to seventy-two, ought I not to compound for the encumbrances of old age? And who has fewer? And who has more cause to be thankful to Providence for his lot? The gout, it is true, comes frequently, but the fits are short, and very tolerable; the intervals are full health. My eyes are perfect, my hearing but little impaired, chiefly to whispers, for which I certainly have little occasion; my spirits never fail; and though my hands and feet are crippled, I can use both, and do not wish to box, wrestle, or dance a hornpipe. In short, I am just infirm enough to enjoy all the prerogatives of old age, and to plead them against anything, that I have not a mind to do. Young men must conform to every folly in fashion: drink when they had rather be sober; fight a duel if somebody else is wrong-headed; marry to please their fathers, not themselves; and shiver in a white waistcoat, because ancient almanacs, copying the Arabian, placed the month of June after May; though, when the style was reformed, it ought to have been intercalated between December and January. Indeed, I have been so childish as to cut my hay for the same reason, and am now weeping over it by the fireside. . . .

238. *Doubtful Pleasures of a Peerage.*

TO HANNAH MORE

My much-esteemed Friend,   Berkeley Square, 1 January 1792.

I have not so long delayed answering your letter from the pitiful revenge of recollecting how long your pen is fetching breath before it replies to mine. Oh! no; you know I love to *heap coals of kindness* on your head, and to draw you into little sins, that you may forgive yourself, by knowing your time was employed on big virtues. On the contrary, you would be revenged; for here have you, according to *your* notions, inveigled me into the fracture of a commandment; for I am writing to you on a Sunday, being the first moment of leisure that I have had since I received your letter. It does not indeed clash with my religious ideas, as I hold paying one's debts as good a deed as praying and reading sermons for a whole day in every week when it is impossible to fix the attention to one course of thinking for so many hours for fifty-two days in every year. Thus you see I can preach too. But seriously, and indeed I am little disposed to cheerfulness now, I am overwhelmed with troubles, and with business – and business that I do not understand; law, and the management of a ruined estate, are subjects ill-suited to a head that never studied anything that in worldly language is called useful. The tranquillity of my remnant of life will be lost, or so perpetually interrupted, that I expect little comfort; not that I am already intending to grow rich, but, the moment one is supposed so, there are so many alert to turn one to their own account, that I have more letters to write to satisfy, or rather to dissatisfy them, than about my own affairs, though the latter are all confusion. I have such missives, on agriculture, pretensions to livings, offers of taking care of my game as I am incapable of it, self-recommendations of making my robes, and round hints of taking out my writ, that at least I may name a proxy, and give my dormant conscience to somebody or other! I trust you think better of my heart and understanding than to suppose that I have listened to any one of these new *friends*. Yet, though I have negatived all, I have been forced to answer some of them before you; and that will convince you how cruelly ill I have passed my time lately, besides having been ill with vexation and fatigue. But I am tolerably well again.

For the other empty metamorphosis that has happened to the outward man, you do me justice in concluding that it can do nothing but teaze me; it is being called names in one's old age.[1] I had rather be my Lord Mayor, for then I should keep the nickname but a year; and mine I may retain a little longer, not that at seventy-four I reckon on becoming my Lord Methusalem. Vainer, however, I believe I am ready become; for I have wasted almost two pages about myself, and said not a tittle about your health, which I most cordially rejoice to hear you are recovering, and as fervently hope you will entirely recover. I have the highest opinion of the element of water as a constant beverage; having so deep a conviction of the goodness and wisdom of Providence, that I am persuaded that when it indulged us in such a luxurious variety of eatables, and gave us but one drinkable, it intended that our sole liquid should be both wholesome and corrective. Your system I know is different; you hold that mutton and water were the only cock and hen that were designed for our nourishment; but I am apt to doubt whether draughts of water for six weeks are capable of restoring health, though some are strongly impregnated with mineral and other particles. Yet you have staggered me: the Bath water by your account is, like electricity, compounded of contradictory qualities; the one attracts and repels; the other turns a shilling yellow, and whitens your jaundice. I shall hope to see you (when is that to be?) without alloy. . . .

I must finish, wishing you three hundred and thirteen days of happiness for the new year that is arrived this morning: the

1 Walpole had become 4th Earl of Orford following the death of his nephew the previous month, and had the responsibility of endeavouring to rescue the estate of Houghton from his nephew's mismanagement.

fifty-two that you hold in commendam,[1] I have no doubt will be rewarded as such good intentions deserve. ... Adieu, my *too* good friend! My direction shall talk superciliously to the postman;[2] but do let me continue unchangeably your faithful and sincere,

Hor. Walpole.

239. *Comforts of Old Age.*

TO HANNAH MORE

Strawberry Hill, 29 August 1796.

You are not only the most beneficent, but the most benevolent of human beings. Not content with being a perfect saint yourself, which (forgive me for saying) does not always imply prodigious charity for others; not satisfied with being the most disinterested, nay, the reverse of all patriots, for you sacrifice your very slender fortune, not to improve it, but to keep the poor honest instead of corrupting them; and you write politics as ill, that is, as simply, intelligibly, and unartfully as you can, not as cunningly as you can to mislead. Well, with all these giant virtues, you can find room and time in your heart and occupations for harbouring and exercising what those mimicking monkeys of pretensions, the French, advertised and called *les petites morales*, which were to supply society with filigrain duties, in the places of all virtues, which they abolished on their road to the adoption of philosophy and atheism. Yes, though for ever busied in exercising services and charities for individuals, or for whole bodies of people, you do leave a cranny empty into which you can slip a kindness. Your inquiry after me to Miss Berry is so friendly, that I cannot trust solely to her thanking you for your letter, as I am sure she will, having sent it to her as she is bathing in the sea at Bognor Rocks, as Lord Chesterfield directed a letter to Lord Pembroke (who was always swimming) to the E. of Pembroke in the Thames, over against Whitehall – but I must with infinite gratitude give you a brief account of myself – a very poor one indeed must I give. Condemned as a cripple to my couch for the rest of my days I doubt I am. Though perfectly healed, and even without a scar, my

---

1 The Sabbath days, as observed by More.
2 Walpole franked his letter by his newly acquired title of Earl of Orford.

leg is so weakened that I have not recovered the least use of it, nor can move across my chamber unless lifted up and held by two servants. This constitutes me totally a prisoner. But why should not I be so? What business had I to live to the brink of seventy-nine? And why should one litter the world at that age? Then, I thank God, I have vast blessings; I have preserved my eyes, ears, and teeth; I have no pain left; and I would bet with any dormouse that day or night it cannot outsleep me. And when one can afford to pay for every relief, comfort, or assistance that can be procured at fourscore, dare one complain? Must not one reflect on the thousands of old poor, who are suffering martyrdom, and have none of those alleviations? O, my good friend, I must consider myself as at my best; for if I drag on a little longer, can I expect to remain even so tolerably? Nay, does the world present a pleasing scene? Are not the devils escaped out of the swine, and overrunning the earth headlong?

What a theme for meditation, that the excellent humane Louis Seize should have been prevented from saving himself by that monster Drouet,[1] and that that execrable wretch should be saved even by those, some of whom one may suppose he meditated to massacre; for at what does a Frenchman stop? But I will quit this shocking subject, and for another reason too: I omitted one of my losses, almost the use of my fingers: they are so lame that I cannot write half a dozen lines legibly, but am forced to have recourse to my secretary. I will only reply by a word or two to a question you seem to ask me; how I like "Camilla"?[2] I do not care to say how little. Alas! she has reversed experience, which I have long thought reverses its own utility by coming at the wrong end of our life when we do not want it. [Miss Burney] knew the world and penetrated characters before she had stepped over the threshold; and, now she has seen so much of it, she has little or no insight at all: perhaps she apprehended having seen too much, and kept the bags of foul air that she brought from the Cave of Tempests[3] too closely tied – well, however I am sincerely [glad] the work has turned out so very profitable.

Adieu, thou who mightest be one of the cleverest of women if

---

1 Jean-Baptiste Drouet (1763–1824), who five years after being responsible for the capture of Louis XVI and Marie Antoinette in the flight to Varennes, had himself escaped from imprisonment.
2 Frances Burney's third novel, *Camilla* (1796).
3 The court, where Burney served from 1786 to 1791.

thou didst not prefer being *one* of the best! And when I say *one* of the best, I have not engaged my vote for the second. Yours most gratefully.

240. *Resignation.*

TO THE COUNTESS OF UPPER OSSORY[1]

My dear Madam,   15 January 1797.

You distress me infinitely by showing my idle notes, which I cannot conceive can amuse anybody. My old-fashioned breeding impels me every now and then to reply to the letters you honour me with writing, but in truth very unwillingly, for I seldom can have anything particular to say; I scarce go out of my own house, and then only to two or three very private places, where I see nobody that really knows anything, and what I learn comes from Newspapers, that collect intelligence from coffee-houses, consequently what I neither believe nor report. At home I see only a few charitable elders, except about four-score nephews and nieces of various ages, who are each brought to me about once a-year, to stare at me as the Methusalem of the family, and they can only speak of their own contemporaries, which interest me no more than if they talked of their dolls, or bats and balls. Must not the result of all this, Madam, make me a very entertaining correspondent? And can such letters be worth showing? or can I have any spirit when so old and reduced to dictate?

Oh! my good Madam, dispense with me from such a task, and think how it must add to it to apprehend such letters being shown. Pray send me no more such laurels, which I desire no more than their leaves when decked with a scrap of tinsel and stuck on twelfth-cakes that lie on the shop-boards of pastry-cooks at Christmas. I shall be quite content with a sprig of rosemary thrown after me, when the parson of the parish commits my dust to dust. Till then, pray, Madam, accept the resignation of your

Ancient servant,

Orford.

---

1 Written some six weeks before his death, Walpole's last letter to Lady Ossory, and virtually the last letter he wrote.

XII
HIS CHARACTER

A NUMBER OF CONTEMPORARY accounts of Walpole have been left by his friends and acquaintances.[1] John Pinkerton, who first met him in 1784 and compiled *Walpoliana* (a miscellany of his conversation with a biographical introduction) in 1799, described him as short and slender with something of a boyish appearance, and stressed "the placid goodness of his eyes, which would often sparkle with sudden rays of wit, or dart forth flashes of the most keen and intuitive intelligence". The novelist Lætitia-Matilda Hawkins who was acquainted with Walpole in her childhood, speaks of his candour and integrity and the enchantment of his conversation, continuing

I speak of him before the year 1772. His eyes were remarkably bright and penetrating, very dark and lively: – his voice was not strong, but his tones were extremely pleasant, and if I may so say highly gentlemanly. I do not remember his common gait; he always entered a room in that style of affected delicacy, which fashion had then made almost natural; – *chapeau bras* between his hands as if he wished to compress it, or under his arm – knees bent, and feet on tip-toe, as if afraid of a wet floor.

George Hardinge was a judge and antiquary who corresponded with Walpole from 1770 until 1795. He was a generation younger than Walpole and his account is revealing if fundamentally unsympathetic:

When I became familiar with his effeminacy of manner, it was lost in his wit, ingenuity and whimsical but entertaining fund of knowledge . . . There was a degree of quaintness in Mr. Walpole's wit, but it was not unbecoming in *him*, for it seemed a part of *his* nature. Some of his friends were as effeminate in appearance and in manner as himself and were as witty. Of these I remember two, Mr. Chute and Mr. George Montagu. But others had effeminacy alone to recommend them.

1 Unless another reference is given, all of the accounts mentioned here are to be found in Peter Sabor's *Horace Walpole: The Critical Heritage* (1987): pp. 274 (Pinkerton), 305 (Hawkins), 290–91 (Hardinge), 310 (Selwyn), and 257–9 (Deffand).

He considered Walpole's relationship with Madame du Deffand to be an attachment of congenial talents and mutual vanity, adding spitefully, "*but she was too young for him*". However, by 1795 Walpole was tired of Hardinge's importunities, describing him in a letter of that year to Mary Berry as "that out-pensioner of Bedlam".[1]

A number of accounts of Walpole by his own friends and contemporaries are less than charitable. His fear of ridicule was widely acknowledged (he said himself in letter 134 that "I hate to be stared at, and the object of whispers before my face"), but it was paired with an interest in what would now be called celebrity, and attracting the public gaze – though without unbecoming ambition. Gilly Williams mocked him in a letter to George Selwyn for his enjoying the society of dowagers who had been Court ladies in their distant youth, and that he "does not see the ridicule which he would so strongly paint in any other character". In another letter to Selwyn, Williams acknowledges that "I can figure no being happier than Horry. *Monstrari digito praetereuntium* has been his whole aim. For this he has wrote, printed and built."[2] And that sense of wanting to be pointed out by the finger of time was carefully deflected by two strategies he habitually employed. One was his affectation of *sprezzatura*, the studied carelessness of the gentleman amateur,[3] and the other was his recurrent self-deprecation (illustrated in letters 241, 242, 244, and 246), layered responses that disguised the seriousness of his literary and antiquarian endeavours.

It would perhaps be surprising if Selwyn had not taken the opportunity to exercise his wit at Walpole's expense, and Lord Ossory relates how he described Strawberry Hill as a catacomb or museum rather than a house, and the master of it as one of the best preserved mummies in the whole collection. Politics also ocasionally coloured the comments of friends such as William Cole, who after a visit to Strawberry Hill in 1774 wrote in his journals that Walpole was "one of the best writers, an admirable poet, one of the most lively, ingenious, and witty persons of the age; but a great share of vanity, eagerness of adulation, as Mr. Gray observed to me, a violence and warmth in party matters, and lately even to enthusiasm,

1 Letter of 10–12 September 1795 (YE 12:163).
2 *George Selwyn and his Contemporaries*, ed. J. H. Jesse [1843], volume 1, pp. 252 and 310.
3 Morris Brownell, *The Prime Minister of Taste: A Portrait of Horace Walpole* (2001), where the theme of *sprezzatura* is introduced at pp. 2–7.

abates, and takes off from, many of his shining qualities"[1].

Macaulay in his damaging *Edinburgh Review* portrait of Walpole (October 1833) saw nothing but affectation: "He was ... the most eccentric, the most artificial, the most fastidious, the most capricious, of men. His mind was a bundle of inconsistent whims and affectations. His features were covered by mask within mask." But this is parody not portraiture. Walpole was principled and honest by the standards of the day, and though he may have sought influence and celebrity, did not pursue power or riches. While he delighted in trivialities, the letters reveal wider concerns – about slavery, for example, which he abhorred, and imperialism, which he denounced. His prejudices too were those of his age. Letter 264 records that he opposed Roman Catholic Emancipation ("I have ever been averse to toleration of an intolerant religion") and the reformation of Parliament ("I do not love removing land-marks").

Walpole's friendships were sincere and generally long-lasting, and he was the most loyal of friends. His manners and breeding did not mean that he was in any way unconscious of his rank: in the words of his most sympathetic biographer, "he could never quite forget, however familiarly he met them in social life, that Reynolds was a painter and Garrick a player".[2] But he treated his servants kindly, and they stayed long in his service. Undeniably malicious and amusingly waspish at the expense of those he disliked, he possessed the more attractive quality of being able to laugh at himself (letters 69 and 113 are random examples), and a pleasant line in gentle teasing (letter 253).

For a psychologically astute overall assessment of Walpole there is no rival to the portrait of him written by Madame du Deffand in 1766. She praises his intelligence and his integrity; observes how pride in his firmness of purpose can turn into obstinacy; describes his friendships as steadfast but not tender, suggesting that he suppresses his emotions for fear of appearing weak. Knowledge of the world has given him a poor opinion of humanity, she deduces, but his manners to all alike are easy and natural, inspired by a genuine desire to please. He has discernment, tact, and taste, high self-esteem but no vanity. Only his fear of ridicule she regards as an unpardonable weakness as it makes him heed the opinion of fools. She appreciates his gift for irony, but feels that his natural gaiety is

1   Volume 2 of the Yale edition of Walpole's Correspondence, Appendix 6, pp. 372–3.
2   R. W. Ketton-Cremer, *Horace Walpole: A Biography* (1940), pp. 21–2.

held in check by too great a sensibility, which drives him to seek extraordinary ways of amusing himself, devoting himself to oddities and building "exotic houses". This is only a brief summary, but even so it makes Macaulay's portrayal look like mere caricature.

1. HIS IMPERFECTIONS
241. *Self Analysis.*

TO SIR HORACE MANN

London, 7 January 1741–2.

I must answer for your brother a paragraph that he showed me in one of your letters: "Mr. W.'s letters are full of wit; don't they adore him in England?" Not at all — and I don't wonder at them; for if I have any wit in my letters, which I do not at all take for granted, it is ten to one that I have none out of my letters. A thousand people can write, that cannot talk; and besides, you know, (or I conclude so, from the little one hears stirring,) that numbers of the English have wit, who don't care to produce it. Then, as to adoring; you now see only my letters, and you may be sure I take care not to write you word of any of my bad qualities, which other people must see in the gross; and that may be a great hindrance to their adoration. Oh! there are a thousand other reasons I could give you, why I am not the least in fashion. I came over in an ill season: it is a million to one that nobody thinks a declining old minister's son has wit. At any time, men in opposition have always most; but now, it would be absurd for a courtier to have even common sense. There is not a Mr. Sturt, or a Mr. Stewart, whose names begin but with the first letters of Stanhope,[1] that has not a better chance than I, for being liked. I can assure you, even those of the same party would be fools, not to pretend to think me one. Sir Robert has showed no partiality for me; and do you think they would commend where he does not? even supposing they had no envy, which, by the way, I am far from saying they have not. Then, my dear child, I am the coolest man of my party, and if I am ever warm, it is by contagion; and where violence passes for parts, what will indifference be called? But how could you

1 Sturt and Stewart are random names. Stanhope is Philip Dormer Stanhope, the accomplished Earl of Chesterfield (for whom see letter 173, p. 238, n. 3).

think of such a question? I don't want money, consequently no old women pay me or my wit; I have a very flimsy constitution, consequently the young women won't taste my wit, and it is a long while before wit makes its own way in the world; especially, as I never prove it, by assuring people that I have it by me. Indeed, if I were disposed to brag, I could quote two or three half-pay officers, and an old aunt or two, who laugh prodigiously at everything I say; but till they are allowed judges, I will not brag of such authorities. . . . Yours ever.

242. *Relinquishing Authorship.*

TO GEORGE MONTAGU, ESQ.

Arlington Street, 24 October 1758.

I am a little sorry that my preface, like the show-cloth to a sight, entertained you more than the bears that it invited you in to see.[1] I don't mean that I am not glad to have written anything that meets your approbation, but if Lord Whitworth's work is not better than my preface, I fear he has much less merit than I thought he had.

Your complaint of your eyes makes me feel for you: mine have been very weak again, and I am taking the bark, which did them so much service last year. I don't know how to give up the employment of them, I mean reading; for as to writing, I am absolutely winding up my bottom for twenty reasons. The first, and perhaps the best, I have writ enough. The next; by what I have writ, the world thinks I am not a fool, which was just what I wished them to think, having always lived in terror of that oracular saying, Ἡρώων παῖδες λῶβοῖ, which Mr. Bentley translated with so much more parts than the vain and malicious *hero* could have done that set him the task – I mean his father,[2] *the sons of heroes are loobies*. My last reason is, I find my little stock of reputation very troublesome, both to maintain and to undergo the consequences – it has dipped me in erudite correspondences – I receive letters every week that compliment my learning now, as there is nothing I hold so cheap as a learned man, except

1 The implication is that Montagu, to whom Walpole had sent his Lord Whitworth's *Account of Russia* (Strawberry Hill Press, 1758), had found Walpole's introduction more entertaining than the text.
2 The father of Walpole's friend Richard Bentley (see letter 15, p. 29, n. 2) was the brilliant but combative classicist Dr. Richard Bentley (1662–1742).

an unlearned one, this title is insupportable to me; if I have not a care, I shall be called learned, till somebody abuses me for not being learned, as they, not I, fancied I was. In short, I propose to have nothing more to do with the world, but divert myself in it as an obscure passenger – pleasure, virtù, politics, and literature, I have tried them all, and have had enough of them. Content and tranquil-lity, with now and then a little of three of them, that I may not grow morose, shall satisfy the rest of a life that is to have much idleness, and I hope a little goodness; for politics – a long adieu! With some of the Cardinal de Retz's experience, though with none of his genius, I see the folly of taking a violent part without any view (I don't mean to commend a violent part with a view, that is still worse); I leave the state to be scrambled for by Mazarine, at once cowardly and enterprising, ostentatious, jealous, and false; by Louvois, rash and dark; by Colbert, the affector of national interest, with designs not much better; and I leave the Abbé de la Rigbiere to sell the weak Duke of Orleans to whoever has money to buy him, or would buy him to get money;[1] at least these are my present reflections – if I should change them to-morrow, remember I am not only a human creature, but that I am I, that is, one of the weakest of human crea-tures, and so sensible of my fickleness that I am sometimes inclined to keep a diary of my mind, as people do of the weather. To-day you see it temperate, to-morrow it may again blow politics and be stormy; for while I have so much quicksilver left, I fear my pas-sionometer will be susceptible of sudden changes. What do years give one? Experience; experience, what? Reflections; reflections, what? nothing that I ever could find – nor can I well agree with Waller, that

> "The soul's dark cottage, batter'd and decay'd,
> Lets in new light through chinks that time has made."[2]

Chinks I am afraid there are, but instead of new light, I find nothing but "darkness visible," that serves only to discover sights of woe. I look back through my chinks – I find errors, follies, faults; forward, old age and death, pleasures fleeting from me, so virtues succeeding

1 The Yale editors make the point that Walpole, like Cardinal de Retz, had a propen-sity to faction, and then suggest that the other 17th-century French politicians listed stand for Newcastle (Mazarine), Fox (Louvois), Pitt (Colbert), Rigby (Abbé de la Rivière, hence Rigbière), and Duke of Bedford (Duke of Orléans).
2 From Edmund Waller's poem "On the Foregoing Divine Poems".

to their place – *il faut avouer*, I want all my quicksilver to make such a background receive any other objects!

I am glad Mr. Frederick Montagu[1] thinks so well of me as to be sure I shall be glad to see him without an invitation. For you, I had already perceived that you would not come to Strawberry this year. Adieu!

Remember, nobody is to see this letter, but yourself and the clerks of the post office.

243. *An Apology.*

TO THE RIGHT HON. LADY HERVEY

12 January 1760.

I am very sorry your ladyship could doubt a moment on the cause of my concern yesterday. I saw you much displeased at what I had said; and I felt so innocent of the least intention of offending you, that I could not help being struck at my own ill-fortune, and with the sensation raised by finding you mix great goodness with great severity.

I am naturally very impatient under praise; I have reflected enough on myself to know I don't deserve it; and with this consciousness you ought to forgive me, Madam, if I dreaded that the person whose esteem I valued the most in the world, should think that I was fond of what I know is not my due. I meant to express this apprehension as respectfully as I could, but my words failed me – a misfortune not too common to me, who am apt to say too much, not too little! Perhaps it is that very quality which your ladyship calls wit, and I call tinsel, for which I dread being praised. I wish to recommend myself to you by more essential merits – and if I can only make you laugh, it will be very apt to make me as much concerned as I was yesterday. For people to whose approbation I am indifferent, I don't care whether they commend or condemn me for my wit; in the former case they will not make me admire myself for it, in the latter they can't make me think but what I have thought already. But for the few whose friendship I wish, I would fain have them see, that under all the idleness of my spirits there are some very serious

1 George Montagu's heir.

qualities, such as warmth, gratitude, and sincerity, which ill returns may render useless or may make me lock up in my breast, but which will remain there while I have a being.

Having drawn you this picture of myself, Madam, a subject I have to say so much upon, will not your good-nature apply it as it deserves, to what passed yesterday? Won't you believe that my concern flowed from being disappointed at having offended one whom I ought by so many ties to try to please, and whom, if I ever meant anything, I had meaned to please? I intended you should see how much I despise wit, if I have any, and that you should know my heart was void of vanity and full of gratitude. They are very few I desire should know so much; but my passions act too promptly and too naturally, as you saw, when I am with those I really love, to be capable of any disguise. Forgive me, Madam, this tedious detail; but of all people living I cannot bear that you should have a doubt about me.

244. *"The Learned Gentleman!"*

TO SIR HORACE MANN

Arlington Street, 6 February 1760, addition to letter begun 3 February.

I am this minute come to town, and find yours of Jan. 12. Pray, my dear child, don't compliment me any more upon my learning; there is nobody so superficial. Except a little history, a little poetry, a little painting, and some divinity, I know nothing. How should I? I, who have always lived in the big busy world; who lie a-bed all the morning, calling it morning as long as you please; who sup in company; who have played at pharaoh half my life, and now at loo till two or three in the morning; who have always loved pleasure; haunted auctions – in short, who don't know so much astronomy as would carry me to Knightsbridge, nor more physic than a physician, nor in short anything that is called science. If it were not that I lay up a little provision in summer, like the ant, I should be as ignorant as all the people I live with. How I have laughed, when some of the Magazines have called me *the learned gentleman!* Pray don't be like the Magazines. . . .

245. *No Ambition.*

TO GEORGE MONTAGU, ESQ.

Strawberry Hill, 14 July 1770.

I see by the papers this morning that Mr. Jenkinson is dead. He had the reversion of my place,[1] which would go away, if I should lose my brother. I have no pretensions to ask it, and you know it has long been my fixed resolution not to accept it. But as Lord North[2] is your particular friend, I think it right to tell you, that you may let him know what it is worth, that he may give it to one of his own sons, and not bestow it on somebody else, without being apprised of its value. I have seldom received less than fourteen hundred a-year in money, and my brother, I think, has four or more from it. There are besides many places in the gift of the office, and one or two very considerable. Do not mention this but to Lord North, or Lord Guilford. It is unnecessary, I am sure, for me to say to you, but I would wish them to be assured that in saying this, I am incapable of, and above any finesse, or view, to myself. I refused the reversion for myself several years ago, when Lord Holland was Secretary of State, and offered to obtain it for me. Lord Bute, I believe, would have been very glad to have given it to me, before he gave it to Jenkinson; but I say it very seriously, and you know me enough to be certain I am in earnest, that I would not accept it upon any account. Any favour Lord North will do for you will give me all the satisfaction I desire. I am near fifty-three; I have neither ambition nor interest to gratify. I can live comfortably for the remainder of my life, though I should be poorer by fourteen hundred pounds a-year; but I should have no comfort if, in the dregs of life, I did anything that I would not do when I was twenty years younger. I will trust to you, therefore, to make use of this information in the friendly manner I mean it, and to prevent my being hurt by its being taken otherwise than as a design to serve those to whom you wish well. Adieu! Yours ever.

1 The sinecure of Collector of Customs. Charles Jenkinson (1729–1808) was a statesman, and later 1st Earl of Liverpool. It was his wife who had died.
2 Lord North, who became prime minister in 1770, was Montagu's cousin.

246. His Mental Attainments.

TO THE REV. WILLIAM MASON

Strawberry Hill, 15 May 1773.

... Mr. Jerningham[1] has just desired my consent to his dedicating a new poem to me. I remonstrated, and advised him to Augustus[2] the patron supreme; he would not be said nay, and modesty, as it always does when folks are pressing, submitted, but it was to be a homage to my *literary merit*. Oh! that was too much, I downright was rude. Sir, says, I, literary merit I have none, literary merit will be interpreted, learning, science, and the Lord knows what, that I have not a grain of. I have forgot half my Latin and all my Greek. I never could learn mathematics; never had patience for natural philosophy or chess; I have read divinity, which taught me that no two persons agree, and metaphysics which nobody understands: and consequently I am little the wiser for either. I know a little modern history of France and England, which those who wrote did not know; and a good deal of genealogy, which could not be true unless it were written by every mother in every family. If I have written any thing tolerable, it was to show I had common sense, not learning. I value my writings very little and many others value them still less, which it would be very unreasonable in me to resent, since nobody forgets them so soon as myself, and, therefore, dear Sir, &c. Well, he has consented, and I hope from his example, I never shall be called the learned author again, as I have been by magazines, when magazines were so cruel as to wish me well. ... Ever yours, H. W.

247. Knows his own Mind.

TO SIR HORACE MANN

Strawberry Hill, 7 May 1775.

... As Strawberry furnishes so little, and this letter is not impatient to set out, I shall carry it to town, and keep it for more bulk. Yet I must commend myself a little first. I have finished this house

1 Edward Jerningham (1737–1812), poet and playwright, and an habitué of Lady Miller's poetical amusements at Batheaston (see letter 153, p. 221, n. 1).
2 George III.

and place these three years, and yet am content with and enjoy it –
a very uncommon case in a country where nobody is pleased but
while they are improving, and where they are tired the moment they
have done.[1] I choose my house should enjoy itself, which poor
houses and gardens seldom do, for people go on mending till they
die, and the next comer, who likes to improve too, begins to mend
all that has been done. I knew what I wished; I have it, and am satisfied – and yet do not forget that I am one of my contemporaries!
I have all my life been blessed with knowing my own mind. I never
wished to be *anybody*, that is, anything; and when the moments have
arrived in which I might have been what I pleased, I resisted them,
and persisted in my nothinghood. I hated Parliament, resolved to
quit it, and did: was told I should repent, but never have. There ends
my panegyric on myself; but pray don't think it very high flown,
when the sum of all is, that I am content with a small house and
garden, and with being nobody. . . .

2. HIS KINDLY NATURE

(i) TO CHILDREN

248. Care for a Sick Child.

TO THE HON. H. S. CONWAY

Strawberry Hill, Saturday, 6 July 1754.

Your letter certainly stopped to drink somewhere by the way,
I suppose with the hearty hostess at the Windmill; for, though written on Wednesday, it arrived here but this morning: it could not have
travelled more deliberately in the Speaker's body-coach.[2] I am concerned, because, your fishmonger not being arrived, I fear you have
stayed for my answer. The fish[3] are apprised that they are to *ride* over
to Park-place, and are ready booted and spurred; and the moment
their pad arrives, they shall set forth. I would accompany them on a
pillion if I were not waiting for Lady Mary [Churchill],[4] who has

1 Walpole in fact added the Beauclerk Tower the following year to receive the drawings of Lady Diana Beauclerk.
2 The State Coach of the Speaker.
3 Gold fish. – WALPOLE.
4 Walpole's half-sister: see letter 101, p. 163, n. 3.

desired to bring her poor little sick girl here for a few days to try the air. You know how courteous a knight I am to distressed virgins of five years old, and that my castle-gates are always open to them. You will, I am sure, accept this excuse for some days; and as soon as ever my hospitality is completed, I will be ready to obey your summons, though you should send a water-pot for me. I am in no fear of not finding you in perfect verdure; for the sun, I believe, is gone a great way off to some races or other, where his horses are to run for the King's plate: we have not heard of him in this neighbourhood. Adieu!

(ii) TO SERVANTS

249. *His Old Gardener.*

TO THE EARL OF HARCOURT

Strawberry Hill, 18 October 1777.

I am sensibly obliged, my dear Lord, by your great goodness, and am most disposed to take the gardener you recommend, if I can. You are so good-natured you will not blame my suspense. I have a gardener that has lived with me above five-and-twenty years; he is incredibly ignorant, and a mule. When I wrote to your Lordship, my patience was worn out, and I resolved at least to have a gardener for flowers. On your not being able to give me one, I half consented to keep my own; not on his amendment, but because he will not leave me, presuming on my long suffering. I have offered him fifteen pounds a year to leave me, and when he pleads that he is old, and that nobody else will take him, I plead that I am old too, and that it is rather hard that I am not to have a few flowers, or a little fruit as long as I live. I shall now try if I can make any compromise with him, for I own I cannot bear to turn him adrift, nor will starve an old servant, though never a good one, to please my nose and mouth. Besides, he is a Scot, and I will not be unjust, even to that odious nation; and the more I dislike him, the less will I allow my partiality to persuade me I am in the right. Every body would not understand this, and the Scotch none of them; but I am sure your Lordship will, and will not be angry that I dally with you. I know how strong my prejudices are, and am always afraid of them. As long as they only hate they are welcome, but prejudices are themselves so much Scots, that I must not let them be my *friends* and govern me. I will take the liberty of letting you know, if I can persuade the Serpent that has reduced my little Eden to be as nasty and barren as the Highlands, to take a pension and a yellow ribbon.

Lady Harcourt or your Lordship may frisk or vagary anywhere separately: I shall not be alarmed, nor think it by choice. Nay, if it were, where could I either mend yourself? I have so high an opinion of Miss Fauquiere,[1] that, with all her regard for your Lordship, I believe you are the last man from whom she would bear to hear a gallantry. So you see, my Lord, how awkwardly you set about mischief. It is plain you are a novice, and have no talent for it, and therefore I advise you as a friend not to attempt what would not become you: you are like a young tragic author, that meaning to draw a politic villain, makes him so very wicked, and lay such gross traps, that they would not catch an elephant. One laughs at his tragedy, but loves his heart. I am sure Miss Fauquiere agrees with me in desiring to remain the confidants of the two perfect characters of the drama.

Your Lordship's most devoted
Hor. Walpole.

250. *Margaret and the Fawn.*

TO THE COUNTESS OF UPPER OSSORY

18 July 1780, addition to letter begun c. 12 July.

. . . I shall conclude this rhapsody with a dismal adventure that happened to me yesterday. The door opened, and Margaret[2] entered with her apron spread over both arms, as a midwife presents a child to be baptized, and bearing, as I thought, the longest, leanest, naked babe I ever beheld. As she approached, I perceived that master or miss had no head, but a bloody neck. "Christ!" said I, "what have you got there?" "A friend of mine has sent me a fawn, if your honour pleases to accept it." "For Heaven's sake," said I, "take it away, I could as soon eat a child:" however, I did call her again, and begged her pardon for having treated her present so brutally; but one must have

1 She lived with the Harcourts, and subsequently married Lady Harcourt's half-brother.
2 Margaret Young, Walpole's housekeeper at Strawberry Hill from about 1760 to 1786.

been a cannibal to have ever borne the sight of it again. . . . Good night, Madam!

(iii) CHARITABLENESS

251. *Objects of Charity.*

TO GROSVENOR BEDFORD, ESQ.[1]

Dear Sir,   17 January 1760.

I wish you would be so good as to give five guineas for me (but without my name) to the subscription for the French prisoners, which I see by the enclosed advertisement has taken place; and put it into the next account.

It is at Mr. Biddulph's, banker, at Charing-cross. Yours ever,

H. W.

252. *Relief for Prisoners.*

TO GROSVENOR BEDFORD

Dear Sir,   29 February 1764.

I will get you to send one of the porters of the Exchequer, in whom you have most confidence, with the enclosed three guineas. Two are for the prisoners that are sick in the new jail, Southwark; the other for those in the common side of the Marshalsea prison. He must not say from whom he comes, but in the name of A. B., and don't let him go into the prison, for the jail distemper[2] is there.

I want some gilt paper and a penknife. Yours ever,

H. W.

253. *A Charitable Subscription.*

TO HANNAH MORE

Berkeley Square, 20 February 1790.

It is very provoking that people must always be hanging or drowning themselves, or going mad, that you forsooth, Mistress,

---

1 Grosvenor Bedford (d. 1771), Walpole's deputy as Usher of the Exchequer.
2 Jail fever, a form of typhus.

may have the diversion of exercising your pity and good-nature, and charity, and intercession, and all that bead-roll of virtues that make you so troublesome and amiable, when you might be ten times more agreeable by writing things that would not cost one above half-a-crown at a time. You are an absolutely walking hospital, and travel about into lone and bye places, with your doors open to house stray casualties! I wish at least that you would have some children yourself, that you might not be plaguing one for all the pretty brats that are starving and friendless. I suppose it was some such goody two or three thousand years ago that suggested the idea of an alma-mater, with dugs enough to suckle the three hundred and sixty-five bant-lings of the Countess of Hainault.[1] Well, as your newly-adopted pensioners have *two* babes, I insist on your accepting *two* guineas for them instead of one at present (that is, when you shall be present). If you cannot circumscribe your own charities, you shall not stint mine, Madam, who can afford it much better, and who must be dunned for alms, and do not scramble over hedges and ditches in searching for opportunities of flinging away my money on good works. I employ mine better at auctions, and in buying pictures and baubles, and hoarding curiosities, that in truth I cannot keep long, but that will last *for ever* in my catalogue, and make me immortal! Alas! will they cover a multitude of sins? Adieu! I cannot jest after *that* sentence. Yours sincerely.

(iv) LOVE OF ANIMALS

254. *Patapan's Fight.*

TO SIR HORACE MANN

9 October 1742, addition to letter begun 8 October.

Well! I have waited till this morning, but have no letter from you; what can be the meaning of it? Sure, if you was ill, Mr. Chute would write to me! Your brother protests he never lets your letters lie at the office.

Sa Majesté Patapanique [Walpole's dog] has had a dreadful misfortune! – not lost his first minister, nor his purse – nor had part of

[1] The Countess of Henneberg, who as a result of a curse was supposed in 1276 to have given birth to 365 children.

his camp equipage burned in the river, nor waited for his secretary of state, who is perhaps blown to Flanders – nay, nor had his chair pulled from under him – worse! worse! quarrelling with a great pointer last night about their Countesses, he received a terrible shake by the back and a bruise on the left eye – poor dear Pat! you never saw such universal consternation! it was at supper. Sir Robert, who makes as much rout with him as I do, says, he never saw ten people show so much *real* concern! Adieu! Yours, ever and ever – but write to me. . . .

255. *His Portrait.*

TO SIR HORACE MANN

25 April 1743.

. . . Patapan sits to Wootton[1] to-morrow for his picture. He is to have a triumphal arch at a distance, to signify his Roman birth, and his having barked at thousands of Frenchmen in the very heart of Paris. If you can think of a good Italian motto applicable to any part of his history send it me. If not, he shall have this antique one – for I reckon him a senator of Rome, while Rome survived, – "O et præsidium et dulce decus meum!"[2] He is writing an Ode on the future campaign of this summer; it is dated from his villa, where he never was, and begins truly in the classic style, "While you, great Sir,"[3] &c. Adieu!

256. *Cruelty to Dogs.*

TO THE EARL OF STRAFFORD

My Dear Lord,   Strawberry Hill, 4 September 1760.
    . . . In London there is a more cruel campaign than that waged by the Russians: the streets are a very picture of the murder of the

---

1 John Wootton (1681/2–1764), landscape and sporting artist. Walpole's *Description* of Strawberry Hill shows that he kept the painting in his bedchamber.
2 From Horace, *Carmina* I. i. 2: My protector and sweet glory.
3 Perhaps related to Pope's "While You, great Patron of Mankind", the opening line of "First Epistle of the Second Book of Horace, Imitated".

360 HORACE WALPOLE'S LETTERS

innocents – one drives over nothing but poor dead dogs![1] The dear, good-natured, honest, sensible creatures! Christ! how can anybody hurt them? Nobody could but those Cherokees the English, who desire no better than to be halloo'd to blood: – one day Admiral Byng, the next Lord George Sackville,[2] and to-day the poor dogs! . . .

257. *Rosette.*

TO SIR HORACE MANN

Arlington Street, 23 March 1770.

. . . You know I have always some favourite, some successor of Patapan.[3] The present is a tanned black spaniel, called Rosette. She saved my life last Saturday night, so I am sure you will love her too. I was undressing for bed. She barked and was so restless that there was no quieting her. I fancied there was somebody under the bed, but there was not. As she looked at the chimney, which roared much, I thought it was the wind, yet wondered, as she had heard it so often. At last, not being able to quiet her, I looked to see what she barked at, and perceived sparks of fire falling from the chimney, and on searching farther perceived it in flames. It had not gone far, and we easily extinguished it. I wish I had as much power over the nation's chimney. Adieu!

258. *Solicitude for Dying Dog.*

TO THE COUNTESS OF UPPER OSSORY

Strawberry Hill, 9 August 1773.

. . . I wish you joy, Madam, of the sun's settling in England. Was ever such a southern day as this? My house is a bower of tuberoses, and all Twitnamshire is passing through my meadows to the races

1 In the summer of 1760 a reward was paid for killing strays because of fears of fatalities caused by bites from mad dogs.
2 Admiral John Byng (bap. 1704–57) and Lord George Sackville (1716–85) had both been disgraced and court-martialled. Byng was subsequently executed despite attempts by Walpole to save him (see letters 284 and 285). Lord George Sackville was court-martialled for disobedience of orders and cowardice at the battle of Minden, and was found guilty of the former and declared unfit for the King's service.
3 A favourite dog Mr. Walpole brought from Rome. – WALPOLE.

at Hampton Court. The picture is incredibly beautiful; but I must quit my joys for my sorrows. My poor Rosette is dying. She relapsed into her fits the last night of my stay at Nuneham, and has suffered exquisitely ever since. You may believe I have too; I have been out of bed twenty times every night, have had no sleep, and sat up with her till three this morning; but I am only making you laugh at me; I cannot help it – I think of nothing else. Without weaknesses I should not be I, and I may as well tell them as have them tell themselves. . . .

259. *Arrival of Tonton.*

TO THE HON. H. S. CONWAY

Strawberry Hill, Sunday evening, 6 May 1781.

. . . I told you in my last that Tonton was arrived. I brought him this morning to take possession of his new villa, but his inauguration has not been at all pacific. As he has already found out that he may be as despotic as at Saint Joseph's,[1] he began with exiling my beautiful little cat; upon which, however, we shall not quite agree. He then flew at one of my dogs, who returned it by biting his foot till it bled, but was severely beaten for it. I immediately rung for Margaret [his housekeeper] to dress his foot; but in the midst of my tribulation could not keep my countenance; for she cried, "Poor little thing, he does not understand my language!" I hope she will not recollect, too, that he is a Papist! . . .

260. *Destruction of Dogs.*

TO THE EARL OF STRAFFORD

29 August 1786.

It has long been my opinion that the out-pensioners of Bedlam are so numerous, that the shortest and cheapest way would be to confine in Moorfields the few that remain in their senses, who would then be safe; and let the rest go at large. They are the out-pensioners

---

1 Mme. du Deffand, Tonton's former owner, had lived at the convent of Saint Joseph in Paris.

who are for destroying poor dogs! The whole canine race never did half so much mischief as Lord George Gordon; nor even worry hares, but when hallooed on by men. As it is a persecution of animals, I do not love hunting; and what old writers mention as a commendation makes me hate it the more, its being an image of war. Mercy on us! that destruction of any species should be a sport or a merit! What cruel unreflecting imps we are! Everybody is unwilling to die; yet sacrifices the lives of others to momentary pastime, or to the still emptier vapour, fame! A hero or a sportsman who wishes for longer life is desirous of prolonging devastation. We shall be crammed, I suppose, with panegyrics and epitaphs on the King of Prussia; I am content that he can now have an epitaph. But, alas! the Emperor will write one for him probably in blood! and, while he shuts up convents for the sake of population,[1] will be stuffing hospitals with maimed soldiers, besides making thousands of widows! . . .

261. *Tonton's Death.*

TO THE COUNTESS OF UPPER OSSORY

Berkeley Square, 26 February 1789, addition to letter begun 24 February.

. . . I would not interrupt my news, or rather, my replies, and therefore delayed telling you that Tonton is dead, and that I comfort myself: he was grown stone deaf, and very nearly equally blind, and so weak that, the two last days, he could not walk upstairs. Happily, he had not suffered, and died close by my side without a pang or a groan. I have had the satisfaction, for my dear old friend's[2] sake and his own, of having nursed him up, by constant attention, to the age of sixteen, yet always afraid of his surviving me, as it was scarcely possible he could meet a third person who would study his happiness equally. I sent him to Strawberry, and went thither on Sunday to see him buried behind the chapel, near Rosette. I shall miss him greatly, and must not have another dog; I am too old, and should only breed it up to be unhappy, when I am gone. My resource is in two marble

1 In his letter to Mann of 18 May 1782 Walpole suggested that a rationale of Joseph II's suppression of convents was that increased copulation would eventually result in more potential soldiers.
2 Mme. du Deffand.

kittens that Mrs. Damer has given me, of her own work, and which are so much alive that I talk to them, as I did to poor Tonton! if this is being superannuated, no matter: when dotage can amuse itself, it ceases to be an evil. I fear, my marble playfellows are better adapted to me, than I am to being your Ladyship's correspondent. . . .

3. PREJUDICES

262. *His Bête Noire.*

TO HON. H.S. CONWAY

25 September 1740.

. . . Did I tell you Lady Mary Wortley[1] is here? She laughs at my Lady Walpole, scolds my Lady Pomfret,[2] and is laughed at by the whole town. Her dress, her avarice, and her impudence must amaze any one that never heard her name. She wears a foul mob, that does not cover her greasy black locks, that hang loose, never combed or curled; an old mazarine blue wrapper, that gapes open and discovers a canvass petticoat. Her face swelled violently on one side with the remains of a pox partly covered with a plaister, and partly with white paint, which for cheapness she had bought so coarse, that you would not use it to wash a chimney. – In three words I will give you her picture as we drew it in the *Sortes Virgilianæ* –

Insanam vatem aspicies.[3]

I give you my honour we did not choose it; but Gray, Mr. Coke, Sir Francis Dashwood,[4] and I, and several others, drew it fairly amongst a thousand for different people, most of which did not hit as you may imagine. . . .

---

1 Lady Mary Wortley Montagu (see letter 213, p. 303, n. 2).
2 Lady Walpole was Margaret Rolle (1709–81), the wife of Walpole's eldest brother, from whom she was separated: Henrietta Fermor, Lady Pomfret (1698–1761) was a letter-writer and diarist and creator of the Gothic Pomfret Castle in Albemarle Street, who had spent time with Lady Mary while travelling in Europe.
3 Virgil, *Æneid* III. 443: you will look on an inspired prophetess.
4 Mr. Coke was Edward Coke (1719–53), the future Viscount Coke of Holkham Hall, and Sir Francis Dashwood (1708–81) was a politician, founder of the Hell-Fire Club at Medmenham Abbey, and creator of the landscape at West Wycombe Park.

263. *A Visit to Lady Mary.*

TO SIR HORACE MANN

29 January 1762.

... I am ashamed to tell you that we are again dipped into an egregious scene of folly. The reigning fashion is a ghost[1] – a ghost, that would not pass muster in the paltriest convent in the Apennine. It only knocks and scratches; does not pretend to appear or to speak. The clergy give it their benediction; and all the world, whether believers or infidels, go to hear it. I, in which number you may guess, go to-morrow; for it is as much the mode to visit the ghost as the Prince of Mecklenburg,[2] who is just arrived. I have not seen him yet, though I have left my name for him. But I will tell you who is come too – Lady Mary Wortley. I went last night to visit her; I give you my honour, and you who know her, would credit me without it, the following is a faithful description. I found her in a little miserable bedchamber of a ready-furnished house, with two tallow candles, and a bureau covered with pots and pans. On her head, in full of all accounts, she had an old black-laced hood, wrapped entirely round, so as to conceal all hair or want of hair. No handkerchief, but up to her chin a kind of horseman's riding-coat, calling itself a *pet-en-l'air*, made of a dark green (green I think it had been) brocade, with coloured and silver flowers, and lined with furs; boddice laced, a foul dimity petticoat sprig'd, velvet muffeteens on her arms, grey stockings and slippers. Her face less changed in twenty years than I could have imagined; I told her so, and she was not so tolerable twenty years ago that she needed have taken it for flattery, but she did, and literally gave me a box on the ear. She is very lively, all her senses perfect, her languages as imperfect as ever, her avarice greater. She entertained me at first with nothing but the dearness of provisions at Helvoet. With nothing but an Italian, a French, and a Prussian, all men servants, and something she calls an *old* secretary, but whose age till he appears will be doubtful; she receives all the world, who go to homage her as Queen Mother,[3] and crams them into this kennel. The Duchess of Hamilton, who came in just after me, was so

1 The Cock Lane Ghost (see letter 56).
2 The Prince was the brother of Queen Charlotte.
3 She was mother of Lady Bute, wife of the Prime Minister. – WALPOLE.

astonished and diverted, that she could not speak to her for laughing. She says that she has left all her clothes at Venice. I really pity
Lady Bute; what will the progress be of such a commencement! ...

264. *Averse to Catholic Emancipation.*

TO SIR HORACE MANN

Berkeley Square, 8 November 1784.

... Ireland, as far as my spare intelligence extends, is a little come
to its senses. Landed property, though no genius, has discovered that
Popery, if admitted to a community of votes, would be apt to inquire
into the old titles of estates; and to remember, that prescription never
holds against any Church militant, especially not against the Church
of Rome. You know I have ever been averse to toleration of an intolerant religion. I have frequently talked myself hoarse with many of
my best friends, on the impossibility of satisfying *Irish* Catholics
without restoring their estates. It was particularly silly to revive the
subject in this age, when Popery was so rapidly declining. The world
had the felicity to see that fashion passing away – for modes of religion are but graver fashions; nor will anything but contradiction
keep fashion up. Its inconvenience is discovered, if let alone; or, as
women say of their gowns, *it is cut and turned*, or variety is sought;
and some mantua-maker or priest that wants business invents a new
mode, which takes the faster, the more it inverts its predecessor.
I shall not wonder if Cæsar, after ravaging, or dividing, or seizing
half Europe, should grow devout, and give it some novel religion of
his own manufacture.

I have had as many disputes on the Reformation of Parliament.
I do not love removing land-marks. Whether it is the leaven of
which my pap was made, or whether my father's *Quieta non movere*
is irradicable, experiments are not to my taste; but I find I am talking
"about it and about it,"[1] because I really have nothing to tell you, and
know nothing. I do worse than live out of the world, for I live with
the old women of my neighbourhood. I read little, not bestowing
my eyes without an object. In short, I am perfectly idle; and such
a glutton of my tranquillity, that I had rather do nothing than

1   A reference to Pope's *Dunciad* IV. 252.

discompose it. I would *go out* quietly; and, as one is sure of being forgotten the monent one is gone, it is as well to anticipate oblivion.

4. LOVE OF RETIREMENT

265. Love of Cambridge.

TO THE REV. WILLIAM COLE

Arlington Street, 22 May 1777.

. . . I have put together some trifles I promised you, and will beg Mr. Lort[1] to be the bearer when he goes to Cambridge, if I know of it. At present I have time for nothing I like. My age and inclination call for retirement: I envied your happy hermitage, and leisure to follow your inclination. I have always *lived post*,[2] and shall not die before I can bait – yet it is not my wish to be unemployed, could I but choose my occupations. I wish I could think of the pictures you mention, or had time to see Dr. Glynn and the master of Emmanuel. I doat on Cambridge, and could like to be often there. The beauty of King's College Chapel, now it is restored, penetrated me with a visionary longing to be a monk in it; though my life has been passed in turbulent scenes, in pleasures – or rather pastimes, and in much fashionable dissipation; still books, antiquity, and *virtù* kept hold of a corner of my heart, and since necessity has forced me of late years to be a man of business, my disposition tends to be a recluse for what remains – but it will not be my lot: and though there is some excuse for the young doing what they like, I doubt an old man should do nothing but what he ought, and I hope doing one's duty is the best preparation for death. Sitting with one's arms folded to think about it, is a very lazy way of preparing for it. If Charles V. had resolved to make some amends for his abominable ambition by doing good, his duty as a King, there would have been infinitely more merit than going to doze in a convent. One may avoid active guilt in a sequestered life; but the virtue of it is merely negative, though innocence is beautiful.

I approve much of your corrections on Sir John Hawkins, and send them to the Magazine.[3] I want the exact blazon of William of

1 Rev. Michael Lort (1724/5–90), antiquary.
2 As in travelling with fresh relays of horses, speedily.
3 Cole had complied some observations on Sir John Hawkins's *History . . . of Music* (1776) for submission to the *Gentleman's Magazine*. They were published in May 1777.

Hatfield[1] his arms, – I mean the Prince buried at York. Mr. Mason
and I are going to restore his monument, and I have not time to look
for them: I know you will be so good as to assist

Yours most sincerely.

5. MATRIMONY

266. *On Marrying Margaret.*

TO THE COUNTESS OF UPPER OSSORY

Strawberry Hill, 4 August 1783.

. . . *A propos* to matrimony, I want to consult your Ladyship very
seriously: I am so tormented by droves of people coming to see my
house, and Margaret[2] gets such sums of money by showing it, that
I have a mind to marry her, and so repay myself that way for what I
have flung away to make my house quite uncomfortable to me. I am
sure Lord Denbigh would have proposed to her had he known of
her riches; and I doubt Margaret could not have resisted the tempta-
tion of being a Countess more than Lady Halford.[3] She certainly
can never have a more disagreeable suitor: and therefore I grow every
day more in danger of losing her and all her wealth. Mr. Williams
[Gilly] said this morning that Margaret's is the best place in England, and wondered Mr. Gilbert[4] did not insist on knowing what it
is worth. Thank my stars, he did not! Colonel Barré or Lord Ash-
burton[5] would propose to suppress housekeepers and then humbly
offer to show my house themselves, and the first would calculate
what he had missed by not having shown it for the last ten years,
and expect to be indemnified; for virtue knows to a farthing what
it has lost by not having been vice. Good night, Madam; my poor
rheumatic shoulder must go to bed.

1 William of Hatfield was the second son of Edward III, and died in infancy.
2 Walpole's housekeeper: see letter 250, p. 356, n. 2.
3 The courtier Basil Feilding (1719–1800), Earl of Denbigh, was said to have acknowledged that he had married Lady Halford because she had £2,700 a year.
4 The M.P. Thomas Gilbert (bap. 1720–98) had been investigating the value of the
pensions of Walpole and others.
5 Both Colonel Isaac Barré (1726–1802) and John Dunning (1731–83), Lord Ashbur-
ton, had been government critics who were criticised for accepting pensions.

6. HIS REGIMEN

267. Spartan Fortitude.

TO GEORGE MONTAGU, ESQ.

Strawberry Hill, 28 July 1765.

... Indeed I shall think myself decrepit, till I again saunter into the garden in my slippers and without my hat in all weathers, – a point I am determined to regain, if possible; for even this experience cannot make me resign my temperance and my hardiness. I am tired of the world, its politics, its pursuits, and its pleasures; but it will cost me some struggles before I submit to be tender and careful. Christ! can I ever stoop to the regimen of old age?[1] I do not wish to dress up a withered person, nor drag it about to public places; but to sit in one's room, clothed warmly, expecting visits from folks I don't wish to see, and tended and flattered by relations impatient for one's death! let the gout do its worst as expeditiously as it can; it would be more welcome in my stomach than in my limbs. I am not made to bear a course of nonsense and advice, but must play the fool in my own way to the last, alone with all my heart, if I cannot be with the very few I wish to see: but, to depend for comfort on others, who would be no comfort to me; this surely is not a state to be preferred to death: and nobody can have truly enjoyed the advantages of youth, health, and spirits, who is content to exist without the two last, which alone bear any resemblance to the first.

You see how difficult it is to conquer my proud spirit: low and weak as I am, I think my resolution and perseverance will get the better, and that I shall still be a gay shadow; at least, I will impose any severity upon myself, rather than humour the gout, and sink into that indulgence with which most people treat it. Bodily liberty is as dear to me as mental, and I would as soon flatter any other tyrant as the gout, my Whiggism extending as much to my health as to my principles, and being as willing to part with life, when I cannot preserve it, as your uncle Algernon when his freedom was at stake. Adieu!

---

1 Walpole was only 47 when he wrote this letter, but the Yale editors point out that he was at the time distressed by Henry Conway's failure to secure him the offer of any position in the new government.

268. *Cold Air and Water.*

TO SIR HORACE MANN

Strawberry Hill, 3 April 1777.

... Though I have been drawn away from your letter by the subject of it and by political reflections, I must not forget to thank you for your solicitude and advice about my health: but pray be assured that I am sufficiently attentive to it, and never stay long here in wet weather, which experience has told me is prejudicial. I am sorry for it, but I know London agrees with me better than the country. The latter suits my age and inclination; but my health is a more cogent reason, and governs me. I know my own constitution exactly, and have formed my way of life accordingly. No weather, nothing gives me cold; because, for these nine and thirty years, I have hardened myself so, by braving all weathers and taking no precautions against cold, that the extremest and most sudden changes do not affect me in that respect. Yet damp, without giving me cold, affects my nerves; and, the moment I feel it, I go to town. I am certainly better since my last fit of gout than ever I was after one: in short, perfectly well; that is, well enough for my age. In one word, I am very weak, but have no complaint; and as my constitution, frame, and health require no exercise, nothing but fatigue affects me: and therefore you, and all who are so good as to interest themselves about me and give advice, must excuse me if I take none. I am preached to about taking no care against catching cold, and am told I shall one day or other be caught – possibly: but I must die of something; and why should not what has done to sixty, be right? My regimen and practice have been formed on experience and success. Perhaps a practice that has suited the weakest of frames, would kill a Hercules. God forbid I should recommend it; for I never saw another human being that would not have died of my darings, especially in the gout. Yet I have always found benefit; because my nature is so feverish, that everything cold, inwardly or outwardly, suits me. Cold air and water are my specifics, and I shall die when I am not master enough of myself to employ them; or rather, as I said this winter, on comparing the iron texture of my inside with the debility of my outside, "I believe I shall have nothing but my inside left!" *Therefore*, my dear Sir, my regard for you will last as long as there is an atom of me remaining.

269. *A Great Nostrum.*

TO THE REV. WILLIAM COLE

Berkeley Square, 14 February 1782.

... On the opposite page I will add the receipt for the diet-drink:[1] as to my regimen I shall not specify it. Not only you would not adopt it, but I should tremble to have you. In fact, I never do prescribe it, as I am persuaded it would kill the strongest man in England, who was not exactly of the same temperament with me, and who had not embraced it early. It consists in temperance to quantity as to eating – I do not mind the quality; but I am persuaded that great abstinence with the gout is dangerous; for, if one does not take nutriment enough, there cannot be strength sufficient to fling out the gout, and then it deviates to palsies. But my great nostrum is the use of cold water, inwardly and outwardly, on all occasions, and total disregard of precaution against catching cold. A hat you know I never wear, my breast I never button, nor wear great-coats, &c. I have often had the gout in my face (as last week) and eyes, and instantly dip my head in a pail of cold water which always cures it, and does not send it anywhere else. All this I dare do, because I have so for these forty years, weak as I look; but Milo would not have lived a week if he had played such pranks. My diet-drink is not all of so Quixote a disposition; any of the faculty will tell you how innocent it is, at least. In a few days, for I am a rapid reader when I like my matter, I will return all your papers and letters; and in the mean time thank you most sincerely for the use of them.

P.S. My old friend, and your acquaintance, Mr. Dodd,[2] died last Saturday – not of cold water. He and I were born on the very same day, but took to different elements. I doubt he had hurt his fortune as well as health.

---

1 Walpole wrote out at the foot of the letter a recipe for herb juices added to boiled roots and grasses.
2 John Dodd, M.P. (1717–82), friend and contemporary of Walpole at Cambridge.

XIII
CURRENT HISTORICAL EVENTS
(GEORGE II'S REIGN)

WALPOLE HAS ALWAYS been celebrated as a recorder of public events. His letters cover a long and critical period of English history and the selections in Sections XIII to XV take the reader from the battle of Dettingen in 1743, with George II riding at the head of his troops, to the French Revolution, the Terror, and finally the failed French invasion of Ireland in 1797. The battles of Dettingen and Fontenoy described in letters 270 and 271 were incidents in the War of the Austrian Succession compiled from despatches or newspaper reports, but are none the less vivid for that. His letters on the Jacobite Rebellion of 1745 – which took place with the blessing of Louis XV, though with little active French support – are an unfolding narrative, recording events as they occurred at a time when the outcome was far from certain. Walpole follows the Pretender's progress from the initial manifestos issued in Scotland (he playfully imagines himself a future exile in Hanover with a deposed George II), the unexpected victory at Prestonpans and invasion of England (which caused real panic in London) to the retreat from Derby and defeat at Culloden in April 1746. At the subsequent trial of the rebel lords, Walpole was there to observe the drama and found himself impressed against his will: "their behaviour melted me!" (letter 278). He declined to attend their execution, relying on friends who did, but it would be impossible to tell from the immediacy of his account – a set-piece remarkable for its very human engagement, relishing the dignity of Lord Kilmarnock and the insouciance of Lord Balmerino – that he was not an eye-witness.

The War of the Austrian Succession was concluded in 1748 by the Treaty of Aix-la-Chapelle (letter 280) but by 1756 the Seven Years' War had broken out, a global conflict fought in Europe, America and India. The selected letters 281 to 291 cover the commencement of hostilities, defeats in America, threats of invasion, the trial and execution of Admiral Byng (whom Walpole made a valiant attempt to save), and the controversy over Lord George Sackville's conduct at the battle of Minden. This is followed by Wolfe's expedition to Quebec. Walpole was initially critical of Wolfe, who had given evidence against Conway following the unsuccessful Rochefort expedition of 1757. In letter 290, which records Wolfe's posthumous triumph, Walpole gives Conway a tortured explanation for Wolfe's conduct that tries to attribute his victory to remorse for his ill-considered criticism of Conway – a view for which there has never been any evidence, but which is revealing as to Walpole's sometimes blinkered loyalty to his friends. The same year, 1759, saw other victories on land at Minden, and on sea at Quiberon Bay and off Lagos, so that it is hardly surprising that Walpole, in writing of "this glorious and wonderful year", said: "It was necessary to ask every morning what new victory there was for fear of missing one."[1]

1. THE WAR OF THE AUSTRIAN SUCCESSION

270. The Battle of Dettingen.[2]

TO SIR HORACE MANN

Friday noon, 24 June 1743.

I don't know what I write – I am all a hurry of thoughts – a battle – a victory! [Battle of Dettingen] I dare not yet be glad – I know no particulars of my friends. This instant my Lord has had a messenger from the Duke of Newcastle, who has sent him a copy of Lord Carteret's[3] letter from the field of battle. The King was in all the heat of the fire, and safe – the Duke [of Cumberland] is wounded in the calf of the leg, but slightly; Duc d'Aremberg in the breast; General Clayton and Colonel Piers are the only officers of note said to be killed – here is all my trust! The French passed the Mayne that morning with twenty-five thousand men, and are driven back. We have lost two thousand, and they four – several of their general officers, and of the Maison du Roi, are taken prisoners: the battle

1 Letter to Mann, 13 December 1759 (YE 21:355).
2 On 27 June 1743 British forces, with troops from Hanover and Hesse and their Austrian allies, defeated a French army commanded by the Duc de Noailles. This was the last occasion that a reigning British monarch led his troops into battle.
3 Newcastle and Carteret had succeeded to government after the fall of Sir Robert Walpole, whom Walpole here refers to as "my Lord".

lasted from ten in the morning till four. The Hanoverians behaved admirably. The Imperialists were the aggressors; in short, in all public views, it is all that could be wished – the King in the action, and his son wounded – the Hanoverians behaving well – the French beaten: what obloquy will not all this wipe off? Triumph, and write it to Rome! I don't know what our numbers were; I believe about thirty thousand, for there were twelve thousand Hessians and Hanoverians who had not joined them. O! in my hurry, I had forgot the place – you must talk of the battle of Dettingen!

After dinner. My child, I am calling together all my thoughts, and rejoice in this victory as much as I dare; for in the raptures of conquest, how dare I think that my Lord Carteret, or the rest of those who have written, thought just of whom I thought? The post comes in to-morrow morning, but it is not sure that we shall learn any particular certainties so soon as that. Well! how happy it is that the King has had such an opportunity of distinguishing himself! what a figure he will make! They talked of its being below his dignity to command an auxiliary army; my Lord says it will not be thought below his dignity to have sought danger. These were the flower of the French troops: I flatter myself they will tempt no more battles. Another such, and we might march from one end of France to the other. So we are in a French war, at least well begun! My Lord has been drinking the healths of Lord Stair and Lord Carteret: he says, "since it is well done, he does not care by whom it was done." He thinks differently from the rest of the world: he thought from the first, that France never missed such an opportunity as when they undertook the German war, instead of joining with Spain against us. If I hear any more to-morrow before the post goes out, I will let you know. Tell me if this is the first you hear of the victory: I would fain be the first to give you so much pleasure. ...

271. *Fontenoy.*

TO SIR HORACE MANN

Arlington Street, 11 May 1745.

I stayed till to-day, to be able to give you some account of the battle of Tournay:[1] the outlines you will have heard already. We don't

1 Since called the battle of Fontenoy. – WALPOLE.

allow it to be a victory on the French side: but that is, just as a woman is not called *Mrs.* till she is married, though she may have had half-a-dozen natural children. In short, we remained upon the field of battle three hours; I fear, too many of us remain there still! without palliating, it is certainly a heavy stroke. We never lost near so many officers. I pity the Duke [of Cumberland], for it is almost the first battle of consequence that we ever lost. By the letters arrived to-day, we find that Tournay still holds out. There are certainly killed Sir James Campbell, General Ponsonby, Colonel Carpenter, Colonel Douglas, young Ross, Colonel Montagu, Gee, Berkeley, and Kellet. Mr. Vanbrugh is since dead.[1] Most of the young men of quality in the Guards are wounded. I have had the vast fortune to have nobody hurt, for whom I was in the least interested. Mr. Conway, in particular, has highly distinguished himself; he and Lord Petersham, who is slightly wounded, are most commended; though none behaved ill but the Dutch horse. There has been but very little consternation here: the King minded it so little, that being set out for Hanover, and blown back into Harwich-roads since the news came, he could not be persuaded to return, but sailed yesterday with the fair wind. ... The whole *hors de combat* is above seven thousand three hundred. The French own the loss of three thousand; I don't believe many more, for it was a most rash and desperate perseverance on our side. The Duke behaved very bravely and humanely; but this will not have advanced the peace. .... Adieu, I am in a great hurry.

2. THE 1745 REBELLION

272. *The Young Pretender's Advance.*

TO SIR HORACE MANN

Arlington Street, 6 September 1745.

It would have been inexcusable in me, in our present circumstances, and after all I have promised you, not to have written to you for this last month, if I had been in London; but I have been at Mount Edgcumbe,[2] and so constantly upon the road, that I neither received your letters, had time to write, or knew what to write.

---

1 Son of the architect and dramatist Sir John Vanbrugh.
2 Seat near Plymouth of Walpole's friend Richard Edgcumbe (1716–61), 2nd Baron Edgcumbe.

I came back last night, and found three packets from you, which I have no time to answer, and but just time to read. The confusion I have found, and the danger we are in, prevent my talking of anything else. The young Pretender,[1] at the head of three thousand men, has got a march on General Cope,[2] who is not eighteen hundred strong; and when the last accounts came away, was fifty miles nearer Edinburgh than Cope, and by this time is there. The clans will not rise for the Government: the Dukes of Argyll and Athol are come post to town, not having been able to raise a man. The young Duke of Gordon sent for his uncle,[3] and told him he must arm their clan. "They are in arms." – "They must march against the rebels." – "They will wait on the Prince of Wales." The Duke flew in a passion; his uncle pulled out a pistol, and told him it was in vain to dispute. Lord Loudon, Lord Fortrose, and Lord Panmure have been very zealous, and have raised some men; but I look upon Scotland as gone! I think of what King William said to Duke Hamilton, when he was extolling Scotland; "My Lord, I only wish it was a hundred thousand miles off, and that you was king of it!"

There are two manifestos published, signed Charles Prince, Regent for his father, King of Scotland, England, France, and Ireland. By one, he promises to preserve every body in their just rights; and orders all persons who have public monies in their hands to bring it to him; and by the other dissolves the union between England and Scotland. But all this is not the worst! Notice came yesterday, that there are ten thousand men, thirty transports and ten men-of-war at Dunkirk. Against this force we have – I don't know what – scarce fears! Three thousand Dutch we hope are by this time landed in Scotland; three more are coming hither. We have sent for ten regiments from Flanders, which may be here in a week, and we have fifteen men-of-war in the Downs. I am grieved to tell you all this; but when it is so, how can I avoid telling you? Your brother is just come in, who says he has written to you – I have not time to expatiate.

---

1 Charles Edward Stuart had landed on the Scottish Isle of Eriskay with a few supporters on 23 July.
2 Sir John Cope (1690–1760), the Commander-in-Chief in Scotland.
3 According to the Yale editors not his uncle but his younger brother, who joined the Pretender.

273. Possible Results.

TO GEORGE MONTAGU, ESQ.

Arlington Street, 17 September 1745.

Dear George,

How could you ask me such a question, as whether I should be glad to see you? Have you a mind I should make you a formal speech, with honour, and pleasure, and satisfaction, &c.? I will not, for that would be telling you I should not be glad. However, do come soon, if you should be glad to see me; for we, I mean we old folks that came over with the Prince of Orange in eighty-eight, have had notice to remove by Christmas-day. The moment I have smugged up[1] a closet or a dressing-room, I have always warning given me, that my lease is out. Four years ago I was mightily at my ease in Downing-street, and then the good woman, Sandys,[2] took my lodgings over my head, and was in such a hurry to junket her neighbours, that I had scarce time allowed me to wrap my old china in a little hay. Now comes the Pretender's boy, and promises all my comfortable apartments in the Exchequer and Custom-house to some forlorn Irish peer, who chooses to remove his pride and poverty out of some large, unfurnished gallery at St. Germain's. Why really Mr. Montagu this is not pleasant; I shall wonderfully dislike being a loyal sufferer in a threadbare coat, and shivering in an ante-chamber at Hanover, or reduced to teach Latin and English to the young princes at Copenhagen. The Dowager Strafford has already written cards for my Lady Nithsdale, my Lady Tullibardine, the Duchess of Perth and Berwick, and twenty more revived peeresses, to invite them to play at whisk, Monday three months: for your part, you will divert yourself with their old taffeties, and tarnished slippers, and their awkwardness, the first day they go to Court in shifts and clean linen. Will you ever write to me at my garret at Herenhausen? I will give you a faithful account of all the promising speeches that Prince George and Prince Edward make whenever they have a new sword, and intend to reconquer England. At least write to me, while you may with acts of parliament on your side: but I hope you are coming. Adieu!

1 Fitted up.
2 The wife of Baron Sandys, who with her husband moved into 10 Downing Street on his appointment as Chancellor of the Exchequer following the fall of Sir Robert Walpole's government in 1742.

274. Prestonpans.

TO SIR HORACE MANN

Arlington Street, 27 September 1745.

I can't doubt but the joy of the Jacobites has reached Florence before this letter. Your two or three Irish priests, I forget their names, will have set out to take possession of abbey-lands here. I feel for what you will feel, and for the insulting things that will be said to you upon the battle[1] we have lost in Scotland; but all this is nothing to what it prefaces. The express came hither on Tuesday morning, but the Papists knew it on Sunday night. Cope lay in face of the rebels all Friday; he scarce two thousand strong, they vastly superior, though we don't know their numbers. The military people say that he should have attacked them. However, we are sadly convinced that they are not such raw ragamuffins as they were represented. The rotation that has been established in that country, to give all the Highlanders the benefit of serving in the independent companies, has trained and disciplined them. Macdonald[2] (I suppose, he from Naples), who is reckoned a very experienced able officer, is said to have commanded them, and to be dangerously wounded. One does not hear the Boy's personal valour cried up; by which I conclude he was not in the action. Our dragoons most shamefully fled without striking a blow, and are with Cope, who escaped in a boat to Berwick. I pity poor him,[3] who with no shining abilities, and no experience, and no force, was sent to fight for a crown! He never saw a battle but that of Dettingen, where he got his red ribbon: Church-ill, whose led-captain he was, and my Lord Harrington, had pushed him up to this misfortune. We have lost all our artillery, five hundred men taken – and *three* killed, and several officers, as you will see in the papers. This defeat has frightened every body but those it

1 The battle of Prestonpans, near Edinburgh, where the Jacobites comprehensively defeated Sir John Cope's forces.
2 The Yale editors suggest this was in fact Archibald Macdonald of Keppoch, who died of his injuries.
3 General Cope was tried afterwards for his behaviour in this action, and it appeared very clearly, that the Ministry, his inferior officers, and his troops, were greatly to blame; and that he did all he could, so ill-directed, so ill-supplied, and so ill-obeyed. – WALPOLE.

rejoices, and those it should frighten most; but my Lord Granville[1] still buoys up the King's spirits, and persuades him it is nothing. He uses his Ministers as ill as possible, and discourages every body that would risk their lives and fortunes with him. Marshal Wade is marching against the rebels; but the King will not let him take above eight thousand men; so that if they come into England, another battle, with no advantage on our side, may determine our fate. Indeed, they don't seem so unwise as to risk their cause upon so precarious an event; but rather to design to establish themselves in Scotland, till they can be supported from France, and be set up with taking Edinburgh Castle, where there is to the value of a million, and which they would make a stronghold. It is scarcely victualled for a month, and must surely fall into their hands.[2] Our coasts are greatly guarded, and London kept in awe by the arrival of the guards. I don't believe what I have been told this morning, that more troops are sent for from Flanders, and aid asked of Denmark.

Prince Charles has called a Parliament in Scotland for the 7th of October; ours does not meet till the 17th, so that even in the show of liberty and laws they are beforehand with us. With all this, we hear of no men of quality or fortune having joined him but Lord Elcho, whom you have seen at Florence; and the Duke of Perth, a silly race-horsing boy, who is said to be killed in this battle. But I gather no confidence from hence: my father always said, "If you see them come again, they will begin by their lowest people; their chiefs will not appear till the end." His prophecies verify every day!

The town is still empty; on this point only the English act contrary to their custom, for they don't throng to see a Parliament, though it is likely to grow a curiosity!

I have so trained myself to expect this ruin, that I see it approach without any emotion. I shall suffer with fools, without having any malice to our enemies, who act sensibly from principle and from interest. Ruling parties seldom have caution or common sense. I don't doubt but Whigs and Protestants will be alert enough in trying to recover what they lose so supinely. ... Adieu, my dear Sir; I hope your spirits, like mine, will grow calm, from being callous with ill-news.

1 Carteret, 2nd Earl Granville since October 1744, who had resigned as Secretary of State in November 1744: see letter 37, p. 64, n. 1.
2 Edinburgh Castle did not fall to the Jacobites.

275. *Carlisle Capitulates.*

TO SIR HORACE MANN

Arlington Street, 22 November 1745.

For these two days we have been expecting news of a battle. Wade marched last Saturday from Newcastle, and must have got up with the rebels if they stayed for him, though the roads are exceedingly bad and great quantities of snow have fallen. But last night there was some notice of a body of rebels being advanced to Penryth. We were put into great spirits by an heroic letter from the mayor of Carlisle, who had fired on the rebels and made them retire; he concluded with saying, "And so I think the town of Carlisle has done his Majesty more service than the great city of Edinburgh, or than all Scotland together." But this hero, who was grown the whole fashion for four-and-twenty hours, had chosen to stop all other letters. The King spoke of him at his *levée* with great encomiums; Lord Stair said, "Yes, sir, Mr. Patterson has behaved very bravely." The Duke of Bedford interrupted him; "My lord, his name is not *Paterson;* that is a Scotch name; his name is *Patinson.*" But, alack! the next day the rebels returned, having placed the women and children of the country in waggons in front of their army, and forcing the peasants to fix the scaling-ladders. The great Mr. Pattinson, or Patterson (for now his name may be which one pleases), instantly surrendered the town, and agreed to pay two thousand pounds to save it from pillage. Well! then we were assured that the citadel could hold out seven or eight days; but did not so many hours. On mustering the militia, there were not found above four men in a company; and for two companies, which the ministry, on a report of Lord Albemarle, who said they were to be sent from Wade's army, thought were there, and did not know were not there, there was nothing but two of invalids. Colonel Durand, the governor, fled, because he would not sign the capitulation, by which the garrison, it is said, has sworn never to bear arms against the house of Stuart. The Colonel sent two expresses, one to Wade, and another to Ligonier at Preston; but the latter was playing at whist with Lord Harrington at Petersham. Such is our diligence and attention! All my hopes are in Wade, who was so sensible of the ignorance of our governors, that he refused to accept the command, till they consented that he should be subject to no kind of orders from hence. The rebels are reckoned up at thirteen thousand; Wade marches with about twelve; but if they come southward, the other army will probably be to fight them; the Duke[1] is to command it, and sets out next week with another brigade of Guards, and Ligonier under him. There are great apprehensions for Chester from the Flintshire-men, who are ready to rise. A quarter-master, first sent to Carlisle, was seized and carried to Wade; he behaved most insolently; and being asked by the General, how many the rebels were, replied, "Enough to beat any army you have in England." A Mackintosh had been taken, who reduces their formidability, by being sent to raise two clans, and with orders, if they would not rise, at least to give out they had risen, for that three clans would leave the Pretender, unless joined by those two. Five hundred new rebels are arrived at Perth, where our prisoners are kept. . . . Adieu!

276. *Derby and the Retreat.*

TO SIR HORACE MANN

Arlington Street, 9 December 1745.

I am glad I did not write to you last post as I intended; I should have sent you an account that would have alarmed you, and the danger would have been over before the letter had crossed the sea. The Duke, from some strange want of intelligence, lay last week for four-and-twenty hours under arms at Stone, in Staffordshire, expecting the rebels every moment, while they were marching in all haste to Derby.[2] The news of this threw the town into great consternation; but his Royal Highness repaired his mistake, and got to Northampton, between the Highlanders and London. They got nine thousand pounds at Derby, and had the books brought to them, and obliged everybody to give them what they had subscribed against them. Then they retreated a few miles, but returned again to Derby, get ten thousand pounds more, plundered the town, and burnt a house of the Countess of Exeter. They are gone again, and go back to Leake, in Staffordshire, but miserably harassed, and, it is said, have left all their cannon behind them, and twenty waggons of

1 The Duke of Cumberland.
2 The consternation was so great as to occasion that day being named *Black Friday.* – WALPOLE.

sick. The Duke has sent General Hawley with the dragoons to harass them in their retreat, and despatched Mr. Conway to Marshal Wade, to hasten his march upon the back of them. They must either go to North Wales, where they will probably all perish, or to Scotland, with great loss. We dread them no longer. We are threatened with great preparations for a French invasion, but the coast is exceedingly guarded; and for the people, the spirit against the rebels increases every day. Though they have marched thus into the heart of the kingdom, there has not been the least symptom of a rising, not even in the great towns of which they possessed themselves. They have got no recruits since their first entry into England, excepting one gentleman in Lancashire, one hundred and fifty common men, and two parsons, at Manchester, and a physician from York. But here in London, the aversion to them is amazing: on some thoughts of the King's going to an encampment at Finchley,[1] the weavers not only offered him a thousand men, but the whole body of the Law formed themselves into a little army, under the command of Lord Chief-Justice Willes, and were to have done duty at St. James's, to guard the royal family in the King's absence. ... Adieu!

277. Culloden.

TO SIR HORACE MANN

Arlington Street, 25 April 1746.

You have bid me for some time send you good news – well! I think I will. How good would you have it? must it be a total victory over the rebels; with not only the Boy, that is here, killed, but the other, that is not here, too; their whole army put to the sword, *besides* an infinite number of prisoners; all the Jacobite estates in England confiscated, and all those in Scotland – what would you have done with them? – or could you be content with something much under this? how much will you abate? will you compound for Lord John Drummond, taken by accident? or for three Presbyterian parsons, who have very poor livings, stoutly refusing to pay a large contribution to

1 The encampment that inspired Hogarth's "The March to Finchley", now at the Foundling Museum.

the rebels? Come, I will deal as well with you as I can, and for once, but not to make a practice of it, will let you have a victory! My friend, Lord Bury,[1] arrived this morning from the Duke, though the news was got here before him; for, with all our victory, it was not thought safe to send him through the heart of Scotland; so he was shipped at Inverness, within an hour after the Duke entered the town, kept beating at sea five days, and then put on shore at North Berwick, from whence he came post in less than three days to London; but with a fever upon him, for which he had been twice blooded but the day before the battle; but he is young, and high in spirits, and I flatter myself will not suffer from this kindness of the Duke: the King has immediately ordered him a thousand pound, and I hear will make him his own aide-de-camp. My dear Mr. Chute,[2] I beg your pardon; I had forgot you have the gout, and consequently not the same patience to wait for the battle, with which I, knowing the particulars, postpone it.

On the 16th, the Duke, by forced marches, came up with the rebels, a little on this side Inverness – by the way, the battle is not christened yet;[3] I only know that neither Prestonpans nor Falkirk are to be godfathers. The rebels, who fled from him after their victory, and durst not attack him, when so much exposed to them at his passage of the Spey, now stood him, they seven thousand, he ten. They broke through Barril's regiment, and killed Lord Robert Kerr, a handsome young gentleman, who was cut to pieces with above thirty wounds; but they were soon repulsed, and fled; the whole engagement not lasting above a quarter of an hour. The young Pretender escaped; Mr. Conway says, he hears, wounded: he certainly was in the rear. They have lost above a thousand men in the engagement and pursuit; and six hundred were already taken; among which latter are their French ambassador and Earl Kilmarnock. The Duke of Perth and Lord Ogilvie are said to be slain; Lord Elcho was in a salivation,[4] and not there. Except Lord Robert Kerr, we lost nobody of note: Sir Robert Rich's eldest son has lost his hand, and about a

1 George Keppel, eldest son of William Anne Earl of Albemarle, whom he succeeded in the title. – WALPOLE.
2 Walpole's friend John Chute was still in 1746 living in Italy.
3 Where the King's troops had been beaten by the rebels. This was called the battle of Culloden. – WALPOLE.
4 The excessive flow of saliva caused by taking mercury.

hundred and thirty private men fell. The defeat is reckoned total, and the dispersion general; and all their artillery is taken. It is a brave young Duke! The town is all blazing round me, as I write, with fireworks and illuminations: I have some inclination to wrap up half-a-dozen skyrockets, to make you drink the Duke's health. Mr. Dodington,[1] on the first report, came out with a very pretty illumination; so pretty, that I believe he had it by him, ready for *any* occasion. . . .

278. *Trial of the Rebel Lords.*

TO SIR HORACE MANN

Arlington Street, 1 August 1746.

I am this monent come from the conclusion of the greatest and most melancholy scene I ever yet saw! you will easily guess it was the Trials of the rebel Lords. As it was the most interesting sight, it was the most solemn and fine: a coronation is a puppet-show, and all the splendour of it idle; but this sight at once feasted one's eyes and engaged all one's passions. It began last Monday; three parts of Westminster-hall were inclosed with galleries, and hung with scarlet; and the whole ceremony was conducted with the most awful solemnity and decency, except in the one point of leaving the prisoners at the bar, amidst the idle curiosity of some crowd, and even with the witnesses who had sworn against them, while the Lords adjourned to their own House to consult. No part of the royal family was there, which was a proper regard to the unhappy men, who were become their victims. One hundred and thirty-nine Lords were present, and made a noble sight on their benches *frequent and full!*[2] The Chancellor [Hardwicke] was Lord High Steward; but though a most comely personage with a fine voice, his behaviour was mean, curiously searching for occasion to bow to the minister [Mr. Pelham] that is no peer, and consequently applying to the other ministers, in a manner, for their orders; and not even ready at the ceremonial. To the prisoners he was peevish; and instead of keeping up to the humane dignity of the law of England, whose character it is to point out favour to the criminal, he crossed them, and almost

1 Bubb Dodington: see letter 20, p. 37, n. 1.
2 Alluding to the Council at the end of the Odyssey where the Seniors sat "frequent and full": Pope, *Odyssey* XXIV, 481–2.

scolded at any offer they made towards defence. I had armed myself with all the resolution I could, with the thought of their crimes and of the danger past, and was assisted by the sight of the Marquis of Lothian in weepers for his son who fell at Culloden – but the first appearance of the prisoners shocked me! their behaviour melted me! Lord Kilmarnock and Lord Cromartie are both past forty, but look younger. Lord Kilmarnock is tall and slender, with an extreme fine person: his behaviour a most just mixture between dignity and submission; if in anything to be reprehended, a little affected, and his hair too exactly dressed for a man in his situation; but when I say this, it is not to find fault with him, but to show how little fault there was to be found. Lord Cromartie is an indifferent figure, appeared much dejected, and rather sullen: he dropped a few tears the first day, and swooned as soon as he got back to his cell. For Lord Balmerino,[1] he is the most natural brave old fellow I ever saw: the highest intrepidity, even to indifference. At the bar he behaved like a soldier and a man; in the intervals of form, with carelessness and humour. He pressed extremely to have his wife, his pretty Peggy, with him in the Tower; the instant she came to him, he stripped her and went to bed. Lady Cromartie only sees her husband through the grate, not choosing to be shut up with him, as she thinks she can serve him better by her intercession without: she is big with child and very handsome: so are their daughters. When they were to be brought from the Tower in separate coaches, there was some dispute in which the axe must go – old Balmerino cried, "Come, come, put it with me." At the bar, he plays with his fingers upon the axe, while he talks to the gentleman-gaoler; and one day somebody coming up to listen, he took the blade and held it like a fan between their faces. During the trial, a little boy was near him, but not tall enough to see; he made room for the child and placed him near himself.

When the trial began, the two Earls pleaded guilty; Balmerino not guilty, saying he could prove his not being at the taking of the castle of Carlisle, as was laid in the indictment. Then the King's counsel opened, and Serjeant Skinner pronounced the most absurd speech imaginable; and mentioned the Duke of Perth, "who," said he, "I see by the papers is dead." Then some witnesses were examined, whom afterwards the old hero shook cordially by the hand.

1 Arthur Elphinstone (1688–1746), Lord Balmerino, who attracted wide attention for his manner at his trial and execution.

The Lords withdrew to their House, and returning, demanded of the judges, whether one point not being proved, though all the rest were, the indictment was false? to which they unanimously answered in the negative. Then the Lord High Steward asked the Peers severally, whether Lord Balmerino was guilty! All said, "guilty upon honour," and then adjourned, the prisoner having begged pardon for giving them so much trouble. While the Lords were withdrawn, the Solicitor-General Murray (brother of the Pretender's minister) officiously and insolently went up to Lord Balmerino, and asked him, how he could give the Lords so much trouble, when his solicitor had informed him that his plea could be of no use to him? Balmerino asked the bystanders who this person was? and being told, he said, "Oh, Mr. Murray! I am extremely glad to see you; I have been with several of your relations; the good lady, your mother, was of great use to us at Perth." Are not you charmed with this speech? how just it was! As he went away, he said, "They call me Jacobite; I am no more a Jacobite than any that tried me: but if the Great Mogul had set up his standard, I should have followed it, for I could not starve." The worst of his case is, that after the battle of Dumblain, having a company in the Duke of Argyll's regiment, he deserted with it to the rebels, and has since been pardoned. Lord Kilmarnock is a presbyterian, with four earldoms in him, but so poor since Lord Wilmington's stopping a pension that my father had given him, that he often wanted a dinner. Lord Cromartie was receiver of the rents of the King's second son in Scotland, which, it was understood, he should not account for; and by that means had six hundred a-year from the Government: Lord Elibank, a very prating, impertinent Jacobite, was bound for him in nine thousand pounds, for which the Duke is determined to sue him.

When the Peers were going to vote, Lord Foley withdrew, as too well a wisher; Lord Moray, as nephew of Lord Balmerino – and Lord Stair, – as, I believe, uncle to his great-grandfather. Lord Windsor, very affectedly, said, "I am sorry I must say, *guilty upon my honour.*" Lord Stamford would not answer to the name of *Henry,* having been christened *Harry* – what a great way of thinking on such an occasion! I was diverted too with old Norsa,[1] the father of my brother's concubine, an old Jew that kept a tavern; my brother

1 Father of Hannah Norsa (see letter 55, p. 90, n. 4.).

[Orford], as Auditor of the Exchequer, has a gallery along one whole side of the court; I said, "I really feel for the prisoners!" old Issachar replied, "Feel for them! pray, if they had succeeded, what would have become of *all us*?" When my Lady Townshend heard her husband vote, she said, "I always knew *my* Lord was *guilty*, but I never thought he would own it *upon his honour*." Lord Balmerino said, that one of his reasons for pleading *not guilty*, was, that so many ladies might not be disappointed of their show.

On Wednesday they were again brought to Westminster-hall, to receive sentence; and being asked what they had to say, Lord Kilmarnock, with a very fine voice, read a very fine speech, confessing the extent of his crime, but offering his principles as some alleviation, having his eldest son (his second unluckily was with him), in the Duke's army, *fighting for the liberties of his country at Culloden, where his unhappy father was in arms to destroy them*. He insisted much on his tenderness to the English prisoners, which some deny, and say that he was the man who proposed their being put to death, when General Stapleton urged that *he* was come to fight, and not to butcher; and that if they acted any such barbarity, he would leave them with all his men. He very artfully mentioned Van Hoey's letter, and said how much he should scorn to owe his life to such intercession. Lord Cromartie spoke much shorter, and so low, that he was not heard but by those who sat very near him; but they prefer his speech to the other. He mentioned his misfortune in having drawn in his eldest son, who is prisoner with him; and concluded with saying, "If no part of this bitter cup must pass from me, not mine, O God, but thy will be done!" If he had pleaded *not guilty*, there was ready to be produced against him a paper signed with his own hand, for putting the English prisoners to death.

Lord Leicester went up to the Duke of Newcastle, and said, "I never heard so great an orator as Lord Kilmarnock? if I was your grace, I would pardon him, and make him *paymaster*."[1]

That morning a paper had been sent to the lieutenant of the Tower for the prisoners; he gave it to Lord Cornwallis, the governor, who carried it to the House of Lords. It was a plea for the prisoners, objecting that the late act for regulating the trials of rebels did not

[1] Alluding to Mr. Pitt, who had lately been preferred to that post, from the fear the ministry had of his abusive eloquence. — WALPOLE.

take place till after their crime was committed. The Lords very tenderly and rightly sent this plea to them, of which, as you have seen, the two Earls did not make use; but old Balmerino did, and demanded council on it. The High Steward, almost in a passion, told him, that when he had been offered council, he did not accept it. Do but think on the ridicule of sending them the plea, and then denying them council on it! The Duke of Newcastle, who never let slip an opportunity of being absurd, took it up as a ministerial point, in defence of his creature the Chancellor [Hardwicke]; but Lord Granville moved, according to order, to adjourn to debate in the chamber of Parliament, where the Duke of Bedford and many others spoke warmly for their having council; and it was granted. I said *their*, because the plea would have saved them all, and affected nine rebels who had been hanged that very morning; particularly one Morgan, a poetical lawyer. Lord Balmerino asked for Forester and Wilbraham; the latter a very able lawyer in the House of Commons, who, the Chancellor said privately, he was sure would as soon be hanged as plead such a cause. But he came as council to-day (the third day), when Lord Balmerino gave up his plea as invalid, and submitted without any speech. The High Steward [Hardwicke] then made his, very long and very poor, with only one or two good passages; and then pronounced sentence!

Great intercession is made for the two Earls: Duke Hamilton, who has never been at Court, designs to kiss the King's hand, and ask Lord Kilmarnock's life. The King is much inclined to some mercy; but the Duke, who has not so much of Cæsar after a victory, as in gaining it, is for the utmost severity. It was lately proposed in the city to present him with the freedom of some company; one of the aldermen said aloud, "Then let it be of the *Butchers!*" ... Adieu!

279. *Execution of Balmerino and Kilmarnock.*

TO SIR HORACE MANN

Windsor, 21 August 1746.

. . . I came from town (for take notice, I put this place upon myself for the country) the day after the execution of the rebel Lords:[1] I was not at it, but had two persons come to me directly who were at the next house to the scaffold: and I saw another who was upon it, so that you may depend upon my accounts.

Just before they came out of the Tower, Lord Balmerino drank a bumper to King James's health. As the clock struck ten, they came forth on foot, Lord Kilmarnock all in black, his hair unpowdered in a bag, supported by Forster, the great Presbyterian, and by Mr. Home, a young clergyman, his friend. Lord Balmerino followed, alone, in a blue coat, turned up with red, (his rebellious regimentals), a flannel waistcoat, and his shroud beneath; their hearses following. They were conducted to a house near the scaffold: the room forwards had benches for spectators, in the second Lord Kilmarnock was put, and in the third backwards Lord Balmerino: all three chambers hung with black. Here they parted! Balmerino embraced the other, and said, "My lord, I wish I could suffer for both!" He had scarce left him, before he desired again to see him, and then asked him, "My Lord Kilmarnock, do you know anything of the resolution taken in our army, the day before the battle of Culloden, to put the English prisoners to death?" He replied, "My lord, I was not present; but since I came hither, I have had all the reason in the world to believe that there was such order taken; and I hear the Duke has the pocket-book with the order." Balmerino answered, "It was a lie raised to excuse their barbarity to us." – Take notice, that the Duke's charging this on Lord Kilmarnock (certainly on misinformation) decided this unhappy man's fate! The most now pretended is, that it would have come to Lord Kilmarnock's turn to have given the word for the slaughter, as lieutenant-general, with the patent for which he was immediately drawn into the rebellion, after having

---

1 Of the third rebel lord, Walpole had written to Mann on 12 August, "Lord Cromartie is reprieved; the Prince [of Wales] asked his life, and his wife made great intercession, though when he was taken, he was actually found in bed with Lady Sutherland" (YE 19:296).

been staggered by his wife, her mother, his own poverty, and the defeat of Cope. He remained an hour and a half in the house, and shed tears. At last he came to the scaffold, certainly much terrified, but with a resolution that prevented his behaving in the least meanly or unlike a gentleman. He took no notice of the crowd, only to desire that the baize might be lifted up from the rails, that the mob might see the spectacle. He stood and prayed some time with Forster, who wept over him, exhorted and encouraged him. He delivered a long speech to the Sheriff, and with a noble manliness stuck to the recantation he had made at his trial; declaring he wished that all who embarked in the same cause might meet the same fate. He then took off his bag, coat and waistcoat, with great composure, and after some trouble put on a napkin-cap, and then several times tried the block; the executioner, who was in white, with a white apron, out of tenderness concealing the axe behind himself. At last the Earl knelt down, with a visible unwillingness to depart, and after five minutes dropped his handkerchief, the signal, and his head was cut off at once, only hanging by a bit of skin, and was received in a scarlet cloth by four of the undertaker's men kneeling, who wrapped it up and put it into the coffin with the body; orders having been given not to expose the heads, as used to be the custom.

The scaffold was immediately new-strewed with saw-dust, the block new-covered, the executioner new-dressed, and a new axe brought. Then came old Balmerino, treading with the air of a general. As soon as he mounted the scaffold, he read the inscription on his coffin, as he did again afterwards: he then surveyed the spectators, who were in amazing numbers, even upon masts of ships in the river; and pulling out his spectacles read a treasonable speech, which he delivered to the Sheriff, and said, the young Pretender was so sweet a Prince, that flesh and blood could not resist following him; and lying down to try the block, he said, "If I had a thousand lives, I would lay them all down here in the same cause." He said, if he had not taken the sacrament the day before, he would have knocked down Williamson, the lieutenant of the Tower, for his ill usage of him. He took the axe and felt it, and asked the headsman how many blows he had given Lord Kilmarnock; and gave him three guineas. Two clergymen, who attended him, coming up, he said, "No, gentlemen, I believe you have already done me all the service you can." Then he went to the corner of the scaffold, and called very loud for the warder, to give him his perriwig, which he took off, and put on a night-cap of Scotch plaid, and then pulled off his coat and waistcoat and lay down; but being told he was on the wrong side, vaulted round, and immediately gave the sign by tossing up his arm, as if he were giving the signal for battle. He received three blows, but the first certainly took away all sensation. He was not a quarter of an hour on the scaffold; Lord Kilmarnock above half a one. Balmerino certainly died with the intrepidity of a hero, but with the insensibility of one too. As he walked from his prison to execution, seeing every window and top of house filled with spectators, he cried out, "Look, look, how they are all piled up like rotten oranges!" ... Adieu!

3. THE TREATY OF AIX-LA-CHAPELLE

280. *Aix-la-Chapelle.*

TO SIR HORACE MANN

Arlington Street, 29 April 1748.

I know I have not writ to you the Lord knows when, but I waited for something to tell you, and I have now what there was not much reason to expect. The preliminaries to the peace are actually signed[1] by the English, Dutch, and French: the Queen [of Hungary],[2] who would remain the only sufferer, though vastly less than she could expect, protests against this treaty, and the Sardinian Minister has refused to sign too, till further orders. Spain is not mentioned, but France answers for them, and that they shall give us a new assiento. The armistice is for six weeks, with an exception to Maestricht; upon which the Duke sent Lord George Sackville to Marshal Saxe, to tell him that, as they are so near being friends, he shall not endeavour to raise the siege and spill more blood, but hopes the Marshal will give the garrison good terms, as they have behaved so bravely.[3] The conditions settled are a general restitution on all sides, as Modena to its Duke, Flanders to the Queen, the Dutch towns to the Dutch,

1 The Treaty of Aix-la-Chapelle, which concluded the War of the Austrian Succession (1740–48).
2 Maria Theresa.
3 The articles of capitulation allowed the defending forces to leave the besieged city with full military honours.

Cape Breton to France, and Final to the Genoese; but the Sardinian to have the cessions made to him by the Queen, who, you see, is to be made [to] observe the treaty of Worms, though we do not. Parma and Placentia are to be given to Don Philip; Dunkirk to remain as it is, on the land-side; but to be *Utrecht'd*[1] again to the sea. The Pretender to be renounced with all his descendants, male and female, even in stronger terms than by the quadruple alliance; and the cessation of arms to take place in all other parts of the world, as in the year 1712. The contracting powers agree to think of means of making the other powers come into this treaty, in case they refuse.

This is the substance; and wonderful it is what can make the French give us such terms, or why they have lost so much blood and treasure to so little purpose! for they have destroyed very little of the fortifications in Flanders. Monsieur de St. Severin told Lord Sandwich, that he had full powers to sign now, but that the same courier that should carry our refusal, was to call at Namur and Bergen-op-zoom, where are mines under all the works, which were immediately to be blown up. There is no accounting for this, but from the King's aversion to go to the army, and to Marshal Saxe's fear of losing his power with the loss of a battle. He told Count Flemming, the Saxon Minister, who asked him if the French were in earnest in their offer of peace, "Il est vrai, nous demandons la paix comme des lâches, et ne pouvons pas l'obtenir."

Stocks rise; the Ministry are in high spirits, and *peu s'en faut* but we shall admire this peace as our own doing! I believe two reasons that greatly advanced it are, the King's wanting to go to Hanover, and the Duke's wanting to go into a salivation.[2]

We had last night the most magnificent masquerade that ever was seen: it was by subscription at the Haymarket: every body who subscribed five guineas had four tickets. There were about seven hundred people, all in chosen and very fine dresses. The supper was in two rooms, besides those for the King and Prince, who, with the foreign ministers, had tickets given them.

You don't tell me whether the seal of which you sent me the impression, is to be sold: I think it fine, but not equal to the price

1 That is, the defensive works removed, as they had been after the Treaty of Utrecht, which had concluded the War of the Spanish Succession in 1713.
2 The Yale editors record that the Duke of Cumberland complained of a kidney infection. For salivation, see letter 277, p. 382, n. 4.

which you say was paid for it. What is it? Homer or Pindar?

I am very miserable at the little prospect you have of success in your own affair:[1] I think the person you employed has used you scandalously. I would have you write to my uncle; but my applying to him would be very far from doing you service. Poor Mr. Chute has got so bad a cold that he could not go last night to the masquerade. Adieu! my dear child! there is nothing well that I don't wish you, but my wishes are very ineffectual!

4. THE SEVEN YEARS' WAR

281. *Hostilities in America. Washington.*

TO SIR HORACE MANN

Arlington Street, 6 October 1754.

You have the kindest way in the world, my dear Sir, of reproving my long silence, by accusing yourself. I have looked at my dates, and though I was conscious of not having written to you for a long time, I did not think it had been so long as three months. I ought to make some excuse, and the truth is all I can make: if you have heard by any way in the world that a single event worth mentioning has happened in England for these three months, I will own myself guilty of abominable neglect. If there has not, as you know my unalterable affection for you, you will excuse me, and accuse the times. Can one repeat often, that everything stagnates? At present we begin to think that the world may be roused again, and that an East Indian war and a West Indian war may beget such a thing as an European war. In short, the French have taken such cavalier liberties with some of our forts, that are of great consequence to cover Virginia, Carolina, and Georgia, that we are actually despatching two regiments thither. As the climate and other American circumstances are against these poor men, I pity them, and think them too many, if the French mean nothing farther; too few, if they do. Indeed, I am one of those that feel less resentment when we are attacked so far off: I think it an obligation to be eaten the last. . . .

You will have observed what precaution I had taken, in the smallness of the sheet, not to have too much paper to fill; and yet you see

1 Mann had written to Walpole on 9 April regarding his efforts to recover his arrears of salary.

how much I have still upon my hands! As, I assure you, were I to fill the remainder, all I should say would be terribly wire-drawn, do excuse me: you shall hear an ample detail of the first Admiral Vernon that springs out of our American war; and I promise you at least half a brick of the first sample that is sent over of any new Porto Bello.[1] The French have tied up the hands of an excellent fanfaron, a Major Washington, whom they took, and engaged not to serve for a year.[2] In his letter, he said, "Believe me, as the cannon-balls flew over my head, they made a most delightful sound." When your relation, General Guise, was marching up to Carthagena, and the pelicans whistled round him, he said, "What would Chloe[3] give for some of these to make a pelican pie?" The conjecture made that scarce a rodomontade; but what pity it is, that a man who can deal in hyperboles at the mouth of a cannon, should be fond of them with a glass of wine in his hand! I have heard Guise affirm, that the colliers at Newcastle feed their children with fire-shovels! Good-night.

282. *Braddock's Defeat.*

TO SIR HORACE MANN

Arlington Street, 28 August 1755.

My last letter to you could not be got out of England, before I might have added a melancholy supplement. Accounts of a total defeat of Braddock and his forces are arrived from America; the purport is, that the General having arrived within a few miles of Fort du Quesne, (I hope you are perfect in your American geography?)[4] sent an advanced party, under Lord Gage's brother: they were fired upon, invisibly, as they entered a wood; Braddock heard guns, and sent another party to support the former; but the first fell back in confusion on the second, and the second on the main body. The whole was in disorder, and it is said, the General himself, though exceedingly brave, did not retain all the *sang froid* that was necessary.

1 Porto Bello had been captured by Admiral Vernon in 1739.
2 Washington was then a major serving in the provincial militia which was fighting with British forces against the French. The capitulation articles do not contain such a provision.
3 The Duke of Newcastle's French cook. – WALPOLE.
4 The battle of Monongahela took place to the south of Fort du Quesne (or Duquesne) on the site of modern Pittsburgh.

The common soldiers in general fled; the officers stood heroically and were massacred: our Indians were not surprised, and behaved gallantly. The General had five horses shot under him, no bad symptoms of his spirit, and at last was brought off by two Americans, no English daring, though Captain Orme, his aide-de-camp, who is wounded too, and has made some noise here by an affair of gallantry, offered sixty guineas to have him conveyed away. We have lost twenty-six officers, besides many wounded, and ten pieces of artillery. Braddock lived four days, in great torment. What makes the rout more shameful is, that instead of a great pursuit, and a barbarous massacre by the Indians, which is always to be feared in these rencontres, not a black or white soul followed our troops, but we had leisure two days afterwards to fetch off our dead. In short, our American laurels are strangely blighted! We intended to be in great alarms for Carolina and Virginia, but the small number of our enemies had reduced this affair to a panic. We pretend to be comforted on the French deserting Fort St. John, and on the hopes we have from two other expeditions which are on foot in that part of the world – but it is a great drawback on English heroism! I pity you who represent the very flower of British courage ingrafted on a Brunswick stock! ... Adieu! Pray don't let any detachment from Pannoni's[1] be sent against us – we should run away!

283. *Preparations against Invasion.*

TO SIR HORACE MANN

Strawberry Hill, 27 October 1755.

When the newspapers swarm with our military preparations at home, with encampments, fire-ships, floating castles at the mouths of the great rivers, &c., in short, when we expect an invasion, you would chide, or be disposed to chide me, if I were quite silent – and yet, what can I tell you more than that an invasion is threatened?[2] that sixteen thousand men are about Dunkirk, and that they are assembling great quantities of flat-bottomed boats! Perhaps they will attempt some landing; they are certainly full of resentment;

1 Pannoni's coffee-house of the Florentine nobility, not famous for their courage of late. – WALPOLE.
2 Invasion was threatened at the beginning of the Seven Years' War.

they broke the peace, took our forts and built others on our boundaries; we did not bear it patiently; we retook two forts, attacked or have been going to attack others, and have taken vast numbers of their ships: this is the state of the provocation – what is more provoking, for once we have not sent twenty or thirty thousand men to Flanders on whom they might vent their revenge. Well! then they must come here, and perhaps invite the Pretender to be of the party; not in a very popular light for him, to be brought by the French in revenge of a national war. You will ask me, if we are alarmed? the people not at all so: a minister or two, who are subject to alarms, are – and that is no bad circumstance. We are as much an island as ever, and I think a much less exposed one than we have been for many years. Our fleet is vast; our army at home, and ready, and two-thirds stronger than when we were threatened in 1744; the season has been the wettest that ever has been known, consequently the roads not very invadeable: and there is the additional little circumstance of the late rebellion defeated; I believe I may reckon too, Marshal Saxe dead. You see our situation is not desperate: in short, we escaped in '44, and when the rebels were at Derby in '45; we must have bad luck indeed, if we fall now!

Our Parliament meets in a fortnight; if no French come, our campaign there will be warm; nay, and uncommon, the opposition will be chiefly composed of men in place. You know we always refine; it used to be an imputation on our senators, that they opposed to get places. They now oppose to get better places! We are a comical nation (I speak with all due regard to our gravity!) – it were a pity we should be destroyed, if it were only for the sake of posterity; we shall not be half so droll, if we were either a province to France, or under an absolute prince of our own. ... Adieu! my dear Sir.

284. *Byng's Cowardice.*

TO SIR HORACE MANN

Arlington Street, 14 June 1756.

Our affairs have taken a strange turn, my dear Sir, since I wrote to you last at the end of May; we have been all confusion, consternation, and resentment! At this moment we are all perplexity! When

we were expecting every instant that Byng[1] would send home
Marshal Richelieu's head to be placed upon Temple-bar, we were
exceedingly astonished to hear that the governor and garrison of
Gibraltar had taken a panic for themselves, had called a council of
war, and in direct disobedience to a positive command, had refused
Byng a battalion from thence. This council was attended, and their
resolution signed, by all the chief officers there, among whom are
some particular favourites, and some men of the first quality. Instead
of being shocked at this disappointment, Byng accompanied it with
some wonderfully placid letters, in which he notified his intention
of retiring under the cannon of Gibraltar, in case he found it dangerous to attempt the relief of Minorca! These letters had scarce struck
their damp here, before D'Abreu, the Spanish minister, received an
account from France, that Galissonière had sent word that the
English fleet had been peeping about him, with exceeding caution,
for two or three days; that on the 20th of May they had scuffled for
about three hours, that night had separated them, and that to his
great astonishment, the English fleet, of which he had not taken one
vessel, had disappeared in the morning. If the world was scandalised
at this history, it was nothing to the exasperation of the Court, who,
on no other foundation than an enemy's report, immediately ordered
Admiral Hawke and Saunders [created an admiral on purpose] to
bridle and saddle the first ship at hand, and post away to Gibraltar,
and to hang and drown Byng and West, and then to send them home
to be tried for their lives: and not to be too partial to the land, and
to be as severe upon good grounds as they were upon scarce any, they
dispatched Lord Tyrawley and Lord Panmure upon the like errand
over the Generals Fowke and Stuart. This expedition had so far a
good effect, that the mob itself could not accuse the ministry of want
of rashness; and luckily for the latter, in three days more the same
canal confirmed the disappearance of the English fleet for four days
after the engagement – but behold! we had scarce had time to jumble
together our sorrow for our situation, and our satisfaction for the
dispatch we had used to repair it, when yesterday threw us into a
new puzzle. Our spies, the French, have sent us intelligence that
Galissonière is disgraced, recalled, and La Motte sent to replace
him, and that Byng has reinforced the garrison of St. Philip's with

1 Byng had been sent to relieve Minorca from invasion by the French.

– 150 men![1] You, who are nearer the spot, may be able, perhaps, to unriddle or unravel all this confusion; but you have no notion how it has put all our politics a-ground! ...

285. *His Execution.*

TO SIR HORACE MANN

Arlington Street, 17 March 1757.

Admiral Byng's tragedy was completed on Monday – a perfect tragedy, for there were variety of incidents, villainy, murder, and a hero! His sufferings, persecutions, aspersions, disturbances, nay, the revolutions of his fate, had not in the least unhinged his mind; his whole behaviour was natural and firm. A few days before, one of his friends standing by him, said, "Which of us is tallest?" He replied, "Why this ceremony? I know what it means; let the man come and measure me for my coffin." He said, that being acquitted of coward-ice, and being persuaded on the coolest reflection that he had acted for the best, and should act so again, he was not unwilling to suffer. He desired to be shot on the quarter-deck, not where common male-factors are; came out at twelve, sat down on a chair, for he would not kneel, and refused to have his face covered, that his countenance might show whether he feared death; but being told that it might frighten his executioners, he submitted, gave the signal at once, received one shot through the head, another through the heart, and fell. Do cowards live or die thus? Can that man want spirit who only fears to terrify his executioners? Has the aspen Duke of Newcastle lived thus? Would my Lord Hardwicke[2] die thus, even supposing he had nothing on his conscience?

This scene is over! what will be the next is matter of great uncer-tainty. The new ministers are well weary of their situation; without credit at court, without influence in the House of Commons, under-mined everywhere, I believe they are too sensible not to desire to be delivered of their burthen, which those who increase yet dread to take on themselves. Mr. Pitt's health is as bad as his situation; confi-dence between the other factions almost impossible; yet I believe

1 The Yale editors note that none of these rumours was true.
2 Philip Yorke (1690–1764), 1st Earl of Hardwicke, former Lord Chancellor and Newcastle's ally.

their impatience will prevail over their distrust. The nation expects a change every day, and being a nation, I believe, desires it; and being the English nation, will condemn it the moment it is made. We are trembling for Hanover, and the Duke [of Cumberland] is going to command the army of observation. . . .

286. *Frederick the Great.*

TO THE HON. H. S. CONWAY

Arlington Street, 19 January 1759.

I hope the treaty of Sluys advances rapidly.[1] Considering that your own court is as new to you as Monsieur de Bareil and his, you cannot be very well entertained: the joys of a Dutch fishing town and the incidents of a cartel will not compose a very agreeable history. In the mean time you do not lose much: though the Parliament is met, no politics are come to town: one may describe the House of Commons like the price of stocks; Debates, nothing done. Votes, under par. Patriots, no price. Oratory, books shut. Love and war are as much at a stand; neither the Duchess of Hamilton, nor the expeditions are gone off yet.[2] Prince Edward[3] has asked to go to Quebec, and has been refused. If I was sure they would refuse me, I would ask to go thither too. I should not dislike about as much laurel as I could stick in my window at Christmas.

We are next week to have a serenata at the Opera-house for the King of Prussia's birthday: it is to begin, "Viva Georgio, e Frederigo viva!" It will, I own, divert me to see my Lord Temple[4] whispering *for* this alliance, on the same bench on which I have so often seen him whisper *against* all Germany. The new opera pleases universally, and I hope will yet hold up its head. Since Vanneschi[5] is cunning

---

1 Mr. Conway was sent to Sluys to settle a cartel for prisoners with the French. M. de Bareil was the person appointed by the French court for the same business. – WALPOLE.
2 The former Elizabeth Gunning (bap. 1733–90), whose husband the Duke of Hamilton had died the previous year, married the future Duke of Argyll two months later, while the expedition to Quebec left one month later.
3 Afterwards created Duke of York. – WALPOLE.
4 Richard Grenville (1711–79), Lord Temple, ally of Pitt and Lord Privy Seal, who had been critical of the interests of Hanover.
5 Abbate Vanneschi, an Italian, and director of the opera. – WALPOLE.

enough to make us sing *the roast beef of old Germany*, I am persuaded it will revive: politics are the only hot-bed for keeping such a tender plant as Italian music alive in England. . . .

287. *Wolfe's Departure for Quebec.*

TO SIR HORACE MANN

Arlington Street, 9 February 1759.

The Dutch have not declared war and interrupted our correspondence, and yet it seems ceased as if we had declared war with one another. I have not heard from you this age – how happens it? I have not seized any ships of yours – you carry on no counterband trade – oh! perhaps you are gone *incognito* to Turin, are determined to have a King of Prussia of your own! I expect to hear that the King of Sardinia, accompanied by Sir Horace Mann, the British minister, suddenly appeared before Parma at the head of an hundred thousand men, that had been *privately* landed at Leghorn. I beg, as Harlequin did when he had a house to sell, that you will send me a brick, as a sample of the first town you take – the Strawberry-press shall be preparing a congratulatory ode.

The Princess Royal has been dead some time; and yet the Dutch and we continue in amity, and put on our weepers together. In the mean time our warlike eggs have been some time under the hen, and one has hatched and produced Gorée.[1] The expedition, called to Quebec, departs on Tuesday next, under Wolfe,[2] and George Townshend, who has thrust himself again into the service, and as far as wrongheadedness will go, very proper for a hero. Wolfe, who was no friend of Mr. Conway last year, and for whom I consequently have no affection, has great merit, spirit, and alacrity, and shone extremely at Louisbourg. I am not such a Juno but I will forgive him after eleven more labours. Prince Edward asked to go with them, but was refused. It is clever in him to wish to distinguish himself; I, who have no partiality to royal blood, like his good-nature and good-breeding. . . .

1 An island off the West African coast that had been captured from the French by Admiral Keppel.
2 James Wolfe (1727–59), Major-General, had appeared as a witness against Walpole's cousin Conway in the inquiry following the failure of the Rochefort expedition.

I long to hear from you; I think I never was so long without a letter. I hope it is from no bad reason. Adieu!

288. *Minden – Sackville's Conduct.*

Arlington Street, 14 August 1759.

I am here in the most unpleasant way in the world, attending poor Mrs. Leneve's[1] death-bed, a spectator of all the horrors of tedious suffering and clear sense, and with no one soul to speak to – but I will not tire you with a description of what has quite worn me out.

Probably by this time you have seen the Duke of Richmond or Fitzroy – but lest you should not, I will tell you all I can learn, and a wonderful history it is. Admiral Byng was not more unpopular than Lord George Sackville. I should scruple repeating his story, if Betty and the waiters at Arthur's did not talk of it publicly, and thrust Prince Ferdinand's orders into one's hand.[2]

You have heard, I suppose, of the violent animosities that have reigned for the whole campaign between him and Lord Granby – in which some other warm persons have been very warm too. In the heat of the battle, the Prince, finding thirty-six squadrons of French coming down upon our army, sent Ligonier to order our thirty-two squadrons, under Lord George, to advance. During that transaction, the French appeared to waver; and Prince Ferdinand, willing, as it is supposed, to give the honour to the British horse of terminating the day, sent Fitzroy to bid Lord George bring up only the British cavalry. Ligonier had but just delivered his message, when Fitzroy came with his. – Lord George said, "This can't be so – would he have me break the line? here is some mistake." Fitzroy replied, he had not argued upon the orders, but those were the orders. "Well!" said Lord George, "but I want a guide." Fitzroy said, he would be his guide. Lord George, "Where is the Prince?" Fitzroy, "I left him at the head of the left wing, I don't know where he is now." Lord

1 See letter 4, p. 10, n. 1.
2 Lord George Sackville was accused of ignoring orders to bring up the cavalry at the battle of Minden (see letter 256, p. 360, n. 2). The Duke of Richmond and Colonel Charles Fitzroy brought the despatches from the battle to London. For Betty, see letter 55, p. 90, n. 5.

George said he would go seek him, and have this explained. Smith then asked Fitzroy to repeat the orders to him; which being done, Smith went and whispered Lord George, who says he then bid Smith carry up the cavalry. Smith is come, and says he is ready to answer anybody any question. Lord George says, Prince Ferdinand's behaviour to him has been most infamous, has asked leave to resign his command, and to come over, which is granted. Prince Ferdinand's behaviour is summed up in the enclosed extraordinary paper: which you will doubt as I did, but which is certainly genuine. I doubted, because, in the military, I thought direct disobedience of orders was punished with an immediate arrest, and because the last paragraph seemed to me very foolish. The going out of the way to compliment Lord Granby with what he would have done, seems to take off a little from the compliments paid to those that have done something; but, in short, Prince Ferdinand or Lord George, one of them, is most outrageously in the wrong, and the latter has much the least chance of being thought in the right.[1]

The particulars I tell you, I collected from the most *accurate* authorities. – I make no comments on Lord George, it would look like a little dirty court to you; and the best compliment I can make you, is to think, as I do, that you will be the last man to enjoy this revenge. . . .

You will be sorry for poor McKinsey[2] and Lady Betty, who have lost their only child at Turin. Adieu!

289. *Failure inevitable at Quebec.*

TO SIR HORACE MANN

Arlington Street, 16 October 1759.

I love to prepare your countenance for every event that may happen, for an ambassador, who is nothing but an actor, should be that greatest of actors, a philosopher; and with the leave of wise men (that is, hypocrites), philosophy I hold to be little more than presence of mind: now undoubtedly preparation is a prodigious help to

---

1 The Yale editors comment that Sackville was associated with Lord Bute and the Leicester House set of the Prince of Wales, while Prince Ferdinand and Granby were close to the government ministers.
2 James Stuart McKenzie (*c.* 1719–1800), brother to Lord Bute.

presence of mind. In short, you must not be surprised that we have
failed at Quebec, as we certainly shall. You may say, if you please, in
the style of modern politics, that your Court never supposed it could
be taken; the attempt was only made to draw off the Russians from
the King of Prussia, and leave him at liberty to attack Daun. Two
days ago came letters from Wolfe, despairing, as much as heroes can
despair. The town is well victualled, Amherst[1] is not arrived, and
fifteen thousand men encamped defend it. We have lost many men
by the enemy, and some by our friends – that is, we now call our nine
thousand only seven thousand. How this little army will get away
from a much larger, and in this season in that country, I don't guess
– yes, I do.

You may be making up a little philosophy too against the invasion, which is again come into fashion, and with a few trifling incidents in its favour, such as our fleet dispersed and driven from their
coasts by a great storm. Before that, they were actually embarking,
but with so ill a grace that an entire regiment mutinied, and they say
is broke. We now expect them in Ireland, unless this dispersion of
our fleet tempts them hither. If they do not come in a day or two,
I shall give them over.

You will see in our gazettes that we make a great figure in the
East Indies. In short, Mr. Pitt and this little island appear of some
consequence even in the map of the world. He is a new sort of Fabius,

> Qui verbis restituit rem.[2]

My charming niece is breeding – you see I did not make my Lord
Waldegrave an useless present. Adieu! my dear Sir.

290. *Victory.*

TO THE HON. H. S. CONWAY

Strawberry Hill, 18 October 1759.

Sir Edward Hawke and his fleet is dispersed, at least driven back
to Plymouth: the French, if one may believe that they have broken

---

1 Lord Amherst (1717–97), who took Canada from the French the following year.
2 "Who by his words restored the State", sourced by the Yale editors as a paraphrase
from the Roman poet Ennius. Fabius Maximus was a Roman general noted for his
defensive strategy in the Second Punic War.

a regiment for mutinying against embarking, were actually embarked at that instant. The most sensible people I know, always thought they would postpone their invasion, if ever they intended it, till our great ships could not keep the sea, or were eaten up by the scurvy. Their ports are now free; their situation is desperate: the new account of our taking Quebec[1] leaves them in the most deplorable condition; they will be less able than ever to raise money, we have got ours for next year; and this event would facilitate it, if we had not: they must try for a peace, they have nothing to go to market with but Minorca. In short, if they cannot strike some desperate blow in this island or Ireland, they are undone: the loss of twenty thousand men to do us some mischief, would be cheap. I should even think Madame Pompadour in danger of being torn to pieces, if they did not make some attempt. Madame Maintenon, not half so unpopular, mentions in one of her letters her unwillingness to trust her niece Mademoiselle Aumale on the road, for fear of some such accident. You will smile perhaps at all this reasoning and pedantry; but it tends to this – if desperation should send the French somewhere, and the wind should force them to your coast, which I do not suppose their object, and you should be out of the way, you know what your enemies would say; and, strange as it is, even you have been proved to have enemies. My dear Sir, think of this! Wolfe, as I am convinced, has fallen a sacrifice to his rash blame of you. If I understand anything in the world, his letter that came on Sunday said this: "Quebec is impregnable; it is flinging away the lives of brave men to attempt it. I am in the situation of Conway at Rochefort; but having blamed him, I must do what I now see he was in the right to see was wrong, and yet what he would have done; and as I am commander, which he was not, I have the melancholy power of doing what he was prevented doing."[2] Poor man! his life has paid the price of his injustice; and as his death has purchased such benefit to his country, I lament him, as I am sure you, who have twenty times more courage and good-nature than I have, do too. . . . Adieu!

---

1 Quebec had capitulated to the British forces a month previously.
2 Walpole's imaginative account of Wolfe's rationale has been criticised as entirely spurious.

291. *A Glorious Year.*

TO GEORGE MONTAGU, ESQ.

Strawberry Hill, 21 October 1759.

Your pictures shall be sent as soon as any of us go to London, but I think that will not be till the Parliament meets. Can we easily leave the remains of such a year as this? It is still all gold. I have not dined or gone to bed by a fire till the day before yesterday. Instead of the glorious and ever-memorable year 1759, as the newspapers call it, I call it this ever-warm and victorious year. We have not had more conquest than fine weather: one would think we had plundered East and West Indies of sunshine. Our bells are worn threadbare with ringing for victories. I believe it will require ten votes of the House of Commons before people will believe it is the Duke of Newcastle that has done this, and not Mr. Pitt. One thing is very fatiguing – all the world is made knights or generals. Adieu! I don't know a word of news less than the conquest of America. Adieu! yours ever.

P. S. You shall hear from me again if we take Mexico or China before Christmas. . . .

XIV
HISTORICAL EVENTS – THE FIRST
HALF OF GEORGE III'S REIGN

WALPOLE WAS PLEASED when the twenty-three-year-old George III succeeded his grandfather in 1760, telling George Montagu of the new King's amiability, grace and good nature. Two weeks later he repeated the compliments, dismissed early claims of the unhealthy influence of the King's mother ("No petticoat ever governed less"), and also distanced himself from attacks on Lord Bute's ministry (letters 42 and 43). He was to change his position dramatically over the next few years and in his Memoirs repeats the unsavoury gossip of the time about the relationship of the Princess Dowager and Bute, now largely discounted.

Bute was deeply unpopular for the compromises made in the Treaty of Paris which concluded the Seven Years' War in February 1763. That unpopularity was fuelled by the *North Briton*, a paper founded in 1762 and largely written by John Wilkes, M.P. for Aylesbury. Immediately after Bute's resignation in April 1763, No. 45 of the *North Briton* attacked the King's speech commending the peace, and so began the long saga of "Wilkes and Liberty" in which Wilkes combined tactical skill, opportunism, and political principle in proportions that are still debated, and turned himself into a popular hero. He was prosecuted for seditious libel, but the government made the mistake of proceeding by means of a general warrant addressed at authors, printers and publishers, without giving specific names. The courts dismissed general warrants as unlawful, but not before Wilkes had been expelled from the House of Commons and had fled to France. He was then in 1764 tried *in absentia*, convicted of libel and outlawed, though his supporters remained vocal and effective in frustrating the government (see letter 397). He spent four years enjoying Parisian society and European travel, until in 1768 – short of funds, a recurrent problem – he returned to London and surrendered himself to the court. He was then sentenced to two

years' imprisonment, one for the libel of the *North Briton*, and
another for his *Essay on Woman*, an obscene parody of Pope's *Essay
on Man*.

From the King's Bench prison he orchestrated his repeated elections as M.P. for the county of Middlesex, while the Commons
repeatedly expelled him. When Grafton's government was able to
procure its own candidate, Colonel Luttrell, Wilkes defeated him
by almost four votes to one, but was declared incapable of election
by the Commons. Letters 292 to 299 tell that story. Wilkes subsequently diverted his attention to the politics of the City of
London, becoming an alderman and then Lord Mayor in 1774, also
re-entering the Commons in that year. What the letters selected do
not record is his efficiency as an administrator in the City, his role
in breaking down the old veto on reporting Parliamentary debates,
and his transition towards political respectability, becoming a government supporter under the younger Pitt in 1784. Nor do they
record that in addition to the philandering for which he was famous,
he was a classicist, a bibliophile, a devoted father, and thoroughly
engaging company – as famously discovered in 1776 by Samuel Johnson, who was seduced by his charm at dinner, despite holding his
politics in as much contempt as his morals. His old foe Lord Mansfield, the Lord Chief Justice, commented in 1783 that "Mr. Wilkes
was the pleasantest companion, the politest gentleman, and the best
scholar he knew".[1]

Twenty-nine letters in this section are concerned with the American War of Independence. As early as 1770 Walpole was writing of
unrest in Boston (letter 300) and speculating perceptively on the
future of the American colonies. They had resented attempts at
taxation by previous governments, but Lord North had persisted in
the policy and his duty on the import of tea provoked the Boston
Tea Party in 1774 (letter 301). Before long war had broken out and
General Gage was defeated by the Americans at Lexington on
19 April 1775. From the beginning Walpole's sympathies were with
the colonists, commenting in letter 303 that "Our conduct has been
that of pert children: we have thrown a pebble at a mastiff, and are
surprised it was not frightened." Letter 306 mentions the Congress's

1 *Letters from the Year 1774 to the Year 1796 of John Wilkes, Esq. addressed to his Daughter*
(London, 1804), volume 1, p. 163.

appointment of General Washington, "allowed a very able officer, who distinguished himself in the last war". One British humiliation followed another. In letter 309 Walpole was able to report a rare victory in the battle of Long Island, but this was followed by Burgoyne's defeat at Saratoga, failed negotiations, the entry of France and Spain into the war, and further threats of invasion. Cornwallis's success at Camden (1780) was not repeated, and he was forced to surrender at Yorktown the following year (letters 310 to 323). As a coda, there is Admiral Rodney's defeat of the French in the battle of the Saintes and General Eliott's relief of Gibraltar after a three-year siege. At last Walpole was able to write on 2 December 1782, "Peace came this morning: thank God!" and express his relief that "the effusion of human gore is stopped, nor are there to be more widows and orphans out of the common course of things" (letter 328). The flow of sympathy for the war's nameless victims is as characteristic of him as the pragmatic qualifying aside of the concluding phrase. The independence of the United States was formally recognised by the belligerents the following September in the Treaty of Paris. Walpole wryly notes the return of French visitors to England, and that "they overflow even upon me, and visit Strawberry as one of our sights" (letter 329).

Britain's problems were not restricted to the colonies. A modest Catholic Relief Act passed in 1778 met with an extraordinary backlash stirred up by the "lunatic apostle" Lord George Gordon, President of the Protestant Association. Parliament was swamped with petitions from the counties, and on 2 June 1780 Gordon led a crowd estimated at 60,000 from St. George's Fields, Southwark to present the Association's London petition to the House of Commons. M.P.s and peers were jostled in the lobby before the Guards dispersed the crowd – who then proceeded to wreck the Bavarian and Sardinian ministers' chapels. Walpole provides two accounts of the events of that day, one to Lady Ossory and a more extended version for Sir Horace Mann, and letters 332 and 333 can be compared to show him reworking and adjusting his material.

Over the next six nights the mob went on the rampage through London destroying Catholic property and setting fire to the houses of those they thought were prominent opponents, including Lord Mansfield (who was known to have repeatedly acquitted Catholic priests accused of saying mass), and M.P.s such as Sir George Savile who had introduced the Relief Act. Newgate prison, the King's Bench and part of the Fleet prison were all burnt before the troops were eventually called with the encouragement of George III. According to the government, some 285 people were killed. Gordon (who had taken no part in the riots) was arrested, and peace was restored. Walpole's curiosity overcame him, and on 7 June he went to London to see the disturbances he would describe to his correspondents, writing rather disingenuously:

I could not bear to sit here [at Strawberry Hill] in shameful selfish philosophy, and hear the million of reports, and know almost all I loved in danger, without sharing it. I went to town on Wednesday, and though the night was the most horrible I ever beheld, I would not take millions not to have been present. (letter 334)

The same letter records that in spite of the dangers he drove around the streets in his coach until two in the morning to observe the tumult, and sent his printer and secretary Kirgate out on to the streets at night for intelligence.

The last eight letters in this section deal with India: Sir Eyre Coote's capture of Pondicherry from the French in 1761; the return to London in 1767 of Lord Clive, victor of Plassey and architect of British imperial expansion in India; the attacks upon him in Parliament, and his acquittal and death, probably by his own hand. Walpole then records the early stages of what would become in 1787 a formal impeachment of Warren Hastings, first Governor-General of India. He deplored British exploitation of India by "that nest of monsters" the East India Company (letter 34), and the greed and corruption of its officers. He correctly forecast that "Mr. Hastings will be honourably acquitted" (though not until 1795) but his own view "is formed more summarily: innocence does not pave its way with diamonds" (letter 341). He was shocked by the human consequences of Company monopolies, announcing to Mann in letter 338, "Oh! my dear sir, we have outdone the Spaniards in Peru! They were at least butchers on a religious principle, however diabolical their zeal. We have murdered, deposed, plundered, usurped" – the result of the Company's greed being three million deaths in the Great Famine in Bengal (1770–72).

1. WILKES AND "THE NORTH BRITON"

292. "The North Briton."

TO SIR HORACE MANN

Arlington Street, 17 November 1763.

The campaign is opened, hostilities begun, and blood shed. Now you think, my dear Sir, that all this is metaphor, and mere eloquence. You are mistaken: our diets, like that approaching in Poland, use other weapons than the tongue; ay, in good truth, and they who use the tongue too, and who perhaps you are under the common error of thinking would not fight, have signalised their prowess. But stay, I will tell you my story more methodically; perhaps you shall not know for these two pages what member of the British Senate, of that august divan whose wisdom influences the councils of all Europe, as its incorrupt virtue recalls to mind the purest ages of Rome, was shot in a duel yesterday in Hyde-Park. The Parliament met on Tuesday. We – for you know I have the honour of being a senator – sat till two in the morning; and had it not been that there is always more oratory, more good sense, more knowledge, and more sound reasoning in the House of Commons, than in the rest of the universe put together, the House of Lords only excepted, I should have thought it as tedious, dull, and unentertaining a debate as ever I heard in my days. The business was a complaint made by one King George of a certain paper called "the North Briton," No. 45, which the said King asserted was written by a much more famous man called Mr. Wilkes. – Well! and so you imagine that Mr. Wilkes and King George went from the House of Commons and fought out their quarrel in Hyde-Park? And which do you guess was killed? Again you are mistaken. Mr. Wilkes, with all the impartiality in the world, and with the phlegm of an Areopagite, sat and heard the whole matter discussed, and now and then put in a word, as if the affair did not concern *him*. The House of Commons, who would be wisdom itself, if they could but all agree on which side of a question wisdom lies, and who are sometimes forced to divide in order to find this out, did divide twice on this affair. The first time, one hundred and eleven, of which I had the misfortune to be one, had more curiosity to hear Mr. Wilkes's story than King George's; but three hundred being of the contrary opinion, it was plain they were in the right, especially as they had

no *private* motives to guide them. Again, the individual one hun-
dred-and-eleven could not see that "the North Briton" tended to
foment treasonable insurrections though we had it argumentatively
demonstrated to us for seven hours together: but the moment we
heard two hundred and seventy-five gentlemen counted, it grew as
plain to us as a pike-staff, for a syllogism carries less conviction than
a superior number, though that number does not use the least force
upon earth, but only walk peaceably out of the house and into it
again. The next day we were to be in the same *numerical* way convinced that we ought to be but one hundred and ten, for that we
ought to expel Mr. Wilkes out of the house: and the majority were
to prove to us (for we are slow of comprehension, and imbibe
instruction very deliberately) that in order to have all London
acquainted with the person and features of Mr. Wilkes, it would be
necessary to set him on a high place called the pillory, where everybody might see him at leisure. Some were even almost ready to think
that, being a very ugly man, he would look better without his ears;
and poor Sir William Stanhope, who endeavoured all day by the
help of a trumpet to listen to these wise debates and found it to no
purpose, said, "If they want a pair of ears they may take mine, for
I am sure they are of no use to me." The regularity, however, of these
systematic proceedings has been a little interrupted. One Mr. Martin,[1] who has much the same quarrel with Mr. Wilkes as King
George, and who chose to suspend his resentment like his Majesty,
till with proper dignity he could notify his wrath to Parliament, did
express his indignation with rather less temper than the King had
done, calling Mr. Wilkes to his face *cowardly scoundrel*, which you,
who represent monarchs, know, is not royal language. Mr. Wilkes,
who, it seems, whatever may have been thought, had rather die com-
pendiously than piecemeal, inquired of Mr. Martin by letter next
morning, if he, Mr. Wilkes, was meant by him, Mr. Martin, under
the periphrasis *cowardly scoundrel*. Mr. Martin replied in the affirmative, and accompanied his answer with a challenge. They immediately went into Hyde-Park; and, at the second fire, Mr. Wilkes

1 Samuel Martin, a West Indian, secretary to the Treasury, when Lord Bute was
First Lord, and treasurer to the Princess Dowager of Wales. – WALPOLE. The Yale
editors state that Martin was said to have been offended by earlier issues of the *North
Briton*; no. 40 had described him as "the most treacherous, base, selfish, mean, abject,
low-lived and dirty fellow, that ever wriggled himself into a Secretaryship".

received a bullet in his body. Don't be frightened, the wound was not mortal – at least it was not yesterday. Being corporally delirious to-day, as he has been mentally some time, I cannot tell what to say to it. However the breed will not be lost, if he should die. You have still countrymen enough left; we need not despair of amusement. . . . Adieu!

293. *Riots for Wilkes.*

TO THE EARL OF HERTFORD

Friday, 9 December 1763.

. . . Well! but we have had a prodigious riot: are not you impatient to know the particulars? It was so prodigious a tumult, that I verily thought half the administration would have run away to Harrowgate.[1] "The North Briton" was ordered to be burned by the hangman at Cheapside, on Saturday last. The mob rose; the greatest mob, says Mr. Sheriff Blunt, that he has known in forty years. They were armed with that most bloody instrument, the mud out of the kennels: they hissed in the most murderous manner; broke Mr. Sheriff Harley's coach-glass in the most frangent manner; scratched his forehead, so that he is forced to wear a little patch in the most becoming manner; and obliged the hangman to burn the paper with a link, though fagots were prepared to execute it in a more solemn manner. Numbers of gentlemen, from windows and balconies, encouraged the mob, who, in about an hour and half, were so undutiful to the ministry, as to retire without doing any mischief, or giving Mr. Carteret Webb[2] the opportunity of a single information, except against an ignorant lad, who had been in town but ten days.

This terrible uproar has employed us four days. The Sheriffs were called before your House on Monday, and made their narrative. My brother Cholmondeley,[3] in the most pathetic manner, and suitably to the occasion, recommended it to your lordships, to search for precedents of what he believed never happened since the world began.

1 Lord Bute had retired to Harrogate.
2 Philip Carteret Webb (?1700–70), politician, antiquary, Solicitor to the Treasury, and a leading figure in the prosecution of Wilkes.
3 George Cholmondeley (1703–70), 3rd Earl of Cholmondeley, who had been the husband of Walpole's elder sister Mary (1705–31).

Lord Egmont, who knows of a plot, which he keeps to himself, though it has been carrying on these twenty years, thought more vigorous measures ought to be taken on such a crisis, and moved to summon the mistress of the Union Coffee-house. The Duke of Bedford thought all this but piddling, and at once attacked Lord Mayor, Common Council, and charter of the City, whom, if he had been supported, I believe he would have ordered to be all burned by the hangman next Saturday. Unfortunately for such national justice, Lord Mansfield, who delights in every opportunity of exposing and mortifying the Duke of Bedford, and Sandwich, interposed for the magistracy of London, and, after much squabbling, saved them from immediate execution. The Duke of Grafton, with infinite shrewdness and coolness, drew from the witnesses that the whole mob was of one mind; and the day ended in a vote of general censure on the rioters. This was communicated to us at a conference, and yesterday we acted the same farce; when Rigby trying to revive the imputation on the Lord Mayor, &c. (who, by the by, *did* sit most tranquilly at Guildhall during the whole tumult), the ministry disavowed and abandoned him to a man, vindicating the magistracy, and plainly discovering their own fear and awe of the City, who feel the insult, and will from hence feel their own strength. ...

294. *Wilkes again in England.*

TO SIR HORACE MANN

Arlington Street, Friday, 1 April 1768, addition to letter begun 31 March.

I was interrupted yesterday. The ghost is laid for a time in a red sea of port and claret. The spectre is the famous Wilkes. He appeared the moment the Parliament was dissolved. The Ministry despised him. He stood for the City of London, and was the last on the poll of seven candidates, none but the mob, and most of them without votes, favouring him. He then offered himself to the county of Middlesex. The election came on last Monday. By five in the morning a very large body of Weavers, &c., took possession of Piccadilly, and the roads and turnpikes leading to Brentford, and would suffer nobody to pass without blue cockades, and papers inscribed "*No. 45, Wilkes and Liberty.*" They tore to pieces the coaches of Sir W. Beauchamp Proctor, and Mr. Cooke, the other candidates, though the latter was not there, but in bed with the gout, and it was with difficulty that Sir William and Mr. Cooke's cousin got to Brentford. There, however, lest it should be declared a void election, Wilkes had the sense to keep everything quiet. But, about five, Wilkes, being considerably a-head of the other two, his mob returned to town and behaved outrageously. They stopped every carriage, scratched and spoilt several with writing all over them "No. 45," pelted, threw dirt and stones, and forced everybody to huzza for Wilkes. I did but cross Piccadilly at eight, in my coach with a French Monsieur d'Angeul, whom I was carrying to Lady Hertford's; they stopped us, and bid us huzza. I desired him to let down the glass on his side, but, as he was not alert, they broke it to shatters. At night they insisted, in several streets, on houses being illuminated, and several Scotch refusing, had their windows broken. Another mob rose in the City, and Harley, the present Mayor, being another Sir William Walworth,[1] and having acted formerly and now with great spirit against Wilkes, and the Mansion House not being illuminated, and he out of town, they broke every window, and tried to force their way into the House. The Trained Bands were sent for, but did not suffice. At last a party of guards, from the Tower, and some lights erected, dispersed the tumult. At one in the morning a riot began before Lord Bute's house, in Audley Street, though illuminated. They flung two large flints into Lady Bute's chamber, who was in bed, and broke every window in the house. Next morning, Wilkes and Cooke were returned members. The day was very quiet, but at night they rose again, and obliged almost every house in town to be lighted up, even the Duke of Cumberland's and Princess Amelia's. About one o'clock they marched to the Duchess of Hamilton's in Argyle Buildings (Lord Lorn[2] being in Scotland). She was obstinate, and would not illuminate, though with child, and, as they hope, of an heir to the family, and with the Duke, her son,[3] and the rest of her children in the house. There is a small court and parapet wall before the house: they brought iron crows, tore down the gates,

---

1 Sir William Walworth (d. c. 1386), the Lord Mayor of London who during the Peasants' Revolt of 1381 had confronted the mob and killed their leader, Wat Tyler.
2 John Campbell, Lord Lorn, eldest son of John, Duke of Argyll, and second husband of the celebrated beauty, Elizabeth Gunning, Duchess-Dowager of Hamilton. – WALPOLE.
3 Duke of Hamilton, her son by her first husband. – WALPOLE.

pulled up the pavement, and battered the house for three hours. They could not find the key of the back door, nor send for any assistance. The night before, they had obliged the Duke and Duchess of Northumberland to give them beer, and appear at the windows, and drink "Wilkes's health." They stopped and opened the coach of Count Seilern, the Austrian ambassador, who has made a formal complaint, on which the Council met on Wednesday night, and were going to issue a Proclamation, but, hearing that all was quiet, and that only a few houses were illuminated in Leicester Fields from the terror of the inhabitants, a few constables were sent with orders to extinguish the lights, and not the smallest disorder has happened since. In short, it has ended like other election riots, and with not a quarter of the mischief that has been done in some other towns.

There are, however, difficulties to come. Wilkes has notified that he intends to surrender himself to his outlawry, the beginning of next term, which comes on the 17th of this month. There is said to be a flaw in the proceedings, in which case his election will be good, though the King's Bench may fine or imprison him on his former sentence. In my own opinion, the House of Commons is the place where he can do the least hurt, for he is a wretched speaker, and will sink to contempt, like Admiral Vernon, who I remember just such an illuminated hero, with two birthdays in one year.[1] You will say, he can write better than Vernon – true; and therefore his case is more desperate. Besides, Vernon was rich: Wilkes is undone; and, though he has had great support, his patrons will be sick of maintaining him. He must either sink to poverty and a jail, or commit new excesses, for which he will get knocked on the head. The Scotch are his implacable enemies to a man. A Rienzi[2] cannot stop: their histories are summed up in two words – a triumph and an assassination. . . . Adieu!

1 The Yale editors note that uncertainty about the date of Admiral Vernon's birthday led to London being illuminated for two nights running in November 1740 to celebrate his victory at Porto Bello. Vernon had been an opponent of Sir Robert Walpole's ministry, hence Walpole's criticism of him.
2 Nicolo Rienzi, a famous demagogue at Rome. – WALPOLE.

295. *Rioting.*

TO SIR HORACE MANN

Arlington Street, Thursday, 12 May 1768.

You sit very much at your ease, my dear Sir, demanding Ribands[1] and settling the conveyance. We are a little more gravely employed. We are glad if we can keep our windows whole, or pass and repass unmolested. I call it reading history as one goes along the streets. Now we have a chapter of Clodius – now an episode of Prynne,[2] and so on. I do not love to think what the second volume must be of a flourishing nation running riot. You have my text; now for the application.

Wilkes, on the 27th of last month, was committed to the King's Bench. The mob would not suffer him to be carried thither, but took off the horses of his hackney-coach and drew him through the City to Cornhill. He there persuaded them to disperse, and then stole to the prison and surrendered himself. Last Saturday his cause was to be heard, but his Counsel pleading against the validity of the outlawry, Lord Mansfield took time to consider, and adjourned the hearing till the beginning of next term, which is in June.

The day before yesterday the Parliament met. There have been constant crowds and mobbing at the prison, but, on Tuesday, they insisted on taking Wilkes out of prison and carrying him to Parliament. The tumult increased so fast, that the Riot Act was read, the soldiers fired, and a young man was shot. The mob bore the body about the streets to excite more rage, and at night it went so far that four or five more persons were killed; and the uproar quashed, though they fired on the soldiers from the windows of houses. The partisans of Wilkes say the young man was running away, was pursued and killed; and the jury have brought it in wilful murder against the officer and men: so they must take their trials; and it makes their case very hard, and lays the Government under great difficulties. On the other side, the young man is said to have been very riotous, and marked as such by the Guards. But this is not all. We have

1 Mann's ambition to be granted the Order of the Bath, which was realised later in 1768.
2 Clodius, Roman demagogue, and William Prynne (1600–69), Puritan pamphleteer convicted of seditious libel.

independent mobs, that have nothing to do with Wilkes, and who only take advantage of so favourable a season. The dearness of provisions incites, the hope of increase of wages allures, and drink puts them in motion. The coal-heavers began, and it is well it is not a hard frost, for they have stopped all coals coming to Town. The sawyers rose too, and at last the sailors, who have committed great outrages in merchant ships, and prevented them from sailing. I just touch the heads, which would make a great figure if dilated in Baker's Chronicle[1] among the calamities at the end of a reign. The last mob, however, took an extraordinary turn; for many thousand sailors came to petition the Parliament yesterday, but in the most respectful and peaceable manner; desired only to have their grievances examined; if reasonable, redressed; if not reasonable, they would be satisfied. Being told that their flags and colours, with which they paraded, were illegal, they cast them away. Nor was this all: they declared for the King and Parliament, and beat and drove away Wilkes's mob. . . .

I wish with all my heart I may have no more to tell you of riots; not that I ever think them very serious things, but just to the persons on whom the storm bursts. But I pity poor creatures who are deluded to their fate, and fall by Gin or Faction, when they have not a real grievance to complain of, but what depends on the elements, or causes past remedy. I cannot bear to have the name of Liberty profaned to the destruction of the cause; for frantic tumults only lead to that terrible corrective, Arbitrary Power, – which cowards call out for as protection, and knaves are so ready to grant. . . .

296. *Wilkes's Trial.*

TO SIR HORACE MANN

Strawberry Hill, 9 June 1768.

. . . Yesterday was fixed for the appearance of Wilkes in Westminster Hall. The Judges went down by nine in the morning, but the mob had done breakfast still sooner, and was there before them; and as Judges stuffed out with dignity and lamb-skins are not absolute sprites, they had much ado to glide through the crowd. Wilkes's

---

1 Sir Richard Baker's *Chronicle of the Kings of England* (1643).

counsel argued against the outlawry, and then Lord Mansfield, in a speech of an hour and a half, set it aside; not on *their* reasons, but on grounds which he had discovered in it himself. I think they say it was on some flaw in the Christian name of the county, which should not have been *Middlesex to wit*, – but I protest I don't know, for I am here alone, and picked up my intelligence as I walked in our meadows by the river. You, who may be walking by the Arno, will, perhaps, think there was some timidity in this; but the depths of the Law are wonderful! So pray don't make any rash conclusions, but stay till you get better information.

Well! now he is gone to prison again, – I mean Wilkes; and on Tuesday he is to return to receive sentence on the old guilt of writing, as the Scotch[1] would *not* call it, *the* 45, though they call the rebellion so. The sentence may be imprisonment, fine, or pillory; but as I am still near the Thames, I do not think the latter will be chosen. Oh! but stay, he may plead against the indictment, and should there be an improper *Middlesex to wit* in that too, why then in that case, you know, he did *not* write *the* 45, and then he is as white as milk, and as free as air, and as good a member of Parliament as if he had never been expelled. In short, my dear Sir, I am trying to explain to you what I literally do not understand; all I do know is, that Mr. Cooke, the other member for Middlesex, is just dead, and that we are going to have another Middlesex election, which is very unpleasant to me, who hate mobs so near as Brentford. Serjeant Glynn,[2] Wilkes's counsel, is the candidate, and I suppose the only one in the present humour of the people, who will care to have his brains dashed out, in order to sit in Parliament. In truth, this enthusiasm is confined to the very mob or little higher, and does not extend beyond the County. All other riots are ceased, except the little civil war between the sailors and coal-heavers, in which two or three lives are lost every week. . . . Adieu! my dear Sir.

---

[1] The Scotch called the rebellion in 1715 "*the* 15," and that in 1745, "*the* 45." – WALPOLE.
[2] Glynn was duly elected for Middlesex.

297. His Expulsion from Parliament.

TO SIR HORACE MANN

Arlington Street, 6 February 1769.

I was not mistaken in announcing to you the approaching expulsion of Wilkes. It passed on Friday night, or rather at three on Saturday morning, by a majority of 219 against 137, after four days of such fatigue and long sittings as never were known together. His behaviour, in every respect but confidence, was so poor, that it confirmed what I have long thought, that he would lose himself sooner in the House of Commons than he can be crushed anywhere else. He has so little quickness or talent for public speaking, that he would not be heard with patience. Now he has all the *éclat* that sufferings, boldness, or his writings can give him – not that I think the latter have other merit than being calculated for the mob and the moment. He stands again for Middlesex, to be again expelled; yet nobody dares oppose him; and he is as sure of recommending his successor. Still there are people so wild and blind, as not to see that every triumph against him is followed by mortification and disgrace. In this country every violence turns back upon its authors. My father, who governed for the longest time, and Mr. Pelham, who enjoyed the quietest administration, always leaned to lenient measures. They who think themselves wiser, have not met with equal success. As worthless a fellow as Wilkes is, the rigours exercised towards him have raised a spirit that will require still wiser heads to allay. Men have again turned seriously to the study of those controversies that agitated this country an hundred years ago; and instead of dipping in Roman and Greek histories for flowers to decorate the speeches of false patriotism, principles are revived that have taken deeper root; and I hope we may not see quarrels of a graver complexion than the dirty squabbles for places and profit. Persecution for politics has just the same issue as for religion; it spreads the oppressed doctrine; and though I think Wilkes as bad a man as if he were a *saint*, he will every day get disciples who will profit of his martyrdom. Thank God, that he has not turned methodist!

298. *Riots Continued.*

Arlington Street, 23 March 1769.

More tempests! Pray, Mr. Minister, keep up your dignity as well as you can; for I doubt that you will be a little laughed at. You are not now representing the conquerors of East and West. Your crest is fallen! Our campaigns do not extend beyond the confines of Middlesex. We will begin with the *third* election at Brentford. One Dingley was sent to oppose Wilkes, but took panic and ran away, and nobody would propose him. The next day he advertised that he had gone thither with all the resolution in the world, provided there had been no danger, and so Wilkes was chosen once more. The House again rejected him; but, lest the country should complain of not being represented, another writ is issued; the Court is to set up somebody, and a new egg is laid for riots and clamours.

Oh! but this is not all. As one or two towns had sent instructions to their members, it was thought wise to procure loyal addresses, and one was obtained from Essex, which, being the great county for calves, produced nothing but ridicule. I foresaw, and said from the first moment, that there could not be a sillier step taken, as it would sow division in every county and great town in England, by splitting the inhabitants into instructors and addressors. Well! the aforesaid Mr. Dingley got an assembly of merchants, and carried an address ready drawn. It produced opposition and hubbub, and Mr. Dingley struck a lawyer in the face and beat out one of his teeth. The man knocked him down, drubbed him, and put him in the Crown Office.[1]

This scheme defeated, an address was left at a public office to be signed by all who pleased, and yesterday was fixed for it to be presented at St. James's by six hundred merchants and others. This imposing cavalcade no sooner set forth than they were hissed and pelted; and when they came to Temple-bar they found an immense mob, who had shut the gates against them, and they were forced to make their escape by any streets and by-lanes that were not occupied. Not a third part reached St. James's, and they were overtaken by a prodigious concourse, attending a hearse drawn by four horses. On

1 That is, liable to criminal prosecution.

one side of the hearse hung a large escutcheon, representing the chairman at Brentford killing Clarke; on the other, the Guards firing on the mob in St. George's Fields and shooting Allen,[1] with streams of blood running down. This procession drove to St. James's Gate, where grenadiers were fixed to prevent their entrance, and the gates towards the park shut. Here the King, Ministers, and Foreign Ministers were besieged till past four, though the Riot-Act was read, and Lord Talbot[2] came down, and seized one man, while the mob broke the steward's wand in his hand. It was near five before they could recover and present the address, which the mob had tried to seize; they had so bepelted the chairman of the committee of merchants, that he was not fit to appear. The Dukes of Northumberland and Kingston were as ill treated. The latter, coming from Bedford House, had been taken for the Duke of Bedford, and had his new wedding-coach, favours, and liveries covered with mud. Fifteen men are taken up, but I don't find that anything can be proved against them. In short, never was a more disgraceful scene! Don't wonder if *I* smile, who have seen more formidable mobs; and something of a better head opposed to them. Many cry out "Shame!" – but half, that cry out, I remember encouraging mobs, and for much worse ends than these poor infatuated people have in view. The Minister[3] of those days would not have seen such a procession arrive in St. James's without having had intelligence of it, nor without being prepared for it. Those great and able persons, the Bedford faction, have conjured up this storm, and now are frightened out of their wits at it. All is perfectly quiet to-day, and the King has been at the House to pass the Bill for the Duke of Grafton's divorce.[4] Luckily, Newmarket begins on Monday, during which holy season there is always a suspension of arms. . . .

1 Allen was the young man killed in the riots of 10 May, as described in letter 295.
2 William, first earl Talbot, lord steward. – WALPOLE.
3 Sir Robert Walpole. – WALPOLE.
4 The Duke of Grafton (for whom see letter 211, p. 299, n. 3), was divorced from his wife Anne, *née* Liddell, Walpole's correspondent, who immediately married John Fitzpatrick, 2nd Earl of Upper Ossory.

299. Colonel Luttrell, M.P.

TO SIR HORACE MANN

Arlington Street, 14 April 1769.

Yesterday, the day of expectation, is over: I mean the election at Brentford, for I must recollect that you have not been thinking of nothing else for a fortnight, as we have. It ended bloodless, both sides having agreed to keep the peace; chance ratified that compromise. Take notice, I engage no farther than for what is past. Wilkes triumphed, as usual, having a majority of between eight and nine hundred. The Court-candidate,[1] who had offered himself for the service, and who was as imprudently accepted, gave no proofs of the determined valour that he had promised. His friends exerted themselves as little; and though he was to have been conveyed by a squadron of many gentlemen, his troop did not muster above twenty, assembled in his father's garden, broke down the wall that they might steal a march, and yet were repulsed at Hyde Park Corner, where the Commander lost his hat, and in self-defence rode over a foot-passenger. He polled under three hundred, and owed his safety to Wilkes's friends. This defeat the House of Commons are at this moment repairing – I believe I may add, by widening the breach; for, as they intend to reject Wilkes and accept Luttrell, they will probably make the county quite mad. In short, they have done nothing but flounder from one blunder into another, and, by an impartial mixture of rashness and timidity, have brought matters to a pass, which I fear will require at last very sharp methods to decide one way or other. We have no heads but wrong ones; and wrong heads on both sides have not the happy attribute of two negatives in making an affirmative. Instead of annihilating Wilkes by buying or neglecting him, his enemies have pushed the Court on a series of measures which have made him excessively important; and now every step they take must serve to increase his faction, and make themselves more unpopular. The clouds all around them are many and big, and will burst as fast as they try violent methods. I tremble at the prospect, and suffer to see the abyss into which we are falling, and the height from whence we have fallen! We were tired of being in a situation to give the law to Europe, and now cannot give it with

1 Colonel Luttrell, eldest son of Lord Irnham. – WALPOLE.

safety to the mob – for giving it, when they are not disposed to receive it, is of all experiments the most dangerous; and whatever may be the consequence in the end, seldom fails to fall on the heads of those who undertake it. I have said it to you more than once; it is amazing to me that men do not prefer the safe, amiable and honourable method of governing the people as they like to be governed, to the invidious and restless task of governing them contrary to their inclinations. If princes or ministers considered, that despair makes men fearless, instead of making them cowards, surely they would abandon such fruitless policy. It requires ages of oppression, barbarism and ignorance, to sink mankind into pusillanimous submission; and it requires a climate too that softens and enervates. I do not think we are going to try the experiment; but as I am sorry the people give provocation, so I am grieved to see that provocation too warmly resented, because men forget from whence they set out, and mutual injuries beget new principles, and open to wider views than either party had at first any notion of. Charles I. would have been more despotic, if he had defeated the republicans, than he would have dreamed of being before the civil war; and Colonel Cromwell certainly never thought of becoming Protector, when he raised his regiment. The King lost his head, and the Colonel his rest; and we were so fortunate, after a deluge of blood, as to relapse into a little better condition than we had been before the contest; but if the son of either had been an active rogue, we might have lost our liberties for some time, and not recovered them without a much longer struggle. . . .

2. THE AMERICAN WAR OF INDEPENDENCE

300. *Vision of a Future America.*

TO SIR HORACE MANN

Strawberry Hill, 6 May 1770.

I don't know whether Wilkes is subdued by his imprisonment, or waits for the rising of Parliament, to take the field; or whether his dignity of Alderman has dulled him into prudence, and the love of feasting; but hitherto he has done nothing but go to City-banquets and sermons, and sit at Guildhall as a sober magistrate. With an inversion of the proverb, "Si ex quovis Mercurio fit lignum!"[1] What do you Italians think of Harlequin Podestà?[2] In truth, his party is crumbled away strangely. Lord Chatham has talked on the Middlesex election till nobody will answer him; and Mr. Burke (Lord Rockingham's governor) has published a pamphlet[3] that has sown the utmost discord between that faction and the supporters of the Bill of Rights. Mrs. Macaulay[4] has written against it. In Parliament their numbers are shrunk to nothing, and the session is ending very triumphantly for the Court. But there is another scene opened of a very different aspect. You have seen the accounts from Boston.[5] The tocsin seems to be sounded to America. I have many visions about that country, and fancy I see twenty empires and republics forming upon vast scales over all that continent, which is growing too mighty to be kept in subjection to half a dozen exhausted nations in Europe. As the latter sinks, and the others rise, they who live between the eras will be a sort of Noahs, witnesses to the period of the old world and origin of the new. I entertain myself with the idea of a future senate in Carolina and Virginia, where their future patriots will harangue on the austere and incorruptible virtue of the ancient English! will tell their auditors of our disinterestedness and scorn of bribes and pensions, and make us blush in our graves at their ridiculous panegyrics. Who knows but even our Indian usurpations and villanies may become topics of praise to American schoolboys? As I believe our virtues are extremely like those of our predecessors the Romans, so I am sure our luxury and extravagance are too.

What do you think of a winter-Ranelagh[6] erecting in Oxford Road, at the expense of sixty thousand pounds? The new bank, including the value of the ground, and of the houses demolished to make room for it, will cost three hundred thousand; and erected, as my Lady Townley says, *by sober citizens too!* I have touched before to you on the incredible profusion of our young men of fashion. I know a younger brother who literally gives a flower-woman half a guinea

1 The Yale editors note that Walpole has adjusted the proverb to read "If from every Mercury a block of wood can be made".
2 Podestà (magistrate).
3 Burke's *Thoughts on the Cause of the Present Discontents* (1770).
4 Catherine Macaulay (1731–91), historian and political polemicist.
5 The Boston Massacre, in which five civilians were killed by British troops, had occurred two months previously.
6 The Pantheon. – WALPOLE. See letter 67, p. 104, n. 1.

every morning for a bunch of roses for the nosegay in his button-
hole. . . .

301. *The Boston Tea-party.*

TO SIR HORACE MANN

2 February 1774.

. . . We have no news public or private; but there is an ostrich-
egg laid in America, where the Bostonians have canted three hundred chests of tea into the ocean, for they will not drink tea with our
Parliament.[1] My understanding is so narrow, and was confined so
long to the little meridian of England, that at this late hour of life it
cannot extend itself to such huge objects as East and West Indies,
though everybody else is acquainted with those continents as well as
with the map of Great Britain. Lord Chatham talked of conquering
America in Germany;[2] I believe England will be conquered some
day or other in New England or Bengal. I think I have heard of such
a form in law, as such an one of the parish of St. Martin's-in-the-
Fields in Asia: St. Martin's parish literally reaches now to the other
end of the globe,[3] and we may be undone a twelve-month before we
hear a word of the matter – which is not convenient, and a little
drawback on being masters of dominions a thousand times bigger
than ourselves. Well! I suppose, some time or other, some learned
Jesuit Needham[4] will find out that Indostan was peopled by a colony
from Cripplegate or St. Mary Axe, which will compensate for a
thousand misfortunes.

You see, my dear Sir, I forget my troubles the moment they are
at an end. Lady Orford concerns me no more than the insurrection
in the Massachusetts. Every year's events are stale by the next. One's
cares, once at an end, are but old accidents, and to be flung by, like
an old almanac. Politicians live by the future; I care only about

1 The Boston Tea Party of 16 December 1773.
2 Chatham was speaking of military victories over the French in Germany damaging
French interests in America.
3 The Yale editors refer to a recent law case in which actions abroad were deemed
to have taken place in England, a legal fiction making them subject to the jurisdiction
of the English courts.
4 The Rev. John Turberville Needham (1713–81) was a naturalist and the first English
Catholic priest to be elected to the Royal Society. He was not, however, a Jesuit.

the present; and the present being very calm, is worth enjoying. Adieu!

302. *Gage's Defeat.*

TO THE REV. WILLIAM MASON

Arlington Street, 12 June 1775.

... By the waters of Babylon we sit down and weep, when we think of thee, O America! Tribulation on Tribulation! Since Gage's defeat,[1] eighteen, some say twenty-eight thousand men have invested Boston; ten thousand more are on their march from Rhode Island. Two ships laden with provisions for him have been destroyed at New York, and all his Majesty's friends turned out thence. *Nous ne scavons plus à quel Saint nous vouer.* The City says there must be a pacification and a change of actors. Much good may it do those who will read their parts! Old *Garrick*[2] perhaps will return to the stage, because he has no time to lose: – however, the manager's company talks of a troop of Hessians, &c. ... Adieu!

303. *Determination of America.*

TO THE HON. H. S. CONWAY

Arlington Street, 15 December 1774.

... The long-expected sloop is arrived at last, and is, indeed, a *man of war!* The General Congress[3] have voted, a non-importation, a non-exportation, a non-consumption; that, in case of hostilities committed by the troops at Boston, the several provinces will march to the assistance of their countrymen; that the cargoes of ships now at sea shall be sold on their arrival, and the money arising thence given to the poor at Boston; that a letter, in the nature of a petition of rights, shall be sent to the King; another to the House of *Commons;* a third to the people of England; a demand of repeal of all the Acts

---

1 The defeat of General Gage (1719/20–87), Governor of Massachusetts, at Lexington on 19 April.
2 Lord Chatham.
3 The sloop "St. Paul" brought news of the resolutions of the Congress that had met at Philadelphia between 5 September and 26 October.

of parliament affecting North America passed during this reign, as also of the Quebec bill: and these resolutions not to be altered till such repeal is obtained.

Well, I believe you do not regret being neither in parliament nor in administration! As you are an idle man, and have nothing else to do, you may sit down and tell one a remedy for all this. Perhaps you will give yourself airs, and say you was a prophet, and that prophets are not honoured in their own country. Yet, if you have any inspiration about you, I assure you it will be of great service – we are at our wit's end – which was no great journey. Oh! you conclude Lord Chatham's crutch will be supposed a wand, and be sent for. They might as well send for *my* crutch; and they should not have it; the stile is a little too high to help them over. His Lordship is a little fitter for raising a storm than laying one, and of late seems to have lost both virtues. The Americans at least have acted like men,[1] gone to the bottom at once, and set the whole upon the whole. Our conduct has been that of pert children: we have thrown a pebble at a mastiff, and are surprised it was not frightened. Now we must be worried by it, or must kill the guardian of the house, which will be plundered the moment little master has nothing but the old nurse to defend it. But I have done with reflections; you will be fuller of them than I.

304. *War Inevitable.*

TO THE COUNTESS OF UPPER OSSORY

21 January 1775, addition to letter begun 19 January.

Alas! the great event was addled, or came to little. I had been told that Lord Chatham was commissioned by Dr. Franklin to offer the King 350,000*l.* a-year from America, if the offensive bills were repealed. The Ministers thought he was to ask for an increase of force, so their intelligence was at last no better than mine! But, indeed, who could guess what he would do? He did appear, and did move to address for a recall of the troops from Boston, a very Pindaric transition from the first step towards a pacification to the last!

1 A view endorsed by Lord Chatham in a letter of 24 December to Stephen Sayre (*Chatham Correspondence* IV, p. 368).

In heroic poems it is a rule to begin in the middle, and great poets and great orators are very like in more instances than one. He was very hostile, and so was Lord Camden; but the generals being braver than the troops, some of the latter ran away, as Colonel Coventry and Cornet Grosvenor.[1] The numbers were 68 to 18. The Duke of Cumberland, who would have joined his regiment if it had been raised, to the vanquished, was among the slain;[2] but in truth the subject is a little too serious for joking. The war on America is determined on. Four regiments more are ordered thither, and every hostile measure is to be pursued. The wise measures of last year have already begotten a civil war. What that will beget,

> The child that is unborn will rue![3]

If Lord Chatham said true yesterday, the Ministers are already checkmated and have not a move to make. . . .

305. *Defeat at Lexington.*

TO THE COUNTESS OF UPPER OSSORY

Arlington Street, 7 July 1775.

It is strange to say, Madam, that I who generally know my own mind as soon as I have a mind, and who am a very methodical general, have not yet settled the plan of my operations for my summer campaign. One of my expeditions will certainly be to Ampthill; but I cannot precisely say when, as I have not fixed the day when my squadron is to sail for the coast of France, which is to be the great *coup* of my measures. I do not stay to join or to watch the Spanish Armada, nor wait for the result of the American Congress; but a little business of my own throws uncertainty into all my deliberations, and is so little a business, that, like greater men, I am forced to disguise the true cause, and give it dignity by a veil of mystery. I have indeed already taken the field, for I came yesterday from Lord Dacre's, in Essex, where I stayed but one night, and am returning to

---

1 Lords Coventry and Grosvenor, usually supporters of Lord Chatham, did not support him and Lord Camden in opposing involuntary taxation of America.
2 That is, voted with Lord Chatham's unsuccessful minority.
3 Adapted from a line in "The More Modern Ballad of Chevy-Chase", from volume 1 of Percy's *Reliques of Ancient English Poetry* (1765).

my head-quarters.[1] I found nobody and heard nothing here, but a new rebuff given us by the Americans – I will not tell you where, because geography is not my forte, nor circumstances my talent; but they have burnt a schooner, and driven General Gage's devils out of a herd of swine, who ran violently into the sea, and lo! is not the place called Hog Island to this day?[2] . . .

306. *Washington in Command.*

TO SIR HORACE MANN

Strawberry Hill, 3 August 1775.

In spite of all my modesty, I cannot help thinking I have a little something of the prophet about me. At least we have not conquered America yet. I did not send you immediate word of our victory at Boston, because the success not only seemed very equivocal, but because the conquerors lost three to one more than the vanquished. The last do not pique themselves upon modern good breeding, but level only at the officers, of whom they have slain a vast number. We are a little disappointed, indeed, at their fighting at all, which was not in our calculation. We knew we could conquer *America in Germany*,[3] and I doubt had better have gone thither now for that purpose, as it does not appear hitherto to be quite so feasible in America itself. However, we are determined to know the worst, and are sending away all the men and ammunition we can muster. The Congress, not asleep neither, have appointed a Generalissimo, Washington, allowed a very able officer, who distinguished himself in the last war. Well! we had better have gone on robbing the Indies: it was a more lucrative trade. . . .

1 Strawberry Hill. The "little business" referred to in the previous sentence was Walpole's projected trip to Paris, for which he left the following month.
2 An American action on 27 May 1775 to destroy the livestock used by General Gage's forces.
3 See letter 301, p. 424, n. 2.

307. *Public Indifference.*

Arlington Street, 17 April 1776.

... I now submit to recall my thoughts to America, for the sake of you Italians and little States, who do not know how superior fashion[1] is in a great nation to national interests. You need not be too impatient for events. The army, that was to overrun the Atlantic continent, is not half set out yet; but it will be time enough to go into winter-quarters. What we have heard lately thence is not very promising. The Congress, that was said to be squabbling, seems to act with harmony and spirit; and Quebec is not thought to be so safe as it was a month ago. However, that is the business of the Ministers; nobody else troubles his head about the matter. Few people knew much of America before; and now that all communication is cut off, and the Administration does not think itself bound to chant its own disappointments, or the praises of the enemy, we forget it as much as if Columbus had not routed it out of the ocean. ...

308. *Charleston.*

22 August 1776, addition to letter begun 20 August.

Since I wrote my letter, an account is come of the total failure of the expedition under General Clinton, Lord Cornwallis, and Sir Peter Parker, against Charleston. The troops landed on Long Island, and then could not act. The fleet attacked a fort, were repulsed, lost a man-of-war, with a captain, lieutenant, and two hundred men, and Sir Peter Parker they say is wounded in six places. They were, besides, forced to burn a store-ship. The provincials are confessed to have behaved remarkably well. This success will not discourage the rest. In what a chaos are we embarked!

---

1 Walpole had been describing the trial for bigamy of the Duchess of Kingston in the House of Lords (see letter 57, p. 92, n. 1).

309. *Victory at Brooklyn.*

TO SIR HORACE MANN

Strawberry Hill, 13 October 1776.

I need not tell you what a splendid Gazette[1] has already told. As I was here before the account arrived, and heard it but imperfectly, I could not write so soon as the first post would set out with the news. The provincials have certainly not behaved up to the haughtiness with which they rejected all overtures of peace. It is said they were outwitted, deceived by feints, and drawn into ambuscade. *That* does no honour to their Generals. Great consequences are expected from this victory. I am too ignorant of war, sieges, and America, to pretend to judge; and really have heard so much from both sides that has not proved true, and at the same time such pains are taken to keep people in the dark, that I have laid it down to myself to believe nothing but what is universally allowed. It is your duty to credit gazettes, and you cannot err while you stick to your Bible. The red Ribbon is to be sent to General Howe, who seems to have acted very sensibly.[2] . . .

I never saw your Duke with the barbarous name – Ostrogothia;[3] nor am longer curious of sights. For the first summer of my life, I have stayed quietly at home; at least not been thirty miles. It has struck fifty-nine with me: which is an hour for thinking of "the great journey," though not for talking of it; in which there always seems a great deal of affectation or unwillingness. Nay, it is silly, too; for how few can one talk to about one's death, that care about it? if they do, it is unkind. My being is so *isolé* and insignificant, that I shall go out, like a lamp in an illumination, that cannot be missed. . . .

---

1 Reporting on the battle of Long Island fought on 27 August 1776, which led ultimately to the British gaining New York.
2 General Howe was invested as a K.B. the following January.
3 A brother of the King of Sweden. – WALPOLE.

310. *Franklin, Envoy to France.*

Arlington Street, 20 December 1776.

. . . It looks very much as if we should know soon whether America is to be subdued or saved by a French war. We heard on Tuesday last that Dr. Franklin[1] himself was landed in France – no equivocal step; and on Wednesday came a full explanation. General Howe had made two movements, that threatened enclosing Washington, and cutting him off from his magazines: a small engagement ensued, in which the Americans were driven from a post without much loss on either side. Washington has since retired with his whole army to other heights, about five miles off, seeming to intend to protract the war, as was always thought would be their wisest way; but, as the Americans do not behave very heroically, and as the King's fleet will now be masters of the coast, it is supposed that Washington must retire northward, and that the Howes will make great progress in the south, if not prevented by the rigour of the season. As nearly as I can make out, Dr. Franklin must have sailed a day or two after Washington's retreat; and therefore it is natural to conclude that he is come to tell France, that she must directly interpose and protect the Americans, or that the Americans must submit to such terms as they can obtain. If I am not wrong in my reasons, the question is thus brought to a short issue, and there I leave it. I am never fond of speculations, and not at all so when I am not quite well. Adieu!

311. *Washington's Masterly Advance.*

Strawberry Hill, 3 April 1777.

. . . I have nothing very new to tell you on public affairs, especially as I can know nothing more than you see in the papers. It is my opinion that the King's affairs are in a very bad position in America. I do not say that his armies may not gain advantages again; though I believe there has been as much design as cowardice in the behaviour

1 Benjamin Franklin (1706–90), arrived in France in December 1776 as a Commissioner representing the United States.

of the provincials, who seem to have been apprised that protraction of the war would be more certainly advantageous to them than heroism. Washington, the dictator, has shown himself both a Fabius and a Camillus. His march through our lines is allowed to have been a prodigy of generalship.[1] In one word, I look upon great part of America as lost to this country! It is not less deplorable, that, between art and contention, such an inveteracy has been sown between the two countries as will probably outlast even the war! Supposing this unnatural enmity should not soon involve us in other wars, which would be extraordinary indeed, what a difference, in a future war with France and Spain, to have the Colonies in the opposite scale, instead of being in ours! What politicians are those who have preferred the empty name of *sovereignty* to that of *alliance*, and forced subsidies to the golden ocean of commerce!

Alas! the trade of America is not all we shall lose! The ocean of commerce wafted us wealth at the return of regular tides: but we had acquired an empire too, in whose plains the beggars we sent out as labourers could reap sacks of gold in three or four harvests; and who with their sickles and reaping-hooks have robbed and cut the throats of those who sowed the grain. These rapacious foragers have fallen together by the ears; and our Indian affairs, I suppose, will soon be in as desperate a state as our American. Lord Pigot [Governor of Madras] has been treacherously and violently imprisoned, and the Company[2] here has voted his restoration. I know nothing of the merits of the cause on either side: I dare to say both are very blameable. I look only to the consequences, which I do not doubt will precipitate the loss of our acquisitions there; the title to which I never admired, and the possession of which I always regarded as a transitory vision. If we could keep it, we should certainly plunder it, till the expense of maintaining would overbalance the returns; and, though it has rendered a little more than the holy city of Jerusalem, I look on such distant conquests as more destructive than beneficial; and, whether we are martyrs or banditti, whether we fight for the holy sepulchre or for lacs of rupees, I detest invasions of quiet

1 This was Washington's attack on Trenton, New Jersey, just over three months earlier. Fabius (see letter 289, p. 402, n. 2) and Camillus (Marcus Furius Camillus, soldier and statesman celebrated as the second founder of Rome) are quoted as exemplars of defensive and attacking generalship.
2 The East India Company.

kingdoms, both for their sakes and for our own; and it is happy for the former, that the latter are never permanently benefitted. . . .

312. *Burgoyne's Defeat at Saratoga.*

TO SIR HORACE MANN

Arlington Street, 4 December 1777.

This letter will not be preceded by nine postilions blowing horns; but should steal into Florence as modestly as a Roman general, who at most hoped to obtain the honour of an ovation. The second part of my despatch will only beg you not to despair of the republic.

After living a whole month upon a New York Gazette, and tired of asking if, *No news yet?* Sir William Howe's aide-de-camp arrived on the first: he confirmed the account of two, not three, engagements between the General and Dictator Washington. In the first, Howe certainly had the advantage; and in the second, so far, that Washington, having attacked him in his post, was repelled, and is retired into the Jerseys, the King having been restored to the sovereignty of Philadelphia. You are to believe that though Howe lost eleven hundred men, particularly Hessians, Washington suffered more: but even the Gazette does not enjoin you to suppose that the latter is totally defeated. On the contrary, for fear too small an army should effect too great things, you are authorised to figure the provincial army in the Jerseys as still consisting of 11,000 men; and there are a few reasons to think that it may now be as large as the Congress or the provinces, no longer checked, may please. Sir William delays the pursuit, as the passage of the Delaware is not yet clear. The Lord his brother is besieging a tough fort, and has already lost a sixty-four-gun ship and a frigate.

General Clinton has marched to relieve or find Burgoyne, but was forced to be content with taking two forts, and showing uncommon valour. The next paragraph will tell you why his expedition was unnecessary.

On Tuesday night came news from Carleton at Quebec, which indeed had come from France earlier, announcing the total annihilation (as to America) of Burgoyne's army.[1] Carleton declares he has

1 At the battle of Saratoga, 19 September and 7 October 1777, where General John Burgoyne (1723–92) was forced to surrender.

no *authentic* information; but from all the intelligence he can get, and which he believes, Burgoyne, after despatching Colonel Fraser with 1000 men to seek provisions, which whole body with their commander was cut off, fought desperately to extricate himself; but, numbers increasing and pouring upon him, he had been forced to lay down his arms, and the whole remaining army, which some say still consisted of 5000, but probably were reduced much lower, surrendered themselves prisoners, and are to be transported to England, on parole of not serving more in America − no bad circumstance for us, if they were but here! Burgoyne is said to be wounded in three places; his vanquisher Arnold is supposed to be dead of his wounds.[1]

You may imagine this occasions some consternation; but none at all, I assure you, in the Temple of Concord.[2] Unless Crœsus besieged the senate with an army of ingots, I do not believe there would be a deserter from the cause of *Sacra Fames*. There have been indeed warm skirmishes in both the Temples of Honour and Virtue,[3] Lord Chatham himself heading the troops of the Opposition, but without making any impression. Lord George Germain has received several wounds from Charles Fox; and Burke and Wedderburn were on the point of a closer engagement; but it was made up. The Parliament is to be adjourned to-morrow till after the holidays.

What will be next, I, the most unwise of men, do not guess. Some, a little wiser, think the wisest could not tell what should be. The Opposition, who, decried as they have been, have at least not been contradicted in their prophecies by events, think that, as Canada is left defenceless, and New York is not overcrowded with defenders, the whole force of New England, which is entire, as Burgoyne experienced, may march to Quebec, or join Washington, and besiege Clinton with as numerous an army as they choose to have. In that case, Sir William Howe must abandon Philadelphia, and march to the succour of New York.

You may be sure the uninformed expect that, as America is so nearly lost, the army will be recalled. You may guess, too, that I, who do not dote on France, nor desire a war at home, should not be sorry we had a little more defence; but who will ask my advice, or take it?

1 Burgoyne was not in fact injured, and Benedict Arnold was only wounded.
2 The House of Commons. − WALPOLE.
3 The Houses of Lords and Commons. − WALPOLE.

We are, in fact, very near the end of the American war, but I doubt we are at the beginning of our troubles. Disgrace is the present chapter, and sufficient to the day is the evil thereof. If disappointment opens our eyes, it has, like a true friend, given us bitter but wholesome counsel. If obstinacy is mistaken for firmness, it will obtain at last, as it generally does, its genuine appellation. ... Adieu!

313. *Attempted Conciliation too Late.*

TO SIR HORACE MANN

Arlington Street, 18 February 1778.

I do not know how to word the following letter; how to gain credit with you! How shall I intimate to you, that you must lower your topsails, waive your imperial dignity, and strike to the colours of the thirteen United Provinces of America? Do not tremble, and imagine that Washington has defeated General Howe, and driven him out of Philadelphia; or that Gates has taken another army; or that Portsmouth is invested by an American fleet. No: no military *new* event has occasioned this revolution. The sacrifice has been made on the altar of Peace. Stop again: peace is not made, it is only implored, – and, I fear, only on this side of the Atlantic. In short, yesterday, *February* 17th, a most memorable era, Lord North opened his Conciliatory Plan, – no partial, no collusive one. In as few words as I can use, it solicits peace with the States of America: it haggles on no terms; it acknowledges the Congress, or anybody that pleases to treat; it confesses errors, misinformation, ill-success, and impossibility of conquest; it disclaims taxation, desires commerce, hopes for assistance, allows the independence of America, not verbally, yet virtually, and suspends hostilities till June 1779. It does a little more: not *verbally*, but *virtually*, it confesses that the Opposition have been in the right from the beginning to the end.

The warmest American cannot deny but these gracious condescensions are ample enough to content that whole continent; and yet, my friend, such accommodating facility had one defect, – it came too late. The treaty between the high and mighty States and France is signed;[1] and instead of peace, we must expect war with the

1 The Treaty of Amity and Commerce and the Treaty of Alliance had been signed in Paris on 6 February.

high allies. The French army is come to the coast, and their officers here are recalled.

The House of Commons embraced the plan, and voted, it *nemine contradicente*. It is to pass both Houses with a rapidity that will do everything but overtake time past. All the world is in astonishment. As my letter will not set out till the day after to-morrow, I shall have time to tell you better what is thought of this amazing step.[1]

314. *Preparations against Invasion.*

TO SIR HORACE MANN

Strawberry Hill, 7 July 1778.

... It is true, we are threatened with invasion. You ask me why I seem to apprehend less than formerly? For many reasons. In the first place, I am above thirty years older. Can one fear anything in the dregs of life as at the beginning? Experience, too, has taught me that nothing happens in proportion to our conceptions. I have learnt, too, exceedingly to undervalue human policy. Chance and folly counteract most of its wisdom. From the "Mémoires de Noailles"[2] I have learnt, that, between the years 1740 and 1750, when I, – ay, and my Lord Chesterfield too, – had such gloomy thoughts, France was trembling with dread of us. These are general reasons. My particular ones are, that, if France meditated a considerable blow, she has neglected her opportunity. Last year, we had neither army nor a manned fleet at home. Now, we have a larger and better army than ever we had in the island, and a strong fleet. Within these three days, our West India and Mediterranean fleets, for which we have been in great pain, are arrived, and bring not only above two millions, but such a host of sailors as will supply the deficiencies in our unequipped men-of-war. The country is covered with camps; General Conway, who has been to one of them, speaks with astonishment of the fineness of the men, of the regiments, of their discipline and manœuvring. In short, the French Court has taught all our young nobility to be soldiers. The Duke of Grafton, who was the most indolent of ministers, is the most indefatigable of officers.

1 Walpole added a postscript on 20 February reflecting on the loss of America.
2 Political memoirs of the reigns of Louis XIV and XV from the papers of the Duc de Noailles, published in 1776–7.

For my part, I am almost afraid that there will be a larger military spirit amongst our men of quality than is wholesome for our constitution: France will have done us hurt enough, if she has turned us into generals instead of senators.

I can conceive another reason why France should not choose to venture an invasion. It is certain that at least five American provinces wish for peace with us. Nor can I think that thirteen English provinces would be pleased at seeing England invaded. Any considerable blow received by us, would turn their new allies into haughty protectors. Should we accept a bad peace, America would find her treaty with them a very bad one: in short, I have treated you with speculations instead of facts. I know but one of the latter sort. The King's army has evacuated Philadelphia, from having eaten up the country, and has returned to New York. Thus it is more compact, and has less to defend.

General Howe is returned, richer in money than laurels. I do not know, indeed, that his wealth is great.

Fanaticism in a nation is no novelty: but you must know, that, though the effects were so solid, the late appearance of enthusiasm about Lord Chatham was nothing but a general affectation of enthusiasm. It was a contention of hypocrisy between the Opposition and the Court, which did not last even to his burial.[1] Not three of the Court attended it, and not a dozen of the Minority of any note. He himself said, between his fall in the House of Lords and his death, that, when he came to himself, not one of his old acquaintance of the Court but Lord Despencer so much as asked him how he did. Do you imagine people are struck with the death of a man, who were not struck with the sudden appearance of his death? We do not counterfeit so easily on a surprise, as coolly; and, when we are cool on surprise, we do not grow agitated on reflection. . . .

1 Lord Chatham had collapsed in the House of Lords on 7 April, and died on 11 May. The funeral was widely attended, but by few peers.

315. *France Declares War.*

Strawberry Hill, 18 July 1778.

As I was going out this evening, I was stopped in Twickenham, and told that France has declared war. I knew the Brest squadron was at sea, and that Admiral Keppel by letters received from him at the Admiralty on Thursday, is off the Land's End, in hourly expectation of being joined by three or four men-of-war, which will make his fleet thirty ships of the line, with which he was determined to seek the enemy, who have thirty-one, two of fifty guns, and eight frigates. Thus the battle may be fought as soon as war is proclaimed; and thus our Ministers may have a full prospect of all their consummately wise measures may produce! What can be expected from two wars when one has been so ignominious? – With an army of fifty thousand men against a rabble, and without being beaten, they have lost a whole continent, and near half that army, and retreated from place to place! Not one General has gained any reputation; our only fleet on this side of the world is to decide whether the two islands are not to be fought for on land. Thus have we, the people, been gamed for; and some few of us against our wills. It is very hard, especially on us that remember other days. I know not what Lord Mansfield's reflections are, when he recollects his sagacious journey to Paris to convince the French cabinet that it was against their interest to protect the Americans, and his famous passage of the Rubicon.[1] I should be sorry to feel what he ought to feel even on the score of folly, – indeed *defendit numerus*;[2] and all that may be left to us few, may be to meet him, *torva tuentes*[3] like the ghost of Dido.

England will one day recollect it had a Minister [Sir Robert Walpole], to whom it owed twenty years of prosperity and happiness, and who left it a motto that would have preserved such halcyon days. *Quieta non movere* was as wise a saying as any my Lord Bolingbroke bequeathed to my Lord Bute. I do not know whether it is true, what has been said, that my father on being advised to tax America,

1 Lord Mansfield had commended the bill to close the port of Boston to shipping, which showed decisively that Britain was "past the Rubicon" in dealing with the colonists.
2 Juvenal, *Satires* II. 46: there is safety in numbers.
3 Looking disdainfully or wildly, from *Æneid* VI. 467.

replied, "It must be a bolder Minister than I am." But that motto of his spoke his opinion.

Well; War proclaimed! and I am near sixty-one. Shall I live to see peace again? and what a peace! I endeavour to compose my mind, and call in every collateral aid. I condemn my countrymen, but cannot, would not divest myself of my love to my country. I enjoy the disappointment of the Scots, who had prepared the yoke for the Americans and for our necks too. I cannot blame the French whom we have tempted to ruin us: yet, to be ruined by France! – there the Englishman in me feels again. My chief comfort is in talking to you, though you do not answer me. I write to vent my thoughts, as it is easier than brooding over them, but allow that it is difficult to be very tranquil when the navy of England is at stake. That thought annihilates resentment. I wish for nothing but victory, and then peace, yet what lives must victory cost! Nor will one victory purchase it. The nation is so frantic that success would intoxicate us more; yet calamity, that alone could sober us, is too near our doors. Resignation to the will of Heaven is the language of reason as well as of religion, when one knows not what would be best for us. It is a dilemma to which the honest are reduced: our gamesters are in a worse situation. The best they can hope for, is to sit down with the *débris* of an empire. What a line they have drawn between them and Lord Chatham! I believe it was modesty made them not attend his funeral. Will the House of Brunswick listen again to the flatterers of prerogative?

My time of life, that ought to give me philosophy, dispirits me. I cannot expect to live to see England revive. I shall leave it at best an insignificant island. Its genius is vanished like its glories; one sees no hero nor statesman arise to flatter hope. Dr. Franklin, thanks to Mr. Wedderburn,[1] is at Paris. Every way I turn my thoughts, the returns are irksome. What is the history of a fallen empire? A transient satire on the vices and follies that hurried it to dissolution. The protest of a few that foretold it, is not registered. The names of Jefferies[2] and two or three principals satisfy the sage moralist who hurries to more agreeable times. I will go to bed and sleep, if I can.

1 Alexander Wedderburn (1733–1805), later Lord Chancellor, had attacked Franklin at a Privy Council meeting in 1774, which Walpole suggests had encouraged the Americans to seek assistance from the French.
2 Judge Jeffreys (1645–89), as an example of a corrupt or vengeful judge.

Pray write to me; tell me how you reconcile your mind to our situation – I cannot. Two years ago I meditated leaving England if it was enslaved. I have no such thought now. I will steal into its bosom when my hour comes, and love it to the last.

316. *Spain Joins France.*

TO SIR HORACE MANN

Strawberry Hill, 16 June 1779.

Alas! my dear Sir, you have been mistaken, and must no more put your trust in the obstinacy of Princes; at least, that of one can surmount that of another. The King of Spain's rescript is arrived and delivered, and the Brest fleet is sailed with both white and red cockades. The declaration is said not to be very injurious; but, after all possible endeavours at pacification, his Catholic Majesty is obliged to take his part, especially as we have made some captures on his subjects. The Ministers were urged even late last night on the hostility of Spain, but would own nothing. This morning they avow everything; and, to your great surprise probably, the Parliament is to rise to-morrow or next day! As events have not proved the wisdom of measures, one can collect no great confidence from such a step: but I don't pretend to reason on what I do not understand; my business is to tell you facts. In short, the Brest fleet has been sailed many days. The Prince of Beauveau[1] is on board – if destined for Ireland, we should probably have heard it by this time; if to meet the Spanish fleet, the object might be Gibraltar.

I shall not boast of having been a better soothsayer than you, when I foretold that the American war would not be of short duration. It is a *triste* honour to be verified a prophet of woes. Were I vain of the character, a Spanish war, added to an American one, were a fine field; but I do not ambition being a Jeremiah, though my countrymen are so like the Jews. Nor does it require inspiration to prophesy, when one has nothing to do but to calculate. Were you here, you would not be alarmed. You would see no panic; you would hear of nothing but diversions. The Ministers affirm the majority of America is with us, and it is credited. Were they to tell us half the Spanish

---

1 He did not go. – WALPOLE.

fleet would come over to us, it would be credited too. When it does not, perhaps they will tell us it has. – Well! what is most to be dreaded is the dissipation of our delusion. When the *réveil* comes, it will be serious indeed!

You see I am not likely to be barren of matter, and you will be sorry that I write oftener than I foresaw. The middle period of our correspondence was the most agreeable. Its early part was the journal of a civil war, and of no glorious one in Flanders. Fifteen years after, I sent you victory upon victory, and conquest upon conquest.[1] For the last five years, my letters have been the records of a mouldering empire. What is now to come I know not: we have, they say, maintained ourselves against France and Spain; true, but with the trifling difference of having America in our scale – now it is in theirs. We had too a Lord Chatham; who does not seem to have been replaced.

I tell you nothing of Parliamentary debates, for I really do not attend to them; especially not to the details of the war, and the conduct of the Generals who have made a very silly figure. There are far mightier objects in question than speeches and votes, and which I *must* learn even here, quiet and abstracted as I sit. My consolation is that I have no particular friend responsible for anything that has happened; and, when one's passions are not concerned, an individual of my age must have learnt to look on the great drama of the world with some indifference. My pride, I own, made me pleased when my country was the most splendid in Europe: I did not imagine I was so singular as I find I was, or we should not have run wild after a phantom of absolute power over a country whose liberty was the source of our greatness. A pretty experiment we have made; and, whenever the hour of peace shall arrive, we shall be able to compute what it has cost us *not* to compass it. . . .

317. *Woeful State of Affairs.*

TO THE COUNTESS OF AILESBURY

Saturday night, 10 July 1779.

. . . Everything has miscarried that has been undertaken, and the worse we succeed, the more is risked; – yet the nation is not angry!

1 1759, the *annus mirabilis* of British victories under Chatham.

How can one conjecture during such a delirium? I sometimes almost think I must be in the wrong to be of so contrary an opinion to most men – yet, when every misfortune that has happened had been fore-told by a few, why should I not think I have been in the right? Has not almost every single event that has been announced as prosperous proved a gross falsehood, and often a silly one? Are we not at this moment assured that Washington cannot possibly amass an army of above 8000 men! and yet Clinton, with 20,000 men, and with the hearts, as we are told, too, of three parts of the colonies, dares not show his teeth without the walls of New York? Can I be in the wrong in not believing what is so contradictory to my senses? We could not conquer America when it stood alone; then France supported it, and we did not mend the matter. To make it still easier, we have driven Spain into the alliance. Is this wisdom? Would it be presumption, even if one were single, to think that we must have the worst in such a contest? Shall I be like the mob, and expect to conquer France and Spain, and then thunder upon America? Nay, but the higher mob do not expect such success. They would not be so angry at the house of Bourbon, if not morally certain that those kings destroy all our passionate desire and expectation of conquering America. We bul-lied, and threatened, and begged, and nothing would do. Yet inde-pendence was still the word. Now we rail at the two monarchs – and when they have banged us, we shall sue to them as humbly as we did to the Congress. All this my senses, such as they are, tell me has been and will be the case. What is worse, all Europe is of the same opin-ion; and though forty thousand *baronesses* may be ever so angry, I venture to prophesy that we shall make but a very foolish figure whenever we are so lucky as to obtain a peace; and posterity, that may have prejudices of its own, will still take the liberty to pro-nounce, that its ancestors were a woful set of politicians from the year 1774 to – I wish I knew when.

The Duke of Ancaster is dead, and Lord Bolingbroke.[1] If I might advise, I would recommend Mr. Burrell to command the fleet in the

---

1 The 2nd Viscount Bolingbroke (see letter 46, p. 76, n. 2) did not die, but was con-fined to a madhouse the following year.

room of Sir Charles Hardy. The fortune of the Burrells is powerful enough to baffle calculation.[1] Good night, Madam!

318. *Invasion Imminent.*

TO THE COUNTESS OF AILESBURY

Strawberry Hill, Friday night, 23 July 1779.

... I am to dine at Ditton[2] to-morrow, and will certainly talk on the subject you recommend; yet I am far, till I have heard more, from thinking with your Ladyship, that more troops and artillery at Jersey would be desirable. Any considerable quantity of either, especially of the former, cannot be spared at this moment, when so big a cloud hangs over this island, nor would any number avail if the French should be masters at sea. A large garrison would but tempt the French thither, were it but to distress this country; and, what is worse, would encourage Mr. Conway to make an impracticable defence. If he is to remain in a situation so unworthy of him, I confess I had rather he was totally incapable of making any defence. I love him enough not to murmur at his exposing himself where his country and his honour demand him; but I would not have him measure himself in a place untenable against very superior force. My present comfort is, as to him, that France at this moment has a far vaster object. I have good reason to believe the Government knows that a great army is ready to embark at St. Malo's, but will not stir till after a sea-fight, which we do not know but may be engaged at this moment. Our fleet is allowed to be the finest ever set forth by this country; but it is inferior in number by seventeen ships to the united squadron of the Bourbons. France, if successful, means to pour in a vast many thousands on us, and has threatened to burn the capital itself. Jersey, my dear Madam, does not enter into a calculation of such magnitude. The moment is singularly awful; yet the vaunts of enemies are rarely executed successfully and ably. Have we trampled America under our foot?

You have too good sense, Madam, to be imposed upon by my

1 Walpole had written to Mann three days earlier, bemused by the fact that the grandchildren of a broken merchant who had been attached to his father had made a series of rich and spectacular aristocratic marriages.
2 Lord Hertford had a property at Thames Ditton.

arguments, if they are insubstantial. You do know that I have had my terrors for Mr. Conway; but at present they are out of the question, from the insignificance of his island. Do not listen to rumours, nor believe a single one till it has been canvassed over and over. Fear, folly, fifty motives, will coin new reports every hour at such a conjuncture. When one is totally void of credit and power, patience is the only wisdom. I have seen dangers still more imminent. They were dispersed. Nothing happens in proportion to what is meditated. Fortune, whatever fortune is, is more constant than is the common notion. I do not give this as one of my solid arguments, but I have always encouraged myself in being superstitious on the favourable side. I never, like most superstitious people, believe auguries against my wishes. We have been fortunate in the escape of Mrs. Damer, and in the defeat at Jersey, even before Mr. Conway arrived; and thence I depend on the same future prosperity. From the authority of persons who do not reason on such airy hopes, I am seriously persuaded, that if the fleets engage, the enemy will not gain advantage without deep-felt loss, enough, probably, to dismay their invasion. Coolness may succeed, and then negotiation. Surely, if we can weather the summer, we shall, obstinate as we are against conviction, be compelled, by the want of money, to relinquish our ridiculous pretensions, now proved to be utterly impracticable; for, with an inferior navy at home, can we assert sovereignty over America? It is a contradiction in terms and in fact. It may be hard of digestion to relinquish it, but it is impossible to pursue it. Adieu, my dear Madam! I have not left room for a line more.

319. *At War with Holland.*

TO SIR HORACE MANN

Berkeley Square, 4 January 1780.

I am going to write a short letter in quantity, but a very serious one in matter. A stroke has been struck that seems pregnant with another war – a war with Holland. Advice had been received of large supplies of naval stores being ready to sail for Brest, furnished by the warm friends of France, the Amsterdamers; stores essential to the re-equipment of the French navy, and as repugnant to the treaties subsisting between us and the States. These merchantmen proposed to take advantage of a convoy going to the Levant and other places, the States not countenancing that manœuvre. It was determined not to wink at such an outrage, but to hazard complaints or resentment, when such a blow could be given to the farther enterprises of our capital enemies. Captain Fielding, with five men-of-war of the line, was ordered to seize the whole counterband trade, and has executed what he could. He has brought into Plymouth eight merchantmen and three men-of-war, with their Admiral. The latter refused to allow a search; some shot were exchanged, but in air, on both sides, and then the Dutchmen struck. Fielding desired him to re-hoist his flag, but he refused, and said he must accompany his convoy; thus creating himself a prisoner.

I have related this event as vaguely – that is, as cautiously – as I could: first, because I know no particulars from authority, for it was but yesterday at noon that the notice arrived; and secondly, because I have heard various accounts; and lastly, because I have been so steeled against sudden belief by lies from all quarters for these five years, that I do not trust my eyes, ears, or reason, and still less those instruments of anybody else.

There are two uncomely features in the countenance of this business. The first is, disappointment. Though the captured stores are counterband, they consist only of hemp and iron, not of masts and timber, as we expected, and which are what the French want. Whether the magazines of those materials have escaped, or have not sailed, we – that is, I – do not know; but, when all the Ratisbons[1] in Europe are to discuss our enterprise, it is not pleasant to have trespassed on punctilios, – if we, and not the Dutch, were the aggressors, – and not to have been crowned with success.

Thus we have involved ourselves fruitlessly in the second inconvenience, of having, perhaps, tapped a new war, without previous indemnification. You diplomatics must canvass all this; and I hope it will be left to such quiet disputants, and not be referred to redcoats and trowsers. I have given you your cue, till you receive better instructions. I am sorry to open the fortieth year of our correspondence by opening another of Janus's temples; better, however, in

---

1 The conference of Ratisbon (1541), which had attempted to restore religious unity in the Holy Roman Empire: referred to by Walpole as an example of a convention or formal meeting at which conflicting interests were discussed.

Holland than in Ireland, where we have got a strong friendly army
instead of a rebellion. . . .

320. *Victory at Camden.*

At night (9 October 1780), addition to letter begun 7 October.

I have just heard some news that you will like to hear, and which
will make you hold up your head again a little *vis-à-vis de M. de
Barbantane.*[1] An express arrived to-day from Lord Cornwallis, who
with two thousand men has attacked General Gates in Carolina at
the head of seven thousand, and entirely defeated him, killed nine
hundred, and taken one thousand prisoners;[2] and there has since
been a little codicil, of all which you will see the particulars in the
to-morrow's "Gazette." – But it is very late, and this must go to town
early in the morning. I allow you to triumph, though Gates is my
godson,[3] and your namesake.

321. *André Executed.*

Berkeley Square, 16 November 1780.

. . . A good courtier, yesterday, sang the praises to me of that atrocious villain, Arnold, who, he said, till he heard of André's execution,
would not discover the persons at New York, with whom Washington was in secret correspondence;[4] then indeed he did. Christ

---

1 The Marquis de Barbantane (1725–*c.* 1800) was the French envoy to Tuscany.
2 Charles, 1st Earl (later 1st Marquis) Cornwallis (1738–1805), lieutenant-general and
second-in-command of the British forces in America, at the battle of Camden on
16 August 1780.
3 The mother of the American general Horatio Gates (1727–1806), victor of Saratoga, was a housekeeper to the Duke of Leeds and intimate with a servant of Walpole's mother: Walpole recorded that he became Gates's godfather at the age of
about twelve.
4 After defecting to the British, Benedict Arnold (1741–1801) had written to Washington threatening retaliation if the English officer and spy Major John André (1750–
80) were executed, but was not in fact aware of the identity of Washington's spies in
New York on whom such retaliation might have been visited. André was hanged as
a spy on 2 October 1780.

Jesus! Only think of the monster! I hope he will be a Privy Councillor! betraying to Sir Harry Clinton, in the height of his indignation for André, the wretched poor souls cooped up in New York, who are guilty of that correspondence. When I expressed my horror at such bloody treachery, and said I did not doubt but Lord Cornwallis's savage executions had hurried on André's fate, and were, besides cruel, indiscreet; the same apologist said, "Oh! we have more prisoners of theirs than they have of ours." How tender to their *own friends*, who they do not care if hanged, provided they can spill more buckets of blood! I know nothing of poor André; he is much commended, but so he would be if as black as Arnold. . . .

322. *Despair.*

TO THE HON. H. S. CONWAY

3 January 1781.

After I had written my note to you last night, I called on * * * *, who gave me the dismal account of Jamaica, that you will see in the "Gazette," and of the damage done to our shipping. Admiral Rowley is safe; but they are in apprehensions for Walsingham.[1] He told me, too, what is not in the "Gazette;" that of the expedition against the Spanish settlements – not a single man survives! The papers to-day, I see, speak of great danger to Gibraltar.

Your brother repeated to me his great desire that you should publish your speech,[2] as he told you. I do not conceive why *he* is so eager for it, for he professes total despair about America. It looks to me as if there was a wish of throwing the blame somewhere; but I profess I am too simple to dive into the objects of shades of intrigues; nor do I care about them. We shall be reduced to a miserable little island; and from a mighty empire sink into as insignificant a country as Denmark or Sardinia! When our trade and marine are gone, the latter of which we keep up by unnatural efforts, to which our debt will put a stop, we shall lose the East Indies as Portugal did; and then France will dictate to us more imperiously than ever

1 Jamaica had suffered a serious hurricane in October 1780. Commodore Walsingham was among those lost.
2 Conway's speech supported the bill to send commissioners to negotiate with the Americans.

we did to Ireland, which is in a manner already gone too.

These are mortifying reflections, to which an English mind cannot easily accommodate itself. But, alas! we have been pursuing the very conduct that France would have prescribed, and more than with all her presumption she could have dared to expect. Could she flatter herself that we would take no advantage of the dilatoriness and unwillingness of Spain to enter into the war? that we would reject the disposition of Russia to support us? and that our still more natural friend, Holland, would be driven into the league against us? All this has happened, and, like an infant, we are delighted with having set our own frock in a blaze! I sit and gaze with astonishment at our frenzy. Yet why? Are not nations as liable to intoxication as individuals? Are not predictions founded on calculation oftener rejected than the prophecies of dreamers? Do we not act precisely like Charles Fox, who thought he had discovered a new truth in figures, when he preached that wise doctrine, that nobody could want money that would pay enough for it? The consequence was, that in two years he left himself without the possibility of borrowing a shilling.[1] I am not surprised at the spirits of a boy of parts; I am not surprised at the people: I do wonder at Government, that games away its consequence. For what are we now really at war with America, France, Spain, and Holland? – Not with hopes of reconquering America; not with the smallest prospect of conquering a foot of land from France, Spain, or Holland. – No; we are at war on the defensive, to protect what is left, or more truly to stave off, for a year perhaps, a peace that must proclaim our nakedness and impotence.

I would not willingly recur to that womanish vision of, Something may turn up in our favour. That something must be a naval victory that will annihilate at once all the squadrons of Europe – must wipe off forty millions of new debt – reconcile the affections of America, that for six years we have laboured to alienate; and that must recall out of the grave the armies and sailors that are perished – and that must make thirteen provinces willing to receive the law, without the necessity of keeping ten thousand men amongst them. The gigantic imagination of Lord Chatham would not entertain such a chimera. Lord * * * *[2] perhaps, would say he did, rather than

1 Walpole compares the national finances to the reckless borrowing of Charles James Fox.
2 The Yale editors speculate Lord North.

not undertake; or Mr. Burke could form a metaphoric vision that would satisfy no imagination but his own; but I, who am *nullius addictus jurare in verba*,[1] have no hopes either in our resources or in our geniuses, and look on my country already as undone! It is grievous – but I shall not have much time to lament its fall.

323. *Cornwallis Defeated at Yorktown.*

TO SIR HORACE MANN

29 November 1781.

. . . I mentioned on Tuesday the captivity of Lord Cornwallis and his army, the Columbus who was to bestow America on us again. A second army taken in a drag-net is an uncommon event, and happened but once to the Romans, who sought adventures everywhere. We have not lowered our tone on this new disgrace, though I think we shall talk no more of insisting on *implicit submission*, which would rather be a gasconade[2] than firmness. In fact, there is one very unlucky circumstance already come out, which must drive every American, to a man, from ever calling himself our friend. By the tenth article of the capitulation, Lord Cornwallis demanded that the loyal Americans in his army should not be punished. This was flatly refused, and he has left them to be hanged.[3] I doubt no vote of Parliament will be able to blanch such a – such a – I don't know what the word is for it; he must get his uncle the Archbishop[4] to christen it; there is no name for it in any Pagan vocabulary. I suppose it will have a patent for being called Necessity. Well! there ends another volume of the American war. It looks a little as if the history of it would be all we should have for it, except forty millions of debt, and three other wars that have grown out of it, and that do not seem so near to a conclusion. They say that Monsieur de Maurepas, who is dying, being told that the Duc de Lauzun had brought the news of Lord Cornwallis's surrender, said, from Racine's "Mithridate" I think: –

1 Horace, *Epistolæ* I. i. 14: not bound to swear by another's precepts.
2 Boast.
3 It was later reported that the captured loyalists were allowed passage to New York.
4 Cornwallis's uncle was the Archbishop of Canterbury.

Mes derniers regards ont vu fuir les Romains.[1]

How Lord Chatham will frown when they meet! for, since I began my letter, the papers say that Maurepas is dead. The Duc de Nivernois, it is said, is likely to succeed him as Minister;[2] which is probable, as they were brothers-in-law and friends, and the one would naturally recommend the other. Perhaps, not for long, as the Queen's influence gains ground.

The warmth in the House of Commons is prodigiously rekindled; but Lord Cornwallis's fate has cost the Administration no ground *there*. The names of most *éclat* in the Opposition are two names to which those walls have been much accustomed at the same period – Charles Fox and William Pitt, second son of Lord Chatham. Eloquence is the only one of our brilliant qualities that does not seem to have degenerated rapidly – but I shall leave debates to your nephew, now an ear-witness: I could only re-echo newspapers. Is it not another odd coincidence of events, that while the father Laurens is prisoner to Lord Cornwallis as Constable of the Tower, the son Laurens signed the capitulation by which Lord Cornwallis became prisoner?[3] It is said too, I don't know if truly, that this capitulation and that of Saratoga were signed on the same anniversary. These are certainly the speculations of an idle man, and the more trifling when one considers the moment. But alas! what would *my* most grave speculations avail? From the hour that fatal egg, the Stamp Act, was laid, I disliked it and all the vipers hatched from it. I now hear many curse it, who fed the vermin with poisonous weeds. Yet the guilty and the innocent rue it equally hitherto! I would not answer for what is to come! Seven years of miscarriages may sour the sweetest tempers, and the most sweetened. Oh! where is the Dove with the olive-branch? Long ago I told you that you and I might not live to see an end of the American war. It is very near its end indeed now – its consequences are far from a conclusion. In some respects, they are commencing a new date, which will reach far beyond *us*. I desire not to pry into that book of futurity. Could

1 Racine, *Mithridate* V. v. 1666: The last thing I saw was the Romans fleeing.
2 Charles Gravier, Comte de Vergennes (1717–87) in fact became chief minister rather than the Duc de Nivernois. For Nivernois, see letter 347, p. 484, n. 1; for Maurepas, see letter 217, p. 309, n. 1.
3 The younger Laurens actually jointly negotiated rather than signed the articles of capitulation. For the elder Laurens, see letter 219.

I finish my course in peace – but one must take the chequered scenes of life as they come. What signifies whether the elements are serene or turbulent, when a private old man slips away? What has he and the world's concerns to do with one another? He may sigh for his country, and babble about it; but he might as well sit quiet and read or tell old stories; the past is as important to him as the future. . . .

324. *Rodney's Victory off St. Lucia.*

TO SIR HORACE MANN

Berkeley Square, 18 May 1782.

. . . To-day we hear that Sir George Rodney has defeated[1] – ay, and taken Monsieur de Grasse – in his own ship, "La Ville de Paris," of a hundred and ten guns, three others of seventy-four, one of sixty-four, and sunk another of the line. We have lost three hundred, have seven hundred wounded (whom, alas! a West India climate will not recover), three captains, and Lord Robert Manners, a fine young fellow, only brother of the Duke of Rutland, who died of his wounds on the passage – but not one ship; yet you see the action must have been bloody. Rodney was recalled by the new Admiralty, but recovers from his falls with marvellous agility. The late Ministers are thus robbed of a victory that ought to have been theirs; but the mob do not look into the almanac. The City of Westminster had just nominated our young Cicero, Mr. William Pitt, to replace Sir George as their representative at the next general election; the latter being a little under a cloud from his rapacity at St. Eustatia.[2] Now, Mr. Pitt must exert some oratorical modesty, and beg not to dethrone a hero!

These naval rostra arrived very opportunely to stay our impatience for a victory over the Dutch, which we have expected a good week from Lord Howe's hands – charming victories, if they facilitate peace! We have two negotiators actually at Paris; the principal, Mr. Thomas Grenville, whom you saw so lately. It will be one of Fortune's caprices, if the son of the author of the Stamp Act and of the war is the mediator of peace.

---

1 At the battle of the Saintes.
2 Rodney had been accused of the plunder of the Caribbean island of St. Eustatia.

Lest we should be too exalted by these successes, we yesterday drank a cup of humiliation. Both Houses, in very few hours, signed the absolute independence of Ireland.[1] I shall not be surprised if our whole trinity is dissolved, and if Scotland should demand a dissolution of the Union. Strange if she alone does not profit of our distresses. It is very true she was grown more fond of availing herself of our prosperity.

There, there is a better cargo of news than I have sent you for some years! . . .

21st.

Lord Howe's victory is not yet hatched; we reckon him in pursuit of the Dutch. The whole town was illuminated to Rodney's health on Saturday night. I was just gone to bed in pain, when a mob, the masters of our ceremonies, knocked outrageously at the door, and would scarce have patience till the servants could put out lights; and till three in the morning there was no sleeping for rockets and squibs. Lord Robert Manners lost one leg and had the other and one arm broken, yet lived three weeks in good spirits till the locked jaw came. How many others of whom one shall not hear, because they were not young Lords!

After dinner.

The Dutch fleet have escaped into the Texel, and Lord Howe is expected back into the Channel.

325. Loss of the "Royal George."

TO THE COUNTESS OF UPPER OSSORY

Strawberry Hill, 31 August 1782.

. . . You are not serious, Madam, that Mr. Fox is going to Gibraltar! Is he to be Alexander at Oxydracæ, as well as at Statira's feet?[2] But he may save himself the trouble; I should think the town gone

---

1 The Repeal Act of 1782, which temporarily gave legislative independence to Ireland.
2 Charles James Fox (who did not go to Gibraltar, which was under siege) is compared to Alexander the Great, who heroically overcame the Oxydracæ tribe, and had married Statira, daughter of the King of Persia – the role of Statira in Racine's *Alexander the Great* having been played by Fox's mistress Mary Robinson.

by this time – which is more than our fleet is. Just this moment I hear the shocking loss of the "Royal George!"[1] Admiral Kempenfelt is a loss indeed; but I confess I feel more for the hundreds of poor babes who have lost their parents! If one grows ever so indifferent, some new calamity calls one back to this deplorable war! If one is willing to content one's self in a soaking autumn with a match broken, or with the death of a Prince Duodecimus,[2] a clap of thunder awakens one, and one hears that Britain herself has lost an arm or a leg. I have been expecting a deluge, and a famine, and such casualties as enrich a Sir Richard Baker;[3] but we have all King David's options at once! and what was his option before he was anointed, freebooting too? . . .

326. *Gibraltar Saved.*

TO THE EARL OF STRAFFORD

Strawberry Hill, 3 October 1782.

I did think it long since I had the honour of hearing from your Lordship; but, conscious how little I could repay you with any entertainment, I waited with patience. In fact, I believe summer-correspondences often turn on complaints of want of news. It is unlucky that that is generally the season of correspondence, as it is of separation. People assembled in a capital contrive to furnish matter, but then they have not occasion to write it. Summer, being the season of campaigns, ought to be more fertile: I am glad when that is not the case, for what is an account of a battle but a list of burials? Vultures and birds of prey might write with pleasure to their correspondents in the Alps of such events; but they ought to be melancholy topics to those who have no beaks or talons. At this moment if I was an epicure among the sharks, I should rejoice that General Eliott has just sent the carcases of fifteen hundred Spaniards down to market under Gibraltar;[4] but I am more pleased that he despatched boats, and saved some of those whom he had overset. What must a

1 Admiral Kempenfelt's flagship sank with much loss of life while being careened for repairs.
2 In fact the 14th child of George III and Queen Charlotte, who had just died before his second birthday.
3 A reference to Baker's *Chronicle* (1643).
4 General Sir George Eliott (1717–90), later Baron Heathfield, the Governor of Gibraltar, had repulsed the Franco-Spanish attack the previous month.

man of so much feeling have suffered at being forced to do his duty so well as he has done! I remember hearing such another humane being, that brave old admiral, Sir Charles Wager, say, that in his life he had never killed a fly.

This demolition of the Spanish armada is a great event: a very good one if it prevents a battle between Lord Howe and the combined fleets, as I should hope; and yet better if it produces peace, the only political crisis to which I look with eagerness. Were that happy moment arrived, there is ample matter to employ our great men, if we have any, in retrieving the affairs of this country, if they are to be retrieved. But though our sedentary politicians write abundance of letters in the newspapers, full of plans of public spirit, I doubt the nation is not sober enough to set about its own work in earnest. When none reform themselves, little good is to be expected. . . .

327. *The Relief by Howe.*

TO SIR HORACE MANN

Strawberry Hill, 4 November 1782, addition to letter begun 2 November.

The great news of the relief of Gibraltar by Lord Howe arrived this day se'nnight, and of the dispersion of the combined fleets by a storm, in which they lost two or three ships, and we none. This is a fine reproof to his Spanish Majesty's obstinacy. What pitiful beings are monarchs, when they knock their heads against winds and seas – yet even then, alas, they knock other heads too! There is something sublime in this little island, beset with foes, calmly despatching its own safeguard to maintain such a distant possession. I do not desire a codicil with a victory, which must be dearly bought: there would be dignity enough in returning, after having performed the intended service. For these two days, indeed, there has been the report of a battle much in our favour, though with the loss of six ships; but I hear it is not credited in London. . . .

328. *Peace.*

TO SIR HORACE MANN

Berkeley Square, Monday evening, 2 December 1782.

The day that I little expected to live to see, is arrived! Peace came this morning: thank God! That is the first thought: the effusion of human gore is stopped, nor are there to be more widows and orphans out of the common course of things.

What the terms are will be known before this goes away to-morrow: they may be public already; but here am I, lying upon a couch and not out of pain, waiting with patience for what I shall learn from the few charitable that I am able to admit. Proud conditions I, nor even you in your representative dignity, can expect. Should they be humiliating, *they* ought to answer who plunged us into a quadruple war, and managed it deplorably for seven years together!

As I have not breath to dictate much, I shall not waste myself on a single reflection: but in truth I am very low; and what are all the great and little affairs of the world to me, who am mouldering away, not imperceptibly!

Just now I received yours of the 16th of November, chiefly on the affairs of Gibraltar; you will find how details on that place, like your preceding occupation for Minorca, will be absorbed in subsequent events. . . .

Friday night, the 6th.

I was much too ill on Tuesday to finish this, and, besides that, recollected that whatever was to be heard you would learn from Paris sooner than from London. I began to write upon the first buzz of the courier being arrived; but all he brought was the Provisional treaty with America, which too is not to take place till the General Peace does. This, however, we are told to expect soon – and there I must leave peace and war, kingdoms and states, and trust to your nephew for saying anything else; for in truth I am not able. The scale of life and death has been vibrating; I believe it is turned to the former. I have had two very good nights, and the progress of the gout seems quite stopped; but I am exceedingly low and weak, and it will take me some time to recover: but I assure you, my dear Sir, you may be easy. I have now a good opinion of myself, and I have spoken so plainly that you may believe me.

Adieu! You shall hear again soon, unless I see your nephew, whom I will desire to give you a more particular account.

329. *Treaty of Versailles.*

TO SIR HORACE MANN

27 August 1783.

It is time to resume my veteran punctuality, and think of writing to you; but alas! correspondence, like matrimonial duty, is but ill performed when only prompted by periodic recollection of a debt to be paid. However, I am so far different from a husband, that my inclination is not decreased: want of matter alone makes me sluggish. The war is at an end, which, like domestic quarrels, animated our intercourse, and, like them, concludes with kissing, and is followed by dullness and inaction. The Definitive Treaty, they say, is signed; the French and we are exceedingly fond. Presents pass weekly between the Duchesses of Polignac and Devonshire; and so many French arrive, that they overflow even upon me, and visit Strawberry as one of our sights. The Marquise de la Jamaique, sister of your *Countess of Albany*,[1] has been here this month, and stays above another. But, are not such articles below even the ingredients of a letter; especially between you and me, who have dealt in the fates of kingdoms? If I would talk politics, I must have recourse to the long-depending topic, whether there will be a war between the Turks and Russians; of which, in good truth, I know as little as of anything else. . . .

---

1 That is, the Marquise was sister-in-law to the Pretender.

3. THE GORDON RIOTS

330. *An Extraordinary Petition.*

Berkeley Square, 29 January 1780.

The weather-cock Marquis has taken his part, or rather his leave, and resigned his key on Thursday.[1] But there was a more extraordinary phenomenon in the closet the same day. Lord George Gordon[2] asked an audience, was admitted, and incontinently began reading his Irish pamphlet, and the King had the patience to hear him do so for above an hour, till it was so dark that the lecturer could not see. His Majesty then desired to be excused, and said he would finish the piece himself. "Well!" said the lunatic apostle, "but you must give me your honour that you will read it out." The King promised, but was forced to pledge his honour. It puts one in mind of Charles II. at Scoon, before his Restoration. It is to be hoped this man is so mad, that it will soon come to perfection, unless my plan is adopted, of shutting up in Bedlam the few persons in this country that remain in their senses. It would be easier and much cheaper than to confine all the delirious. . . .

331. *Petitions from the Counties.*

Strawberry Hill, 6 February 1780.

I write only when I have facts to send. Detached scenes there have been in different provinces: they will be collected soon into a drama in St. Stephen's Chapel. One or two and twenty counties, and two or three towns, have voted petitions.[3] But in Northamptonshire Lord Spencer was disappointed, and a very moderate petition was ordered. The same happened at Carlisle. At first, the Court was struck dumb, but have begun to rally. Counter-protests have been signed in Hertford and Huntingdon shires, in Surrey and Sussex.

1 Francis Godolphin Osborne (1751–99), Marquis of Carmarthen, resigned his position at court where his support of the Yorkshire Association (which urged economical and parliamentary reform) made him unacceptable.
2 Lord George Gordon (see letter 194, p. 275, n. 1).
3 Petitions on the expenditure of public money, critical of the government.

Last Wednesday a meeting was summoned in Westminster Hall: Charles Fox harangued the people finely and warmly; and not only a petition was voted, but he was proposed for candidate for that city at the next general election, and was accepted joyfully. Wilkes was his zealous advocate:[1] how few years since a public breakfast was given at Holland House to support Colonel Luttrell against Wilkes! Charles Fox and his brother rode thence at the head of their friends to Brentford. Ovid's Metamorphoses contains not stranger transformations than party can work.

I must introduce a new actor to you, a Lord George Gordon – metamorphosed a little too, for his family were Jacobites and Roman Catholics: he is the Lilburne of the Scottish Presbyterians, and an apostle against the Papists. He dresses, that is, wears long lank hair about his shoulders, like the first Methodists; though I take the modern ones to be no Anti-Catholics. This mad lord, for so all his family have been too, and are, as likewise assumed the patronage of Ireland. Last Thursday he asked an audience of the King, and, the moment he was admitted into the closet, began reading an Irish pamphlet, and continued for an hour, till it was so dark he could not see; and then left the pamphlet, exacting a promise on royal honour that his Majesty would finish it. Were I on the throne, I would make Dr. Monro[2] a Groom of my Bedchamber: indeed it has been necessary for some time; for, of the King's lords, Lord Bolingbroke is in a mad-house, and Lord Pomfret and my nephew ought to be there. The last, being fond of onions, has lately distributed bushels of that root to his Militia; Mr. Windham[3] will not be surprised.

By the tenor of the petitions you would think we were starving; yet there is a little coin stirring. Within this week there has been a cast at hazard at the Cocoa tree, the difference of which amounted to an hundred and four-score thousand pounds. Mr. O'Birne, an Irish gamester, had won one hundred thousand pounds of a young Mr. Harvey[4] of Chigwell, just started from a midshipman into an

1 That is, Charles James Fox, supported by Wilkes, was adopted as parliamentary candidate for Westminster.
2 Physician of Bedlam. – WALPOLE.
3 Mr. Windham [William Windham (1750–1810), statesman] had been Lieutenant-Colonel [Major] of the Norfolk Militia under Lord Orford, and had resigned on the trouble he gave them. – WALPOLE.
4 The Cocoa Tree was a Club in Pall-Mall. Harvey [Sir Eliab Harvey (1758–1830)] was to distinguish himself at Trafalgar and eventually became an admiral.

estate by his elder brother's death. O'Birne said, "You can never pay me." "I can," said the youth; "my estate will sell for the debt." "No," said O.; "I will win ten thousand – you shall throw for the odd ninety." They did, and Harvey won.

332. *Beginning of the Riots.*

TO THE COUNTESS OF UPPER OSSORY

Berkeley Square, 3 June 1780.

I know that a governor or a gazetteer ought not to desert their posts, if a town is besieged, or a town is full of news; and therefore, Madam, I resume my office. I smile to-day – but I trembled last night; for an hour or more I never felt more anxiety. I knew the bravest of my friends were barricaded into the House of Commons, and every avenue to it impossible. Till I heard the Horse and Foot Guards were gone to their rescue,[1] I expected nothing but some dire misfortune; and the first thing I heard this morning was that part of the town had had a fortunate escape from being burnt after ten last night. You must not expect order, Madam; I must recollect circumstances as they occur; and the best idea I can give your Ladyship of the tumult will be to relate it as I heard it.

I had come to town in the morning on a private occasion, and found it so much as I left it, that though I saw a few blue cockades[2] here and there, I only took them for new recruits. Nobody came in; between seven and eight I saw a hack and another coach arrive at Lord Shelburne's, and thence concluded that Lord George Gordon's trumpet had brayed to no purpose. At eight I went to Gloucester House; the Duchess told me, there had been a riot, and that Lord Mansfield's glasses had been broken, and a bishop's, but, that most of the populace were dispersed. About nine his Royal Highness and Colonel Heywood arrived; and then we heard a much more alarming account. The concourse had been incredible, and had by no means obeyed the injunctions of their apostle, or rather had interpreted the spirit instead of the letter. The Duke had reached the House with the utmost difficulty, and found it sunk from the temple of dignity to

1 The Gordon rioters had marched from St. George's Fields into the lobby of the House of Commons.
2 The symbol adopted by Gordon's supporters.

an asylum of lamentable objects. There were the Lord Hillsborough, Stormont, Townshend, without their bags, and with their hair dishevelled about their ears, and Lord Willoughby without his periwig, and Lord Mansfield, whose glasses had been broken, quivering on the woolsack like an aspen. Lord Ashburnham had been torn out of his chariot, the Bishop of Lincoln ill-treated, the Duke of Northumberland had lost his watch in the holy hurly-burly, and Mr. Mackenzie his snuff-box and spectacles. Alarm came that the mob had thrown down Lord Boston, and were trampling him to death; which they almost did. They had diswigged Lord Bathurst on his answering them stoutly, and told him he was the pope, and an old woman; thus splitting Pope Joan into two. Lord Hillsborough, on being taxed with negligence, affirmed that the Cabinet had the day before empowered Lord North to take precautions; but two Justices that were called denied having received any orders. Colonel Heywood, a very stout man, and luckily a very cool one, told me he had thrice been collared as he went by the Duke's order to inquire what was doing in the other House; but though he was not suffered to pass he reasoned the mob into releasing him, – yet, he said, he never saw so serious an appearance and such determined countenances.

About eight the Lords adjourned, and were suffered to go home; though the rioters declared that if the other House did not repeal the Bill, there would at night be terrible mischief. Mr. Burke's name had been given out as the object of resentment. General Conway I knew would be intrepid and not give way; nor did he, but inspired the other House with his own resolution. Lord George Gordon was running backwards and forwards, and from the windows of the Speaker's Chamber denouncing all that spoke against him to the mob in the lobby. Mr. Conway tasked him severely both in the House and aside, and Colonel Murray told him he was a disgrace to his family. Still the members were besieged and locked up for four hours, nor could divide, as the lobby was crammed. Mr. Conway and Lord Frederick Cavendish, with whom I supped afterwards, told me there was a moment when they thought they must have opened the doors and fought their way out sword in hand. Lord North was very firm, and at last they got the Guards and cleared the pass.

Blue banners had been waved from tops of houses at Whitehall as signals to the people, while the coaches passed, whom they should applaud or abuse. Sir George Savile's and Charles Turner's coaches were demolished. Ellis, whom they took for a Popish gentleman, they carried prisoner to the Guildhall in Westminster, and he escaped by a ladder out of a window. Lord Mahon harangued the people from the balcony of a coffee-house and begged them to retire; but at past ten a new scene opened. The mob forced the Sardinian Minister's Chapel in Lincoln's Inn Fields, and gutted it. He saved nothing but two chalices; lost the silver lamps, &c., and the benches being tossed into the street, were food for a bonfire, with the blazing brands of which they set fire to the inside of the chapel, nor, till the Guards arrived, would suffer the engines to play. My cousin, T. Walpole, fetched poor Madam Cordon,[1] who was ill, and guarded her in his house till three in the morning, when all was quiet.

Old Haslang's Chapel[2] has undergone the same fate, all except the ordeal. They found stores of mass-books and run tea.

This is a slight and hasty sketch, Madam. On Tuesday the House of Commons is to consider the Popish laws. I forgot to tell you that the Bishops not daring to appear, the Winchester Bill, which had passed the Commons, was thrown out.

No saint was ever more diabolic than Lord George Gordon. Eleven wretches are in prison for the outrage at Cordon's, and will be hanged instead of their arch-incendiary. One person seized is a Russian officer, who had the impudence to claim acquaintance with the Sardinian Minister, and desired to be released. Cordon replied, "*Oui, Monsieur, je vous connoissois, mais je ne vous connais plus.*" I do not know whether he is an associate of Thalestris,[3] who seems to have snuffed a revolution in the wind. . . .

1 The wife of the Sardinian ambassador.
2 The Bavarian Chapel, which was destroyed as, like the Sardinian Minister's Chapel, it was a Catholic place of worship.
3 Amazon Queen who according to legend presented herself and 300 other women to Alexander the Great in order to have daughters by him so as to breed new Amazons.

333. *The Riots.*

TO SIR HORACE MANN

Strawberry Hill, 5 June 1780.

Not a syllable yet from General Clinton. There has been a battle at sea in the West Indies, which we might have gained; know we did not, but not why: and all this is forgotten already in a fresher event. I have said for some time that the field is so extensive, and the occurrences so numerous, and so much pains are taken to involve them in falsehoods and mystery, and opinions are so divided, that all evidences will be dead before a single part can be cleared up; but I have not time, nor you patience, for my reflections. I must hurry to the history of the day. The Jack of Leyden[1] of the age, Lord George Gordon, gave notice to the House of Commons last week, that he would, on Friday, bring in the petition of the Protestant Association; and he openly declared to his disciples, that he would not carry it unless a *noble army of martyrs, not fewer than forty thousand*, would accompany him. Forty thousand, led by such a lamb, were more likely to prove butchers than victims; and so, in good truth, they were very near being. Have you faith enough in me to believe that the sole precaution taken was, that the Cabinet Council on Thursday empowered the First Lord of the Treasury to give proper orders to the civil magistrates to keep the peace, – and his Lordship forgot it!

Early on Friday morning the conservators of the Church of England assembled in *St. George's* Fields to encounter the dragon, the old serpent, and marched in lines of six and six – about thirteen thousand only, as they were computed – with a petition as long as the procession, which the apostle himself presented; but, though he had given out most Christian injunctions for peaceable behaviour, he did everything in his power to promote a massacre. He demanded immediate repeal of toleration, told Lord North he could have him torn to pieces, and, running every minute to the door or windows, bawled to the populace that Lord North would give them no redress, and that now this member, now that, was speaking against them.

In the mean time, the Peers, going to their own Chamber, and as

1   16th-century Anabaptist leader.

yet not concerned in the petition, were assaulted;[1] many of their glasses were broken, and many of their persons torn out of the carriages. Lord Boston was thrown down and almost trampled to death; and the two Secretaries of State, the Master of the Ordnance, and Lord Willoughby were stripped of their bags or wigs, and the three first came into the House with their hair all dishevelled. The chariots of Sir George Savile and Charles Turner, two leading advocates for the late toleration, though in Opposition, were demolished; and the Duke of Richmond and Burke were denounced to the mob as proper objects for sacrifice. Lord Mahon laboured to pacify the tempest, and towards eight and nine, prevailed on so many to disperse, that the Lords rose and departed in quiet; but every avenue to the other House was besieged and blockaded, and for four hours they kept their doors locked, though some of the warmest members proposed to sally out, sword in hand, and cut their way. Lord North and that House behaved with great firmness, and would not submit to give any other satisfaction to the rioters, than to consent to take the Popish laws into consideration on the following Tuesday; and, calling the Justices of the Peace, empowered them to call out the whole force of the country to quell the riot.

The magistrates soon brought the Horse and Foot Guards, and the pious ragamuffins soon fled; so little enthusiasm fortunately had inspired them; at least all their religion consisted in outrage and plunder; for the Duke of Northumberland, General Grant, Mr. Mackinsy, and others, had their pockets picked of their watches and snuff-boxes. Happily, not a single life was lost.

This tumult, which was over between nine and ten at night, had scarce ceased before it broke out in two other quarters. Old Haslang's Chapel was broken open and plundered; and, as he is a Prince of Smugglers as well as Bavarian Minister, great quantities of run tea and contraband goods were found in his house. This one cannot lament; and still less, as the old wretch has for these forty years usurped a hired house, and, though the proprietor for many years has offered to remit his arrears of rent, he will neither quit the house nor pay for it.

Monsieur Cordon, the Sardinian Minister, suffered still more.

---

1 Walpole here gives a more detailed account to Mann than that he had provided to Lady Ossory two days previously, in letter 332.

The mob forced his chapel, stole two silver lamps, demolished everything else, threw the benches into the street, set them on fire, carried the brands into the chapel, and set fire to that; and, when the engines came, would not suffer them to play till the Guards arrived, and saved the house and probably all that part of the town. Poor Madame Cordon was confined by illness. My cousin, Thomas Walpole, who lives in Lincoln's Inn Fields, went to her rescue, and dragged her, for she could scarce stand with terror and weakness, to his own house.

I doubt this narrative will not re-approach you and Mr. Windham. I have received yours of the 20th of last month.

You will be indignant that such a mad dog as Lord George should not be knocked on the head. Colonel Murray did tell him in the House, that, if any lives were lost, his Lordship should join the number. Nor yet is he so lunatic as to deserve pity. Besides being very debauched, he has more knavery than mission. What will be decided on him, I do not know; every man that heard him can convict him of the worst kind of sedition: but it is dangerous to constitute a rascal a martyr. I trust we have not much holy fury left; I am persuaded that there was far more dissoluteness than enthusiasm in the mob: yet the episode is very disagreeable. I came from town yesterday to avoid the birthday [June 4]. We have a report here that the Papists last night burnt a Presbyterian meeting-house, but I credit nothing now on the first report. It was said to be intended on Saturday, and the Guards patrolled the streets at night; but it is very likely that Saint George Gordon spread the insinuation himself. . . .

Thursday, 8th.

I am exceedingly vexed. I sent this letter to Berkeley Square on Tuesday, but by the present confusions my servant did not receive it in time. I came myself yesterday, and found a horrible scene. Lord Mansfield's[1] house was just burnt down, and at night there were shocking disorders. London and Southwark were on fire in six places; but the regular troops quelled the sedition by daybreak, and everything now is quiet. A camp of ten thousand men is formed in Hyde Park, and regiments of horse and foot arrive every hour.

1 William Murray (1705–93), 1st Earl of Mansfield, Lord Chief Justice. His house was in Bloomsbury Square and contained a particularly valuable library.

Friday morn, 9th.

All has been quiet to-night. I am going to Strawberry for a little rest. Your nephew told me last night that he sends you constant journals just now.

334. *Further Details.*

TO THE REV. WILLIAM MASON

Strawberry Hill, 9 June at night, 1780.

I have not had a moment's time, or one calm enough, to write you a single line, and now am not only fatigued, but know not where to begin, or how to arrange the thousand things I have in my mind. If I am incoherent, you must excuse it, and accept whatever presents itself.

I could not bear to sit here in shameful selfish philosophy, and hear the million of reports, and know almost all I loved in danger, without sharing it. I went to town on Wednesday, and though the night was the most horrible I ever beheld, I would not take millions not to have been present; and should I have seen the conflagration as I must from these windows, I should have been distracted for my friends.

At nine at night, on notice of fire, I went with the Duchess and her daughters to the top of Gloucester House, and thence beheld the King's Bench, which was a little town, and at a distance the New Prison in flames.[1] At past ten I went to General Conway's: in a moment we were alarmed by the servants, and rushing to the street-door saw through Little Warwick-street such an universal blaze, that I had no doubt the Mews, at least St. Martin's-lane, was on fire. Mr. Conway ran, and I limped after him, to Charing Cross, but, though seemingly close, it was no nearer than the Fleet Market.

At past twelve I went up to Lord Hertford's: two of his sons came in from the Bridge at Blackfriars, where they had seen the toll-houses plundered and burnt. Instantly arrived their cook, a German Protestant, with a child in his arms, and all we could gather was that the mob was in possession of his house, had burnt his furniture, and

---

1 The rioters burnt the King's Bench prison and New Bridewell prison, Fleet Street, on the evening of 7 June.

had obliged him to abandon his wife and another child. I sent my own footman, for it was only in Woodstock-street, and he soon returned and said it had been only some apprentices who supposed him a Papist on his not illuminating his house, and that three of them and an Irish Catholic Chairman had been secured, but the poor man has lost his all! I drove from one place to another till two, but did not go to bed till between three and four, and ere asleep heard a troop of horse gallop by. My printer [Thomas Kirgate], whom I had sent out for intelligence, came not home till past nine the next morning: I feared he was killed, but then I heard of such a scene. He had beheld three sides of the Fleet Market in flames, Barnard's Inn at one end, the prison on one side and the distiller's on the other, besides Fetter and Shoe Lanes, with such horrors of distraction, distress, &c., as are not to be described; besides accounts of slaughter near the Bank. The engines were cut to pieces, and a dozen or fourteen different parts were burning. It is incredible that so few houses and buildings in comparison are in ashes. The papers must tell you other details, and of what preceded the total demolition of Lord Mansfield's, &c.

Yesterday was some slaughter in Fleet-street by the Horse-Guards, and more in St. George's Fields by the Protestant Association, who fell on the rioters, who appear to have been chiefly apprentices, convicts, and all kinds of desperadoes; for Popery is already out of the question, and plunder all the object. They have exacted sums from many houses to avoid being burnt as Popish. The ringleader Lord George is fled.[1] The Bank, the destruction of all prisons and of the Inns of Court, were the principal aims.

The Magistrates, intimidated by demolition of Fielding's and Justice Hyde's houses,[2] did not dare to act. A general Council was summoned at Buckingham House, at which the twelve Judges attended. It was determined not to shut up the Courts but to order military execution. Both Houses are adjourned to Monday sevennight, which hurt General Conway so much, who intended yesterday to move for the repeal of the Toleration, and found the

---

1 In fact Gordon had been arrested at his London house on the day that Walpole wrote this letter.
2 Their houses were destroyed because they were magistrates, and in the case of Hyde because he had summoned the Horse Guards against the rioters.

House adjourned before he could get to it, though early, that he is gone out of town.

The night passed quietly, and by this evening there will be eighteen thousand men in and round the town. As yet there are more persons killed by drinking than by ball or bayonet. At the great Popish distiller's they swallowed spirits of all kinds, and Kirgate saw men and women lying dead in the streets under barrows as he came home yesterday.

We have now, superabundantly, to fear robbery: 300 desperate villains were released from Newgate. Lady Albemarle was robbed at Mrs. Keppel's door in Pall Mall at twelve at night. Baron D'Aguilar's coach was shot at here last night, close to the Crown.

I have so much exerted my no strength, and had so little sleep these two nights, that I came hither to-day for some rest. It will be but *grim repose*. It is said that this insurrection was expected in France a month ago. Just as I came away Mr. Griffith told me the French were embarking. In short, what may not be expected? Then one turns from what is to come, to helpless misery, that will soon be forgotten but by the sufferers; whole families ruined, wives that tried to drag their husbands out of the mobs and have found them breathless, the terrors of the Catholics, indeed of all foreigners, but one. That Scythian heroine, the Princess Daskiou,[1] is here; her natural brother Rantzau was taken in Monsieur Cordon's Chapel, and was reclaimed by Simonin, and released. *She* herself on Wednesday, I *know*, sent Lord Ashburnham word that his house was marked for destruction. Merciful tigress! it is proof he is not an Emperor.

My bosom, I think, does not want humanity, yet I cannot feel pity for Lord Mansfield. I did feel joy for the four convicts who were released from Newgate within twenty-four hours of their execution; but ought not a man to be taught sensibility, who drove us cross the Rubicon?[2] I would not hurt a hair of his head: but if I sigh for the afflicted innocent, can I blend him with them? . . . Adieu!

---

1 Ekaterina Romanovna Vorontsova (1743–1810), Princess Dashkov, to whom Walpole was not sympathetic as she was a friend of Catherine the Great, the purchaser of the Houghton pictures and alleged murderer of her husband.
2 See letter 315, p. 438, n. 1.

4. INDIAN AFFAIRS

335. Pondicherry and the King's Marriage.

TO GEORGE MONTAGU, ESQ.

Strawberry Hill, 22 July 1761.

For my part, I believe Mademoiselle Scuderi[1] drew the plan of this year. It is all royal marriages, coronations, and victories; they come tumbling so over one another from distant parts of the globe, that it looks just like the handywork of a lady romance writer, whom it costs nothing but a little false geography to make the Great Mogul in love with a Princess of Mecklenburg, and defeat two marshals of France as he rides post on an elephant to his nuptials. I don't know where I am. I had scarce found Mecklenburg Strelitz with a magnifying-glass before I am whisked to Pondicherry – well, I take it, and raze it. I begin to grow acquainted with Colonel Coote,[2] and to figure him packing up chests of diamonds, and sending them to his wife against the King's wedding – thunder go the Tower guns, and behold, Broglio and Soubise are totally defeated; if the mob have not much stronger heads and quicker conceptions than I have, they will conclude my Lord Granby is become nabob. How the deuce in two days can one digest all this? Why is not Pondicherry in Westphalia? I don't know how the Romans did, but I cannot support two victories every week. Well, but you will want to know the particulars. Broglio and Soubise united, attacked our army on the 15th, but were repulsed; the next day, the Prince Mahomet Alli Cawn – no, no, I mean Prince Ferdinand, returned the attack, and the French threw down their arms and fled,[3] run over my Lord Harcourt, who was going to fetch the new Queen; in short, I don't know how it was, but Mr. Conway is safe, and I am as happy as Mr. Pitt himself. We have only lost a Lieutenant-colonel Keith; a Colonel Marlay and Harry Townshend are wounded.

I could beat myself for not having a flag ready to display on my round tower, and guns mounted on all my battlements. Instead of

1 Madeleine de Scudéry (1607–1701), French novelist.
2 Lieutenant-Colonel Eyre Coote (1726–83) had taken Pondicherry in January.
3 The battle of Kirch-Denckern, in which the French army was led by the Duc de Broglie and the Prince de Soubise, was according to the Yale editors not as decisive as Walpole thought.

that, I have been foolishly trying on my new pictures upon my gallery. However, the oratory of our Lady of Strawberry[1] shall be dedicated next year on the anniversary of Mr. Conway's safety. Think with his intrepidity, and delicacy of honour wounded, what I had to apprehend; you shall absolutely be here on the sixteenth of next July. Mr. Hamilton tells me your King[2] does not set out for his new dominions till the day after the Coronation; if you will come to it, I can give you a very good place for the procession; where, is a profound secret, because, if known, I should be teazed to death, and none but my first friends shall be admitted. I dined with your secretary [Single-speech Hamilton] yesterday;[3] there were Garrick and a young Mr. Burke, who wrote a book in the style of Lord Bolingbroke, that was much admired.[4] He is a sensible man, but has not worn off his authorism yet, and thinks there is nothing so charming as writers, and to be one. He will know better one of these days. I like Hamilton's little Marly; we walked in the great *allé*, and drank tea in the arbour of triellage; they talked of Shakspeare and Booth, of Swift and my Lord Bath, and I was thinking of Madame Sévigné. Good night – I have a dozen other letters to write; I must tell my friends how happy I am – not as an Englishman, but as a cousin.

336. *Clive's Return.*

TO SIR HORACE MANN

20 July 1767.

... Lord Clive[5] is arrived, has brought a million for himself, two diamond drops worth twelve thousand pounds for the Queen, a scimitar, dagger, and other matters, covered with brilliants, for the King, and worth twenty-four thousand more. These *baubles* are presents from the deposed and imprisoned Mogul, whose poverty can still afford to give such bribes. Lord Clive refused some overplus,

---

1 The Oratory to the right of the entrance door to Strawberry Hill, where Walpole placed a 15th-century bronze statue of a saint.
2 Montagu's cousin Lord Halifax, who was about to leave for Dublin: see letter 46, p. 75, n. 1.
3 At Hamilton's house near Bushy Park.
4 Burke's *Vindication of Natural Society* ... (1756), a satire of Bolingbroke.
5 Robert Clive, 1st Baron Clive of Plassey (1725–74), army officer and Indian administrator, had arrived at Portsmouth a week earlier.

and gave it to some widows of officers: it amounted to ninety thousand pounds. He has *reduced* the appointments of the Governor of Bengal to thirty-two thousand pounds a-year; and, what is better, has left such a chain of forts and distribution of troops as will entirely secure possession of the country – till we lose it. Thus having composed the Eastern and Western worlds, we are at leisure to kick and cuff for our own little island, which is great satisfaction; and I don't doubt but my Lord Temple hopes that we shall be so far engaged before France and Spain are ripe to meddle with us, that when they do come, they will not be able to re-unite us.

Don't let me forget to tell you, that of all the friends you have shot flying, there is no one whose friendship for you is so little dead as Lord Hillsborough's. He spoke to me earnestly about your Riband[1] the other day, and said he had pressed to have it given to you. Write and thank him. You have missed one by Lord Clive's returning alive, unless he should give a hamper of diamonds for the Garter. . . .

337. *East India Company Corrupt.*

TO SIR HORACE MANN

Arlington Street, 19 July 1769.

. . . The East-India Company is all faction and gaming. Such fortunes are made and lost every day as are past belief. Our history will appear a gigantic lie hereafter, when we are shrunk again to our own little island. People trudge to the other end of the town to vote who shall govern empires at the other end of the world. Panchaud, a banker from Paris, broke yesterday for seventy thousand pounds, by buying and selling stock; and Sir Laurence Dundas[2] *paid in* an hundred and forty thousand pounds for what he had bought. The Company have more and greater places to give away than the First Lord of the Treasury. Riches, abuse, cabals, are so enormously overgrown, that one wants conception and words to comprehend or describe them. Even Jewish prophets would have found Eastern hyperboles

1 Wills Hill (1718–93), 1st Earl of Hillsborough, joint Postmaster-General in Chatham's government, was encouraging Mann's ambition to obtain the Order of the Bath; see letter 295, p. 415, n. 1.
2 Sir Lawrence Dundas (1712–81), "the Nabob of the North", financier and M.P.

deficient, if Nineveh had been half so extravagant, luxurious, and rapacious as this wicked good town of London. I expect it will set itself on fire at last, and light the match with India bonds and bank-bills. As I pass by it and look at it, I cannot help talking to it, as Ezekiel would do, and saying, "with all those combustibles in thy bowels, with neither government, police, or prudence, how is it that thou still existeth?" ...

338. *Effects of a Monopoly.*

TO SIR HORACE MANN

Arlington Street, 5 March 1772.

... We have another scene coming to light, of black dye indeed. The groans of India have mounted to heaven, where *the heaven-born General Lord Clive* will certainly be disavowed. Oh! my dear sir, we have outdone the Spaniards in Peru! They were at least butchers on a religious principle, however diabolical their zeal. We have murdered, deposed, plundered, usurped – nay, what think you of the famine in Bengal, in which three millions perished, being caused by a mono-poly of the provisions, by the servants of the East India Company? All this is come out, is coming out – unless the gold that inspired these horrors can quash them. Voltaire says, learning, arts, and philosophy have softened the manners of mankind: when tigers can read they may possibly grow tame – but man! –

What shall I tell you to clear up your brow and make you smile again? Shall it be that Lord Chatham hunts and makes verses? He has written a copy to Garrick, in which he disclaims ambition.[1] Recollect what I have said to you, that *this world is a comedy to those who think, a tragedy to those who feel!* This is the quintessence of all I have learnt in fifty years! Adieu!

---

1 Lord Chatham wrote a poetical invitation to Garrick to visit him at his seat, Burton Pynsent.

339. *Attack on Clive.*

TO THE REV. WILLIAM MASON

Strawberry Hill, 15 May 1773.

... The House of Commons has embarked itself in a wilderness of perplexities. Though Lord Clive was so frank and high-spirited as to confess a whole folio of his Machiavelism; they are so ungenerous as to have a mind to punish him for assassination, forgery, treachery, and plunder, and it makes him very indignant. 'Tother night, because the House was very hot, and the young members thought it would melt their rouge and shrivel their nosegays, they all on a sudden, and the old folks too, voted violent resolutions, and determined the great question of the right of sovereignty, though, till within half an hour of the decision, the whole House had agreed to weigh and modify the questions a little more. Being so fickle, Lord Clive has reason to hope that after they have voted his head off, they will vote it on again the day after he has lost it.[1] ...

340. *Death of Clive.*

TO SIR HORACE MANN

Strawberry Hill, 24 November 1774.

... A great event happened two days ago – a political and moral event; the sudden death of that second Kouli Khan, Lord Clive. There was certainly illness in the case; the world thinks more than illness. His constitution was exceedingly broken and disordered, and grown subject to violent pains and convulsions. He came unexpectedly to town last Monday, and they say, ill. On Tuesday his physician gave him a dose of laudanum, which had not the desired effect. On the rest, there are two stories;[2] one, that the physician repeated the dose; the other, that he doubled it himself, contrary to advice. In short, he has terminated at fifty a life of so much glory, reproach,

1 They did. After two speeches by Clive on 19 and 21 May, the motion condemning Clive was defeated and the House instead resolved that Clive did "render great and meritorious services to this country".
2 Subsequent speculation has suggested as cause of death an apoplectic fit, a seizure brought on by a double dose of opium, or perhaps that his death may have been by his own hand.

art, wealth, and ostentation. He had just named ten members for the new Parliament. . . .

341. *Warren Hastings's Trial.*

TO SIR HORACE MANN

Berkeley Square, 30 April 1786.

. . . The tragedy, or rather, I suppose, the farce, of Mr. Hastings's Trial is also to commence to-morrow, when he is to make his defence before the House of Commons;[1] where the majority of his judges are *ready* to be astonished at his eloquence, and the transparency of his innocence, and the lustre of his merit. In the mean time, the charges are enormous, and make numbers, who are not to be his jury, marvel how he will clear himself of half; and, if he does, what he will do with the remainder. I have not yet looked into the charge, which fills a thick octavo. My opinion is formed more summarily: innocence does not pave its way with diamonds, nor has a quarry of them on its estate. . . .

4 May.

. . . Mr. Hastings used two days in his defence, which was not thought a very modest one, and rested rather on Machiavel's code than on that of rigid moralists. The House is now hearing evidence; and as his counsel, Mr. Machiavel, will not challenge many of the jury, I suppose Mr. Hastings will be honourably acquitted. In fact, who but Machiavel can pretend that we have a shadow of title to a foot of land in India; unless, as our Law deems that what is done extraparochially is deemed to have happened in the parish of St. Martin's in the Fields, India must in course belong to the Crown of Great Britain. Alexander distrained the goods and chattels of Popes upon a similar plea; and the Popes thought all the world belonged to them, as heirs-at-law to one who had not an acre upon earth. We condemned and attainted the Popes without trial, which was not in fashion in the reign of Henry the Eighth, and, by the law of forfeiture, confiscated, all their injustice to our own use; and thus till we shall be ejected, have we a right to exercise all the tyranny and rapine

1 Warren Hastings (1732–1818), colonial administrator, who was obliged to answer Edmund Burke's call for his impeachment.

that ever was practised by any of our predecessors anywhere, – as it was in the beginning, is now, and ever shall be, world without end.

342. *Sheridan's Great Speech.*

TO THE COUNTESS OF UPPER OSSORY

Berkeley Square, 9 February 1787.

... In short, I doubt I shall never make my fortune by turning courtier or comedian; and therefore I may as well adhere to my old principles, as I have always done, since you yourself, Madam, would not be flattered in a convert that nobody would take off your hands. If you could bring over Mr. Sheridan,[1] he would do something: he talked for five hours and a half on Wednesday, and turned everybody's head. One heard everybody in the streets raving on the wonders of that speech; for my part, I cannot believe it was so supernatural as they say – do you believe it was, Madam? I will go to my oracle, who told me of the marvels of the pamphlet, which assures us that Mr. Hastings is a prodigy of virtue and abilities; and, as you think so too, how should such a fellow as Sheridan, who has no diamonds to bestow, fascinate all the world? – Yet witchcraft, no doubt, there has been, for when did simple eloquence ever convince a majority? Mr. Pitt and 174 other persons found Mr. Hastings guilty last night, and only sixty-eight remained thinking with *the pamphlet* and your Ladyship, that he is as white as snow. Well, at least there is a new crime, sorcery, to charge on the Opposition! and, till they are cleared of that charge, I will never say a word in their favour nor think on politics more, which I would not have mentioned but in answer to your Ladyship's questions; and therefore I hope we shall drop the subject and meet soon in Grosvenor-place in a perfect neutrality of good humour.

---

1   Richard Brinsley Sheridan (1751–1816), playwright and politician.

XV
FRANCE AND THE FRENCH
REVOLUTION

THIS SECTION FALLS into three distinct parts of radically different character. The first (letters 343 to 359) recounts and reflects on Walpole's visits to Paris between 1765 and 1771; the second (letters 360 to 370) records premonitions of revolt up to 1789; and the third (letters 371 to 388) shows Walpole recoiling from the horrors of the Revolution.

When Walpole stayed in Paris for seven months from September 1765 he had not been to the city since his Grand Tour of 1739–41. His letters show us Walpole the Francophile and habitué of the salons, the celebrated guest moving with ease and charm through Parisian society. The life suited him: "Suppers please me extremely," he wrote to Montagu in letter 346; "I love to rise and breakfast late, and to trifle away the day as I like. There are sights enough to answer that end, and shops you know are an endless field for me." As a group, these letters present as fine a picture of salon society as can be found. Anglomania was then at its height in Paris, ranging from enthusiastic imitation of English gardens and a passion for English fashions to adulation of Richardson and lionising of Hume. If to be English alone was fashionable, Walpole further enhanced his status by the *succès de scandale* of a letter he concocted, ostensibly from Frederick the Great to Rousseau (see letter 351). It was during this visit that he met Madame du Deffand (see Section X, Part II), and he returned to see her four times over the following decade. After his second visit to Paris he corresponded with Voltaire, who had written to him asking for a copy of *The Historic Doubts*, which Walpole sent together with *The Castle of Otranto*.

Whatever his somewhat sceptical religious views, Walpole found the open atheism of sections of French society shocking. "Freethinking is for oneself, surely not for society ... I dined to-day with a dozen *savans*, and though all the servants were waiting, the conversation was much more unrestrained, even on the Old Testament, than I would suffer at my own table in England, if a single footman was present" (letter 346). He disapproved of the *philosophes* – "solemn, arrogant, dictatorial coxcombs" (letter 359) – and of the dirt that lay so close beneath the surface glitter of the metropolis. Nevertheless he relished his triumphs in Parisian society: as he announced to George Selwyn in December 1765, at the age of forty-eight, "it is charming to totter into vogue" (letter 349).

Walpole made several visits to the court at Versailles, the first occasion in 1765 inspiring one of his classic set-pieces (letter 347). Here he was presented to Louis XV – glaring at strangers as he dressed – "the good old Queen", the fading Dauphin, and the King's four unmarried daughters – "clumsy plump old wenches, with a bad likeness to their father, [who] stand in a bed-chamber in a row, with black cloaks and knotting-bags, looking good-humoured, not knowing what to say, and wriggling as if they wanted to make water" – as well as to the Dauphin's three sons, "who only bow and stare" and his little girl, "fat as a pudding". At Versailles again in 1769 he observed "the amorous and still handsome King. One could not help smiling at the mixture of piety, pomp, and carnality" (letter 356). In 1774 the King died and was succeeded by his grandson, Louis XVI. At court the following year Walpole was dazzled by the young Queen, Marie Antoinette: "Hebes and Floras, and Helens and Graces, are street-walkers to her. She is a statue of beauty, when standing or sitting; grace itself when she moves . . . They say she does not dance in time, but then it is wrong to dance in time" (letter 365).

Letters 360 to 369 note the darkening clouds in France, as bills and pensions remained unpaid, the noble gallery in the Louvre was abandoned to the elements, and ministers of finance supplanted each other in dizzying succession. As for the Revolution itself, Walpole was clear-headed from the beginning. "No man living is more devoted to liberty than I am," he told Mary Berry in letter 370, "yet blood is a terrible price to pay for it!" He was aware of the failings and cruelties of the Ancien Régime, the grossness of the wealth of bankers like La Borde (letter 350), the scandal of *lettres de cachet* (letter 366), and the bizarre mixture of parade and poverty as the French economy crumbled. But he was also a child of the English revolution of 1688, applauding its "integrity, wisdom, and temper" (letter 383), and of the eighteenth-century Whig supremacy; a wealthy member of the establishment, naturally compassionate but no friend to radical social or political change. He had nothing but contempt for men like Paine and Priestley who actively supported the French Revolution. The Gordon Riots of 1780 (letters 330 to 334) had given the merest hint of what chaos the breakdown of social order could let loose; like Burke the now ageing Walpole (he was seventy-one when the Bastille was stormed) feared the terrible consequences of mob-law in France, and his sympathies lay entirely with its victims, the royal family and those he had known in the salons. The implosion of French society, the bloodletting and wanton cruelty, were anathema to his privileged but civilised Whig values.

1. VISITS TO FRANCE

343. *Arrival in France.*

TO THE HON. H. S. CONWAY

Beau Cousin,   Amiens, Wednesday, 11 September 1765.

I have had a very prosperous journey till just at entering this city. I escaped a Prince of Nassau at Dover, and sickness at sea, though the voyage lasted seven hours and a half. I have recovered my strength surprisingly in the time; though almost famished for want of clean victuals, and comfortable tea and bread and butter. Half a mile from hence I met a coach and four with an equipage of French, and a lady in pea-green and silver, a smart hat and feather, and two *suivantes*. My reason told me it was the Archbishop's concubine; but luckily my heart whispered that it was Lady Mary Coke.[1] I jumped out of my chaise – yes, jumped, as Mrs. Nugent said of herself,[2] fell on my knees, and said my first *Ave Maria, gratiâ plena*. We just shot a few politics flying – heard that Madame de Mirepoix had toasted me t'other day in tea – shook hands, forgot to weep, and parted; she to the Hereditary Princess, I to this inn, where is actually resident the Duchess of Douglas. We are not likely to have an intercourse, or I would declare myself a Hamilton.[3]

1   See letter 213, p. 303, n. 1.
2   The Yale editors note that this refers to a standing joke between Walpole, Conway and Lady Ailesbury about a very fat Mrs. Nugent.
3   A reference to the famous litigation between the Douglas and Hamilton families known as the Douglas Cause.

I find this country wonderfully enriched since I saw it four-and-twenty years ago. Boulogne is grown quite a plump snug town, with a number of new houses. The worst villages are tight, and wooden shoes have disappeared. Mr. Pitt and the city of London may fancy what they will; but France will not come a-begging to the Mansion-house this year or two. In truth, I impute this air of opulence a little to ourselves. The crumbs that fall from the chaises of the swarms of English that visit Paris, must have contributed to fatten this province. It is plain I must have little to do when I turn my hand to calculating: but here is my observation. From Boulogne to Paris it will cost me near ten guineas; but then consider, I travel alone, and carry Louis most part of the way in the chaise with me. *Nous autres milords Anglois* are not often so frugal. Your brother,[1] last year, had ninety-nine English to dinner on the King's birth-day. How many of them do you think dropped so little as ten guineas on this road? In short, there are the seeds of a calculation for you; and if you will water them with a torrent of words, they will produce such a dissertation, that you will be able to vie with George Grenville next session in plans of national economy[2] – only be sure not to tax travelling till I come back, loaded with purchases; nor, till then, propagate my ideas. It will be time enough for me to be thrifty of the nation's money, when I have spent all my own. . . .

344. *Paris.*

Paris, 15 September 1765.

I am but two days old here, Madam, and I doubt I wish I was really so, and had my life to begin, to live it here. You see how just I am, and ready to make *amende honorable* to your ladyship. Yet I have seen very little. My Lady Hertford has cut me to pieces, and thrown me into a cauldron with tailors, periwig-makers, snuff-box-wrights, milliners, &c. which really took up but little time; and I am come out quite new, with everything but youth. The journey recovered me

---

1 Conway's brother Lord Hertford had until July 1765 been British Ambassador in Paris.
2 George Grenville (1712–70) was, following the resignation in 1763 of Lord Bute, the First Lord of the Treasury.

with magic expedition. My strength, if mine could ever be called strength, is returned; and the gout going off in a minuet step. I will say nothing of my spirits, which are indecently juvenile, and not less improper for my age than for the country where I am; which, if you will give me leave to say it, has a thought too much gravity. I don't venture to laugh or talk nonsense, but in English.

Madame Geoffrin[1] came to town but last night, and is not visible on Sundays; but I hope to deliver your ladyship's letter and packet to-morrow. Mesdames d'Aiguillon, d'Egmont, and Chabot, and the Duc de Nivernois are all in the country. Madame de Boufflers is at l'Isle Adam, whither my Lady Hertford is gone to-night to sup, for the first time, being no longer chained down to the incivility of an ambassadress. She returns after supper; an irregularity that frightens me, who have not yet got rid of all my barbarisms. There is one, alas! I never shall get over – the dirt of this country: it is melancholy, after the purity of Strawberry! The narrowness of the streets, trees clipped to resemble brooms, and planted on pedestals of chalk, and a few other points, do not edify me. The French Opera, which I have heard to-night, disgusted me as much as ever; and the more for being followed by the "Devin de Village,"[2] which shows that they can sing without cracking the drum of one's ear. The scenes and dances are delightful: the Italian comedy charming. Then I am in love with *treillage* and fountains, and will prove it at Strawberry. Chantilly is so exactly what it was when I saw it above twenty years ago, that I recollected the very position of Monsieur le Duc's chair and the gallery.[3] The latter gave me the first idea of mine; but, presumption apart, mine is a thousand times prettier. I gave my Lord Herbert's compliments to the statue of his friend the Constable; and, waiting some time for the concierge, I called out *Où est Vatel?*[4]

In short, Madam, being as tired as one can be of one's own country, – I don't say whether that is much or little, – I find myself wonderfully disposed to like this. Indeed I wish I could wash it. Madame

1 See letter 217, p. 309, n. 2.
2 With words and music by Rousseau.
3 Louis-Henri, Duc de Bourbon and Prince de Condé (1692–1740), prime minister of France 1723–6, whose château at Chantilly Walpole had visited with Gray in 1739. The gallery there, as at Strawberry Hill, had a series of mirrors on one wall facing a line of windows on the other.
4 The Constable was Henri, Duc de Montmorency (1534–1614), whom Lord Herbert describes visiting in his memoirs, as printed at Strawberry Hill in 1764. Vatel was

de Guerchy[1] is all goodness to me; but that is not new. I have already been prevented by great civilities from Madame de Bentheim and my old friend Madame de Mirepoix;[2] but am not likely to see the latter much, who is grown a most particular favourite of the King, and seldom from him. The Dauphin is ill, and thought in a very bad way. I hope he will live, lest the theatres should be shut up. Your ladyship knows I never trouble my head about royalties, farther than it affects my own interest. In truth, the way that princes affect my interest is not the common way.

I have not yet tapped the chapter of baubles, being desirous of making my revenues maintain me here as long as possible. It will be time enough to return to my Parliament when I want money.

Mr. Hume, that is *the Mode*,[3] asked much about your ladyship. I have seen Madame de Monaco, and think her very handsome, and extremely pleasing. The younger Madame d'Egmont, I hear, disputes the palm with her; and Madame de Brionne is not left without partisans. The nymphs of the theatres are *laides à faire peur*, which at my age is a piece of luck, like going into a shop of curiosities, and finding nothing to tempt one to throw away one's money.

There are several English here, whether I will or not. I certainly did not come for them, and shall connect with them as little as possible. The few I value, I hope sometimes to hear of. Your ladyship guesses how far that wish extends. Consider too, Madam, that one of my unworthinesses is washed and done away, by the confession I made in the beginning of my letter.

345. *Anglomania.*

TO THE COUNTESS OF SUFFOLK

Paris, 20 September 1765.

I obey your commands, Madam, though it is to talk of myself. The journey has been of great service to me, and my strength

---

chef to Louis de Bourbon, Prince de Condé (1621–86), "the Great Condé", and had killed himself during a visit to Chantilly of Louis XIV because he feared that the fish would be late for Friday's feast.
1 Wife to the Comte de Guerchy, for whom see letter 61, p. 98, n. 3.
2 See letter 207, p. 291, n. 4.
3 David Hume had been Lord Hertford's unofficial secretary in Paris.

returned sensibly in two days. Nay, though all my hours are turned topsy-turvy, I find no inconvenience, but dine at half an hour after two, and sup at ten, as easily as I did in England at my usual hours. Indeed breakfast and dinner, now and then jostle one another, but I have found an excellent preservative against sitting up late which is by not playing at whist. They constantly tap a rubber before supper, get up in the middle of a game, finish it after a meal of three courses and a dessert; add another rubber to it; then take their knotting-bags, draw together into a little circle, and start some topic of literature or irreligion, and chat till it is time to go to bed; that is, till you would think it time to get up again. The women are very good humoured and easy; most of the men disagreeable enough. However as everything English is in fashion, our bad French is accepted into the bargain. Many of us are received everywhere. Mr. Hume is fashion itself, although his French is almost as unintelligible as his English; Mr. Stanley is extremely liked, and, if liking them, good humour and spirits can make anybody please, Mr. Elliot will not fail: for my own part I receive the greatest civilities, and in general am much amused. But I could wish there was less whist, and somewhat more cleanliness. My Lady Brown and I have diverted ourselves with the idea of Lady Blandford here.[1] I am convinced she would walk upon stilts for fear of coming near the floors, and that would rather be a droll sight.

The town is extremely empty at present, our manners having gained so much in that respect too, as to send them all into the country till winter. Their country houses would appear to me no more rural than those in Paris. Their gardens are like *deserts* with no more verdure or shade. What trees they have are stripped up, and cut straight at top; it is quite the massacre of the innocents. Their houses in town are all white, and gold and looking-glass: I never know one from another. Madame de Mirepoix's, though small, has the most variety and a little leaven of English.

You see, Madam, it will take some time to make me a perfect Frenchman. Upon the whole I am very well amused, which is all I seek besides my health. I am a little too old to be inquiring into their government or politics, being come hither, not to finish my studies, but to forget them. One may always take one's choice here,

---

1   Lady Browne and Lady Blandford were dowagers visited at home by Walpole.

old folks may be as young as they please, and the young, as wise as they will. The former not only suits my age better, but my inclination, though the *bon ton* here is to be grave and learned. When Miss Hotham,[1] to whom I beg my best compliments, is so good as to acknowledge the receipt of this, I must desire her to direct to her and your Ladyship's most obedient humble servant,

Hor. Walpole.

346. *French Life.*

TO GEORGE MONTAGU, ESQ.

Paris, 22 September 1765.

. . . Nothing can be more obliging than the reception I meet with everywhere. It may not be more sincere (and why should it?) than our cold and bare civility; but it is better dressed, and looks natural; one asks no more. I have begun to sup in French houses, and as Lady Hertford has left Paris to-day, shall increase my intimacies. There are swarms of English here, but most of them are going, to my great satisfaction. As to the greatest part are very young, they can no more be entertaining to me than I to them, and it certainly was not my countrymen that I came to live with. Suppers please me extremely; I love to rise and breakfast late, and to trifle away the day as I like. There are sights enough to answer that end, and shops you know are an endless field for me. The city appears much worse to me than I thought I remembered it. The French music as shocking as I knew it was. The French stage is fallen off, though in the only part I have seen Le Kain I admire him extremely. He is very ugly and ill made, and yet has an heroic dignity which Garrick wants, and great fire. The Dumenil I have not seen yet, but shall in a day or two. It is a mortification that I cannot compare her with the Clairon, who has left the stage. Grandval[2] I saw through a whole play without suspecting it was he. Alas! four-and-twenty years make strange havoc with us mortals! You cannot imagine how this struck me! The Italian comedy now united with their *opera comique*, is their most perfect

<hr>

1 Amanuensis to Lady Suffolk.
2 Walpole summarises some leading Parisian actors of the day: Henri-Louis Cain or Lekain, Marie-Françoise Dumesnil, Mlle. Clairon, and François-Charles Racot de Grandval.

diversion; but alas! harlequin, my dear favourite harlequin, my passion, makes me more melancholy than cheerful. Instead of laughing,
I sit silently reflecting how everything loses charms when one's own
youth does not lend it gilding! When we are divested of that
eagerness and illusion with which our youth presents objects to us,
we are but the *caput mortuum* of pleasure.

Grave as these ideas are, they do not unfit me for French company. The present tone is serious enough in conscience. Unluckily,
the subjects of their conversation are duller to me than my own
thoughts, which may be tinged with melancholy reflections, but
I doubt from my constitution will never be insipid.

The French affect philosophy, literature, and free-thinking: the
first never did, and never will possess me; of the two others I have
long been tired. Freethinking is for one's self, surely not for society;
besides one has settled one's way of thinking, or knows it cannot be
settled, and for others I do not see why there is not as much bigotry
in attempting conversions from any religion as to it. I dined to-day
with a dozen *savans*, and though all the servants were waiting, the
conversation was much more unrestrained, even on the Old Testament, than I would suffer at my own table in England, if a single
footman was present. For literature, it is very amusing when one has
nothing else to do. I think it rather pedantic in society; tiresome
when displayed professedly; and, besides, in this country one is sure
it is only the fashion of the day. Their taste in it is worst of all: could
one believe that when they read our authors, Richardson and Mr.
Hume should be their favourites? The latter is treated here with perfect veneration. His History, so falsified in many points, so partial
in as many, so very unequal in its parts, is thought the standard of
writing.

In their dress and equipages they are grown very simple. We
English are living upon their old gods and goddesses; I roll about in
a chariot decorated with cupids, and look like the grandfather of
Adonis.

Of their parliaments and clergy I hear a good deal, and attend
very little: I cannot take up any history in the middle, and was too
sick of politics at home to enter into them here. In short, I have done
with the world, and live in it rather than in a desert, like you. Few
men can bear absolute retirement, and we English worst of all.
We grow so humoursome, so obstinate and capricious, and so

prejudiced, that it requires a fund of good-nature like yours not to grow morose. Company keeps our rind from growing too coarse and rough; and though at my return I design not to mix in public, I do not intend to be quite a recluse. My absence will put it in my power to take up or drop as much as I please. Adieu! I shall inquire about your commission of books, but having been arrived but ten days, have not yet had time. Need I say? – no I need not – that nobody can be more affectionately yours than, &c.

347. *French Society and the Court.*

TO JOHN CHUTE, ESQ.

Paris, 3 October 1765.

I don't know where you are, nor when I am likely to hear of you. I write at random, and, as I talk, the first thing that comes into my pen.

I am, as you certainly conclude, much more amused than pleased. At a certain time of life, sights and new objects may entertain one, but new people cannot find any place in one's affection. New faces with some name or other belonging to them, catch my attention for a minute – I cannot say many preserve it. Five or six of the women that I have seen already are very sensible. The men are in general much inferior, and not even agreeable. They sent us their best, I believe, at first, the Duc de Nivernois.[1] Their authors, who by the way are everywhere, are worse than their own writings, which I don't mean as a compliment to either. In general, the style of conversation is solemn, pedantic, and seldom animated, but by a dispute. I was expressing my aversion to disputes: Mr. Hume, who very greatfully admires the tone of Paris, having never known any other tone, said with great surprise, "Why, what do you like, if you hate both disputes and whisk?"

What strikes me the most upon the whole is, the total difference of manners between them and us, from the greatest object to the least. There is not the smallest similitude in the twenty-four hours. It is obvious in every trifle. Servants carry their lady's train,

1 Louis-Jules Barbon Mancini-Mazarini (1716–98), Duc de Nivernais, diplomat and writer, who had negotiated the Treaty of Paris in 1763 as Ambassador Extraordinary to London. For Walpole's account of him, see letter 352.

and put her into her coach with their hat on. They walk about the streets in the rain with umbrellas to avoid putting on their hats; driving themselves in open chaises in the country without hats, in the rain too, and yet often wear them in a chariot in Paris when it does not rain. The very footmen are powdered from the break of day, and yet wait behind their master, as I saw the Duc of Praslin's do, with a red pocket-handkerchief about their necks. Versailles, like everything else, is a mixture of parade and poverty, and in every instance exhibits something most dissonant from our manners. In the colonnades, upon the staircases, nay in the antechambers of the royal family, there are people selling all sorts of wares. While we were waiting in the Dauphin's sumptuous bedchamber, till his dressing-room door should be opened, two fellows were sweeping it, and dancing about in sabots to rub the floor.

You perceive that I have been presented. The Queen took great notice of me; none of the rest said a syllable. You are let into the King's bedchamber just as he has put on his shirt; he dresses and talks good-humouredly to a few, glares at strangers, goes to mass, to dinner, and a-hunting. The good old Queen, who is like Lady Primrose in the face, and Queen Caroline in the immensity of her cap, is at her dressing-table, attended by two or three old ladies, who are languishing to be in Abraham's bosom, as the only man's bosom to whom they can hope for admittance. Thence you go to the Dauphin, for all is done in an hour. He scarce stays a minute; indeed, poor creature, he is a ghost, and cannot possibly last three months. The Dauphiness is in her bedchamber, but dressed and standing; looks cross, is not civil, and has the true Westphalian grace and accents. The four Mesdames,[1] who are clumsy plump old wenches, with a bad likeness to their father, stand in a bedchamber in a row, with black cloaks and knotting-bags, looking good-humoured, not knowing what to say, and wriggling as if they wanted to make water. This ceremony too is very short; then you are carried to the Dauphin's three boys, who you may be sure only bow and stare. The Duke of Berry looks weak and weak-eyed: the Count de Provence is a fine boy; the Count d'Artois[2] well enough. The whole concludes

1 The four unmarried daughters of Louis XV.
2 The Dauphin's three boys, grandsons of Louis XV: the Duc de Berry became Louis XVI, the Comte de Provence became Louis XVIII, and the Count d'Artois became Charles X.

with seeing the Dauphin's little girl dine, who is as round and as fat as a pudding.

In the Queen's antechamber we foreigners and the foreign ministers were shown the famous beast of the Gevaudan,[1] just arrived, and covered with a cloth, which two chasseurs lifted up. It is an absolute wolf, but uncommonly large, and the expression of agony and fierceness remains strongly imprinted on its dead jaws.

I dined at the Duc of Praslin's[2] with four-and-twenty ambassadors and envoys, who never go but on Tuesdays to court. He does the honours sadly, and I believe nothing else well, looking important and empty. The Duc de Choiseul's[3] face, which is quite the reverse of gravity, does not promise much more. His wife is gentle, pretty, and very agreeable. The Duchess of Praslin, jolly, red-faced, looking very vulgar, and being very attentive and civil. I saw the Duc de Richelieu in waiting, who is pale, except his nose, which is red, much wrinkled, and exactly a remnant of that age which produced General Churchill, Wilks the player, the Duke of Argyll, &c. ... Adieu!

348. *The Same.*

TO THE HON. H. S. CONWAY

Paris, 2 October 1765.

... For so reasonable a person as I am, I have changed my mind very often about this country. The first five days I was in violent spirits; then came a dismal cloud of whisk and literature, and I could not bear it. At present I begin, very *Englishly* indeed, to establish a right to my own way. I laugh, and talk nonsense, and make them hear me. There are two or three houses where I go quite at my ease, am never asked to touch a card, nor hold dissertations. Nay, I don't pay homage to their authors. Every woman has one or two planted in her house, and God knows how they water them. The old President

---

1 A large wolf that had ravaged the Auvergne and the Gévaudan. It had been killed two weeks earlier.
2 César Gabriel de Choiseul, Duc de Praslin (1712–85) was then Secretary of State for Foreign Affairs.
3 The Duc de Choiseul (for whom see letter 217, p. 309, n. 1), first minister and cousin of the Duc de Praslin.

Hénault[1] is the pagod at Madame du Deffand's, an old blind debauchée of wit, where I supped last night.[2] The President is very near deaf, and much nearer superannuated. He sits by the table: the mistress of the house, who formerly was his, inquires after every dish on the table, is told who has eaten of which, and then bawls the bill of fare of every individual into the President's ears. In short, every mouthful is proclaimed, and so is every blunder I make against grammar. Some that I make on purpose, succeed; and one of them is to be reported to the Queen to-day by Hénault, who is her great favourite. I had been at Versailles; and having been much taken notice of by her Majesty, I said, alluding to Madame Sévigné, *La Reine est le plus grand roi du monde.*[3] You may judge if I am in possession by a scene that passed after supper. Sir James Macdonald had been mimicking Hume: I told the women, (who, besides the mistress, were the Duchess de la Valière, Madame de Forcalquier, and a demoiselle,) that to be sure they would be glad to have a specimen of Mr. Pitt's manner of speaking; and that nobody mimicked him so well as Elliot.[4] They firmly believed it, teased him for an hour, and at last said he was the rudest man in the world not to oblige them. It appeared the more strange, because here everybody sings, reads their own works in public, or attempts any one thing without hesitation or capacity. Elliot speaks miserable French; which added to the diversion.

I had had my share of distress in the morning, by going through the operation of being presented to the Royal Family, down to the little Madame's pap-dinner, and had behaved as sillily as you will easily believe; hiding myself behind every mortal. The Queen called me up to her dressing-table, and seemed mightily disposed to gossip with me; but instead of enjoying my glory like Madame de Sévigné, I slunk back into the crowd after a few questions. She told Monsieur de Guerchy of it afterwards, and that I had run away from her, but said she would have her revenge at Fontainbleau. So I must go

1 Charles-Jean-François Hénault (1685–1770), writer and historian, superintendent of the Queen's household, and friend of Mme. du Deffand. Walpole printed his tragedy *Cornélie, Vestale* in 1768.
2 For Mme. du Deffand see introduction to letter 215.
3 A comment attributed to Mme. de Sévigné after her being noticed by Louis XIV at Versailles.
4 Sir Gilbert Elliot of Minto (1722–77), politician, of whom Walpole was not an admirer.

thither, which I did not intend. The King, Dauphin, Dauphiness, Mesdames, and the wild beast did not say a word to me. Yes, the wild beast, he of the Gevaudan. He is killed, and actually in the Queen's antechamber, where he was exhibited to us with as much parade as if it was Mr. Pitt. It is an exceedingly large wolf, and, the connoisseurs say, has twelve teeth more than any wolf ever had since the days of Romulus's wet-nurse. The critics deny it to be the true beast; and I find most people think the beast's name is *legion, for there are many*. He was covered with a sheet, which two chasseurs lifted up for the foreign ministers and strangers. I dined at the Duke of Praslin's with five-and-twenty tomes of the *corps diplomatique;* and after dinner was presented, by Monsieur de Guerchy, to the Duc de Choiseul. The Duc de Praslin is as like his own letters in D'Eon's book as he can stare; that is, I believe, a very silly fellow. His wisdom is of the grave kind. His cousin, the first minister, is a little volatile being, whose countenance and manner had nothing to frighten me for my country. I saw him but for three seconds, which is as much as he allows to any one body or thing. Monsieur de Guerchy,[1] whose goodness to me is inexpressible, took the trouble of walking everywhere with me, and carried me particularly to see the new office for state papers.[2] I wish I could send it you. It is a large building, disposed like an hospital, with the most admirable order and method. Lodgings for every officer; his name and business written over his door. In the body is a perspective of seven or eight large chambers: each is painted with emblems, and wainscotted with presses with wired doors and crimson curtains. Over each press, in golden letters, the country to which the pieces relate, as Angleterre, Allemagne, &c. Each room has a large funnel of bronze with *or moulu*, like a column, to air the papers and preserve them. In short, it is as magnificent as useful.

From thence I went to see the reservoir of pictures at M. de Marigny's.[3] They are what are not disposed of in the palaces though sometimes changed with others. This *refuse*, which fills many rooms from top to bottom, is composed of the most glorious works of

---

1 He had been ambassador in England. – WALPOLE (see letter 61, p. 98, n. 3).
2 Dépôt des Archives des Affaires Étrangères at Versailles, designed by Berthier.
3 Abel-François Poisson de Vandières (1727–81), Marquis de Marigny, younger brother of Mme. de Pompadour, Director-General of the King's buildings, gardens, arts and manufactures, and an important collector.

Raphael, L. da Vinci, Giorgione, Titian, Guido, Correggio, &c. Many pictures, which I knew by their prints, without an idea where they existed, I found there.

The Duc de Nivernois is extremely obliging to me. I have supped at Madame de Bentheim's, who has a very fine house, and a woful husband. She is much livelier than any Frenchwoman. The liveliest man I have seen is the Duc de Duras: he is shorter and plumper than Lord Halifax, but very like him in the face. I am to sup with the Dussons on Sunday. In short, all that have been in England are exceedingly disposed to repay any civilities they received there. Monsieur de Caraman wrote from the country to excuse his not coming to see me, as his wife is on the point of being brought to bed, but begged I would come to them. So I would, if I was a man-midwife: but though they are easy on such heads, I am not used to it, and cannot make a party of pleasure of a labour. . . . Adieu!

349. *Madame du Deffand.*

TO GEORGE SELWYN

Dear George,   Paris, 2 December 1765.

In return for your kind line by Mr. Beauclerk[1] I send you a whole letter, but I was in your debt before, for making over Madame du Deffand to me, who is delicious; that is, as often as I can get her fifty years back; but she is as eager about what happens every day as I am about the last century. I sup there twice a week, and bear all her dull company for the sake of the Regent.[2] I might go to her much oftener, but my curiosity to see every body and every thing is insatiable, especially having lost so much time by my confinement. I have been very ill a long time, and mending much longer, for every two days undo the ground I get. The fogs and damps, which, with your leave, are greater and more frequent than in England, kill me. However, it is the country in the world to be sick and grow old in. The first step towards being in fashion is to lose an eye or a tooth. Young people I conclude there are, but where they exist I don't guess: not that I complain; it is charming to totter into vogue. If I could but run

1 See letter 224, p. 319, n. 2.
2 Mme. du Deffand had briefly in about 1721 been mistress to the Regent, the Duc d'Orléans.

about all the morning, I should be content to limp into good company in the evening. They humour me and fondle me so, and are so good-natured, and make me keep my armed-chair, and rise for nobody, and hand out nobody, and don't stare at one's being a skeleton, that I grow to like them exceedingly, and to be pleased with living here, which was far from the case at first: but then there was no soul in Paris but philosophers, whom I wished in heaven, though they do not wish themselves so. They are so overbearing and so underbred!

Your old flame, the Queen, was exceedingly kind to me at my presentation. She has been ever since at Fontainbleau, watching her son, whose death is expected every day,[1] though it is as much the fashion not to own it, as if he was of the immortal House of Brunswick. Madame Geoffrin is extremely what I had figured her, only with less wit and more sense than I expected. The Duchess d'Aiguillon is delightful, frank, and jolly, and handsome and good-humoured, with dignity too. There is another set in which I live much, and to my taste, but very different from all I have named, Madame de Rochfort, and the set at the Luxembourg. My newest acquaintance is Monsieur de Maurepas,[2] with whom I am much taken, though his countenance and person are so like the late Lord Hardwicke. From the little I have seen of him, we have reason, I believe, to thank Madame de Pompadour for his disgrace. At the Marquis de Brancas' I dined with the Duke de Brissac, in his red stockings: in short, I think my winter will be very well amused, whether Mr. Garrick and Mr. Pitt act or not.

Pray tell Lord Holland, that I have sent him the few new things that I thought would entertain him for a moment, though none of them have much merit. I would have written to him, had I had anything to tell him; which, you perceive by what I said, I had not. The affair of the Parliament of Brétagne, and the intended trial of the famous Mons. de la Chalotais by *commission*, against which the Parliament of Paris strongly inveighs, is the great subject in agitation;[3] but I know little of the matter, and was too sick of our own Parliaments to interest myself about these. The Hôtel de Carnavalet sends

1 The Dauphin died later that month.
2 See letter 217, p. 309, n. 1.
3 A dispute between the *parlement* of Brittany at Rennes, whose leader was Louis-René de Caradeuc de la Chalotais (1701–85), and the central government.

its blessings to you. I never pass it without saying an Ave Maria de Rabutin-Chantal, gratiâ plena! The Abbé de Malherbe has given orders that I should see Livry whenever I please. Pray tell me which convent was that of *nos Sœurs de Sante Marie*, where our friend used to go on the evening that Madame de Grignan set out for Provence?[1] . . .

I beg your pardon, my dear sir, for this idle letter; yet don't let it lie in your work-basket. When you have a quarter of an hour awake, and to spare, I wish you would bestow it on me. There are no such things as *bons-mots* here to send you, and I cannot hope that you will send me your own. Next to them, I should like Charles Townshend's, but I don't desire Betty's.[2]

I forgot to tell you that I sometimes go to Baron d'Olbach's;[3] but I have left off his dinners, as there was no bearing the authors, and philosophers, and savants, of which he has a pigeon-house full. They soon turned my head with a new system of ante-diluvian deluges, which they have invented to prove the eternity of matter. The Baron is persuaded that Pall Mall is paved with lava or deluge stones. In short, nonsense for nonsense, I like the Jesuits better than the philosophers. Were ever two men so like in their persons, or so unlike in their dispositions, as Dr. Gem and Brand?[4] Almost the first time I ever saw Gem, he said to me, "Sir, I am serious, I am of a very serious turn!" Yes, truly! Say a great deal for me to Lord March, and to the Rena's dogs *touffe ébourifée*.[5] The old President [Henault] would send his compliments to you, if he remembered you or anything else.

When we three meet again at Strawberry, I think I shall be able at least to divert Mr. Williams; but till then you must keep my counsel. Madame du Deffand says I have *le fou mocquer*, and I have not hurt myself a little by laughing at *whisk* and Richardson, though I have

---

1 The Hôtel de Carnavalet had been the Paris home of Mme. de Sévigné, who was admired by Selwyn as well as by Walpole. Livry was the house outside Paris where she had spent much of her youth, and Mme. de Grignan was her daughter and correspondent.
2 Charles Townshend (1725–67), politician and wit. For Betty, see letter 55, p. 90, n. 5.
3 Paul-Henri Thiry, Baron d'Holbach (1723–89), philosopher and encyclopedist.
4 Dr. Richard Gem (c. 1717–1800) and Thomas Brand (1718–70), M.P.: both occasional correspondents of Walpole. For Gem see also letter 367, note p. 519, n. 1.
5 A reference to one of Mme. de Sévigné's letters.

steered clear of the chapter of Mr. Hume; the only Trinity now in fashion here. *A propos*, I see by the papers that the Bishop of London [Terrick] is suppressing mass-houses. When he was Bishop of Peterborough and Parson of Twickenham, he suffered one under his nose. Did the Duchess of Norfolk[1] get him translated to London? I should conclude so; and that this was the first opportunity he had of being ungrateful. Adieu! my dear sir, yours most sincerely,

Horace Walpole.

350. *A French Mansion.*

TO THE COUNTESS OF SUFFOLK

Paris, 5 December 1765.

... Yesterday I dined at La Borde's,[2] the great banker of the Court. Lord! Madam, how little and poor all your houses in London will look after his! In the first place, you must have a garden half as long as the Mall, and then you must have fourteen windows, each as long as the other half, looking into it, and each window must consist of only eight panes of looking-glass. You must have a first and second ante-chamber, and they must have nothing in them but dirty servants. Next must be the grand cabinet, hung with red damask, in gold frames, and covered with eight large and very bad pictures, that cost four thousand pounds. I cannot afford them you a farthing cheaper. Under these, to give an air of lightness, must be hung bas-reliefs in marble. Then there must be immense *armoires* of tortoise-shells and ormolu, inlaid with medals. And then you may go into the petit-cabinet, and then into the great *salle*, and the gallery, and the billiard-room, and the eating-room; and all these must be hung with crystal lustres and looking-glass from top to bottom, and then you must stuff them fuller than they will hold with granite tables and porphyry urns, and bronzes, and statues, and vases, and the Lord or the devil knows what. But, for fear you should ruin yourself or the nation, the Duchess de Grammont must give you *this*, and Madame de Marseu *that;* and if you have anybody that has any taste to advise you, your eating-room must be hung with huge hunting-pieces in

1 She was a Catholic.
2 Marquis de La Borde (1724–94), financier. In his Paris Journals Walpole described the mansion as a "most magnificent house and large garden".

frames of all coloured golds, and at top of one of them you may have a setting-dog, who, having sprung a wooden partridge, it may be flying a yard off against the wainscot. To warm and light this palace it must cost you eight and twenty thousand livres a-year in wood and candles. If you cannot afford that, you must stay till my Lord Clive returns with the rest of the Indies.

The mistress of this Abrabian Night's Entertainment is very pretty, and Sir Laurence la Borde[1] is so fond of her, that he sits by her at dinner, and calls her *Pug*, or *Taw*, or I forget what.

Lady Mary Chabot always charges me to mention her to your Ladyship, with particular attention. There are some to whom I could wish your Ladyship would do me the same good office; but I have been too troublesome already, and will only mention Miss Hotham, Mr. Chetwynd, Lady Blandford, and St. James's Square.

351. *A "Letter" to Rousseau.*

TO THE HON. H. S. CONWAY

Paris, 12 January 1766.

I have received your letter by General Vernon, and another, to which I have writ an answer, but was disappointed of a conveyance I expected. You shall have it with additions, by the first messenger that goes; but I cannot send it by the post, as I have spoken very freely of some persons you name, in which we agree thoroughly. These few lines are only to tell you I am not idle in writing to you.

I almost repent having come hither; for I like the way of life and many of the people so well, that I doubt I shall feel more regret at leaving Paris than I expected. It would sound vain to tell you the honours and distinctions I receive, and how much I am in fashion; yet when they come from the handsomest women in France, and the most respectable in point of character, can one help being a little proud? If I was twenty years younger, I should wish they were not quite so respectable. Madame de Brionne, whom I have never seen, and who was to have met me at supper last night at the charming Madame d'Egmont's, sent me an invitation by the latter for

---

1 Previous editors have suggested that Walpole is here conflating La Borde with the extremely rich British financier Sir Lawrence Dundas (for whom see letter 337, p. 470, n. 2).

Wednesday next. I was engaged, and hesitated. I was told, "Comment! savez-vous que c'est qu'elle ne feroit pas pour toute la France?"[1] However, lest you should dread my returning a perfect old swain, I study my wrinkles, compare myself and my limbs to every plate of larks I see, and treat my understanding with at least as little mercy. Yet, do you know, my present fame is owing to a very trifling composition, but which has made incredible noise. I was one evening at Madame Geoffrin's joking on Rousseau's affectations and contradictions, and said some things that diverted them. When I came home, I put them into a letter,[2] and showed it next day to Helvetius and the Duc de Nivernois; who were so pleased with it, that, after telling me some faults in the language, which you may be sure there were, they encouraged me to let it be seen. As you know I willingly laugh at mountebanks, *political* or literary, let their talents be ever so great, I was not averse. The copies have spread like wildfire; *et me voici à la mode!* I expect the end of my reign at the end of the week with great composure. Here is the letter: –

LE ROI DE PRUSSE À MONSIEUR ROUSSEAU

Mon Cher Jean Jacques,

Vous avez renoncé à Génève votre patrie; vous vous êtes fait chasser de la Suisse, pays tant vanté dans vos écrits; la France vous a décreté. Venez donc chez moi; j'admire vos talents; je m'amuse de vos rêveries, qui (soit dit en passant) vous occupent trop, et trop longtemps. Il faut à la fin être sage et heureux. Vous avez fait assez parler de vous par des singularités peu convenables à un véritable grand homme. Démontrez à vos ennemis, que vous pouvez avoir quelquefois le sens commun: cela les fâchera, sans vous faire tort. Mes états vous offrent une retraite paisible; je vous veux du bien, et je vous en ferai, si vous le trouvez bon. Mais si vous vous obstiniez à rejetter mon secours, attendez-vous que je ne le dirai à personne.

1 Louise-Julie-Constance de Rohan-Montauban (1734–1815), Comtesse de Brionne, was a great beauty, hence the surprised response at the suggestion of refusing such a sought-after invitation.
2 Walpole's letter purported to be from Frederick the Great, offering the philosopher Rousseau an asylum in Prussia, and teasing him for his sense of persecution. It was circulated and then published shortly after David Hume had escorted Rousseau to England, but when Rousseau learned of it he convinced himself that the letter was the result of a conspiracy against him by Hume, Voltaire and d'Alembert, resulting in a total breach between himself and Hume.

Si vous persistez à vous creuser l'esprit pour trouver de nouveaux malheurs, choisissez les tels que vous voudrez. Je suis roi, je puis vous en procurer au gré de vos souhaits: et ce qui sûrement ne vous arrivera pas vis à vis de vos ennemis, je cesserai de vous persécuter quand vous cesserez de mettre votre gloire à l'être.

Votre bon ami,
FRÉDÉRIC ...

352. *French Friends.*

TO THOMAS GRAY

Paris, 25 January 1766.

I am much indebted to you for your kind letter, and advice; and though it is late to thank you for it, it is at least a stronger proof that I do not forget it. However, I am a little obstinate, as you know, on the chapter of health, and have persisted through this Siberian winter in not adding a grain to my clothes, and in going open-breasted without an under waistcoat. In short, though I like extremely to live, it must be in my own way, as long as I can: it is not youth I court, but liberty; and I think making oneself tender is issuing a *general warrant* against one's own person. I suppose I shall submit to confinement when I cannot help it; but I am indifferent enough to life not to care if it ends soon after my prison begins.

I have not delayed so long to answer your letter, from not thinking of it, or from want of matter, but from want of time. I am constantly occupied, engaged, amused, till I cannot bring a hundredth part of what I have to say into the compass of a letter. You will lose nothing by this: you know my volubility, when I am full of new subjects; and I have at least many hours of conversation for you at my return. One does not learn a whole nation in four or five months; but, for the time, few, I believe, have seen, studied, or got so much acquainted with the French as I have.

By what I said of their religious or rather irreligious opinions, you must not conclude their people of quality atheists – at least, not the men. Happily for them, poor souls! they are not capable of going so far into thinking. They assent to a great deal, because it is the fashion, and because they don't know how to contradict. They are ashamed to defend the Roman Catholic religion, because it is quite exploded; but I am convinced they believe it in their hearts. They hate the Parliaments and the philosophers, and are rejoiced that they may still idolize royalty. At present, too, they are a little triumphant: the Court has shown a little spirit, and the Parliaments much less: but as the Duc de Choiseul, who is very fluttering, unsettled, and inclined to the philosophers, has made a compromise with the Parliament of Bretagne, the Parliaments might venture out again, if, as I fancy will be the case, they are not glad to drop a cause, of which they began to be a little weary of the inconveniences.

The generality of the men, and more than the generality, are dull and empty. They have taken up gravity, thinking it was philosophy and English, and so have acquired nothing in the room of their natural levity and cheerfulness. However, as their high opinion of their own country remains, for which they can no longer assign any reason, they are contemptuous and reserved, instead of being ridiculously, consequently pardonably, impertinent. I have wondered, knowing my own countrymen, that we had attained such a superiority. I wonder no longer, and have a little more respect for English *heads* than I had.

The women do not seem of the same country: if they are less gay than they were, they are more informed, enough to make them very conversable. I know six or seven with very superior understandings; some of them with wit, or with softness, or very good sense.

Madame Geoffrin,[1] of whom you have heard much, is an extraordinary woman, with more common sense than I almost ever met with. Great quickness in discovering characters, penetration in going to the bottom of them, and a pencil that never fails in a likeness – seldom a favourable one. She exacts and preserves, spite of her birth and their nonsensical prejudices about nobility, great court and attention. This she acquires by a thousand little arts and offices of friendship: and by a freedom and severity, which seem to be her sole end of drawing a concourse to her; for she insists on scolding those she inveigles to her. She has little taste and less knowledge, but protects artisans and authors, and courts a few people to have the credit of serving her dependents. She was bred under the famous Madame Tencin, who advised her never to refuse any man; for, said her mistress, though nine in ten should not care a farthing for you,

1 See letter 217, p. 309, n. 2.

the tenth may live to be an useful friend. She did not adopt or reject the whole plan, but fully retained the purport of the maxim. In short, she is an epitome of empire, subsisting by rewards and punishments. Her great enemy, Madame du Deffand, was for a short time mistress of the Regent, is now very old and stone-blind, but retains all her vivacity, wit, memory, judgment, passions, and agreeableness. She goes to Operas, Plays, suppers, and Versailles; gives suppers twice a-week; has everything new read to her; makes new songs and epigrams, ay, admirably, and remembers every one that has been made these fourscore years. She corresponds with Voltaire, dictates charming letters to him, contradicts him, is no bigot to him or anybody, and laughs both at the clergy and the philosophers. In a dispute, into which she easily falls, she is very warm, and yet scarce ever in the wrong: her judgment on every subject is as just as possible; on every point of conduct as wrong as possible: for she is all love and hatred, passionate for her friends to enthusiasm, still anxious to be loved, I don't mean by lovers, and a vehement enemy, but openly. As she can have no amusement but conversation, the least solitude and ennui are insupportable to her, and put her into the power of several worthless people, who eat her suppers when they can eat nobody's of higher rank; wink to one another and laugh at her; hate her because she has forty times more parts – and venture to hate her because she is not rich. She has an old friend whom I must mention, a Monsieur Pondeveyle,[1] author of the "Fat puni," and the "Complaisant," and of those pretty novels, the "Comte de Cominge," the "Siege of Calais," and "Les Malheurs de l'Amour." Would not you expect this old man to be very agreeable? He can be so, but seldom is: yet he has another very different and very amusing talent, the art of parody, and is unique in his kind. He composes tales to the tunes of long dances: for instance, he has adapted the Regent's "Daphnis and Chloe" to one, and made it ten times more indecent; but is so old, and sings it so well, that it is permitted in all companies. He has succeeded still better in *Les Caractères de la danse*, to which he has adapted words that express all the characters of love. With all this he has not the least idea of cheerfulness in conversation; seldom speaks but on grave subjects, and not often on them; is a humourist, very supercilious, and wrapt up in admiration of his own country, as

1 Antoine de Ferriol de Pont de Veyle (1697–1774), playwright.

the only judge of his merit. His air and look are cold and forbidding; but ask him to sing, or praise his works, his eyes and smiles open and brighten up. In short, I can show him to you: the self-applauding poet in Hogarth's Rake's Progress, the second print, is so like his very features and very wig, that you would know him by it, if you came hither – for he certainly will not go to you.

Madame de Mirepoix's[1] understanding is excellent of the useful kind, and can be so when she pleases of the agreeable kind. She has read, but seldom shows it, and has perfect taste. Her manner is cold, but very civil; and she conceals even the blood of Lorraine, without ever forgetting it. Nobody in France knows the world better, and nobody is personally so well with the King. She is false, artful, and insinuating beyond measure when it is her interest, but indolent and a coward. She never had any passion but gaming, and always loses. For ever paying court, the sole produce of a life of art is to get money from the King to carry on a course of paying debts or contracting new ones, which she discharges as fast as she is able. She advertised devotion to get made *dame du palais* to the Queen; and the very next day this Princess of Lorrain was seen riding backwards with Madame Pompadour in the latter's coach. When the King was stabbed, and heartily frightened, the mistress took a panic too, and consulted D'Argenson, whether she had not best make off in time. He hated her, and said, "By all means." Madame de Mirepoix advised her to stay. The King recovered his spirits, D'Argenson was banished, and La Maréchale inherited part of the mistress's credit. – I must interrupt my history of illustrious women with an anecdote of Monsieur de Maurepas,[2] with whom I am much acquainted, and who has one of the few heads which approach to good ones, and who luckily for us was disgraced, and the marine dropped, because it was his favourite object and province. He employed Pondeveyle to make a song on the Pompadour: it was clever and bitter, and did not spare even Majesty. This was Maurepas absurd enough to sing at supper at Versailles. Banishment ensued; and lest he should ever be restored, the mistress persuaded the King that he had poisoned her predecessor Madame de Châteauroux. Maurepas is very agreeable, and

1 See letter 207, p. 291, n. 4.
2 See letter 217, p. 309, n. 1.

exceedingly cheerful; yet I have seen a transient silent cloud when politics are talked of.

Madame de Boufflers,[1] who was in England, is a *savante*, mistress of the Prince of Conti, and very desirous of being his wife. She is two women, the upper and the lower. I need not tell you that the lower is gallant, and still has pretensions. The upper is very sensible, too, and has a measured eloquence that is just and pleasing – but all is spoiled by an unrelaxed attention to applause. You would think she was always sitting for her picture to her biographer.

Madame de Rochfort[2] is different from all the rest. Her understanding is just and delicate; with a finesse of wit that is the result of reflection. Her manner is soft and feminine, and though a *savante*, without any declared pretensions. She is the *decent* friend of Monsieur de Nivernois; for you must not believe a syllable of what you read in their novels. It requires the greatest curiosity, or the greatest habitude, to discover the smallest connexion between the sexes here. No familiarity, but under the veil of friendship, is permitted, and Love's dictionary is as much prohibited, as at first sight one should think his ritual was. All you hear, and that pronounced with nonchalance, is, that *Monsieur un tel* has had *Madame une telle*.

The Duc de Nivernois[3] has parts, and writes at the top of the mediocre, but, as Madame Geoffrin says, is *manqué par tout; guerrier manqué, ambassadeur manqué, homme d'affaires manqué*, and *auteur manqué* – no, he is not *homme de naissance manqué*. He would think freely, but has some ambition of being governor to the Dauphin, and is more afraid of his wife and daughter, who are ecclesiastic fagots. The former out-chatters the Duke of Newcastle; and the latter, Madame de Gisors, exhausts Mr. Pitt's eloquence in defence of the Archbishop of Paris. Monsieur de Nivernois lives in a small circle of dependent admirers, and Madame de Rochfort is high-priestess for a small salary of credit.

The Duchess of Choiseul,[4] the only young one of these heroines, is not very pretty, but has fine eyes, and is a little model in waxwork,

1 In 1763 Mme. de Boufflers had visited Strawberry Hill (see letter 106) and had also visited Dr. Johnson at his chambers in the Temple.
2 Marie-Thérèse de Brancas (1716–82), Comtesse de Rochefort. She later married the Duc de Nivernais.
3 See letter 347, p. 484, n. 1.
4 Louise-Honorine Crozat du Châtel (1735–1801), who in 1750 married the Duc de Choiseul.

which not being allowed to speak for some time as incapable, has a hesitation and modesty, the latter of which the Court has not cured, and the former of which is atoned for by the most interesting sound of voice, and forgotten in the most elegant turn and propriety of expression. Oh! it is the gentlest, amiable, civil little creature that ever came out of a fairy egg! so just in its phrases and thoughts, so attentive and good-natured! Everybody loves it but its husband, who prefers his own sister the Duchesse de Grammont, an Amazonian, fierce, haughty dame, who loves and hates arbitrarily, and is detested. Madame de Choiseul, passionately fond of her husband, was the martyr of this union, but at last submitted with a good grace; has gained a little credit with him, and is still believed to idolize him. But I doubt it – she takes too much pains to profess it.

I cannot finish my list without adding a much more common character – but more complete in its kind than any of the foregoing, the Maréchale de Luxembourg.[1] She has been very handsome, very abandoned, and very mischievous. Her beauty is gone, her lovers are gone, and she thinks the devil is coming. This dejection has softened her into being rather agreeable, for she has wit and good-breeding; but you would swear, by the restlessness of her person and the horrors she cannot conceal, that she had signed the compact, and expected to be called upon in a week for the performance.

I could add many pictures, but none so remarkable. In those I send you there is not a feature bestowed gratis or exaggerated. For the beauties, of which there are a few considerable, as Mesdames de Brionne, de Monaco, et d'Egmont, they have not yet lost their characters, nor got any. . . .

---

1 Madeleine-Angélique de Neufville-Villeroy (1707–87), whose late husband, the Duc de Luxembourg, had been a Maréchal de France.

353. *Presentation of Books to Voltaire.*

TO MONSIEUR DE VOLTAIRE[1]

Sir,   Strawberry Hill, 21 June 1768.

You read English with so much more facility than I can write French, that I hope you will excuse my making use of my own tongue to thank you for the honour of your letter. If I employed your language, my ignorance in it might betray me into expressions that would not do justice to the sentiments I feel at being so distinguished.

It is true, Sir, I have ventured to contest the history of Richard the Third, as it has been delivered down to us: and I shall obey your commands, and send it to you, though with fear and trembling; for though I have given it to the world, as it is called, yet, as you have justly observed, Sir, *that* world is comprised within a very small circle of readers – and undoubtedly I could not expect that you would do me the honour of being one of the number. Nor do I fear you, Sir, only as the first genius in Europe, who have illustrated every science; I have a more intimate dependence on you than you suspect. Without knowing it, you have been my master, and perhaps the sole merit that may be found in my writings is owing to my having studied yours; so far, Sir, am I from living in that state of barbarism and ignorance with which you tax me when you say *que vous m'êtes peut-être inconnu.* I was not a stranger to your reputation very many years ago, – though I was at school, and had not the happiness of seeing you but remember to have then thought you honoured our house by dining with my mother: and yet my father was in a situation that might have dazzled eyes older than mine. The plain name of that father, and the pride of having had so excellent a father, to whose virtues truth at last does justice, is all I have to boast. I am a very private man, distinguished by neither dignities nor titles, which I have never done anything to deserve – but as I am certain that titles

---

1   "1768. June 20. Received a letter from Voltaire desiring my 'Historic Doubts.' I sent them and 'The Castle of Otranto' that he might see the preface, of which I told him. He did not like it, but returned a very civil answer defending his opinion. I replied with more civility, but dropping the subject, not caring to enter into a controversy; especially on a matter of opinion, on which, whether right or wrong, all France would be on his side, and all England on mine." – *Walpole's "Short Notes"* [see volume 13 of the Yale edition, pp. 1–51].

alone would not have procured me the honour of your notice, I am
content without them.

But, Sir, if I can tell you nothing good of myself, I can at least
tell you something bad; and, after the obligation you have conferred
on me by your letter, I should blush if you heard it from anybody but
myself. I had rather incur your indignation than deceive you. Some
time ago I took the liberty to find fault in print with the criticisms
you had made on our Shakspeare. This freedom, and no wonder,
never came to your knowledge. It was in a preface to a trifling
romance, much unworthy of your regard, but which I shall send you,
because I cannot accept even the honour of your correspondence,
without making you judge whether I deserve it. I might retract,
I might beg your pardon; but having said nothing but what
I thought, nothing illiberal or unbecoming a gentleman, it would be
treating you with ingratitude and impertinence, to suppose that you
would either be offended with my remarks, or pleased with my
recantation. You are as much above wanting flattery as I am above
offering it to you. You would despise me, and I should despise myself
– a sacrifice I cannot make, Sir, even to you. . . .

354. *Voltaire and Shakespeare.*

TO MONSIEUR DE VOLTAIRE

Strawberry Hill, 27 July 1768.

One can never, Sir, be sorry to have been in the wrong, when one's
errors are pointed out to one in so obliging and masterly a manner.
Whatever opinion I may have of Shakspeare, I should think him to
blame, if he could have seen the letter you have done me the honour
to write to me, and yet not conform to the rules you have there laid
down. When he lived, there had not been a Voltaire both to give
laws to the stage, and to show on what good sense those laws were
founded. Your art, Sir, goes still farther: for you have supported your
arguments, without having recourse to the best authority, your own
Works. It was my interest perhaps to defend barbarism and irregularity. A great genius is in the right, on the contrary, to show that
when correctness, nay, when perfection is demanded, he can still
shine, and be himself, whatever fetters are imposed on him. But
I will say no more on this head; for I am neither so unpolished as to

tell you to your face how much I admire you, nor, though I have taken the liberty to vindicate Shakspeare against your criticisms, am I vain enough to think myself an adversary worthy of you. I am much more proud of receiving laws from you, than of contesting them. It was bold in me to dispute with you even before I had the honour of your acquaintance; it would be ungrateful now when you have not only taken notice of me, but forgiven me. The admirable letter you have been so good as to send me, is a proof that you are one of those truly great and rare men who know at once how to conquer and to pardon. . . .

355. *French Trees and Philosophy.*

TO THE EARL OF STRAFFORD

Paris, 8 September 1769.

T'other night, at the Duchess of Choiseul's at supper, the intendant of Rouen asked me, if we have roads of communication all over England and Scotland? – I suppose he thinks that in general we inhabit trackless forests and wild mountains, and that once a year a few legislators come to Paris to learn the arts of civil life, as to sow corn, plant vines, and make operas. If this letter should contrive to scramble through that *desert* Yorkshire, where your Lordship has *attempted* to improve a dreary hill and uncultivated vale, you will find I remember your commands of writing from this capital of the world, whither I am come for the benefit of my country, and where I am intensely studying those laws and that beautiful frame of government, which can alone render a nation happy, great, and flourishing; where *lettres de cachet* soften manners, and a proper distribution of luxury and beggary ensures a common felicity. As we have a prodigious number of students in legislature of both sexes here at present, I will not anticipate their discoveries; but, as your particular friend, will communicate a rare improvement on nature, which these great philosophers have made, and which would add considerable beauties to those parts which your Lordship has already recovered from the waste, and taught to look a little like a Christian country. The secret is very simple, and yet demanded the effort of a mighty genius to strike it out. It is nothing but this: trees ought to be educated as much as men, and are strange awkward productions when not taught to hold themselves upright or bow on proper occasions. The academy *de belles-lettres* have even offered a prize for the man that shall recover the long-lost art of an ancient Greek, called *le sieur Orphée*, who instituted a dancing-school for plants, and gave a magnificent ball on the birth of the Dauphin of Thrace, which was performed entirely by forest-trees. In this whole kingdom there is no such thing as seeing a tree that is not well-behaved. They are first stripped up and then cut down; and you would as soon meet a man with his hair about his ears as an oak or an ash. As the weather is very hot now and the soil chalk, and the dust white, I assure you it is very difficult, powdered as both are all over, to distinguish a tree from a hair-dresser. Lest this should sound like a travelling hyperbole, I must advertise your Lordship, that there is little difference in their heights; for, a tree of thirty years' growth being liable to be marked as royal timber, the proprietors take care not to let their trees live to the age of being enlisted, but burn them, and plant others as often almost as they change their fashions. This gives an air of perpetual youth to the face of the country, and if adopted by us would realise Mr. Addison's visions, and

> "Make our bleak rocks and barren mountains smile."[1]

What other remarks I have made in my indefatigable search after knowledge must be reserved to a future opportunity; but as your Lordship is my friend, I may venture to say without vanity to you, that Solon nor any of the ancient philosophers who travelled to Egypt in quest of religions, mysteries, laws, and fables, never sat up so late with the ladies and priests and *presidents de parlement* at Memphis, as I do here – and consequently were not half so well qualified as I am to new-model a commonwealth. I have learned how to make remonstrances, and how to answer them. The latter, it seems, is a science much wanted in my own country – and yet it is as easy and obvious as their treatment of trees, and not very unlike it. It was delivered many years ago in an oracular sentence of my namesake – "Odi profanum vulgus, et arceo."[2] You must drive away the vulgar, and you must have an hundred and fifty thousand men to drive them

---

1 Slightly misquoted from Joseph Addison, "A Letter from Italy, to the Right Honourable Charles Lord Halifax in the Year 1701", line 140; *The Works of the Right Honourable Joseph Addison, Esq.* (1721), volume 1, p. 53.
2 Horace, *Carmina* III. i. 1: I hate the vulgar crowd, and keep them away.

away with – that is all. I do not wonder the intendant of Rouen thinks we are still in a state of barbarism, when we are ignorant of the very rudiments of government. . . .

356. *Versailles and St. Cyr.*

TO GEORGE MONTAGU, ESQ.

Paris, Sunday night, 17 September 1769.

I am heartily tired; but, as it is too early to go to bed, I must tell you how agreeably I have passed the day. I wished for you, the same scenes strike us both, and the same kind of visions has amused us both ever since we were born.

Well then; I went this morning to Versailles with my niece Mrs. Cholmondeley, Mrs. Hart, Lady Denbigh's sister, and the Count de Grave, one of the most amiable, humane, and obliging men alive. Our first object was to see Madame du Barri.[1] Being too early for mass, we saw the Dauphin and his brothers at dinner. The eldest is the picture of the Duke of Grafton, except that he is more fair, and will be taller. He has a sickly air, and no grace. The Count de Provence has a very pleasing countenance, with an air of more sense than the Count d'Artois, the genius of the family.[2] They already tell as many *bons-mots* of the latter as of Henri Quatre and Louis Quatorze. He is very fat, and the most like his grand-father of all the children. You may imagine this royal mess did not occupy us long: thence to the Chapel, where a first row in the balconies was kept for us. Madame du Barri arrived over against us below, without rouge, without powder, and indeed *sans avoir fait sa toilette;* an odd appearance, as she was so conspicuous, close to the altar, and amidst both Court and people. She is pretty, when you consider her; yet so little striking, that I never should have asked who she was. There is nothing bold, assuming, or affected in her manner. Her husband's sister was along with her. In the Tribune above, surrounded by prelates, was the amorous and still handsome King. One could not help smiling at the mixture of piety, pomp, and carnality. From chapel we

---

1 Jeanne Bécu (1743–93), Comtesse du Barry, mistress of Louis XV.
2 The grandsons of Louis XV: see letter 347, p. 485, n. 2. The Duc de Berry is now the Dauphin, his father having died in December 1765.

went to the dinner of the elder Mesdames.[1] We were almost stifled
in the ante-chamber, where their dishes were heating over charcoal,
and where we could not stir for the press. When the doors are
opened, everybody rushes in, princes of the blood, *cordons bleus*,
abbés, housemaids, and the Lord knows who and what. Yet, so used
are their highnesses to this trade, that they eat as comfortably and
heartily as you or I could do in our own parlours.

Our second act was much more agreeable. We quitted the Court
and a reigning mistress, for a dead one and a Cloister. In short, I had
obtained leave from the Bishop of Chartres to enter *into* St. Cyr;[2]
and, as Madame du Deffand never leaves anything undone that can
give me satisfaction, she had written to the abbess to desire I might
see everything that could be seen there. The Bishop's order was to
admit me, *Monsieur de Grave, et les dames de ma compagnie:* I begged
the abbess to give me back the order, that I might deposit it in the
archives of Strawberry, and she complied instantly. Every door flew
open to us: and the nuns vied in attentions to please us. The first
thing I desired to see was Madame de Maintenon's apartment. It
consists of two small rooms, a library, and a very small chamber, the
same in which the Czar saw her, and in which she died. The bed is
taken away, and the room covered now with bad pictures of the royal
family, which destroys the gravity and simplicity. It is wainscotted
with oak, with plain chairs of the same, covered with dark blue damask. Everywhere else the chairs are of blue cloth. The simplicity and
extreme neatness of the whole house, which is vast, are very remarkable. A large apartment above (for that I have mentioned is on the
ground-floor), consisting of five rooms, and destined by Louis
Quatorze for Madame de Maintenon, is now the infirmary, with
neat white linen beds, and decorated with every text of Scripture by
which could be insinuated that the foundress was a Queen. The hour
of vespers being come, we were conducted to the chapel, and, as it
was *my* curiosity that had led us thither, I was placed in the Maintenon's own tribune; my company in the adjoining gallery. The pensioners, two and two, each band headed by a man, march orderly to
their seats, and sing the whole service, which I confess was not a
little tedious. The young ladies, to the number of two hundred and

1 The daughters of Louis XV: see letter 347, p. 485, n. 1.
2 The convent school founded by Mme. de Maintenon, and to which she retired.

fifty, are dressed in black, with short aprons of the same, the latter and their stays bound with blue, yellow, green or red, to distinguish the classes; the captains and lieutenants have knots of a different colour for distinction. Their hair is curled and powdered, their coiffure a sort of French round-eared caps, with white tippets, a sort of ruff and large tucker: in short, a very pretty dress. The nuns are entirely in black, with crape veils and long trains, deep white handkerchiefs, and forehead cloths and a very long train. The chapel is plain but very pretty, and in the middle of the choir under a flat marble lies the foundress. Madame de Cambis, one of the nuns, who are about forty, is beautiful as a Madonna. The abbess has no distinction but a larger and richer gold cross: her apartment consists of two very small rooms. Of Madame de Maintenon we did not see fewer than twenty pictures. The young one looking over her shoulder has a round face, without the least resemblance to those of her latter age. That in the royal mantle, of which you know I have a copy, is the most repeated; but there is another with a longer and leaner face, which has by far the most sensible look. She is in black, with a high point head and band, a long train, and is sitting in a chair of purple velvet. Before her knees stands her niece Madame de Noailles, a child; at a distance a view of Versailles or St. Cyr, I could not distinguish which. We were shown some rich *reliquaires*, and the corpo santo that was sent to her by the Pope. We were then carried into the public room of each class. In the first, the young ladies, who were playing at chess, were ordered to sing to us the choruses of Athaliah; in another, they danced minuets and country-dances, while a nun, not quite so able as St. Cecilia, played on a violin. In the others, they acted before us the proverbs or conversations written by Madame de Maintenon for their instruction; for she was not only their foundress but their saint, and their adoration of her memory has quite eclipsed the Virgin Mary. We saw their dormitory, and saw them at supper; and at last were carried to their archives, where they produced volumes of her letters, and where one of the nuns gave me a small piece of paper with three sentences in her handwriting. I forgot to tell you, that this kind dame who took to me extremely, asked me if we had many converts and relics in England. I was much embarrassed for fear of destroying her good opinion of me, and so said we had but few now. Oh! we went too to the *apothecairie*, where they treated us with cordials, and where one of the ladies told me inoculation was a sin, as it was a voluntary detention from mass, and as voluntary a cause of eating *gras*. Our visit concluded in the garden, now grown very venerable, where the young ladies played at little games before us. After a stay of four hours we took our leave. I begged the abbess's blessing; she smiled, and said, she doubted I should not place much faith in it. She is a comely old gentlewoman, and very proud of having seen Madame de Maintenon. Well! was not I in the right to wish you with me? – could you have passed a day more agreeably. . . .

Yours ever.

357. *English Gardening Fashionable.*

TO JOHN CHUTE, ESQ.

Paris, 5 August 1771.

It is a great satisfaction to me to find by your letter of the 30th, that you have had no return of your gout. I have been assured here, that the best remedy is to cut one's nails in hot water. It is, I fear, as certain as any other remedy! It would at least be so here, if their bodies were of a piece with their understandings; or if both were as curable as they are the contrary. Your prophecy, I doubt, is not better founded than the prescription. I may be lame; but I shall never be a duck, nor deal in the garbage of the Alley.

I envy your *Strawberry tide*, and need not say how much I wish I was there to receive you. Methinks, I should be as glad of a little grass, as a seaman after a long voyage. Yet English gardening gains ground here prodigiously – not much at a time, indeed – I have literally seen one, that is exactly like a tailor's paper of patterns. There is a Monsieur Boutin, who has tacked a piece of what he calls an English garden to a set of stone terraces, with steps of turf. There are three or four very high hills, almost as high as, and exactly in the shape of, a tansy pudding. You squeeze between these and a river, that is conducted at obtuse angles in a stone channel, and supplied by a pump; and when walnuts come in I suppose it will be navigable. In a corner enclosed by a chalk wall are the samples I mentioned; there is a stripe of grass, another of corn, and a third *en friche*, exactly in the order of beds in a nursery. They have translated Mr. Whately's book,[1] and the Lord knows what barbarism is going to be laid at our door. This new *Anglomanie* will literally be *mad English.*

New *arrêts*, new retrenchments, new misery, stalk forth every day. The Parliament of Besançon is dissolved; so are the *grenadiers de France.* The King's tradesmen are all bankrupt; no pensions are paid, and everybody is reforming their suppers and equipages. Despotism makes converts faster than ever Christianity did. Louis *Quinze* is the true *rex Christianissimus,* and has ten times more success than his dragooning great grandfather. Adieu, my dear Sir! Yours most faithfully. . . .

358. *Madame de Sévigné.*

TO THE COUNTESS OF UPPER OSSORY

Strawberry Hill, Christmas night, 1773.

. . . Your reflection on Madame de Grignan's[2] letter after her mother's death is just, tender, and admirable, and like the painter's[3] hiding Agamemnon's face, when he despaired of expressing the agony of a parent. No, Madame de Sévigné could not have written a letter of grief, if her daughter had died first. Such delicacy in sentiment women only can feel. *We* can never attain that sensibility, which is at once refined and yet natural and easy, and which makes your sex write letters so much better than men ever did or can; and which if you will allow me to pun in Latin, though it seems your ladyship does not understand that language, I could lay down as an infallible truth in the words of my godfather,

"Pennis non homini datis,"[4]

the English of which is, "it was not given to *man* to write letters." For example, how tiresome are Corbinelli's[5] letters, and how he wears out the *scélérat* and the jealousy! . . .

1 Thomas Whately, *Observations on Modern Gardening, Illustrated by Descriptions* (1770).
2 Daughter of Mme. de Sévigné.
3 Pliny recounts that the artist Timanthes showed Agamemnon covering his face as his daughter Iphigenia was about to be sacrificed.
4 Horace, *Carmina* I. iii. 35: with wings not granted to men.
5 Jean Corbinelli (1622–1716), French writer.

359. *The Character of the French.*

Strawberry Hill, 7 July 1779.

... I have been often and much in France. In the provinces they may still be gay and lively; but at Paris, bating the pert *étourderie* of very young men, I protest I scarcely ever saw anything like vivacity – the Duc de Choiseul alone had more than any hundred Frenchmen I could select. Their women are the first in the world in everything but beauty; sensible, agreeable, and infinitely informed. The *philosophes*, except Buffon, are solemn, arrogant, dictatorial coxcombs – I need not say superlatively disagreeable. The rest are amazingly ignorant in general and void of all conversation but the routine with women. My dear and very old friend [Madame du Deffand] is a relic of a better age, and at nearly eighty-four has all the impetuosity that *was* the character of the French. They have not found out, I believe, how much their nation is sunk in Europe; – probably the Goths and Vandals of the North will open their eyes before a century is past. I speak of the swarming empires that have conglomerated within our memories. *We* dispelled the vision twenty years ago: but let us be modest till we do so again. ...

2. THE FRENCH REVOLUTION

360. *Heavy Expenses at the French Court.*

Arlington Street, 29 September 1755.

It is not I that am perjured for not writing to you oftener, as I promised; the war is forsworn. We do all we can; we take, from men-of-war and Domingo-men, down to colliers and cock-boats and from California into the very Bay of Calais. The French have taken but one ship from us, the Blandford, and that they have restored – but I don't like this drowsy civil lion; it will put out a talon and give us a cursed scratch before we are aware. Monsieur de Seychelles, who grows into power, is labouring at their finances and marine: they have struck off their *sous-fermiers*, and by a reform in what they call the King's pleasures, have already saved 1,200,000*l*.

sterling a year. Don't go and imagine that 1,200,000*l.* was all sunk in the gulph of Madame Pompadour,[1] or even in suppers and hunting; under the word the King's pleasures, they really comprehended his civil list; and in that light I don't know why our civil list might not be called *another King's pleasures*[2] too, though it is not all entirely squandered. In short, the single article of coffee for the Mesdames amounted to 3000*l.* sterling a year – to what must their rouge have amounted? ...

361. *Financial Straits.*

TO SIR HORACE MANN

Arlington Street, 31 December 1769.

... It is not less fortunate that the extreme distress of France prevents her from interfering (take notice I say *openly*) in our confusions. Monsieur du Châtelet is returned, as mild and pacific as if Sir Edward Hawke was lying before Brest with our late thunderbolt in his hand. Their distress for money is certainly extreme. Dinvaux (Choiseul's favourite Comptroller-General) has been forced to resign, *re infectâ*, and it is said that the Duc declined to name another, urging, that having recommended the two last to no purpose, he desired the chancellor might find one. As Maupeou[3] is of the opposite faction, his naming the new Comptroller-General has but an ill look for the minister – at least it is plain that Choiseul sees the impossibility of making brick without straw, and chooses to miscarry no more. I have been told here, that even their army is unpaid. I may add, to the amendment of our prospect, that the city itself has taken alarm, and does not care to give itself up to the new levellers. The latter having attempted to change the Common-Council this Christmas, have not succeeded in carrying above eight new members.[4] ...

---

1 Jeanne Antoinette Poisson, Marquise de Pompadour (1721–64), mistress of Louis XV from 1745 to 1751.
2 Alluding to the King's love of money. – WALPOLE.
3 René-Nicolas-Charles-Augustin de Maupeou (1714–92), Chancellor.
4 A reference to the increased numbers of supporters of Wilkes on the Common Council of the City of London.

362. *Bankruptcy.*

TO THE HON. H. S. CONWAY

Paris, 30 July 1771.

I do not know where you are, nor where this will find you, nor when it will set out to seek you, as I am not certain by whom I shall send it. It is of little consequence, as I have nothing material to tell you, but what you probably may have heard.

The distress here is incredible, especially at Court. The King's tradesmen are ruined, his servants starving, and even angels and archangels cannot get their pensions and salaries, but sing "Woe! woe! woe!" instead of Hosannahs. Compiegne is abandoned; Villiers-Coterets and Chantilly[1] crowded, and Chanteloup[2] still more in fashion whither everybody goes that pleases; though, when they ask leave, the answer is, "Je ne le défends ni le permets." This is the first time that ever the will of a King of France was interpreted against his inclination. Yet, after annihilating his Parliament, and ruining public credit, he tamely submits to be affronted by his own servants. Madame de Beauveau, and two or three high-spirited dames, defy this Czar of Gaul. Yet they and their cabal are as inconsistent on the other hand. They make epigrams, sing vaudevilles against the mistress, hand about libels against the Chancellor [Maupeou], and have no more effect than a sky-rocket; but in three months will die to go to Court, and to be invited to sup with Madame du Barry. The only real struggle is between the Chancellor [Maupeou] and the Duc d'Aiguillon.[3] The first is false, bold, determined, and not subject to little qualms. The other is less known, communicates himself to nobody, is suspected of deep policy and deep designs, but seems to intend to set out under a mask of very smooth varnish; for he has just obtained the payment of all his bitter enemy La Chalotais' pensions and arrears. He has the advantage, too, of being but moderately detested in comparison of his rival, and,

1 The country palaces of the Duke of Orleans and the Prince of Condé; who were in disgrace at court for having espoused the cause of the Parliament of Paris, banished by the Chancellor Maupeou. – WALPOLE.
2 The country seat of the Duc de Choiseul, to which, on his ceasing to be first minister, he was banished by the King. – WALPOLE.
3 Emmanuel-Armand Vignerot du Plessis-Richelieu, Duc d'Aiguillon (1720–88), Governor of Brittany. For La Chalotais see letter 349, p. 490, n. 3.

what he values more, the interest of the mistress.[1] The Comptroller-General serves both, by acting mischief more sensibly felt; for he ruins everybody but those who purchase a respite from his mistress.[2] He dispenses bankruptcy by retail, and will fall, because he cannot even by these means be useful enough. They are striking off nine millions from *la caisse militaire*, five from the marine, and one from the *affaires étrangères:* yet all this will not extricate them. You never saw a great nation in so disgraceful a position. Their next prospect is not better: it rests on an *imbécille* [Louis XVI.], both in mind and body. . . .

363. *Louvre Neglected.*

TO THE EARL OF STRAFFORD

Paris, 25 August 1771.

. . . Everybody feels in their own way. My grief is to see the ruinous condition of the palaces and pictures. I was yesterday at the Louvre. Le Brun's noble gallery, where the battles of Alexander are, and of which he designed the ceiling, and even the shutters, bolts, and locks, is in a worse condition than the old gallery at Somerset-house. It rains in upon the pictures, though there are stores of much more valuable pieces than those of Le Brun. Heaps of glorious works by Raphael and all the great masters are piled up and equally neglected at Versailles. Their care is not less destructive in private houses. The Duke of Orleans' pictures and the Prince of Monaco's have been cleaned, and varnished so thick that you may see your face in them; and some of them have been transported from board to cloth, bit by bit, and the seams filled up with colour; so that in ten years they will not be worth sixpence. It makes me as peevish as if I was posterity! I hope your lordship's works will last longer than these of Louis XIV. The glories of his *siècle* hasten fast to their end, and little will remain but those of his authors.

---

1 Madame du Barry. – WALPOLE.
2 The Baronne de la Garde, who was the mistress of the Comptroller-General, the Abbé Terrai (1715–78), was notorious for the sale of public offices.

364. *Promise of Better Times.*

Strawberry Hill, 2 September 1774.

... The King of France[1] has at last spoken out; both the Chancellor[2] and Terray are banished, and the old Parliament restored, or to be restored. As little as I care about the revolutions of the great planets, I am mightily pleased with this convulsion. I like old constitutions recovering themselves; and I abhorred the Chancellor, a consummate villain, who would have served Alexander VI. and Cæsar Borgia too, and wished no better than to have restored St. Ignatius and St. Nero. This young King is exceedingly in my good graces; and may gain my whole heart whenever he pleases, if he will but release Madame du Barri, for, though the tool of a vile faction, I would not be angry with a street-walker; nor make no difference between Thais and Fredegonde; between Con Phillips and the Czarina.[3]

By the way, one hears no more of my friend Pugatscheff;[4] yet perhaps he contributed to this peace. It is now part of my plan that the King of France should dethrone that woman, and their Majesties of Prussia and Sweden, and restore Corsica – not to the Genoese, but to themselves. You may think all this a great deal, but it is not a quarter so difficult as conquering one's-self, and relinquishing despotism. It is a greater victory to make happy than miserable; but then what glorious rewards! Think, how contemptible the end of Louis the Well-beloved, how bright the dawn of Louis XVI.! Can any power taste so sweet as this single word on the statue of Henri Quatre, *Resurrexit?* And then, what a blessed retirement the Chancellor's! How he must enjoy himself, when the loss of power is sweetened with the curses of a whole nation, who have not cursed him in vain! My whole heart makes a bonfire on this occasion. What

1 Louis XVI, who had just succeeded his grandfather.
2 De Maupeou (see letter 361, p. 511. n. 3).
3 Walpole here groups together the royal mistress Mme. du Barry; the London courtesan Teresia Constantia Phillips (1709–65); the cruel and murderous Fredegond, consort of the Frankish king of Soissons; the Athenian courtesan Thaïs, blamed for the burning of the palace of Persepolis; and Catherine the Great.
4 A Cossack leader and imposter who led an unsuccessful revolt against Catherine the Great; Walpole's friend in the sense of his opposing the Empress.

a century, which sees the Jesuits annihilated, and absolute power relinquished! I begin to believe in the Millennium, when the just shall reign on earth. I scorn to say a word more, or profane such a subject with heathen topics. Adieu! . . .

365. *Marie Antoinette.*

TO THE COUNTESS OF UPPER OSSORY

Paris, 23 August 1775, addition to letter begun 18 August.

I should have a heart of adamant, Madam, if I was not become a perfect Frenchman. Nothing could exceed my reception. I do not talk only of my dear old friend,[1] whose kindness augments with the century. The Marechales de Luxembourg and Mirepoix came to Paris to see me; the Duchesse de la Valière[2] met me in the outward room and embraced me. I am smeared with red, like my own crest the Saracen, and, in short, have been so kissed on both cheeks, that had they been as large as Madame de Virri's, they would have lost leather; but enough of vanity. I have landed on the moment of pomp and diversion. Madame Clotilde[3] was married on Monday morning, and at night was the banquet *royal*, – the finest sight *sur la terre*, – I believe, for I did not see it. I husband my pleasures and my person, and do not expose my wrinkles *au grand jour*. Last night I did limp to the *Bal Paré*, and as I am the hare with many real friends, was placed on the *banc des ambassadeurs*, just behind the royal family. It was in the theatre, the bravest in the universe; and yet taste predominates over expense. What I have to say, I can tell your Ladyship in a word, for it was impossible to see anything but the Queen![4] Hebes and Floras, and Helens and Graces, are street-walkers to her. She is a statue of beauty, when standing or sitting; grace itself when she moves. She was dressed in silver, scattered over with laurierroses; few diamonds, and feathers much lower than the Monument. They say she does not dance in time, but then it is wrong to dance in time.

1 Mme. du Deffand.
2 The widows of the Duc de Luxembourg and the Duc de Mirepoix, both Marshals of France, and Anne-Julie-Françoise de Crussol (1713–93), Duchesse de la Valière.
3 Marie-Adélaïde-Clotilde-Xavière (1759–1802), sister of Louis XVI, married the Prince of Piedmont, the future Charles Emmanuel IV of Sardinia.
4 Marie Antoinette.

Four years ago I thought her like an English Duchess, whose name
I have forgotten *for some years*. Horrible! but the Queen has had the
cestus[1] since. The King's likeness to a Duke, whose name is equally
out of my books, remains; and as if there was a fatality that chained
the two families together, Madame is as like Lady Georgiana as two
peas.[2] As your Ladyship and Lord Ossory cannot be so engrossed
with gazing on the Queen as I was, you will want to hear more of
the Court. I will try what I can remember of it. The new Princess
of Piedmont has a glorious face, the rest about the dimensions of
the last Lord Holland, which does not do so well in a stiff-bodied
gown. Madame Elizabeth is pretty and genteel; Mademoiselle a
good figure and dances well. As several of the royal family are *drapés*[3]
for the Princess of Conti, there were besides, only the King's two
brothers, the three elder Mesdames, the Princess de Lamballe, and
the Prince of Condé. Monsieur is very handsome; the Comte
d'Artois a better figure and better dancer. Their characters approach
to those of two other royal dukes.[4]

There were but eight minuets, and, except the Queen and Princesses, only eight lady dancers. I was not so struck with the dancing
as I expected, except with a *pas de deux* by the Marquis de Noailles
and Madame Nolstein. For beauty, I saw none, or the Queen effaced
all the rest. After the minuets were French country dances, much
encumbered by the long trains, longer tresses, and hoops. As the
weather was excessively sultry, I do not think the clothes, though of
gauze and the lightest silks, had much taste. In the intervals of dancing, baskets of peaches, China oranges (a little out of season), biscuits, ices, and wine and water, were presented to the royal family
and dancers. The ball lasted but just two hours. The Monarch did
not dance, but for the first two rounds of the minuets even the
Queen does not turn her back to him; yet her behaviour is as easy as
divine. To-night is a banquet for three hundred persons, given by
the Count de Virri,[5] and on Friday he gives a *bal masqué* to the

1 A bridal girdle acquired on her marriage to the Dauphin in 1770.
2 Walpole is pointing out similarities in appearance with Lady Ossory (formerly
Duchess of Grafton) and her family.
3 In court mourning.
4 The Yale editors suggest that the royal dukes referred to are the Dukes of Gloucester and Cumberland.
5 Francesco Maria Giuseppe Giustino, Conte di Viri (1736–1813), the Sardinian
Minister in Paris.

universe in a Colisée erected on purpose. I have excused myself from the first, as I have no curiosity to see how three hundred persons eat, but shall go for a moment to the other *fête*, as nothing but dominos are used, except the grand habit for the dancers. On Saturday is to be acted, in the same great theatre at Versailles, the "Connêtable de Bourbon," a new piece by Monsieur Guibert (author of the "Tactique")[1] graciously indulged to the Queen, and not to be profaned but there and at Fontainebleau, *car cela derogeroit;* and, besides, his father is a *vieux militaire,* who would not condescend to hear his son's play read, even to the Queen! The Prince de Beauvau is to place me, and there end the spectacles, for Monsieur Turgot[2] is *œconome.*

I am rejoiced, for the heat was so great last night, and I traversed so many corridors, that I would not have so much pleasure often for all the world. Thus, Madam, I have given your Ladyship a full account of my travels in this my second life; and you are relieved by my letters from England. I cannot help telling you the French are a little amazed at our sacrificing the substance of America to the sovereignty, for they grow as English in their ideas as we grow French. Well, I will go read our papers, that I may be able to dispute with them.

366. *The Bastile.*

TO THE REV. WILLIAM MASON

Strawberry Hill, 25 October 1775.

I am returned to my own Lares and Penates[3] – to my dogs and cats; and was not a little edified by my journey. I saw a king who accords everything that is asked for the good of his people, and I saw two ministers, Messieurs de Malesherbes[4] and Turgot, who do not let their master's benevolent disposition rust. The latter is

---

1 Jacques-Antoine-Hippolyte, Comte de Guibert (1743–90), author of *L'essai général de Tactique* (1772), whose tragedy *Le Connêtable de Bourbon* was said to be reserved for the royal stage.
2 Anne-Robert-Jacques Turgot, Baron de l'Aulne (1727–81), appointed Comptroller-General of Finances in 1774.
3 Roman household deities.
4 Chétrien-Guillaume de Lamoignon de Malesherbes (1721–94) had become Minister of the King's Household in July.

attempting to take off *corvées*,[1] that *quintesse* of cruel and ostentatious despotism, but the *country gentlemen*, that race of interested stupidity, will baffle him. Monsieur de Malesherbes, in the most simple and unaffected manner, gave me an account of his visitation of the Bastile, whence he released the prisoners, half of whom were mad with their misfortunes, and of many of whom he could not find even the causes of their commitment. One man refused his liberty: he said he had been prisoner fifteen years, and had nothing in the world left; that the King lodged and fed him, and he would not quit the Bastile unless they would give him half his pension. M. de Malesherbes reported it to the King, who replied, "*C'est juste*," and the man has fifteen hundred livres a year and his freedom. This excellent magistrate, who made my tears run down my cheeks, added, that what the prisoners complained of most was the want of pen and ink. He ordered it. The demons remonstrated and said the prisoners would only make use of the pen to write memorials against the Ministers; he replied, "*Tant mieux*." He is going to erect a court of six masters of Request to examine the petitions of those who demand *lettres de cachet* for their relations. Under the late Duc de la Vrillière, his mistress, Madame Sabatin, had a bureau of printed *lettres de cachet* with blanks, which she sold for twenty-five louis a piece.[2] When a great Scotch judge[3] was last in France, at the restoration of the old parliament, he said, "If the Ministers mean the good of the people, they are doing right, but if they regard the prerogative of the Crown, very wrong." What a diabolical But! Do not imagine these Ministers will hold their places long; they will soon be epigrammatised out of them. The first event since my return, after hearing of this gaol-delivery, is Mr. Sayer[4] being sent to the Bastile; but it is not the prisoners in this country that are mad, but the Ministers. They have committed him for designing to steal the Tower and the King, he and one more; and I suppose send them to New York;

---

1 An historic system of forced labour required of tenants by their landlords, not abolished in France until 1789.
2 *Lettres de cachet* were royal orders, whether of exile or of imprisonment, which were often requested by relatives in matters of family honour. Louis Phélypeaux, Duc de la Vrillière (1705–77), had ceased to be Minister of the King's Household earlier in 1775.
3 Lord Mansfield (see letter 333, p. 464, n. 1).
4 American revolutionary Stephen Sayre (1736–1818), a former sheriff of London, had just been committed to the Tower on a charge of treason for an alleged plot to capture George III.

not to Halifax, for that is gone, and Quebec too, and Boston by this time. So now we know what we have to do; only, retake all America, which is very easy, from three hundred thousand cowards. ...

367. *Malesherbes and Turgot.*

TO DR. GEM [1]

Arlington Street, 4 April 1776.

It is but fair, when one quits one's party, to give notice to those one abandons – at least, modern patriots, who often imbibe their principles of honour at Newmarket, use that civility. You and I, dear Sir, have often agreed in our political notions; and you, I fear, will die without changing your opinion. For my part, I must confess I am totally altered; and, instead of being a warm partisan of liberty, now admire nothing but despotism. You will naturally ask, what place I have gotten or what bribe I have taken? Those are the criterions of political changes in England – but, as my conversion is of foreign extraction, I shall not be the richer for it. In one word, it is the *relation du lit de justice*[2] that has operated the miracle. When two ministers[3] are found so humane, so virtuous, so excellent, as to study nothing but the welfare and deliverance of the people; when a king listens to such excellent men; and when a parliament, from the basest, most interested motives, interposes to intercept the blessing, must I not change my opinions, and admire arbitrary power? or can I retain my sentiments, without varying the object?

Yes, Sir, I am shocked at the conduct of the Parliament – one would think it was an English one! I am scandalised at the speeches of the *Avocat-général*,[4] who sets up the odious interests of the nobility and clergy against the cries and groans of the poor; and who employs his wicked eloquence to tempt the good young monarch, by personal views, to sacrifice the mass of his subjects to the privileges of the few. -- But why do I call it eloquence? The fumes of

---

1 An English physician long settled at Paris, no less esteemed for his professional knowledge, than for his kind attention to the poor who applied to him for medical assistance. – WALPOLE.
2 The first lit de justice held by Louis XVI. – WALPOLE.
3 Messieurs de Malesherbes and Turgot. – WALPOLE.
4 Antoine-Louis Séguier (1726–92), the Advocate-General of the *parlement* of Paris.

interest had so clouded his rhetoric, that he falls into a downright Iricism.[1] – He tells the King, that the intended tax on the proprietors of land will affect the property not only of the rich, but of the poor. I should be glad to know what is the property of the poor? Have the poor landed estates? Are those who have landed estates the poor? Are the poor that will suffer by the tax, the wretched labourers who are dragged from their famishing families to work on the roads? – But *it is* wicked eloquence when it finds a reason, or gives a reason for continuing the abuse. The Advocate tells the King, those abuses are *presque consacrés par l'ancienneté;* indeed, he says all that can be said for nobility, it is *consacrée par l'ancienneté;* and thus the length of the pedigree of abuses renders them respectable!

His arguments are as contemptible when he tries to dazzle the King by the great names of Henri Quatre and Sully, of Louis XIV. and Colbert,[2] two couple whom nothing but a mercenary orator would have classed together. Nor, were all four equally venerable, would it prove anything. Even good kings and good ministers, if such have been, may have erred; nay, may have done the best they could. They would not have been good, if they wished their errors should be preserved, the longer they had lasted.

In short, Sir, I think this resistance of the Parliament to the adorable reformation planned by Messrs. de Turgot and Malesherbes is more phlegmatically scandalous than the wildest tyranny of despotism. I forget what the nation was that refused liberty when it was offered. This opposition to so noble a work is worse. A whole people may refuse its own happiness; but these profligate magistrates resist happiness for others, for millions, for posterity! – Nay, do they not half vindicate Maupeou, who crushed them? And you, dear Sir, will you now chide my apostasy? Have I not cleared myself to your eyes? I do not see a shadow of sound logic in all Monsieur Séguier's speeches, but in his proposing that the soldiers should work on the roads, and that passengers should contribute to their fabric; though, as France is not so luxuriously mad as England, I do not believe passengers could support the expense of the roads. That argument, therefore, is like another that the Avocat proposes to the King, and which, he modestly owns, he believes would be impracticable.

1   As in Irish-ism.
2   The Duc de Sully (1560–1641) and Jean-Baptiste Colbert (1619–83) were respectively chief ministers to Henri IV and Louis XIV.

I beg your pardon, Sir, for giving you this long trouble; but I could not help venting myself, when shocked to find such renegade conduct in a Parliament that I was rejoiced had been restored. . . . Adieu, dear Sir. Yours most sincerely.

368. *Their Downfall.*

TO SIR HORACE MANN

Strawberry Hill, 18 May 1776, addition to letter begun 17 May.

. . . A great revolution has happened in France. Monsieur de Maurepas and Vergennes, either not to burn their own fingers, or to involve Turgot (of whom the former was grown jealous) and Malesherbes in a scrape, set the latter on representing to the Queen that she ought to abandon M. de Guisnes.[1] Her Majesty, and consequently the public, laughed at him. He, who hated his place, asked to resign, and it was at last granted. But to-day's letters add, that Turgot is also dismissed, and the King has thanked M. de Guisnes for his services and made him a *Duc à brevet*. This implies what I have said these six months, that a woman who passes every night with a man, however unmanly and unwomanly, would prevail at last, if he passed no moments with any other woman. Malesherbes is the best of men, but void of all ambition. Turgot has the ambition of reforming the nation, and blessing the people; is intrepid, indifferent to fortune, and determined to carry his points, or fall. Such men, friends of human kind, could not think of war, however fair the opportunity we offered to them. Poor France, and poor England! Choiseul, if not Choiseul, some Louvois[2] or other, will rise out of this fall of patriot philosophers; and then we shall be forced to see the wisdom of the Stamp Act, and of persisting in taxing America! Somebody rings at the gate, but I have said enough to furnish you with reflections. Monsieur de Noailles[3] is named ambassador hither, but that does not comfort me. . . .

1 Adrien-Louis de Bonnières (1735–1806), Duc de Guisnes. He had been appointed Ambassador to London in 1770.
2 François-Michel le Tellier, Marquis de Louvois (1641–91), Louis XIV's aggressive Secretary of State for War.
3 Emmanuel-Marie-Louis, Marquis de Noailles (1743–1822), Ambassador to England 1776–8.

369. *Necker About to Resign.*

TO THE HON. H. S. CONWAY

Berkeley Square, 28 May 1781.

... At the same time with yours I received a letter from another cousin at Paris, who tells me Necker[1] is on the verge, and in the postscript says, he has actually resigned. I heard so a few days ago: but this is a full confirmation. Do you remember a conversation at your house, at supper, in which a friend of yours spoke very unfavourably of Necker, and seemed to wish his fall? In my own opinion they are much in the wrong. It is true, Necker laboured with all his shoulders to restore their finances; yet I am persuaded that his attention to that great object made him clog all their military operations. They will pay dearer for money; but money they will have: nor is it so dear to them, for, when they have gotten it, they have only not to pay. A Monsieur Joly de Fleury is comptroller-general. I know nothing of him; but as they change so often, some able man will prove Minister at last – and there they will have the advantage again. ...

370. *French Revolution Imminent.*

TO MARY BERRY

Strawberry Hill, 9 July 1789.

You are so good and punctual, that I will complain no more of your silence, unless you are silent. You must not relax, especially until you can give me better accounts of your health and spirits. I was peevish before with the weather; but, now it prevents your riding, I forget hay and roses, and all the comforts that are washed away, and shall only watch the weather-cock for an east wind in Yorkshire.[2] What a shame that *I* should recover from the gout and from bruises, as I assure you I am entirely, and that *you* should have a complaint left! One would think that it was I was grown young again; for just now, as I was reading your letter in my bedchamber, while some of my *customers*[3] are seeing the house, I heard a gentleman in the

1 Jacques Necker (1732–1804), Director-General of Finances 1777–81.
2 Where Mary Berry was staying.
3 The name given by Mr. Walpole to parties coming to view his house. – BERRY.

Armoury ask the housekeeper as he looked at the bows and arrows, "Pray, does Mr. Walpole shoot?" No, nor with pistols neither. I leave all weapons to Lady Salisbury and Mr. Lenox; and, since my double marriage,[1] have suspended my quiver in the Temple of Hymen. Hygeia shall be my goddess, if she will send you back blooming to this region. Lady Cecilia thinks the house at Bushy Gate Park will be untenanted by the time of your return.

I wish I had preserved any correspondence in France, as you are curious about their present history; which I believe very momentous indeed. What little I have accidentally heard, I will relate, and will learn what more I can. On the King's being advised to put out his talons, Necker desired leave to resign, as not having been consulted, and as the measure violated his plan. The people, hearing his intention, thronged to Versailles; and he was forced to assure them from a balcony, that he was not to retire. I am not accurate in dates, nor warrant my intelligence, and therefore pretend only to send you detached scraps. Force being still in request, the Duc du Châtelet[2] acquainted the King that he could not answer for the French Guards. Châtelet, who, from his hot arrogant temper, I should have thought would have been one of the proudest opposers of the people, is suspected to lean to them. In short, Marshal Broglio is appointed commander-in-chief, and is said to have sworn on his sword, that he will not sheathe it till he has plunged it into the heart of *ce gros banquier Genevois*.[3] I cannot reconcile this with Necker's stay at Versailles. That he is playing a deep game is certain. It is reported that Madame Necker tastes previously everything he swallows. A vast camp is forming round Paris; but if the army is mutinous – the tragedy may begin on the other side. They do talk of an engagement at Metz, where the French troops, espousing the popular cause, were attacked by two German regiments, whom the former cut to pieces. The Duke and Duchess of Devonshire, who were at Paris, have thought it prudent to leave it; and my cousin, Mr. Thomas Walpole,

1 Walpole refers to his affectionate relationship with the two Berry sisters. The Yale editors note that Emily Cecil, Marchioness of Salisbury (1751–1835) was fond of archery and that Charles Lennox (1764–1819), later 4th Duke of Richmond, had recently fought two duels.
2 Louis-Marie-Florent de Lomont d'Haracourt, Duc du Châtelet (1727–93), formerly Ambassador to England, and the son of Emilie du Châtelet, author, scientist, and mistress of Voltaire.
3 Necker, who was dismissed by the King two days after the date of this letter.

who is near it, has just written to his daughters, that he is glad to be out of the town, that he may make his retreat easily.

Thus, you see the crisis is advanced far beyond orations, and wears all the aspect of civil war. For can one imagine that the whole nation is converted at once, and in some measure without provocation from the King, who, far from enforcing the prerogative like Charles the First, cancelled the despotism obtained for his grandfather by the Chancellor Maupeou, has exercised no tyranny, and has shown a disposition to let the constitution be amended? It did want it indeed; but I fear the present want of temper grasps at so much, that they defeat their own purposes; and where loyalty has for ages been the predominant characteristic of a nation, it cannot be eradicated at once. Pity will soften the tone of the moment; and the nobility and clergy have more interest in wearing a royal than a popular yoke; for great lords and high-priests think the rights of mankind a defalcation of their privileges. No man living is more devoted to liberty than I am; yet blood is a terrible price to pay for it! A martyr to liberty is the noblest of characters; but to sacrifice the lives of others, though for the benefit of all, is a strain of heroism that I could never ambition. . . .

371. *Storming of the Bastile.*

TO THE HON. H. S. CONWAY

Strawberry Hill, Wednesday night [15 July 1789].

I write a few lines only to confirm the truth of much of what you will read in the papers from Paris. Worse may already be come, or is expected every hour.

Mr. Mackenzie and Lady Betty called on me before dinner, after the post was gone out; and he showed me a letter from Dutens,[1] who said two couriers arrived yesterday from the Duke of Dorset and the Duchess of Devonshire, the latter of whom was leaving Paris directly. Necker had been dismissed, and was thought to be set out for Geneva. Breteuil,[2] who was at his country-house, had been sent for to succeed him. Paris was in an uproar; and, after the couriers had

1 Rev. Vincent-Louis Dutens (1730–1812), antiquary.
2 Louis-Auguste le Tonnelier (1733–1807), Baron de Breteuil, was chief minister only until 16 July, as he fled France after the fall of the Bastille.

left it, firing of cannon was heard for four hours together. That must have been from the Bastile, as probably, the *tiers état* were not so provided. It is shocking to imagine what may have happened in such a thronged city! One of the couriers was stopped twice or thrice, as supposed to pass from the King; but redeemed himself by pretending to be despatched by the *tiers état*. Madame de Calonne told Dutens, that the newly encamped troops desert by hundreds.

Here seems the egg to be hatched, and imagination runs away with the idea. I may fancy I shall hear of the King and Queen leaving Versailles, like Charles the First, and then skips imagination six-and-forty years lower, and figures their fugitive Majesties taking refuge in this country. I have besides another idea. If the Bastile conquers, still is it impossible, considering the general spirit in the country, and the numerous fortified places in France, but some may be seized by the *dissidents*, and whole provinces be torn from the Crown? On the other hand, if the King prevails, what heavy despotism will the *états*, by their want of temper and moderation, have drawn on their country! They might have obtained many capital points, and removed great oppression. No French monarch will ever summon *états* again, if this moment has been thrown away.

Though I have stocked myself with such a set of visions for the event either way, I do not pretend to foresee what will happen. Penetration argues from reasonable probabilities; but chance and folly are apt to contradict calculation, and hitherto they seem to have full scope for action. One hears of no genius on either side, nor do symptoms of any appear. There will perhaps: such times and tempests bring forth, at least bring out, great men. I do not take the Duke of Orleans or Mirabeau to be built *du bois dont on les fait;* no, nor Monsieur Necker. He may be a great traitor, if he made the confusion designedly: but it is a woful evasion, if the promised financier slips into a black politician! I adore liberty, but I would bestow it as honestly as I could; and a civil war, besides being a game of chance, is paying a very dear price for it.

For us, we are in most danger of a deluge; though I wonder we so frequently complain of long rains. The saying about St. Swithin is a proof of how often they recur; for proverbial sentences are the children of experience, not of prophecy. Good night! In a few days I shall send you a beautiful little poem from the Strawberry press.[1]

1 Hannah More's *Bishop Bonner's Ghost* (1789).

372. *Lafayette.*

TO THE COUNTESS OF UPPER OSSORY

Strawberry Hill, 4 August 1789.

I have had my house so filled lately by detachments of my family, that I had not a moment's time to answer your Ladyship's last.

For myself, I can say that I am not glad, in your Ladyship's sense of the words, that *Monsieur de la Fayette*[1] *governs France instead of their King;* nor do my principles lead me at all to approve of government violently wrenched, or violently exercised by anybody; nor do I believe that Monsieur de la Fayette's government will be lasting. I still less like liberty displayed by massacre, and without legal trials; and abhor the savage barbarity that the French have always shown on all commotions. The factions in the reign of Charles VI., and St. Bartelemi, and the Ligue, were all ferociously cruel; and their bearing the heads of those they have now murdered in triumph, is of a piece with their tearing the heart of the Maréchal d'Ancre[2] with their teeth.

The *États Généraux* are, in my opinion, the most culpable. The King had restored their old constitution, which all France has so idolised; and he was ready to amend that Constitution. But the *États*, with no sense, prudence, or temper, and who might have obtained a good government, and perhaps permanently, set out with such violence to overturn the whole frame, without its being possible to replace it at once with a sound model entirely new, and the reverse of every law and custom of their whole country, – have deposed not only their King, but, I should think, their own authority, for they are certainly now trembling before the populace, and have let loose havoc through every province, which sooner or later will end in worse despotism than that they have demolished. Weak their late monarch is, I have no doubt, and irresolute; but I cannot look on a King, who offers to soften and meliorate a constitution, as deserving to be compared with those princes, who have encroached on the liberties of their people.

1   Gilbert de Motier (1757–1834), Marquis de Lafayette had become Commander-in-Chief of the National Guard.
2   The Italian politician Concino Concini, Marquis d'Ancre, adviser of Louis XIII, assassinated in 1617.

Give me leave to conclude this chapter, Madam, with observing, that acute as you intended your present of Monsieur de la Fayette to me for my hero, I presume to think my principles as sound and as free from prejudice, faction, and personality as those of persons who, from pique to some, or partiality to others, applaud or condemn wholesale, whatever can be wire-drawn into a kind of parallel.

It is out of respect that I have presumed to defend myself, Madam, against your sarcasm on Lord Ossory and myself. When ladies are politicians, and love to attack, like the unfortunate Camilla in Virgil,[1] it is irreverent not to skirmish with them a little. Lord Ossory, like an ill-bred husband, is not so attentive, but in silence lets you ascribe to him what bad notions you please; but he is so temperate and reasonable, that I am persuaded his sentiments on French politics are not very different from mine.

In one point I perfectly agree with your Ladyship: every morning when I wake, and France rushes on my mind, I think I have been dreaming; nor can I at once conceive so total an inversion of a whole nation's character. Perhaps it is but a bloody fashion, momentary, like their other modes; and when they have deposed their monarch, or worse, and committed ten thousand outrages, they will rebound to loyalty, and out of penitence, confer on whoever shall be their king, unbounded power of punishing their excesses. . . .

373. *French Revolution and Slavery.*

TO HANNAH MORE

Strawberry Hill, *c.* 10 September 1789.

. . . I congratulate you on the demolition of the Bastile; I mean as you do, of its functions. For the poor soul itself, I had no ill will to it: on the contrary, it was a curious sample of ancient castellar dungeons, which the good folks the founders took for palaces: yet I always hated to drive by it, knowing the miseries it contained. Of itself it did not gobble up prisoners to glut its maw, but received them by command. The destruction of it was silly, and agreeable to the ideas of a mob, who do not know stones and bars and bolts from a

---

1 In the *Æneid*, Camilla, the leader of the Vulscians, killed many enemies, before being herself killed.

lettre de cachet. If the country remains free, the Bastile would be as tame as a ducking-stool, now that there is no such thing as a scold. If despotism recovers, the Bastile will rise from its ashes! – recover, I fear, it will. The *États* cannot remain a mob of kings, and will prefer a single one to a larger mob of kings and greater tyrants. The nobility, the clergy, and people of property will wait, till by address and money they can divide the people; or, whoever gets the larger or more victorious army into his hands will be a Cromwell or a Monk. In short, a revolution procured by a national vertigo does not promise a crop of legislators. It is time that composes a good constitution: it formed ours. We were near losing it by the lax and unconditional Restoration of Charles the Second. The Revolution was temperate and has lasted; and, though it might have been improved, we know that with all its moderation it disgusted half the nation, who would have brought back the old sores.

I abominate the Inquisition as much as you do; yet if the King of Spain receives no check like his cousin Louis, I fear he will not be disposed to relax any terrors. Every crowned head in Europe must ache at present; and the frantic and barbarous proceedings in France will not meliorate the stock of liberty, though for some time their Majesties will be mighty tender of the rights of their subjects.

According to this hypothesis, I can administer some comfort to you about your poor Negroes. I do not imagine that they will be emancipated at once; but their fate will be much alleviated, as the attempt will have alarmed their butchers enough to make them gentler, like the European monarchs, for fear of provoking the disinterested, who have no sugar plantations, to abolish the horrid traffic. . . .

374. *Conduct of the États Généraux.*

TO THE COUNTESS OF UPPER OSSORY

Strawberry Hill, Sunday night, 8 November 1789.

I have not yet received that essential consolation, Madam, of Lady Waldegrave's being safely delivered; and they even think she may go on a month longer – a cruel suspense! But the Duchess says she is stronger, and in no danger of not being able to go through her labour; but after the false hopes we had of her

Lord for three days, I am daunted, and dare not be sanguine.

Your Ladyship's letter, which I could not answer then, was very judicious, indeed, on the French *distractions. Distracted* they really seem, and, worse than savages, for in a state of nature the hurt one man can do to his neighbour is very limited; but a whole nation turned loose to their passions, with all the implements of mischief that have been devised during the improvements of society, and groaning with resentments for oppression, is a million of times worse. Still I can excuse the mob sooner than the *États*, who proceed in rending all ties, and overturning all systems, without repairing or replacing any; and increase the confusion by new demolitions, so that I am sometimes tempted to refine so much as to suppose that the concealed friends of the Crown, the nobility and the Church, encourage the general extravagance, in hopes that all orders but the populace will unite, through interest and indignation, to restore the old system. This would have some meaning, though not easily put in practice, as the whole army has been inspired with the same fury as the mob.

Perhaps I am too candid, for the *États* set out so foolishly, that I know not why I should suspect them of any sense. Their early debate on the title of the King of Spain to the crown, and their discussion on their own King's style, were such characteristics of absurdity, that it is too charitable to impute a grain of sense to them. They might as well have agitated a question whether Louis-Seize should be called Louis-le-Gros, or Louis-le-Simple. One would think he had convoked his heralds, not his *États*. What would Europe have thought, if, when Sir E. Hawke burnt so many of their men-of-war,[1] the French Academy had consulted how their new ships should be christened? That would have been a puerility worthy of the *Quarante*, and a theme for an epigram on them. The Jews, I see, have addressed those sage legislators – I do not wonder. *They* crucified their King, and called him, on his cross, King of the Jews, not of Judæa; and no doubt, if the *poissardes* offered to deliver King Louis, the Hebrews would cry out, "Not him, but Lord George Barabbas."[2] ...

1 At the battle of Quiberon Bay in 1759.
2 Perhaps a reference to Lord George Gordon, who in Newgate prison had in 1787 converted to Judaism.

375. *Sublime Empirics.*

TO THE EARL OF STRAFFORD

Strawberry Hill, 26 June 1790.

I do not forget your Lordship's commands, though I do recollect my own inability to divert you. Every year at my advanced time of life would make more reasonable my plea of knowing nothing worth repeating, especially at this season. The general topic of elections is the last subject to which I could listen: there is not one about which I care a straw; and I believe your Lordship quite as indifferent. I am not much more *au fait* of war or peace; I hope for the latter, nay and expect it, because it is not yet war. Pride and anger do not deliberate to the middle of the campaign; and I believe even the great incendiaries are more intent on making a good bargain than on saving their honour. If they save lives, I care not who is the better politician; and, as I am not to be their judge, I do not inquire what false weights they fling into the scales. Two-thirds of France, who are not so humble as I, seem to think they can entirely new-model the world with metaphysical compasses; and hold that no injustice, no barbarity, need to be counted in making the experiment. Such legislators are sublime empirics, and in their universal benevolence have very little individual sensibility. In short, the result of my reflections on what has passed in Europe for these latter centuries is, that tyrants have no consciences, and reformers no feeling; and the world suffers both by the plague and by the cure. What oceans of blood were Luther and Calvin the authors of being spilt! The late French government was detestable; yet I still doubt whether a civil war will not be the consequence of the revolution, and then what may be the upshot? Brabant[1] was grievously provoked; is it sure that it will be emancipated? For how short a time do people who set out on the most just principles, advert to their first springs of motion, and retain consistency? Nay, how long can promoters of revolutions be sure of maintaining their own ascendant? They are like projectors, who are commonly ruined; while others make fortunes on the foundation laid by the inventors.

---

1 The unsuccessful revolt of the province of Brabant against Austrian control.

376. *An Outrageous Crime.*

TO THE COUNTESS OF UPPER OSSORY

Strawberry Hill, 30 August 1790.

... At Marseilles – I think it was at Marseilles – a Monsieur Caz-alet, and of his name I am not sure, to secure himself (being known, I suppose, for no friend to the Chaos), had just taken the civic oath, and thereupon had been invited to dine with the *maire!* On a sudden they heard a violent clamour in the street, and, opening the window, beheld a furious mob, who being asked what they wanted, answered, "The head of Cazalet." On that he was concealed; but the savages broke in, found him, dragged him down stairs by his hair, and then by one leg through the streets, till he lost his senses, when, putting a rope round his neck, they were going to despatch him; but two grenadiers, shocked at such barbarities, drew their sabres, rescued the sufferer, kept off the ruffians, and conveyed the poor martyr into a house: but he expired the moment he arrived!

At Paris, I have told you, Madam, confusion increases. A formal denunciation has been made to the domineering tribunal against Necker, who is accused of having advanced a million of livres to La Fayette, for the purpose of exciting or promoting the revolt in Brab-ant – how justly I know not; but when anarchy is abroad, its centur-ions are not a whit more safe than their antagonists. There is a sentence in Juvenal that Lord Ossory will translate, that comprises the whole code of such times,

> "——Verso pollice vulgi
> Quemlibet occidunt populariter –"[1]

What a nation are the French! Sometimes carrying slavery to idol-atry of their tyrants; sometimes gorging their native insolence with all the extravagance of cruelty!

---

1 Juvenal, *Satires* III. 36–7: They kill by turning down their thumbs when the mob demands it.

377. *L'Égalité.*

TO SIR DAVID DALRYMPLE

Strawberry Hill, 21 September 1790.

. . . My sentiments on French politics concur as much with yours as they do on the subjects above. The National Assembly set out too absurdly and extravagantly, not to throw their country into the last confusion; which is not the way of correcting a government, but more probably of producing a worse, bad as the old one was, and thence they will have given a lasting wound to liberty: for what king will ever call *États* again, if he can possibly help it? The new legislators were pedants, not politicians, when they announced the equality of all men. We are all born so, no doubt, abstractedly; and physically capable of being kept so, were it possible to establish a perfect government, and give the same education to all men. But are they so in the present constitution of society, under a bad government, where most have had no education at all, but have been debased, brutified, by a long train and mixture of superstition and oppression, and witnesses to the luxury and vices of their superiors, which they could only envy and not enjoy? It was turning tigers loose; and the degradation of the nobility pointed out the prey. Could it be expected that savages so hallooed on to outrage and void of any notions of reciprocal duties and obligations, would fall into a regular system of acting as citizens under the government of reason and justice? It was tearing all the bonds of society, which the experience of mankind had taught them were necessary to the mutual convenience of all; and no provision, no security, was made for those who were levelled, and who, though they enjoyed what they had by the old constitution, were treated, or were exposed to be treated, as criminals. They have been treated so: several have been butchered; and the National Assembly dare not avenge them, lest they should lose the favour of the intoxicated populace. That conduct was senseless, or worse. With no less folly did they seem to expect that a vast body of men, more enlightened, at least, than the gross multitude, would sit down in patience under persecution and deprivation of all they valued; I mean the nobility and clergy, who might be stunned, but were sure of reviving and of burning with vengeance. The insult was the greater, as the subsequent conduct of the National Assembly has proved more shamefully dishonest, in their paying themselves daily more than two-thirds of them ever saw perhaps in a month; and that flagitious self-bestowed stipend, as it is void of all patriotic integrity, will destroy their power too; for, if constitution-making is so lucrative a trade, others will wish to share in the plunder of their country too; and, even without a civil war, I am persuaded the present Assembly will neither be septennial, nor even triennial.[1]

378. *Mob Law.*

TO THE COUNTESS OF UPPER OSSORY

Berkeley Square, 30 April 1791.

. . . The uproar is begun at Paris, and everybody that can is leaving it. Three or four of their *late* dukes[2] are arrived, and La Fayette is expected. The Duke of Orleans[3] gains ground, for he has some money left; but having neither character nor courage, it shows how little exists of either. Mobs can destroy a government for a time, but it requires the greatest talents and the greatest firmness – ay, and time too, to recompose and establish one. The French might have had a good government, if the National Assembly had had sense, experience, moderation, and integrity; but wanting all, they have given a lasting wound to liberty. They have acted, as that nation has always done, from the fashion of the hour, and with their innate qualities, cruelty and insolence: and when this hurricane is blown over, the anarchy of France will always be quoted as worse than despotism; and it should be remembered that an attempt to suppress general prejudices by violence and a total change, does but inflame and root those prejudices more deeply in the sufferers. What hundred thousands of lives did *the Reformation* cost? And was it general at last? What feeling man would have been Luther if he could have foreseen the blood he should occasion to be spilt? For Calvin, he was a monster. His opposing the Papacy, and burning Servetus,[4] proved

1 It was dissolved a year later.
2 Hereditary nobility and titles had been abolished by the National Assembly in June 1790.
3 Louis-Philippe-Joseph de Bourbon, Duc d'Orléans (1747–93). He supported the early stages of the Revolution and adopted the name Philippe Égalité.
4 A Spanish reformer burned in 1553 on Calvin's orders.

him as bad, if not worse, than any of the popes. How different are English and French! How temperate are the Americans! How unlike the villain Mirabeau to Washington! How odious is a reformer who acts from ambition or interest! – and what are moments of gratified ambition or interest to endless obloquy!

Our constitution proves that no good government can be formed at once, or at once reformed; and reason, without experience, would tell one the same, for nature does not produce at the same period a number of great men enough to comprehend all the abuses that ought to be corrected in any system, and at the same time to foresee the greater evils that would arise from various alterations; for good and evil are so intermixed in human affairs in a series of ages, that it would require the omnipotent hand of the Creator to separate the bran from the chaff; and since he has permitted the intermixture, and not revealed his secret, it becomes us, though bound to aim at the amendment of abuses, to proceed with diffidence and a timid hand. A presumptuous Alexander may cut a Gordian knot with his sword; and I wish it had never been worse occupied – but perhaps the poor knot hurt nothing but *his* pride; and to be sure his time would have been better employed in continuing to try to unravel it than in drawing his sword on any other occasion. . . .

379. *Tom Paine – Flight and Recapture of Louis XVI.*

TO MARY BERRY

Strawberry Hill, 26 July 1791.

. . . Lady Cecilia tells me, that her nephew, Mr. West,[1] who was with you at Pisa, declares he is in love with you both; so I am not singular. You too may like to hear this, though no novelty to you; but it will not satisfy Mr. Berry, who will be impatient for news from Birmingham: but there are no more, nor any-whence else. There has not been another riot in any of the three kingdoms. The villain Paine came over for the Crown and Anchor;[2] but, finding that his

1 The Hon. Septimus West, who died two years later, according to earlier editors of consumption.
2 Thomas [Tom] Paine (1737–1809), writer and revolutionary, had come for the dinner of the Revolution Club at the Crown and Anchor tavern in the Strand, held on 14 July 1791.

pamphlet had not set a straw on fire, and that the 14th of July was as little in fashion as the ancient gunpowder-plot, he dined at another tavern with a few quaking conspirators; and probably is returning to Paris, where he is engaged in a controversy with the Abbé Sieyes, about the *plus* or *minus* of rebellion. The rioters in Worcestershire, whom I mentioned in my last, were not a detachment from Birmingham, but volunteer incendiaries from the capital; who went, *according to the rights of men*, with the mere view of plunder, and threatened gentlemen to burn their houses, if not ransomed. Eleven of these disciples of Paine are in custody; and Mr. Merry, Mrs. Barbauld, and Miss Helen Williams[1] will probably have subjects for elegies. Deborah and Jael,[2] I believe, were invited to the Crown and Anchor, and had let their nails grow accordingly; but, somehow or other, no *poissonnières* were there, and the two prophetesses had no opportunity that day of exercising their talents or talons. Their French allies, cock and hen, have a fairer field open; and the Jacobins, I think, will soon drive the National Assembly to be better royalists than ever they were, in self-defence.

Wednesday evening, 27th.

… You have indeed surprised me by your account of the strange credulity of poor King Louis's escape *in safety!* In these villages we heard of his flight late in the evening, and, the very next morning, of his being retaken.[3] Much as he, at least the Queen, has suffered, I am persuaded the adventure has hastened general confusion, and will increase the royal party; though perhaps their Majesties, for their personal safeties, had better have awaited the natural progress of anarchy. The enormous deficiencies of money, and the total insubordination of the army, both apparent and uncontradicted, from the reports made to the National Assembly, show what is coming. Into what such a chaos will subside, it would be silly to attempt to guess. Perhaps it is not wiser in the exiles to expect to live to see a re-settlement in their favour. One thing I have for these two years thought probable to arrive – a division, at least, a dismemberment, of France. Despotism could no longer govern so unwieldy a machine; a

1 Robert Merry (1755–98), Anna Lætitia Barbauld (1743–1825), and Helen Maria Williams (1759–1827), writers sympathetic to the French Revolution.
2 Barbauld and Williams.
3 The flight to Varennes of 20–21 June 1791.

republic would be still less likely to hold it together. If foreign powers should interfere, they will take care to pay themselves with what is *à leur bienséance;* and that, in reality, would be serving France too. So much for my speculations! and they have never varied. We are so far from intending to new-model our government and dismiss the Royal Family, annihilate the peerage, cashier the hierarchy, and lay open the land to the first occupier, as Dr. Priestley, and Tom Paine, and the Revolution Club humbly proposed, that we are even encouraging the breed of princes. It is generally believed that the Duke of York is going to marry the Princess of Prussia, the King's daughter by his first wife, and his favourite child.[1] I do not affirm it; but many others do. . . .

380. *On Travelling in France.*

TO MARY AND AGNES BERRY

> Berkeley Square, Monday night, 19 September 1791,
> addition to letter begun 16 September.

You have alarmed me exceedingly, by talking of returning through France, against which I thought myself quite secure, or I should not have pressed you to stir, yet. I have been making all the inquiries I could amongst the foreign ministers at Richmond, and I cannot find any belief of the march of armies towards France. Nay, the Comte d'Artois[2] is said to be gone to Petersburg; and he must bring back forces in a balloon, if he can be time enough to interrupt your passage through Flanders. One thing I must premise, if, which I deprecate, you should set foot in France; I beg you to burn, and not bring a scrap of paper with you. Mere travelling ladies, as young as you, I know have been stopped and rifled, and detained in France to have their papers examined: and one was rudely treated, because the name of a French lady of her acquaintance was mentioned in a private letter to her, though in no political light. Calais is one of the worst places you can pass; for, as they suspect money being remitted through that town to England, the search and delays there are

1 The marriage of the Duke of York and the daughter of the King of Prussia took place later that year.
2 Younger brother of Louis XVI, later Charles X. He was in fact at Koblenz, where he declared the intention to invade France.

extremely strict and rigorous. The pleasure of seeing you sooner would be bought infinitely too dear by your meeting with any disturbance; as my impatience for your setting out is already severely punished by the fright you have given me. One charge I can wipe off; but it were the least of my faults. I never thought of your settling at Cliveden[1] in November, if your house in town is free. All my wish was, that you would come for a night to Strawberry, and that the next day I might put you in possession of Cliveden. I did not think of engrossing you from all your friends, who must wish to embrace you at your return.

Tuesday.

I am told that on the King's acceptance of the constitution, there is a general amnesty published, and passports taken off. If this is true, the passage through France, for mere foreigners and strangers, may be easier and safer; but be assured, of all, I would not embarrass your journey unnecessarily; but, for Heaven's sake! be well informed. I advise nothing; I dread everything where your safeties are in question, and I hope Mr. Berry is as timorous as I am. My very contradictions prove the anxiety of my mind, or I should not torment those I love so much; but how not love those who sacrifice so much for me, and who, I hope, forgive all my unreasonable inconsistencies. Adieu! adieu!

381. *Ex Uno Disce Omnes!*

TO THE HON. H. S. CONWAY

Strawberry Hill, 27 September 1791.

... I can say nothing to comfort them,[2] but what I firmly believe, which is, that total anarchy must come on rapidly. Nobody pays the taxes that are laid; and which, intended to produce eighty millions a month, do not bring in six. The new Assembly will fall on the old,[3] probably plunder the richest, and certainly disapprove of much they have done; for can eight hundred new ignorants approve of what has

1 Little Strawberry Hill, formerly occupied by Mrs. Clive, which Walpole made available to the Berrys.
2 The French *émigrés*.
3 The National Assembly was on 1 October replaced by the Legislative Assembly.

been done by twelve hundred almost as ignorant, and who were far from half agreeing? And then their immortal constitution (which, besides, is to be mightily mended nine years hence) will die before it has cut any of its teeth but its grinders. The exiles are enraged at their poor King for saving his own life by a forced acceptance:[1] and yet I know no obligation he has to his noblesse, who all ran away to save their own lives; not a gentleman, but the two poor gendarmes at Versailles, having lost their lives in his defence. I suppose La Fayette, Barnave, the Lameths, &c., will run away, too,[2] when the new tinkers and cobblers, of whom the present elect are and will be composed, proceed on the levelling system taught them by their predecessors, who, like other levellers, have taken good care of themselves. Good Dr. Priestley's friend, good Monsieur Condorcet,[3] has got a place in the Treasury of one thousand pounds a year: — *ex uno disce omnes!*[4] And thus a set of rascals, who might, with temper and discretion, have obtained a very wholesome constitution, witness Poland! have committed infinite mischief, infinite cruelty, infinite injustice, and left a shocking precedent against liberty, unless the Poles are as much admired and imitated as the French ought to be detested. . . .

382. *Atrocities in Paris.*

TO HANNAH MORE

Strawberry Hill, 21 August 1792.

. . . This *second*[5] massacre of Paris has exhibited horrors that even surpass the former. Even the Queen's women were butchered in the Tuileries, and the tigers chopped off the heads from the dead bodies,

1 Louis XVI had before the National Assembly sworn fidelity to the Constitution on 14 September.
2 The brothers Charles-Malo-François de Lameth (1757–1832) and Alexandre-Théodore-Victor de Lameth (1760–1829), both members (and Charles the former President) of the National Assembly, left France with Lafayette in August 1792. Antoine-Pierre-Joseph-Marie Barnave (1761–93) was guillotined.
3 Marie-Jean-Antoine-Nicolas de Caritat, Marquis de Condorcet (1743–94), philosopher and mathematician, member of the Legislative Assembly and National Convention, later guillotined. The English theologian and natural philosopher Joseph Priestley (1733–1804) is mentioned by Walpole because of his radical views.
4 From one learn to know them all: a play on Virgil, *Æneid* II, 66.
5 The first being the St. Bartholomew's Day Massacre of 1572.

and tossed them into the flames of the palace. The tortures of the poor King and Queen, from the length of their duration, surpass all example; and the brutal insolence with which they were treated on the 10th, all invention. They were dragged through the Place Vendome to see the statue of Louis the Fourteenth in fragments, and told it was to be the King's fate; and he, the most harmless of men, was told he is a monster; and this after three years of sufferings. King, and Queen, and children, were shut up in a room, without nourishment, for twelve hours. One who was a witness has come over, and says he found the Queen sitting on the floor, trembling like an aspen in every limb, and her sweet boy the Dauphin asleep against her knee! She has not one woman to attend her that she ever saw, but a companion of her misery, the King's sister, an heroic virgin saint, who, on the former irruption into the palace, flew to and clung to her brother, and being mistaken for the Queen, and the hellish fiends wishing to murder her, and somebody aiming to undeceive them, she said, "Ah! ne les détrompez pas!" Was not that sentence the sublime of innocence? But why do I wound your thrilling nerves with the relation of such horrible scenes? Your *blackmanity* must allow some of its tears to these poor victims. For my part, I have an abhorrence of politics, if one can so term these tragedies, which make one harbour sentiments one naturally abhors; but can one refrain without difficulty from exclaiming such a nation should be exterminated? They have butchered hecatombs of Swiss, even to *porters* in private houses, because they often are, and always are called, *Le Suisse*. Think on fifteen hundred persons, probably more, butchered on the 10th, in the space of eight hours. Think on premiums voted for the assassination of several princes, and do not think that such execrable proceedings have been confined to Paris; no, Avignon, Marseilles, &c., are still smoking with blood! Scarce the Alecto of the North,[1] the legislatress and the usurper of Poland, has occasioned the spilling of larger torrents!

I am almost sorry that your letter arrived at this crisis; I cannot help venting a little of what haunts me. But it is better to thank Providence for the tranquillity and happiness we enjoy in this country, in spite of the philosophising serpents we have in our bosom, the Paines, the Tookes, and the Woolstoncrafts. I am glad you have not

---

1 Catherine the Great (Alecto being one of the Furies in Greek mythology).

read the tract of the last-mentioned writer.[1] I would not look at it, though assured it contains neither metaphysics nor politics; but as she entered the lists on the latter, and borrowed her title from the demon's book, which aimed at spreading the *wrongs* of men, she is excommunicated from the pale of my library. We have had enough of new systems, and the world a great deal too much, already. . . .

Orford.

383. *Contrast between the French and English Revolutions.*

TO THE COUNTESS OF UPPER OSSORY

Strawberry Hill, 4 September 1792.

. . . When your Ladyship's querist will show me a glimpse of resemblance between the Diet of Poland and the former National Assembly in France, even from their outset, I will for that moment of similitude, if it can be discovered, admire the latter as I adore the former: but I am no dupe to words, nor honour the term Revolution for the mere sound. A revolution is not to be commended for simply overturning a government, though as bad as that of France was. A mob, or a czarina, or janizaries, can destroy good or bad. A revolution, before it has any claim to praise, must give a better government, and that can only be done by integrity, wisdom, and temper, as our revolution did, and as the generous and disinterested Poles would have done – *sed diis alter visum!*[2] I should rather say *diabolis.* Pedantry, actuated by envy and every species of injustice and barbarity, and impregnated with vanity and insolence, and void of any plan but that of seizing power, and, I believe, plunder, were not likely to produce patriots, and, still less, legislators. Accordingly, beginning by disregarding and disobeying that first ground-work of liberty, the intentions and instructions of the whole nation their constituents, they hurried into contradicting their own decrees as fast as they made them, pronounced property sacred and seized it everywhere, declared for universal peace, and usurped Papal and German

---

1 Probably a reference to *A Vindication of the Rights of Men* (1790) by Mary Wollstonecraft (1759–97), though Walpole may be referring to her *A Vindication of the Rights of Woman* (1792). Walpole groups her along with Tom Paine and John Horne Tooke (1736–1812) as insidious revolutionary authors.
2 From Virgil, *Æneid* II, 428: the Gods saw otherwise.

dominions, proclaimed everybody at liberty to live where they pleased, but burnt their houses and forced them to fly, and then confiscated their estates if they did not return at the hazard of their lives. The option of perjury or starving was another benefit bestowed on all the conscientious clergy. The Bastille (where only six prisoners were found, rather a moderate number for such a capital as Paris) was destroyed, and every other prison was crammed, nay, the city of Orleans was turned into a vast jail, whence nobody was even indulged with a trial; and, at last, by every species of artifice, falsehood, and imposture, the philosophic legislators, and their excrements the clubs, have worked themselves and the people up to such a pitch of infernal frenzy, that they have produced a second St. Barthélemi, and realised what has been thought a legend in history – in short, a whole senate has assumed the accursed dignity of the "old man of the mountain,"[1] and spawned a legion of assassins! and with still more impudence, for he did not proclaim his mandates openly for the murder of princes and generals.

The *former* National Assembly did not commit *all* these atrocious enormities, but they led the way, and checked none. Did they punish the barbarities at Avignon and at other places? What excesses did they disapprove? What liberty did they confer but that of leaving every man free to hang and murder whom he pleased? In short, madam, they have blasted and branded liberty – perhaps for centuries – and for that and their barbarity, I abhor them; and by destroying their own country – who can foresee for how long? Posterity will look on them with horror; and their not having in three years of convulsions produced one man, but the villainous Mirabeau,[2] eminent for abilities, on the contrary, legions of folly, absurdity, and ignorance, will give future generations as much contempt for the French, as devout people have for the Jews.

If anybody from such a mass of detestable proceedings can pick out a moment where I am to stop and admire, and where I am to divide my partiality to the Poles with the revolutionists in France, or to rank the Barnaves, Lameths, and Noailleses with that true patriot Malachowski,[3] whose honest and humane protest brought the tears

1 The leader of the sect of assassins based in eleventh- and twelfth-century Lebanon.
2 Honoré-Gabriel Riquetti (1749–91), Comte de Mirabeau, revolutionary.
3 Count Stanislaw Malachowski (1736–1809), Polish patriot, one of the principal authors of the constitution of 1791, which was overthrown the following year.

into my eyes, I will confess that I have been blind for a moment; or I will even go so far as to say for the term *revolution* –

> "Quod si non aliam venturo fata *Neroni*
> Invenere viam –
>   Scelera ipsa nefasque
> Hac mercede placent."[1]

The Polish revolution and ours were noble, wise, and moderate – wise because moderate; but to subvert all justice and order for pedantic and speculative experiments, without having anything to substitute in their places, as their contradictions have demonstrated, is the acme of folly, incapacity, and ignorance of human nature; and I shall take leave to despise the late august Diet – the present is below contempt; and if the nation ever recovers its senses, it will be ashamed of descending from such progenitors. Adieu, Madam; but pray set me on writing no more declamations.

384. *Execution of Louis XVI.*

TO HANNAH MORE

My holy Hannah,   Berkeley Square, 9 February 1793.

    With your innate and usual goodness and sense, you have done me justice by guessing exactly at the cause of my long silence. You have been apt to tell me that my letters diverted you. How then could I write, when it was impossible but to attrist you! when I could speak of nothing but unparalleled horrors! and but awaken your sensibility, if it slumbered for a moment! What mind could forget the 10th of August and the 2nd of September;[2] and that the black and bloody year 1792 has plunged its murderous dagger still deeper, and already made 1793 still more detestably memorable! though its victim has at last been rewarded for four years of torture by forcing from him every kind of proof of the most perfect character that ever sat on a throne. Were these alas! themes for letters? Nay, am I not sure that *you* have been still more shocked by a crime that passes even the guilt of shedding the blood of poor Louis, to hear of atheism avowed, and the avowal tolerated by monsters calling themselves

1 Lucan, *Pharsalia* I, 33–4 and 37–8: Yet, if Fate could find no other way for the advent of Nero . . . even such crimes and such guilt are not too high a price to pay.
2 The massacres in Paris of those dates.

a National Assembly! But I have no words that can reach the criminality of such *inferno-human* beings, but must compose a term that aims at conveying my idea of them. For the future it will be sufficient to call them *the French* – I hope no other nation will ever deserve to be confounded with them!

Indeed, my dear friend, I have another reason for wishing to burn my pen entirely: all my ideas are confounded and overturned; I do not know whether all I ever learned in the seventy-first years of my seventy-five was not wrong and false: common sense, reasoning, calculation, conjecture from analogy and from history of past events, all, all have been baffled; nor am I sure that what used to be thought the result of experience and wisdom was not a mass of mistakes. Have I not found, do I not find, that the invention of establishing metals as the *signs* of property was an useless discovery, or at least only useful till the art of making paper was found out? Nay, the latter is preferable to gold and silver. If the ores were adulterated and cried down, nobody would take them in exchange. Depreciate paper as much as you will, and it will still serve all the purposes of barter. Tradesmen still keep shops, stock them with goods, and deliver their commodities for those coined rags. Poor Reason, where art thou?

To show you that memory and argument are of no value, at least with me, I thought a year or two that this paper-mint would soon blow up, because I remembered that when Mr. Charles Fox and one or two more youths of brilliant genius first came to light, and into vast debts at play, they imparted to the world an important secret which they had discovered. It was, that nobody needed to want money, if they would pay enough for it. Accordingly, they borrowed of Jews at vast usury; but as they had made but an incomplete calculation, the interest so soon exceeded the principal, that the system did not maintain its ground for above two or three years. Faro has proved a more substantial speculation. But I miscarried in applying my remembrance to the Assignats, which still maintain their ground against that long-decried but as long adored corrupter of virtue, gold. Alack! I do not hear that virtue has flourished more for the destruction of its old enemy!

Shall I add another truth? I have been so disgusted and fatigued by hearing of nothing but French massacres, &c., and found it so impossible to shift conversation to any other topic, that before I had been a month in town, I wished Miss Gunning[1] would revive, that people might have at least one other subject to interest the ears and tongues of the public. But no wonder universal attention is engrossed by the present portentous scene! It seems to draw to a question, whether Europe or France is to be depopulated; whether civilisation can be recovered, or the republic of Chaos can be supported by assassination. We have heard of the golden, silver, and iron ages; the brazen one existed, while the French were only predominantly insolent. What the present age will be denominated, I cannot guess. Though the paper age would be characteristic, it is not emphatic enough, nor specifies the enormous sins of the fiends that are the agents. I think it may be styled the diabolic age: the Duke of Orleans has dethroned Satan, who since his fall has never instigated such crimes as Orleans has perpetrated.

Let me soften my tone a little, and harmonise your poor mind by sweeter accents. In this deluge of triumphant enormities, what traits of the sublime and beautiful may be gleaned! Did you hear of Madame Elizabeth, the King's sister? a saint like yourself. She doted on her brother, for she certainly knew his soul. In the tumult in July, hearing the populace and the poissardes had broken into the palace, she flew to the King, and by embracing him tried to shield his person. The populace took her for the Queen, cried out "Voilà cette chienne, cette Autrichienne!" and were proceeding to violence. Somebody, to save her, screamed "Ce n'est pas la Reine, c'est——." The Princess said, "Ah! mon Dieu! ne les détrompez pas." If that was not the most sublime instance of perfect innocence ready prepared for death, I know not where to find one. Sublime indeed, too, was the sentence of good father Edgeworth, the King's confessor, who, thinking his royal penitent a little dismayed just before the fatal stroke, cried out, "Montez, digne fils de St. Louis! Le ciel vous est ouvert." The holy martyr's countenance brightened up, and he submitted at once. Such victims, such confessors as those, and Monsieur de Malesherbes,[2] repair some of the breaches in human nature made by Orleans, Condorcet, Santerre, and a legion of evil spirits. . . .

---

1 A scandal of 1790 in which Elizabeth Gunning (1769–1823), novelist and niece of the beautiful Gunning sisters, allegedly used forged letters to try to ensnare the heir of the Duke of Marlborough into marriage.
2 Senior counsel to Louis XVI at his trial: for Malesherbes see letter 366, p. 517, n. 4).

385. *Marie Antoinette.*

TO MARY BERRY

Strawberry Hill, Tuesday evening, eight o'clock, 15 October 1793.

Though I do not know when it will have its whole lading, I must begin my letter this very moment, to tell you what I have just heard. I called on the Princesse d'Hennin, who has been in town a week. I found her quite alone, and I thought she did not answer quite clearly about her two knights: the Prince de Poix has taken a lodging in town and she talks of letting her house here, if she can. In short, I thought she had a little of an Ariadne-air[1] – but this was not what I was in such a hurry to tell you. She showed me several pieces of letters, I think from the Duchesse de Bouillon: one says, the poor Duchesse de Biron is again arrested and at the Jacobins,[2] and with her "une jeune étourdie, qui ne fait que chanter toute la journée;" and who, think you, may that be? – only our pretty little wicked Duchesse de Fleury![3] by her singing and not sobbing, I suppose she was weary of her *Tircis*, and is glad to be rid of him. This new blow, I fear, will overset Madame de Biron again. The rage at Paris seems to increase daily or hourly; they either despair, or are now avowed banditti. I tremble so much for the great and most suffering victim of all, the Queen, that one cannot feel so much for many, as several perhaps deserve: but her tortures have been of far longer duration than any martyrs, and more various; and her courage and patience equal to her woes!

My poor old friend, the Duchesse de la Valière,[4] past ninety and stone-deaf, has a guard set upon her, but in her own house; her daughter, the Duchesse de Chatillon, mother of the Duchesse de la Tremouille, is arrested; and thus the last, with her attachment to the Queen, must be miserable indeed! – but one would think I feel for nothing but Duchesses: the crisis has crowded them together into

1 That is, Walpole thought she might have been deserted by her "two knights".
2 Amélie de Boufflers, Duchesse de Biron (1751–94), was guillotined the following year.
3 Anne-Françoise-Aimée Franquetot de Coigny, Duchess de Fleury (1769–1820) was in fact released, and survived the Revolution. Walpole described her to Lady Ossory on 8 October 1792 as "much the prettiest Frenchwoman I ever beheld".
4 See letter 365, p. 515, n. 2. The Yale editors note that she was not yet 80.

my letter, and into a prison; – and to be a prisoner among cannibals is pitiable indeed! . . .

386. *War with France.*

TO MARY BERRY

Saturday, 14 December 1793, addition to letter begun 13 December.

I am glad this is to be the last of my gazettes. I am tired of notifying and recalling the articles of news: not that I am going to dislaurel the Duke of Brunswick; but not a sprig is yet come in confirmation. Military critics even conjecture, by the journals from Manheim and Frankfort, that the German victories have not been much more than repulses of the French, and have been bought dearly. I am inclined to believe the best from Wurmser; but I confess my best hopes are from the factions of Paris. If the gangrene does not gain the core, how calculate the duration? It has already baffled all computation, all conjecture. One wonders now that France, in its totality, was not more fatal to Europe than even it was. Is not it astonishing, that after five years of such havoc, such emigrations, expulsions, massacres, annihilation of commerce, evanition of specie, and real or impending famine, they can still furnish and support armies against us and the Austrians in Flanders, against the Duke of Brunswick and Wurmser, against us at Toulon, against the King of Sardinia, against Spain, against the Royalists in La Vendée, and along the coast against our expedition under Lord Moira; and though we have got fifteen of their men-of-war at Toulon, they have sixteen, or more, at Brest, and are still impertinent with a fry of privateers? Consider too, that all this spirit is kept up by the most extravagant lies, delusions, rhodomontade; by the extirpation of the usual root of enthusiasm, religion; and by the terror of murder, that ought to revolt all mankind. If such a system of destruction does not destroy itself, there is an end of that *ignis fatuus*, human reason; and French policy must govern, or exterminate mankind. . . .

387. *Death of Robespierre.*

TO THE COUNTESS OF UPPER OSSORY

Park Place, 4 September 1794.

I could not thank your Ladyship sooner for giving me notice of your campaign, as you did not specify your head-quarters, and I am sadly ignorant of military stations; but Marshal Conway tells me I may safely direct my letter to Lord Ossory, at the camp near Harwich, and that it will certainly reach the commandant's lady.

I love discussions, that is, conjectures, on French affairs no more than you, Madam; yet I cannot but look on Robespierre's death[1] as a very characteristic event, I mean as it proves the very unsettled state of that country. It is the fifth Revolution in the governing power of that country in five years; and as faction in the capital can overturn and destroy the reigning despots in the compass of twelve months, I see no reason for expecting anything like durability to a system compounded of such violent and precarious ingredients. Atrocious a monster as Robespierre was, I do not suppose the alleged crimes were true, or that his enemies, who had all been his accomplices, are a whit better monsters. If his barbarities, which were believed the sole engines of his success, should be relaxed, success will be less sure; and though lenity may give popularity to his successors, it will be but temporary – and terror removed, is a negative sensation, and produces but very transient gratitude; and then will revive unchecked, every active principle of revenge, ambition, and faction, with less fear to control them. I will prophesy no farther, nor will pretend to guess how long a genealogy of revolutions will ensue, when they breed so fast, before chaos is extinct. . . .

388. *Failure of Attempt to Invade Ireland.*

TO THE COUNTESS OF UPPER OSSORY

Berkeley Square, 4 January 1797.

Well, Madam, little as I expected it would happen, the French have seriously intended to invade *us*, or rather *you*, but so clumsily, that we may rejoice at the experiment; and had we had a little more

1   Robespierre had been guillotined on 28 July 1794.

luck, we might have captured half their expedition, and may still hear of their having lost many of their ships.[1] Seven had nearly fallen into the mouth of Colpoys, but were saved by a fog; those that lay for three days in Bantry Bay took a sudden panic and fled, as if they had just recollected that no venomous creature can live in Ireland. Indeed, whatever invitation they might have received, they were received very inhospitably, not a single crew of a ship was asked to land and drink a glass of whiskey, but the whole country was ready to rise and knock their brains out. Those that retired were pursued by two violent storms, and have probably suffered like a mightier Armada. It is supposed that this disappointed invasion was one motive to the interruption of the pacification, though so wretchedly equipped, and so little consonant to the poverty of which they have talked so much lately, and which has made me recollect an expression which my father used on the mobs which were raised by the distillers against his Excise bill, whom he called *sturdy beggars*, words re-echoed in a thousand libels. . . .

1   An unsuccessful French invasion of Ireland where the Yale editors note that Lord Ossory owned extensive property.

XVI
SOCIAL HISTORY ILLUSTRATED

WALPOLE INTENDED HIS letters to paint a portrait of his age, and would no doubt have been gratified that generations of writers and social historians have mined them for anecdote and incident. Lord Holland, who edited Walpole's *Memoirs of King George II* (1822) recalled of him that "His conversation, like his written compositions, displayed a sprightly mind and a memory stored with anecdotes, historical and literary, the result of much antiquarian research and the fruit of a long life spent in the company of statesmen, authors, artists, and wits."[1] Reading Walpole's letters is one remove from being regaled by his flow of conversation at Strawberry Hill.

The selection in this concluding section is arbitrary, and any number of selections could be made to comment on different topics. Duelling is the subject of letters 389 to 392, opening with the rather unlikely figure of Walpole's uncle Horace as combatant. Letters 394 and 395 address very different aspects of clandestine marriages, while in letter 398 Walpole recounts his experience of being robbed by a highwayman (not for the first time – he had in 1749 been robbed by the famous James Maclaine, a year before his capture and execution).

It has already been noted that Walpole found the emotional excesses of revealed religion absurd. Whereas an established church might be seen as an essential part of the fabric of an ordered society, what personal engagement religion had to offer was in his view purely a matter of individual preference. It is no surprise then that he regarded the Methodists with disdain, describing Wesley as being "as evidently an actor as Garrick", who at the end of his sermon "exalted his voice, and acted very ugly enthusiasm", while Whitfield was simply an "arch-rogue" (letters 402 to 405).

There are then reflections on English travel and English inns (for which see also letter 80), the English countryside, urban growth, the uncertain attractions of spas and the excesses of fashion. Walpole discusses the astronomical discoveries of Hershel and the wonders

1 *Horace Walpole: The Critical Heritage*, Sabor, p. 309.

of the first manned flights in balloons, and finally the selection concludes in the minor key with familiar complaints of the English summer.

1. DUELLING

389. *A Duel in Parliament.*

TO SIR HORACE MANN

Arlington Street, 14 March 1743.

I don't at all know how to advise you about mourning; I always think that the custom of the country, and what other foreign ministers do, should be your rule. But I had a private scruple rose with me: that was, whether you should show so much respect to the late woman[1] as other ministers do, since she left that legacy to *Quello à Roma.*[2] I mentioned this to my lord, but he thinks that the tender manner of her wording it, takes off that exception; however, he thinks it better that you should write for advice to your commanding officer.[3] That will be very late, and you will probably have determined before. You see what a casuist I am in ceremony; I leave the question more perplexed than I found it.

Pray, Sir, congratulate me upon the new acquisition of glory to my family! We have long been eminent statesmen; now that we are out of employment we have betaken ourselves to war – and we have made great proficiency in a short season. We don't run, like my Lord Stair, into Berg and Juliers, to seek battles where we are sure of not finding them – we make shorter marches; a step across the Court of Requests brings us to engagement. But not to detain you any longer with flourishes which will probably be inserted in my uncle Horace's[4] patent when he is made a field-marshal; you must know that he has fought a duel, and has scratched a scratch three inches long on the side of his enemy – *Io Pæan!* The circumstances of this memorable engagement were, in short, that on some witness being to be examined the other day in the House upon remittances to the army,

1 The Electress Palatine Dowager. – WALPOLE.
2 She left a legacy to the Pretender, describing him only by these words, *To him at Rome.* – WALPOLE.
3 The Duke of Newcastle, following the fall of Sir Robert Walpole ("my Lord").
4 Horatio Walpole, Baron Walpole of Wolterton: see letter 126, p. 194, n. 2.

my uncle said, "He hoped they would *indemnify* him, if he told any-thing that affected himself." Soon after he was standing behind the Speaker's chair, and Will. Chetwynd,[1] an intimate of Bolingbroke, came up to him, and said, "What, Mr. Walpole, are you for rubbing up old sores?" He replied, "I think I said very little, considering that you and your friends would last year have hanged up me and my brother at the lobby door without a trial." Chetwynd answered, "I would still have you both have your deserts." The other said, "If you and I had, probably I should be here and you would be some-where else." This drew more words, and Chetwynd took him by the arm and led him out. In the lobby, Horace said, "We shall be observed, we had better put it off till to-morrow." "No, no, now! now!" When they came to the bottom of the stairs, Horace said, "I am out of breath, let us draw here." They drew; Chetwynd hit him on the breast, but was not near enough to pierce his coat. Horace made a pass, which the other put by with his hand, but it glanced along his side – a clerk, who had observed them go out together so arm-in-armly, could not believe it amicable, but followed them, and came up just time enough to beat down their swords, as Horace had driven him against a post, and would probably have run him through at the next thrust. Chetwynd went away to a surgeon's, and kept his bed the next day; he has not reappeared yet, but is in no danger. My uncle returned to the House, and was so little moved as to speak immediately upon the *Cambrick Bill*, which made Swinny say, "That it was a sign he was not *ruffled*." Don't you delight in this duel? I expect to see it daubed up by some circuit-painter, on the ceiling of the saloon at Woolterton. . . . Adieu!

390. *Spitting in a Hat.*

TO SIR HORACE MANN

Strawberry Hill, 25 February 1750.

. . . You will be delighted with a *bon-mot* of a chair-maker, whom he[2] has discarded for voting for Lord Trentham; one of his black-caps was sent to tell this Vaughan that the Prince would employ him

1 William Richard Chetwynd (?1683–1770), later Viscount Chetwynd, M.P., and Master of the Mint.
2 The Prince of Wales.

no more; "I am going to bid another person make his Royal Highness a chair." – "With all my heart," said the chair-maker; "I don't care what they make him, so they don't make him a throne."

The Westminster election, which is still scrutinising, produced us a parliamentary event this week, and was very near producing something much bigger. Mr. Fox and Mr. Pitt moved to send for the High-Bailiff to inquire into the delay. The Opposition took it up very high, and on its being carried against them the Court of Requests was filled next day with mob, and the House crowded, and big with expectation. Nugent had flamed and abused Lord Sandwich[1] violently, as author of this outrageous measure. When the Bailiff appeared, the pacific spirit of the other part of the administration had operated so much, that he was dismissed with honour; and only instructed to abridge all delays by authority of the House – in short, "we spit in his hat on Thursday, and wiped it off on Friday." This is a new fashionable proverb which I must construe to you. About ten days ago, at the new Lady Cobham's[2] assembly, Lord Hervey[3] was leaning over a chair talking to some women, and holding his hat in his hand. Lord Cobham came up and spit in it – yes, spit in it! – and then, with a loud laugh, turned to Nugent, and said, "Pay me my wager." In short, he had laid a guinea that he committed this absurd brutality, and that it was not resented. Lord Hervey, with great temper and sensibility, asked if he had any farther occasion for his hat? – "Oh! I see you are angry!" – "Not very well pleased." Lord Cobham took the fatal hat, and wiped it, made a thousand apologies, and wanted to pass it for a joke. Next morning he rose with the sun, and went to visit Lord Hervey; so did Nugent: he would not see them, but wrote to the Spitter, (or, as he is now called, Lord Gob'em,) to say, that he had affronted him very grossly before company, but having involved Nugent in it, he desired to know to which he was to address himself for satisfaction. Lord Cobham wrote him a most submissive answer, and begged pardon both in his own and Nugent's name. Here it rested for a few days; till getting wind, Lord

---

1 Robert Nugent (1709–88), later Earl Nugent, M.P., and John Montagu, 4th Earl of Sandwich (for whom see letter 199, p. 282, n. 1).
2 Anna Chamber, wife of Richard Temple, Lord Cobham, afterwards Earl Temple. – WALPOLE.
3 George, eldest son of John, late Lord Hervey, son of the Earl of Bristol; whom this George succeeded in the title. – WALPOLE.

Hervey wrote again to insist on an explicit apology under Lord Cobham's own hand, with a rehearsal of the excuses that had been made to him. This too was complied with, and the *fair conqueror*[1] shows all the letters. Nugent's disgraces have not ended here: the night of his having declaimed so furiously against Lord Sandwich, he was standing by Lady Catherine Pelham, at the masquerade, without his mask: she was telling him a history of a mad dog, (which I believe she had bit herself,) young Leveson,[2] the Duchess of Bedford's brother, came up, without his mask too, and looking at Nugent, said, "I have seen a mad dog to-day, and a silly dog too." – "I suppose, Mr. Leveson, you have been looking in the glass." – "No, I see him now." Upon which they walked off together, but were prevented from fighting, (if Nugent would have fought,) and were reconciled at the side-board. You perceive by this that our factions are ripening. The Argyll carried all the Scotch against the turnpike: they were willing to be carried, for the Duke of Bedford, in case it should have come into the Lords, had writ to the sixteen Peers to solicit their votes; but with so little deference, that he enclosed all the letters under one cover, directed to the British Coffee-house![3]

The new Duke of Somerset is dead: that title is at last restored to Sir Edward Seymour, after his branch had been most unjustly deprived of it for about one hundred and fifty years.[4] Sir Hugh Smithson and Sir Charles Windham are Earls of Northumberland and Egremont, with vast estates; the former title, revived for the blood of Percy, has the misfortune of being coupled with the blood of a man that either let or drove coaches – such was Sir Hugh's grandfather![5] This peerage vacates his seat for Middlesex, and has opened a contest for the county, before even that for Westminster is decided. The Duchess of Richmond takes care that house shall not be extinguished: she again lies in, after having been with child seven-and-twenty times: but even this is not so extraordinary as the Duke's

1 A comment on Hervey's alleged effeminacy.
2 Hon. Richard Leveson-Gower (1726–53), M.P.
3 A coffee-house in Cockspur Street frequented by Scotsmen. The Argyll was Archibald Campbell, 3rd Duke of Argyll (1682–1761).
4 Lord Protector Somerset (executed 1552) had disinherited his sons by his first wife in favour of the descendants of his second.
5 The modest ancestry of Sir Hugh Smithson (see letter 211, p. 300, n. 1), who acquired following his marriage the title and estates of the Percys, was a jibe repeated not just by Walpole, but more sarcastically by William Beckford in his *Liber Veritatis*.

fondness for her, or as the vigour of her beauty: her complexion is as fair and blooming as when she was a bride.

We expect some chagrin on the new Regency, at the head of which is to be the Duke; "An Augustum fessâ ætate totiens in Germaniam commeare potuisse," say the mutineers in Tacitus – *Augustus* goes in April.[1] He has notified to my Lord Orford his having given the reversion of New Park to his daughter Emily;[2] and has given him leave to keep it in the best repair. One of the German women, Madame Munchausen, his minister's wife, contributes very kindly to the entertainment of the town. She is ugly, devout, and with that sort of coquetry which proceeds from a virtue that knows its own weakness so much as to be alarmed, even when nothing is meant to its prejudice. At a great dinner which they gave last week, somebody observed that all the sugar-figures in the dessert were girls: the Baron replied, "Sa est frai; ordinairement les petits cupitons sont des garsons; mais ma femme s'est amusée toute la matinée à en ôter tout sà par motestie." This improvement of hers is a curious refinement, though all the geniuses of the age are employed in designing new plans for desserts. The Duke of Newcastle's last was a baby Vauxhall, illuminated with a million of little lamps of various colours.

We have been sitting this fortnight on the African Company: *we*, the British Senate, that temple of liberty, and bulwark of Protestant Christianity, have this fortnight been pondering methods to make more effectual that horrid traffic of selling negroes. It has appeared to us that six-and-forty thousand of these wretches are sold every year to our plantations alone! – it chills one's blood. I would not have to say that I voted in it for the continent of America! The destruction of the miserable inhabitants by the Spaniards was but a momentary misfortune, that flowed from the discovery of the New World, compared to this lasting havoc which it brought upon Africa. We reproach Spain, and yet do not even pretend the nonsense of butchering these poor creatures for the good of their souls!

I have just received your long letter of Feb. 13th, and am pleased that I had writ this volume to return it. I don't know how almost to

---

1 A reference to George II travelling to Hanover. The Duke [of Cumberland] was not among his listed regents. The quote from Tacitus, *Annals* I. xlvi, relates to Augustus visiting Germany in his declining years.
2 Princess Amelia succeeded Sir Robert as Ranger.

avoid wishing poor Prince Craon dead, to see the Princess end upon a throne. I am sure she would invert Mr. Vaughan's[1] wish, and compound to have nothing else made for her, provided a throne were.

I despise your literati enormously for their opinion of Montesquieu's book.[2] Bid them read that glorious chapter on the subject I have been mentioning, the selling of African slaves. Where did he borrow that? In what book in the world is there half so much wit, sentiment, delicacy, humanity?

I shall speak much more gently to you, my dear child, though you don't like Gothic architecture. The Grecian is only proper for magnificent and public buildings. Columns and all their beautiful ornaments, look ridiculous when crowded into a closet or a cheese-cake-house. The variety is little, and admits no charming irregularities. I am almost as fond of the *Sharawaggi*, or Chinese want of symmetry, in buildings, as in grounds or gardens.[3] I am sure, whenever you come to England, you will be pleased with the liberty of taste into which we are struck, and of which you can have no idea! Adieu!

391. *Lord Byron's Duel.*

TO THE EARL OF HERTFORD

Arlington Street, 27 January 1765.

... Since I wrote my letter, the following is the account nearest the truth that I can learn of the fatal duel last night: a club of Nottinghamshire gentlemen had dined at the Star and Garter, and there had been a dispute between the combatants, whether Lord Byron, who took no care of his game, or Mr. Chaworth, who was active in the association, had most game on their manor.[4] The company, however, had apprehended no consequences, and parted at eight o'clock; but Lord Byron stepping into an empty chamber, and

1 The chair-maker mentioned in the anecdote in the first paragraph of this letter.
2 Montesquieu's *De l'Esprit des lois* (1748).
3 An important statement of taste in relation to Strawberry Hill.
4 The Yale editors record that the issue between them was whether to prosecute poachers vigorously (the view of William Chaworth) or treat them with leniency (that of Lord Byron). William Byron, 5th Baron Byron (1722–98), was found guilty of manslaughter by the House of Lords but was able to plead privilege and was only required to pay a small fine.

sending the drawer for Mr. Chaworth, or calling him thither himself, took the candle from the waiter, and bidding Mr. Chaworth
defend himself, drew his sword. Mr. Chaworth, who was an excellent fencer, ran Lord Byron through the sleeve of his coat, and then
received a wound fourteen inches deep into his body. He was carried
to his house in Berkeley-street, – made his will with the greatest
composure, and dictated a paper, which, they say, allows it was a fair
duel, and died at nine this morning. Lord Byron is not gone off, but
says he will take his trial, which, if the Coroner brings in a verdict
of manslaughter, may, according to precedent, be in the House of
Lords, and without the ceremonial of Westminster Hall. George
Selwyn is much missed on this occasion, but we conclude it will
bring him over.[1] I feel for both families, though I know none of
either, but poor Lady Carlisle,[2] whom I am sure you will pity. . . .

392. *Fox's Duel.*

TO THE REV. WILLIAM MASON

Berkeley Square, 29 November 1779.

. . . As Lord Lyttelton had spoken *against* the Ministers, Mr.
Adam,[3] nephew of the architects, spoke *for* them. It is supposed that
when ever Scotland was dissatisfied with, pooh! I mean, not satisfied
by, Lord North, Adam was delegated to run at him; and now and
then might have a plenary indulgence from the Pope for talking the
language of opposition, in order to worm out secrets – poor souls!
as if they had any!

Well, on Thursday he made a most absurd speech in favour of
the Court, which Charles Fox tore piecemeal with infinite humour
and argument, which tortured the patient so much that next day he
asked an explanation. Fox assured him he had meant nothing personal, but had a right to dislocate his arguments, and he was satisfied; but on Sunday he sent a Scotch major to Fox to complain of the
state of the debate in the newspapers, and to desire Mr. Fox would
contradict and declare his good opinion of him. Fox returned for
answer, that he was not responsible for accounts in newspapers; that

1 A reference to Selwyn's fascination with trials and executions.
2 The sister of Lord Byron, who had fought in the duel.
3 William Adam (1751–1839), son of John Adam, subsequently Attorney-General.

it was harder still if on their misrepresentation he must give a good character of any man they abused: he again declared he had intended no offence, and that Mr. Adam was welcome to show that declaration to anybody. After consult had, Adam returned that Mr. Fox must print that recantation. "Hold!" said Fox, "not so far neither." —Oh! I forgot the principal circumstance of all: Adam added that his *friends* would not be satisfied under less than publication. At eight this morning they went into Hyde Park, Fox with Fitzpatrick, Adam with his Major Humberston for seconds. Adam fired, and the ball wounded Charles Fox's side, though very slightly: he then fired, missed, and said, "Now, Mr. Adam, are you satisfied?"

Near as you are to the Tweed you will not guess the reply. "No," said Adam; "you must still print your letter." Nothing could be more unjust, more unfair. They had fought because Fox would *not* consent to that pretension. Fox with the same firmness and temper with which he had conducted himself through the whole affair peremptorily refused, and the bloodhound again fired, but missed, and then Fox fired into the air and it ended. . . . Adieu, or the bellman will be gone.

2. LAW AND CRIME

393. *The Drunken Constables.*

TO SIR HORACE MANN

c. 21 July 1742.

. . . There has lately been the most shocking scene of murder imaginable; a parcel of *drunken* constables took it into their heads to put the laws in execution against *disorderly* persons, and so took up every woman they met, till they had collected five or six-and-twenty, all of whom they thrust into St. Martin's round-house, where they kept them all night, with doors and windows closed. The poor creatures, who could not stir or breathe, screamed as long as they had any breath left, begging at least for water: one poor wretch said she was worth eighteen pence, and would gladly give it for a draught of water, but in vain! So well did they keep them there, that in the morning four were found stifled to death, two died soon after, and a dozen more are in a shocking way. In short, it is horrid to think what the poor creatures suffered: several of them were beggars, who, from having no lodging, were necessarily found in the street, and others honest labouring women. One of the dead was a poor washer-woman, big with child, who was returning home late from washing. One of the constables is taken and others absconded; but I question[1] if any of them will suffer death, though the greatest criminals in this town are the officers of justice; there is no tyranny they do not exercise, no villany of which they do not partake. These same men, the same night, broke into a bagnio in Covent-Garden and took up Jack Spencer, Mr. Stewart, and Lord George Graham,[2] and would have thrust them into the round-house with the poor women, if they had not been worth more than eighteen-pence! . . . Adieu!

394. *The Attorney's Wife. "Handsome" Tracy.*

TO GEORGE MONTAGU, ESQ.

Strawberry Hill, Saturday night, 3 September 1748.

. . . Since I came home I have been disturbed with a strange, foolish woman, that lives at the great corner house yonder; she is an attorney's wife, and much given to the bottle. By the time she has finished that and daylight, she grows afraid of thieves, and makes the servants fire minute guns out of the garret windows. I remember persuading Mrs. Kerwood that there was a great smell of thieves, and this drunken dame seems literally to smell it. The divine Ashton,[3] whom I suppose you will have seen when you receive this, will give you an account of the astonishment we were in last night at hearing guns; I, began to think that the Duke had brought some of his defeats from Flanders.

I am going to tell you a long story, but you will please to remember that I don't intend to tell it well; therefore, if you discover any beauties in the relation when I never intended them, don't conclude, as

---

1 The keeper of the round-house [William Bird] was tried, but acquitted of wilful murder. – WALPOLE. The Yale editors note that Bird was in fact convicted and transported, but died on shipboard.

2 Spencer was the grandson of the 1st Duke of Marlborough, and Graham was the son of the Duke of Montrose.

3 For Ashton see letter 1, p. 6, n. 4.

you did in your last, that I know they are there. If I had not a great command of my pen, and could not force it to write whatever nonsense I had heard last, you would be enough to pervert all one's letters, and put one upon keeping up one's characters, but as I write merely to satisfy you, I shall take no care but not to write well; I hate letters that are called good letters.

You must know then, – but did you know a young fellow that was called Handsome Tracy? He was walking in the Park with some of his acquaintance, and overtook three girls; one was very pretty; they followed them; but the girls ran away, and the company grew tired of pursuing them, all but Tracy. (There are now three more guns gone off; she must be very drunk.) He followed to Whitehall gate, where he gave a porter a crown to dog them: the porter hunted them – he the porter. The girls ran all round Westminster, and back to the Haymarket, where the porter came up with them. He told the pretty one she must go with him, and kept her talking till Tracy arrived, quite out of breath, and exceedingly in love. He insisted on knowing where she lived, which she refused to tell him; and after much disputing, went to the house of one of her companions, and Tracy with them. He there made her discover her family, a butterwoman in Craven Street, and engaged her to meet him the next morning in the Park; but before night he wrote her four love-letters; and in the last offered two hundred pounds a-year to her, and a hundred a-year to Signora la Madre. Griselda made a confidence to a staymaker's wife, who told her that the swain was certainly in love enough to marry her, if she could determine to be virtuous and refuse his offers. "Ay," says she, "but if I should, and should lose him by it." However, the measures of the cabinet council were decided for virtue; and when she met Tracy the next morning in the Park, she was convoyed by her sister and brother-in-law, and stuck close to the letter of her reputation. She would do nothing; she would go nowhere. At last, as an instance of prodigious compliance, she told him, that if he would accept such a dinner as a butterwoman's daughter could give him, he should be welcome. Away they walked to Craven Street: the mother borrowed some silver to buy a leg of mutton, and they kept the eager lover drinking till twelve at night, when a chosen committee waited on the faithful pair to the minister of May-fair. The doctor was in bed, and swore he would not get up to marry the King, but that he had a brother over the way who perhaps would, and who did. The mother borrowed a pair of sheets, and they consummated at her house; and the next day they went to their own place. In two or three days the scene grew gloomy; and the husband coming home one night, swore he could bear it no longer. "Bear! bear what?" – "Why, to be teased by all my acquaintance for marrying a butterwoman's daughter. I am determined to go to France, and will leave you a handsome allowance." – "Leave me! why, you don't fancy you shall leave me? I will go with you." – "What, you love me, then?" – "No matter whether I love you or not, but you shan't go without me." And they are gone! If you know anybody that proposes marrying and travelling, I think they cannot do it in a more commodious method. . . . Adieu!

395. *The Marriage Act.*

TO THE HON. H. S. CONWAY

Strawberry Hill, 24 May 1753.

It is well you are married! How would my Lady Ailesbury have liked to be asked in a parish church for three Sundays running? I really believe she would have worn her weeds for ever rather than have passed through so impudent a ceremony! What do *you* think? – But you will want to know the interpretation of this preamble. Why, there is a new bill, which, under the notion of preventing clandestine marriages, has made such a general rummage, and reform in the office of matrimony, that every Strephon and Chloe, every dowager and her Hussey,[1] will have as many impediments and formalities to undergo as a treaty of peace. Lord Bath invented this bill, but had drawn it so ill, that the Chancellor was forced to draw a new one, and then grew so fond of his own creature, that he has crammed it down the throats of both Houses – though they gave many a gulp before they could swallow it. The Duke of Bedford attacked it first with great spirit and mastery, but had little support, though the Duke of Newcastle did not vote. The lawyers were all ordered to nurse it through our House; but, except the poor Attorney-General [Ryder], who is nurse indeed to all intents and purposes, and did

1 A reference to Edward Hussey (*c.* 1721–1802), later Earl of Beaulieu, who had in 1743 secretly married the Dowager Duchess of Manchester.

amply gossip over it, not one of them said a word. Nugent shone extremely in opposition to the bill, and, though every now and then on the precipiece of absurdity, kept clear of it, with great humour and wit and argument, and was unanswered – yet we were beat. Last Monday it came into the committee: Charles Townshend acted a very good speech with great cleverness, and drew a picture of his own story and his father's tyranny, with at least as much parts as modesty. Mr. Fox[1] mumbled the Chancellor and his lawyers, and pinned the plan of the bill upon a pamphlet he had found of Dr. Gally's,[2] where the Doctor, recommending the French scheme of matrimony, says, "It was found that fathers were too apt to forgive." "The Gospel, I thought," said Mr. Fox, "enjoined forgiveness; but pious Dr. Gally thinks fathers are too apt to forgive." Mr. Pelham, extremely in his opinion against the bill, and in his inclination too, was forced to rivet it, and, without speaking one word for it, taught the House how to vote for it; and it was carried against the Chairman's leaving the chair by 165 to 84. . . .

396. *An Execution.*

TO GEORGE MONTAGU, ESQ.

Arlington Street, 6 May 1760.

The extraordinary history of Lord Ferrers is closed: he was executed yesterday.[3] Madness, that in other countries is a disorder, is here a systematic character: it does not hinder people from forming a plan of conduct, and from even dying agreeably to it. You remember how the last Ratcliffe[4] died with the utmost propriety; so did this horrid lunatic, coolly and sensibly. His own and his wife's relations had asserted that he would tremble at last. No such thing; he shamed

1 Henry Fox, later Lord Holland (see letter 15, p. 29, n. 3). The Yale editors note that his opposition to the Marriage Bill was partly based on opposition to Hardwicke, the Lord Chancellor, who promoted the Bill, and was partly a reflection of his own happy marriage in 1744 to Lady Caroline Lennox – without the consent of her parents, the Duke and Duchess of Richmond.
2 Dr. Henry Gally (1696–1769), rector of St. Giles in the Fields, had written *Some Considerations upon Clandestine Marriages* (1750).
3 Laurence Shirley, 4th Earl Ferrers (1720–60), was hanged at Tyburn on 5 May 1760 after being convicted in a trial by his peers for the murder of his steward.
4 Charles Radclyffe, Earl of Derwentwater, English Jacobite, one of the rebel lords executed in 1746.

heroes. He bore the solemnity of a pompous and tedious procession of above two hours, from the Tower to Tyburn, with as much tranquillity as if he was only going to his own burial, not to his own execution. He even talked on indifferent subjects in the passage and if the sheriff and the chaplain had not thought that they had parts to act, too, and had not consequently engaged him in more particular conversation, he did not seem to think it necessary to talk on the occasion; he went in his wedding-clothes, marking the only remaining impression on his mind. The ceremony he was in a hurry to have over: he was stopped at the gallows by the vast crowd, but got out of his coach as soon as he could, and was but seven minutes on the scaffold, which was hung with black, and prepared by the undertaker of his family at their expense. There was a new contrivance for sinking the stage under him, which did not play well; and he suffered a little by the delay, but was dead in four minutes. The mob was decent, and admired him, and almost pitied him; so they would Lord George,[1] whose execution they are so angry at missing. I suppose every highwayman will now preserve the blue handkerchief they have about their necks when they are married, like a lord. With all the frenzy of his blood, he was not mad enough to be struck with his aunt Huntingdon's sermons. The Methodists have nothing to brag of his conversion, though Whitfield[2] prayed for him and preached about him. Even Tyburn has been above their reach. I have not heard that Lady Fanny[3] dabbled with his soul; but I believe she is prudent enough to confine her missionary zeal to subjects where the body may be her perquisite.

When am I likely to see you? The delightful rain is come – we look and smell charmingly. Adieu!

1 Lord George Sackville, who was not executed following his court martial: see letter 256, p. 360, n. 2.
2 See letter 214, p. 305, n. 1.
3 Lady Frances Shirley (c. 1706–78), a neighbour of Walpole's in Twickenham, had been a great beauty when young, celebrated by Pope and painted by Charles Jervas. In later life she converted to Methodism: she was related to Selina Hastings, Countess of Huntingdon (1707–91), whose religious persuasion was anathema to Walpole.

397. *The Pillory.*

TO THE EARL OF HERTFORD

14 February 1765, addition to letter begun 12 February.

... Williams, the reprinter of the "North Briton," stood in the pillory to-day in Palace Yard. He went in a hackney-coach, the number of which was 45. The mob erected a gallows opposite him, on which they hung a boot[1] with a bonnet of straw. Then a collection was made for Williams, which amounted to near 200*l*. In short, every public event informs the Administration how thoroughly they are detested, and that they have not a friend whom they do not buy. Who can wonder, when every man of virtue is proscribed, and they have neither parts nor characters to impose even upon the mob! Think to what a government is sunk, when a Secretary of State is called in Parliament to his face "the most profligate sad dog in the kingdom,"[2] and not a man can open his lips in his defence. Sure power must have some strange unknown charm, when it can compensate for such contempt! I see many who triumph in these bitter pills which the Ministry are so often forced to swallow; I own I do not; it is more mortifying to me to reflect how great and respectable we were three years ago, than satisfactory to see those insulted who have brought such shame upon us. 'Tis poor amends to national honour to know, that if a printer is set in the pillory, his country wishes it was my Lord This, or Mr. That. They will be gathered to the Oxfords, and Bolingbrokes, and ignominious of former days; but the wound they have inflicted is perhaps indelible. That goes to *my* heart, who had felt all the Roman pride of being one of the first nations upon earth! – Good night! – I will go to bed and dream of Kings drawn in triumph; and then I will go to Paris, and dream I am proconsul there: pray, take care not to let me be wakened with an account of an invasion having taken place from Dunkirk! Yours ever, H. W.

1 The symbol used to mock Lord Bute.
2 Isaac Barré's not unreasonable description of "Jemmy Twitcher," Lord Sandwich (for whom see letter 199, p. 282, n. 1).

398. *A Highwayman Outwitted.*

TO THE COUNTESS OF UPPER OSSORY

Strawberry Hill, 7 October 1781.

... The night I had the honour of writing to your Ladyship last, I was robbed – and, as if I were a sovereign or a nation, have had a discussion ever since whether it was not a *neighbour* who robbed me – and should it come to the ears of the newspapers, it might produce as ingenious a controversy amongst our anonymous wits as any of the noble topics I have been mentioning. *Voici le fait.* Lady Browne and I were, as usual, going to the Duchess of Montrose at seven o'clock.[1] The evening was very dark. In the close lane under her park-pale, and within twenty yards of the gate, a black figure on horseback pushed by between the chaise and the hedge on my side. I suspected it was a highwayman, and so I found did Lady Browne, for she was speaking and dropped. To divert her fears, I was just going to say, Is not that the apothecary going to the Duchess? when I heard a voice cry "Stop!" and the figure came back to the chaise. I had the presence of mind, before I let down the glass, to take out my watch and stuff it within my waistcoat under my arm. He said, "Your purses and watches!" I replied, "I have no watch." "Then your purse!" I gave it to him; it had nine guineas. It was so dark that I could not see his hand, but felt him take it. He then asked for Lady Browne's purse, and said, "Don't be frightened; I will not hurt you." I said, "No; you won't frighten the lady?" He replied, "No; I give you my word I will do you no hurt." Lady Browne gave him her purse, and was going to add her watch, but he said, "I am much obliged to you! I wish you good night!" pulled off his hat, and rode away. "Well," said I, "Lady Browne, you will not be afraid of being robbed another time, for you see there is nothing in it." "Oh! but I am," said she, "and now I am in terrors lest he should return, for I have given him a purse with only bad money that I carry on purpose." "He certainly will not open it directly," said I, "and at worst he can only wait for us at our return; but I will send my servant back for a horse and a blunderbuss," which I did. The next distress was not to terrify the Duchess, who is so paralytic and nervous. I therefore made Lady

1 Frances Sheldon (1714–90), Lady Browne, Walpole's neighbour and correspondent. For the Duchess of Montrose, see letter 220, p. 313, n. 2.

Browne go into the parlour, and desired one of the Duchess's servants to get her a glass of water, while I went into the drawing-room to break it to the Duchess. "Well," said I, laughing to her and the rest of the company, "you won't get much from us to-night." "Why," said one of them, "have you been robbed?" "Yes, a little," said I. The Duchess trembled; but it went off. Her groom of the chambers said not a word, but slipped out, and Lady Margaret and Miss Howe having servants there on horseback, he gave them pistols and despatched them different ways. This was exceedingly clever, for he knew the Duchess would not have suffered it, as lately he had detected a man who had robbed her garden, and she would not allow him to take up the fellow. These servants spread the story, and when my footman arrived on foot, he was stopped in the street by the hostler of the "George," who told him the highwayman's horse was then in the stable; but this part I must reserve for the second volume, for I have made this no story so long and so tedious that your Ladyship will not be able to read it in a breath. . . .

399. *Robberies Wholesale.*

TO SIR HORACE MANN

Strawberry Hill, 8 September 1782.

. . . I am perfectly ignorant of the state of the war abroad; they say we are in no pain for Gibraltar:[1] but I know that we are in a state of war at home that is shocking. I mean, from the enormous profusion of housebreakers, highwaymen, and footpads and, what is worse, from the savage barbarities of the two latter, who commit the most wanton cruelties. This evil is another fruit of the American war. Having no vent for the convicts that used to be transported to our late colonies, a plan was adopted for confining them on board of lighters for the term of their sentences. In those colleges, undergraduates in villainy commence Masters of Arts, and at the expiration of their studies issue as mischievous as if they had taken their degrees in laws physic, or divinity, at one of our regular universities; but, having no profession, nor testimonial to their characters they

---

1 The siege of Gibraltar, defended by Sir George Eliott (see letter 326, p. 453, n. 4), was lifted the following February.

can get no employment, and therefore live upon the public. In short, the grievance is so crying, that one dare not stir out after dinner but well-armed. If one goes abroad to dinner, you would think one was going to the relief of Gibraltar. You may judge how depraved we are, when the war has not consumed half the reprobates, nor press-gangs thinned their numbers! But no wonder – how should the morals of the people be purified, when such frantic dissipation reigns above them? Contagion does not mount, but descend. A new theatre is going to be erected merely for people of fashion, that they may not be confined to vulgar hours – that is, to day or night. Fashion is always silly, for, before it can spread far, it must be calculated for silly people; as examples of sense, wit, or ingenuity could be imitated only by a few. All the discoveries that I can perceive to have been made by the present age, is to prefer riding about the streets rather than on the roads or on the turf, and being too late for everything. Thus, though we have more public diversions than would suffice for two capitals, nobody goes to them till they are over. This is literally true. Ranelagh, that is, the music there, finishes at half an hour after ten at night; but the most fashionable set out for it, though above a mile out of town, at eleven or later. Well! but is not this censure being old and cross? were not the charming people of my youth guilty of equivalent absurdities? Oh, yes; but the sensible folks of my youth had not lost America, nor dipped us in wars with half Europe, that cost us fifteen millions a year. I believe the Jews went to Ranelagh at midnight, though Titus was at Knightsbridge. But Titus demolished their Ranelagh as well as Jerusalem. Adieu!

400. *The Same.*

TO THE HON. H. S. CONWAY

Strawberry Hill, 14 August 1784.

As Lady Cecilia Johnston offers to be postman, I cannot resist writing a line, though I have not a word to say. In good sooth, I know nothing, hear of nothing, but robberies and housebreaking; consequently never think of Ministers, India Directors, and such honest men. Mrs. Clive has been broken open, and Mr. Raftor miscarried and died of the fright. Lady Browne has lost all her liveries and her temper, and Lady Margaret Compton has cried her eyes out on losing a lurch[1] and almost her wig. In short, as I do not love exaggeration, I do not believe there have been above threescore highway robberies within this week, fifty-seven houses that have been broken open, and two hundred and thirty that are to be stripped on the first opportunity. We are in great hopes, however, that the King of Spain, now he has demolished Algiers,[2] the metropolitan see of thieves, will come and bombard Richmond, Twickenham, Hampton Court, and all the suffragan cities that swarm with pirates and banditti, as he has a better knack at destroying vagabonds than at recovering his own.

Ireland is in a blessed way; and, as if the climate infected everybody that sets foot there, the viceroy's aides-de-camp have blundered into a riot, that will set all the humours afloat.[3] I wish you joy of the summer being come now it is gone, which is better than not coming at all. I hope Lady Cecilia will return with an account of your all being perfectly well. Adieu!

401. *Newspapers.*

TO HANNAH MORE

Strawberry Hill, 4 July 1788.

… No botanist am I ; nor wished to learn from *you*, of all the Muses, that *piping* has a new signification. I had rather that you handled an oaten pipe than a carnation one; yet setting layers, I own, is preferable to reading newspapers, one of the chronical maladies of this age. Everybody reads them, nay, quotes them, though everybody knows they are stuffed with lies or blunders. How should it be otherwise? If any extraordinary event happens, who but must hear it before it descends through a coffee-house to the runner of a daily paper? They who are always wanting news, are wanting to hear they don't know what. A lower species, indeed, is that of the scribes you mention, who every night compose a journal for the satisfaction of such *illiterati*, and feed them with all the vices and misfortunes of every private family; nay, they now call it a *duty* to publish all those

1 Lady Margaret Compton (*c.* 1703–86) was one of the Walpole's dowager friends, who was very fond of cards: a lurch is in some games an unassailable lead.
2 The Spanish attacked Algiers in July 1784.
3 Some aides-de-camp of the Lord Lieutenant of Ireland had initiated a drunken brawl which led to a riot.

calamities which decency to wretched relations used in compassion to suppress, I mean self-murder in particular. Mr. [Hesse's] was detailed at length; and to-day that of Lord [Saye and Sele's].[1] The pretence is, *in terrorem*, like the absurd stake and highway of our ancestors; as if there were a precautionary potion for madness, or the stigma of a newspaper were more dreadful than death. Daily journalists, to be sure, are most respectable magistrates! Yes, much like the cobblers that Cromwell made peers.[2] . . .

3. METHODISM

402. Increasing Popularity.

TO SIR HORACE MANN

Strawberry Hill, 3 May 1749.

. . . Here is another *bon-mot* of my Lady Townshend:[3] we were talking of the Methodists; somebody said, "Pray, Madam, is it true that Whitfield has *recanted?*" "No, Sir, he has only *canted.*"

If you ever think of returning to England, as I hope it will be long first, you must prepare yourself with Methodism. I really believe that by that time it will be necessary: this sect increases as fast as almost ever any religious nonsense did. Lady Fanny Shirley[4] has chosen this way of bestowing the dregs of her beauty upon Jesus Christ; and Mr. Lyttelton[5] is very near making the same sacrifice of the dregs of all those various characters that he has worn. The Methodists love your big sinners, as proper subjects to work upon – and indeed they have a plentiful harvest – I think what you call flagrancy was never more in fashion. Drinking is at the highest wine-mark; and gaming joined with it so violent, that at the last Newmarket meeting, in the rapidity of both, a bank-bill was thrown down, and nobody immediately claiming it, they agreed to give it to a man that was standing by. . . .

1 George Hesse (*c.* 1748–88), a friend of the Prince of Wales, and Thomas Twisleton, Lord Saye and Sele (*c.* 1735–88) had both recently committed suicide: the Yale editors note that lurid accounts of both deaths had appeared in the newspaper *The World.*
2 Walpole exaggerates the low birth of the peers created by Cromwell.
3 Etheldreda, *née* Harrison, Viscountess Townshend (*c.* 1708–88), society figure and friend of Walpole.
4 See letter 396, p. 562, n. 3.
5 Lord Lyttelton (see letter 130, p. 197, n. 2) became a Christian, but not a Methodist.

403. *Whitfield in Disgrace.*

TO THE EARL OF STRAFFORD

My dear Lord, Strawberry Hill, 5 July 1761.

... The apostle Whitfield is come to some shame: he went to Lady Huntingdon lately, and asked for forty pounds for some distressed saint or other. She said she had not so much money in the house, but would give it him the first time she had. He was very pressing, but in vain. At last he said, "There's your watch and trinkets, you don't want such vanities; I will have that." She would have put him off: but he persisting, she said, "Well, if you must have it you must." About a fortnight afterwards, going to his house, and being carried into his wife's chamber, among the paraphernalia of the latter the Countess found her own offering. This has made a terrible schism: she tells the story herself – I had not it from Saint Frances,[1] but I hope it is true. Adieu, my dear lord!

P.S. My gallery sends its humble duty to your new front, and all my creatures beg their respects to my lady.[2]

404. *Wesley.*

TO JOHN CHUTE, ESQ.

Bath, 10 October 1766.

I am impatient to hear that your charity to me has not ended in the gout to yourself – all my comfort is, if you have it, that you have good Lady Brown[3] to nurse you.

My health advances faster than my amusement. However, I have been at one opera, Mr. Wesley's. They have boys and girls with charming voices, that sing hymns, in parts, to Scotch ballad tunes; but indeed so long, that one would think they were already in eternity, and knew how much time they had before them. The chapel is very neat, with true Gothic windows (yet I am not converted) but

1 Lady Frances Shirley. – WALPOLE.
2 Walpole compares his Gallery at Strawberry Hill with the south-east façade of Wentworth Castle, designed by Lord Strafford, both then under construction.
3 Margaret, *née* Cecil, Lady Brown (*c.* 1696–1782), who was celebrated for her Sunday-evening concerts.

I was glad to see that luxury is creeping in upon them before persecution; they have very neat mahogany stands for branches, and brackets of the same in taste. At the upper end is a broad *hautpas* of four steps, advancing in the middle: at each end of the broadest part are two of *my* eagles,[1] with red cushions for the parson and clerk. Behind them rise three more steps, in the midst of which is a third eagle for pulpit. Scarlet armed chairs to all three. On either hand, a balcony for elect ladies. The rest of the congregation sit on forms. Behind the pit, in a dark niche, is a plain table within rails; so you see the throne is for the apostle. Wesley is a lean elderly man, fresh-coloured, his hair smoothly combed, but with a *soupçon* of curl at the ends. Wondrous clean, but as evidently an actor as Garrick. He spoke his sermon, but so fast, and with so little accent, that I am sure he has often uttered it, for it was like a lesson. There were parts and eloquence in it; but towards the end he exalted his voice, and acted very ugly enthusiasm; decried learning, and told stories, like Latimer, of the fool of his college, who said, "I *thanks* God for everything." Except a few from curiosity, and *some honourable women*, the congregation was very mean. There was a Scotch Countess of Buchan, who is carrying a pure rosy vulgar face to heaven, and who asked Miss Rich, if that was *the author of the poets*. I believe she meant me and the "Noble Authors."

The Bedfords[2] came last night. Lord Chatham was with me yesterday two hours; looks and walks well, and is in excellent political spirits.

405. *Whitfield, a Rogue.*

TO THE REV. WILLIAM COLE

Strawberry Hill, 16 April 1768.

. . . I hope the Methodist, your neighbour,[3] does not, like his patriarch Whitfield, encourage the people to forge, murder, &c., in

---

1 That is, reminiscent of the Boccapadugli eagle, an antique sculpture found in Rome and secured by Chute for Walpole in 1745.
2 John Russell (1710–71), 4th Duke of Bedford and his wife Gertrude Leveson Gower (1715–94).
3 John Berridge (1716–93), a Methodist clergyman near Cole's home at Waterbeach, Cambridge.

order to have the benefit of being converted at the gallows. That arch-rogue preached lately a funeral sermon on one Gibson, hanged for forgery, and told his audience, that he could assure them Gibson was now in heaven, and that another fellow, executed at the same time, had the happiness of touching Gibson's coat as he was turned off. As little as you and I agree about a hundred years ago, I don't desire a reign of fanatics. Oxford has begun with these rascals, and I hope Cambridge will wake. I don't mean that I would have them persecuted, which is what they wish; but I would have the clergy fight them and ridicule them. Adieu! dear Sir. Yours ever.

4. TRAVEL

406. *English Inns.*

TO SIR HORACE MANN

Newmarket, 3 October 1743.

I am writing to you in an inn on the road to London. What a paradise should I have thought this when I was in the Italian inns! in a wide barn with four ample windows, which had nothing more like glass than shutters and iron bars! no tester to the bed, and the saddles and portmanteaus heaped on me to keep off the cold. What a paradise did I think the inn at Dover when I came back! and what magnificence were twopenny prints, salt-sellers, and boxes to hold the knives; but the *summum bonum* was small-beer and the newspaper.

"I bless'd my stars, and call'd it luxury!"[1]

Who was the Neapolitan ambassadress[2] that could not live at Paris, because there was no maccaroni? Now am I relapsed into all the dissatisfied repinement of a true English grumbling voluptuary. I could find in my heart to write a Craftsman[3] against the Government, because I am not quite so much at my ease as on my own sofa. I could persuade myself that it is my Lord Carteret's fault that I am only sitting in a common arm-chair, when I would be lolling in a

---

1 From Addison's *Cato* I. iv: "Blesses his stars, and thinks it luxury".
2 The Princess of Campoflorido. – WALPOLE.
3 The leading opposition journal to the government of Sir Robert Walpole.

péché-mortel.[1] How dismal, how solitary, how scrub does this town look; and yet it has actually a street of houses better than Parma or Modena. Nay, the houses of the people of fashion, who come hither for the races, are palaces to what houses in London itself were fifteen years ago. People do begin to live again now, and I suppose in a term we shall revert to York Houses, Clarendon Houses, &c. But from that grandeur all the nobility had contracted themselves to live in coops of a dining-room, a dark back-room, with one eye in a corner, and a closet. Think what London would be, if the chief houses were in it, as in the cities in other countries, and not dispersed like great rarity-plums in a vast pudding of country. Well, it is a tolerable place as it is! Were I a physician, I would prescribe nothing but recipe, CCCLXV, drachm. Londin. Would you know why I like London so much? Why, if the world must consist of so many fools as it does I choose to take them in the gross, and not made into separate pills, as they are prepared in the country. Besides, there is no being alone but in a metropolis: the worst place in the world to find solitude is the country: questions grow there, and that unpleasant Christian commodity, neighbours. Oh! they are all good Samaritans, and do so pour balms and nostrums upon one, if one has but the toothache, or a journey to take, that they break one's head. A journey to take – ay! they talk over the miles to you, and tell you, you will be late in. My Lord Lovel says, *John* always goes two hours in the dark in the morning to avoid being one hour in the dark in the evening. I was pressed to set out to-day before seven: I did before nine; and here am I arrived at a quarter past five, for the rest of the night. . . .

5. THE COUNTRY

407. *Boredom in Norfolk.*

TO JOHN CHUTE, ESQ.

Houghton, 20 August 1743.

Indeed, my dear Sir, you certainly did not use to be stupid, and till you give me more substantial proof that you are so, I shall not believe it. As for your temperate diet and milk bringing about such

---

1 A *péché-mortel* was a form of *chaise longue*. Lord Carteret (see letter 37, p. 64, n. 1) with the Duke of Newcastle (see letter 14, p. 28, n. 2) led the ministry following the fall of Walpole's father, hence a figure open to criticism.

a metamorphosis, I hold it impossible. I have such lamentable proofs every day before my eyes of the stupifying qualities of beef, ale, and wine, that I have contracted a most religious veneration for your spiritual nouriture. Only imagine that I here every day see men, who are mountains of roast beef, and only seem just roughly hewn out into the outlines of human form, like the giant-rock at Pratolino![1] I shudder when I see them brandish their knives in act to carve, and look on them as savages that devour one another. I should not stare at all more than I do, if yonder Alderman at the lower end of the table was to stick his fork into his neighbour's jolly cheek, and cut a brave slice of brown and fat. Why, I'll swear I see no difference between a country gentleman and a sirloin; whenever the first laughs, or the latter is cut, there run out just the same streams of gravy! Indeed, the sirloin does not ask quite so many questions. I have an Aunt here, a family piece of goods, an old remnant of inquisitive hospitality and economy, who, to all intents and purposes, is as beefy as her neighbours. She wore me so down yesterday with interrogatories, that I dreamt all night she was at my ear with "who's" and "why's," and "when's" and "where's," till at last in my very sleep I cried out, "For God in heaven's sake, Madam, ask me no more questions!"

Oh! my dear Sir, don't you find that nine parts in ten of the world are of no use but to make you wish yourself with that tenth part? I am so far from growing used to mankind by living amongst them, that my natural ferocity and wildness does but every day grow worse. They tire me, they fatigue me; I don't know what to do with them; I don't know what to say to them; I fling open the windows, and fancy I want air; and when I get by myself, I undress myself, and seem to have had people in my pockets, in my plaits, and on my shoulders! I indeed find this fatigue worse in the country than in town, because one can avoid it there and has more resources; but it is there too. I fear 'tis growing old; but I literally seem to have murdered a man whose name was Ennui, for his ghost is ever before me. They say there is no English word for *ennui*; I think you may translate it most literally by what is called "entertaining people," and "doing the honours:" that is, you sit an hour with somebody you

1 Walpole here compares the squires of Norfolk, entertained by his father at Houghton, to the giant rock figure carved by Giambologna at the Grand Duke of Tuscany's estate at Pratolino, which he had visited with Gray and Chute in April 1741.

don't know and don't care for, talk about the wind and the weather, and ask a thousand foolish questions, which all begin with, "I think you live a good deal in the country," or, "I think you don't love this thing or that." Oh! 'tis dreadful! . . . Yours most sincerely.

408. *The English Countryside.*

TO THE HON. H. S. CONWAY

Strawberry Hill, Wednesday night, late, 17 July 1793.

. . . It is much cooler to-day, yet still delicious; for be it known to you that I have enjoyed weather worthy of Africa, and yet without swallowing mouthfuls of mosquitoes, nor expecting to hear hyænas howl in the village, nor to find scorpions in my bed. Indeed, all the way I came home, I could but gaze at the felicity of my countrymen. The road was one string of stage-coaches, loaded within and without with noisy jolly folks, and chaises and gigs that had been pleasuring in clouds of dust; every door and every window of every house was open, lights in every shop, every door with women sitting in the street, every inn crowded with jaded horses, and every ale-house full of drunken topers; for you know the English always announce their sense of heat or cold by drinking. Well! it was impossible not to enjoy such a scene of happiness and affluence in every village and amongst the lowest of the people; and who are told by villanous scribblers, that they are oppressed and miserable. New streets, new towns, are rising every day and everywhere; the earth is covered with gardens and crops of grain.

How bitter to turn from this Elysium to the Temple at Paris! The fiends there have now torn her son from the Queen! Can one believe that they are human beings, who 'midst all their confusions sit coolly meditating new tortures, new anguish for that poor, helpless, miserable woman, after four years of unexampled sufferings?[1] Oh! if such crimes are not made a dreadful lesson, this world might become a theatre of cannibals! . . .

---

1 The National Convention had ordered that the Dauphin be taken away from Marie Antoinette, who was imprisoned in the Temple. Three months later she was guillotined.

6. INCREASING POPULATION

409. Bristol.

TO GEORGE MONTAGU, ESQ.

Strawberry Hill, 22 October 1766.

They may say what they will, but it does one ten times more good to leave Bath than to go to it. I may sometimes drink the waters, as Mr. Bentley used to say I invited company hither that I did not care for, that I might enjoy the pleasure of their going away. My health is certainly mended, but I did not feel the satisfaction of it till I got home. I have still a little rheumatism in one shoulder, which was not dipped in Styx, and is still mortal; but, while I went to the rooms, or stayed in my *chambers* in a dull court, I thought I had twenty complaints. I don't perceive one of them.

Having no companion but such as the place afforded, and which I did not accept,[1] my excursions were very few; besides that the city is so guarded with mountains, that I had not patience to be jolted like a pea in a drum, in my chaise alone. I did go to Bristol, the dirtiest great shop I ever saw, with so foul a river, that, had I seen the least appearance of cleanliness, I should have concluded they washed all their linen in it, as they do at Paris. Going into the town, I was struck with a large Gothic building, coal-black, and striped with white; I took it for the Devil's cathedral. When I came nearer, I found it was an uniform castle, lately built, and serving for stables and offices to a smart false Gothic house on the other side of the road.[2]

The real Cathedral is very neat, and has pretty tombs, besides the two windows of painted glass, given by Mrs. Ellen Gwyn. There is a new church besides of St. Nicholas, neat and truly Gothic, besides a charming old church at the other end of the town.[3] The cathedral,

1 The Yale editors note that Walpole wrote "except", but probably meant "accept".
2 Arno's Court and its stables, built for William Reeve, a brass manufacturer. The house was a classical block to which Gothic trimmings were added *c.* 1764, and at the same time the stables opposite were designed as a mock-Gothic castle, built of black compressed slag from Reeve's brass foundry.
3 Bristol Cathedral contains the monument to the wife of Walpole's correspondent William Mason, who died at Bristol the year after this letter. The church of St. Nicholas had recently been Gothicised; the charming old church at the other end of the town was probably St. Mary Redcliffe, in whose muniment room Thomas Chatterton claimed to have found the manuscripts of the Rowley poems (see letters 140–44).

or Abbey, at Bath, is glaring and crowded with modern tablet-monuments; among others, I found two, of my cousin Sir Erasmus Phillips, and of Colonel Madan. Your cousin Bishop Montagu decked it much. I dined one day with an agreeable family, two miles from Bath, a Captain Miller and his wife, and her mother, Mrs. Riggs.[1] They have a small new-built house [Bath-Easton Villa], with a bow-window, directly opposite to which the Avon falls in a wide cascade, a church behind it in a vale, into which two mountains descend, leaving an opening into the distant country. A large village, with houses of gentry, is on one of the hills to the left. Their garden is little, but pretty, and watered with several small rivulets among the bushes. Meadows fall down to the road; and above, the garden is terminated by another view of the river, the city, and the mountains. 'Tis a very diminutive principality, with large pretensions. . . .

410. *Growth of London.*

TO SIR HORACE MANN

Strawberry Hill, 17 July 1776, addition to letter begun 16 July.

. . . I did flatter myself with being diverted at your surprise from so general an alteration of persons, objects, manners, as you would have found; but there is an end of all that pleasing vision! I remember when my father went out of place, and was to return visits, which Ministers are excused from doing, he could not guess where he was, finding himself in so many new streets and squares. This was thirty years ago. They have been building ever since, and one would think had imported two or three capitals. London could put Florence into its fob-pocket; but as they build so slightly, if they did not rebuild, it would be just the reverse of Rome, a vast circumference of city surrounding an area of ruins. As its present progress is chiefly north, and Southwark marches south, the metropolis promises to be as broad as long. Rows of houses shoot out every way like a polypus; and, so great is the rage of building everywhere, that, if I stay here a fortnight, without going to town, I look about to see if no new house is built since I went last. America and France must tell us how

1 For the poetical amusements held by Anna Riggs Miller at her villa, see letter 153, p. 221, n. 1. Walpole was subsequently more critical of the pretensions of the establishment.

long this exuberance of opulence is to last! The East Indies, I believe, will not contribute to it much longer. Babylon and Memphis and Rome, probably, stared at their own downfall. Empires did not use to philosophise, nor thought much but of themselves. Such revolutions are better known now, and we ought to expect them – I do not say we do. This little island will be ridiculously proud some ages hence of its former brave days, and swear its capital was once as big again as Paris, or – what is to be the name of the city that will then give laws to Europe – perhaps New York or Philadelphia.

411. *Camden Town – Dulwich College.*

TO MARY BERRY

Berkeley Square, 8 June 1791.

... The Duke of St. Albans has cut down all the brave old trees at Hanworth, and consequently reduced his park to what it issued from – Hounslow-heath: nay, he has hired a meadow next to mine, for the benefit of embarkation; and there lie all the good old corpses of oaks, ashes, and chestnuts directly before *your* windows, and blocking up one of my views of the river! but so impetuous is the rage for building, that his Grace's timber will, I trust, not annoy us long. There will soon be one street from London to Brentford; ay, and from London to every village ten miles round! Lord Camden has just let ground at Kentish Town for building fourteen hundred houses[1] – nor do I wonder; London is, I am certain, much fuller than ever I saw it. I have twice this spring been going to stop my coach in Piccadilly, to inquire what was the matter, thinking there was a mob – not at all; it was only passengers. Nor is there any complaint of depopulation from the country: Bath shoots out into new crescents, circuses, squares every year: Birmingham, Manchester, Hull, and Liverpool would serve any King in Europe for a capital, and would make the Empress of Russia's mouth water. .... This morning I went with Lysons the Reverend to see Dulwich College, founded in 1619 by Alleyn, a player, which I had never seen in my many days. We were received by a smart divine, *très bien poudré*, and with black satin breeches – but they are giving new wings and red satin breeches to

---

1 The origins of Camden Town.

the good old hostel too, and destroying a gallery with a very rich ceiling; and nothing will remain of ancient but the front, and an hundred mouldy portraits, among apostles, sibyls, and Kings of England.[1] On Sunday I shall settle at Strawberry; and then woe betide you on post-days! I cannot make news without straw. The Johnstones are going to Bath, for the healths of both; so Richmond will be my only staple. Adieu all three!

7. INDUSTRIAL UNREST
412. *A Strike.*

TO SIR HORACE MANN

Strawberry Hill, 1 July 1762.

... I am in distress about my Gallery and Cabinet: the latter was on the point of being completed, and is really striking beyond description. Last Saturday night my workmen took their leave, made their bow, and left me up to the knees in shavings. In short, the journeymen carpenters, like the cabinet-makers, have entered into an association not to work unless their wages are raised; and how can one complain? The poor fellows, whose all the labour is, see their masters advance their prices every day, and think it reasonable to touch their share. You would be frightened at the dearness of everything; I build out of economy, for unless I do now, in two years I shall not be able to afford it. I expect that a pint of milk will not be sold under a diamond, and then nobody can keep a cow but my Lord Clive. Indeed your country's fever is almost at the height every way. Adieu! ...

---

1 The gift of the Bourgeois collection of paintings to Dulwich College did not take place until twenty years after this letter. The Rev. Daniel Lysons (1762–1834) was a topographer, occasional correspondent of Walpole and author of *The Environs of London* (1792–1811), of which the first volume was dedicated to Walpole.

8. HEALTH RESORTS

413. *Bath.*

TO THE COUNTESS OF SUFFOLK

Madam,   Bath, 6 October 1766.

Your ladyship ordered me to give you an account of myself, and I can give you a very good one. The waters agree with me as well as possible, and do not heat me. All I have to complain of is, that they have bestowed such an appetite upon me, that I expect to return as fat as a hog; that is, something bigger than a lark. I hope this state of my health will content your ladyship, and that you are not equally anxious about my pleasure, which does not go on quite so rapidly. I am tired to death of the place, and long to be at home, and grieve to lose such a delightful October. The waters agree so well with the trees in this country, that they have not a wrinkle or a yellow leaf, and the sun shines as brightly as it can possibly through such mists. I regret its beams being thrown away on such a dirty ditch as their river.

I have not yet been at ball-rooms[1] or pump-rooms, for I steal my glass at the Cross Bath. We have all kind of folk here: Lord Chatham, the Chancellor [Camden], the Dowager Chancellor [Northington], Lady Rockingham, Lady Scarborough, Lord and Lady Powis, Lord and Lady Spencer, judges, bishops, and Lady Vane. It is my own fault if I do not keep the best company, for the mayor of the town has invited me to his feast. But as I cannot be inconstant to the Mayor of Lynn,[2] I have sent an excuse, with such a deplorable account of my health, that it will require all my paleness and leanness to bear me out.

Lord Chatham has still a little gout in his arm, but takes the air. My Lord President [Northington] goes to the balls, but I believe had rather go to the ale-house. Lady Vane, I hear, opens the balls; since it is too late for her now to go anywhere else. This is all I know of people I have not seen.

As I shall not stay above a fortnight longer, I do not propose to learn the language. I hope to find your ladyship in perfect health at my return; but though the banks of the Thames are a little pleasanter

1 The Yale editors have the reading "ball, rooms", with "rooms" as in "public rooms".
2 Walpole was M.P. for King's Lynn until 1768.

than those of the Avon, I beg you will not sit by the former till midnight. The Bath is sure of doing me some good; for I shall take great care of myself, for fear of being sent hither again. I am, &c.

414. *Sea-Bathing.*

TO SIR HORACE MANN

Berkeley Square, 19 May 1780, addition to letter begun 13 May.

. . . I am grieved to hear you complain of your nerves, and know how to pity you. My own are so shattered, that the sudden clapping of a door makes me tremble for some minutes. I should think seabathing might be of use to you. I know, though I have neglected it myself, that the sea-air, even for four-and-twenty hours, is incredibly strengthening. I would not have you bathe without advice; but I do beg you to go to Leghorn, if but for three days. I will communicate yours to your nephew. I think his conduct, as far as I know, is very proper. I am sure it is, if it pleases you; for it is you I wish him to study. I have not time to say more now. Only remember to be easy when you do not hear from me, as you may be sure I have nothing material to tell you.

9. FASHION AND THE FASHIONABLE

415. *The Beautiful Miss Gunnings.*[1]

TO SIR HORACE MANN

Arlington Street, 18 June 1751.

. . . The two Miss Gunnings, and a late extravagant dinner at White's,[2] are twenty times more the subject of conversation than the two brothers [Newcastle and Pelham] and Lord Granville. These are two Irish Girls, of no fortune, who are declared the handsomest women alive. I think their being two so handsome and both such perfect figures is their chief excellence, for singly I have seen much handsomer women than either; however, they can't walk in the park,

1 Mary Gunning was to marry the Earl of Coventry, and Elizabeth Gunning married first the Duke of Hamilton, and later the Duke of Argyll. See letter 182, p. 257, n. 1, and letter 286, p. 398, n. 2.
2 White's Club in St. James's, of which Walpole was a member.

or go to Vauxhall, but such mobs follow them that they are generally driven away. The dinner was a folly of seven young men, who bespoke it to the utmost extent of expense: one article was a tart made of duke cherries from a hot-house; and another, that they tasted but one glass out of each bottle of champagne. The bill of fare is got into print, and with good people has produced the apprehension of another earthquake. Your friend St. Leger[1] was at the head of these luxurious heroes – he is the hero of all fashion. I never saw more dashing vivacity and absurdity, with some flashes of parts. He had a cause the other day for ducking a sharper, and was going to swear: the judge said to him, "I see, Sir, you are very ready to take an oath." "Yes, my lord," replied St. Leger, "my father was a judge." ...

416. *The Wigmaker's Complaint.*

TO THE EARL OF HERTFORD

Arlington Street, 12 February 1765.

... If it was not too long to transcribe, I would send you an entertaining petition of the perriwig-makers to the King, in which they complain that men will wear their own hair. Should one almost wonder if carpenters were to remonstrate, that since the peace their trade decays, and that there is no demand for wooden legs?[2] Apropos my Lady Hertford's friend, Lady Harriot Vernon has quarrelled with me for smiling at the enormous head-gear of her daughter, Lady Grosvenor.[3] She came one night to Northumberland-house with such display of friz, that it literally spread beyond her shoulders. I happened to say it looked as if her parents had stinted her in hair before marriage, and that she was determined to indulge her fancy now. This, among ten thousand things said by all the world, was reported to Lady Harriot, and has occasioned my disgrace. As she

1 This may be Barry Matthew St. Leger (1733–93) or Anthony St. Leger (1731–86), sons of the Irish judge Sir John St. Leger (d. 1743), and brothers of Mann's friend John St. Leger.
2 The peruke-makers' petition to the King was parodied in a mock-petition from carpenters, complaining that their trade in making wooden legs had fallen away since the Treaty of Paris had brought the Seven Years' War to an end.
3 Harriet or Henrietta, *née* Vernon (d. 1828), then married to the Earl of Grosvenor. There were many contemporary criticisms and caricatures of extravagant female hair fashions.

never found fault with anybody herself, I excuse her! I You will be less surprised to hear that the Duchess of Queensberry[1] has not yet done dressing herself marvellously: she was at Court on Sunday in a gown and petticoat of red flannel. The same day the Guerchys made a dinner for her, and invited Lord and Lady Hyde, the Forbes's, and her other particular friends: in the morning she sent word she was to go out of town, but as soon as dinner was over, arrived at Madame de Guerchy's, and said she had been at Court. ...

417. *The Present Folly.*

TO SIR HORACE MANN

Strawberry Hill, 18 June 1777.

... One effect the American war has not had, that it ought to have had; it has not brought us to our senses. Silly dissipation rather increases, and without an object. The present folly is late hours. Everybody tries to be particular by being too late; and, as everybody tries it, nobody is so. It is the fashion now to go to Ranelagh two hours after it is over. You may not believe this, but it is literal. The music ends at ten; the company go at twelve. Lord Derby's cook lately gave him warning. The man owned he liked his place, but he should be killed by dressing suppers at three in the morning. The Earl asked him coolly at how much he valued his life? That is, he would have paid him for killing him. You see we have brought the spirit of calculation to perfection! I do not regret being old, for I see nothing I envy. To live in a crowd, to arrive everywhere too late, and to sell annuities for forty times more than I can ever pay, are not such supreme joys as to make me wish myself young again: indeed, one might execute all these joys at four-score. I am glad the Emperor[2] did not visit us. I hope he is gone home, thinking France the most trifling nation in Europe. ...

1 For the Duchess of Queensberry see letter 95, p. 156, n. 1. Guerchy was the French Ambassador (see letter 61, p. 98, n. 3).
2 Joseph II, Holy Roman Emperor and brother of Marie Antoinette, had been in Paris.

418. *Extravagance.*

TO THE REV. WILLIAM MASON

12 May 1778.

I now and then write a letter for, rather than to, you; that is, when they will bear delay, and be equally fresh, and when they contain anecdotes that I do not care to send by the post if they are too personal, and I have not a prospect of sudden conveyance. The following will have all these ingredients, and will rather be an epitome of the manners of the time, than a letter. The characteristics of the age are frenzy, folly, extravagance, and insensibility; no wonder when such stars are predominant, that Ruin both stalks on, and is not felt or apprehended.

About ten days ago, I wanted a housemaid, and one presented herself very well recommended. I said, "But, young woman, why do you leave your present place?" She said she could not support the hours she kept; that her lady never went to bed till three or four in the morning. "Bless me, child," said I, "why, you tell me you live with a bishop's wife: I never heard that Mrs. North[1] gamed or raked so late." "No, Sir," said she, "but she is three hours undressing." Upon my word, the edifice that takes three hours to demolish, must at least be double the time in fabricating! Would not you for once sit up till morning to see the destruction of the Pyramid and distribution of the materials? Do not mention this, for I did not take the girl, and she still assists at the daily and nightly revolutions of Babel.

On Tuesday I supped after the Opera at Mrs. Meynel's with a set of the most fashionable company, which, take notice, I very seldom do now, as I certainly am not of the age to mix often with young people. Lady Melbourne[2] was standing before the fire, and adjusting her feathers in the glass, says she, "Lord! they say the stocks will blow up: that will be very comical."

These would be features for Comedy, if they would not be thought caricatures, but to-day I am possessed of a genuine paper,

1 Henrietta, *née* Bannister (1750–96), wife of Brownlow North (1741–1820), then Bishop of Worcester, and later of Winchester.
2 Elizabeth Lamb, *née* Milbanke (bap. 1751–1818), Lady Melbourne, and mother of the future prime minister. Mrs. Meynell was the wife of Hugo Meynell, the famous fox hunter.

that I believe I shall leave to the Museum,[1] and which, though its object will, I suppose, to-morrow become record, cannot be believed authentic an hundred years hence. It would in such a national satire as Gulliver be deemed too exaggerated. In short, Lord Foley and his brother have petitioned the House of Lords to set aside their father's Will, as it seems he intended to have raised an hundred thousand pounds to pay their debts, but died before he could execute his intention. All the ladies, Melbournes, and all the Bishops' wives that kill their servants by vigils are going about the town lamenting these poor orphans, and soliciting the peers to redress their grievances; but no words, no ridicule, can attain to the ridiculous pathetic of the printed case itself, which now lies before me, and of which the four first lines are these – upon my honour they are exactly these: –

"The present Lord Foley and his brother Mr. Edward Foley having contracted large bond debts to the amount of about – *l.*, and encumbered themselves by granting annuities for their lives to the amount of about seventeen thousand four hundred and fifty pounds a *year*, explained their situation to their father the late Lord――."

Poor unfortunate children! before thirty, the eldest had spent an estate (to the possession of which he was not arrived) of twenty thousand a year; at least, forfeited his father's affections, who left him but six thousand a year and a palace; and the youngest brother had been dipped in the same extravagance with him, and the legislature is desired to set aside so just a punishment, and if it does will deserve that every lad in England should waste his father's estate before his face. Tell it not in Gath, where all the shekels that ever were in the country would give no idea of the debt, though Jews are the creditors! Burn your sermon instead of printing it. Do you think you can preach up to the enormities of the times? Hyperbole is baffled, and if the fine ladies of Jerusalem were so gallant that the prophets were obliged to pass all bounds of decency in censuring Duchess Aholah and Countess Aholibah,[2] where would they have found figures even in eastern rhetoric to paint the enormity of two sons *explaining to their father* that they paid seventeen thousand pounds a year to usurers for money they had borrowed to pay gaming

1 The British Museum.
2 Two sisters who "committed whoredoms" in Egypt (Ezekiel 23).

debts? and what tropes, what metaphors drawn from asses would describe a sanhedrim that suffered such a petition to be laid before it?

These have been my collections in a single fortnight in the flagrancy of a civil war. History shall not revert to Athens for decrees against diverting the revenues of the theatre to the service of the state.[1] London shall be the storehouse hereafter, whence declamations shall be drawn on the infatuation of falling empires. Nay, so potent is the intoxication, that in two companies this evening I have been thought singular for seeing *this petition* in the light I do: at York perhaps I may not be held so antediluvian in my opinions. With such obsolete prejudices I certainly am not very proper at modern suppers, yet with such *entremets* one would not wholly miss them. Nations at the acme of their splendour, or at the eve of their destruction, are worth observing. When they grovel in obscurity afterwards, they furnish neither events nor reflections; strangers visit the vestiges of the Acropolis, or may come to dig for capitals among the ruins of St. Paul's; but nobody studies the manners of the pedlars and banditti, that dwell in mud huts within the precincts of a demolished temple. Curio and Clodius[2] are memorable as they paved the way to the throne of Cæsar, but equal scoundrels are not entitled to infamy after a constitution is overturned. What we shall retain, I do not conjecture. The constitution might recover – the nation cannot; but though its enemies have miscarried in their attacks on the former, is there sense or virtue enough left to restore it, though the assailants have betrayed such wretched, despicable incapacity? Unless sudden inspiration should seize the whole island, and make it with one voice invite Dr. Franklin to come over and new model the government, it will crumble away in the hands that still hold it. They feel, they own their insufficiency. Everybody is sensible of it, and everybody seems to think, like Lady Melbourne, that if we are blown up it will be very comical.

---

1 The Yale editors speculate that this is a reference to the strict laws in Athens against diverting for other purposes the Theoric fund, which was set aside for religious festivals.
2 The profligate Caius Scribonius Curio (d. 49 B.C.) and the turbulent politician Publius Clodius Pulcher (*c.* 93–52 B.C.).

419. *Late Hours.*

TO SIR HORACE MANN

Arlington Street, 18 December 1778.

Having so many lonely vacant hours (if pain leaves vacancy), I should seem unpardonable in having left such a chasm in our correspondence, when I know you are extremely impatient for news. Solitary hours, to be sure, I have had innumerable, even in my best intervals; for fashion has pushed the day so far into the night, that I have been forced to conform my sick regularity a little to the watches of the town, and dine later than I choose, or dine in public: for nobody will make me a morning's visit before two in the afternoon, nor leave me to go home to dress for dinner before four. They come not again till eight or nine at night, when they would keep me out of bed till twelve, if I would let them. . . .

420. *Excessive Gambling.*

TO SIR HORACE MANN

Strawberry Hill, 17 May 1781, addition to letter begun 16 May.

. . . Dissipation is at high-water mark; but it is either without variety, novelty, and imagination, or the moroseness of age makes me see no taste in their pleasures. Lateness of hours is the principal feature of the times, and certainly demands no stress of invention. Every fashionable place is still crowded; no instance of selection neither. Gaming is yet general; though money, the principal ingredient, does not abound. My old favourite game, faro, is lately revived. I have played but thrice, and not all night, as I used to do; it is not decent to end where one began, nor to sit up with a generation by two descents my juniors. Mr. Fox[1] is the first figure in all the places I have mentioned; the hero in Parliament, at the gaming-table, at Newmarket. Last week he passed four-and-twenty hours without interruption at all three, or on the road from one to the other; and ill the whole time, for he has a bad constitution and treats it as if he

1 Charles James Fox. Walpole's concern as to his constitution appears to have been ill-founded.

had been dipped in the immortal river: but I doubt his heel at least will be vulnerable. . . .

421. *Head-dresses.*

Berkeley Square, 7 September 1781.

. . . The decree[1] you sent me against high heads diverted me. It is as necessary here, but would not have such expeditious effect. The Queen has never admitted feathers at Court; but, though the nation has grown excellent courtiers, Fashion remained in opposition, and not a plume less was worn anywhere else. Some centuries ago, the Clergy preached against monstrous head-dresses; but Religion had no more power than our Queen. It is better to leave the Mode to its own vagaries; if she is not contradicted, she seldom remains long in the same mood. She is very despotic; but, though her reign is endless, her laws are repealed as fast as made. . . .

422. *New Fashions and Late Hours.*

TO MARY BERRY

Berkeley Square, 26 May 1791.

I am rich in letters from you: I received that by Lord Elgin's[2] courier first, as you expected, and its elder the next day. You tell me mine entertain you; *tant mieux*. It is my wish, but my wonder; for I live so very little in the world, that I do not know the present generation by sight; for, though I pass by them in the streets, the hats with valences, the folds above the chin of the ladies, and the dirty shirts and shaggy hair of the young men, who have levelled nobility almost as much as the mobility in France have, have confounded all individuality. Besides, if I did go to public places and assemblies, which my going to roost earlier prevents, the bats and owls do not begin to fly abroad till far in the night, when they begin to see and be seen.

1 An ordinance of the Great-Duke against high head-dresses. – WALPOLE. See letter 416, p. 581, n. 2.
2 Thomas Bruce, 7th Earl of Elgin (1766–1841), and later the acquirer of the Elgin marbles, who had been on a mission to the Emperor Leopold II.

However, one of the empresses of fashion, the Duchess of Gordon,[1] uses fifteen or sixteen hours of her four-and-twenty. I heard her journal of last Monday. She first went to Handel's music in the Abbey; she then clambered over the benches, and went to Hastings' trial in the Hall; after dinner, to the play; then to Lady Lucan's assembly; after that to Ranelagh, and returned to Mrs. Hobart's faro-table; gave a ball herself in the evening of that morning, into which she must have got a good way; and set out for Scotland the next day. Hercules could not have achieved a quarter of her labours in the same space of time. What will the Great Duke think of our Amazons, if he has letters opened, as the Emperor[2] was wont! One of our Camillas, but in a freer style, I hear, he saw (I fancy, just before your arrival); and he must have wondered at the familiarity of the Dame, and the nincompoophood of her Prince.[3] Sir William Hamilton is arrived − his Nymph of the Attitudes[4] was too prudish to visit the rambling peeress. . . .

10. INVENTIONS AND DISCOVERIES

423. *The Delineator.*

TO THE REV. WILLIAM MASON

Strawberry Hill, 21 September 1777.

This is but a codicil to my last, but I forgot to mention in it a new discovery that charms me more than Harlequin did at ten years old, and will bring all paradise before your eyes more perfectly than you can paint it to the good women of your parish. It will be the delight

---

1 Jane Gordon, *née* Maxwell (1748–1812), Duchess of Gordon, a society hostess and wit.
2 Emperor Leopold II, who had formerly been Grand Duke of Tuscany, in which he was succeeded by his son Ferdinand III.
3 The Dame was Lady Craven, *née* Lady Elizabeth Berkeley (1750–1828), society hostess and travel writer, who in 1791 married "her Prince", the Margrave of Brandenburg-Ansbach.
4 The celebrated Emma Hart (bap. 1765–1815), then mistress of Sir William Hamilton (1730/31–1803), Plenipotentiary at Naples and celebrated archaeologist and collector. She married Hamilton in September 1791, and was famous for the portraits of her by George Romney, for her "Attitudes" (poses representing characters from antiquity), and for her later liaison with Lord Nelson. Walpole's point is that although she was Hamilton's mistress, she distanced herself from the unconventional figure of Lady Craven.

of your solitude, and will rival your own celestinette.[1] It is such a perfecting of the camera obscura, that it no longer depends on the sun, and serves for taking portraits with a force and exactness incredible; and serves almost as well by candlelight as by day. It is called *the delineator*, and is invented within these eighteen months by a Mr. Storer,[2] a Norfolk man, one of the modestest and humblest of beings. Sir Joshua Reynolds and West[3] are gone mad with it, and it will be their own faults if they do not excel Rubens in light and shade, and all the Flemish masters in truth. It improves the beauty of trees, – I don't know what it does not do – everything for me, for I can have every inside of every room here drawn minutely in the size of this page. Mr. Storer fell as much in love with Strawberry Hill as I did with his instrument. The perspectives of the house, which I studied so much, are miraculous in this camera. The Gallery, Cabinet, Round Drawing Room, and Great Bed Chamber, make such pictures as you never saw. The painted glass and trees that shade it are Arabian tales. This instrument will enable engravers to copy pictures with the utmost precision: and with it you may take a vase or the pattern of a china jar in a moment; architecture and trees are its greatest beauty; but I think it will perform more wonders than electricity, and yet it is so simple as to be contained in a trunk, that you may carry in your lap in your chaise, for there is such contrivance in that trunk that the filbert in the fairy tales which held such treasures was a fool to it. In short it is terrible to be threescore when it is just invented; I could play with it for forty years; when will you come up and see it? I am sure you will not go back without one. . . .

---

1 A musical instrument invented by Mason, a version of a harpsichord in which a form of bow was also used.
2 The Yale editors note that the bankruptcy of the inventor William Storer, optician of Saham Toney, near Swaffham, Norfolk, was recorded in 1785. Storer's images of Strawberry Hill have not survived.
3 Benjamin West (see letter 88, p. 144, n. 4).

424. *Herschel's Discovery – The New Planet.*

TO THE COUNTESS OF UPPER OSSORY

5 November 1782.

. . . The planet's distance from the sun is 1,710 millions of miles – I revere a telescope's eyes that can see so far! What pity that no Newton should have thought of improving instruments for hearing too! If a glass can penetrate seventeen hundred millions of miles beyond the sun, how easy to form a trumpet like Sir Joshua Reynolds's,[1] by which one might overhear what is said in Mercury and Venus, that are within a stone's throw of us! Well, such things will be discovered – but alas we live in such an early age of the world, that nothing is brought to any perfection! I don't doubt but there will be invented spying-glasses for seeing the thoughts – and then a new kind of stucco for concealing them; but I return to my new favourite, astronomy. Do but think, Madam, how fortunate it is for us that discoveries are not reciprocal. If our superiors of the great planets were to dabble in such minute researches as we make by microscopes, how with their infinitely greater facilities, they might destroy us for a morning's amusement! They might impale our little globe on a pin's point, as we do a flea, and take the current of the Ganges or Oroonoko for the circulation of our blood – for with all due respect for philosophy of all sorts, I humbly apprehend that where people wade beyond their sphere, they make egregious blunders – at least we do, who are not accustomed to them. I am so vulgar, that when I hear of 17 millions of miles, I fancy astronomers compute by livres like the French, and not by pounds sterling, I mean, not by miles sterling. Nay, as it is but two days that I have grown wise, I have another whim. I took it into my head last night that our antediluvian ancestors, who are said to have lived many hundred years, were not inhabitants of this earth but of the new planet, whence might come the account, which we believe came from heaven. Whatever came from the skies, where the new planet lives, would, in the apprehension of men at that time be deemed to come from heaven. Now, if a patriarch lived ten of their years, which may be the term of their existence, and which according to our computation make 800 of our

---

1   Sir Joshua Reynolds was in later life deaf and used an ear trumpet.

years, he was pretty nearly of the age of Methusalem; for what signifies a fraction of an hundred years or so? – Yet I offer this only as a
conjecture; nor will I weary your Ladyship with more, though I am
not a little vain for my new speculations. . . .

425. *Cook's Voyages.*

TO THE COUNTESS OF UPPER OSSORY

Strawberry Hill, 19 June 1784.

. . . Captain Cook's "Voyage"[1] I have neither read nor intend to
read. I have seen the prints – a parcel of ugly faces, with blubber lips
and flat noses, dressed as unbecomingly as if both sexes were ladies
of the first fashion; and rows of savages, with backgrounds of palm-
trees. Indeed I shall not give five guineas and a half – nay, they sell
already for nine, for such uncouth lubbers; nor do I desire to know
how unpolished the north or south poles have remained ever since
Adam and Eve were just such mortals. My brother's death has made
me poor, and I cannot now afford to buy every thing I see. It is late,
to be sure, to learn economy, but I must do it, though a little grievous
as I never was able to say the multiplication table. Well! before
I come to the Rule of Three it will be all over; and then an obolus[2]
will serve to pay the ferryman. How he will stare if I cry, "No, stay,
I cannot give you that; it is a Queen Anne's farthing." . . .

426. *Herschel's Investigations.*

TO THE EARL OF BUCHAN

Strawberry Hill, 23 September 1785.

. . . I have heard formerly, that numbers of papers, of various sorts,
were transported at the Reformation to Spain and Portugal but, if
preserved there, they probably are not accessible *yet.* If they were,
how puny, how diminutive, would all such discoveries, and others

1 The account of Captain Cook's third voyage, *A Voyage to the Pacific Ocean . . . in . . .
the Resolution and Discovery . . .* had been published two weeks earlier in three volumes
with a further folio volume of plates.
2 An ancient Greek coin, placed in the mouth of the deceased when buried so it
could be used to pay Charon for transporting them over the River Styx.

which we might call of far greater magnitude, be to those of
Herschel,[1] who puts up millions of coveys of worlds at a beat! My
conception is not ample enough to take in even a sketch of his
glimpses; and, lest I should lose myself in attempting to follow his
investigations, I recall my mind home, and apply it to reflect on what
we thought we knew, when we imagined we knew something (which
we deemed a vast deal) pretty correctly. Segrais,[2] I think, it was, who
said with much contempt, to a lady who talked of her star, "Your
star! Madam, there are but two thousand stars in all; and do you
imagine that you have a whole one to yourself?" The foolish dame,
it seems, was not more ignorant than Segrais himself. If our system
includes twenty millions of worlds, the lady had as much right to
pretend to a whole ticket as the philosopher had to treat her like a
servant-maid who buys a chance for a day in a state lottery.

Stupendous as Mr. Herschel's investigations are, and admirable
as are his talents, his expression *of our retired corner of the universe*,
seems a little improper. When a little emmet, standing on its ant-
hill, could get a peep into infinity, how could he think he saw a *corner*
in it? – a retired corner? Is there a bounded side to infinitude? If
there are twenty millions of worlds, why not as many, and as many,
and as many more? Oh! one's imagination cracks! I long to bait
within distance of home, and rest at the moon. Mr. Herschel will
content me if he can discover thirteen provinces[3] there, well inhabited by men and women, and protected by the law of nations; that
law which was enacted by Europe for its own emolument, to the
prejudice of the other three parts of the globe, and which bestows
the property of whole realms on the first person who happens to espy
them, who can annex them to the Crown of Great Britain, in lieu
of those it has lost beyond the Atlantic.

I am very ignorant in astronomy, as ignorant as Segrais or the
lady, and could wish to ask many questions; as, Whether our celestial
globes must not be infinitely magnified? Our orreries, too, must not
they be given to children and new ones constructed, that will at least
take in *our retired corner*, and all its outflying constellations? Must not
that host of worlds be christened? Mr. Herschel himself has stood

---

1 William Herschel (1738–1822), musician and astronomer.
2 Jean Regnauld de Segrais (1624–1701), French poet.
3 That is, the newly independent American states.

godfather for his Majesty to the new Sidus.[1] His Majesty, thank God! has a numerous issue; but they and all the princes and princesses in Europe cannot supply appellations enough for twenty millions of new-born stars: no, though the royal progenies of Austria, Naples, and Spain, who have each two dozen saints for sponsors, should consent to split their bead-rolls of names among the foundlings. But I find I talk like an old nurse, and your Lordship at last will, I believe, be convinced that it is not worth your while to keep up a correspondence with a man in his dotage, merely because he has the honour of being, my Lord, your Lordship's most obedient servant.

11. BALLOONS

427. Balloons and Astley's Circus.

TO SIR HORACE MANN

Berkeley Square, 2 December 1783.

... Do not wonder that we do not entirely attend to the things of earth: Fashion has ascended to a higher element. All our views are directed to the air. *Balloons* occupy senators, philosophers, ladies, everybody. France gave us the *ton*;[2] and, as yet, we have not come up to our model. Their monarch is so struck with the heroism of two of his subjects who adventured their persons in two of these new *floating batteries*, that he has ordered statues of them, and contributed a vast sum towards their marble immortality. All this may be very important: to me it looks somewhat foolish. Very early in my life I remember this town at gaze on a man who *flew down* a rope from the top of St. Martin's steeple;[3] now, late in my day, people are staring at a voyage to the moon. The former Icarus broke his neck at a subsequent flight: when a similar accident happens to modern knights-errant, adieu to air-balloons.

1 The planet Uranus, discovered by Herschel in March 1781, and originally named by him "Novum Sidus Georgium".
2 The first hot-air balloon had been launched by the Montgolfier brothers in June, and the first free manned flight had taken place in November.
3 An Italian called Violante on 31 May 1727 descended head-first down a rope from the top of the steeple of St. Martin in the Fields, before a considerable crowd.

Apropos, I doubt these new kites have put young Astley's[1] nose out of joint, who went to Paris lately under their Queen's protection, and expected to be Prime Minister, though he only ventured his neck by dancing a minuet on three horses at full gallop, and really in that attitude has as much grace as the Apollo Belvedere. When the arts are brought to such perfection in Europe, who would go, like Sir Joseph Banks, in search of islands in the Atlantic, where the natives have in six thousand years not improved the science of carving fishing-hooks out of bones or flints! Well! I hope these new mechanic meteors will prove only playthings for the learned and the idle, and not be converted into new engines of destruction to the human race, as is so often the case of refinements or discoveries in science. *The wicked wit of man always studies to apply the result of talents to enslaving, destroying, or cheating his fellow-creatures.* Could we reach the moon, we should think of reducing it to a province of some European kingdom. . . .

428. *His First Balloon.*

TO THE HON. H. S. CONWAY

Strawberry Hill, 30 June 1784.

. . . I have, at last, seen an air-balloon; just as I once did see a tiny review, by passing one accidentally on Hounslow-heath. I was going last night to Lady Onslow at Richmond, and over Mr. Cambridge's field I saw a bundle in the air not bigger than the moon,[2] and she herself could not have descended with more composure if she had expected to find Endymion fast asleep. It seemed to 'light on Richmond-hill; but Mrs. Hobart[3] was going by, and her *coiffure* prevented my seeing it alight. The papers say, that a balloon has been made at Paris representing the castle of Stockholm, in compliment to the King of Sweden; but that they are afraid to let it off: so, I suppose, it will be served up to him in a dessert. No great progress,

1 John Astley (1768–1821), equestrian performer, son of Philip Astley, founder and proprietor of Astley's Amphitheatre.
2 Walpole was visiting Henrietta, *née* Shelley, Baroness Onslow (1731–1809). For Richard Owen Cambridge: see letter 159, p. 225, n. 3.
3 The Yale editors note that there were two Mrs. Hobarts living in the neighbourhood, either of whom Walpole could have intended.

surely, is made in these airy navigations, if they are still afraid of risking the necks of two or three subjects for the entertainment of a visiting sovereign. There is seldom a *feu de joie* for the birth of a Dauphin that does not cost more lives. I thought royalty and science never haggled about the value of blood when experiments are in the question.

I shall wait for summer before I make you a visit. Though I dare to say that you have converted your smoke-kilns[1] into a manufacture of balloons, pray do not erect a Strawberry castle in the air for my reception, if it will cost a pismire a hair of its head. Good night! I have ordered my bed to be heated as hot as an oven, and Tonton and I must go into it.

429. *Lunardi.*

TO SIR HORACE MANN

Strawberry Hill, 30 September 1784.

I do not recollect having ever been so totally at a stand for want of matter since our correspondence began. The Duchess of Gloucester,[2] in her last to me, told me that my letters contain nothing but excuses for having nothing to say; so, you see, my silence is not particular to you. I can only appeal to my usual vouchers, the newspapers, who let no event escape them; and I defy you to produce one they have told you that was worth knowing. I cannot fill my paper, as they do, with air-balloons; which, though ranked with the invention of navigation, appear to me as childish as the flying kites of schoolboys. I have not stirred a step to see one; consequently, have not paid a guinea for gazing at one, which I might have seen by only looking up into the air. An Italian, one Lunardi,[3] is the first *airgonaut* that has mounted into the clouds in this country. So far from respecting him as a Jason, I was very angry with him: he had full right to venture his own neck, but none to risk the poor cat, who, not having proved a martyr, is at least better entitled to be a confessor

1 Conway had obtained a patent for a coke-oven to burn lime.
2 Walpole's niece Maria, Duchess of Gloucester, formerly Lady Waldegrave (see letter 31, p. 53, n. 2).
3 Vincenzo Lunardi (1759–1806) had ascended from the Artillery-ground, Moorfields, on 15 September.

than her master Dædalus. I was even disappointed *after* his expedition had been prosperous: you must know, I have no ideas of space: when I heard how wonderfully he had soared, I concluded he had arrived within a stone's throw of the moon – alas! he had not ascended above a mile and a-half: so pitiful an ascension degraded him totally in my conceit. As there are mountains twice as high, what signifies flying, if you do not rise above the top of the earth? any one on foot may walk higher than this man-eagle! Well! now you know all that I know – and was it worth telling? ...

430. *Aerial News.*

TO THE HON. H. S. CONWAY

Strawberry Hill, 16 October 1784.

... As I was writing this, my servants called me away to see a balloon; I suppose Blanchard's, that was to be let off from Chelsea this morning.[1] I saw it from the common field before the window of my round tower. It appeared about a third of the size of the moon, or less, when setting, something above the tops of the trees on the level horizon. It was then descending; and, after rising and declining a little, it sunk slowly behind the trees, I should think about or beyond Sunbury, at five minutes after one. But you know I am a very inexact guesser at measures and distances, and may be mistaken in many miles; and you know how little I have attended to those *airgonauts:* only t'other night I diverted myself with a sort of meditation on future *airgonation*, supposing that it will not only be perfected, but will depose navigation. I did not finish it, because I am not skilled, like the gentleman that used to write political ship-news, in that style which I wanted to perfect my essay: but in the prelude I observed how ignorant the ancients were in supposing Icarus melted the wax of his wings by too near access to the sun, whereas he would have been frozen to death before he made the first post on that road. Next, I discovered an alliance between Bishop Wilkins's[2] art of flying and his plan of universal language; the latter of which

1 The ascent of the French balloonist Jean-Pierre Blanchard (1753–1809).
2 John Wilkins (1614–72), Bishop of Chester, a founder member of the Royal Society, had in his writings speculated on the possibilities of flying and of a universal language.

he no doubt calculated to prevent the want of an interpreter when he should arrive at the moon.

But I chiefly amused myself with ideas of the change that would be made in the world by the substitution of balloons to ships. I supposed our seaports to become *deserted villages;* and Salisbury Plain, Newmarket Heath, (another canvass for alteration of ideas,) and all downs (but *the* Downs) arising into dock-yards for aërial vessels. Such a field would be ample in furnishing new speculations. But to come to my ship-news: –

"The good balloon Dædalus, Captain Wing-ate, will fly in a few days for China; he will stop at the top of the Monument to take in passengers.

"Arrived on Brand-sands, the Vulture, Captain Nabob; the Tortoise snow, from Lapland; the Pet-en-l'air, from Versailles; the Dreadnought, from Mount Etna, Sir W. Hamilton, commander; the Tympany, Montgolfier; and the Mine-A-in-a-bandbox, from the Cape of Good Hope. Foundered in a hurricane, the Bird of Paradise, from Mount Ararat. The Bubble, Sheldon, took fire, and was burnt to her gallery; and the Phœnix is to be cut down to a second-rate."

In those days Old Sarum will again be a town and have houses in it. There will be fights in the air with wind-guns and bows and arrows; and there will be prodigious increase of land for tillage, especially in France, by breaking up all public roads as useless. But enough of my fooleries; for which I am sorry you must pay double postage.

431. *A Balloon Disaster.*

TO SIR HORACE MANN

Berkeley Square, 24 June 1785.

... You will find by our and the French Gazettes, that *air-navigation* has received a great blow; the first *air*onaut, poor Pilâtrier,[1] and his companions, having broken their necks. He had the Croix de St. Louis in his pocket, and was to have put it on the

---

1 Jean-François Pilâtre de Rozier (1754–85), who had made the first balloon ascent in November 1783, was killed with his companion near Boulogne on 15 June.

moment he should have crossed the Channel and landed in England. I have long thought that France has conceived hopes of annihilating our Pyrenees by these flying squadrons. Here they have been turned into a mere job for getting money from gaping fools. One of our adventurers, named Sadler, has been missing, and is supposed lost in the German Ocean. . . .

P. S. 28th.

Notwithstanding Pilâtrier's miscarriage, Balloonation holds up its head. Colonel Fitzpatrick,[1] Lord Ossory's brother, has ascended in one from Oxford, and was alone. Sadler, whom I thought lost, is come to light again, and was to have been of the voyage; but the vessel not being potent enough for two, the Colonel went alone, had a brush with a high hill in his descent, but landed safe about fifteen miles from the University. How Posterity will laugh at us, one way or other! If half a dozen break their necks, and Balloonism is exploded, we shall be called fools for having imagined it could be brought to use: if it should be turned to account, we shall be ridiculed for having doubted.

12. ENGLISH WEATHER

432. An Earthquake.

TO SIR HORACE MANN

Arlington Street, 11 March 1750.

"Portents and prodigies are grown so frequent,
That they have lost their name."[2]

My text is not literally true; but as far as earthquakes go towards lowering the price of wonderful commodities, to be sure we are overstocked. We have had a second, much more violent than the first; and you must not be surprised if by next post you hear of a burning mountain sprung up in Smithfield. In the night between Wednesday and Thursday last, (exactly a month since the first shock,) the earth had a shivering fit between one and two; but so slight that, if no

1 Hon. Richard Fitzpatrick (1748–1813), M.P., brother-in-law of Walpole's correspondent Lady Ossory.
2 The opening line of Dryden's play *All for Love* (1677).

more had followed, I don't believe it would have been noticed – one or two husbands pretended to be frightened; but in general the business of the night went on much as usual, till half an hour after five – I had been awake, as was scarce dozed again – pray mind, I lie alone, and what I have been saying don't at all relate to myself – on a sudden I felt my bolster lift up my head; I thought somebody was getting from under my bed, but soon found it was a strong earthquake, that lasted near half a minute, with a violent vibration and great roaring. I rang my bell; my servant came in, frightened out of his senses: in an instant we heard all the windows in the neighbourhood flung up. I got up and found people running into the streets, but saw no mischief done: there has been some; two old houses flung down, several chimneys, and much china-ware. The bells rung in several houses. Admiral Knowles, who has lived long in Jamaica, and felt seven there, says this was more violent than any of them; Francesco prefers it to the dreadful one at Leghorn.[1] The wise say, that if we have not rain soon, we shall certainly have more. Several people are going out of town, for it has nowhere reached above ten miles from London: they say, they are not frightened, but that it is such fine weather, "Lord! one can't help going into the country!" The only visible effect it has had, was on the Ridotto, at which, being the following night, there were but four hundred people. A parson, who came into White's the morning of earthquake the first, and heard bets laid on whether it was an earthquake or the blowing up of powder-mills, went away exceedingly scandalised, and said, "I protest, they are such an impious set of people, that I believe if the last trumpet was to sound, they would bet puppet-show against Judgment." If we get any nearer still to the torrid zone, I shall pique myself on sending you a present of cedrati and orange-flower water: I am already planning *a terreno* for Strawberry Hill. . . .

---

1 Admiral Sir Charles Knowles (*c.* 1704–77). Francesco was John Chute's Italian servant.

433. *A Cold Summer.*

TO GEORGE MONTAGU, ESQ.

Strawberry Hill, 15 June 1768.

No, I cannot be so false as to say I am glad you are pleased with your situation.[1] You are so apt to take root, that it requires ten years to dig you out again when you once begin to settle. As you go pitching your tent up and down, I wish you were still more a Tartar, and shifted your quarters perpetually. Yes, I will come and see you; but tell me first, when do your Duke and Duchess[2] travel to the north? I know that he is a very amiable lad, and I do not know that she is not as amiable a *laddess*, but I had rather see their house comfortably when they are not there.

I perceive the deluge fell upon you before it reached us. It began here but on Monday last, and then rained near eight-and-forty hours without intermission. My poor hay has not a dry thread to its back. I have had a fire these three days. In short, every summer one lives in a state of mutiny and murmur, and I have found the reason: it is because we will affect to have a summer, and we have no title to any such thing. Our poets learnt their trade of the Romans, and so adopted the terms of their masters. They talk of shady groves, purling streams, and cooling breezes, and we get sore throats and agues with attempting to realise these visions. Master Damon writes a song, and invites Miss Chloe to enjoy the cool of the evening, and the deuce a bit have we of any such thing as a cool evening. Zephyr is a north-east wind, that makes Damon button up to the chin, and pinches Chloe's nose till it is red and blue; and then they cry, *This is a bad summer!* as if we ever had any other. The best sun we have is made of Newcastle coal, and I am determined never to reckon upon any other. We ruin ourselves with inviting over foreign trees, and making our houses clamber up hills to look at prospects. How our ancestors would laugh at us, who knew there was no being comfortable, unless you had a high hill before your nose, and a thick warm wood at your back! Taste is too freezing a commodity for us, and, depend upon it, will go out of fashion again. . . .

1 Montagu was at Adderbury, Oxfordshire, a house of the Duke of Buccleuch.
2 Henry Scott, 3rd Duke of Buccleuch (1746–1812) and his wife, Lady Elizabeth Montagu (1743–1827).

434. *An English June.*

TO MARY BERRY

Strawberry Hill, 14 June 1791.

I pity you! what a dozen or fifteen uninteresting letters are you going to receive! for here I am unlikely to have anything to tell you worth reading. You had better come back incontinently – but pray do not prophesy any more; you have been the death of our summer, and we are in close mourning for it in coals and ashes. It froze hard last night: I went out for a moment to look at my haymakers, and was starved. The contents of an English June are, hay and ice, orange-flowers and rheumatisms! I am now cowering over the fire. Mrs. Hobart had announced a rural breakfast at Sans-Souci[1] last Saturday; nothing being so pastoral as a fat grandmother in a row of houses on Ham Common. It rained early in the morning: she despatched post-boys, for want of Cupids and zephyrs, to stop the nymphs and shepherds who tend their flocks in Pall Mall and St. James's-street; but half of them missed the couriers and arrived. ...

1 Albinia Bertie (*c.* 1738–1816), wife of the Hon. George Hobart, later Earl of Buckinghamshire. The Yale editors note had she had several grandchildren, and that she had a villa on Ham Common. She named this Sans-Souci after the summer palace of Frederick the Great, and entertained there.

APPENDIX A

The purpose of this index is to list all the letters and selections from letters in this volume in the order in which they appear, and to cross-reference them to the Yale edition of Walpole's Correspondence. Yale Edition references are by volume and page numbers.

V. VIRTUOSO AND ANTIQUARIAN

76	West	2 October 1740	13:229–34
77	Montagu	11 August 1748	9:67–73
78	Montagu	20 July 1749	9:91–95
79	Montagu	22 July 1751	9:117–22
80	Bentley	5 August 1752	35:131–46
81	Bentley	23 February 1755	35:207–11
82	Bentley	August 1756	35:266–72
83	Montagu	20 August 1758	9:222–25
84	Montagu	19 July 1760	9:288–90
85	Montagu	1 September 1760	9:293–300
86	Montagu	23 July 1763	10:88–92
87	Montagu	10 May 1764	10:123–24
88	Mann	6 May 1770	23:208–13
89	Cole	28 July 1772	1:270–71
90	Cole	15 August 1774	1:340–45
91	Lord Harcourt	8 October 1777	35:477–78
92	Cole	5 January 1780	2:183–85
93	Rev. William Mason	19 May 1780	29:32–39
94	Richard Gough	24 August 1789	42:259–60

VI. STRAWBERRY HILL

95	Conway	8 June 1747	37:269–71
96	Mann	26 December 1748	20:16–21
97	Montagu	28 September 1749	9:101–03
98	Montagu	6 June 1752	9:132–36
99	Mann	27 April 1753	20:371–74
100	Mann	12 June 1753	20:379–84
101	Bentley	18 May 1754	35:172–76
102	Bentley	10 June 1755	35:226–31
103	Mann	4 August 1757	21:118–22
104	Mann	9 September 1758	21:237–40
105	Montagu	2 June 1759	9:237–39
106	Montagu	17 May 1763	10:69–74
107	Montagu	1 July 1763	10:84–85
108	Montagu	16 July 1764	10:128–31
109	Hertford	3 August 1764	38:414–23
110	Montagu	10 June 1765	10:156–57
111	Montagu	11 May 1769	10:277–80
112	Cole	23 October 1771	1:243–44
113	Conway	7 January 1772	39:152–53
114	Conway	30 June 1776	39:275–78
115	Ossory	2 August 1786	33:521–23

VII. HIS LITERARY WORKS

116	Montagu	4 May 1758	9:218–21
117	Rev. Henry Zouch	12 January 1759	16:24–26
118	Cole	28 February 1765	1:84–85
119	Cole	9 March 1765	1:88–91

14 Sterne
    151   Dalrymple   4 April 1760   15:64–67

15 Burney
    152   Ossory   1 October 1782   33:355–58

16 Johnson
    153   Ossory   19 January 1775   32:224–30
    154   Ossory   1 February 1779   33:85–89
    155   Mason   27 January 1781   29:95–99
    156   Mason   3 February 1781   29:100–03
    157   Mason   19 February 1781   29:108–12
    158   Mason   14 April 1781   29:128–31

17 Boswell
    159   Gray   18 February 1768   14:166–71
    160   Mason   22 May 1781   29:143–45
    161   Berry   26 May 1791   11:272–79

18 Goldsmith
    162   Ossory   27 March 1773   32:108–13
    163   Mason   27 March 1773   28:76–81
    164   Ossory   14 December 1773   32:166–71

19 Sheridan
    165   Robert Jephson   13 July 1777   41:361–4
    166   Mason   16 May 1777   28:307–10

20 Gibbon
    167   Edward Gibbon   14 February 1776   41:334–36
    168   Mason   18 February 1776   28:241–47
    169   Mason   27 January 1781   29:95–99

21 Burke
    170   Mason   27 May 1775   28:201–05
    171   Berry   8 November 1790   11:130–36
    172   Ossory   1 December 1790   34:97–99

22 Chesterfield
    173   Mason   7 April 1774   28:143–47

23 General Criticism
    174   Mason   21 July 1772   28:38–41
    175   Pinkerton   26 June 1785   16:267–73

IX. HIS FAMILY

1 Sir Robert Walpole, his father
    176   Zouch   21 October 1758   16:18–21
    177   Governor Pownall   27 October 1783   42:77–82
    178   Mann   26 August 1785   25:602–06

2 Sir Edward Walpole, his brother
    179   Sir Edward Walpole   17 May 1745   36:21
    180   Mann   23 March 1749   20:38–42
    181   Mason   2 February 1784   29:326–33

287	Mann	9 February 1759	21:266–68
288	Conway	14 August 1759	38:20–24
289	Mann	16 October 1759	21:335–37
290	Conway	18 October 1759	38:37–40
291	Montagu	21 October 1759	9:250–51

XIV. HISTORICAL EVENTS – THE FIRST HALF OF GEORGE III'S REIGN

1 Wilkes and "The North Briton"

292	Mann	17 November 1763	22:181–86
293	Hertford	9 December 1763	38:253–60
294	Mann	31 March 1768	23:5–8
295	Mann	12 May 1768	23:19–22
296	Mann	9 June 1768	23:28–32
297	Mann	6 February 1769	23:86–88
298	Mann	23 March 1769	23:97–101
299	Mann	14 April 1769	23:104–07

2 The American War of Independence

300	Mann	6 May 1770	23:208–13
301	Mann	2 February 1774	23:548–52
302	Mason	12 June 1775	28:205–07
303	Conway	15 December 1774	39:225–28
304	Ossory	19 January 1775	32:224–230
305	Ossory	7 July 1775	32:238–40
306	Mann	3 August 1775	24:119–21
307	Mann	17 April 1776	24:191–95
308	Mann	20 August 1776	24:234–37
309	Mann	13 October 1776	24:248–50
310	Mann	20 December 1776	24:268–69
311	Mann	3 April 1777	24:286–89
312	Mann	4 December 1777	24:338–43
313	Mann	18 February 1778	24:354–56
314	Mann	7 July 1778	24:390–93
315	Mason	18 July 1778	28:414–17
316	Mann	16 June 1779	24:482–85
317	Ailesbury	10 July 1779	39:331–34
318	Ailesbury	23 July 1779	39:335–37
319	Mann	4 January 1780	25:3–5
320	Mann	7 October 1780	25:89–92
321	Ossory	16 November 1780	33:237–40
322	Conway	3 January 1781	39:352–56
323	Mann	29 November 1781	25:210–15
324	Mann	18 May 1782	25:277–81
325	Ossory	31 August 1782	33:352–55
326	Strafford	3 October 1782	35:366–68
327	Mann	2 November 1782	25:334–37
328	Mann	2 December 1782	25:346–48
329	Mann	27 August 1783	25:426–28

3 The Gordon Riots

| 330 | Ossory | 29 January 1780 | 33:162–65 |
| 331 | Mann | 6 February 1780 | 25:10–15 |

APPENDIX B

This Appendix lists the letters appearing in this volume by correspondent, and by date order for each correspondent. It also shows in the 'Letter Number' column where a letter has been used more than once in this selection.

CORRESPONDENT	DATE	LETTER NUMBER
Ailesbury, Countess	10 October 1761	20
	10 July 1779	317
	23 July 1779	318
Bedford, Grosvenor	c. 17 January 1760	251
	29 February 1764	252
Bentley, Richard	5 August 1752	80
	19 December 1753	148
	17 March 1754	15
	18 May 1754	101
	23 February 1755	81
	10 June 1755	102
	August 1756	82
Berry, Mary	2 February 1789	229
	9 July 1789	370
	10 October 1790	230
	8 November 1790	171
	12 May 1791	35
	26 May 1791	161 and 422
	8 June 1791	411
	14 June 1791	434
	26 July 1791	379
	23 August 1791	70
	16 September 1791	380
	15 October 1793	385
	13 December 1793	386
Buchan, Earl of	23 September 1785	426
Chatterton, Thomas	28 March 1769	140
Chute, John	20 August 1743	407
	3 October 1765	347
	10 October 1766	404
	5 August 1771	196 and 357
Cole, Rev. William	28 February 1765	118
	9 March 1765	119 and 136
	16 April 1768	405
	26 June 1769	211
	23 October 1771	112
	28 January 1772	132
	28 July 1772	89
	15 August 1774	90

INDEX

AUGUSTINE
The Confessions

JANE AUSTEN
Emma
Mansfield Park
Northanger Abbey
Persuasion
Pride and Prejudice
Sanditon and Other Stories
Sense and Sensibility

SIMONE DE BEAUVOIR
The Second Sex

SAUL BELLOW
The Adventures of Augie March

WILLIAM BLAKE
Poems and Prophecies

GIOVANNI BOCCACCIO
Decameron

JORGE LUIS BORGES
Ficciones

JAMES BOSWELL
The Life of Samuel Johnson
The Journal of a Tour to
the Hebrides

CHARLOTTE BRONTË
Jane Eyre
Villette
Shirley and The Professor

EMILY BRONTË
Wuthering Heights

MIKHAIL BULGAKOV
The Master and Margarita

ITALO CALVINO
If on a winter's night a traveler

ALBERT CAMUS
The Plague, The Fall, Exile and
the Kingdom, and Selected Essays
The Outsider (UK)
The Stranger (US)

BENVENUTO CELLINI
The Autobiography of
Benvenuto Cellini

MIGUEL DE CERVANTES
Don Quixote

RAYMOND CHANDLER
The novels (2 vols)
Collected Stories

GEOFFREY CHAUCER
Canterbury Tales

ANTON CHEKHOV
The Complete Short Novels
My Life and Other Stories
The Steppe and Other Stories

CONFUCIUS
The Analects

JOSEPH CONRAD
Heart of Darkness
Lord Jim
Nostromo
The Secret Agent
Typhoon and Other Stories
Under Western Eyes
Victory

DANTE ALIGHIERI
The Divine Comedy

CHARLES DARWIN
The Origin of Species
The Voyage of the Beagle
(in 1 vol.)

DANIEL DEFOE
Moll Flanders
Robinson Crusoe

CHARLES DICKENS
Barnaby Rudge
Bleak House
A Christmas Carol and Other
Christmas Books
David Copperfield
Dombey and Son
Great Expectations
Hard Times
Little Dorrit
Martin Chuzzlewit
The Mystery of Edwin Drood
Nicholas Nickleby
The Old Curiosity Shop
Oliver Twist
Our Mutual Friend
The Pickwick Papers
A Tale of Two Cities